SERMONS

AND

MISCELLANEOUS PIECES

BY

ARCHBISHOP SANDYS.

The Parker Society.

Instituted A.D. M.DCCC.XL.

For the Publication of the Works of the Fathers and Early Writers of the Reformed English Church.

THE SERMONS

OF

EDWIN SANDYS, D.D.,

SUCCESSIVELY BISHOP OF WORCESTER AND LONDON, AND
ARCHBISHOP OF YORK;

TO WHICH ARE ADDED

SOME MISCELLANEOUS PIECES,

BY

THE SAME AUTHOR.

EDITED FOR

The Parker Society,

BY THE

REV. JOHN AYRE, M.A.,

MINISTER OF ST JOHN'S CHAPEL, HAMPSTEAD.

Wipf & Stock
PUBLISHERS
Eugene, Oregon

Wipf and Stock Publishers
199 W 8th Ave, Suite 3
Eugene, OR 97401

The Sermons of Edwin Sandys, D.D.,
Successively Bishop of Worcester and London, and Archbishop of York
To Which Are Added Some Miscellaneous Pieces by the Same Author
By Sandys, Edwin
ISBN 13: 978-1-55635-046-7
ISBN 10: 1-55635-046-5
Publication date 10/19/2006
Previously published by Cambridge, 1842

CONTENTS.

	PAGE
BIOGRAPHICAL Notice of Archbishop Sandys	i
Epistle to the Reader	1
Order and Matter of the Sermons	5
Sermons	7

MISCELLANEOUS PIECES.

Advice concerning Rites and Ceremonies in the Synod 1562	433
Orders for the Bishops and Clergy	434
Advertisement to the translation of Luther's Commentary on Galatians	435
Epistola Pastoralis Episcopo Cestrensi	436
The same translated	439
Prayers to be used at Hawkshead School	443
Preamble to the Archbishop's will	446
Notes	453

BIOGRAPHICAL NOTICE

OF

ARCHBISHOP SANDYS.

EDWIN SANDYS or Sandes was born in the year 1519, near Hawkshead, in the part of Lancashire called Furness Fells. He was the third son of William Sandys, Esq, and Margaret his wife, a descendant of the ancient barons of Kendal. As Easthwaite Hall was the principal residence of the father, it is probable that it was in this house that Edwin first saw the light.

It is not certainly known at what seminary the future archbishop received the rudiments of his education: it has however been conjectured with some plausibility by a biographer that, as the school of Furness Abbey was then highly distinguished, and as his family were feudatories of that house, he was a pupil of the monks. It is also ascertained that he was at one time instructed by Mr Bland, who, being rector of Adesham in Kent, was apprehended for his religion and burned at Canterbury, July 12, 1555. In 1532 or 3 he was removed to the University of Cambridge, and placed at St John's College, a house deeply tinctured with the principles of the Reformation; and here doubtless the religious views of Sandys were, if not implanted, at least confirmed. Though never either scholar or fellow of his college, he served the office of proctor, and was in 1547 elected master of Catharine Hall. This was just after his father's decease. He is said to have been at this time vicar of Haversham in Buckinghamshire, his first considerable preferment: in 1549 he was made prebendary of Peterborough, and obtained in 1552 the second stall at Carlisle, both on the presentation of the crown. He had previously married a lady of his own name. In 1553, when he was vice-chancellor of the University of Cambridge, king Edward VI. died: the troubles that ensued to Sandys shall be narrated in the words of Fox.

"King Edward died, the world being unworthy of him: the duke of Northumberland came down to Cambridge with an army of men, having commission to proclaim lady Jane queen, and by power to suppress lady Mary, who took upon her that dignity, and was proclaimed queen in Norfolk. The duke sent for Doctor Sandys, being vice-chancellor, for Doctor Parker, for Doctor Bill, and Master Leaver to sup with him. Amongst other speeches he said, Masters, pray for us, that we speed well: if not, you shall be made bishops, and we deacons. And even so it came to pass: Doctor Parker and Doctor Sandys were made bishops; and he, and Sir John Gates who was then at the table, were made deacons ere it was long after, on the Tower-hill. Doctor Sandys being vice-chancellor was required to preach on the morrow. The warning was short for such an auditory, and to speak of such a matter: yet he refused not the thing, but went into his chamber, and so to bed. He rose at three of the clock in the morning, took his bible in his hand, and after that he had prayed a good space, he shut his eyes, and, holding his bible before him, earnestly prayed to God that it might fall open where a most fit text should be for him to entreat of. The bible, as God would have it, fell open upon the first chapter of Josua, where he found so convenient a piece of scripture for that time, that the like he could not have chosen in all the bible. His text

Josh. i. 16—18. was thus: *Responderuntque ad Josue atque dixerunt, Omnia quæ præcepisti nobis faciemus, et quocunque miseris ibimus:*

sicut obedivimus in cunctis Mosi, ita obediemus et tibi; tantum sit Dominus Deus tuus tecum sicut fuit cum Mose: qui contradixerit ori tuo, et non obedierit cunctis sermonibus quos præceperis ei, moriatur: tu tantum confortare et viriliter age. Who shall consider what was concluded by such as named themselves by the state, and withal the auditory, the time, and other circumstances, he shall easily see that this text most fitly served for the purpose. And as God gave the text, so gave he such order and utterance, as pulled many tears out of the eye of the biggest of them.

"In the time of his sermon one of the guard lift up to him into the pulpit a mass book and a graile, which Sir George Haward with certain of the guard had taken that night in Master Hurlestone's[1] house, where Lady Mary had been a little before, and there had mass. The duke with the rest of the nobility required Doctor Sandys to put his sermon in writing, and appointed Master Leaver to go to London with it, and to put it in print. Doctor Sandys required one day and a half for writing of it. At the time appointed he had made it ready; and Master Leaver was ready booted to receive it at his hands and carry it to London. As he was delivering of it, one of the beadles, named Master Adams, came weeping to him, and prayed him to shift for himself, for the duke was retired and queen Mary proclaimed.

"Doctor Sandys was not troubled herewithal, but gave the sermon written to Master Layfield. Master Leaver departed home; and he went to dinner to one Master Moore's, a beadle, his great friend. At the dinner Mistress Moore, seeing him merry and pleasant (for he had ever a man's courage, and could not be terrified), drank unto him, saying, Master vice-chancellor, I drink unto you; for this is the last time that ever I shall see you.

[[1] Compare p. vi. l. 17.—ED.]

And so it was; for she was dead before Doctor Sandys returned out of Germany. The duke that night retired to Cambridge, and sent for Doctor Sandys to go with him to the market-place to proclaim queen Mary. The duke cast up his cap with others, and so laughed, that the tears ran down his cheeks for grief. He told Doctor Sandys that queen Mary was a merciful woman, and that he doubted not thereof; declaring that he had sent unto her to know her pleasure, and looked for a general pardon. Doctor Sandys answered, My life is not dear unto me, neither have I done or said any thing that urgeth my conscience. For that which I spake of the state, I have instructions warranted by the subscription of sixteen counsellors; neither can speech be treason, neither yet have I spoken further than the word of God and the laws of the realm doth warrant me, come of me what God will. But be you assured, you shall never escape death: for if she would save you, those that now shall rule will kill you.

"That night the guard apprehended the duke; and certain grooms of the stable were as busy with Doctor Sandys as if they would take a prisoner. But Sir John Gates, who lay then in Doctor Sandys his house, sharply rebuked them, and drave them away. Doctor Sandys, by the advice of Sir John Gates, walked into the fields. In the mean time the university, contrary to all order, had met together in consultation, and ordered, that Doctor Mouse and Doctor Hatcher should repair to Doctor Sandys' lodging, and fet[1] away the statute book of the university, the keys, and such other things that were in his keeping: and so they did; for Doctor Mouse being an earnest protestant the day before, and one whom Doctor Sandys had done much for, now was he become a papist, and his great enemy. Certain of the university had appointed

[1 Fet—fetch.]

a congregation at afternoon. As the bell rang to it, Doctor Sandys cometh out of the fields; and sending for the beadles, asketh what the matter meaneth, and required them to wait upon him to the schools, according to their duty. So they did. And so soon as Doctor Sandys, the beadles going before him, came into the regent-house and took his chair, one Master Mitch with a rabble of unlearned papists went into a bye school, and conspired together to pull him out of his chair, and to use violence unto him. Doctor Sandys began his oration, expostulating with the university, charging them with great ingratitude, declaring that he had said nothing in his sermon but that he was ready to justify, and that their case was all one with his; for they had not only concealed, but consented to that which he had spoken.

"And thus while he remembered unto them how beneficial he had been to the university, and their unthankfulness to him again, in cometh Master Mitch with his conspirators about twenty in number. One layeth hand upon the chair, to pull it from him; another told him that that was not his place; and another called him traitor. Whereat he perceiving how they used violence, and being of great courage, groped to his dagger, and had dispatched some of them as God's enemies, if Doctor Bill and Doctor Blith had not fallen upon him, and prayed him for God's sake to hold his hands and be quiet, and patiently to bear that great offered wrong. He was persuaded by them; and after that tumult was ceased, he ended his oration, and, having some money of the university's in his hand, he there delivered the same every farthing. He gave up the books, reckonings, and keys, pertaining to the university, and withal yielded up his office, praying God to give the university a better officer, and to give them better and more thankful hearts; and so repaired home to his own college.

"On the morrow after there came unto him one Master Gerningham, and one Master Thomas Mildmay. Gerningham told him, that it was the queen's pleasure that two of the guard should attend upon him, and that he must be carried prisoner to the Tower of London with the duke. Master Mildmay said, he marvelled that a learned man would speak so unadvisedly against so good a prince, and wilfully run into such danger. Doctor Sandys answered, I shall not be ashamed of bonds; but if I could do as Master Mildmay can, I needed not to fear bonds. For he came down in payment against queen Mary, and armed in the field, and now he returneth in payment for queen Mary; before a traitor, and now a great friend. I cannot with one mouth blow hot and cold after this sort.

"Upon this his stable was robbed of four notable good geldings: the best of them Master Huddlestone took for his own saddle, and rode on him to London in his sight. An inventory was taken of all his goods by Master Moore, beadle for the university. He was set upon a lame horse that halted to the ground, which thing a friend of his perceiving prayed that he might lend him a nag. The yeomen of the guard were contented. As he departed forth at the town's end, some papists resorted thither to jeer at him, some of his friends to mourn for him. He came in the rank to London, the people being full of outcries. And as he came in at Bishopsgate, one like a milkwife hurled a stone at him, and hit him on the breast with such a blow, that he was like to fall off his horse. To whom he mildly said, Woman, God forgive it thee. Truth is, that journey and evil entreating so mortified him, that he was more ready to die than to live.

"As he came through Tower-hill-street, one woman standing in her door cried, Fie on thee, thou knave, thou knave, thou traitor, thou heretic. Whereat he smiled. Look, the desperate heretic (saith she) laugheth at this gear. A woman on the other side of the street answered, saying, Fie on thee, neighbour! thou art not worthy to be called a woman, railing upon this gentleman whom thou knowest not, neither yet the cause why he is thus entreated. Then she said, Good gentleman, God be thy comfort, and give thee strength to stand in God's cause even to the end! And thus he passed through fire and water into the Tower, the first prisoner that entered in that day, which was St. James' day. The yeomen of the guard took from him his borrowed nag, and what else soever he had. His man, one Quinting Suainton brought after him a bible and some shirts, and such like things. The bible was sent in to him; but the shirts and such like served the yeomen of the guard.

"After he had been in the Tower three weeks in a bad prison, he was lift up into Nuns' bower, a better prison, where was put to him Master John Bradford.

"At the day of queen Mary's coronation, their prison door was set open, ever shut before. One Master Mitchell, his old acquaintance, which had been prisoner before in the same place, came in to him, and said, Master Sandys, there is such a stir in the Tower, that neither gates, doors, nor prisoners, are looked to this day. Take my cloak, my hat, and my rapier, and get you gone: you may go out of the gates without questioning: save yourself, and let me do as I may. A rare friendship; but he refused the offer, saying, I know no just cause why I should be in prison: and thus to do were to make myself guilty. I will expect God's good will; yet must I think myself most bound unto you. And so Master Mitchell departed.

"While Doctor Sandys and Master Bradford were thus in close prison together twenty-nine weeks, one John Bowler was their keeper, a very perverse papist; yet by often persuading of him, (for he would give ear,) and by gentle using of him, at the length he began to mislike popery, and to favour the gospel, and so persuaded in true religion, that on a Sunday, when they had mass in the chapel, he bringeth up a service book, a manchet, and a glass of wine, and there Doctor Sandys ministered the communion to Bradford and to Bowler. Thus Bowler was their son begotten in bonds. When Wyat was in arms, and the old duke of Norfolk sent forth with a power of men to apprehend him; that room might be made in the Tower for him and other his complices, Doctor Cranmer, Doctor Ridley, and Master Bradford were cast into one prison, and Doctor Sandys with nine other preachers were sent into the Marshalsea.

"The keeper of the Marshalsea appointed to every preacher a man to lead him in the street: he caused them to go far before, and he and Doctor Sandys came behind, whom he would not lead, but walked familiarly with him. Yet Doctor Sandys was known; and the people everywhere prayed to God to comfort him and to strengthen him in the truth. By that time the people's minds were altered: popery began to be unsavoury. After they passed the bridge, the keeper, Thomas Way, said to Doctor Sandys, I perceive the vain people would set you forward to the fire. Ye are as vain as they, if you being a young man will stand in your own conceit, and prefer your own knowledge before the judgment of so many worthy prelates, ancient, learned, and grave men, as be in this realm. If you so do, you shall find me as strait a keeper, as one that utterly misliketh your religion. Doctor Sandys answered, I know my years young and my learning small: it is enough to know Christ crucified; and he hath learned nothing, that seeth not the great blasphemy that is in popery. I will yield unto God and not unto man: I have read in the scriptures of many godly and courteous keepers: God may make you one. If not, I trust he will give me strength and patience to bear your hard dealing with me. Saith Thomas Way, Do ye then mind to stand to your religion? Yea, saith Doctor Sandys, by God's grace. Truly, saith the keeper, I love you the better: I did but tempt you. What favour I can shew you ye shall be sure of, and I shall think myself happy if I may die at the stake with you. The said keeper shewed Doctor Sandys ever after all friendship: he trusted him to go into the fields alone, and there met with Master Bradford, who then was removed into the Bench and there found the like favour of his keeper. He laid him in the best chamber in the house: he would not suffer the knight marshal's man to lay fetters on him, as others had. And at his request he put Master Sanders in to him, to be his bedfellow; and sundry times suffered his wife, who was Master Sandys' daughter of Essex, a gentlewoman beautiful both in body and soul, to resort to him. There was great resort to Doctor Sandys and Master Sanders: they had much money offered them, but they would receive none. They had the communion there three or four times, and a great sort of communicants. Doctor Sandys gave such exhortation to the people (for at that time being young he was thought very eloquent) that he moved many tears, and made the people abhor the mass, and defy all popery.

"When Wyat with his army came into Southwark, he sent two gentlemen into the Marshalsea to Doctor Sandys, saying, that Master Wyat would be glad of his company and advice, and that the gates should be set open for all the prisoners. He answered, Tell Master Wyat, if this his rising be of God, it will take place; if not, it will fall. For my part I was committed hither by order: I will be discharged by like order, or I will never depart hence. So answered Master Sanders, and the rest of the preachers being there prisoners.

"After that Doctor Sandys had been nine weeks prisoner

in the Marshalsea, by the mediation of Sir Thomas Holcroft, then knight marshal, he was set at liberty. Sir Thomas sued earnestly to the bishop of Winchester, Doctor Gardiner, for his deliverance: after many repulses, (except Doctor Sandys would be one of their sect, and then he could want nothing,) he wrung out of him that, if the queen could like of his deliverance, he would not be against it: for that was Sir Thomas' last request. In the mean time he had procured two ladies of the privy chamber to move the queen in it; who was contented if the bishop of Winchester could like of it. The next time that the bishop went into the privy chamber to speak with the queen, Master Holcroft followed, and had his warrant for Doctor Sandys' remission ready; and prayed the two ladies, when as the bishop should take his leave, to put the queen in mind of Doctor Sandys. So they did; and the queen said, Winchester, what think you by Doctor Sandys, is he not sufficiently punished? As it please your majesty, saith Winchester. That he spake, remembering his former promise to Master Holcroft, that he would not be against Doctor Sandys, if the queen should like to discharge him. Saith the queen, Then truly, we would that he were set at liberty. Immediately Master Holcroft offered the queen the warrant; who subscribed the same, and called Winchester to put to his hand; and so he did. The warrant was given to the knight marshal again, Sir Thomas Holcroft. As the bishop went forth of the privy chamber door, he called Master Holcroft to him, commanding him not to set Doctor Sandys at liberty, until he had taken sureties of two gentlemen of his country with him, every one bound in five hundred pounds, that Doctor Sandys should not depart out of the realm without licence. Master Holcroft immediately after met with two gentlemen of the north, friends and cousins to Doctor Sandys, who offered to be bound in body, goods, and lands for him. After dinner the same day, Master Holcroft sent for Doctor Sandys to his lodging at Westminster, requiring the keeper to company with him. He came accordingly, finding Master Holcroft alone, walking in his garden. Master Holcroft imparted his long suit, with the whole proceeding, and what effect it had taken, to Doctor Sandys; much rejoicing that it was his good hap to do him good, and to procure his liberty, and that nothing remained, but that he would enter into bonds with his two sureties for not departing out of the realm. Doctor Sandys answered, I give God thanks, who hath moved your heart to mind me so well, and I think myself most bound unto you. God shall requite, and I shall never be found unthankful. But as you have dealt friendly with me, I will also deal plainly with you. I came a free man into prison, I will not go forth a bondman. As I cannot benefit my friends, so will I not hurt them. And if I be set at liberty, I will not tarry six days in this realm if I may get out. If therefore I may not go free forth, send me to the Marshalsea again, and there ye shall be sure of me.

"This answer much misliked Master Holcroft: he told Doctor Sandys that the time would not long continue, a change would shortly come; the state was but a cloud, and would soon shake away: and that his cousin Sir Edward Bray would gladly receive him and his wife into house, where he should never need to come at church; and how the Lady Bray was a zealous gentlewoman, who hated popery: adding, that he would not so deal with him, to lose all his labour. When Doctor Sandys could not be removed from his former saying, Master Holcroft said, Seeing you cannot be altered, I will change my purpose and yield unto you. Come of it what will, I will set you at liberty; and seeing you mind to go over sea, get you gone so quick like as you can. One thing I require of you, that while you are there you write nothing to come hither; for so ye may undo me. He friendly kissed Doctor Sandys, bade him farewell, and commanded the keeper to take no fees of him, saying, Let me answer Winchester as I may. Doctor Sandys returning with the keeper to the Marshalsea tarried all night; there on the morrow gave a dinner to all the prisoners, bade his bed-fellow and sworn stake-fellow, if it had so pleased God, Master Sanders, farewell, with many tears and kissings, the one falling on the other's neck; and so departed, clearly delivered without examination or bond. From thence he went to the Bench, and there talked with Master Bradford, and Master Farrar, bishop of Saint David's, then prisoners. Then he comforted them; and they praised God for his happy deliverance. He went by Winchester's house, and there took boat, and came to a friend's house in London called William Banks, and tarried there one night. On the morrow at night he shifted to another friend's house, and there he learned that search was made for him.

"Doctor Watson and Master Christopherson, coming to the bishop of Winchester, told him that he had set at liberty the greatest heretic in England, and one that had of all other most corrupted the university of Cambridge, Doctor Sandys. Whereupon the bishop of Winchester, being chancellor of England, sent for all the constables of London, commanding them to watch for Doctor Sandys, who was then within the city, and to apprehend him; and whosoever of them should take him and bring him to him, he should have five pounds for his labour. Doctor Sandys, suspecting the matter, conveyed him by night to one Master Bartie's house, a stranger, who was in the Marshalsea with him prisoner awhile: he was a good protestant and dwelt in Mark-lane. There he was six days, and had one or two of his friends that repaired unto him. Then he repaired to an acquaintance of his, one Hurlestone, a skinner, dwelling in Cornhill: he caused his man Quinting to provide two geldings for him, minding on the morrow to ride into Essex to Master Sandys, his father-in-law, where his wife was.

"At his going to bed in Hurlestone's house, he had a pair of hose newly made that were too long for him. For while he was in the Tower, a tailor was admitted him to make him a pair of hose. One came unto him whose name was Benjamin, a good protestant, dwelling in Birchin-lane: he might not speak to him, or come unto him to take measure of him, but only look upon his leg: he made the hose, and they were two inches too long. These hose he prayed the goodwife of the house to send to some tailor, to cut his hose two inches shorter. The wife required the boy of the house to carry them to the next tailor to cut. The boy chanced (or rather God so provided) to go to the next tailor, which was Benjamin that made them, which also was a constable, and acquainted with the lord chancellor's commandment. The boy required him to cut the hose. He said, I am not thy master's tailor. Saith the boy, Because you are our next neighbour, and my master's tailor dwelleth far off, I came to you, for it is far night, and he must occupy them timely in the morning. Benjamin took the hose and looked upon them: he knew his handy work, and said, These are not thy master's hose, but Doctor Sandys': them I made in the Tower. The boy yielded and said, it was so. Saith he, Go to thy mistress, pray her to sit up till twelve of the clock; then I will bring the hose, and speak with Doctor Sandys to his good.

"At midnight the goodwife of the house and Benjamin the tailor cometh into Doctor Sandys' chamber: the wife prayeth him not to be afraid of their coming. He answered, Nothing can be amiss: what God will, that shall be done. Then Benjamin telleth him that he made his hose, and by what good chance they now came to his hands. God used the means that he might admonish him of his peril, and advise him how to escape it; telling him that all the constables of London, whereof he was one, watched for him, and some were so greedily set, that they prayed him, if he took him, to let them have the carriage of him to the bishop of Winchester, and he should have the five pound. Saith Benjamin, It is known that your man hath provided two geldings, and that you mind to ride out at Aldgate to-morrow, and there then you are sure to be taken. Follow mine advice; and by God's grace ye shall escape their hands. Let your man walk all the day to-morrow in the street where your horses stand, booted and ready to ride. The goodman's servant of the house shall take the horses and carry them to Bethnal-green. The goodman shall be booted, and follow after as if he would ride. I will be here with you to-morrow about eight of the clock: it is both term and parliament time: here we will break our fast, and, when the street is full, we will go forth. Look wildly, and if you meet your brother in the street, shun him not, but outface him and know him not. Accordingly Doctor Sandys did, clothed like a gentleman in all respects, and looked wildly as one that had been long kept in prison out of the light. Benjamin carried him through Birchin-lane, and from one lane to another, till he came at Moorgate. There they went forth until they came to Bethnal-green, where the horses were ready, and Master Hurlestone, to ride with him as his man. Doctor Sandys pulled on his boots, and, taking leave of his friend Benjamin, with tears they kissed each other; he put his hand in his purse, and would have given Benjamin a great part of that little he had, but Benjamin would take none. Yet since, Doctor Sandys hath remembered him thankfully. He rode that night to his father-in-law, Master Sandys, where his wife was: he had not been there two hours but it was told Master Sandys, that there was two of the guard which would that night apprehend Doctor Sandys, and so they were appointed.

"That night Doctor Sandys was guided to an honest farmer near the sea, where he tarried two days and two nights in a chamber without all company. After that he shifted to one James Mower a shipmaster, who dwelt at Milton shore, where he expected wind for the English fleet ready into Flanders. While he was there, James Mower brought to him forty or fifty mariners, to whom he gave an exhortation: they liked him so well, that they promised to die for it, or that he should be apprehended.

"The sixth of May, being Sunday, the wind served. He took his leave of his host and hostess, and went towards the ship. In taking his leave of his hostess, who was barren, and had been married eight years, he gave her a fine handkerchief and an old royal of gold in it, thanking her much, and said, Be of good comfort; ere that an whole year be past, God shall give you a child, a boy. And it came to pass, for that day twelvemonth lacking one day God gave her a fair son.

"At the shore Doctor Sandys met with Master Isaac of Kent, who had his eldest son there; who, upon the liking he had to Doctor Sandys, sent his son with him, who afterward died in his father's house in Frankfort. Doctor Sandys and Doctor Cox were both in one ship, being one Cockrel's ship. They were within the kenning, when two of the guard came thither to apprehend Doctor Sandys. They arrived at Antwerp, being bid to dinner to Master Locke. And at dinner time one George Gilpin, being secretary to the English house, and kinsman to Doctor Sandys, came to him and rounded him in his ear, and said, King Philip hath sent to make search for you, and to apprehend you. Hereupon they rose from their dinner in a marvellous great shower, and went out at the gate toward the land of Cleve. They found a waggon and hasted away, and came safe to Ausburg in Cleveland, where Doctor Sandys tarried fourteen days, and then journeyed towards Strausborough, where, after he had lived one year, his wife came unto him. He fell sore sick of a flux, which kept him nine months, and brought him to death's door. He had a child which fell sick of the plague and died. His wife at length fell sick of a consumption, and died in his arms: no man had a more godly woman to his wife.

"After this, Master Sampson went away to Emmanuel, a man skilful in Hebrew. Master Grindall went into the country to learn the Dutch tongue. Doctor Sandys still remained in Strausborough, whose sustentation then was chiefly from one Master Isaac, who loved him most dearly, and was ever more ready to give than he to take. He gave him in that space above one hundred marks, which sum the said Doctor Sandys paid him again, and by his other gifts and friendliness shewed himself to be a thankful man. When his wife was dead, he went to Zurich, and there was in Peter Martyr's house for the space of five weeks. Being there, as they sat at dinner, word suddenly came that queen Mary was dead, and Doctor Sandys was sent for by his friends at Strausborough. That news made Master Martyr and Master Jarret, then there, very joyful, but Doctor Sandys could not rejoice: it smote into his heart that he should be called to misery.

" Master Bullinger and the ministers feasted him, and he took his leave and returned to Strausborough, where he preached; and so Master Grindall and he came towards England, and came to London the same day that queen Elizabeth was crowned."

When Sandys returned to England, he was graciously received by the queen, and was soon employed in the various matters which regarded the reformation of religion. He was one of the divines in commission for reviewing the Common Prayer, who met at Sir Thomas Smith's in Westminster. His name is also found in some lists of those who, selected from the Romish and reformed parties, were to hold a solemn disputation before the privy council; but it appears that he was not one of the disputants, though it is very probable he was present as an auditor. And when visitors were sent throughout the country, he was one of those appointed to travel through and preach in the northern counties.

Sandys was of course marked out for preferment; and indeed he stood in absolute need of something for his maintenance, for he declares in a letter to Parker[1], "in the time of our exile were we not so bare as we are now brought." Yet he had some scruples to overcome before he consented to occupy the place intended for him. He, with some others, had an objection to the use of the vestments that had been customary in the Romish church, and he urged the abrogation as much as possible of ceremonies. Being unsuccessful in his endeavours, he consulted with those of his friends who were in a like position with himself as to what was their proper course of conduct. After full deliberation, they concluded that it would be unbecoming and injurious for them to desert their ministry on account of rites, which were but few and not abstractedly evil, especially as purity of doctrine was obtained. They felt that, if they retired, it would perhaps open the door to concealed papists; and therefore they determined that they would agree to the order established; and this determination nothing afterwards occurred to shake. Worcester was the see designed for Sandys, and to this he was consecrated at Lambeth, Dec. 21, 1559, by Parker, archbishop of Canterbury, Barlow, Scory, and Hodgkin as-

---

[1] Burnet, Hist. of Ref. Records, Vol. II. Book III. No. XXII.

sisting. There were also consecrated the same day, Grindall as bishop of London, Cox of Ely, and Merick of Bangor. Nowell, Grindall's chaplain, preached the consecration sermon from Acts xx. 28. The oath of allegiance and homage was soon after taken by Sandys, on the same day as by Parker and several other bishops.

Shortly after his consecration he visited his diocese by commission for the archbishop. In the course of this visitation a circumstance occurred, which probably gave occasion to much future discomfort to the bishop. When he came to the parish where Sir John Bourne lived, a presentment was made of an altar-stone standing in the church. This Sandys ordered to be pulled down and defaced. But Bourne, who was a Romanist, and had borne the office of principal secretary of state under queen Mary, resisted the order and had the altar carried to his own house. The bishop very soon visited his diocese a second time as ordinary, and deprived two persons. By this proceeding he gave offence to the archbishop of Canterbury, who censured him for visiting again after so short an interval, and conceived that he had acted with too great rigour. Sandys vindicated himself in a letter, which, (dated Oct. 24, 1560,) has been preserved[1]. It would seem that the bishop of Worcester's reply was satisfactory to the archbishop, as the friendship between these eminent persons was terminated only by Parker's death.

In 1563, the dispute between bishop Sandys and Sir John Bourne was heard before the privy council. Bourne had, it appears, taken every opportunity of insulting the bishop and deriding his wife; for he was now married a second time to Cecilia, daughter of Sir Thomas Wilford; and a tumult had once arisen between the retainers of both parties, in which several persons were wounded. Bourne preferred a series of accusations against the bishop

[1] Strype's Life of Parker, Appendix, No. XIII.

to which Sandys replied; and after much discussion Sir John having been committed to the Marshalsea was compelled to make his submission to the bishop. It was made however with little sincerity, for we find up to the last year of his continuance in the see of Worcester, that the prelate had reason to complain of his enmity[1].

Sandys was one of those employed upon the Bishops' Bible. The books allotted to him were 1 and 2 Kings and 1 and 2 Chronicles. He applied himself diligently to these, and sent them completed to the archbishop, as appears by his letter that accompanied them, Feb. 6, 1565.

In 1570 the see of London was vacant by the promotion of Grindall to that of York. The bishop of Worcester was selected, chiefly through secretary Cecil, as a proper person to be Grindall's successor. The grounds for his appointment were, that he was known to be a man of spirit and determination, and a warm promoter of the queen's ecclesiastical commands; that he had been a bishop many years, and had therefore full experience of the episcopal office; and that, having formerly resided much in London, he was well known to and beloved by the citizens. But on the proposal being made him he shrunk from it, alleging his insufficiency, both as respected mind and body, for such a place. He was however told that the queen had in special favour fixed upon him, and misliked to alter her determination, and that the people were grieved at his unwillingness. He felt it therefore now his duty to comply.

Shortly after his translation he visited his new diocese and issued injunctions:

1. To keep strictly the book of common prayer.
2. No man to preach without a licence.

[1] Large particulars of the dispute with Sir John Bourne may be seen in Strype's Annals, Vol. I. Chap. 35.

3. To observe the appointed apparel; that is, to wear the square cap, the scholar's gown, &c.; and in all divine service to wear the surplice.

4. None to receive strangers, that is, any of other parishes, to their communion.

5. All clerks' tolerations to be called in[1].

6. That parish clerks intrude not into the priests' duty, as before they had sometimes done.

In 1571 Sandys was present at the convocation, and signed the book of canons then made. We also find him afterwards taking a part in the ecclesiastical commission, and administering his episcopal authority with characteristic vigour. He claimed the superintendence of the Dutch church in London. He suppressed (in 1572) the mass celebrated at the Portuguese ambassador's in Tower Street, which was a favourite resort of the Romanists. He was equally desirous of restraining those who contravened the established order of the church. In a letter written Aug. 5, 1573[2], to lord treasurer Burghley and the earl of Leicester, he complains of the seditious preachers at St Paul's cross, to whom the people flocked, as in the time of popery they had run on pilgrimage. Field, Wilcox, and Cartwright he names as their leaders, and speaks of the great favour shewn especially to Cartwright by the city. As he found himself too weak to check their proceedings, he prays the lords to interfere and to enjoin the French ministers, who it seems had put in, not to meddle

---

[1] To explain this article it must be understood that private preaching and administration of the sacraments had been held in houses after a different form than that appointed in the Liturgy, which, and the government, were in these assemblies condemned. Some persons were imprisoned for this. But bishop Grindall had by permission and order of the privy council, after about a year's restraint, granted them their liberty and some toleration to their practices on a promise of peaceable behaviour. The promise however had not been kept, and hence the indulgence was withdrawn.

[2] Strype's Life of Whitgift, Appendix, No. xvi.

in such matters, and also to write a letter to the city against shewing countenance to these men.

About the same time the bishop was brought into a more personal collision with Deering. This individual had been suspended by the privy council from his lectureship in St Paul's: but on the recommendation of Sandys, for which he was afterwards rebuked by the queen, he was restored without consulting the ecclesiastical commissioners. His party thereupon triumphed; and Deering himself relying on his popularity held out a kind of threat to the bishop against his interference. The prelate was not a man to be daunted: he replied with spirit; and ere long Deering was on the bishop's complaint a second time silenced.

To end such divisions Sandys conceived the best course would be to summon a national synod. "I humbly pray your lordship," he wrote to the treasurer, "to be a means unto her majesty that a national council may be called, wherein these matters now in question may be thoroughly debated, and that concluded, and by her majesty confirmed, which may most tend to the true serving of God and the good ordering of this church of England. If your lordship travail herein, you shall travail in God's cause, and for the quiet of his church; and the sooner the better. For it is time to cut off these troubles. I have earnestly moved the archbishop of Canterbury in this matter."

Archbishop Parker died May 17, 1575, and Sandys was the principal mourner at his funeral. He received by the deceased prelate's will a walking-staff as a token of friendly remembrance. The vacancy thus made in the primacy prepared the way for the bishop of London's advancement to a higher post. For Grindall, archbishop of York, was selected to succeed Parker; and Sandys, who had followed Grindall to London, was also his successor in the see of York. He was translated thither March 8, 1576. His farewell sermon to his charge in London is the 22nd in the present volume.

It may be doubted whether the change was advantageous to either prelate. At Canterbury Grindall found little else but sorrow; and Sandys was vexed during almost the whole remainder of his life with perpetual contention. Before he was fully installed in the see, an attempt was made to alienate Bishopthorp from it. This was urged indeed merely as a temporary measure, in order that the lord president of the north might occupy it; but Sandys perceived that if this house once fell into other hands, there would be little probability of its ever being restored: he therefore stoutly resisted the proposal[1] on the grounds, that Bishopthorp was absolutely necessary to the archbishop as a residence near York, and that if he yielded to the alienation he should appear to have consented to a spoliation of the see. But this was not his only trouble. He had a disagreement with Grindall about dilapidations; which being referred to the lord treasurer was, as it should seem, at length peaceably settled by him. And, to put these matters all together, he disputed with the same prelate two or three years afterwards about the possession of the lease of a house at Battersea, intended for the convenience of the archbishops of York when they came to London. Grindall's full reply may be found in Strype[2]. But these were not the worst contentions. His successor, Aylmer, in the see of London demanded of him the income of the see from the Michaelmas preceding up to Lady-day, which Sandys refused, alleging that, if he yielded up the revenues as far back as the Purification, it was as much as he had expected, or as in reason could be required. Aylmer appealed to the lord treasurer; and Sandys, provoked at his

---

[1] His reasons at length dated Jan. 28, 1576, are given by Strype, Annals, Vol. II. Book II. Chap. 2.

[2] Life of Grindall, Book II. Chap. 10.

pertinacity, reflected upon him in severe terms, especially as he had, he said, himself been instrumental in furthering his preferment. It is not known how eventually this affair was settled. In 1579 he had another dispute with the same bishop about dilapidations. Aylmer would not, as had been agreed by the two archbishops, refer the dispute to the lord treasurer, but insisted on a commission. When at length, (for the controversy lasted some years;) a sentence was given, it seems to have been not so favourable to the archbishop as he had anticipated, and to have called forth from him a statement of reasons why it should be modified.

In his ecclesiastical proceedings also Sandys met with opposition. In 1577 he visited Durham (the see being vacant); but the dean, W. Whittingham, who had been ordained by the English exiles at Geneva, refused his visitation. A contest ensued; and the archbishop, who was thought in some measure wrong by the lord treasurer, proceeded to excommunication. The proceedings were protracted through several years: two commissions of inquiry and visitation were at different times granted; but before the whole was brought to a conclusion, the dean of Durham died. It added to Sandys' disquietude that his own dean, Hutton, took part with Whittingham, and also protested against the archbishop's right to visit the chapter of York cathedral.

Proceeding on his metropolitan visitation, the archbishop gave in 1578 an account to the lord treasurer of some of his proceedings. He had found, he said, two sorts of precisians; some who objected to the public service as then established, while others maintained the continued obligation of the Mosaic law. He added that "the people were very ignorant, and yet willing and of capacity to learn. Whereupon he set the preachers on work, to preach at every market and great town every second Sunday. And that he took his part and did as much as the rest. And that besides, for the increase of learning in the ministry, he gave order that every archdeacon should keep four synods in the year. And the ministers there assembled (some principal points of religion having been before propounded to them) all should be prepared to speak, but such only should speak as should be called thereunto by some grave persons appointed moderators; and that they should speak to the matter and not *vagari* [i. e. stray from it.] And this to be done among the ministers themselves." Sandys was thus, it would seem, not unfavourable to what were called the prophesyings, provided they were kept within due limits. He had already given evidence of this by having, while bishop of London, in 1574, signed an order in council in recommendation of them in the diocese of Norwich.

The archbishop was, it appears, found fault with in the visitation just referred to. He was accused of being too lordly, of being solicitous to get money; but the great cause of offence he gave was, his questioning the canonical ordination of Whittingham. It may here be mentioned to his honour, that he never, though once urgently applied to by his friend lord treasurer Burghley, would grant an advowson before it fell void. He was anxious, he said, to prefer men of merit, and he did not choose to give to others that which more reasonably should be the reward of those trained under his immediate eye. Neither would he ever take a resignation. In his archiepiscopal see he was as zealous against popery, as he has already been shewn to be while bishop of London.

In May 1581 a diabolical plot was hatched against him, which would, had it not been detected, have for ever stained his moral character, and driven him in disgrace from society. It was contrived by Sir Robert Stapleton, who had conceived a grudge against the archbishop, and was stimulated with the hope of appropriating some of the property of the see. At Doncaster, while on a visitation, the inn-keeper's wife introduced herself at night into the archbishop's chamber, where her husband pretending to discover her threatened the prelate with his dagger. Stapleton, who was at hand, affected to interpose, expressed his concern for the honour of the church, and charged all present to secresy. Sandys, wakened with the tumult, and dreading lest, as appearances were against him, he might not be able to establish his innocence, consented to give money to the inn-keeper and to yield to Stapleton's demands. But as these grew with every concession, till at last he required even the manor of Southwell, the archbishop, no longer able to bear the thraldom he suffered, revealed the matter to the lord treasurer, and entreated his help in vindicating himself. The queen and the earl of Leicester interested themselves for him: the conspirators were examined before the star chamber, and obliged to confess their guilt. They were hereupon compelled, besides other punishments, to acknowledge the archbishop's innocence at the assizes at York. But as this submission, particularly on the part of Sir Robert, was made with little appearance of contrition, the prelate for his own justification rightly insisted on further satisfaction. And it was not till after a long confinement in the Tower and the Fleet, that in 1584 Stapleton shewed himself really penitent for his crime. This the archbishop called, with justice, the great trouble of his life[1].

In 1583, the see of Canterbury was vacant by Grindall's death; but Sandys was not called on again to succeed him, both on account of his warmth of temper, and also because the queen did not like the primate to be a married man.

In 1584, Sandys had the honour of recommending

[1] For full particulars see Strype's Annals, Vol. III. Book I. Chap. 9, and Appendix Nos. xx. xxi.

Hooker, whom he had previously appointed tutor to his son Edwin, to the mastership of the Temple. In the same year we find him actively exerting himself in parliament, on the presentation of a petition of sixteen articles by the Commons to the Lords, reflecting on the present government of the church and on the bishops. Some of these articles he deemed reasonable; but to others he strongly objected. He promised that non-residence should be checked, and candidates for the ministry diligently examined; but wholly disallowed the demands, that at every ordination there should be six ministers to lay hands on those ordained; that none should be preferred without requiring the approval of the parish, which he thought likely to breed controversies; that oaths and subscriptions should not be imposed; and that such as had been suspended should be restored, except on submission. He approved however, he said, and he added that he spoke in the name of many of his brethren, of the exercises or prophesyings, provided they were conducted under due order[1].

It was about this time that archbishop Sandys founded and endowed the grammar school at Hawkshead in Lancashire, the letters patent for the establishment of which are dated April 10, 1585. He drew up a code of statutes for this school, which have been printed in Abingdon's Antiquities of the cathedral church of Worcester. It may be added, that he was a benefactor to the school of Highgate, Middlesex.

In 1585, the archbishop was involved in fresh troubles. He wrote to the lord treasurer against usury, which was at an excessive rate at York; but his dean opposed him in his endeavours to redress the grievance. Articles were exhibited against the dean; and mutual recriminations ensued, the dean charging the archbishop with providing for his family out of the revenues of the see, which

[1] Strype, Life of Whitgift, Book III. Chap. 10.

Sandys strenuously denied, declaring that he had but granted leases to his sons, which he must have granted to some, and that he was justified in giving to his own children rather than to strangers. In the end the dean was compelled to make a submission.

Attempts were afterwards, in 1587, made to alienate Southwell from the see of York. The earl of Leicester, it would seem, wanted it, and the queen was persuaded to favour the plan. The proposal was, that the archbishop should lease it out for 70 years; but he could not be prevailed on to consent. After this he was engaged in a controversy with the new dean, Matthew, of Durham; and in 1588 he was urged to give up his episcopal house in London. He refused; but so many troubles preyed deeply on his mind, and this last is supposed to have hastened his death. He died July 10 in that year, and was buried in the collegiate church of Southwell.

Archbishop Sandys' family consisted of six sons and two daughters. His widow survived till 1610.

His epitaph is as follows:

"Edwinus Sandes sacræ theologiæ doctor, postquam Wigorniensem episcopatum xi annos totidemque tribus demptis Londinensem gessisset; Eboracensis sui archiepiscopatus anno xii°, vitæ autem lxix°, obiit Julii x°, anno Dom. 1588. [Round edge of monument.]

"Cujus hic conditum cadaver jacet, genere non humilis, [At the head.] vixit dignitate locoque magnus; exemplo major; duplici functus episcopatu, archiepiscopali tandem amplitudine etiam illustris; honores hosce mercatus grandi pretio, meritis virtutibusque. Homo hominum a malitia et vindicta innocentissimus, magnanimus, apertus, et tantum nescius adulari; summè liberalis atque misericors, hospitalissimus, optimus, facilis, et in sola vitia superbus: scilicet haud minora quàm locutus est, vixit; et fuit in evangelii prædicandi laboribus ad extremum usque halitum mirabiliter assiduus. A sermonibus ejus nunquam non melior discederes. Facundus volebat esse, et videbatur. Ignavos, sedulitatis suæ conscius, oderat. Bonas literas auxit pro facultatibus. Ecclesiæ patrimonium, velut rem Deo consecratam decuit, intactum defendit. Gratia, quâ floruit apud illustrissimam mortalium Elizabetham, effecit, ne hanc, in qua jaces, ecclesiam tu jacentem cerneres, venerande præsul. Utriusque memorandum fortunæ exemplar, qui tanta cum gesseris, multo his majora animo ad omnia semper impavido perpessus es; carceres, exilia, amplissimarum facultatum amissiones, quodque omnium difficillimè innocens perferre animus consuevit, immanes calumnias; et hac re una votis tuis minor, quod Christo testimonium etiam sanguine non præbueris. Attamen qui in prosperis tantos fluctus, et post agonum tot adversa, tandem quietis sempiternæ portum, fessus mundi, Deique sitiens reperisti, æternum lætare; vice sanguinis sunt sudores tui. Abi lector, nec ista scias tantum ut sciveris, sed ut imitere.

At the feet under the arms.

Verbum Domini manet in æternum[1]."

[1] Edwin Sandes, doctor of sacred theology, after he had held the bishopric of Worcester eleven years, and that of London three years less, died July 10, 1588, in the twelfth year of his incumbency of the see of York and the sixty-ninth of his life.

He whose body lies buried here was of a family not mean, of a rank and station great, in the example he set still greater, having filled two bishoprics, and been at last distinguished with the archiepiscopal dignity, obtaining these honours at a high price, namely, his merits and virtues. He was of all men most free from malice and revenge, magnanimous, open, and ignorant only how to flatter; very liberal and compassionate, most hospitable, virtuous, affable, and proud to vices alone: his life was in no degree inferior to his teaching; and he was wonderfully assiduous in the labour of preaching the gospel, even to his last breath. You could not but depart improved from his sermons. He desired to be eloquent, and so he was seen to be. Conscious of his own industry he disliked the slothful. He encouraged literature according to his means. The patrimony of the church, as that which is dedicated to God ought to be, he preserved untouched. It was the influence enjoyed with the most illustrious Elizabeth which preserved you, venerable prelate, from seeing this church in which you now lie itself lying prostrate. You were a memorable example of every kind of fortune, who did so much,

The following notice of Sandys may be added: it is taken from Dr Whitaker's life of this prelate.

From a MS. Catalogue of Bishops who have belonged to the Society of St John's College, Cambridge.

"EDWINUS SANDYS, natus in Furness Fells, in Com. Lanc. ex familia antiqua in agro Cumbr. apud villam St Begæ, Grindallo archiepiscopo natalem, eique ex vicinia notus, et ex morum ac studiorum cognatione amicus, per cætera fere gemelli; uterque enim incepit in artibus eodem anno 1540,—ac in theologia an. 1549.—Uterque procurator Academiæ, Collegiorum quoque præfecti uterque; uterque episcopus eodem anno et postea ejusdem sedis archiepiscopus.

"Vixit noster in Collegio Io. pensionarius per septennium aut eo amplius.—Inter socios aulæ Catherinæ non occurrit: admissus ibi præfectus circa annum 1547.—Canonicus Eccl. Cath. Petriburg. ad præsentationem Regiæ Majest. Decem. 23. an. 1549, ejectus inde—Canonicus Carleolensis ad præsent. Reg. Maj. Sept. an. 1552. Procan. an. 1553.

"Sub eodem tempore duce Northumbr. adveniente et procancellario jussu ducis concionante de re dubia et ancipite, incurrit in offensam reginæ ac compingitur in turrem Lond.; ubi diu detentus tandem amicorum ope et

and suffered yet more, with a mind always fearless against all things, prisons, exile, the loss of ample possessions, and what the innocent mind can least of all endure, atrocious slanders, and in this thing alone did you fail in your desires, that you did not seal your testimony for Christ with your blood. But, as at length after so many fluctuations in prosperity, and so many contests of adversity, weary of the world and thirsting for God, you have found the haven of everlasting rest, rejoice eternally: your labours are instead of your blood. Go, reader, think it not enough to know these things, but imitate.

The word of the Lord abideth for ever.

reginæ gratia evasit ac fugit in Germaniam.—Reversus inde an. 1559, designatus Episcopus Vigorn. Sacratus Dec. 21. ejusdem anni, ac Grindallo translato, primo a sede Lond. deinde a sede Eborac. ei utrobique successit, tam Londini quam Eboraci: ob. Julii 10. 1588. Southwelliæ tumulatus cum splendido epitaphio[1]."

It only remains to notice the archbishop's works. These, as enumerated by Tanner, whose list is given in the note[2], are

[1] Edwin Sandys, born in Furness Fells, in the county of Lancaster, of an ancient family in Cumberland, near St Bees, the birthplace of archbishop Grindall, was known to him by neighbourhood and attached to him by similarity of manners and pursuits: in other things they were almost twins: for each incepted in arts in the same year, 1540, and in divinity in 1549. Each was proctor of the university, each a master of a college, each a bishop in the same year, and afterwards archbishop of the same see.

Vice-chancellor in the year 1553. Our Sandys lived in St John's as a pensioner for seven years or more. He is not found among the fellows of Catherine Hall; but was made master there about the year 1547. He was canon of the cathedral church of Peterborough, on the presentation of the king's majesty, Dec. 23, 1549, ejected thence,—canon of Carlisle on the presentation of the king's majesty, Sept. 1552.

At the time when the duke of Northumberland came, the vice-chancellor, having by the duke's command preached on a matter doubtful and uncertain, incurred the queen's anger and was thrown into the Tower of London: where having been long detained, he at length, by the help of friends and the favour of the queen, was liberated, and fled into Germany. Returning thence in 1559 he was appointed bishop of Worcester. He was consecrated Dec. 21, of the same year, and on Grindall's translation first from the see of London, then from that of York, he succeeded him in each, both at London and at York. He died July 10, 1588, and was buried at Southwell, with a splendid epitaph.

[2] Sandys [Edwinus] filius Gulielmi, patria Lancastrensis (Cumbriensis natus apud S. Begæ fanum, Strype in *Vita Grindal* 2.) apud Conisby natus ex antiquo et generoso stemmate. Fuit collegii S. Johannis academiæ Cantabrig. alumnus, ubi procurator A. MDXLII. dein S. th. doctor A. MDXLIX. Aulæ S. Catharinæ magister et vice-cancellarius A. MDLII. et renunciabatur. Regnante Maria in turrim Londinensem detruditur; et tandem inde liberatus in Germaniam trajecit, ubi exul Argentorati et Tiguri degit, quoad vixit Maria. In patriam

* I. Sermons.
II. Vindication of himself against Sir John Bourne.
* III. Advice concerning Rites and Ceremonies in the Synod of 1562.
* IV. Orders for the Bishops and Clergy.
* V. Pastoral Epistle to the Bishop of Chester.
VI. A share in the Bishops' Bible.
* VII. Advertisement to the Translation of Luther on the Galatians.
VIII. Various Letters.

Those marked * will be found in the present volume. There have also been added the preamble to his will, and the prayers he composed for his school at Hawkshead. Some letters of Sandys, together with those of other eminent men to foreign reformers, will appear in a volume now preparing for the press by the Parker Society, from

rediens ab Elizabetha A. MDLIX episcopus Wigorniensis, anno MDLXX Londinensis, et A. MDLXXVI archiepiscopus Eboracensis constitutus est. Scripsit Anglice, *Sermons on several occasions*, num. XXII. Pr. præf. "Of other things besides." Pr. concionis i. "Our evangelical prophet Esaias." Lond. MDLXXXV. 4to. quæ sæpius impressæ extant. Lond. MDCXVI. 4to. *Long Vindication of himself against Sir John Bourne*, MDLXIII. Strype, *Elizab.* p. 348. *His advice concerning rites and ceremonies in the Synod* MDLXII. Ibid. p. 297. *Orders for the Bishops and Clergy*, Ibid. p. 300. *Epistolas varias ad M. Parkerum*, Strype in *Vita Parker, App.* **n**. 13. Burnet. *Hist. Reform.* Tom. II. Append. p. 332, MS. Coll. Corp. Chr. Cantabr. Miscell. I. 455, vid. Strype in *Vita Grindal*, p. 299. *Epistolam Parkhursto episc. Norwicensi*, Strype in *Vita Parker*, p. 333. *Epistolam Bernardo Gilpin de episcopatu Carliol.* Fuller. *Ch. Hist.* XVI. 63. *Epistolam pastoralem episcopo Cestrensem*, Latine. MDLXXXIII. 13 Febr. Pr. "Intuenti mihi." MS. Caio Gonvil. Cantabr. D. 37, p. 471. In *Bibliis sacris* in sermonem Anglicum convertendis suas egit partes MDLX. Ideo ante primum librum *Regum* et post secundum librum *Chronicorum* in *Bibliis* episcopalibus (*the Bishops' Bible*) dantur literæ E. W. pro Edwinus Wigorn. qui libros hos proculdubio in Anglicum sermonem transtulit. *Epistolam præf. translationi M. Lutheri super Galatas.* Lond. MDLXXVII. 4to. Obiit. A. MDLXXXVIII. Augusti 8, [Jul. 10, A Wood MS. C. 38. Et *Reg.* Ebor.] et in ecclesia collegiata Southwelliæ humatus jacet. Blofeild. Godwin. MS. Wood. H. Holland. *Heroolog.* p. 207. Fox. 2086. Hollinsh. 545.

the originals preserved at Zurich; and, if it be thought desirable to print any more of his letters, they will be comprised in a volume, hereafter to be compiled, of Letters of the Reformers.

It may be proper to state that the Sermons are printed from the first edition of 1585, with the necessary correction of typographical errors. The quotations from the fathers have been given at length, with a very few unimportant exceptions, in which the editor, though enjoying the assistance of friends, has been unable to trace out the passage intended. Additional references have been included within brackets.

SERMONS

OF

ARCHBISHOP SANDYS.

SERMONS

Made by the most reue-

rende Father in God, Edwin, Arch-

bishop of Yorke, Primate of England

and Metropolitane.

DAN. 12. 3.

They that be wise shall shine as the brightnesse of the firmament: and they that turne many to righteousnesse, as the starres for euer and euer.

AT LONDON,
Printed by Henrie Midleton,
for Thomas Charde
1585.

TO THE CHRISTIAN READERS,

GRACE AND PEACE THROUGH JESU CHRIST OUR LORD.

"Of other things besides these, my son, take thou heed: for there is none end of making many books, and much reading is a weariness of the flesh. Let us hear the end of all: fear God and keep his commandments; for this is the whole duty of every man." By which words of weight, proceeding from the oracle, not of Apollo, but of God himself, what effect hath been wrought, both in the hearts and in the hands of many great learned clerks, both here and elsewhere, both heretofore and at this day, to make them withdraw their minds from writing, and to withhold their pens from paper, some witnesses worthy credit could testify, but that daily experience needeth no farther proof. Howbeit, when it is well known, and ought accordingly to be considered, that the place alleged should rather correct the bookish humour of common writers and idle discoursers, than controul the writing of necessary and needful works, which, to the singular advancement of kingdoms and commonweals, to the most excellent service of Almighty God, to the inestimable benefit and blessing of his church, many hundred years sithens that saying of Solomon, have been printed and published notwithstanding; (as by large volumes innumerable, of scriptures and fathers, of histories and arts in all kinds of knowledge, may evidently appear;) every man of ability should rather by those examples encourage himself, than suffer himself by these words to be dissuaded, to employ the talent, as well of his hand as of his tongue, to meet with and overtake all

[Eccles. xii. [12, 13.]

[SANDYS.]

practices and inconveniences, and as it were to apply a salve to every sore, to minister a medicine to every malady that may occur. Again, when we perceive Sanballat, Tobiah, Geshem, Noadiah the prophetess, and their accomplices, continually to hinder and impeach, as much as in them lieth, the work of God's temple; that is papists, Jesuits, and malcontents, with their adherents, all adversaries and enemies to the everlasting truth of the gospel, without intermission to abuse their great leisure and small learning, to plant error and heresy in the hearts of our brethren, thereby to supplant all religious worship of Almighty God, all audience of his word and reverence to his sacraments, all humble obedience to lawful magistrates, all dutiful regard of wholesome laws, all careful observation of ancient discipline, all sincere and seemly conversation of christian life and honest manners; how can the Holy Ghost (who reproveth the world of sin) but require us to bestow all the forces and habiliments we have, not only, as good Zacharias and Aggeus[1], to prophesy, but, as godly Zorobabel and Salathiel, to re-edify, that is, as well by writing as by preaching, as well by our books as by our sermons, and as it were with a trowel in the one hand and a sword in the other to raise and erect the new Jerusalem, supplying the decays, repairing the ruins, filling up the breaches, building up the walls and towers of Sion in perfect beauty? The consideration whereof, together with some other earnest and vehement persuasions to the like effect used, did at the last, though long first, induce the most reverend author of this book, even another Esdras or Nehemias, to suffer these his labours to come to light: as well for that he mought leave behind him a witness and warrant of his godly and zealous affection, that the profession of his faith mought become the sweet savour of life to life in all, rather than the savour of death to death in any; as also for

[[1] Aggeus—Haggai.—ED.]

that words spoken are soon come soon gone, but written withal may make a deeper impression, and so, by striking as well the eye of the reader as the ear of the hearer, may pierce his heart the better and save his soul the sooner.

Of the book itself I will say but this; that, for mine own part, I am verily persuaded, there is no work written in this kind wherein men of principal estate, or particular callings, may be either more sufficiently informed to know, or more plainly directed to perform, their several duties: the superior how to govern, the inferior how to obey; the minister what to teach, the people what to learn; the parliament what to establish, the realm what to embrace; her majesty and council what to hear, court, city, and country what to amend: why patrons especially professing godliness should be uncorrupt; why pastors undergoing such a charge should keep the flock from the fox and wolf; why bishops should be more vigilant and precise not to admit ministers hand over head; why the rich should be open-handed, and poor Christ in his needy members competently relieved: how the church to be deciphered by her proper marks, of the word to be heard with diligence, and the sacraments with reverence to be frequented: how the temple to be purged of idolatry, superstition, and superfluity; the churchmen of ignorance, negligence, and simony; the commonweal of unmercifulness, covetousness, and usury; the judgment-seats, both civil and ecclesiastical, of bribery, extortion, and partiality: why the gospel to be preached with favour, the law with terror, yet both with a caveat: how God to be worshipped, our neighbours entreated, our children and families catechised, ourselves conformed to Christ his image, the simple advised, the subtil prevented, the weak supported, the obstinate corrected: what patience to be used under the cross, what thankfulness to be shewed for God's great mercies, what prayers in our extremest necessities to be poured out: what sorrow must throw down the sinful man, what faith raise him up, what hope sustain him, what charity inflame him, what worthy fruits commend him to the world : finally, how the truth may be confirmed, falsehood refelled, vice reproved, virtue advanced, and so the child of God made a man wise unto salvation, and perfectly enabled unto every good work: besides many other most profitable observations, sooner taught than learned, yet sooner learned than followed, such and so many, as in so few sermons you shall hardly find, I believe, but in the same. Nor is this my single opinion only, but many men's censure of greater learning and better judgment; who know what belongs to matter and method, to times and persons, to place and occasions, with other due circumstances of well and wise meaning, speaking, and writing. But, as those sermons be best praised ever that be ever best practised; so, if these shall be received into the good ground of your hearts, with the same affection and spirit they were preached first and now be published, no doubt but the sower, the seed, the soil, the increase and all, will be found to the glory of his grace that worketh all in all. Wherefore, as not only Paul, Apollos, and Cephas, but all are ours, and we are Christ's, and Christ is God's; so let us comfort and strengthen one another in our holy faith, holding nothing more dear unto us than the salvation each of others: and in God's holy fear commend we one another to that faithful Creator, who is Father of all, above us all, and through us all, and in us all. To him be rendered all thanks, and all honour given for ever and for ever.

THE

ORDER AND MATTER OF THE SERMONS.

SERMON
I. Ho, every one that thirsteth, come to the waters; &c.
Esay LV. 1.

II. Be this sin against the Lord far from me, that I should cease to pray, &c. 1 Sam. xii. 23.

III. Take us the little foxes which destroy the vines: for our vine hath flourished. Cant. ii. 15.

IV. I exhort therefore before all things that requests, supplications, &c. 1 Tim. ii. 1.

V. Be like-minded, having the same love, being of one accord, &c.
Phil. ii. 2.

VI. Teach me thy way, O Lord, and I will walk in thy truth.
Psal. LXXXVI. 11.

VII. Draw near to God, and he will draw near to you.
Jac. iv. 8.

VIII. Seek the Lord while he may be found, call upon him while he is near. Esay LV. 6.

IX. All the days of this my warfare do I wait, till my changing come. Job xiv. 14.

X. That being delivered out of the hands of our enemies we may serve him, &c. Luke i. 74.

XI. Owe nothing to any man, but this, to love one another: for he that loveth, &c. Rom. xiii. 8.

XII. He hath shewed thee, O man, what is good; and what the Lord requireth of thee, &c. Mic. vi. 8.

XIII. And Jesus went into the temple of God, and cast out all them that sold and bought, &c. Matt. xxi. 12.

XIV. Then Peter opened his mouth and said, Of a truth I perceive that God, &c. Acts x. 34.

XV. We therefore as helpers beseech you that ye receive not the grace of God in vain, &c. 2 Cor. vi. 2.

SERMON
XVI. Marriage is honourable in all. Heb. xiii. 4.
XVII. After these things Jesus went his way over the sea of Galilee, &c. Joh. vi. 1.
XVIII. Then there shall be signs in the sun and in the moon, &c. Luke xxi. 25.
XIX. And when he was entered into the ship, his disciples followed him, &c. Matt. viii. 23.
XX. The end of all things is at hand: be ye therefore sober, &c. 1 Pet. iv. 7.
XXI. Offer the sacrifices of righteousness, &c. Psal. iv. 5.
XXII. For the rest, brethren, fare ye well, be perfect, be of good comfort, &c. 2 Cor. xiii. 11.

THE FIRST SERMON.

A SERMON
MADE IN PAUL'S, ON THE DAY OF CHRIST'S NATIVITY.

Esay LV.

1. *Ho, every one that thirsteth, come to the waters; and ye that have no silver, come, buy and eat: Come, I say, buy wine and milk without silver, and without money.*
2. *Wherefore do ye lay out silver, and not for bread; and your labour, without being satisfied? Hearken diligently unto me, and eat that which is good, and let your soul delight in fatness.*
3. *Incline your ears, and come unto me; hear, and your souls shall live; and I will make an everlasting covenant with you, even the sure mercies of David.*

Our evangelical prophet Esaias, through the spirit of revelation, hath in the former part of this his prophecy, eight hundred years before the birth of Christ (even as if the thing had already been performed, such is the certainty of his prophecy) most lively described and set forth the nativity, the preaching, the persecution, the apprehension, the death, the resurrection, the ascension, yea, and the latter coming of our Saviour Christ to judge the quick and the dead; in such wise, that, for the substance thereof, no evangelist hath more perfectly or plainly set forth this great mystery of our salvation. He foretelleth that Christ shall be born of a Virgin; that his name shall be Immanuel; that his office shall be to preach the glad tidings of salvation to the poor in spirit; that he shall be led as a sheep to the shambles to be slain; that he shall be stricken for our sakes, and bear the burden of all our sins upon his back. Christ, and those things which he should do and suffer, foretold by Esaias.

2. His birth, foreshewed so long ago by this heavenly prophet, was in fulness of time accomplished, as this day, in Bethlem, a city of David, according to the testimony of that angel sent from heaven to proclaim the birth of the Son of God at the same time, saying: "Behold, I His birth according to that which was spoken before by the prophet. Luke ii. [10, 11.]

bring you tidings of great joy, that shall be unto all the people; because this day is born unto you a Saviour, which is Christ our Lord, in the city of David." This is that Seed of the woman which breaketh the Serpent's head, that meek Abel murdered by his brethren for our sin, that true Isaac whom his Father hath offered up to be a sacrifice of pacification and atonement between him and us. This is that Melchisedec, both a king and a priest, that liveth for ever, without father or mother, beginning or ending. This is Joseph that was sold for thirty pieces of money. This is that Samson full of strength and courage, who, to save his people and destroy his enemies, hath willingly brought death upon his own head. This is that Lord and Son of David, to whom the Lord said, [Psal. cx. [1.]] "Sit thou on my right hand." This is that Bridegroom in the Canticle, whose heart is so inflamed with heavenly love towards his dear spouse, which is his church. This is he, whom holy Simeon embracing prophesied that he [Luke ii. 32.] should be "a light to the Gentiles, and a glory to his people Israel;" he upon whom the Holy Ghost descended, [Matt. iii. 16, 17.] and of whom the Father testified from heaven, "This is my well-beloved Son." This is that Lamb of God, pointed [John i. 29.] at by John, and sent to "take away the sins of the world;" to redeem us from thraldom, not with gold, nor silver, but with the inestimable price of his precious blood; to be made our wisdom, justification, sanctification, and [Isai. ix. [6.]] redemption. This is the Child that is born for us, the Son that is given for our cause, the King whose rule is upon his shoulders, whose name is Marvellous, the Giver of Counsel, the Mighty God, the Everlasting Father, the Prince of Peace; the same Messias which was shadowed in the ceremonies and sacrifices of old, which was prefigured in the law, and is presented in the gospel, and hath been approved to the world by signs and wonders, by so clear evidence as cannot be either dissembled or denied. Let us therefore embrace this babe with joy, let us kiss the Son, let us, with the angels of heaven, praise the Lord; let us sing their psalm to the honour of [Luke ii. [14.]] his name, "Glory be to God on high, and on earth peace."

All men invited unto Christ.

3. The prophet Esaias having in spirit espied Christ, and seen the day, though far off, wherein the Saviour of

the world should be born, calleth all the nations of the earth together, and exhorteth them to come, to behold, to believe, to embrace, to taste of the mercies of Christ Jesus, which are as water to refresh their thirsty spirits, and as milk to nourish and comfort their hearts. "All you that thirst, come to the waters," &c. In which exhortation the prophet observeth this order: first, he exhorteth the people to come: secondly, he telleth whither and to whom they should come: thirdly, he teacheth after what sort they must come: fourthly, what commodity such as come shall receive.

4. "Come all that are thirsty." God's mercy is great and general; he hath no partial respect unto any person: no country, no kindred, no age, no condition, no sex is excluded. He calleth Jew and Gentile, young and aged, rich and needy, bond and free, man and woman. He commanded his gospel to be preached to all: "Go your ways, preach the gospel to every creature." In the parable all are invited to that magnificent marriage and kingly supper. Christ himself crieth, in general words, "Come to me all that labour." If all be called and exhorted to come, what cause can any man allege sufficient to excuse his not coming? The buying of farms, or the trying of oxen, or the marrying of wives? They have base minds, that are withheld by these means. But, if any have a fearful and a trembling heart, who being called stand still afar off, not because they will not, but because they dare not approach near; them God pitieth, yea unto them especially, or rather only unto them, he saith, "Come you." Be thy sins never so great, fear not to come; for he that calleth thee hath stretched out his arms of mercy at length; they are wide open to embrace thee: mercy is ready to all that will receive it; and to them that need it most, most ready. A comfortable lesson to all sinners.

1. Who are called: generally, all; but specially the thirsty.

Mark xvi. [15.]

Matt. xi. [28.]

5. Come all that are "thirsty." He calleth not them which are full, and need neither meat nor drink, but such as be hungry and thirsty, them he calleth. The proud Pharisee, that was full of his own righteousness, hungered not after remission of sins; and they, who are over-filled with works of supererogation, and have store to serve themselves and others, never thirst to drink of the cup

of salvation: in general, such as are drunk with the vain trust of their own merits will neither taste of this bread, nor drink of this water. The covetous man thirsteth after money, even with the sale of his own soul to get it; the lewd after fleshly delights and pleasures, to the wasting of his patrimony upon them; the proud after glory, that his itching ears may be tickled with his own praise: but what thirst the prophet doth mean Christ sheweth in the gospel, where he also blesseth it: "Blessed are they which hunger and thirst for righteousness." Such as see their own nakedness, as feel their own infirmities, as groan under the heavy burden of their sin, as confess with David, "I know mine own iniquities;" as make request with the publican, "God be merciful to me a sinner;" as cry with the leper, "Lord, if thou wilt, thou canst make me clean:" such are invited, unto such our prophet speaketh. He calleth not the just, but unto sinners he saith, Come; go not away, but come.

<small>Matt. v. [6.]</small>

<small>Psal. li. [3.]</small>
<small>Luke xviii. [13.]</small>
<small>Luke v. [12.]</small>

<small>2. Whither and to whom they are called. To the waters, wine and milk.
John vi. [68.]</small>
6. Whither, and to whom? "Come to the waters." Not to such waters, as either the well or the river yieldeth; but to those that issue from the Son of God, to those that shall be in him which tasteth them a well of water springing unto everlasting life. "Unto whom shall we go? Thou hast the words of everlasting life." Come to these waters, buy this wine and this milk. Other bread is no bread; eat that which is good. Under these names of water, wine, and milk, all things necessary to a spiritual life are comprehended. For as with these corporal meats and drinks the body is nourished, so in Christ, through the believing of the gospel, our soul is refreshed, and perfectly fed unto everlasting life. Christ is the fresh fountain, whereof whoso drinketh shall never thirst. Christ is that bread which descended from heaven. He that eateth that bread, which is his flesh, shall live for ever. Christ is that wine which maketh merry the heart of man, and quieteth the troubled conscience. Christ is that milk which nourisheth and feedeth us, that we may grow to a perfect man. Milk is fit for infants, water is convenient for young men, wine agreeth with old age. So in the scriptures there is food, both for such as are simple and weak, and also for such as are learned and strong.

7. This grace of God which saveth, hath appeared to all men: this heavenly food, Christ Jesus, by preaching the gospel is offered to all, as manna the heavenly bread, by faith to feed upon; and as a lively fountain to drink of to everlasting life. All are of mercy, grace, and favour freely called; all may come and freely feed, without penny or penny-worth. The grace of God is free, remission of sins is free—freely granted, freely given without money. "The price of our redemption is neither gold nor silver: Through grace ye are freely saved." For "it cannot be grace any way, which is not every way free[1]," saith St Augustine. *(margin: Water, wine, milk, freely offered by Christ. Contra Pelag. de origin. peccat. cap. 24.)*

8. "Wherefore do ye lay out your silver for that which is no bread, and your labour on that which is not to satisfy?" As before he exhorted us to come and buy freely without money, because God is no money-man, neither can any man deserve favour at his hands, but whatsoever we have of him, we have it of mercy; so now he sharply reproveth all such as by money or merchandize, by desert or merit, seek after salvation. He dehorteth us from false teachers, crafty seducers, which offer to sell the grace and mercy of God for money. Christ proposeth his heavenly treasures, remission of sins, justification, sanctification, mercy, grace, and salvation, freely. He that sitteth in the temple of God, and termeth himself Christ's vicar, doth in like sort offer unto the people bread, water, wine, milk, pardon of sins, grace, mercy, and eternal life; but not freely: he is a merchant, he giveth nothing, and that is nothing which he selleth. For although he make large promises to the buyer, he selleth that which he hath not to deliver. "Eternal life is the gift of God." The pope therefore selleth but wind and smoke for fire, shadows for truths: he deceiveth the buyers with false sleights, false measures, false weights. Beware of this merchant, lose not your labour, cast not away your money: it is not meat but poison which he offereth you. His physic cannot heal your diseases; his holy water cannot wash away the spots of a sullied and defiled soul, as he untruly *(margin: The contrary sold by antichrist for money.)*

[1 Non enim Dei gratia erit ullo modo, nisi gratuita fuerit omni modo.—August. Op. Par. 1696, Cont. Pelag. et Cœlest. Lib. II. De Peccato Originali. 28. Tom. x. col. 265.—ED.]

would bear you in hand; his blasphemous masses do not appease, but provoke God's wrath; they cannot benefit the quick, much less the dead, which either need no help, or are past all help; his rotten relics cannot comfort you; his blind, dumb, and worm-eaten idols can do you no good. It is cast away which is spent upon his shameless pardons; they will not prevail—God will not admit them: by his Latin service ye cannot be edified, or made wiser. Yet this trumpery they sell for money, and upon this trash they cause silly men to waste their substance, and to these to commit their souls. Thus you see a manifest difference between Christ and antichrist, the doctrine of God and the learning of man, true teachers and false, sound and counterfeited religion. The one offereth true bread freely: the other, that which is no bread, for bread, and that not freely neither, but for money. The diversity of religion professed in these our times is here most plainly and lively depainted. For the better clearing whereof, I will in three notes lay before your eyes the whole difference which is between them.

Three differences between the doctrine professed by true Christians, and that which is maintained by their adversaries, the pope and his adherents.

9. First, we disagree in the very foundation. They lay one ground, and we another. We lay no one stone but only upon that foundation of the prophets and apostles, whereupon whosoever is builded, groweth into an holy temple in the Lord—a temple, which no wind, no waves, no storm, no tempest is able to overthrow. The foundation of our religion is the written word, the scriptures of God, the undoubted records of the Holy Ghost. We require no credit to be given to any part or parcel of our doctrine, further than the same may be clearly and manifestly proved by the plain words of the law of God, which remaineth in writing, to be seen, read, and examined of all men. This we do, first, because we know that God hath caused his whole law to be written: secondly, because we see that it hath been the practice of all the defenders of the truth since the beginning to rely their faith only upon the scripture and written word: thirdly, because it is evident and plain that we cannot receive any other foundation of heavenly truth without the overthrow of christian faith.

The first difference is in the ground and foundation of doctrine. Reasons why religion should be grounded only upon scripture.

The whole law of God, which is the

10. There was never any law-maker so simple, as to make statutes for perpetuity, and not to register them in

books, or engrave them in tables. When Memucan was desirous to have a law made for the bringing of women in subjection under their husbands, his persuasion was this, "If it may please the king, let a royal decree proceed from him, and let it be written." The laws of the Medes and Persians, that might never be altered, were for ever recorded. When God delivered his first law unto his people, the law which commonly we call moral, he gave it them written in tables of stone. Again, when he delivered them civil ordinances for the administration of justice between man and man, Moses first proclaimed all those laws and ordinances amongst the people; afterward he took and wrote in a book all the words of the Lord. As for the laws of rites and ceremonies, they are likewise written in this book. To these we must add that law, which the blessed apostle doth call the "law of faith." This law God preached unto Adam by himself, "The seed of the woman shall break the serpent's head:" unto Abraham by his angel, "In thee shall all the nations of the earth be blessed:" to the children of Abraham by his prophets, "Behold, a virgin shall conceive and bear a Son:" finally, unto us by his Son, and by them whom his Son hath sent into the world to make it known, "That through this man is preached remission of sins; and from all things from which ye could not be justified by the law of Moses, by him every one that believeth is justified." And the statutes of this law are also written. God, being moreover desirous to have his servants not only taught by doctrine, but provoked also by examples, gave them a fifth sort of laws and testimonies, called historical, not leaving these neither to men, to deliver unto their children by word of mouth, but all by writing. If God have committed his laws moral, civil, ceremonial, evangelical, and historical also, unto writing, where should we seek for the statutes of the Almighty but in his written word?

rule of religion, committed to writing.

Esther i. [19.]

Rom. iii. [27.]
Gen. iii. [15.]

Gen. xii. [3.]

Isai. vii. [14.]

Acts xiii. [38, 39.]

11. The ancients of the house of God knew no fountain of his truth but this. They never inquired what had been whispered in men's ears; that which they believed and taught, they read it out of the book. In the history of Josua it is recorded, how he did assemble the tribes, elders, heads, judges, and officers of Israel together, shewing them

The true professors of all ages have rested their faith upon scripture only.
Josh. xxiv.

what God had spoken unto them by Moses, but uttering to them no speech which was not written. Josias, with all the men of Judah, and all the inhabitants of Jerusalem, the priests, prophets, and all the people, small and great, made a covenant before the Lord, to keep his commandments, and his testimonies, and his statutes, with all their heart and with all their soul: but what statutes? what testimonies? "The words of the covenant written in this book." Christ speaketh many things, his apostles many things, concerning the doctrine of the prophets, but no one point of doctrine which is not found in their books and writings. The prophet Esay crieth, *Ad legem et testimonium,* "To the law and to the testimony." If they teach not "according to this law, it is because there is no light in them." Consider the practice of Christ Jesus. His proofs are, *Scriptum est,* "It is written:" his demands are, *Quomodo legis?* "How dost thou read?" His apologies are, *Scrutamini scripturas,* "Search the scriptures, they bear me record." His apostles tread in the same path; they go not the breadth of an hair, not a whit from that which is written. Thus St Paul protesteth, "I delivered unto you that which I received, how Christ died for our sins according to the scriptures, and that he was buried, and that he rose the third day according to the scriptures." It is not lightly to be marked, which is twice repeated. He delivered nothing but "according to the scriptures." "I would hear the voice of my pastor" (saith St Augustine); "read this out of some prophet, read it out of some psalm, recite it out of the law, recite it out of the gospel, recite it out of some apostle: read it, and we will believe it[1]." These be good precedents for us to follow, till sufficient reason be alleged why we should lay another foundation than that which hath been laid by so many, so wise, so reverend builders.

12. Especially sith this foundation is so peculiar to the

[1] Non invidemus alicui: legite nobis hoc de lege, de prophetis, de psalmis, de ipso evangelio, de apostolicis literis: legite, et credimus.—August. Op. Par. 1694. Contra Donatistas Epist., vulg. De Unit. Eccles. Liber Unus. Tom. IX. col. 345. The archbishop appears to have had also in his mind the following passage: Ego vocem pastoris inquiro. Lege hoc mihi de propheta, lege mihi de psalmo, recita mihi de lege, recita de evangelio, recita de apostolo.—Sermo xlvi. De Pastoribus in Ezek. xxxiv. Tom. v. col. 242.—ED.]

truth, that we cannot rest upon any other without manifest danger of the utter overthrow of christian faith. For first, what certainty or assurance can we have of any of those things which are believed, if our faith do not lean only upon the scriptures? If once a religious credit be given to unwritten verities and to men's reports, the undoubted articles of our belief cannot choose but at the length become doubtful and uncertain, like a tale that passeth from man to man, and is told as many ways as there are men to tell it. Again, if once it be granted that there is any part of the law of God unwritten, if entrance once be given to laws that pass by the word of mouth, I would know when we should be able to say, "Now we have all the statutes of God, these we must observe, but more we may not receive." The Marcionites, they have a doctrine, as they say, received from the apostles by tradition, without book: Valentinus, he likewise urgeth very stoutly, "Christ had many things to tell his disciples, which as then they could not bear," and therefore his doctrine may not be tried by the book, "it is a tradition[1]." Let any thing but the written word of God take place in matters of faith; and who seeth not that the very main sea of heresies must needs break in upon the church of Christ? These are, as we suppose, causes just and allowable, and sufficient in the indifferent judgment of reasonable men, why we should deliver you no doctrine concerning faith and religion, but only that which is in scripture; why we should admonish you to beware of bread soured with pharisaical leaven, and to feed upon that which ye know came down from heaven; to shun broken cisterns, and to come to the well of living waters, as here ye are exhorted by the prophet.

13. At this the adverse part doth greatly storm: they cannot abide to have controversies judged only by the scriptures. They which make scripture only the ground and foundation of faith, are no fit builders for the church of Rome. When Constantinus required that those matters, about which the church was then very hot in contention, might be decided "only according to those things which are written," the answer of Hilary was, *Hoc qui repudiat,*

^{margin:} The pope will not have his doctrine tied unto this ground; and why.

^{margin:} Hil. ad Constan. lib. quem ipse tradidit.

[1 Marcion and Valentinus were heretics of the second century.—ED.]

antichristus est[1]: "He which refuseth this is antichrist." Why then do our adversaries fly this kind of trial? Why refuse they to go to the "law and testimonies," there to be judged? The reason is rendered by the prophet, "It is because there is no light in them." They have chosen to themselves another foundation than that of the prophets and apostles. Wherefore, as Herod, to cover the baseness of his stock, and to the end that in time he might be thought to be of the blood royal, burned the sacred monuments and books of the Jews, wherein the lineal descents, pedigrees, and genealogies of the kings of Israel were described[2]; so they, to strengthen the authority of their base and ill-favoured grounds, do endeavour not only in word and writing, by contumelious and reproachful terms, to discountenance, but also (if the power of God were not greater than theirs) by fire and flame to destroy for ever the eternal testament of the Son of God. We charge them with no corner attempts: we have seen the burning of these heavenly records, we have seen the very handling of the book of life punished with bitter and cruel death. May we not justly say to that man of sin, as St Augustine to Petilian? *Judas Christum carnalem tradidit, tu spiritualem: furens evangelium sanctum flammis sacrilegis tradidisti*[3]. "Judas betrayed Christ in the flesh, but thou in the spirit. In thy fury thou hast delivered the holy gospel unto heinous flames."

Ambros. in Luc. lib. iii. cap. 3.

August. contra liter. Petilia. lib. ii. cap. 7.

The grounds of popery.

14. But what are the grounds, for which they have thus furiously bent themselves against the writings of the Holy Ghost? The grounds, whereupon they build such doctrines as cannot stand with the scriptures of God, are feigned miracles, the record and witness of foul spirits, precepts of men, muddy legends, uncertain traditions; which grounds, so long as the light of the gospel shineth in men's

---

[1] Hilar. Pictavor. Episc. Op. Par. 1693. Ad Constant. Aug. Lib. II. 8. col. 1229.—ED.]

[2] Ambros. Op. Par. 1686. Expos. Ev. sec. Luc. Lib. III. 41. Tom. I. col. 1329.—ED.]

[3] Judas Christum carnaliter tradidit, tu spiritaliter furens evangelium sanctum flammis sacrilegis tradidisti.—August. Op. Par. 1694. Contra Literas Petiliani Lib. II. 17. Tom. IX. col. 221. This charge is made by Petilian against Augustine, not by Augustine against Petilian. —ED.]

eyes, so long as we have the scriptures to direct us in our judgment, are easily perceived to be but bogs and false grounds: but take away the scriptures, put out the light, and in darkness who can descry what they are? This is the only reason why antichrist doth so much strive to hoodwink the world, by conveying the scriptures out of sight.

15. By the scriptures we learn that the coming of that wicked one shall be "with power, and signs, and lying wonders, and in all deceivableness of unrighteousness;" which when we hear, it giveth us plainly to understand, that miracles are rather to be taken for causes of reasonable suspicion, than infallible proofs of true doctrine. But the pope well perceiveth that, if the scriptures may be buried, his miracles will then stand him in good stead. As soon as Philip preached "the things that concerned the kingdom of God, and the name of Jesus Christ," to the people of Samaria, they forsook the sorceries of Simon Magus, and believed the doctrine of the scriptures. But till then they all gave heed to witchcraft, and their general judgment of Magus was, "This man is the power of the great God." Miracles.
2 Thess. ii. [9, 10.]

Acts viii. [12.]

16. In the scriptures we are charged to hear Moses and the prophets. In the scriptures we find that Christ refused the testimony of an unclean spirit. In the scriptures we have learned how to answer them, which send us either to devils, or dead men's ghosts, to be schooled and taught. "Should not a people inquire at their God? From the living to the dead?" But let it be provided that such sentences as these may be no more remembered, and then what is it which the pope may not confirm by his pale and grisly witnesses? When men do not hear of these scriptures, they will easily find as good reason as Saul to open their ears, and to listen unto Satan, "God answereth me no more neither by prophets, nor by dreams: therefore I have called thee, that thou mayest tell me what to do." Foul spirits.

Isai. viii. [19.]

1 Sam. xxviii. [15.]

17. How often are we warned in scriptures to take heed that we build not religion upon doctrines of men! How sharply are the Corinthians taken up by the apostle, for pinning themselves upon men's sleeves, saying, "I am of Paul, and I of Apollos!" But if this were concealed, who would control the pope for dividing his train; for appointing some to be of Benedict, some of Francis, some of Precepts of men.

1 Cor. iii. [4.]

Dominick; for exacting more rigorously the strict observation of their rules, than the keeping of the laws and statutes of God?

Legends.

18. So long as the mist of popery was thick enough to stop the light of the scriptures of God, the fabulous legends of saints' lives were thought as true as the gospel. There they had, with marvellous cunning conveyance, interlaced all points of popish doctrine; which, being barely taught, would, by reason of the grossness of them, have been loathed in short time; but being mingled with strange and pleasant fables, and so poured both into young and tender wits as the first liquor wherewith their minds were seasoned, and into old heads as the only thing that might hold them, even then when all other entries of delight were shut up, so long as they had but an ear left, were so effectual to deceive all sorts of men, that, knowing this, we cannot marvel if popery were spread far and wide. He did the pope very profitable service, which first found out this ground to build on. It bare up their building a great while. But after that the light began a little to appear, when men had gotten once a sight of the scriptures in a known tongue, they wondered to see the world so deluded, insomuch that, even amongst themselves, such as had any small freedom of judgment spared not plainly to avouch that this ground was but mire and slough, altogether unfit for spiritual building. "Why that book should be called a Golden legend," saith Vives, (for so it was intituled) "I do not know, sith it was written by a man of an iron mouth and a leaden heart, and is altogether full of most shameless lies[1]." Erasmus likewise, "At this day," saith he, "every body's dreams, yea the dotages of silly women, are read amongst divine scriptures[2]."

Vives.

Annot. in Hieron. de Ecclesiast. scriptorib.

[[1] Quam indigna est divis et hominibus Christianis illa sanctorum historia, quæ Legenda aurea nominatur, quam nescio cur auream appellent, quum scripta sit ab homine ferrei oris, plumbei cordis. Quid fœdius dici potest illo libro? ò quam pudendum est nobis Christianis, non esse præstantissimos nostrorum divorum actus verius et accuratius memoriæ mandatos!—Lodovici Vivis Op. Basil. 1555. De Causis Corruptarum Artium, Lib. II. Tom. I. pp. 371, 2.—Ed.]

[[2] Hinc apparet non nisi apostolicas litteras olim legi solitas in templis, aut certe virorum apostolicæ authoritatis; cum hodie mona-

19. The last ground which they have, and the fairest to the eye, is their traditions. Under the name of doctrine received from Moses by word of mouth, without writing, that is to say tradition, the scribes and Pharisees were able smoothly to carry away any thing, till Christ recalled all things to the law, the psalms, and the prophets, till he opened the scriptures. And as in other grounds, so in this, the pope hath found by good experience, that they cannot stand longer than the scriptures lie secret and unknown. *Traditions.*

20. He therefore that buildeth upon these grounds hath cause, I think, to bestir hand and foot, that men may be always kept off from the scriptures. For whatsoever is builded upon these grounds, by the scripture it is overthrown. The scriptures have prescribed an holy communion: they upon their foundation have reared a blasphemous mass. The scripture maketh baptism the consecrated seal of man's salvation: they upon their foundation have builded the baptism of bells and ships. The scripture saith, Christ was offered up but once: they upon their foundation have erected an altar, whereupon he is daily offered up. The scripture will have the scriptures to be read of all men, prayer to be made with understanding, Christ to be a full satisfaction for sin, worship to be done unto God alone: they upon their foundations have built a doctrine that forbiddeth God's people to read his word, that teacheth them to pour out their prayer in a tongue which they cannot understand, that hath found out a way to satisfy the wrath of Almighty God in this life by penance, and after this life by endurance in purgatory; a doctrine that commandeth them to call upon saints and souls departed, to worship the work of their own hands, to say to a piece of bread, "My Lord and my God." If these doctrines of theirs did not contain, as they do, most manifest impiety, yet all religion builded upon such grounds must needs be vain and frivolous. For, although we offer up never so many sacrifices; though we keep all the days in the year holy; though we pray, and give thanks, and do alms; yet, except we know that herein we shew obedience to the laws and *Doctrines builded upon the foresaid grounds against scripture.* *Religion builded upon such grounds, though it were not injurious, is notwithstanding frivolous and uncertain.*

chorum somnia, imo muliercularum deliramenta legantur inter divinas scripturas.—Hieron. Op. Basil. 1516. Erasmi Roterod. in Catal. Script. Ecclesiast. Scholia. Tom. I. p. 141.—ED.]

statutes of our God, we do but tire out ourselves in vain. Will God reward those things wherein he taketh no delight? Or taketh he delight in any thing, and hath not shewed it? Or hath he shewed it, and not in scripture? Doubtless they worship him but in vain, which either teach or practise the precepts of men for the laws of God. That they teach or practise the precepts of men, they will not grant; yet the most that possibly they can allege to prove any one of these things to be of God is this, "Such or such a father saith, that this or this, being not written, is nevertheless apostolical." And they know that the witnesses, whom they cite in matters of tradition, do sometimes check and contrary one another. In the controversy that was between the East and West churches concerning the feast of Easter, the one part alleged tradition to prove their custom; and the other part, tradition to prove the contrary. It might be that neither was apostolical: both could not be, when each gainsaid other. Yet both must be, if all be apostolical which the fathers have said is apostolical. If all be not, where is the certainty of these grounds? Why do they murder, burn, and persecute from place to place as many as make any doubt of these things, which are grounded upon so fickle and weak foundation?

The second difference between true Christianity and popery is in the end.

21. But, to leave the foundation whereupon they build their doctrine, if in the rest we find them as corrupt, as in this they have been declared weak; surely then we may boldly affirm that the church of Rome is rather a sink of all abomination, than a fountain from whence those living waters, or a store-house wherein that heavenly food, whereof the prophet Esay speaketh, may be had. Let us therefore now consider the end, as well of our religion, as of theirs. Let us view the mark whereat each part doth shoot. Whatsoever men do, they do it to some end. And the quality of things which are done to any end is judged to be good or bad by the end whereunto they are done. Hereof it is, that in scripture things otherwise highly commended, as prayer, fasting, and alms deeds, are most bitterly reproved when they tend to bad ends. As there is but one Author, from whom all things are, so there is but one end, unto whom all things should incline and bend themselves. "God is Alpha, the first, from whom

all other things have their being and beginning; wherefore in reason he is Omega, the end and final cause of all things: upon him they must attend, and seeing they are not of themselves therefore they may not serve themselves, but for the glory of him by whom they are. From hence a rule may be gathered, to judge between pure religion in deed, and that which is untruly so called. For that religion no doubt is best, which most advanceth the glory of God; and that which taketh most from him, the worst. *Ipsi gloria in ecclesia:* In the church of God all glory is given, not to men, but to him. This is the song of the true church of Christ, "Righteousness, O Lord, belongeth unto thee, but unto us open shame." Eph. iii. [21.]
Dan. ix. [7.]

22. Wherefore, touching ourselves, we teach with the blessed apostles and prophets, "that by nature we are the children of wrath;" that corruption is bred and settled within our bones: that we are both born and begotten in it; that with it all the powers and faculties of our nature are infected; that still it cleaveth fast unto our souls, and, although the deadly sting be taken from it, yet there it sticketh as long as life doth endure, so irksome and so grievous, that it forceth the most upright and perfect to cry, "Miserable man, who shall deliver me?" Man is humbled by true doctrine touching original sin. Eph. ii. [3.]
Rom. vii. [24.]

23. By this inbred corruption our understanding is so darkened, that naturally we cannot perceive the things which are of God; no, we count them foolishness: our will is in such thraldom and slavery unto sin, that it cannot like of any thing spiritual and heavenly, but is wholly carried unto fleshly desires. Thraldom of will.

24. If therefore we perceive the things that are of God, and do like of them; if our hearts be inclined to do his will; because this cannot come of ourselves (our nature bending a clean contrary way), we acknowledge most willingly and unfeignedly, the good we do is his, it is not ours: our beginning to do, and our continuance in doing well, proceedeth only and wholly from him. If any man receive the grace of God offered, it is because God hath framed his heart thereto. If any man come when God calleth, it is because his grace, which calleth, draweth. If being brought unto Christ we continue in him, we have no other reason to yield of our doing, but Grace.

only this, he hath linked us and fastened us unto himself. We neither rise when we are fallen, nor stand when we are risen, by our own strength. When we are in distress, we are of ourselves so far from ability to help ourselves, that we are not able to crave help of him, unless his Spirit wrest out "Abba, Father," from us. We cannot moan our own case, unless he do groan and sigh for us: we are not able to name Jesus, unless by the special grace of his Spirit our mouths be opened: no, we cannot of ourselves so much as think of naming him, if to think of naming him be a good thought.

Works.

25. When against our natural inclination to evil his Spirit, which worketh all in all, hath so prevailed, that we now begin to hate the works of the flesh, having an earnest desire to abound in "love, joy, peace, long-suffering, gentleness, goodness, faith, meekness, temperance," and all other fruits of the Spirit; yet, by reason of the strength of that body of sin which ever fighteth against the Spirit, our inward man is so weakened, that we cannot do the things which we would; and the things which we do, even the best of them, are so far beneath that perfection which the law of God requireth, that, if he should rigorously examine them in justice, no flesh could ever be accounted righteous in his sight. The loathsomest things that can be imagined, the clothes that be most unclean, are not so foul as our very righteousness is unrighteous. Whereupon we conclude, that whatsoever we receive by way of reward at God's hand, either in this life or in the life to come, we receive it as a thing freely given by him, without any merit or desert of ours: we do not say in our hearts,

Gal. v. [22, 23.]

[Deut. ix. 4.] "The Lord hath given us these good things to possess for our righteousness." For seeing it is he which giveth both to will and to do, he crowneth indeed his own work, when he rewardeth ours; and he never rewardeth any work of his own, wherein there is not somewhat of ours which he pardoneth.

The truth seeketh to throw down men, and to advance Christ.

26. Thus being naked and utterly destitute in ourselves, we seek all things in Christ Jesus. Him only we acknowledge to be our wisdom, our justification, our sanctification, our redemption, our priest, our sacrifice, our king, our head, our mediator, our physician, our way, our truth,

our life. In ourselves we find nothing but poverty and weakness: praise, and honour, and glory, we give to him. The only mark we aim at is to set up his throne, to advance his kingdom, to make it known that in him the Father hath laid up all the treasures of heaven; to the end that unto him the thirsty may repair for water, the hungry for bread, the naked for clothes, and we all for all things needful to the safety of our souls and bodies.

27. This is not the scope which the church of Rome proposeth: they direct all things to another end. "How can ye believe," saith Christ to the Jews, "which receive honour one of another, and seek not that honour which cometh of God alone?" And how can the faith of the church of Rome be sound, sith they hold such doctrines as tend wholly to their own glory, their own gain, and not to the praise and honour of God? *The church of Rome seeketh her own glory and gain. John v. [44.]*

28. That they seek not his glory but their own, it may appear unto any man which throughly considereth of their doctrine. First, they will not acknowledge that poverty and nakedness, those filthy garments of corruption and sin, wherein Adam hath wrapped his posterity: but in the pride of their hearts they dissemble it, diminish it, and make light of it. For although they deny not but that man's nature is corrupted, yet mark how they pare and lessen this corruption. The prophet David doth term it "wickedness" and "sin;" but they make it only an inclination unto sinning. The Lord himself doth witness that by it "all the imaginations of the thoughts of man's heart are only evil:" they restrain it to the inferior part of the soul, and make it only a mother of some grosser desires. The blessed apostle prayed, groaned, and wept against it, as a thing which made him altogether weary of his life: but after baptism they make no more account of those inward rebellious motions against the Spirit, than they do of the beating of a man's pulse. *She pareth and diminisheth man's original corruption. Psal. li. [5.] Gen. vi. [5.]*

29. And as they hide that weakness which indeed they have, so they boast of that strength which is not in them. For being subject unto miserable bondage under sin, by reason of that corruption which hath spread itself over all flesh, they brag notwithstanding of the freedom of their will; as if sin had not utterly bereaved us there- *She boasteth of freewill.*

of, but still it were in us to frame and fashion our own hearts unto good things. For proof whereof, their manner is to make long discourses, teaching that God's foreknowledge doth not take away free-will, that men are not violently drawn to good or evil. Which things we easily and willingly grant; neither do we teach, or ever did, that the freedom of our will is taken away by the eternal decree of his unsearchable purpose: but this we say, and all that have the truth do say the same—that the will of man, being free unto natural and civil actions, hath of itself no freedom to desire things heavenly and spiritual; not because the eternal purpose of God, but because the corruption of our nature, hath addicted us only unto evil. We do not teach, or ever did, that any man is the servant either of sin or of righteousness by constraint; for whether we obey the one unto death and condemnation, or unto life and salvation the other, our obedience is always voluntary; it is not wrested from us against our wills. But the question being, how we are made willing unto that which is good, this is the difference between our answer and theirs: We say, only by the grace of God; they say, partly by grace, but principally by the power and strength of their own nature. For, being ashamed to affirm with Pelagius that a man may do the works of righteousness by nature without the grace of God, they hold his grace to be a thing indeed necessary; but how? As a bird that is tied, or a man that is in fetters, needeth only to have those incumbrances removed, having then a natural ability to fly and walk without any further help; so man, as they say, hath in himself ability to do good, if the grace of God do but remove lets. Is not this to make nature the principal cause of our well doing? whereas in truth, without the special motion of God's Spirit, and that in every particular action, we are no more able to walk in the ways which God hath commanded, than a drunken man to go without leading, who staggereth even in the plainest ground, though all stumblingblocks be removed, though his way lie never so smooth before him: such is our weakness. In consideration whereof the blessed apostle saith plainly, "It is not in him that willeth, or in him that runneth, but

in God that sheweth mercy." We drag and are not able
of ourselves to set one foot before another. "Draw me," <small>Cant. i. [4.]</small>
saith the spouse in the Canticles, "and then we will run
after thee." But these men, little considering of what
frail metal they are made, perceiving not how sin hath
weakened the faculties of the soul, vaunt of freedom, of
strength, of inward power, and make their own will the
chiefest cause of their well doing.

30. And when they have done any thing which to <small>Justification by works.</small>
their seeming is well done, they prize it so high, and
esteem so much of it, that God, as they think, should do
them injury, if in judgment he did not pronounce them
just and righteous for their works' sake. If it were possible that God, entering into judgment, should find any
so upright and perfect that by their works they might
be justified in his sight, doubtless he should find his own
servants to be such, or else none; if any of his servants,
surely his prophets; if any prophet, rather David than
any other. But David crieth out, "Enter not into judg- <small>Psal. cxliii. [2.]</small>
ment," no, not "with thy servant, O Lord: for in thy sight
shall none that liveth be justified." For, whether we consider works forbidden or commanded by the law, what
man is there living, which can say in the one, "My
heart is pure"? in the other, "I have done all that is
enjoined me"? For if it were so, that we knew nothing
wherein we had transgressed the laws and statutes of the
Almighty, yet herein could we in no wise be justified,
because of secret sins, hidden even from our own selves.
For which if God shall call us to our reckoning, and
mark straitly what is done amiss, "O Lord," saith the <small>Psal. cxxx. [3.]</small>
prophet, "who shall stand?" Again, if we had done
whatsoever we could; yet, because we cannot do so much
as we should, we ought to acknowledge ourselves unprofitable: whereas we, even the best of us, are far from doing
that which, if we would, we might do.

31. Now, if God notwithstanding, for his Son's sake, <small>Of merits and works of supererogation.</small>
do so allow and accept the work of our hands, that he
bountifully rewardeth our weak service with an excellent
and an eternal weight of glory, how much are we bound
both to praise his mercy, and to hate the insolency of
those men, who, besides all this, swelling in the proud con-

ceit of their works, will have eternal life, which is his gift, to be their merit! nor only that, but the worthiness of their deserts to be so great, that many of them, doing God more service than can be sufficiently rewarded in their own persons, deserve heaven, not only for themselves, but for others too. These shipwrecks of faith they have made by reason of their inward pride.

She desireth excessively outward pomp.

32. The excessive desire of outward pomp hath furthermore caused them to disdain the baseness of Christ Jesus and of his apostles, to be ashamed of the mean and low estate wherein they lived; to make of their deacons and priests cardinals, exceeding the kings of the earth in glory; of their bishop a monarch, under whose foot the emperor himself hath been a footstool, whose stirrup the greatest sovereigns have scarce been deemed worthy to hold, at whose bridle kings have attended as servants; that *Eccles. x. [6, 7.]* the words of the Preacher might be justified, "Folly is set in great excellency, and the rich set in the low place. I have seen servants on horses, and princes walking as servants on the ground."

She maintaineth it by vile merchandize.

33. This pomp cannot be maintained with nothing: it must have strong sinews. And therefore, whatsoever man's wit might possibly devise for gain, they have both found it out, and put it in ure; setting offices, masses, prayers, pardons, sacraments, heaven and earth, all the treasures of the house of God, to sale; if we may term it the house of God, which they have made a shop of so vile merchandise. It were infinite to recite what huge sums of money they have heretofore, by religious pretences, every year gathered within the compass of this one island: what heaps then have they raked out of other parts of Christendom? Which offals and profits if once men begin, as here, so in other kingdoms also, to withhold from them; if men leave off buying their wares any more; if things which are fat and excellent depart; doubtless that city, which now is clothed in fine linen and purple and scarlet, which now is gilded with gold, and decked with precious stones and pearls, shall in one hour be made desolate. This they know, and it maketh them careful to maintain whatsoever is commodious and gainful to them. As for the glory of God, it is the least part of their care: nay, they care not how heinous

sacrilege they commit in spoiling and robbing him of his honour.

34. It is an honour unto God, when all men by faith point their fingers, as it were, at Christ Jesus, naming him the only Lamb which taketh away the sins of the world; when he is acknowledged the only Mediator between God and us; when we confess, that he is that Priest according to the order of Melchisedec, which, having offered one sacrifice for sins, hath therewith, because it was a perfect sacrifice, consecrated for ever them that are sanctified; when our faith is so ascertained and grounded upon his promises, that we can be "bold as lions," assuring ourselves that "the eye of the Lord is on them which trust in his mercy, to deliver their souls from death," as the prophet witnesseth. But how do they give unto him this honour, who have devised so many ways to take away sin, besides the blood of the Lamb of God?—who, as though we might not be bold "to enter into the holy place by the new and lively way which he hath prepared for us through the vail, which is his flesh;" or as though there were some others, without whom the Father in him is not pleased, some others more willing to hear our requests than he who gave himself to death for our sakes, have made their intercessors infinite in number; and, as though his sacrifice were so unperfect that by being once offered it could not perfectly consecrate those which are sanctified, renew their oblations day by day; finally, as though the prophet were over-presumptuous which saith, "God is our hope, and strength, and help, therefore will not we fear," go about by all means to strike a servile terror into the hearts of the faithful, to keep them always wavering and doubting, to take away all assurance of the mercy and favour of God towards them; which when we have lost, what courage can we have to withstand the fiery assaults of Satan? what comfort or consolation in the midst of those sharp and bitter conflicts, which we must endure if we will live godly in Christ Jesus?

She robbeth God of the honour which he should have by faith, invocation, and obedience.

Heb. x. [12, 14.]

Prov. xxviii. [1.]
Psal. xxxiii. [18, 19.]

[Heb. x. 19, 20.]

Psal. xlvi. [1, 2.]

35. It is an honour unto God, when his name only is called upon, when we worship and fall down before none but him. This honour he getteth not at their hands, which have gotten to themselves legions of angels to whom they pray, and millions of idols which they daily adore. Their differ-

ences between an idol and an image are but shifts. Call them what ye will, they are similitudes of things in heaven or things in earth, which is sufficient to condemn them of idolatry that worship such things. Their distinctions between the honour which they give to images, and the worship which they do to God alone, may serve to blear the eyes of mortal men: but the eternal God doth know, that they honour creatures with that honour which is forbidden them in the law; that they "bow down to them," and that "they serve them."

<small>Exod. xx. [5.]</small>

36. It is an honour unto God, when reverence and obedience is shewed unto his law. But is this performed in that synagogue, where he sitteth which is an adversary, and exalteth himself against all that is called God, or that is worshipped; making himself supreme judge of all nations; requiring his own words to be heard of all men as the words of God; bereaving magistrates of their lawful power; exempting his clergy from the civil sword, what villainy soever they commit; changing at pleasure the government of Christ established in his church; dispensing with sin, be it never so directly against the express commandment of God; forbidding his clergy marriage, under colour of severing them from the world, but indeed to ease them of such cares and troubles as are necessarily joined with that honourable estate which God commendeth; and both secretly with concubines, and openly in stews, permitting them fornication, which God doth hate? Seeing therefore that this their synagogue is nothing but a sink of all uncleanness, seeing that all their endeavours tend to no other end, but only to the advancement of themselves, the dishonour of God, and the disgrace of Christ, doubtless they are not, they cannot be, the men which minister the waters of eternal life unto thirsty souls.

<small>The third difference between true Christianity and popery is in the means and manner of proceeding.</small>

37. Now that we have seen both the ground, and the end, as well of that faith which we profess, as of the doctrine which is held by them who are deadly enemies to us and our profession; it remaineth that a word be spoken of the means which are used on both parts to set forward that for which we strive. Touching ourselves, as the mark which we shoot at is to set up the kingdom of Christ Jesus, a kingdom which is not of the world; so the means which herein we

use are not worldly, but altogether heavenly and spiritual. What the proceedings of the gospel have been, ye are not ignorant: ye know very well, how without force, without cruelty, without treachery and deceit, without all wisdom of flesh and blood, in naked simplicity, in truth uncoloured, and, as the apostle speaketh, in foolishness of preaching, we have laboured to prepare you for one husband; to present you as a pure virgin to Christ, not outwardly arrayed in purple and scarlet, gilded with gold, precious stones, and pearl, like the strumpet that sitteth upon many waters; but, like the spouse of Solomon, glorious within, full of Christ, rich in faith and in good works, fulfilled with knowledge of his will in all wisdom and spiritual understanding, strengthened mightily in the inward man, rooted and grounded in sincere love, enabled to comprehend with all saints what is the breadth and length and depth and height of the love of Christ, strengthened with all patience and long-suffering, blessed with all spiritual blessings in heavenly things.

38. Contrariwise they, desiring no such thing, but seeking to build an earthly kingdom for themselves, use the means which are fittest for that purpose. They feed men's eyes with all glorious and glittering shews: they invent to themselves instruments of music to delight the ear; but of the work of the Lord, of preaching the gospel, of instructing the heart, of building the faith, of exhorting and comforting God's people, who seeth not how little regard they have? They keep men occupied always in corporal and bodily exercise, which profiteth little; but are they careful to train men up in the knowledge of Christ, which is eternal life? in true godliness, which is profitable unto all things, which hath the promise of the life present, and of that which is to come? No, their practice from time to time doth shew that most profane and godless men, only siding themselves with the church of Rome, and defending by all means the pope's honour, may both be counted as catholics, and even canonized as saints among them. If they pass the days of their life lewdly, after death at a reasonable price they may purchase rest for their souls. If their hearts be set upon adultery, incest, theft, murder; consider¹

1 Tim. iv. [8.]

[¹ Consider—give a consideration or fee to.—ED.]

the holy father for his parchment and lead; and what more easily granted in the court of Rome than full and free liberty to commit sin? Hence it cometh to pass, that as every man is most licentiously bent, so he joineth himself most willingly to the church of Rome, and warreth most earnestly for that faith, which faith if the rich men of this world be for the most part ready to embrace, what marvel [Mark x.23.] is it? For whereas Christ hath said, "It is hard for a rich man to enter into heaven," their doctrine and practice maketh the way expedite only for the rich: but by the way which they teach, for a poor man to enter into the kingdom of heaven, it is a hard matter. It were too much to recite all the means whereby that kingdom of darkness hath grown: it were a thing too full of horror to discourse of all the treacheries, poisonings, murderings, massacres, which they have used to maintain their power; never any tyrant in the world more. Did Christ, did Peter, did the blessed apostles, thus subdue and conquer nations? Did they thus enlarge the kingdom of God? As verily as he doth live, it is not the goodness of their religion, but the strength of their faction and the wiliness of flesh, by which they stand.

39. Wherefore, briefly to conclude this matter, and in few words to knit up that which remaineth; I have, as you see, set before you life and death, truth and error, wholesome food and noisome poison. If ye tender the safety of your own souls, be not as children ready to take whatsoever is offered you: learn to judge between good and evil: lay not out money for that which is no bread: spend not your labour in that which cannot satisfy: come to the waters whereunto God calleth you.

3.
After what sort men must come to the waters of life.
Jer. xxiii. [16.]

40. The manner of coming is set down by the prophet in many words: the sum of all is this: we must not give ear unto lying spirits; "Hear not the words of the prophets that prophesy unto you, and teach you vanity: they speak the vision of their own heart, and not out of the mouth of the Lord:" turn away your ears from such, and "hearken unto me," saith the Lord. "Hearken diligently," carefully, attentively. The word of life is of power and strength to save your souls. But if ye be as vessels that leak and run out, how should the doctrine

of salvation profit you? This food, refusing all other, we are exhorted both to take and to eat. If sinners, heretics, enemies of the truth, say, Come with us; shun them, turn away your feet from their paths, offer not you their offerings of blood, present not yourselves in their temples, taste not things sacrificed unto their idols; "Eat that which is good." Labour not for the meat which perisheth, much less for that whereby men perish; but labour for the meat that endureth to everlasting life, which meat the Son of man shall give you, for "him hath God the Father sealed." He is the bread of life: his flesh is meat indeed, and his blood is drink indeed: his word is the power of God unto salvation: his sacraments are seals of righteousness by faith: in him are all the treasures of peace, joy, rest, comfort: no eye hath seen, no ear hath heard, no heart hath conceived the things which are hidden and laid up in him. Whereupon if we feed in such sort that our souls take joy, pleasure, and "delight in fatness," then the fruit which hereby we shall reap is this: [John vi. 27.]

41. "Your soul," saith God, "shall live, and I will make an everlasting covenant with you, even the sure mercies of David." What? Shall they then which hearken unto him, and put their trust in his mercy, deliver their lives for ever from the hand of the grave? Shall they live, and not see death? There is a first and a second death: the one only severeth the soul from the body for a time; the other tormenteth, first the soul severed, and afterward both body and soul for ever. The second death shall not touch them of whom the prophet here speaketh. But of the first Job hath said, "Death is the house appointed for all the living." Wherefore God doth not promise to prolong the days of his children continually here on earth; but his promise is, that their souls shall live. For touching outward things, we cannot certainly judge the hatred or love of God by them. In these external events, "The same condition is to the just and to the wicked, to the good and pure, and to them that are polluted, to him that sacrificeth, and to him that sacrificeth not. As is the good, so is the sinner; he that sweareth as he that feareth an oath." "How 4. What commodities such as come shall receive. [Job xxx. 23.] [Eccles. ix. 2. ii. 16.]

dieth the wise man? Even as the fool," saith the Preacher. Nay, one is wicked, and liveth in ease and prosperity; another feareth God, and dieth in the bitterness of his soul: they sleep both in the dust together, the worms cover them both alike. This only is the difference, "The wicked is kept to the day of destruction, and shall be brought forth to the day of wrath." But "the just shall live by faith;" his soul shall live. The foundation from whence this life floweth is that covenant, which was made with David: "I will set up thy seed after thee, which shall proceed out of the[1] body, and I will stablish his kingdom: he shall build an house for my name, and I will stablish the throne of his kingdom for ever." Now as David, so the children of David after him, fulfilled their days, and fell asleep: the throne of David was not established in them for ever. But of Christ the angel of the Lord hath said, "The Lord shall give unto him the throne of his father David, and he shall reign over the house of Jacob for ever, and of his kingdom shall be no end." Wherefore in Christ this covenant with David is fulfilled. The mercies which were promised unto David are the benefits, and, as the apostle termeth them, "the holy things," which we receive by Christ Jesus. This covenant is everlasting. "If," saith God by the prophet Jeremy, "you can break my covenant of the day, and my covenant of the night, that there should not be day and night in their season, then may my covenant be broken with David." As the covenant made with David is everlasting, so the mercies therein contained are "sure." Of the sure mercies of David thus he speaketh in the book of Psalms: "Mine hand shall be established with him, and mine arm shall strengthen him: the enemy shall not oppress him; neither shall the wicked do him hurt; but I will destroy his foes before his face, and plague them that hate him: my mercy will I keep for him for evermore, and my covenant shall stand fast with him." The covenant made with David is made with us: his mercies are our mercies, if so be we perform that which here is required at our hands. If we hearken diligently unto him that crieth, "Come to the waters," if we cleave fast unto his truth,

[[1] "The," probably an error for "thy."—Ed.]

if we embrace his promises with joy, eating that which is good, shunning and loathing that which is evil; surely his hand shall be established with us as with David, his arm shall be our strength, the enemy shall not oppress us, neither shall the wicked do us harm: but God shall destroy all our enemies before us, and plague them that hate us; his mercies he shall keep towards us for ever, his covenant shall stand fast with us, our souls shall live, he shall make an everlasting covenant with us, even the sure mercies of David. Which mercies the God of all mercy grant us; unto whom, with the Son by whose blood they are purchased, together with that glorious Spirit which hath sealed in our hearts full assurance that they cannot fail, be honour and glory for ever and ever. Amen.

THE SECOND SERMON.

A SERMON

MADE BEFORE THE PARLIAMENT AT WESTMINSTER.

1 SAMUEL XII.

23. Be this sin against the Lord far from me, that I should cease to pray for you: but I will shew you the good and the right way.
24. Therefore fear you the Lord, and serve him in the truth.

<small>The use of parliaments.</small>   HISTORIES, as well sacred as profane, at large record, that good princes have ever vigilantly looked into the state of the commonwealth which is their charge; and perceiving disorder, or foreseeing danger, have speedily caused consultation to be had, as well for the reformation, as for the preservation thereof. In which consultation three especial things are commonly offered to consider of: the state of religion; the state of the prince; and the state of the commonwealth. Three most necessary things to be regarded and provided for. If religion be not sound, men's souls cannot be safe: if the head be not preserved, the body of necessity must decay: if good government want[1], the commonwealth falleth into confusion. Our prophet, that good prince and ruler of the people, in the great assembly of the Israelites, remembered unto them these self-same things, as, by the words which I have chosen to treat of, it will appear. Our Samuel, our good and gracious governor, moved with like affection, hath called this honourable and high court of parliament for like end. Wherein that things well intended may the better proceed and take best effect, let us in our prayers crave help and assistance from above. Wherein let us not forget Christ's universal church, this particular church of England and Ireland, the Queen's excellent majesty, our most sovereign Lady and chief Governor, that God, remembering us in his mercy, may grant her majesty a

[¹ Want—be wanting.—ED.]

long happy life, with the increase of all godly honour and felicity, to the great praise of his name and great good of his church. Let us also remember in our prayers the honourable privy council, the clergy, the nobility, with the whole people of this realm; that God may grant every one grace in his calling sincerely to serve him. And especially at this time let us call upon God for wisdom and grace from above, that in this consultation of parliament, all private affections and respects to our own commodities laid aside, God's glory and the good of his church and this commonwealth only and sincerely may be sought. For these, and grace, let us pray unto God as our Saviour Christ hath taught us: "Our Father," &c.

2. The better to convey myself to the matter which I have in hand, I shall crave leave that I may speak somewhat of this princely prophet Samuel; who, descending of noble parentage, was by his mother consecrated to the ministry. Of which calling though Christ himself thought so highly and honourably that, refusing to be a king, he chose the office of a minister; yet so perverse is the judgment of the world, that they think no condition more base or vile. The minister with his master Christ is contemned: this holy office is become odious: "All men seek their own," and serve themselves: it is accounted slavery to serve the Lord. *Things to be considered in the person of Samuel. He was a minister.* *John vi.[15.]* *Phil. ii. [21.]*

3. Samuel was called of God to be a magistrate, wherein he was so faithful and upright, that his adversaries were forced to justify his doings, and to bear him record that he neither was a bribe-taker, nor an extortioner, nor one that had injured any man. It were well with our commonwealth, if all officers could carry away the like testimony. But evil subjects cannot away with good magistrates. The prodigal, which have consumed their substance in lewdness and vanity, long for a change; supposing that their state will be bettered thereby, and persuading themselves that it cannot be made worse. "All change is perilous;" and an old saying is it, "Seldom comes the better." A better this people could hardly have had: yet so unquiet and discontented they were, that (the good and peaceable government of Samuel notwithstanding) they misliked their present state, and desired another governor to be given them. The worthy magistrate Moses was *He was a godly magistrate; yet misliked by them over whom he was placed.* *Exod. xv. [24.]*

muttered against; the noble king David for a time deposed; our faithful Samuel rejected. Behold the hard state of good princes, who are, for the most part rewarded with great ingratitude. Moses' dear cousins became his deadly enemies: David's familiar friends became his most fierce and violent foes: Samuel was rejected of such as he most favoured. Chrysippus, observing the course of these things, saith that which experience proveth true: "Thou shalt be sure, if thou govern amiss, to purchase God's, if well, the people's anger and displeasure." The danger of this office, by reason of the great ingratitude of the people, made Moses say to God, "Send whom thou wilt send." It caused Demosthenes rather to wish banishment, than place of government; and Themistocles to prefer hell itself to the judgment-seat. When Antigonus should put on a royal diadem, he brake forth into this speech, "O cloth of more honourable than happy estate; wherewith if a man were so throughly acquainted that he could tell the number of cares and miseries wherewith thou art fraught, he would not stoop for thee, though he might have thee for the taking up." Wherefore it grieved not Samuel to be eased of so heavy a burthen: but God was much grieved to see so great disgrace offered to his anointed. "They have not rejected thee, but me," saith the Lord. To dislike and cast off a good magistrate is to dislike and cast off God; because "all power is of God." God, in his wrath for godly Samuel, gave them wicked Saul. I pray God in his justice serve all such alike, as seek after such change, as cannot submit themselves with loving and obedient hearts to the good government of worthy Samuel, their natural prince, their good and faithful magistrate; whom for conscience sake they ought to honour and obey.

2 Sam. xvii.
Psal. lxx. [2, 3.]
Chrysippus.
Exod. iv. [13.]
Demosthenes.
Themistocles.
Valer. Max. lib. vii. cap. ii.
1 Sam. viii. [7.]
Rom. xiii. [1.]

4. Samuel was both a prophet and a prince, a minister and a magistrate: so was Melchisedec, Moses, David, Christ. He had need to be a rare man, that should well answer sundry offices. When *Redde rationem*, "Give account," cometh, then one office such as the least of these will be thought a burthen heavy enough for any one, besides these, to have borne. But the matching of these two offices doth teach, what agreement, love, and liking

He was both a prophet and a prince.
Luke xvi. [2.]

should be between these two officers. They are God's two hands to build up withal the decayed walls of Jerusalem. If the one hand set forward, and the other put backward, God's work will be ill wrought. The wisdom of God matched Moses and Aaron, two brethren; the one the minister, the other the magistrate; that, knit together in brotherly love, they might labour together with both hands for the furtherance of God's building. When the word and the sword do join, then is the people well ruled, and then is God well served. So long as king Joas and the good priest Jehoida lived together, God was served according to his word: the priest rightly counselled, the king gladly followed. [Exod. iv. [14, 16.]] [2 Kings xii. [2.]]

5. Samuel, zealous for the glory of God, and careful for the commonwealth, preacheth to the parliament assembled after this sort: "Be this sin against the Lord far from me, &c." Wherein first, he putteth the ministers in mind of their duty; secondly, he telleth the prince and people of their office; lastly, he sheweth, if they do it not, what punishment will follow. [Things contained in the words of Samuel. 1. The duty of the minister. 2. The duty of the prince. 3. The duty of the people. 4. The punishment, if this duty be not performed.]

6. Samuel, rejected and put from the office of a magistrate by this froward and rebellious people, yet was not so froward himself, as to forsake the office of a minister. Neither minded he to revenge this wrong offered him; but with a mild mind he was content, not only to pray for them, but to teach them faithfully, and lovingly to admonish them. A pattern for all princes to be mild in their own matters, yet earnest and zealous in the quarrel of God. He prayed for the people his enemies—the cause was his own: he took the sword in his hand, and cut king Agag in pieces—the cause was God's. Moses in his own cause was a man most mild; he quietly suffered wonderful wrongs: but when he perceived idolatry committed, God's glory coming into question, he with his partakers, for worshipping of that calf, put to the sword three thousand men. Christ our Saviour and Master suffered, though undeservedly, yet meekly, all reproof, yea reproach, yea death itself: but when his Father's cause came in hand, that the house of God was made a den of thieves, he bestirred him with his whip, coursed those simoniacal choppers and changers, buyers and sellers, out of the temple, and make havock of whatsoever they had. [Samuel zealous in God's cause, but mild in his own.] [1 Sam. xv. [33.]] [Exod. xxxii. [28.]] [John ii. [15.]]

7. This mild and zealous Samuel, zealous in God's cause, and mild in his own, first by his own example putteth the ministers in mind of their duty: in whom he requireth two things, as principal points concerning them, to pray, and to teach. "God forbid that I should sin against the Lord, and cease praying for you: I will shew you the good and right way."

<small>1. By his own example he giveth ministers to understand that it is their duty to pray and to teach.</small>

8. Christ, that good pastor, was earnest in prayer for the people, "Holy Father, keep them:" yea for his enemies, "Father, forgive them." Paul, the good apostle, "prayed without intermission." James, the good bishop of Jerusalem, made his knees as hard as the hoof of a camel with continual praying[1]. Our good prophet Samuel thinketh it a great sin not to pray for the people: *Absit a me hoc peccatum,* "Be this sin far from me." Christ, Peter, Paul, Jeremy, prayed with many tears. God is delighted with an hearty prayer, both in the minister, in the prince, and in the people. Christ was so fervent herein, that he sweat water and blood. King David, in his earnest prayer, nightly watered his bed with tears. The Israelites in Babylon, in pouring out their hearty prayers, poured out also tears abundantly. Moses was so earnest with God in his prayers, that God said unto him, "Why dost thou hold me?" Anna[2] was so eager, that she poured out her very heart before God in prayer. The very ethnicks[3] would not dally with their false gods in prayer. Plutarch reporteth, that when they met in the house of their idols to pray, one openly pronounced, *Hoc agite;* "Do this." Talk not, trifle not, let not your minds wander. Do that ye come for. For "prayer is the lifting up of the mind to God." And Christ complaineth of this lip-labour: "This people honour me with their lips." God seeth thy heart, and he requireth it.

<small>His prayer was earnest, as appeareth by his words, "Be this sin far from me, that I should cease to pray."

Luke xxii. [44.]

Psal. vi. [6.]
2 Chron. xxxiii. [12, 13.]
Exod. xxxii. [10.]
1 Sam. i. [10.]

Plutarch.

Matt. xv. [8.]</small>

9. The persons for whom Samuel did pray, are specified in the latter end of his speech. For to whom he saith, "if ye do wickedly, ye shall perish, both you and your king;" for them, that they might not do wickedly, he prayed. We must pray "first for kings, and all that are

<small>He prayed for the prince and the people.

1 Tim. ii. [1, 2.]</small>

[1 Euseb. Pamph. Hist. Eccl. Amst. 1695. Lib. II. 23. p. 50.—Ed.]
[2 Anna—Hannah.—Ed.]
[3 Ethnicks—heathen.—Ed.]

placed in authority;" that God may give them understanding hearts, rightly to rule; faithful counsellors, from whom they may receive wise and grave advice; careful minds, to put good counsels in execution. Evil counsel given and followed hath wrought much woe to many princes, and utter ruin to sundry commonwealths. King Hanan hearkened to evil counsel, and executed it; but it turned to the confusion of him and his people. Absolon likewise followed Achitophel's wicked counsel; and destruction likewise followed them both. Solomon, he gave ear to foolish women, and followed their idolatrous devices; whereby he procured to himself the wrath of God. Roboam rejected the counsel of the grave and wise, and followed the light and lusty devices of young brains; but it spoiled him of the most part of his kingdom. Zedekias would not hear the good counsel of Jeremy, but gave ear to the evil advice of his bad counsellors; which in the end turned to his confusion. Happy is that prince, that hath wise and godly counsellors; and thrice happy, that will follow them. Then may the people live a quiet and a peaceable life in all godliness and honesty. Samuel prayed for the prince and the people. This is one principal part of the minister's office. [2 Sam. x. [3, 4.]] [2 Sam. xvi. [20—23.]] [1 Kings xi. [1—10.]] [1 Kings xii. [13, 14.]] [Jer. xxxviii. [19.]]

10. The other is to teach. "If I teach not, woe worth me," saith St Paul. But what is it that the minister should teach? The pope to be head of the universal church? No: that Christ claimeth as his own right. To abstain from marriage and meat, as not lawful to be used? That St Paul termeth the "doctrine of devils." Shall we teach purgatory and prayer to the dead, or for the dead? But St John teacheth, that we are purged by the blood of Christ. And God commandeth us to call upon him in our prayer. Other commandment have we none. To be short, shall we teach the doctrine of men? Then all our "worshipping of God shall be in vain." Samuel therefore telleth us what we shall teach, namely, "the good and right way." Esay, speaking of God's word, saith, "This is the way, walk in it." The prophet Jeremy hath the like, "Stand upon the ways and see, and inquire of the old way, which is the good way, and walk in it." We ought to walk in the old path of God's ancient word: for that is the good and the right way. [The next duty of the minister is to teach; not what they list, but the good and right way. Col. i. [18.] Eph. iv. [15.] 1 Tim. iv. [1, 3.] 1 John i. [7.] Matt. xv. [9.] Isai. xxx. [21.] Jer. vi. [16.]]

"Ye shall not do that which seemeth right unto you." "But what I command, that only do: neither add nor detract any thing." Christ taught not his own ways, but the ways of his Father: "The words which I have spoken are not mine, but his that sent me, the Father's." St Paul durst not teach any other thing than what he had received of the Lord. Yea, he curseth the very angels of heaven, if they teach any other way than that which he had already delivered, as right and good. It is the office therefore of the minister to teach the word. "He that speaketh, let him speak as the words of God." The good emperor Constantinus was so careful of this, that he required of the synod over which he was set to decide matters of religion, that they should order all things by the book of God, which book he placed for the same purpose in the midst of them: and what the bishops in synod did so conclude to be godly and behoveful, that he did ratify and confirm.

Deut. xii. [8, 32.]
John xiv. [10.]
1 Cor. xi. [23.]
Gal. i. [8.]
1 Pet. iv. [11.]

11. The ministers, you see, should teach the right way. He which beareth that name, and performeth not this office, is but an "idol:" "Let another take his bishoprick." Such drones were better smothered, than suffered in that hive, where none should live that will not labour. Such as sow not, why should they reap? Neither is it any new thing to cast out unworthy ministers who cast off care of their duty. Solomon deposed Abiathar the high priest: and Justinian deprived Sylverius and Vigilius, bishops of Rome. These are good precedents for princes in like case to follow.

Such as do not this work, should not be suffered to bear this office.
Zech. xi. [17.]
Acts i. [20.]
1 Kings ii. [27.]

12. Again, such as teach, but teach not the good and right way; such as are open and public maintainers of errors and heresy; such, in the judgment of God, are thought unworthy to live. *Falsus propheta moriatur.* Elias and Jehu did not think themselves imbrued, but rather sanctified with such blood. I have no cruel heart: blood be far from me: I mind[1] nothing less. Yet needs must it be granted that the maintainers and teachers of errors and heresy are to be repressed in every christian commonwealth. Such troublers of the quiet of the church, such deceivers of the people, are at least wise, according

Punishment due unto such as teach ways contrary to that which is good and right.
Deut. xiii. [5.]
1 Kings xviii. [40.]
2 Kings x. [24, 25.]

[1 Mind—desire.—Ed.]

to the ancient commendable custom of the church, to be removed from the ministry. It is no reason that the church enemies should be fostered in the bosom of the church. The histories of things done by good princes and rulers in these cases are so many and manifest, that I need not trouble you with recital of them. Amphilochius the bishop sharply reproved Theodosius the emperor, that he so long winked at Arius, and suffered him to spread his pestilent heresy far and wide over the body of the church: the emperor was not angry at the words of just reproof; but forthwith banished Arius, and gave him some part of his just deserts. The ministers, what room soever they have in the church of God, ought to pray, and teach the good and right way, or else to give place to others that can and will. And thus much for the duty of the ministers. Trip. hist.
lib. ix. cap.
25.

13. It followeth, "Fear the Lord, and serve him in the truth with all your hearts." The prophet, in these words, putteth the prince and people in remembrance of their duty. Wherein double service is required; the service due unto God, and the service due unto the commonwealth. The service which we owe unto God is fear: which fear is ever joined with love, and for that cause called a son-like fear; to distinguish it from that servile fear, the end whereof is desperation, as the fruit of the former is love, which maketh not ashamed. Fear God; for they which fear him shall not feel his power. All things be naked and open before him. He doth see, and will judge. Fear him therefore: but love him too, who hath so loved thee, that he hath not spared his only Son, but given him to death for thee. 2.
The duty of the prince towards God and the commonwealth.

14. God putteth the heads in mind of this duty; knowing that, as they go before, so the people will follow after. Jeroboam gave evil example, and he made the people sin. Josias feared and zealously served God; and the people did the like. *Quomodo reges Domino serviunt in timore, nisi ea quæ contra Domini jussa sunt religiosa severitate prohibendo atque plectendo? Aliter rex servit ut homo, aliter ut rex: ut homo, fideliter timendo; ut rex, leges justa præcipientes et contraria prohibentes sanciendo*[1]. "How do How princes do serve God as princes.
2 Kings xxii.
Aug. Ep. 50.

[1] Quomodo ergo reges Domino serviunt in timore, nisi ea, quæ contra jussa Domini fiunt, religiosâ severitate prohibendo atque plectendo?

princes serve the Lord in fear," saith St Augustine, "unless with religious rigour they forbid and punish things wherein the statutes of the Lord are broken? The king serveth God as a man one way, and another way as a king; as a man by leading a faithful life; as a king by making laws, such as enjoin things that are just, and forbid the contrary." Ezekias did God the service of a king in destroying the groves and temples of idols, which were builded against the commandment of God. Josias did the like in reforming the church, in dispatching all idolatry and superstition. Darius did God royal service, when he gave the idol into Daniel's hands, and cast his enemies into the den of lions. Nebuchodonazer did the like, when by strait law he commanded that none should blaspheme, but that all should serve the God of Sydrach, Mysach, and Abednago. Herein princes do rightly serve God as princes, when to serve him they do such things, "as unless they were princes they could not do."

<small>2 Chron. xxxi. [1.]</small>

<small>2 Chron. xxxiv.</small>

<small>Dan. vi. [24.]</small>

<small>Dan. iii. [28, 29.]</small>

<small>The first point of kingly service unto God is to purge his church.</small>

15. The first point of kingly service unto God is to purge and cleanse his church. Christ teacheth this by that which he did at his entering into that foully defiled temple of Jerusalem. It appertaineth to princes, to magistrates, to them which are now assembled in this honourable court of parliament, by all good means and laws to see God's house made clean; that it may be the house of prayer, and not a den of thieves.

<small>From false doctrine and idolatry.</small>

16. First it must be purged from all false doctrine; from all idolatry and superstition. The good kings Ezekias and Josias were careful in this behalf. They could not abide idolatry to be committed, or God to be blasphemed, within their dominions. It had been hard to have purchased such a thing as a mass at Moses' hands with a mass of money. That zealous prince king Asa deposed Maacha his grandmother wholly from all government, for setting up a foul idol in a grove. He that dealt so sharply with his grandmother for this, surely would in no

<small>2 Chron. xv. [16.]</small>

---

tendo? Aliter enim servit, quia homo est, aliter quia etiam rex est. Quia homo est, ei servit vivendo fideliter: quia vero etiam rex est, servit leges justa præcipientes et contraria prohibentes convenienti vigore sanciendo.—August. Op. Par. 1679. Ep. clxxxv. Tom. II. col. 651. —Ed.]

case or respect have tolerated a blasphemous mass in his reformed church and kingdom. The evil, which others do by our sufferance, is ours. We do it, when we suffer it to be done. Princes, to please princes, may not displease the Prince of all princes. Fear the Lord and serve him in zeal and in truth: cast out of the church of England all leaven of blasphemy and idolatry. So shall you glorify God, "and he shall glorify you." Paul's heart was set on fire, his spirit was kindled within him, when he saw the city of Athens given to idolatry. Ye know the history of that worthy man Mattathias. We pray daily, "Hallowed be thy name;" but with what minds, if wittingly we suffer his name to be profaned and blasphemed? 1 Sam. ii. [30.]
Acts xvii. [16.]
1 Mac. ii.

17. "Fear the Lord:" purge his church: remove all stones of offence out of his vineyard. St Paul's rule is, "Let all things in the church be done seemly." What that seemliness is, he himself expoundeth in these words, "Let all things be done unto edification." The primitive church, casting away Judaical and heathenish rites, was simple in her ceremonies. The pope hath polluted and burthened the church with both. We may have no other than such as are comely, and serve for the furtherance of true religion. From occasions of offence.
1 Cor. xiv. [40.]
1 Cor. xiv. [26.]

18. The church had need to be purged of another enormity; or else it cannot be safe. The sin of Magus must be removed. This disease spreadeth far. Patrons gape for gains; and hungry fellows, utterly destitute of all good learning or godly zeal, yea, scantly clothed with common honesty, having money, find ready entrance into the church. These are thieves and robbers: they creep into the church of Christ by stealth. They are not called of God, as Aaron was. This sin is universally complained of. Surely, if simoniacal affection have corrupted the heart of any bishop (as some will not let openly to say), it were not amiss if his heart were given him in his hand. He is easily dealt withal if he be disbishoped. If the lot fall on the layman, the loss of his patronage is but a light punishment for a fault so heinous. But whosoever is this money-man, I will say unto him, in the words of St Peter, "Thy money be with thee unto perdition." Shifts are but shifts in these matters. It is all one to go plainly to work with Judas, "What will ye give me?" and to give thy patronage to thy servant to From simony.

John x. [1.]
Heb. v. [4.]

Acts viii. [20.]

sell, and so to divide Christ's coat between you. Ambrose, in his book *De Pastore*, seemeth to touch bishops of his time with simony, saying, *Quod dedit cum episcopus ordinaretur, aurum fuit; et quod perdidit, anima fuit: cum alium ordinaret, quod accepit, pecunia fuit; quod dedit, lepra fuit*[1]. "That which he gave when he was ordained bishop was gold; and that which he lost was his soul: that which he took when he ordained another was money; and that which he gave was a leprosy." This is the hole whereat so many unfit and unworthy persons have crept in. "Lay not thy hands on any man quickly," is worn out of remembrance. Such as cannot feed the flock are now dispensed withal to be owners of the fleece. God no doubt will find out the fault; and the blood of such as perish will be required at somebody's hands. God grant speedy reformation herein! Such in authority, as truly fear God, will purge his church from false doctrine, from idolatry, from superstition, and from simony.

Ambrosius.

1 Tim. v. [22.]

19. The next point of princely service done to God is to nurse the church with wholesome food, till we all grow up to a perfect man in Christ Jesus. That this food may be ministered, that this word may be preached every where to God's people, good princes, and such as are in authority, must take special care. For this is truly to serve and fear God. It is not enough that princes and magistrates embrace the gospel, that they feed upon the food of salvation themselves; but they, as heads and pastors, must see this bread broken and delivered to the people. Christ had care of all the people, and sent his disciples abroad with this charge, "Go your ways into the whole world." The will of Christ is, "that all be saved, and come to the knowledge of the truth." The preaching of the gospel is called the kingdom of Christ; for by that means Christ is planted, groweth, and reigneth in the hearts and souls of the people. If the flock want their pastor, and by reason thereof through famine perish, doubtless that blood of souls will be required. Laws provide for many matters of small importance. This weighty matter of man's salvation is not lightly to be passed over. The harvest no doubt is great, many

The next point of princely service to God is to provide that his people may be taught the way of salvation.

Matt. xxviii. [19.] 1 Tim. ii. [4.]

Luke x. [2.]

[1 Ambros. Op. Par. 1690. De Dignit. Sacerdot. Tom. II. Appendix, col. 363.—This treatise is placed by the Benedictine editors among the Tractatus Supposititii.—Ed.]

willing to hear the word: few there be that labour, but many idle lookers-on, who take the wages, but either will not or cannot work. They have learned of the evil steward to play the thief, both to rob their master Christ of his glory, and the church of Christ of their salvation. But woe be to those shepherds which feed themselves, and suffer the flock of Christ to want their meat. [Luke xvi. [1—8.]]

20. The want of reward hindereth this work. But this will be answered, Some have enough, and some have too much. I am acquainted with these speeches; but let me say again: A great sort[1] have too little, and some that are worthy to have have stark nothing. No man hath too much, that well doeth his duty: for he is worthy of double that honour which he hath. And he that can justly be charged with want of duty, let his candlestick, in God's name and for God's sake, be removed. Now if it be alleged that, if equal division were made, all might be sufficiently provided for: But who shall make the division? There is cause, why men may think it scant safe for the church of Christ to put her patrimony to arbitrement; lest, while division be pretended, some Quintus Fabius adjudge a good part thereof to the senate of Rome. Rome hath robbed Christ of his honour, and by impropriations given his patrimony to idle fat monks to feed upon. We have restored Christ to his honour and dignity: but we still hold from him his lands and living, like a ward. The ethnick and idolatrous priests of Egypt, of Jupiter, of Baal, of Bel, were liberally provided for. The priests of Aaron, the scribes and Pharisees, the monks, friars, and sacrificing popish priests, were in high authority, and had the wealth of the world. Shall idle service be preferred to the true service of God? Shall false prophets be better regarded and rewarded than true preachers? Then just is our condemnation. For we shew that, "light being come into the world," we love it not so much as they loved darkness. The gospel hath evil luck: it is never preached, but the patrimony thereof is pinched. Such as will pretend the gospel, and labour to pull away the patrimony of the gospel, may well profess Christ in words, but they deny him in their deeds. [Provision to be made for teachers to that purpose.] [1 Tim. v. [17.]] [Rev. ii. [5.]] [Cic. de Off. lib. 1. [10.]] [John iii. [19.]] [Tit. i. [16.]]

[¹ Sort—number, multitude.—ED.]

21. As the ministers are to be provided for, that the word may be preached; so the people must be brought to conform themselves to the thankful receiving thereof, that from thence they may learn truly to serve and fear God. And this care also pertaineth to godly princes and good magistrates, to provide good laws for the same, and to see those laws put in execution. Although conscience cannot be forced, yet unto external obedience, in lawful things, men may lawfully be compelled. God the great King, who worketh all things well, sent forth his officers to compel men to come in and eat of his great supper. Hereupon St Augustine saith, *Qui compellitur, quo non vult cogitur; sed cum intrarit, jam volens pascitur*[1]. "He that is constrained, is driven whither he would not go willingly; but when he is entered by constraint, then he feedeth with a good will." Paul never embraced the gospel until he was cast off his horse flat upon the earth; and then he cried, "Lord, what wilt thou have me to do?" It is profitable for men to be constrained unto those things which are good. And as it is profitable for them to be constrained, so is it a thing very reasonable to constrain them. For why should not the church enforce her lost children to return to salvation, if lost children enforce others to turn to destruction? Seeing that the whole service in our church is no other than God's written word; as there can be alleged no just cause why any man should withdraw himself from this word, so appertaineth it unto princes that fear God, within their dominions, to compel every subject to come and hear this word, lest the church by this evil example should be greatly offended. God's causes are zealously to be seen unto; and the winning of men's souls is religiously to be sought. And thus much briefly touching the service of God. To see the gospel every where preached, the ministers provided for, and the people compelled to come hear the word—this is the fear of God which Samuel requireth.

22. Whereunto must be added a special regard to the commonwealth. It is commonly said that the commonwealth is sore diseased, and that every member of that body seemeth to be grieved. Remedy would be sought in time, lest remedy come too late. But I am no physician for that

[[1] August. Op. Par. 1679. Ep. clxxiii. Tom. II. col. 616.—ED.]

body; and therefore is it not fit for me to minister any medicine to it. But I shall pray for the health thereof, and set it over to such as have skill and can help. The care of the commonwealth chiefly appertaineth to the head of the commonwealth, who is *Parens Patriæ*, the mother of this sick child. It is required at our hands to fear and serve the Lord in truth. That prince doth serve God in truth and in deed, which is careful that the evil may be punished and repressed, and that the good may be defended and advanced. When generally all men are seen unto, that every man do his duty, then God is in truth and sincerity served.

23. The prince is set as the head over the body, as the chief shepherd over the flock. These titles are given to princes and governors, to put them in mind, not only of their honour and pre-eminence, but of their charge and office also. But the prince cannot do this alone: it is a burthen too heavy for one to wield. And therefore he must, according to the counsel which Jethro gave unto Moses, " choose out of all the people men wise and fearing God, lovers of the truth, such as hate covetousness, and out of them make rulers over thousands, hundreds, fifties, and tens, that they may sit and judge the people at all seasons." Magistrates should be chosen out of all the people for their worthiness. It is unmeet that such things as should follow deserts be procured by other sinister means. Magistrates should be wise men, furnished with learning, understanding, good skill, and long experience; men that fear God, religious lovers of his truth, favourers of the gospel, and of all such as live in the fear of God; true and upright dealers, such as will stedfastly fasten their eyes upon the causes brought before them, and not regard the face of any man; lastly, haters of covetousness, bribes, and rewards. Good officers should thus be qualified. And, to the end that magistrates may be such, it must be provided that there may be choice of officers without sale of offices. It is not probable that he, which obtaineth such a room for a price, will leave it freely, or deal justly in it. A greater corruption than this cannot enter into a commonwealth. For by this mean both the prince and people are deceived. To punish the evil, to maintain the good, to overlook the

marginal notes: With the prince other officers must be joined, of whose choice how great care should be had. Exod. xviii. [21, 22.]

whole, and to choose and appoint forth worthy officers for the government of the commonwealth, this is the duty of a prince that feareth God. That prince which doth this serveth God in truth.

The power of princes, if they list to use it unto good purposes.

24. Homer bringeth in Jupiter sitting in the midst of the assembly of gods, whom he menaceth and threateneth on this wise: "Let not any god or goddess attempt the breach of my mandate. If I understand that any do, I will give him small joy of this place, or provide him another far enough hence, a dwelling-place, the gates whereof are iron, and the ground brass. I will plunge him as deep under hell, as heaven is over earth. He shall well know his might to be somewhat beneath mine. For if ye think yourselves to be stronger than I am, make trial of your strength, fasten a chain in heaven, and join all your force at the end thereof. But ye shall never be able to pull Jupiter out of heaven, no, though ye sweat much about it: whereas if I list to put but my finger to the haling of you, I will pluck up sea and land with you; so much am I superior unto gods and men[1]." Kings and princes in their several dominions have such power through the providence of Almighty God, by whose appointment they wear their crowns, that their ordinances be not lightly broken, unless themselves be careless to have them kept. For, by reason of the majesty that God hath given them, they are feared of all estates and conditions of men. They can throw down whom they will; and whom they will they can advance. They have the chain and the rein in their hands: they can draw others whither they will, but others are not able to draw them unless they list. This power, and strength, and glory, which God hath given unto kings, and whereby they are able to lead the world as it were in a string, leaveth them utterly without excuse, if they use it not to the benefit of the commonwealth. They cannot serve God in truth, and give the bridle to their subjects to sin without restraint. These times of greatest and gravest consultation are fit occasions, wherein princes may most effectually shew how heartily and truly they fear the Lord. These are the times to provide chains, that is to say,

[1 Hom. Il. Θ. 7—27.—ED.]

good statutes and laws to hold all men within compass, and to bind together the scattered parts of the commonwealth. When the great council of Rome entered into the senate, to consult for the good government and defence of the empire; first they went and sacrificed to Jupiter, and there every man offered up and left behind him his private affections, promising that their consultation should only tend to the common benefit. Leave you all private affections likewise: cast them behind you: seek not your own commodity. Let it appear that you love your country. God, the prince, and the commonwealth, require a faithful performance of this service at your hands. Seek by law the sincere setting forth, the maintenance and continuance, of God's true religion. Let this be your first and principal care; and so shall ye serve the Lord in truth. *{Making of laws to remedy abuses in the commonwealth.}*

25. Seek by law to repress the gainsayers, and the enemies of this truth. This liberty, that men may openly profess diversity of religion, must needs be dangerous to the commonwealth. What stirs diversity of religion hath raised in nations and kingdoms, the histories are so many and so plain, and our times in such sort have told you, that with further proof I need not trouble your ears. One God, one king, one faith, one profession, is fit for one monarchy and commonwealth. Division weakeneth: concord strengtheneth. The story of Scilurus the Scythian is known, who upon his death-bed taught his fourscore sons the force of unity by the strength of sticks, weak by themselves, when they are tied in a bundle. Let conformity and unity in religion be provided for; and it shall be as a wall of defence unto this realm. *{Liberty of professing divers religions is dangerous to the state.}*

26. And as these things are especially to be regarded; as our principal care must be for the highest matters, sincerity and unity in religion; so we may not neglect or pass over smaller things, which need redress. For, as diseases and sores in the basest and vilest parts of the body do grieve and may endanger the chiefest, unless they be cured betimes; so the least abuses, by sufferance, may work the greatest harm. Gorgeous apparel and sumptuous diet, with such like matters, may seem small things; but they are the causes of no small *{Smaller abuses in attire, diet, &c.}*

[SANDYS.]

evils. They eat up England; and are therefore to be repressed by strait laws. It is a part of true service done unto God to see even unto these things.

Corruptions in officers under the prince.
27. We may seem to cast our eyes very low, when we look into the dealings of every officer under the prince. Yet every one must be seen unto. They wax suddenly rich by the spoil of the prince. Reform it by law, that all may walk in truth. If merchants, with other artificers, and meaner trades, do enrich themselves by impoverishing others through deceitful shifts; the commonwealth suffereth damage by their uneven dealings. If we will have God served in truth, we must by law reform them.

Deceit in the meaner trades of life.

Usury.
28. That biting worm of usury, that devouring wolf, hath consumed many: many it hath pulled upon their knees, and brought to beggary; many such as might have lived in great wealth, and in honour not a few. This canker hath corrupted all England. It is become the chief chaffer and merchandise of England. We shall do God and our country true service, by taking away this evil. Repress it by law; else the heavy hand of God hangeth over us and will strike us.

Adultery.
29. That vile sin of adultery, in God's commonwealth punished with death, so overfloweth the banks of all chastity, that, if by sharp laws it be not speedily cut off, God from heaven with fire will consume it. Prevent God's wrath: bridle this outrage: so shall you serve the Lord in truth.

Corner contracts, without consent of parents.
30. There is nothing more hurtful to the commonwealth than these corner contracts, without consent of parents; contrary to the word of God, the law of nature, the law civil, and all right and reason. The inconveniences that follow are not sufferable. Euaristus, a bishop of Rome, saith, "It is not wedlock, but whoredom, when the consent of parents is wanting[1]." God cannot be better

[1 ... legitimum... non fit conjugium, nisi ab his qui super ipsam feminam dominationem videntur habere, et a quibus custoditur, uxor petatur, et a parentibus aut propinquioribus sponsetur... Aliter vero præsumpta, non conjugia, sed aut adulteria, aut contubernia, aut stupra, vel fornicationes, potius quam legitima conjugia esse non dubitet.—Evaristi Epist. i. in Concil. Stud. Labbei. Lut. Par. 1671. Tom. i. col. 534.— The epistle is spurious: Evaristus having been bishop of Rome about

served, than if by law ye restrain this unlawful contracting. The children of this inconvenient marriage may scarcely be termed lawful. The devil, that hath ever hated wedlock, and loveth whoredom, was the first author of this great disorder. God grant you understanding hearts and willing minds, faithfully and in truth to travail to repress and take away these evils.

31. And, as evil is to be controuled by law, so that which is good is also by law to be procured. God hath made us many ways rich. For what we have, freely at his hands we have it. But he himself is become very poor; insomuch that, for want of relief, he is forced to beg; and, for want of lodging and meat, he lieth and dieth in our streets. This great ingratitude God cannot but revenge. O, what shame is this to a christian commonwealth, in a reformed country! Obstinate Jews would never shew themselves so unthankful. Their ancient law, forbidding beggars, is even to this day most straitly kept amongst them. Laws in this behalf have been provided; but as they wanted perfection, so have they in manner in no point or any where had execution. Serve God in truth: provide that Christ crave not. Such as will not feed him here he will never feed in his kingdom. Thus have I, point by point, let you see disorders and wants in the commonwealth. Ye have authority by law to reform them. Consider dutifully of it, and serve God truly as ye ought, always remembering the saying of the prophet Esay, "Woe be to them that make wicked laws." *The poor.* *Deut. xv. [7.]* *Isai. x. [1.]*

32. When good laws are made, they must be put in execution. Law is the life of the commonwealth; and execution the life of the law. And better not to make laws, than not to execute laws when they are once made. This is the duty of the public ministers of the commonwealth. They must first keep laws themselves; and then see that others in like sort may observe them. If the officers and ministers of the commonwealth contemn laws, doubtless the people will never reverence them: if they *Execution of laws.*

A. D. 100; while his letter quotes writings of the fourth century, and makes use of Jerome's version of the scriptures. See Prolegomena, p. 63, to Blondell's Epist. Decretalium Examen.—ED.]

break them, the people will never keep them. Which Solon wisely considering, wisely answered, being demanded what was chief safety for a commonwealth; "If the citizens obey the magistrate, and the magistrate the laws." You that are appointed to this purpose, and put in trust therewith, lay aside dread and meed, favour and friendship, gift and gain; and with simplicity of heart punish the transgressor of the law, according to the law.. Make not Anacharsis' web of the law: let not the hornet escape, and the little fly be caught. Few laws, well made and well kept, would serve the turn. This is God's service: the execution thereof he hath set over to your hands. Serve him in truth and singleness of heart. "Cursed is he that negligently doeth the work of the Lord."

Solon.

Valer. lib. vii. c. 2.

Jer. xlviii. [10.]

3. The duty of the people towards God.

33. Thus much hath been spoken concerning higher powers, and of their duty in the service of God. Samuel speaketh not to them alone: to the people it is spoken, as well as to the prince, "Fear and serve ye the Lord in truth." Fear God: embrace the gospel: lead your lives in holiness and righteousness according to the word of truth. The Lord is a strong defence to them that fear him. "They that fear him, want nothing."

Psal. xxxiv. [10.]

Towards higher powers. Rom. xiii. [1.]

34. Give unto the Lord's anointed due reverence and honour. "Let every soul be subject," not by constraint but for conscience sake. Imitate those worthy Israelites, who were so willingly obedient to Joshua, that they cried with one voice, "Whosoever shall rebel against thy commandment, and will not obey thy words in all that thou commandest him, let him die." Grudge not, repine not at higher powers: say not in your hearts, "Let us break their bands, and cast away their chains from us."

Josh. i. [18.]

Psal. ii. [3.]

Towards the commonwealth. Jer. xxix. [7.]

35. Seek the peace of the commonwealth, and the safety thereof; "for in the peace thereof your peace doth stand." In this sort God is to be feared: in this sort of all sorts he is to be served; and by this mean the commonwealth is to be maintained and preserved. If we, linked together in the fear of God, and in true concord and amity among ourselves, put to our helping hands, every one dutifully in his calling, to the supporting of this state and defending thereof, doubtless no enemy, no foreign power can hurt us, no bull of Basan shall prevail

against us: but we and our commonwealth, in despite of all both corporal and spiritual enemies, shall be strengthened and stablished for ever. So true is it, "That kingdom which is grounded upon goodwill standeth fast and sure for ever." Greg. Nazian.

36. But as the natural body without sinews cannot grow, wax strong, or continue; no more can a civil body without his sinews. The sinews of the commonwealth are the treasures. Tributes therefore and subsidies are due to the prince. "Give unto Cæsar those things that are Cæsar's;" "tribute unto whom tribute belongeth." It is not given to the prince, but to the commonwealth: it is in truth bestowed upon ourselves. The prince, in respect of private use, neither needeth neither requireth our money. It is the commonwealth, whereunto we owe not our goods only, but our lives also: it requireth this at our hands for our own safety. The prince will be but a steward hereof, seasonably to lay it out for public use. Good commonwealths-men have not spared to give their very lives for their country; as Themistocles, Curtius, Codrus, and others. And who can so little regard the commonwealth as, by pinching at a piece of money, to pinch it? He that seeth his house ruinous, and for sparing will not repair it; if it fall upon his head, let him fault himself. Moses found his subjects marvellous ready in this behalf: when a voluntary contribution was required towards the building of the tabernacle, they brought in so much, that he was forced to cry, *Sufficit;* "now enough." Cyrus was a gentle and a good prince, and he had thankful subjects: their voluntary gift at one subsidy surmounted all the long-heaped treasure of rich Crœsus. The prince's treasure is wasted in our defence: our duty is to repair it again for our safety. This duty God and our commonwealth require at our hands. Let us pay frankly this debt: so shall we work our own safety, strengthen the commonwealth, and serve God and our country in truth. Subsidies.
Matt. xxii. [21.]
Rom. xiii. [7.]
Valer. lib. v. c. 6.
Exod. xxxvi. [5.]

37. And thus we learn, that if the ministers earnestly pray for, and faithfully teach the prince and the people; if the prince and the people sincerely fear and serve God— fear him as an omnipotent Lord and just Judge, and withal love him as a most loving Father; serve him 4. The punishment, if by the minister, the prince, and the people, the foresaid duties be not performed.

in cleansing and feeding his church—cleansing it from false doctrine, idolatry, superstition, and simony, feeding it with the word, by causing it every where to be preached, which will be by providing maintenance for the preachers thereof, and compelling all subjects to hear God's word, and receive his sacraments: further, if the prince carefully consider of the commonwealth, to repress the evil, encourage and strengthen the good, and overlook the whole; and do choose wise, religious, lovers of the truth, and haters of covetousness under him to govern it: if in this great and stately council of the kingdom (banishing private affections) it sincerely be sought by law to set forth and prefer true religion, and withal to bridle the desperate tongues of gainsayers: if by strength of good laws they repress monstrous apparel and excessive diet, deceitful bargaining, usury, adultery, unlawfully stolen contracts; and so provide for the poor, that Christ in his members may be relieved: if the officers of the commonwealth keep good laws themselves; and faithfully, without foolish pity (which is cruelty), see them executed upon others: if the people, like good subjects, fear God, honour the prince, live peaceably, and seek the safety of their country: lastly, if we all, linked together in love, liberally relieve the commonwealth, and frankly supply the want thereof, for our own safety—then doubtless the Lord will bless and preserve our prince and us, and stablish this kingdom in peace and prosperity, to flourish and to continue. But if we be cold and negligent in God's cause; if we be unthankful and disobedient to our good Samuel, to our gracious sovereign; then let us look for that which God threateneth here by his prophet, "Both you and your king shall perish." God grant in his mercy that, assisted with his grace, we may sincerely seek and serve him, to his great glory and our great safety in this life, and eternal salvation in the world to come! To that immortal, only wise, and most gracious God, &c.

THE THIRD SERMON.

A SERMON

PREACHED IN YORK, AT THE CELEBRATION OF THE DAY OF THE QUEEN'S ENTRANCE INTO HER REIGN.

CANTICLES II.

15. Take us the little foxes which destroy the vines: for our vine hath flourished.

SUCH solemn assemblies in so sacred a place, to give God thanks for great benefits received, are no rare things among God's people; but are confirmed by sundry examples in the scriptures. Nehemias, after that the house of God was re-edified, assembled the people, caused the law of the Lord to be openly read, gave thanks unto the Lord for their deliverance from Babylon and for restitution of religion, and with great rejoicing and feasting kept that day holy unto the Lord. When, by the means of queen Hester, the Jews had gotten rest, and given a great overthrow to their enemies, she likewise, with the advice of her godly uncle, Mardocheus[1], commanded the people to keep that day, the fourteenth of the month Adar, holy unto the Lord yearly, to feast and give thanks for God's great mercies and their marvellous deliverance. When God had delivered his people Israel from the tyranny of Triphon by the means of Simon the high priest, a governor and prince of the Jews, Simon ordained that the same day of their deliverance should yearly be kept holy unto the Lord with gladness, feasting, and thanksgiving. The feasts of Passover, Pentecost, Tabernacles, and such other, were commanded to be kept holy in remembrance of great benefits received at the Lord's hands. The people of Israel, with thankful hearts remembering what a great benefit they had received, when he chose and anointed David to be their king, gathered together

Solemn assemblies ordained in the church, to the praise of God for special benefits.
Nehem. viii.

Esther ix. [29—32.]

1 Mac. xiii. [51, 52.]

Deut. xvi.

[¹ Mardocheus—Mordecai.—ED.]

in a solemn assembly to celebrate that happy day, and to give God thanks, sang with joyful acclamation unto the Lord, "This is the day which the Lord hath made, let us rejoice and be glad in it."

Psal. cxviii. [24.]

2. Greater cause to assemble together, and to give God thanks for blessings and benefits received, had never nation or people than we presently have. For as this day, now twenty years fully finished, the Lord in his mercy remembering us, when we little hoped and less deserved, delivered us from the state of miserable servitude, and gave us our gracious sovereign, his own elect, Elizabeth by his grace our prince and governor; the restorer of our religion and liberty. Lord, shew us the light of thy favourable countenance: multiply these good days: grant us many of these happy years: O Lord, I pray thee, save now: O Lord, I pray thee, how give prosperity: Lord, preserve whom thou hast given: give her, O Lord, good success and prosperity. Eusebius, the bishop of Cesarea, thought himself much honoured, that he was appointed to celebrate with a sermon the inauguration of Constantinus the emperor. Even so I take it for my great good hap, that it falleth to my lot at this present to put you in remembrance of the great happiness which hath befallen us as on this day, that we may rejoice and be thankful for it.

As great cause of the like assemblies presently in England as ever any where.

3. And for the better performance hereof, as the public minister of the church, I bring unto you the voice of the church, a part of the most excellent Song of Solomon. Which at the first sight although it may seem a strange piece of scripture, and scantly fit for this time; yet, when it shall be throughly considered of, it will appear very pertinent to our time and purpose. For herein is contained a doctrine touching the mercies of God towards us, the malicious frowardness of his and our enemies, and our duty towards him concerning them. "Our vineyard hath flourished;" behold the mere grace and favour of God towards his church: "Little foxes devour it;" behold the ingratitude of the people, resisting the grace of God, and abusing his mercy: "Take us these little foxes;" behold the commandment of God, and the duty of his servants. Of these three things in order as they lie, my purpose is, by God's assistance, to speak.

Three things contained in this parcel of scripture above written.

4. The church of God, by a metaphor, is many times in the scriptures termed a vineyard; neither can there be a better resemblance in any thing, and that in divers respects. But because it were more curious than profitable particularly to follow the comparison, I will only remember unto you the chief parts. The vineyard that shall fructify must fall into the hands of a skilful and laboursome husbandman, who first must weed it, stone it, and prepare it; then he must in season, and with cunning, plant a good vine that will bear a pleasant grape in it, water, underprop, and prune it; and lastly compass it about with a ditch, a strong wall, or a sure hedge for defence. Such a vineyard must needs bring forth good fruit. God of his goodness hath provided for this vineyard, his church of England, all these helps abundantly: he hath beautified it and furnished it most plentifully with rare and wonderful blessings.

1. Our vineyard hath flourished. The church of God like a vineyard, which must first be cleansed, then planted, and thirdly fenced; to the end it may flourish.

5. He hath given it a skilful overseer, one endued with all gifts and qualities fit for government. "An unwise king destroyeth his people: but where they that be in authority are men of understanding, there the city prospereth." "Be wise therefore, O ye kings; be learned, ye judges of the earth," saith the prophet. It pleased the Lord greatly that Solomon asked rather wisdom than riches, knowledge than honour: "Give unto thy servant, O Lord, an understanding heart, to judge thy people, that I may discern between good and bad." If learning and wisdom be so necessarily required in a governor, how great is the goodness of Almighty God to us-ward, which hath so plentifully bestowed this gift of knowledge and wisdom upon our sovereign; not far inferior to Mithridates for diversity of languages, but far surmounting all former English princes in learning, knowledge, and understanding! which rare and excellent gift dwelleth not in her royal breast alone, but is beautified and accompanied with sundry other most singular graces. She is the very patroness of true religion, rightly termed "the Defender of the Faith;" one that before all other things seeketh the kingdom of God. If the threatenings of men could have terrified her, or their allurements enticed her, or any crafty persuasions have prevailed, she had revolted long ere this; so fiercely by great potentates her constancy hath been assaulted. But God hath strengthened his royal handmaid:

The church of England blessed with an overseer, wise, and learned, religious, just, peaceful, performing the aforesaid duties therein. Ecclus. x. [3.] Psal. ii. [10.] 1 Kings iii. [9.]

the fear of God hath put to flight the fear of men: her religious heart is accepted of the Lord, and glorious it is also in the eyes of the world. A prince so zealous for God's house, so firmly settled in his truth, that she hath constantly determined, and oftentimes vowed, rather to suffer all torments, than one jot to relent in matter of religion. She is not fraudulent and treacherous, but dealeth justly and truly in word and deed with all men, promiseth and performeth. Herein her majesty passeth all princes; and therefore in credit she is far before others. And her great desire is, that all men placed in authority under her should deal truly, judge rightly, and give to every man his own according to justice, matching always with justice mercy; which two are so linked and coupled together, that they may not be severed. Justice without mercy is too sharp and rigorous; and mercy without justice is not mercy but folly. That no prince of this realm, inclining so much to mercy, did ever less hinder the course of justice than her highness hath done, such as are placed in judicial rooms must needs confess. So truly it may be said, "The sceptre of thy kingdom is a righteous sceptre; thou lovest justice, and hatest sin." Of nature a prince most merciful, in judgment upright and just. A prince void of all corruption, an hater of bribes, free in bestowing, in taking close-handed: one that hath learned and doth practise our Saviour's lesson, "It is a more blessed thing to give, than to receive." A right Samuel, that cannot be charged with indirect dealing. A prince mild as Moses, just as Samuel, peaceful as Solomon, zealous as David. Neither speak I this in flattery, which thing be far from me, but in an upright conscience; not of guess, but of knowledge; not seeking myself, but the glory of God; that, being put in mind of your happiness, ye may praise God for his mercy, and glorify him in his gracious gifts. Thus hath God blessed this vineyard his church with a learned, wise, religious, just, uncorrupt, mild, merciful, peaceful, and zealous prince to govern it. A great blessing: the Lord continue it, and make us thankful for it!

Psal. xlv. [6.]

Acts xx. [35.]

The vineyard of England purged of idolatry and superstition.

6. This skilful manurer of the vineyard must first rid the ground, purge the church. The barn floor must be cleansed, before the harvest be brought in. Jeremy commandeth the thorns first to be rooted out, and then the seed

to be cast into the ground. Moses gave charge to cast out all leaven, before the people might celebrate the passover. Joshua willed the Canaanites to be expelled, ere he would establish his commonwealth of Israel. Jacob would not sacrifice unto God, till he had purged his house of idols. The like might be shewed in David, Ezekias, Nehemias, Mattathias. But one example may serve for all, being of our Saviour, who is above all and Lord of all. Christ, at his first entry into the temple, purged it by casting out buyers and sellers. Our gracious governor, following Christ's example, hath laboured most earnestly first to cleanse this ground, and to purge this church of England; hath caused the stones to be picked out, brambles and briars to be pulled up, all rubbidge and whatsoever was hurtful to be removed, the den of thieves to be dispersed, buyers and sellers of popish trash, monks, friars, massmongers, with like miscreants, to be hurled and whipped out; the stumbling stones of superstition, the baggage of man's traditions, with all monuments of idolatry, vanity, and popery, to be cast out of the house of God and vineyard of the Lord; so that the field of God is cleared, the vineyard cleansed, the church purged, ready for the seed to be sown, and the vine to be planted. And all this without resistance or tumult. It was the work of God: it is marvellous to as many as duly consider it.

7. Now it behoveth the vinitor to take great heed what vine he planteth in this vineyard. Thorns will not bring forth grapes, nor thistles figs. If thou sow the giddy darnel of human traditions, look for like fruit; for he that conceiveth vanity shall bring forth wind. But our skilful householder, our wise governor, hath planted in this our vineyard neither thorns nor thistles, but the true vine Christ, growing in the hearts of his elect. This vine hath been diligently watered with the dew of God's truth sincerely preached: it hath been cherished with his sacraments, reverently administered according to his will: it hath been under-propped with the continuance of authority, and defence of zealous christian magistrates; pruned with the two-edged sword of God's Spirit, working by the ministry of his servants, who with the sweet promises of the gospel have reared up the drooping branches overburthened with sin, and with the

Christ planted in the vineyard of England.

sharp threatenings of the law have cut off the lascivious wild boughs of wickedness. No flock better fed, no people more instructed, no vineyard in the world more beautiful or goodly to behold.

The vineyard fenced with laws of discipline.

8. This vineyard so prepared, this vine so planted, watered, and underset, hath also been strongly hedged, and fenced with godly laws of good discipline, to put back all enemies, to punish all transgressors, to bridle the unruly, and to keep men in order, that the church of God may live in all peace and tranquillity, with all piety and honesty. This is the flourishing vineyard of the Lord; the beautiful ark of covenant, wherein are reposed the treasures of God, the golden pot with manna, the rod of Aaron, and the tables of Moses. No church under heaven more enriched with treasures and gifts of God; so that we may truly say, "We are enriched by him in all knowledge, and in all speech, insomuch that we are not destitute of any gift." The Lord may justly say to us, as to his people of old, "What might I do for my vine, which I have not done?" and we may well sing the song which the Spirit hath indited, even of purpose as it seemeth for us, *Vinea nostra floruit.* " Our vine hath flourished."

1 Cor. i. [5, 7.]

Isai. v. [4.]

The fruits of this vineyard many; one special, which is peace both spiritual and civil.

9. And, although the ground where this vine is planted hath been very barren, yet hath it brought forth many goodly and pleasant grapes. The gospel hath chased away walking spirits: it hath cast out devils, banished much ignorance and blindness, put horrible blasphemy in manner to flight, utterly cleansed that sink, the stews, made vain and filthy songs less current than they have been in former times, and caused sin to be more shunned, although it be, God knoweth, too much still frequented. But one pleasant grape especially the gospel, the word of reconciliation, hath brought forth, and that is the sweet fruit of peace; peace towards God, and peace amongst ourselves. The gospel preacheth Christ. Christ is our peace, and peace-maker. He that hath Christ hath peace with God; and he that believeth in him hath him. By this means we have peace of conscience, peace with God. The other peace is civil peace among men. This is a pleasant fruit and a great blessing. He that knoweth the hurt of war can best judge of the worth of this benefit. The God of peace hath done this for

us, to our singular commodity and comfort: he hath given peace in our days: England never so long tasted the like. War heretofore hath torn this realm in pieces: all nations round about us starve in the field, tumble in war, wallow in blood, expecting no end of their troubles, but utter ruin and desolation. In the mean while we sit safe under our vine: every man in peace may quietly follow his vocation. God hath not dealt thus with all nations as he hath dealt with us, the least nation of all. It must be granted, some storms have been stirred up to disturb this our happy rest. But the Prince of peace and Lord of our tranquillity hath ceased the waves of the sea, stilled the rage of the people, marvellously prevented their wicked devices, and confounded the devisers of them. There is neither power nor counsel against the Lord. God taketh away the hearts of the enemies, and then as fearful hares they flee at the wagging of every leaf; yea, they fear where there is nothing to be feared. For this great calm, for this miraculous peace, we have to praise our God.

10. This peace hath fructified and brought forth his natural fruit, which is plenty. War is a locust, devouring all fruits: peace, as a sweet and pleasant dew, maketh all things fruitful. Peace hath made this land flow, like Canaan, with milk and honey. God hath opened his merciful hand, and replenished us with all his blessings: the Lord hath shewed us his loving kindness, and our land hath brought forth her increase. *The fruit of civil peace, plenty.*

11. These earthly blessings God hath given to try us whether, provoked by his gracious benignity, we will walk in his law or no. "I will rain down bread out of heaven, that I may try you whether ye will walk in my law or no." After this sort he proved Adam, giving him all dominion over his creatures, with all the fruit and plenty of the earth. So proved he the Sodomites with a country, for pleasure and plenty, termed "the Lord's garden." So proved he Israel, when he gave them Canaan: but they were forgetful of the Giver, and abused his gifts, both their peace and plenty: they provoked God unto wrath, and they felt his heavy hand: their peace was turned into war, their plenty into distress, their pleasure into pain, their joy into sorrow. *The end why God sendeth these temporal blessings. Exod. xvi. [4.] Gen. xiii. [10.]*

The plagues which follow temporal blessings when they are abused.

12. These things are written to warn us, that we should beware of the like sins, lest we feel the like plagues. For if we regard not the favour of God, if we contemn his word, the word of salvation; if we refuse to hear it, read it, follow it; if the seed of God do not fructify in our hearts; if the peace we have with God bring not forth piety; if our civil peace bring forth no better fruit than beastly security; if plenty work nothing in us but pride; if with Adam in our presumption we disobey the Lord; if with Sodom, when we are full, our care be only to satisfy our lust; if we neglect the poor, and deride the just; if, with Israel, we lust after flesh, and despise angels' food; if we hunger after popery, and thirst not after the water of life; if we fall away from God, and fall down to creatures; if we run a whoring, and defile the flesh, and profane the temple of God; if we tempt God, being weary of our profession, having wavering minds and backsliding hearts; if we despise government, and speak evil of them that be in authority; if we mutter and murmur against the principality of Moses and Aaron; if we loathe the present state, and seek after alterations; then shall all these godly blessings of God turn into cursings; the message of life shall be unto us a savour of death; the words of the Son of God, spoken unto us for our salvation, shall bear witness against us and condemn us; our vineyards shall be laid waste; we shall be made a bye-word and a wonder to the world; and, for a just reward of this our wickedness, our former benefits shall but add a greater weight unto our wo. But this be far from us, and from our children, for evermore. Wherefore, to return and to conclude this part, when we shall behold the great mercies of God so plentifully poured upon us; how he hath regarded his vineyard, blessed and enriched this his church with so great gifts, and so marvellous treasures, you see how truly we may say, *Vinea nostra floruit,* "Our vine hath flourished." This is the goodness of God towards us.

2. The vineyard devoured by little foxes. Why the church enemies are termed foxes, and why little.

13. Let us now cast our eyes another way, and see how men have dealt with the Lord's vineyard. Great hath been the favour of God towards it: and great also hath been the malice of Satan, and the ingratitude of man, in labouring by all means to lay it waste. These enemies of the vineyard are termed "foxes;" under which name be comprised all

heretics, all schismatics, all hypocrites, atheists, epicures, conspirators, persecutors, with all the rabble of the wicked. They are termed "little foxes," either for that they are more rash, more wilful, and more hurtful to the vineyard than the old foxes, because they shun no peril; or else they are so called in contempt. For although they seem mighty, strong, and fierce, yet, when God shall arm himself against them, then they will appear silly weak cubs, not able to kick against the prick. There is no wiliness, no force, no power, no counsel against our God. If Christ say, "It is I," all his enemies do stagger and fall flat to the ground. The little cubs perhaps are animated by reason of their wiliness, and because they know they are many in number. It is true, "The children of this world are wise in their generation;" subtile they are as serpents. But God confoundeth the counsels of all crafty Achitophels, and taketh foxes in the snares they set for others. The number is great; and, as the manner is of evil weeds, it groweth apace: they are ten for one. But one David is worth not only ten, but ten thousand Philistines, because he cometh in the name of the Lord. He that fighteth under Christ's banner, and is protected under the shadow of the wings of the Almighty, he is safe, be he in never so great perils. Gedeon with three hundred, crying, "The sword of the Lord and Gedeon," slew and put to flight an infinite number, the huge army of the Madianites. It is all one with God to overcome with few or many. So the enemies then of God, the enemies of the church, they are but silly weak cubs; be they never so wily, never so many.   [John xviii. [6.]]   [Luke xvi. 8.]   [Judg. vii. [20.]]

14. But the enemies of God's vineyard are therefore chiefly called foxes, because they are of like condition unto foxes, whom they singularly resemble in four peculiar properties. The fox is ravenous, greedy on his prey. And these cubs, enemies to the cross of Christ, have under pretence of long prayer devoured widows' houses; spared no estate or condition of men; beguiled princes of their possessions; gotten to themselves the riches and wealth of the whole world with false merchandise, selling that for bread which is no bread, making their gain of masses, merits, pardons, and such like stuff. Unsatiable dogs they are, ever barking and never satisfied. The old grey fox   [The church enemies resemble foxes in four properties.   In ravening.]

is become the lord of the whole earth, the king of kings; his cardinals, abbots, and bishops, great princes, and lords of whole countries; the little foxes, as monks, friars, and massing priests, what with singing, and what with begging, have raked no small heaps together.

In cruelty.

15. Foxes do feed on blood, in desire whereof they kill more than they can devour. Christ calleth Herod "fox," partly for his savage and cruel murdering of infants. What thousands of the children and lambs of God these Herodians, these Romanists, these ravening wolves and bloody foxes, have devoured, look into the histories of all times, you shall wonder at it and abhor them. Doubtless the righteous blood which they have shed upon the earth shall come upon them: the blood of the saints, whom they have cruelly butchered, crieth unto the Lord against them for revenge, and the Lord will hear it. "Whomsoever thou shalt see take delight in the blood of persecution, he is a fox."

In wiliness.

16. As they lively resemble foxes in greediness and cruelty; so in wiliness also they are like unto them: crafty they are and subtile, as false as a fox. The fox will not worry near his bele[1], but rangeth far abroad, lest he be espied. So these subtile deceivers go far off: they compass sea and land to make a proselyte of their own profession: they shut themselves up in their beles in the daytime: they dare not abide the light, but seek lurking-holes and corners, disguising themselves in strange apparel, lest their wonted attire should bewray them; wily foxes, deep dissemblers, double-hearted, double-tongued, double-faced; speaking them full fair whom they hate full deadly; promising and not performing; shifting off and seeking time; now humble as sheep, but when time serveth, as fierce as lions. By subtile sleights and breach of faith they brought John Huss to the council at Constance, and there cruelly murdered him: they promised him a safe conduct to come and to go; but those holy fathers agreed upon a new point of religion, that "Promise is not to be kept with heretics," and so cruelly and treacherously consumed with fire the saint of God. These faith-breakers be no more to be trusted than foxes.

[1 Bield—den, or covert—is still used in Scotland.—ED.]

17. The last property that I note in the fox is that he casteth an evil savour. I will not remember unto you, for offending your chaste ears, the horrible filthiness wherewith those learned scribes, those holy fathers, those maiden priests, those foxes, were infected; the smell whereof ascended up into heaven, and cried out for vengeance against them. Spiritual and corporal whoredom for the most part go together. Who was more hot in the service of Baal than Jezebel, that devout hypocrite? And yet she was but a painted harlot. When Israel gave themselves to idolatry, they forthwith fell unto whoredom. Men's life and religion are for the most part like; a sound faith, a sweet behaviour: men gather not figs of thorns; neither can their outward conversation be pure, whose inward persuasion is not good. These are they that destroy the vines. Whereunto even now they have prepared themselves: for this end and purpose they gather themselves together; they boldly have their conventicles; they contrive treachery, and devise how to destroy the vineyard and church of God. In the late evil times the professors of the gospel found no such liberty. But the saying of Christ is verified, "Foxes have holes, but the Son of man hath not where to hide his head." *In casting an evil savour.* *Matt. viii. [20.]*

18. Two especial means they use in seeking to destroy the vineyard; force, and persuasion. Force of two sorts; open, and secret. Open force of persecution that cruel beast hath always practised from time to time. What prince hath he not stirred up, what nation hath he not armed, to persecute the professors of true religion with fire and sword? The red bloody dragon doth still vex the woman with her child, Christ with his church. The practice hereof all nations have felt, and England cannot forget. The late rebellion in this realm, raised for no other cause but by force to subvert religion, by no other man than the father of these foxes, is fresh in memory[1]. *The means which they use to destroy the church, force and fraud; force open, and secret. Open, by fire and sword.* *Rev. xii. [13—17.]*

19. When by open force this beast cannot quench his thirst with the blood of his saints, then he practiseth by secret devices. Sometimes, under pretence of marriage and faithful affinity, he leadeth princes blindfold to the *Secret force, by treacheries, sorceries, poisonings.*

[[1] The rebellion in the northern counties headed by the earls of Northumberland and Westmoreland in 1569.—Ed.]

[SANDYS.]

house of slaughter: sometimes, under colour of giving aid to possess kingdoms, he dispossesseth them both of their state and of their life: sometimes he offereth league and confederacy with such as in heart he deadly hateth, thereby to stay their force, till he may fitly practice his purposed mischief. When these practices will not serve, then they sell themselves to Satan, as did pope Silvester[1]: they enter into an execrable league with the devil; and labour by incantation, conjuration, magic, sorcery, and witchcraft, to consume, kill, and destroy the Lord's anointed by picturing, &c. When enchantments will not serve, that no poisoned device be left unattempted, they fly to poisonings, which practice of theirs hath taken effect in divers. Henry[2] the emperor received poison in sacramental bread, Victor[3] the pope in sacramental wine. Wherein it is to be noted by the way, that if they did offer the body and blood of Christ indeed, as they pretend to do, they could not mingle that sacred and glorified substance with poison. Of late noble Dandelot[4], with others, have drunk of the like cup. So these foxes conceive mischief, and bring forth most monstrous and cruel wickedness, both by open violence and by secret treachery.

Their fraud in persuading by arguments drawn from antiquity.

20. The other mean, whereby they labour to hinder the course of the gospel and to subvert religion, is fraud, the natural property of a fox. This fraud is practised after sundry sorts. First they labour to seduce the simple by persuasion. Of persuasion they have sundry kinds. As, first, the antiquity of their religion, their fathers' old faith. But they should remember that their religion is as new as false; six hundred years after Christ unknown. The substance of our religion is most ancient, and shall be most permanent: it was from the beginning; it shall remain to the end; no jot nor tittle thereof shall perish. In matter of religion we may not follow our fathers further than they have followed our master Christ. We must think, not what others have said or done before, but what he which is before all others hath said and done.

[[1] Silvester II. was believed to be a magician.—ED.]
[[2] Henry VII. emperor of Germany.—ED.]
[[3] Victor II.—ED.]
[[4] Francis d'Andelot, a brother of Coligni, admiral of France.—ED.]

"Hear him." The scripture hath given us warning to be wary in this point. God fed Israel with wormwood, and gave them waters of gall to drink, because they walked after "Baalims, which their fathers taught them." *Jer. ix. [14.]*

21. Another ground whereupon they build their persuasion, is the "authority of the church," and of the pope, which cannot err. There is a church of God, and a synagogue of Satan. The church of God is builded upon the doctrine of the apostles and prophets. The true church hath her marks whereby she is known; the gospel truly preached, the sacraments sincerely ministered, discipline duly executed. The popish church hath neither the true foundation nor yet the right marks of the church of God: her foundation is man: her marks are blasphemy, idolatry, superstition. Christ is "the head of his body the church." This Head cannot err: the head of the church antichristian is the pope, that man of sin, a liar, yea, a very father of lies. *From the authority of their church and pope.* *Col. i. [18.]*

22. From these general persuasions they train the people to particulars, teaching many other shameful things; but this above all other, as most needful to be held of all, that the mass is a sacrifice available for quick and dead, strong and effectual to take away sin, forcible in ridding souls out of purgatory pains. But St Paul teacheth, that Christ was offered up once to take away all sin, and by that one oblation, because it was perfect, obtained the full delivery and redemption of his church. "The blood of Christ doth cleanse us from all sin." Therefore we need not their after-cleansings, which in truth are defilings. With these and other like false and subtile persuasions, they lead the simple people to the pit of destruction. *From the excellency of their sacrifice.* *[Heb. x. 12. 14.]* *[1 John i. 7.]*

23. Or, if they cannot prevail by such persuasions, they find out prophecies, and therewith fill the people's ears: they have the books of Merlin, and other fantastical spirits, full of doubtful sayings and deceitful dreams; of these they make such constructions and expositions, as may serve their purpose; all tending to this end, that alteration is near, that the state will not continue, that religion cannot endure long. Such and such times when this change should be, they have presumed more than once *From feigned prophecies.*

to appoint. But their times-master hath deceived them: they have found him a lying spirit in the mouth of his prophets. This practice of Satan and of his imps hath brought sundry great persons and noble houses to confusion. Let their posterity take example and warning by them.

Their fraud in persuading by promises of reconciliation. 24. They have left no means unattempted, whereby the hearts of the people might any way be seduced. Wherefore unto other their deceitful practices they have joined the offer of reconciliation. The pope hath sent his proctors abroad to pardon whatsoever is already past, so that men will now forsake the church of Christ, and join themselves unto that harlot inseparably henceforward; which to do they must take a solemn oath, and in token thereof wear some mark of the beast, as a cross, an *Agnus Dei*, a medal, or some such badge of recognisance. These popish proctors have poisoned many; and the observing of this most wicked oath hath made many silly souls, especially women, break their faith to Christ, their loyalty to their prince, and their promised obedience to their husbands. A wicked promise is best unmade, but being made is better broken than performed. It had been a less offence for Herod to break his oath than to behead an innocent. We may neither make nor keep any promise, oath, or vow against the Lord. As for reconciliation, 2 Cor. v.[20.] "Be reconciled unto God." He it is which alone remitteth sin; and they only which are reconciled to him shall be saved.

Their stratagem of raising up slanderous reports. 25. But these destroyers and subverters of the Lord's vineyard cease not thus. Some credit they think to win to their own cause, if they can work the discredit of such as are maintainers of the contrary. To this end they raise up slanderous reports against our magistrates and ministers, that the people, first misliking them, may afterwards be brought with more ease to mislike of that religion whereof they are. This is an old practice of the ancient enemy. Daniel was charged to contemn the decree of Nebuchadnezzar, Micheas[1] to be a liar, Jeremy to be an enemy to the commonwealth, Elias to be a disturber of the state, Christ to be an enemy unto Cæsar,

[¹ Micheas—Micaiah.—ED.]

Paul to be factious and seditious, the Christians in the days of Trajan the emperor to have their women common in their night-assemblies, to worship an ass's head instead of God, with many such like shameless reports. How these foxes have falsely slandered both magistrates and ministers of God in these our days, it shall be needless here to recite. Their books are extant as full of lies as lines. Thus you see how they labour by all means to hinder the passage of the gospel, and utterly to subvert true religion. We see also how the Lord of hosts fighteth for us; how the Almighty is our defence; how he that keepeth us slumbereth not; how strangely and miraculously he preserveth his anointed David, both from the bloody hands of Saul abroad, and Absolon at home, in the midst of so many conspiracies, treacheries, snares, and traps, which these foxes have devised and laid. We see how God preserveth his vineyard, how he maintaineth his church so many ways assaulted, maugre all his and all our enemies. It is his only work, marvellous in our eyes: it is the Lord, let us praise his name.

26. But although God hitherto hath preserved his vineyard from the spoil of these foxes, yet his will and commandment is, that we should not live in security, but beware of them; watch them, and catch them, if we can: "Take us the little foxes." This last and most necessary part, for order sake, may be thus divided. First we learn, that foxes are to be taken; secondly, to whom; thirdly, by whom; and lastly, how they are to be taken.

3. The foxes must be taken. To whom, by whom, how.

27. These foxes are to be taken. For so the spouse of Christ, or rather Christ himself, commandeth. And why? Because they are hurtful to his vineyard. God commandeth false prophets not only to be taken, but also to die the death: "Let the false prophet die." Paul wisheth that the disturbers of the peace of the church were cut off. He laid an heavy hand upon Elymas the sorcerer, when he stroke him stark blind. Moses, at the commandment of God, made a speedy dispatch of idolaters. The apostle would that dogs, evil workmen, sect-makers, should be shunned, that all heretics not recalling themselves by admonition should be avoided. The scabbed sheep must be removed out of the flock,

Why foxes must be taken.

Deut. xiii. [5.]
Gal. v. [12.]
Acts xiii. [11.]
Exod. xxxii. [27, 28.]
Phil. iii. [2.]
Tit. iii. [10.]

the leper should be severed, the adulterer cast out, the leaven put away, foxes taken and tied short. This is the will of God, the request of the spouse, the commandment of Christ. The law of nature, God, and man, crieth, "Take these foxes."

They must be taken, if it may be, to the church; if not, then from the church.

28. But unto whom? *Nobis.* Catch them unto us, saith the spouse of Christ. Christ came into the world to save sinners: he willeth not the death of a sinner, but rather that he should convert and live. He came to recall the lost sheep of the house of Israel: his will is, that stony hearts be turned into fleshy; that foxes be changed into sheep; that enemies be reconciled, and made friends; that strangers be made citizens with his saints; that all come unto him, that all may find rest for their souls. He created man for himself, for himself he redeemed him: his will is, that foxes be taken and brought to him, that he himself may be glorified in them.

They must be taken by the friends of the bridegroom, ministers and magistrates.

29. But who should take them? The friends of the spouse, the servants and officers of the bridegroom Christ. There be two especial servants, whom the Lord hath appointed to hunt for these cubs; the magistrate, and the minister. These are to join their force together, to be as brethren, Moses and Aaron, knit in love and liking, to give all diligence and mutual endeavour for the apprehension of these foxes. For why? the vineyard of the Lord is set over to their oversight and government. Kings and queens should be as nurses, to tender and cherish the church of Christ, to keep every noisome and hurtful thing from it. Ministers are they whom God hath set to sweat and labour in the vineyard; to govern and feed the flock, which he hath purchased with his own blood. These are the Lord's two hands; to both these he speaketh when he saith, "Take the foxes." But all the craft is in the catching. We must therefore learn how they are to be taken.

The minister taketh them by doctrine.

[2 Tim. iv. 2.]

Luke iii. [3—14.]

30. The minister hath his nets to take withal, the magistrate hath his traps. The first is the net of God's word, to cast into the sea for fishes, or to set upon the land for foxes. "Preach the word; be instant in season, and out of season." The law of the Lord converteth souls. With this net John Baptist caught at one time a great

number of foxes; scribes, Pharisees, publicans, soldiers, and sinners: they came confessing their sins, and asking, "What shall we do?" Peter cast out this net, and in one sermon brought three thousand unto Christ. With this net at Cesarea he took Cornelius the captain, with a great multitude. Paul, by spreading this net, gat huge numbers in Asia, in Africa, in Europe, in all parts and quarters of the world. Christ himself with this net took so many that they said, "Behold, the whole world goeth after him." Philip took the eunuch in this net; in the same net Lydia, Dionysius, Paulus Sergius, was caught. Ambrose set this net for Augustine, and took him in it. Verily, if this net were diligently set, it would catch these cubs apace. For they err, because they know not the scriptures; and they cannot know, because they are not taught. Wo therefore to the idle and idol pastor, to the dumb dog, to the unpreaching minister! For the blood of all these that perish for lack of taking, through his negligence, shall be required at his hands. *Acts ii. [41.] Acts x. [34—44.] John xii. [19.] Acts viii. [35—38.]*

31. The second net is godly conversation, good example of life. This net holdeth hard. Examples are a great deal stronger than words, and the voice doth not so fully instruct as the life. Therefore Peter saith, "Be a platform for the flock to follow." "He that liveth otherwise than he speaketh, teacheth God to punish him," saith St Chrysostom. Paul termeth such teachers as are fertile in speech and barren in life, tinkling cymbals. They send forth a sound, and inwardly are hollow. Christ did what he taught. His innocency and patience changed the hearts of the very soldiers that put him to death. And as the godly example of a good life draweth many to Christ, so an evil life giveth great offence. The bad demeanour of Heli's sons caused men to loath the offering of the Lord. "And you," saith Jacob to his two sons, Simeon and Levi, "have made me to be abhorred among the inhabitants of the land." Let us therefore have our conversation honest among these men, that, as now they speak evil of us as evil doers, so hereafter they may by our good works, which they shall see, glorify God in the day of visitation. *By example of life. 1 Pet. v. [3.] 1 Cor. xiii. [1.] Gen. xxxiv. [30.] 1 Pet. ii. [12.]*

32. The third net to take these foxes in is discipline. Where the former nets fail, this will take hold: it held that *By ecclesiastical discipline.*

incestuous Corinthian, whom no other way could have taken. Hereby Ambrose brought the emperor Theodosius himself to unfeigned humility and hearty repentance[1]. "Doth it not appertain unto pastoral diligence," saith St Augustine, "with fear, yea, if they resist, with feeling of stripes, to recall to the fold of the Lord those sheep, when we find them, which have not been violently carried away, but, by fair and soft usage being seduced, have gone astray and began to be held in possession of strangers[2]?" Those wilful cubs, which neither by teaching nor by example will be reformed, must feel the smart of the rod. "We have," saith Paul, "in a readiness punishment against all disobedience." Such as will not come to feed with Christ willingly, must be compelled against their wills. "Constrain them to come in." Thus the minister should take these little foxes, and win them unto the Lord with the net of God's word, of good example, and of discipline. Now, if they cannot be so recalled that themselves perish not, they are to be cut off or tied up, that they destroy not others.

1 Cor. v. [1—5.]
Aug. de cor. c. viii.
2 Cor. x. [6.]
Luke xiv. [13.]

The magistrate taketh foxes by civil punishments.

33. The magistrate therefore must also set traps to catch these foxes withal. The chief trap the magistrate hath is the law. Artaxerxes writeth his letter unto Esdras, whom he sent to Jerusalem to see the people governed, and requireth him both to place magistrates and judges over the people, and to see that they might live according to the laws of God and the king, adding thereunto a sharp commination against transgressors: "Whosoever will not do the law of thy God, and the king's law, let him have judgment without delay, whether it be unto death, or to banishment, or to confiscation of goods, or to imprisonment." The kinds of punishment here set down are four, death, exile, confiscation, incarceration. These lawful means are wisely to be used of christian magistrates, as traps to take these little foxes.

Ezra vii. [26.]

By death.
[Deut. xiii. 5. Lev. xx. 10. xxiv. 16.]

34. The first is death. It is the Lord's commandment, "Let the false prophet die," "Let the adulterer and the adulteress be put to death," "Let the blasphemer be

[1 Theod. Hist. Eccl. Amst. 1695. Lib. v. c. 18. pp. 220—3.—ED.]
[2 August. Op. Par. 1679. De Correct. Donatist. Lib. ad Bonifac. seu Epist. clxxxv. Tom. II. cols. 652, 3.—ED.]

stoned." Moses observed this in destroying idolaters, and hanging up them that committed whoredom. The magistrate beareth not the sword in vain. Asa the good king of Judah gave commandment, that "if any would not seek the Lord God of Israel, he should die, from the least to the greatest, from the man to the woman." Thus zealous magistrates have endeavoured to take rebellious foxes. 2 Chron. xv. [13.]

35. Exile is also a punishment fit for foxes. Zerubabel and Jeshua, together with the rest of the fathers of Israel, agreed not to suffer the enemies of their religion, those wily foxes, to join with them, but banished them out of their company: "It is not for us and you to build a house to our God." The emperor Theodosius likewise, being moved thereunto by that zealous bishop Amphilochius, drave all the Arians out of his dominion[1]. These foxes must be removed, the further the better. And it were well with Christ's church, if they were all as far as Rome hence, from whence many of them came, who now wander and range amongst us. God spared not to expel angels out of heaven, men out of paradise. And when Absolon had put off the dutiful mind of a natural son, then David, laying aside the tender affection of a loving father, banished him his country. By exile. Ezra iv. [3.] 2 Sam. xiii. [37.]

36. The third trap to take withal is confiscation of goods; which way is the easiest, and not the worst. For the most men love mammon better than God, their riches more than their religion. When the rich man heard that he and his wealth must part, he went away very sorrowful; if he from Christ, it is to be hoped these will from antichrist. There can be no sharper punishment to a worldly-minded man, than to be taken in this trap. God therefore commanded the Egyptians to be spoiled, than which there could be no plague more grievous unto them, being so greedily set upon their gain. When the Philistines would keep the Jews in good order, and disable them to rebel, they took their weapons and instruments of war from them. It is no evil or unlawful policy to weaken these enemies, which are ready to use the strength of their wealth to the overthrow of the church, if occasion By confiscation. 1 Sam. xiii. [19.]

[1 Theod. Hist. Eccl. Amst. 1695. Lib. v. c. 16, p. 218.—ED.]

did serve. Touch them by the purse: it is the most easy and ready way, whereby to take and tame these foxes.

By incarceration.

37. The last way set down by wise Artaxerxes is incarceration. When Joseph had cast his brethren in prison, then they remembered their fault and repented: then they thought, "We suffer these things deservedly for the hardness of our hearts against our brother." Manasses was never reclaimed until he was inclosed in prison. He was miserable in his kingdom, and blessed in his captivity. Thus it is the duty as well of the magistrate as the minister to obey the commandment of the Almighty, and by all means to prevent wicked enterprises, to root out evil, and to seek the safety of God's vineyard, his beloved church. Which God grant them once effectually to do, for their own discharge, and benefit of the people so dearly redeemed by the blood of Christ. To whom, &c.

[Gen. xlii. 21.]
2 Chron. xxxiii. [10—13.]

THE FOURTH SERMON.

A SERMON

PREACHED IN THE SAME PLACE, AND UPON THE SAME OCCASION WITH THE FORMER.

1 TIM. II.

1. *I exhort therefore before all things, that requests, supplications, intercessions, and givings of thanks, be made for all men;*
2. *For kings, and for all that are in authority, that we may lead a quiet and a peaceable life, in all godliness and honesty.*

MOSES, speaking to the people of God concerning the institution of the passover to be kept at the appointed season, from year to year, saith, "When thy son shall ask thee, What is this? thou shalt say unto him, With a mighty hand the Lord brought us out of Egypt, out of the house of bondage; and in remembrance hereof we celebrate this feast." In like sort, when your children shall ask you what this our assembly meaneth, you shall answer, that it is to give God thanks for that great benefit which we received at his hands as this day, when in his mercy he gave us our gracious elect Elizabeth, whom he hath used as his mighty arm, to work our deliverance, to bring us out of Egypt, the house of Romish servitude. "This is the day which the Lord hath made," this is that our happy day, the Lord in his mercy hath made it; let us be thankful for it, let us rejoice and be glad in it. This is the acceptable time, the day of salvation, the happy time of our deliverance. This day God shewed us the light of his gracious countenance, and had mercy on us in bestowing upon us so great a treasure, so good a governor, so worthy a prince. The Lord grant us many of these days, and long continuance of these happy years! And, as our apostle doth exhort us, let us both praise the Lord, and pray unto him, that under so good a government we may live a quiet, a godly, and an honest

The cause of the assembly, and the matters which this scripture offereth to be spoken of. Exod. xiii. [14.]

Psal. cxviii. [24.]

life, as the Lord's goodness towards us, and our duty towards him, and profession of his name, require. "I exhort you therefore before all things," &c. Here are two things offered to our consideration, first, an exhortation, "Pray for all men, especially for princes and rulers;" secondly, a reason of this exhortation, "that by their good government we may live a quiet, a godly, and an honest life."

<small>1.
An exhortation unto prayer.</small>

2. In exhorting us to pray, he sheweth the benefit and fruit of our prayer. We must pray to God to give us good princes and rulers: under a good prince we ought to lead a good life: a good prince should procure peace, piety, and honesty to the people: a good people should live peaceably, godlily, and honestly under their prince. The exhortation is, "Pray for all men, especially princes and rulers." In this part we have to consider, What prayer is; To whom we should pray; What be the parts of prayer; When, where, and how we should pray; For whom we should pray.

<small>What prayer is, and what parts it hath.</small>

3. Prayer is a lifting up of the mind unto God, or a friendly talking with the Lord, from an high and a kindled affection of the heart. In the word God speaketh unto us, in prayer we speak unto him. Prayer is the pouring out of a contrite heart, with a sure persuasion that God will grant our requests, and give ear to the suits which we make unto him. This prayer must be only unto God. It is prayer unto God that only hath <small>Psal. l. [15.]</small> promise, that only hath example in the scriptures. "Call <small>John xvi. [23, 24.] Matt. vi. [9.]</small> upon me," saith God; "Ask the Father in my name," saith our Saviour, "ask, and ye shall have." "When ye shall pray," saith Christ, "pray thus, Our Father which art in heaven." So and none otherwise prayed all the patriarchs, prophets, apostles, and Christ himself, and all true Christians in all ages. In prayer no creature may be joined with God. "God and our Lady help us," is no allowable prayer.

<small>Petitions, or requests.</small>

4. This prayer, which must be made only to God, our apostle divideth into his parts, "requests," "supplications," "intercessions," "thanksgivings." Requests or petitions are when we pray for the increase of God's good gifts in us, and that of his mercy and favour he would

give us whatsoever is necessary for body or soul; and, forasmuch as we cannot obtain any thing for our own merits, that he would grant us all things for his Son our Saviour's sake.

5. Supplications, when we pray to be delivered from evil; as when we pray that the wrath of God, which we have deserved, may through his mercy be removed from us as far as the east is from the west, that our sin may be remitted and blotted out of God's books. Supplications.

6. Intercessions are when we pray for such as do afflict and wrong us, for our enemies which persecute us; that God would forgive them, turn their hearts, and better them. Or when we pray for others; either for removing of evil from them, or for God's favour and blessing towards them. Intercessions.

7. Thanksgivings are when we praise and thank God for the great mercies, graces, and gifts, which we have received at his hands. For we must acknowledge that "every good and perfect gift cometh down from above, from the Father of lights," and is by his mercy freely given. Prayer generally may be divided into two parts, petition and thanksgiving: in the one we ask of God; in the other we offer unto God: both are accepted as sweet-smelling sacrifices; pure, and through the merit of his Son pleasant in his sight. I shall not need to put you in remembrance, that we must pray both for ourselves and others; that there is a private, and a public prayer; that we must pray for things pertaining to salvation absolutely, and for things that pertain to this life conditionally. These are matters wherewith ye are throughly acquainted. Thanksgivings. James i. [17.]

8. The next thing to be considered in prayer, is when, where, and how to pray. When? Always, "without ceasing." Where? In all places, especially that place which, being sanctified to this use, is therefore called the house of prayer. How? From the heart; "lifting up pure and clean hands;" that is to say, in faith, and in love. Our prayer, feathered with these two wings, flieth straight into heaven. When, where, and how to pray. 1 Thess. v. [17.] 1 Tim. ii. [8.]

9. Thus we are by the apostle willed to pray before all things, according to the commandment of our Saviour, "Seek first the kingdom of God." Let us begin all our Prayer before all things. [Matt. vi. 33.]

works, our enterprises, our actions, our journeys, our lying down, our rising up, our eating, our drinking, and all our studies, with prayer. So our bread shall be multiplied, our oil increased, our meat sanctified, all our endeavours and actions blessed. If the very ethnicks in the beginning of their books first prayed unto their gods, to prosper and give good success to their labours; it were a shame for us not to pray to our God before all things, knowing that the prayer of the just is greatly available before him. Prayer is a succour unto us, a sacrifice to God, and a scourge to Satan. Examples are infinite. Israel in prayer groaned unto God, and was delivered out of Egypt. Moses by prayer so held God, that he could not destroy his idolatrous people. The blast of prayer overthrew the walls of Jericho. At the prayer of Josua the sun stood still. The young men prayed in the burning furnace, and their prayer took away the force of the fire. The scriptures are full of examples of all sorts: kings, prophets, apostles, faithful Christians, have called upon the Lord in the time of their troubles: he hath heard them, granted their requests, and delivered them from their distresses. Wherefore, before all things the apostle here exhorteth us unto prayer.

Exod. iii. [9, 10.]
Exod. xxxii. [9—14.]
Josh. vi. [20.]
Josh. x. [13, 14.]
Dan. iii. [27.]

For whom we must pray, and for whom not.

10. But for whom? First, generally for all men; then specially for kings, and them that are placed in authority. It seemeth, some were of opinion that prayers should be made only for the faithful, for the brethren, for Christians, and not for infidels. Paul, to meet with this uncharitable error, saith, "Let supplications be made for all men." St John in his canonical epistle seemeth to make exception against this general doctrine: "There is a sin unto death, I say not that thou shouldest pray for it." This is that sin which Christ calleth sin against the Holy Ghost, which never shall be remitted, and therefore is not to be prayed for. But, because it is hard for us to discern who sin unto eternal death, christian charity will that we hope well of all, and observe the general rule to pray "for all." There were secrets revealed to the apostles of Christ, which are hidden from us: they had the gift of prophesying and discerning of spirits, to foresee, and know; which gifts these times have not. Paul, rapt into the third heaven,

1 John v. [16.]

2 Cor. xii. [4.]

learned secrets not to be revealed: he knew that Hymenæus and Alexander were reprobates. We may not so judge of others. "Who art thou that judgest another man's servant?" In outward shew, after the judgment of man, Paul, being a violent persecutor of Christ, sinned unto death; yet was he the elect vessel and glorious instrument of God. Christ is "the propitiation for the sins of the whole world:" he will have all men to be saved, and to come to the knowledge of the truth. We must therefore have a charitable meaning towards all, and pray for all, as he hath died for all. Pray even for your enemies, for them that persecute and slander you: "Bless them that curse you:" Wish well to them that do ill to you. For God suffereth his rain to fall and his light to shine both upon good and bad. Abraham prayed for Abimelech, Moses for idolaters, Samuel for Saul, Stephen for them that stoned him, and Christ for them that cruelly put him to shameful death. Let us imitate these holy patterns.

1 Tim. i. [20.]

Rom. xiv. [4.]

[1 John ii. 2.]

[Matt. v. 44.]

11. As we should pray for all men, so chiefly for kings, and such as are in authority, because they chiefly need it. In Paul's time the kings and rulers of the people were ethnicks, tyrants, enemies to Christ, and cruel persecutors of the gospel: whereupon some thought it not convenient for the church to pray for them who sought to destroy it. St Paul abateth this opinion, teaching them that they should chiefly pray for such, as for men in greatest danger, and most needing the help of their prayer. Pray for him that prayeth not for himself. The prophet Jeremy requireth the Israelites to pray for the cruel persecutor of God's people, Nebuchadnezzar. For God in his mercy giveth good princes, and in his ire he giveth "wantons," as Esay saith, and "hypocrites," as Job writeth. Both evil and good are the ordinance of God. We must pray for ill princes, because the king's heart is in God's hand; that he may turn their minds, and stay their persecutions, of evil make them good, and of strangers from the commonwealth of his saints make them pillars and stays unto the church. For good princes we ought heartily to praise the Lord, for them especially to pray, as the prophet did for Solomon, "Give thy judgments to the king, O God, and thy righteousness to the king's son." For it is the

Prayer to be made especially for kings and such as are in authority.

Jer. xxix. [7.]

Isai. iii. [4.]

Job xxxiv. [30.]

Psal. lxxii. [1.]

singular gift of God not only to set up rightful government in the world, but also to cherish and preserve the same. Even they whom he hath furnished with the spirit of righteousness and of judgment, are unable further forth to execute their charge, than they be specially directed by the hand of God, and assisted from heaven with all helps necessary for their calling. If the Christians did pray for the wealth and prosperity of those princes, which bent all their force and power against the kingdom of Christ[1], surely for such as are defenders of the faith, and zealous patrons of God's people, we ought daily and hourly to pour out supplications, that God would grant them a long life, a safe government, a sure dwelling, valiant soldiers, faithful counsellors, a good people, a quiet world, and whatsoever the hearts of men or kings do desire. And let all such as will not say Amen to those prayers, assure themselves that they are neither dutiful Christians nor faithful subjects, but disloyal contemners of God's ordinance, and rebellious despisers of his commandment, who spake by the mouth of his apostle, saying, "Pray for kings, and all such as be in authority."

Tertul. in Apologet.

12. If any church, any people, any nation in the world, have cause to praise the Lord for their prince; this land hath more than any, in respect of the wonderful blessings wherewith God, by the ministry of his handmaid, hath enriched us far beyond all that we are possibly able to conceive. Israel was well apaid with the good government of Deborah, Judith, and Hester. But they thought themselves twice happy when God gave them Moses, Samuel, David, Solomon, Jehosaphat, Ezekias, Josias, to govern them. England liked well, and took it for no small blessing of God, when Henry the first, Henry the second, Edward the first, Edward the third, Edward the fourth, Henry the fifth, Henry the sixth, Henry the seventh, Henry the eighth, Edward the sixth, bare rule over it. But did God ever bless the throne of any man as he hath done the royal seat of his anointed at this day?

No nation more occasioned than the English to praise the Lord for their prince.

[[1] Inspice Dei voces...scitote ex illis præceptum esse nobis, ad redundantiam benignitatis, etiam pro inimicis Deum orare, et persecutoribus nostris bona precari.—Tertull. Op. Lutet. 1641. Apologet. adv. Gentes, 31. p. 30.—ED.]

Hath the like ever been heard of in any nation to that which in ours is seen? Our Deborah hath mightily repressed the rebel Jaben: our Judith hath beheaded Holophernes, the sworn enemy of Christianity: our Hester hath hanged up that Haman, which sought to bring both us and our children into miserable servitude. And, if we may compare with the ancients of Israel, Moses was not more mild, nor Samuel more just, nor David more faithful, nor Solomon more peaceful, nor Jehosaphat more ready to assist his neighbours, nor Ezekias more careful for God's cause, nor Josias more zealous to restore sincere religion: if ye make the comparison between her own predecessors, neither was Henry the first better learned, nor Henry the second more easy to forgive and put up injuries, nor Edward the first more chaste, nor Edward the third more loth to accept of foreign dominion being offered, nor Edward the fourth more just in yielding all men their own, nor Henry the fifth more happy, nor Henry the sixth more holy, nor Henry the seventh more prudent, nor Henry the eighth more valiant in quelling the pope, nor Edward the sixth more sincerely affected towards the gospel of Christ. Look upon other princes at this day: some are drunken with the poisoned cup of that harlot, whose venom her highness doth abhor; some have imbrued themselves in blood, wherewith her majesty did never yet stain the tip of her finger: when they tumble in war, she sitteth in peace; when they break oaths and covenants, she keepeth promise: therefore God hath blessed the work of her hands: she found this realm in war, she hath established it in peace: she found it in debt, which she hath discharged; she hath changed dross into silver and gold; she hath, by living within compass and sparing wasteful expences, without pressing the people, or seeking more than ordinary and usual tribute, furnished this land with so great a navy, with such store of armour and warlike munition, both for defence and offence, as England never had in former times. This I speak not of flattery, (it was never my fault) but rather in sincerity testifying the truth, that seeing your happiness you may be thankful, and considering the wonderful mercies of God ye may fall into that meditation of the prophet, "What shall I render unto the Lord? All [Psal. cxvi. 12—14.]

his benefits are upon me. I will receive the cup of salvation, and call upon the name of the Lord. I will pay my vows unto the Lord, even now in the presence of all his people." God hath loaden us with all his benefits. Far be it from us that our unthankfulness should bereave us of this felicity. That we hear the sound of bells, and not the thundering of guns; that our goods are not spoiled, our houses razed, our lands extended[1], our bodies imprisoned, our wives and children murdered before our eyes; that mercy and truth are met together; that righteousness and peace have kissed each other; that in liberty of body and freedom of conscience we may assemble thus together in the house of God, to make our prayers, to hear his word, to receive these holy and heavenly mysteries; do we think it a small, or a light, or a common benefit? How should we requite the Lord? We have nothing in us worthy the name of recompence. All that we can render or repay for that which we have received is, before we crave more, to be mindful and thankful of that we have obtained already, to take up the cup of salvation, call upon the name of the Lord in the presence of all the people: let supplications, prayers, intercessions, and giving of thanks, be made for kings: this one payment doth abundantly satisfy God for all graces, benefits, and blessings, which by the means of good kings have been poured upon us.

All that are in authority under the prince must also be prayed for; be they good or bad; be their authority ecclesiastical or civil.

13. Neither let us pray for our prince only, but also for all such as God hath placed in authority under her. For every power is of God, whether it be ecclesiastical or civil power. We must pray for all those that be in authority, be they good or bad; for the continuance of the one, and the amendment of the other. Our prayer for ecclesiastical powers must be, that God would place over his people good guides, loving and wise shepherds, such as may carefully govern the flock, over which the Holy Ghost doth make them overseers; such as Peter, that will feed as much as in them lieth; such as Paul, that will preach in season and out of season, that will soundly instruct, sharply improve, severely correct, and diligently guide; such as John, that fear not to reprove kings to their faces; as Elias, which will not spare to punish trans-

[1 Extended=confiscated, seized.—ED.]

gressors: that the church may be delivered from such as Judas and Magus, buyers and sellers, from false prophets, from sacrificing Balaamites, from devouring wolves, wily foxes, insatiable dogs, dumb curs, deceitful workmen, makers of division, idle pastors, unsavoury salt, such as make their belly their God, their preferment their religion, lewdly and worldly minded men. Our prayer for them in whose hands civil government lieth must be that, forasmuch as one is unable to bear the burthen of a commonwealth alone, such, according to the counsel of Jethro, may be chosen, as be Solomons, not Nabals; men of wisdom, and not dottrels; men of experience that can, and of courage that will, both wisely and boldly discharge their duty; men like to Gedeon, and not to Pilate, such as will not fear the face of Cæsar, when they should do right; men able mightily to put down sin; men that fear God sincerely, being lovers of the truth, not secret fosterers of superstition; men that hate covetousness, and are not takers of bribes to pervert judgment; men like to Samuel, not the sons of Samuel. Wo be to that people which is led with blind guides, and wo be to that commonwealth, which is ruled with base, bad, and evil governors!

14. Let us therefore bless God, if we have good rulers, and pray that we may reap the good fruit of them: that is to say, that we may lead a peaceable and quiet life under them, with all godliness and honesty. Herein we have two things to be considered, the duty of rulers, and the duty of them which live under rulers. Kings, and such as are in authority, must seek the peace, piety, and honesty of the people: the people thus governed must lead a peaceable, a godly, and honest life under them. It was said to the Jews which lived in captivity, but may serve as a profitable lesson for all that have sovereignty over others: "Seek the prosperity of the city; in the peace thereof you shall have peace." Solomon hath this commendation especially given him in scripture, as a notable effect of his wonderful wisdom: "He had peace on all sides: Judah and Israel dwelt without fear: every man sat quiet under his vine, and under his fig-tree, all the days of Solomon." Our Saviour Christ is called the "Prince of peace:" he brought peace into the world: at his na-

2. The reason why we pray for all men and for princes putteth both princes and all other men in mind of their duties. Princes that they should study to make the people live in peace.

Jer. xxix. [7.]

1 Kings iv. [24, 25.]

Isai. ix. [6.]

Luke ii. [14.] tivity the angels sung "Peace on earth:" at what time he was born, there was peace amongst all people. Ezekias likewise sought the peace of his country by earnest and hearty prayer: *Isai. xxxix. [8.]* "Let there be peace and truth in my days."

In piety. 15. The long and honourable peace which we have enjoyed and do enjoy, is in the eyes of all that do behold it wonderful; the more, because the procurer of our peace hath been careful therewithal to have piety and true religion planted and continued amongst us. Doubtless they that so watch over the people committed unto their charge, shew that they are neither coldly affected towards God, nor uncharitably towards their people. David, Solomon, Jehosaphat, Asa, Ezekias, Josias, are commended of God for good rulers, because they were religious and feared God. These, loving the law of the Lord themselves, laboured by all means to make the people partakers also of the like love. These were indeed the nurses of the church, having the same affection and kind-hearted inclination, *1 Thess. ii. [8.]* which the blessed apostle had towards them of Thessalonica, unto whom he was not only content to give the milk of the gospel of Christ, but willing that they might suck even blood out of his breast, so it were for their benefit. So dear and precious they were unto him. Such a nurse was Moses, which fed the people with the law of God, the food of life, meat sweeter than honey or the honey-comb. Such a one Jehosaphat, in sending abroad preachers to feed the people. Such a one Ezekias, in washing and cleansing the church from idolatry; Josias, in reforming the house of God; Solomon, in deposing evil priests and placing better, in labouring by all means to enlarge the glorious kingdom of God. These did the parts of good and faithful nurses, and God did highly requite their service.

In honesty. 16. After piety, honesty and order must be sought. This is attained unto by seeing good laws both made and put in execution. For the execution of the law is the life of the law; and a law not executed is but a dead law. And here let rulers first learn to observe laws themselves, and so with greater courage and better countenance they may punish by law the transgressors of the law. For this cause St. Paul would have a bishop, whose office it is to reprove others, himself to be unreprovable. Judah gave sentence against Thamar for her incontinency: "Bring her forth, and let her be burnt." But when he once understood it was his own offence, the case was altered. The prophet David was driven to the like. Those magistrates do both wickedly and shamefully, which prescribe a law of honest life unto others, and keep it not themselves. It is a foul thing, when he that punisheth is more worthy punishment than the party punished. Paul himself, being blameless, executed discipline with great authority upon that lewd incestuous person. Samuel, a faultless magistrate, was not afraid to cut off the head of Agag the king with his own hands. Moses could not with that courage have hanged up those gentlemen-fornicators, had not his own life that way been without stain or blemish. When magistrates themselves be clear, they may boldly punish others, and see diligently to the strait execution of laws. For want whereof it cometh to pass, that for the most part laws are accounted like to cobwebs, which take small flies and hold them fast, but suffer hornets to break through. In execution of laws, we may not respect the person of the rich, or of the poor: neither fear nor pity must remove us: that which is just must take place in both. For if laws be not executed without respect of person, if sin be not severely repressed, if the people be not kept in order, it will shake the state, all will be in an uproar, no man shall be master of his own, or in any safety of his life, all iniquity will abound, all honesty will be exiled, and the magistrate shall bear the sword in vain. To neglect it is to neglect that thing for which this ordinance of God was first appointed. For if men without these means might be kept in order, surely God would never have established government to keep them in order by these means. Barbarous, therefore, and wicked is the opinion of the anabaptists, which condemn all superiority, authority, and government in the church. For what is this else, but utterly to expel, both out of church and commonwealth, all godliness, all peace, all honesty?

<small>Gen. xxxviii. [24.]</small>

17. Now, as magistrates and rulers should by good government procure peace, promote religion, and preserve <small>The duty of the people under their princes is to</small>

honesty amongst men; so our apostle requireth at the people's hands, that they under government lead a peaceable, quiet, and honest life. There is a double peace, the one outward, the other inward; peace with men, and peace with God. With God there is no peace, but in Christ. Through faith in him we have peace with God, and not otherwise. He hath peace with God, whose sins are remitted: for, "Blessed are they whose iniquities are pardoned." But our sins are remitted only in the blood of Christ Jesus: "His blood doth purge us from all sin." Christ therefore is our only peace-maker with God. This is that peace which passeth all understanding: he that will enjoy it must be careful to keep a good conscience. "Have a good conscience, that, when men speak evil of you as of ill doers, they may be ashamed." For if our own heart condemn us, God is greater and will more sincerely judge us. A good conscience maketh a strong faith. Many, by loosing their hold of the one, have made shipwreck of the other.

<small>lead a peaceable, a godly, and an honest life.</small>

<small>Rom. iv. [7.]</small>

<small>1 John i. [7.]</small>

<small>1 Pet. iii. [16.]</small>

18. The peaceable and quiet life, which St Paul in this place doth chiefly require, is to have outward peace with men. "If it be possible, and as much as in you lies, have peace with all men." Yet not peace with all men so, but that we may be always ready for God's cause to sustain the hatred of all men in the world. We may not for peace sake flatter men in their sin; for that is to be partakers of evil. We must have peace with all, if it may be, and so far as in us lieth, ever preferring a good conscience and a christian mind. For it may not be, which may not be honestly. Follow those things that belong unto peace, but unto godly peace. For our God is the God of true and of good peace. He detesteth them that sow discord, yea, the soul of the Lord abhorreth them. Doeg was hated of God for setting dissention between Saul and David; Achitophel likewise for stirring up Absolon to strive against his father. For as peace makers are blessed, so cursed are all disturbers of peace, all breeders and maintainers of sedition. Unto peace we must join holiness, true and religious worshipping of God. So saith the apostle: "Follow peace and holiness, without which no man shall see the Lord." "Thou shalt worship the Lord thy God, and

<small>What it is to live peaceably.</small>
<small>Rom. xii. [18.]</small>

<small>Heb. xii. [14.]</small>

<small>Matt. iv. [10.]</small>

him only shalt thou serve." He is a spirit, and will be worshipped in spirit and truth; in inward holiness, not in outward shew of holiness only; in sincerity, and not in ceremony alone; according to his own will and commandment, not according to the fancy or invention of man. "Every god," saith Socrates, "is so to be worshipped as himself hath appointed[1]." Aug. de consen. Evang. lib. i. cap. 18.

19. This our serving of God in the church of God in true holiness consisteth chiefly in true and earnest prayer unto God, in diligent and dutiful hearing of his word, in faithful and reverent receiving of his sacraments. In prayer we beg of God those things which we wish and hope to receive, and we praise him for things already received. This is a sweet and an acceptable sacrifice. The hearing of his word is also a service wherewith he is pleased. The principal public duties of godliness are prayer, hearing of the word, and receiving of the sacraments.

20. And as praying and hearing, so the worthy receiving of his sacraments, is not only a sealing of his grace unto us, but also a testifying of our godliness towards him. His sacraments are two in number, instituted by Christ to be received of Christians: by the one, which is baptism, we are received and incorporated into the church of Christ; by the other, which is the eucharist, or Lord's supper, we are nourished and fed unto life everlasting. These are pledges and assurances of remission of sins, and salvation, purchased by the death of Christ. These are God's seals, added unto his most certain promises for the confirmation of our weak faith, weak by reason of the infirmity of our flesh. "For, if we were spiritual," saith Chrysostom, "we should not need these corporal signs[2]." We being now prepared and purposed to be partakers of this holy mystery, the sacrament of the body and blood of Christ, it standeth us upon to have that due consideration which the weight of a matter so nearly concerning our salvation doth require, to the end that we may to our comfort and profit receive the same. Deeply to enter into this matter Two sacraments, baptism and the supper of the Lord. Hom. 80. super Matt.

[[1] Socratis enim sententia est, unumquemque deum sic coli oportere, quomodo se ipse colendum esse præceperit.—August. Op. Par. 1680. De Consensu Evangelistarum, Lib. i. 26. Tom. iii. Pars ii. col. 12.—Ed.]

[[2] Εἰ μὲν γὰρ ἀσώματος εἶ, γυμνὰ ἄν αὐτά σοι τὰ ἀσώματα παρέδωκε δῶρα.—Chrysost. Op. Par. 1727. In Matt. Hom. lxxxii. Tom. vii. p. 787.—Ed.]

Of the outward signs in the eucharist, and how the inward grace thereof is reaped, not by carnal and gross devouring, but by spiritual and heavenly feeding upon the body and blood of Christ Jesus.

the shortness of this time will not permit: yet somewhat I will say, and give you a taste of things needful.

21. In this sacrament there are two things, a visible sign, and an invisible grace: there is a visible sacramental sign of bread and wine, and there is the thing and matter signified, namely, the body and blood of Christ: there is an earthly matter, and an heavenly matter. The outward sacramental sign is common to all; as well the bad, as the good. Judas received the Lord's bread; but not that bread, which is the Lord to the faithful receiver. The spiritual part, that which feedeth the soul, only the faithful do receive. For he cannot be partaker of the body of Christ, which is no member of Christ's body. This food offered us at the Lord's table is to feed our souls withal: it is meat for the mind, and not for the belly. Our souls, being spiritual, can neither receive nor digest that which is corporal; they feed only upon spiritual food. *John vi.[63.]* It is the spiritual eating that giveth life. "The flesh," saith Christ, "doth nothing profit." We must lift up ourselves from these external and earthly signs, and like eagles fly up and soar aloft, there to feed on Christ, which sitteth on the right hand of his Father, whom the heavens shall keep until the latter day. From thence and from no other altar shall he come, in his natural body, to judge both quick and dead. His natural body is local, for else it were not a natural body: his body is there, therefore not here: for a natural body doth not occupy sundry places at once. Here we have a sacrament, a sign, a memorial, a commemoration, a representation, a figure effectual, of the body and blood of Christ. These terms the ancient fathers, Irenæus, Tertullian, St Augustine, St Jerome, St Chrysostom, do use[1]. Seeing then that Christ in his natural body is absent from hence; seeing he is risen, and is not here; seeing he hath left the world, and is gone to his Father; "how shall I," saith St Augustine, "lay hold on him which is absent? how shall I put my hand into heaven? Send up thy faith, and thou hast taken hold." "Why preparest thou thy teeth? Believe, and thou hast eaten[2]."

[1] See Note A.—ED.

[2] Quomodo tenebo absentem? Quomodo in cœlum manum mittam, ut ibi sedentem teneam? Fidem mitte, et tenuisti.—August. Op. Par.

Thy teeth shall not do him violence, neither thy stomach contain his glorious body. Thy faith must reach up into heaven. By faith he is seen, by faith he is touched, by faith he is digested. Spiritually by faith we feed upon Christ, when we stedfastly believe that his body was broken, and his blood shed for us, upon the cross; by which sacrifice, offered once for all, as sufficient for all, our sins were freely remitted, blotted out, and washed away. This is our heavenly bread, our spiritual food. This doth strengthen our souls and cheer our hearts. Sweeter it is unto us than honey, when we are certified by this outward sacrament of the inward grace given unto us through his death; when in him we are assured of remission of sins and eternal life. Better food than this thy soul can never feed upon. This is the bread of everlasting life. They which truly eat it shall live by it.

22. Thus I have briefly, simply, and plainly unfolded unto you the meaning of this most holy mystery. Time will not suffer me to let you see the absurdities of the popish unsavoury opinions in this matter; neither to confute their vain allegations and false collections; abusing the scriptures, dreaming evermore, with the gross Capernaites, of a carnal and a fleshly eating. Behold the one part of this sacrament consecrated is termed bread, the other a cup, by the apostle himself: "Because what they were according to the substance of their natures before consecration, the same they remain after," saith Bertram[1]. The like hath Theodoret: "Those mystical tokens, after they be sanctified, do not leave their proper nature: for they abide in their former substance, figure, and shape[2]." This sacra-

The visible elements of bread and wine are neither changed in substance by virtue of consecration, and they should in administration be given both unto all, not one without the other, unto priest or people.

Bert. l. 4 de cor. et sang. Chr.

1680. In Joh. Ev. Tract. L. Tom. III. Pars II. col. 630.—Ut quid paras dentes et ventrem? Crede, et manducasti.—Id. Tract. XXV. col. 489.—Ed.]

[1 Nam secundum creaturarum substantiam, quod fuerunt ante consecrationem, hoc et postea consistunt.—Ratr. Lib. de Corp. et Sang. Dom. Oxon. 1838. c. LIV. p. 27.—Ed.]

[2 Οὐδὲ γὰρ μετὰ τὸν ἁγιασμὸν τὰ μυστικὰ σύμβολα τῆς οἰκείας ἐξίσταται φύσεως. μένει γὰρ ἐπὶ τῆς προτέρας οὐσίας, καὶ τοῦ σχήματος καὶ τοῦ εἴδους, καὶ ὁρατά ἐστι καὶ ἁπτὰ, οἷα καὶ πρότερον ἦν.—Theodor. Op. Lut. Par. 1642. Inconfusus Dialog. II. Tom. IV. p. 85.—Ed]

ment was delivered to the Corinthians in both kinds. As Christ saith, so saith Paul, *Bibite ex hoc omnes.* "Drink ye all of this." That the whole sacrament should be received of the people, and no mutilation permitted, the ancient writers are most clear; as Ambrose, Jerome, Chrysostom, Gelasius, Cyprian, &c.[1] This sacrament is to be received in remembrance of Christ crucified. "As oft as ye shall eat this bread, and drink of this cup, ye shew the Lord's death until his coming."

[1 Cor. xi. 26.]

Of preparation required to the worthy receiving of this blessed sacrament.

23. In what manner we ought to prepare ourselves thereunto, Paul teacheth, saying, "Let a man prove himself, and so eat of that bread, and drink of that cup." This condemneth anabaptists, which, thinking themselves to be without sin, communicate with none but such as they think like to themselves. Every man shall bear his own burthen: it behoveth therefore every man to try himself and not other men. "Try whether ye be in the faith, or no." Faith hath his fruits: it worketh repentance, it causeth sorrow for sins committed, fear of sinning again, and hope of pardon. It breedeth love towards God, and love towards our brethren. If incredulity, if impenitency, if hatred and malice have possessed thine heart, then abstain from the Lord's table, lest with Judas thou receive the Lord's bread against the Lord, the food of salvation to thy condemnation. But, if thou believe, repent thee of thy sin, purpose to live a charitable and godly life; if thou be clothed with the sweet garment of the Son of God, then sit thee down at the table of the Lord and at the feast of the Lamb. For this is his feast; this is done only in remembrance of him; this is the blessed eucharist, a sacrament of praise and thanksgiving, as for all other godly benefits, so particularly and principally for the death and passion of Jesus Christ, God's only Son, and our only Saviour.

[1 Cor. xi. [28.]]

[2 Cor. xiii. 5.]

Honest life and conversation amongst men.

24. These duties being thus performed unto God, we must also endeavour to live and lead an honest life. Peace is a great mean to procure piety, and piety should breed honesty in us. The one cannot be where the other is not. Walk honestly, because the days are evil: deny impiety and worldly lusts: "live soberly, justly, godlily in this present world; looking for that blessed hope, and appearing of the

[Tit. ii. 12, 13.]

[1 See Note B.—ED.]

glory of the mighty God, and our Saviour Jesus Christ." If we will be Christ's disciples, let us tread in his footsteps. If we follow him here in peace, piety, and honesty, we shall receive in his kingdom that crown of eternal glory, which God the Father for his Son's sake grant us; to whom, with the Holy Ghost, three Persons and one God, be all honour and glory, now and for ever. Amen.

THE FIFTH SERMON.

A SERMON

PREACHED BEFORE THE QUEEN.

PHILIPPIANS II.

2. *Be like minded, having the same love, being of one accord and of one judgment:*
3. *That nothing be done through contention or vain glory, but that in meekness of mind every man esteem other better than himself.*
4. *Look not every man on his own things, but every man also on the things of other men.*
5. *Let the same mind be in you, that was in Christ Jesus.*

<small>The apostle's vehemency in exhorting to brotherly concord.</small>

THE apostle of our Lord and Saviour Jesus Christ, with a most vehement spirit, and most earnest obtestation, doth here exhort the Philippians, if there were any consolation in Christ, any comfort of charity, any communion of the Spirit, any bowels of tender affections, or any compassion in them, they would, to the fulfilling of his joy, follow peace, unity, love, and brotherly concord; removing withal the lets thereof, and shewing the means how unity, love, and concord, may be continued and preserved. And, that his exhortation might be of greater authority, and so take better effect, he setteth down our Saviour Christ as an example; who is the God of unity and peace, the Lord of love, and the liveliest pattern of all piety and sweetness of manners; requiring of us, as we profess Christ in name and word, so in mind and in deed to be so affected as Jesus Christ himself was.

<small>Three things performed in the words of St Paul: he moveth unto unity, taketh away lets which hinder unity, sheweth the means whereby unity is maintained.</small>

2. "Be like minded, having the same," &c. We have here an exhortation and an example, so linked and tied together, the one depending upon the other, that they cannot well be sundered. My purpose therefore is jointly to lay them both before you, and in explicating the one to propose the other. The exhortation is this: "Be like minded, having the same love, being of one accord, and

of one judgment: that nothing be done through contention or vain glory, but in meekness of mind every man esteem other better than himself. Look not every man on his own things, but every man also on the things of other men." Upon this exhortation followeth the example: "Let the same mind be in you, that was in Christ Jesus." The exhortation standeth upon three parts. First, he moveth unto unity, saying "Be ye like minded, having the same love;" and this unity, by way of interpretation, he divideth into two members, be of "one accord" and of "one judgment:" of "one judgment" in matters of religion; and of "one accord" in brotherly love. In the second part he removeth the lets of this unity and concord, saying, "Let nothing be done through contention and vain glory." These are great hindrances to unity and concord. Lastly, he telleth the means whereby agreement and love may be upholden and maintained, saying, "In meekness of mind let every man esteem other better than himself: look not every man to his own things, but every man also to the things of other men." Here he setteth down two preservatives and defences of unity and love: the one, "in humbleness of mind, to think better of others than of ourselves;" the other, "not to look upon our own things only, but every man also on the things of other men."

3. The apostle requireth of us a double unity, in "religion" and in "brotherly concord." Both are so necessary, that the one cannot stand long, if the other fall. Unity in religion is a thing most to be desired. "What is the worst thing of all others? Dissention. What the best? Unity, peace, and agreement[1]." Thus thought Gregory. And we read that the gospel had his beginning in unity: "The multitude of them which believed had one heart and one soul." Schism had his beginning of dissention: "I am of Paul, I of Apollos, I of Cephas:" this was that which rent the church of God in pieces. The church is called the "kingdom of God." the "ark of Noah;" the "body of Christ;" to teach us that it should

1. The apostle requireth unity both in religion and affection.
Greg. Nazian.
Acts iv. [32.]
1 Cor. i. [12.]

[1 Τί τοῦ ἡμετέρου λόγου τὸ κάλλιστον; ἡ εἰρήνη· προσθήσω δ' ὅτι καὶ τὸ λυσιτελέστατον. τί δαὶ τὸ αἴσχιστον καὶ τὸ βλαβερώτατον; ἡ διχόνοια.—Greg. Naz. Op. Par. 1778. Orat. xxxii. De Moderatione, Tom. I. p. 580.—ED.]

be at unity in itself. For a house, a ship, a body divided cannot continue: by themselves they are brought to ruin. Wherefore, together with the blessed apostle, "I beseech you, brethren, by the name of our Lord Jesus Christ, that ye all speak one thing, and that there be no dissentions among you: but be ye knit together in one mind and in one judgment."

1 Cor. i. [10.]

4. But we must consider which is true unity. For every agreement is not that concord whereunto we are in this place exhorted. Lucifer with other angels consented together; Eve and Adam and the serpent were all of one mind; so were the builders of the tower of Babel; so were they of Sodom *a puero usque ad senem*, "from the child to the man of grey hairs"; so were Dathan and Abiram, with their complices; so were the worshippers of the golden calf; so were the sacrificers in Dan and Bethel; so were Pilate and Herod; so were the Jews that cried with one voice, "Let him be crucified;" and so are they which have joined themselves in holy league with no other intent than those wicked confederates had, of whom the prophet saith, "They assembled themselves together against the Lord, and against his Christ." But it is unity of the Spirit, unity in the truth, unity in Christ and in his gospel, whereunto our apostle here exhorteth us. "The name of peace is goodly, and the opinion of consent," saith Hilary, "is a fair and a beautiful thing: but who doubteth that the linked peace of the church and of the gospel is that peace only which is of Christ, which he spake of to his apostles after his glorious passion, which he commended at his departure as the pawn[1] of his everlasting commandment[2]?" All other peace is no peace indeed. "Nor is he joined to the church," saith Cyprian, "who is severed and sundered from the

Every agreement is not that unity whereunto we are exhorted.
Gen. iii. [6.]
Gen. xi. [1—4.]
Gen. xix. [4.]
Numb. xvi. [2, 3.]
Exod. xxxii. [3, 4.]

Psal. ii. [2.]

Hilar. contra Auxent.

[1 Pawn—pledge.—Ed.]

[2 Speciosum quidem nomen est pacis, et pulcra est opinio unitatis: sed quis ambigat eam solam ecclesiæ atque evangeliorum unitatem pacem esse, quæ Christi est? Quam ad apostolos post passionis suæ gloriam est locutus, quam ad æterni mandati sui pignus commendavit abiturus, hanc nos, fratres dilectissimi, et amissam quærere, et turbatam componere, et repertam tenere curavimus.—Hil. Pictavor. Episc. Op. Par. 1693. Cont. Arianos vel Auxent. Mediolan. Liber. col. 1263. —Ed.]

gospel[1]." St Paul, moving men to unity in religion, saith, "This is all one thing;" but he addeth further, "according to Jesus Christ." The city whereof the prophet speaketh, which is at unity within itself, must be builded upon the foundation of the apostles and of the prophets. For what a concord is that which is at strife with Christ? Unity must be in verity: "Thy word is verity;" in this we must agree. "Let us not hear, This I say, this thou sayest, but, This saith the Lord[2]." For unity in religion not grounded upon Christ and his gospel is not concord, but conspiracy.

_{Rom. xv. [5.]}

_{John xvii. [17.] Augustine.}

5. And here we have to praise our God, that in public doctrine touching the substance of religion we all agree in one truth; we all build upon one foundation, Christ Jesus slain and offered up for our full redemption according to the doctrine of the scriptures. So much the greater pity it is that there should be such dissent in matters of small importance, in rites and circumstances, that by contention in such things the course of the gospel should be hindered, Christ's adversaries strengthened, and his church offended. The ministry cannot be well executed without her rites; which rites are left indifferent to every policy, so that they be not disagreeing from the word, so that they tend unto edification, so that they be seemly and according to decent order. Be it granted that some rites upon some consideration might be bettered, or omitted; yet can I not say, neither any man, I suppose, can prove, that any thing is set down to be observed in the church, wicked, or contrary to the word. And it were scarce wisdom, when as in many years a beautiful and a costly house is builded, if a window be set a little awry, or some small like eye-sore do appear, in respect thereof to disturb the whole house, to pull it down, and lay it flat with the ground. For, every change being so full of peril, surely these great alterations upon so light advice, these new commonwealths, howsoever they be shadowed with the plausible name of reformation, yet in seeking (for

_{The unity which is in the church of England at this day touching religion: the disagreement about some smaller things outwardly appertaining to religion.}

[1 Nec ecclesiæ jungitur, qui ab evangelio separatur.—Cypr. Op. Oxon. 1682. De Lapsis, p. 129.—Ed.]

[2 Non audiamus, Hæc dicis, hæc dico: sed audiamus, Hæc dicit Dominus.—August. Op. Par. 1694. Cont. Don. Epist., vulgo De Unit. Eccles. Liber Unus. Tom. ix, col. 340.—Ed.]

undoubtedly this is sought, and that by many) to have the patrimony of the church divided, mangled, and impaired, they threaten the utter overthrow of learning and religion. For take away living, at which root this axe especially striketh, and ye take away learning: take away learning, and ye overthrow teaching: take away teaching, and what shall become of the church of Christ? "Where there is no vision," there the people cannot choose but come to decay. There is no state (no, not the state of a prince excepted, to whom fear, honour, obedience, and tribute is due) that may more rightly challenge a competent and sufficient living, than the minister of the word of God. They seem to have put out the very light of nature in themselves, which repine at the reasonable maintenance of them that minister before the Lord in these sanctified labours. For who doth plant a vineyard, and doth not eat of the fruit thereof? or who feedeth a flock, and eateth not of the milk of the flock? Mark how the scriptures both in the law and in the gospel do beat upon this point. "In the law it is said, Thou shalt not muzzle the mouth of the ox. Doth God take care for oxen?" No, his care is for us. For our cause it is that he hath said, "The labourer is worthy of his hire." For our cause he hath "ordained that they which preach the gospel, should live of the gospel." He had a care of his church, and therefore gave charge: "Let him that is taught in the word make him that taught him partaker of all his goods." This is large, yet but reasonable. For, "if we have sown unto you spiritual things, is it a great matter if we reap your carnal things?" is it much to make us partakers of all your goods? "The elders that rule well are worthy of double honour, specially they which labour in the word and doctrine." "They which labour amongst you, and are over you in the Lord, and admonish you, have them," saith the apostle, "we beseech you, in singular love, for their work's sake." It was foreseen no doubt by the Spirit, how God's portion should be pinched, how the ministers of the word should be contemned, how injuriously men in these last uncharitable days would seek for the havoc and spoil of the church: this moved him in so large and ample sort to speak of maintenance and honour due to his ministers. If any man be slow and retchless in doing his office, if there be any idle shepherd, that feedeth himself only, and not his flock, let him be reformed or removed: but for the fault of a few that the whole state should be subverted, and the patrimony of the church of Christ spoiled and devoured, it were very hard. No prince nor people, christian or heathen, could ever consent to such a thing without sacrilege. Well: as we are at unity in substance of religion, so God grant that at length in these things also we may agree and be as one, even as becometh the congregation of Christ, which is a society linked and knit together, not sundered by division, and rent in pieces by variety of opinions and judgments. To this unity Paul exhorteth: "Be of one meaning." This unity Christ commendeth to his disciples, saying, "Be one." [2 Cor. xiii. 11.] [Mark ix. 50.]

6. Of this unity and conjunction of men agreeing in the truth ariseth that brotherly concord, whereof St Paul, in the words that follow, saith, "Be like minded, having the same charity." Where dissent in religion is, there can hardly be consent in love. Diversity of religion sundered the Jew and Gentile; caused the one to be an abomination to the other. Wherefore he, that came to bring religion into the world, came not to bring with it peace, but a sword; a sword to divide asunder not only kingdoms and cities, but even the man and the wife, the father and the child; a sword to cut off one brother from another. For there can be no agreement between Christ and Belial; the light of the one, and the other's darkness: such as are not of one true religion with us, their profession may be friendship, but their practice is deceit: they may with speech and countenance flatter and fawn, but they carry for the most part a malicious heart, set upon mischief. Cain spake Abel fair enough; but for the diversity of his sacrifice he hated him, and, spying opportunity, shed his blood. Herod pretended to worship Christ, whose death he fully purposed in his malicious mind. There was never therefore wise Israelite that would trust an Amorite. It is and will be true for ever, that Constantius said; *Qui perfidi sunt in Deum, in principem fideles esse non possunt*[1]. [Of unity in religion cometh that unity which linketh men's minds in mutual affection each towards other.] [Gen. iv. [3–8.]] [Matt. ii. [8.]] [Sozom. l. 1. c. 6.]

[¹ Λογισάμενος μή ποτε ἔσεσθαι περὶ βασιλέα εὔνους τοὺς ὧδε ἑτοίμους προδότας θεοῦ γεγενημένους.—Soz. Hist. Eccl. Amst. 1700. p. 333.—ED.]

[SANDYS.]

"They cannot be sure to their prince, who to God-ward are not sincere." They count truth heresy; and No PROMISE TO BE KEPT WITH HERETICS is their posy[1]. Children they are like to their father, which is a murderer and liar from the beginning. But when we speak of love and charity, we speak of the badge of Christianity, of the virtues of true Christians; who, consenting in faith, bring forth the fruit of faith, which is love; without which, how near soever we approach unto Christ in word and in outward profession, we are indeed none of his. He cannot agree with Christ, that is at discord with a Christian. God is so delighted with this affection, that he professeth himself to hate them that are enemies of it: yea, "the soul of the Lord abhorreth him that raiseth up contentions amongst brethren." Love is the livery-coat of Christ: whosoever will be numbered with his servants, must put it on. "By this men shall know you to be my disciples, if ye love one another." In those very creatures which God hath left empty and void of understanding, there is a kind of love: a consent we see there is in the stars, in the elements, in times and seasons, amongst the beasts of the field, the fowls of the air, the fishes of the sea, and fruits of the earth: every beast doth love his like, to our shame and reproach, if, having so many schoolmasters to teach us one thing, we learn it not; especially being so necessary as it is. For in love and concord our prayers are accepted in the sight of God, and without them abhorred: "Verily I say unto you, that if two of you shall agree in earth upon any thing, whatsoever they shall desire, it shall be given them of my Father which is in heaven."

Prov. vi. [16, 19.]

John xiii. [35.]

Matt. xviii. [19.]

The love and unity, which should be in the mystical body of Christ, which is the company of men professing the christian faith, shewed by comparison of that unity which is seen in the parts

7. St Paul therefore, to persuade men to this concord, useth a similitude drawn from the members of a natural body: wherein he noteth, that the body by nature is a thing whole and perfect, consisting of all his members; if any part be wanting or cut off, it is maimed: even so in this mystical body of Christ, in this spiritual society of the faithful, if any part be cut off, the whole is defaced and deformed. All the members, and every one of them, labour not for themselves only, but for the use and preservation of the whole body. So are we born, not for ourselves alone,

[1 Posy—motto.—ED.]

but for others also, for whom we should travail as for ourselves. The members strive not, but are content with their placing, be it honourable, be it base: even so should not we strive for equality or superiority, but every man content himself with his own calling. The members rejoice and suffer together: even so should we be kindly affected each to other, mourning with them that mourn, and being glad with them that do rejoice. That member which hath not this sympathy, this mutual suffering, this feeling of other men's hurts, is dead and rotten. "Remember them," saith the apostle, "that are in bonds, as though ye yourselves were bound with them, and them that are in affliction, as if ye yourselves were afflicted in their bodies." The members are sundry, and have sundry offices. For if all were an eye, where were the hearing? if all did command, which should obey? even so in this resembled body, and civil society, there must be diversity, as of members, so of functions. The prince is as the head, without whose discreet and wise government the laws would cease, and, the people being not ruled by order of laws, ruin and confusion would soon follow: each contending and striving against other, the end would be the utter subversion of all. The ministers of the word are as the eyes to watch, and not to wink or sleep, and as the mouth to speak, and not be dumb: for then they perform not their allotted function. They are placed as watchmen over the church, for the good and godly direction thereof; to take heed both to themselves, and to all the flock, whereof the Holy Ghost hath made them overseers; to feed the church of God, which he hath purchased with his own blood; to warn the people of the enemy ever at hand, always ready to assault; to teach and instruct the people of God in the way of their salvation, to tell them of their sins, to cry unto them, and not to cease. The judges are as ears, who should sit in open places, to hear the causes and complaints of the people, opening the one ear to the plaintiff, and reserving the other to the defendant's answer. The nobility are as the shoulders and arms to bear the burthen of the commonwealth, to hold up the head, and defend the body with might and force, with wise counsel and good advice. Men of lower degrees are set as inferior parts in the body, pain-

and members of a natural body.
1 Cor. xii. [12—27.]

Heb. xiii. [3.]

fully to travail for the necessary sustentation both of themselves and others. All these members are so necessary, that none can want[1] without the ruin of the whole. For every one hath need of other, and by the help of the other is maintained. This necessary conjunction should cause the prince to love the people, as Moses, which wished rather to be blotted out of the book of life, than that they should perish; and as David, which besought the Lord to turn his wrathful hand against him, and to spare the people. It should cause such love in the people towards the prince, as was both in the people of Israel towards their prince and governor Josua, when they said, "All that thou hast commanded us, we will do; and whithersoever thou sendest us, we will go;" and in David's subjects towards him, when they stood fast by him at such time as he fled from his rebellious and unnatural son; not suffering that he should adventure himself in the field, but they rather for him to bear the brunt and burthen of the battle: "Thou shalt not go, thou art worth ten thousand of us." This should cause the pastor to love his flock, as Paul did love his brethren, "I would wish myself separated from Christ for my brethren:" and again, "Our good will was to have dealt unto you not the gospel of God only, but even our own souls too, because ye were dear unto us." This should cause the people to love their pastor dearly, as the Galatians loved Paul, to whom he giveth this testimony: "I bear you record, that, if it had been possible, you would have plucked out your own eyes, and have given them to me." Finally, this should cause all men to walk in love, even as Christ our example hath loved us.

[Exod. xxxii. 32.]
[2 Sam. xxiv. 17.]
Josh. i. [16.]
2 Sam. xviii. [3.]
Rom. ix. [3.]
1 Thess. ii. [8.]
Gal. iv. [15.]

2.
The first hinderance of unity is contention.

8. It followeth: "Let nothing be done through contention or vain-glory." After that St Paul hath exhorted us to love and unity, now he removeth the lets and enemies of them. The breach of all concord is contention; and the daughter of contention is dissipation. Wherefore our God is not the God of contention, but of peace; not of confusion, but of order: his apostles are not breeders of stirs and mutinies, they are messengers sent to make peace: to this they provoke and exhort every where: "I beseech you, let there be no contentions amongst you, fol-

Heb. xii. [14, 15.]

[1 Want—be wanting.—ED.]

low peace; let no root of bitterness spring up and trouble you." Where the man and the wife, the parents and the children, strive one against another, that house needeth no foreign enemy to bring it to nought; it will be devoured of itself. A kingdom, a city, divided by contention, how should it stand? All times and examples are our witnesses. Contention between Roboam and Jeroboam brought the kingdom of Israel first to a division, and then to confusion. The contention between Simon, John, and Eleazar, chief men in the city of Jerusalem, was the last and utter destruction of that city. If counsellors emulate and contend amongst themselves, it must needs tear the state of the commonwealth in pieces. It was great wisdom therefore in M. Æmilius and Fulvius Flaccus, that, being at enmity, yet when they were chosen censors of Rome together, they joined hands and buried all injuries; lest through their contention the state should come to ruin. Abraham, knowing the hurt of contention, gave place to his nephew Lot: "Let there be no strife, I pray thee, between thee and me, neither between mine herdmen and thine; for we are brethren." The scripture termeth us sheep, meek and patient: let us not therefore be currish like unto dogs, contending, barking, and biting at our brethren. "If ye bite one another, beware lest ye be consumed one of another." [Gen. xiii. [8.]] [Gal. v. [15.]]

9. And as the bane of unity is contention, so the breeder of contention is vain-glory. What else caused John, bishop of Constantinople, to contend to be called, "The universal bishop"? *Superbum nomen hoc est*[1] : "This is a proud name," saith Gregory. What else made the angel to contend to advance himself above measure? Adam to seek to be wise as God? Absolon to strive for his father's kingdom? Cæsar to brook no man to be his better? Pompey no man to be his peer? Wherefore, "let us not be desirous of vain-glory, provoking one another, envying one another." The proud and vain-glorious are compared to the cedar-trees of Libanus, which are higher than others, not of themselves, but by reason of the high mountain whereupon they grow. [Another hinderance is vain-glory, the mother and breeder of contention.] [Gal. v. [26.]] [Isai. ii. 13.]

[[1] Tantoque major efficeris, quanto te à superbi et stulti vocabuli usurpatione restringis.—Greg. Papæ I. Mag. Op. Par. 1705. Lib. v. Epist. xviii. Ad Johannem Episc. Constantin. Tom. ii. col. 742.—ED.]

10. It is madness for men to glory in that which is not their own. "What hast thou, that thou hast not received? And if thou hast received, why dost thou glory?" Dost thou glory in thy good works and righteousness? They are as the clothes of a woman in her blood. Dost thou glory in thy nobility and great authority? "By me kings do reign:" neither is there any power but from God. Rule is given you of the Lord, and power by him that is most high. Glory not, but fear, knowing that he which hath received much, hath much to reckon for; and "a hard judgment shall they have that bear rule." Dost thou glory in thy riches? Fool, this night thy life is taken from thee, and then whose are they? They are as grass unto all, but unto most men as thorns: many have been pierced to the heart by them: they spare neither prophet nor apostle, as we see by the examples of Balaam and Judas: they are every where unquiet guests. Sigismundus the emperor could not sleep so long as a chest full of gold remained in his bed-chamber. Dost thou glory in form and fashion? in favour? in beauty? "All flesh is grass, and the glory of it is as the flower of the field." To-day it flourisheth, to-morrow it vanisheth. Dost thou glory in thy worldly wisdom and policy? The wisdom of the world is but foolishness before the Lord. "Let not the wise man glory in his wisdom: let him that glorieth glory in this, that he understandeth and knoweth me, that I am the Lord which shew mercy, judgment, and righteousness in the earth." Dost thou glory, with insolent Haman, that thou art in exceeding grace and favour with Assuerus the king, and canst have whatsoever thy heart doth wish at his hands? Dost thou in this thy loftiness envy unto death godly Mardocheus, because he honoureth not thee, which art in thyself altogether unworthy of honour? His pride had a fall, his insolency ended in ignominy and shame. Let such as are lifted up into such favour fear: let them learn to be so much lowlier, as they are higher than others, remembering that the wrath of a prince is death; and what is more easily kindled than wrath?

11. It is hard to bridle the haughty affections of vain-glorious men. This vanity staineth our best and purest actions; our prayer, when we pray that we may

[Marginal notes: There is nothing in us whereof we may boast. 1 Cor. iv. [7.] — Isai. lxiv. [6.] — Prov. viii. [15.] — Wisd. vi. [6.] — Num. xxii. — Matt. xxvi. — Isai. xl. [6.] — Jer. ix. [23, 24.] — Esther v. [11.] — Vain-glory hardly bridled.]

be seen and thought holy; our alms, when we give that we may have a praise; our fasting, when we use it either to merit unto ourselves, or thereby to seem devout unto others; our preaching, when we seek our own commendation, when we study not so much to please God as men, when much learning puffeth us up, when we take a pride in our picked words and pleasant utterance, when we rejoice with Herod to hear the people shout and cry, "The voice of a God." Thus, as the goodliest trees in a garden are soonest blasted with red winds, so men endued with the rarest qualities and best gifts are soonest infected with this poison. That great and blessed apostle himself was in some danger of this disease. Wherefore thus he speaketh: "Lest I should be exalted above measure through abundance of revelations, there was given unto me a sting in the flesh, the messenger of Satan to buffet me, that I might not be exalted above measure." He only was quite and clean void of this sin, who is our example, who saith in the gospel, "I do not seek mine own glory." [Acts xii. 22.] [2 Cor. xii. 7.] [John viii. 50.]

12. Now the lets of unity, which are contention and vain-glory, being removed, St Paul teacheth in the last place, by what means unity and concord may be preserved. Wherein he setteth down two strong preservatives. The first is, "In humbleness of mind every man to esteem others better than himself." To esteem others better than ourselves is a lesson hard to be learned, a lesson which never can enter into the brain of a proud-hearted man. And therefore St Paul requireth humbleness of mind in him, that shall thus frame and fashion his judgment; according to that whereunto he exhorteth in another place, "Walk worthy of the vocation whereunto ye are called, with all humbleness of mind and meekness, with long suffering, supporting one another through love, endeavouring to keep the unity of the Spirit in the bond of peace." For upon whom shall the Spirit of the Lord rest, but only upon them that are humble and lowly? To whom should he give grace, but unto men of a meek and gentle spirit? But there are sundry sorts of humility. [Eph. iv. 1—3.]

3. The first mean to preserve unity is humbleness of mind.

13. There is an humility which is constrained, an humility perforce, such as that whereof the prophet saith: *Divers kinds of humility.*

Psal. cxlvii.
[6.]
"The Lord relieveth the meek, and humbleth the wicked to the ground." Such are then humble, only when God hath humbled them by afflicting them. There is a counterfeit humility, such as was in Absolon, when he stole *Ecclus. xix.*
[22, 23.] away the people's hearts from the king. For it is the usual manner of some to bow down themselves, and to look most demurely, when their inward parts are full of deceit, and their heads most occupied about wicked purposes. Again, there is a superstitious humility, such as *Col. ii.* [21.] that was, "Touch not, taste not, handle not:" touch not the chalice, taste not an egg in Lent, handle not the bread that by consecration is made holy: which things had a shew of religious holiness, but were indeed mere dalliances, devised by Satan, to no other end but only to noozle the deceived in their blindness. But true humility *Luke xviii.* [13.] is the lowliness of a pensive and contrite heart. This humility was in the publican, which thought so basely of himself that he durst not lift up his eyes towards heaven: this humility was in Paul, when he confessed himself the [1 Cor. xv. 9.]
1 Tim. i.
[15.] "least" amongst the apostles, and "the chiefest amongst sinners." A man of this disposition, which thinks so basely of himself, will easily esteem others better than himself. But what? Should a king then, in dignity, place, and authority, prefer a mean artificer or a day-labourer before himself? or should a wise man esteem a natural fool wiser than himself? No: St Paul is no author of confusion, neither will he in any wise have God's good gifts debased. He descendeth not to these extremities, but only persuadeth us not to think so arrogantly of ourselves, as in respect of ourselves to condemn others. Every man hath the mind of a king in himself. Goliah thought bigly of himself, but of David how basely! This self-liking hath infected and possessed all flesh.

The way to redress that overweening which we have of ourselves. 14. The way to redress it is to look upon ourselves and upon others, but not upon both with the same eyes; upon ourselves with the eyes of strait judgment, upon our neighbours with a favourable and a charitable eye. Whosoever therefore thou art that depisest another, consider in thyself these two things. First, whatsoever thou hast that good is, it is of God, the author of all goodness; and as all that thou hast is from him, so to him thou dost stand accountable for it. Thou art but a steward of his goods, which will call thee to a strict and a hard reckoning for every mite. If thou consider this, thou shalt find small cause to boast and glory of thyself, but shalt give all glory to the King of glory. But open thine other eye, and look down to thy sins; there shalt thou see an ugly sight: thou shalt be forced to leave off glorying, and to cry with the prophet David, "Mine ini- Psal.xxxviii. quities are gone over my head, and as a weighty burthen [4.] they are too heavy for me." Yea, if thou rightly look upon thy sins, thou shalt see in that glass God's face turned away from thee, and his ears shut up against thy prayers: "Your iniquities," saith God, "have made a division be- Isai. lix. [2.] tween you and me." If thou truly enter into thyself, and consider of thy sin, thou shalt say with the prodigal child, "Lord, I am not worthy to be called thy son;" Luke xv. [21.] and with Peter, "Depart from me, for I am a sinner;" Luke v. [8.] and with David, "It is I that have sinned; as for these 2 Sam. xxiv. sheep, what have they done?" Thou wilt think of others, [17.] as Saul did say of David, "Thou art more righteous than 1 Sam. xxiv. I." But the prince of darkness hath dimmed, or rather [17.] put out both these eyes: we can neither see our gifts that be good to be of God, nor our sin, as we should, to be of ourselves; and therefore we esteem most highly of ourselves, and most vilely of others. Which we would not do, if we did lovingly and charitably behold with reverence the graces and gifts of God which are in them. For who is there in whom some commendable thing doth not appear? Lazarus seemed a contemptible thing in the eyes of that rich glutton; yet was his patience to be preferred before the other's riches. The publican seemed ugly and odious to the Pharisee; yet his humbleness was much more worthy praise, than the other's supposed purity and holiness of life. There is no man so base, but a charitable eye may find out in him some good and precious thing. And no man may be despised, in whom there is any appearance at all of that which is good. At the least this we may see in all men, that they shew the workmanship of him which made them, they carry the image of him by whom they were created; and in them which are our brethren, how high soever we bear our heads, yet thus much we may consider more, that they are as dearly bought as we: the precious blood of the Son of God was shed for them, as well as for us: we have not a foot more than they in that eternal inheritance which God hath provided for his humble-minded children. If these considerations do not make us to esteem others better than ourselves, yet somewhat they will abate and take down that proud humour which causeth us to lift up ourselves so much above others. And, as in looking upon our brethren we must have one eye open, to behold the graces of God which are in them, so the other must be shut and closed up, that those things wherein they are weak may be hidden. For "charity doth cover sins." There can be no charity in that man's heart, whose eyes are fed with beholding the infirmities of his brethren. Sem and Japhet turned away their faces when they went to cover their father's nakedness, for which charitable deed they received a blessing: but Cham, for looking upon his father's fall, brought a curse upon himself and his posterity—to teach us, that he which looketh upon other men's faults with pleasure and delight, doth well deserve that other men should look upon his plagues without compassion. St Paul therefore would have us to be favourable censurers of our brethren, ready to pardon scapes, "considering," saith he, "thyself, lest thou also be tempted." And it is a good meditation which Augustine prescribeth in these cases: "Such we were or may be[1]." Wherefore, as Christ doth not only cover our manifold sins, but also forgive, as it

1 Pet. iv. [8.]

Gal. vi. [1.]

Augustine.

[1 Hunc compatientis affectum in eadem epistola ad Galatas præcipit, dicens, "Si præoccupatus fuerit homo in aliquo delicto, vos qui spirituales estis, instruite hujusmodi in spiritu lenitatis, intendens teipsum, ne et tu tenteris." Vide si non dixit, Fiere tanquam ille, ut illum lucrifacias. Non utique, ut ipsum delictum fallaciter ageret, aut se id habere simularet: sed ut in alterius delicto, quid etiam sibi accidere posset, adtenderet, atque ita alteri, tamquam sibi ab altero vellet, misericorditer subveniret: hoc est non mentientis astu, sed compatientis affectu. Sic Judæo, sic gentili, sic cuilibet homini Paulus in errore vel peccato aliquo constituto, non simulando quod non erat, sed compatiendo, quia esse potuisset, tamquam qui se hominem cogitaret, omnibus omnia factus est, ut omnes lucrifaceret.—August. Op. Par. 1679. Epist. lxxxii. Ad Hieron. Tom. II. col. 201.—ED.]

were, and quite forget them; so let us, like good and pitiful surgeons, hide the sores of our wounded brethren from the wind. This the law of charity and love requireth, and this neither taketh away the sword from the magistrate, nor yet the rod from the minister; but that each of them severally according to the order of his vocation may punish sin, as he must pity sinners.

15. The other preservative of unity is, "Not to look upon our own things only, but every man upon the things of others." These words do suffer a double exposition. They may be referred to the words before by way of pre-occupation, as if he should say, "You think it hard to prefer others before yourselves, but you may make it easy. Look not upon your own things, such as minister occasion of overweening, but look upon the virtues, qualities, and graces, that be in others." Another exposition is, to make this a proper mean to keep and conserve unity, rather than a way only to diminish loftiness and pride: so that the words are to this effect, "Without unity there can be no Christianity; and a chief mean to live in unity is, that men be not every one for himself, but each careful to do good to other, that we seek not greedily our own commodity, and neglect the commodity of our brethren. Love seeketh not her own." But in these evil days charity is grown so cold that every man's song is, "I am nearest to myself." Men scrape and scratch, they heap together and lay up for them and theirs; but the bowels of tender mercy towards others are withered and dried up. Of these self-seekers we have too many examples Of this crew were the Sichemites: for to obtain substance, wealth, and cattle, and friends, they sticked not to alter their religion. But whilst they thus sought themselves, they lost themselves. Nabal was one of the same note; and the rich man, whose heart was set only upon the enlarging of his barns, was another. *The second mean to maintain concord is care not only for ourselves but for others also.* *Gen. xxxiv. [24.]* *1 Sam. xxv. [3.] Luke xii. 18.]*

16. There be that seem to be far from this fault, and are not; that seem to look upon others, but do it not with a single eye. And of this kind I note four sorts. There be that give to others for a *Ne noceat*, which, although it be not simple, yet is it more sufferable than *Many seem to have a care of others, whose care in deed is for themselves.*

the rest. Achaz spoiled the temple of God, to give rewards to the king of Assyria, and so bought his own quietness with a stolen price. Yea, Jacob is fain and glad to send his brother Esau great gifts, that he may pass quietly by him without hurt. The needier sort are forced to consider of the richer for their better safety. The poor servant in the comedy complaineth of it: "It is a hard case," saith he, "that the poor must still offer to the rich man's box[1]." There be others, that sometime look upon others with some part of liberality. But either they do it to avoid an evil name, and lest they should be noted for niggards; or else they do it when it is wrung out from them by clamour and importunity. The poor widow, by wearying the wicked judge, brought him at length to shew her justice. The disciples may seem to have had a spice of this fault by that speech of theirs concerning the Canaanite, "Send her away, she crieth after us." Another sort give, not because they are, but because they would seem to be, bountiful and liberal, as the Pharisees, which made a trumpet to be blown, that men might know when they gave alms. The last and worst sort give, but they give to gain. Jason gave Antiochus the king a grand sum of money: but he knew the office of the high priest to be well worth it.

margin: 2 Chron. xxviii. [21.]
margin: Gen. xxxii. [13—20.]
margin: Matt. xv. [23.]
margin: [2 Macc. iv. 7, 8.]

17. Our apostle's meaning is not that we should in this wise consider one another, but he exhorteth us sincerely, heartily, and in deed, to seek the commodity and safety of others, even as Christ hath sought ours. He sought not himself; but being equal with God, became man for us; and being Lord of all, for us became a servant; to exalt us, he humbled himself; he made himself a curse, to take away the curse which was due unto us. Let that affection therefore be in us, which was in him. He is our example. Him we must follow in the path of his virtues, if we will follow him in at the gate of his kingdom. Every Christian ought so to be affected towards others that he may say with St Paul in sincerity and truth, "I seek you, not yours."

margin: Our care for others must be hearty and sincere, as Christ's is for us.
margin: [2 Cor. xii. 14.]

18. Princes are not exempted from this rule of Christian duty. "Love thy neighbour as thyself," is

margin: This care of caring for others doth principally concern princes. [Luke x. 27.]

[1 Ter. Phorm. I. i. 8, 9.—Ed.]

spoken unto them. All Christians are our neighbours, which do need our help. To suffer such to perish for want of help is to be guilty of their blood. Moses, in consideration hereof, when he saw an Israelite in danger to be murdered of an Egyptian, in defence of his brother slew the enemy of God. Abraham sat not still when Lot was in danger. When the Christians were persecuted by the Persian, Constantinus wrote letters in their behalf, that they might peaceably enjoy the freedom of their conscience and the liberty of the gospel[1]. The same emperor waged war against Licinius, his own sister's husband, in the quarrel of the poor afflicted Christians[2]. Constans likewise wrote a menacing letter to Constantius his brother, wherein he proclaimed open war against him, unless he did presently surcease his enterprises against the Christians[3]. These zealous and worthy princes, being nearly touched with those afflictions which others suffered for God's cause, studied for their safety, as for their own. This they did for strangers: what would they have done if their subjects had claimed succour at their hands? would they have put their own sheep in the mouths of bloody and ravening wolves, which were so careful to deliver a strange flock from the butcher's knife? As it is treason for the subjects to forsake their prince; so for the prince to forsake his subjects, it is a fault not sufferable. If Christ made himself poor to enrich us, if he humbled himself to the death of the cross for our deliverance, when we were his enemies held in captivity under sin and death, shall we spare our pains, our purses, or our lives, for the relieving of our brethren, the afflicted members of Christ Jesus? It was a plain lesson which Mardocheus gave queen Hester, "If she neglected the people of God, God would find a way to deliver his people, but she and her father's house should perish." Kings and princes should consider that they are God's ministers, furnished with power and might from above to stand with him against his enemies, to serve him both

Exod. ii. [11, 12.]

Gen. xiv. [14—16.]

Sozom. lib. ii. c. 15.

Euseb. lib. x. c. ult.

Theod. lib. ii. c. 9. Socr. lib. ii. c. 22.

[Esther iv. 14.]

[1 Soz. Hist. Eccl. Amst. 1700. pp. 377, 8.—Ed.]
[2 Euseb. Pamph. Hist. Eccl. Amst. 1695. p. 326.—Ed.]
[3 Theod. Hist. Eccl. Amst. 1695. Lib. ii. c. 8. p. 83: Socr. Hist. Eccl. Amst. 1700. p. 88.—Ed.]

with sceptre and with sword, to be patrons and defenders of all his servants. It is a glorious thing for a prince to fight, as David did, the Lord's wars against the Philistines, to be in the field under Christ's banner. But to draw in one yoke with infidels, to be in league with antichrist, it is both an impious and a base thing. By joining with Achaz[1], Jehosaphat gained nothing, and Ochozias[2] as little by joining with Joram. Joas and Jehu, worthy princes, regarded God's cause, and had singular care of the safety of their people: the one took away that cruel murderer of the king's blood, the conspiring and traitorous queen Athaliah; the other brake the neck of that idolatrous, proud, and lascivious queen Jezebel. Moses and David, most worthy princes, looked not only on themselves, but provided for their posterity, when the one appointed Josua, and the other Solomon to reign after them. The prince, that hath not a special and singular care over his people, hath denied the faith, and is worse than an infidel.

[1 Kings xxii.]
2 Kings viii. [28, 29.]
2 Kings ix. [27.]

2 Kings xi. [15, 16.]

2 Kings ix. [33.]

It concerneth also counsellors, ministers, and generally all men.

19. Neither doth this concern the duty of princes only, but of counsellors also. Their care should be greater for the prince and commonwealth, than for their own commodity. I will not remember unto you Codrus, and Decius, Curtius, Brutus, with such like, who loved their country more than themselves. I will not put you in mind of those two precepts set down by Tully out of Plato; the one, of not seeking for private commodity; the other, of not leaning to one part, and neglecting another, of the commonwealth. I like not so well to deal with profane things in this place; the word of God being so plentiful, and of great power to move the hearts of such as believe. In the scriptures of God, counsellors have examples laid before them of both sorts; as well such as have referred all their counsels to their own private gain, as also such as have faithfully employed their travails to the benefit of others. Achitophel being a man of a traitorous heart, gave treacherous advice, tending to the king's confusion; but Chusa[3] the Archite directed faithfully his counsel to the safety of his lord and master the king. Let him be followed, who is most to be

2 Sam. xvii. [1—3.]

[¹ An error for Ahab.—Ed.]
[² Ochozias—Ahaziah.—Ed.]
[³ Chusa—Hushai.—Ed.]

commended, and was best rewarded. This lesson must be delivered unto them also, which have charge to deliver it unto others. For wo be to those pastors that feed themselves, and not their flock! Paul had care of all churches. Christ preferred the safety of his flock before his own soul: he gave his precious life for his beloved sheep. To be short, this must teach every member to travail for the benefit of the whole body, that the glory of God may be sought of all: which that all may seek sincerely and heartily, God the Father grant, for his Son our Saviour's sake: to whom, &c.

THE SIXTH SERMON.

A SERMON

PREACHED BEFORE THE QUEEN.

Psalm LXXXVI.

11. *Teach me thy way, O Lord, and I will walk in thy truth.*

<small>A petition to be taught the way of God, and a promise to walk in his truth.</small>

I WILL not meddle with the argument of this psalm, nor make any general discourse of the whole: this one verse shall suffice, being plentiful and rich in matter, most fit for these our times, and not unfit for this most honourable audience: they are the words of a most worthy prince, pertinent to all princes, and convenient for all Christians. This short sentence consisteth partly of a petition, and partly of a promise. For, first, he prayeth to be taught of God: secondly, he promiseth to walk in his truth. In the former part are these things chiefly to be considered: first, a request to be taught, "Teach me;" secondly, to be taught of God, "Teach me, O Lord;" thirdly, what he would be taught, "Teach me thy ways."

<small>In praying to be taught he confesseth his ignorance.</small>

2. The king, in praying to be taught, confesseth his ignorance; and if the great prophet of God plead ignorance, who is he that dare boast of knowledge? If St Paul, after so long study and after so many heavenly revelations, did confess, "We know in part;" then the best learned of all may learn. Yea, when a man hath done his best, he must then begin again, as if all which hath been done already were in comparison of perfection nothing. It is too much arrogancy in that proud man, who thinketh himself to have all knowledge hid in the chest of his bosom, and all truth chained to his tongue, so that he can neither deceive nor be deceived. No man hath attained to the knowledge of any thing, which will not confess with Socrates, "This one thing I know, that I know nothing." "Brethren," saith the apostle, "I would not have you ignorant."

<small>1 Cor. xiii. [9.]</small>

<small>1 Cor. x. [1.]</small>

Ignorance is the mother, not of devotion, but of superstition; not of truth, but of error and sin. If we desire therefore rather to walk in light, than to dwell in blindness, we must learn of this princely prophet to become scholars in God's school: we must with Solomon prefer knowledge and wisdom before riches, honour and long life. 1 Kings iii. [9, 11.]

3. God hath appointed good means to lead men to knowledge: he hath caused the scriptures to be written for our learning. Without the knowledge whereof, neither can kings bear rule, neither subjects obey and live in order as they should. Wherefore Josua was commanded not to lay aside the volume of the law at any time, night nor day. The prophet David made it his continual study. The wisest governors of Israel would not enterprise any matter of weight till they had turned the leaves of this book, thence to take advice for their better direction. This most precious jewel is to be preferred before all treasure. If thou be hungry, it is meat to satisfy thee; if thou be thirsty, it is drink to refresh thee; if thou be sick, it is a present remedy; if thou be weak, it is a staff to lean unto; if thine enemy assault thee, it is a sword to fight withal; if thou be in darkness, it is a lanthorn to guide thy feet; if thou be doubtful of the way, it is a bright shining star to direct thee; if thou be in displeasure with God, it is the message of reconciliation; if thou study to save thy soul, receive the word ingrafted, for that is able to do it: it is the word of life. Whoso loveth salvation will love this word, love to read it, love to hear it; and such as will neither read nor hear it, Christ saith plainly, they are not of God. For the spouse gladly heareth the voice of the bridegroom; and "my sheep hear my voice," saith the Prince of pastors. The means whereby God doth lead men to knowledge.
Josh. i. [8.]
Psal. cxix. [97, 148.]
John x. [27.]

4. But the world seemeth to be glutted with the word: there be many stomachs that cannot digest it, and many that loathe it. I stand in fear that God in his justice will give us, instead of plenty of this bread, a famine, and, for wholesome food, meat that shall rot between our teeth. There is not that desire in us to know the wisdom of Christ, which was in the queen of Saba to hear the wisdom of Solomon. There were of the The contempt of the means whereby knowledge is attained.
Luke xi. [31.]

[SANDYS.]

Jews no small numbers that heard Christ three days together in the wilderness, and that fasting: but he hath fed us so full that we care not for him. The servants of Solomon were thought happy, that they might stand daily to hear his wisdom. Happy it were both for the servants of Solomon, and for Solomon too, if but every sabbath they would hear him which is far both greater and wiser than Solomon. There is no want, except it be of willingness only: for both we have leisure enough to hear, and there are store of them whom God hath very well enabled to speak. No time can be better spent; nothing more necessary for a christian court. What more prince-like, than to honour the Prince of all princes with that service, wherein he is so highly delighted? The belly is daily and daintily fed: O suffer not the soul to want that food which abideth for ever. They are not blessed that feed and pamper the flesh: they are, that "hear the word and keep it." This word, attentively and carefully heard, would convert our souls, correct our lives, soften our hearts, inflame our minds with the love of God: it would root out vice and ingraft virtue, banish vain, and cherish good desires in us: it would lay our sins before our faces, humble our proud and haughty looks, bring us unto true and hearty repentance, throw us down with godly sorrow, and raise us up again with heavenly comfort, in the merits and mercies of Christ Jesus: it would perfectly perfect us unto every good work.

Luke xi. [28.]

2 Tim. iii. [17.]

Unto knowledge prayer is as needful as meditation.

[Psal. cxix. 33, 34.]

5. The prophet, being inflamed with a desire of knowledge and understanding, saw no other way to attain thereunto, but by joining with continual meditation earnest prayer. "Teach me thy ways, O Lord: Give me understanding: Shew me thy law." He knew that praying was as needful altogether as reading; that, if there be any difference at all, it is this: by praying we profit more than by reading.

No man learneth wisdom except God be his teacher.

Rev. v. [9.]

6. As he desireth to be taught, so it is especially to be noted that his desire is to be taught of God. Teach thou me, "O Lord." There is none that can open the sealed book of God, but only the Lion of the tribe of Judah, the Root of David, the Lamb of God. For "Thou art worthy to take the book, and to open the seven seals thereof;

because thou wast slain, and hast redeemed us to God by thy blood." It is he that hath the key of David, which openeth and no man shutteth, shutteth and no man openeth. For the outward reading of the word, without the inward working of his Spirit, is nothing. The precise Pharisees, the learned scribes, read the scriptures over and over again: they not only read them in books, but wore them on their garments: they were not only taught, but were able themselves to teach others. But because this heavenly teacher had not instructed them, their understanding was darkened, their knowledge was but vanity: they were ignorant altogether in that saving truth, which the prophet David is so desirous to learn. The mysteries of salvation were so hard to be conceived of the very apostles of Christ Jesus, that he is forced many times sharply to rebuke them for their dulness; which unless he himself had removed by opening the eyes of their minds, they could never have attained to the knowledge of salvation in Christ Jesus. The ears of that woman Lydia would have been as close shut against the preaching of Paul as any others, if the finger of God had not touched and opened her heart. As many as learn, they are "taught of God;" and "no man knoweth the Father, but he to whom it pleaseth the Son to reveal him." There is but one teacher in the school of Christ: he it is "that leadeth unto all truth." *Luke xxiv. [27.]* *Acts xvi. [14.]* *John vi. [45.]* *Matt. xi. 27.* *John xvi. [13.]*

7. Now, although Christ only openeth the book of knowledge, giveth understanding, and revealeth unto us the will of his Father; although the Spirit only be the schoolmaster that inwardly guideth the heart in the way of truth; yet may we not gape for revelations, as the anabaptists do, or think that God hath revealed unto us whatsoever we do vainly imagine and conceive in our brains. For as there is a Spirit of truth, so there is also a lying spirit. St John therefore giveth us a caveat not to credit every spirit; but to "try [the]¹ spirits, whether they be of God or no." We are to be taught of God, yet by such means as God hath appointed. The rich man, being in torments, craved revelations for his brethren: *Dangerous to look for instruction by revelations.* *1 John iv. [1.]*

[¹ The word "the," which is not in the first edition of 1585, is inserted from the second edition of 1616.—ED.]

to whom it was answered, "They have Moses and the prophets." God doth teach inwardly, but by outward means. He spake in old time by angels, by dreams, by visions, by revelations. But now in these latter days he hath spoken by his Son; and he by his ministers. He taught the eunuch, but it was by Philip: he taught Cornelius, but it was by Peter: he taught Paul, but it was by Ananias.

Luke xvi. [29.]
Acts viii. [26—39.]
Acts x.
Acts ix. [10—19.]

8. But howsoever or by whomsoever we be taught, the thing which we must learn is the word of God; not the decrees and decretals of popes, not the quiddities of too curious schoolmen, not lying legends, not amorous arts, not the dangerous discourses of politics, void of the fear of God, denying and defacing christian religion. This is not our school, these are not our studies. What we should desire to learn, the prophet sheweth by the words following, "thy ways."

The thing which the prophet desireth to learn is the way of the Lord.

9. This word *way*, by a translation or metaphor in the scripture, hath sundry significations. Sometime it is taken for doctrine, as "Thou teachest the *way* of God truly;" sometimes for religion, as when St Paul saith, "I persecuted this *way*;" and again, "According to this *way* which they call heresy, I worship the God of my fathers;" sometimes it is taken for the course and order of a man's life, as in the words of the prophet Esay, "The Lord taught me that I should not walk in the *way* of this people;" sometimes for the counsels and purposes of men, so Elihu meant it, saying, "His eyes are upon the *ways* of man, and he seeth all his goings." The way which the prophet here would learn of God is true religion, the doctrine of his holy will in his word revealed, but chiefly the doctrine of the true Messias promised, the way of truth itself, he only being the way, the truth, and the life, having given us an example that we should follow his steps who did no sin. Now, as God hath his way, so man hath his. "My ways are not your ways." The ways of Christ and antichrist, of the church of God and the synagogue of Satan, of religion and superstition, these are contrary each to other. Christ saith of himself, "I am the way." In the knowledge of this way St Paul glorieth: "I esteemed to know nothing but Christ Jesus, and him

The word way taken diversely in scripture.
Matt. xxii. [16.]
[Acts xxii. 4.]
Acts xxiv. [14.]

Isai. viii. [11.]

Job xxxiv. [21.]

Isai. lv. [8.]

[John xiv. 6.]

1 Cor. ii. [2.]

crucified;" and in the knowledge of this way the prophet desireth to be taught of God: "Teach me thy way, O Lord."

10. To this petition he addeth a promise, first, to "walk," and secondly, to walk "in truth." We may not be idle: "We are created unto good works, which God hath prepared, that we might walk in them." We are redeemed and "bought with a price," not to do nothing, or to live as we list, but "to serve him" which hath redeemed us. Our Saviour could in no wise abide idleness: "Why stand ye still?" St Paul would have all men to be stirring: "Let every man walk." Not one is excepted, not one can be dispensed withal: "Whosoever he be that will not labour, let him not eat." For it is good that every man should eat his bread in the sweat of his brows. And work, in the wise man's judgment, is even as needful for men as meat. There is no such bane to a commonwealth or kingdom, no such poison to the manners of every particular man, as idleness is. Examples we have too many in all ages. Idleness in David was a cause of lewdness: so that it is not good, no not for princes, to be idle. Idleness was the root of all that filth in Sodoma. Israel, in the absence of Moses, being idle, fell to feasting, dancing, and idolatry. And therefore, seeing that such as be idle are subject to so many noisome temptations, St Jerome's counsel is this: "See thou be always doing somewhat, that the devil may find thee occupied: he that is out of good exercise is easily snared of the devil[1]." And "idleness," saith St Bernard, "is the mother of toys, (he might have said of vices) and the step-dame of virtues[2]." Amasis king of Egypt made provision by law against idleness, once a year calling every man to a reckoning, what he had gotten, and what he had spent. In this reckoning was neither the gain of carding, dicing, usury, bribery, cozenage, nor extortion allowed. "Let every man walk in that vocation

The promise of the prophet to walk.
Eph. ii. [10.]

1 Cor. vi. [20.]

Matt. xx. [6.]
1 Cor. vii. [17.]

2 Thess. iii. [10.]

1 Cor. vii. [20.]

[1 Facito aliquid operis; ut te semper diabolus inveniat occupatum.—Hieron. Op. Par. 1706. Ad Rusticum Monach. Epist. xcv. Tom. iv. col. 773.—Ed.]

[2 Fugienda proinde otiositas, mater nugarum, noverca virtutum.—Bernard. Op. Par. 1690. De Consider. Lib. ii. c. 13. Tom. ii. Vol. i. col. 425.—Ed.]

wherewith God hath called him." God hath called no man with these vocations. Yet dare I not say, neither will I, that for any man, at any time, in any sort, to recreate himself with cards or dice, is sin. I am not of that opinion. Yet it falleth out too often that these exercises are occasions of much sin. And when they are so, it were no doubt much better to be altogether idle than so ill occupied. We must not play, but walk.

Our walking must be in truth.

11. And, lest in walking we should wander out of the way, the prophet now teacheth us wherein we should walk: "In truth." We must beware of crooked by-walks: the way of the Lord is the straight path of truth. Therefore the prophet maketh this promise: "I will walk in thy truth." Truth comprehendeth both soundness of doctrine and integrity of life. Solomon declareth that David walked after this sort: "My father walked in truth and justice before thee:" in "truth" of doctrine, and in "justice" of life. He faithfully performed his promise unto the Lord.

1 Kings iii. [6.]

Walking in heresy. Phil. iii. [18.]

12. St Paul complaineth grievously of some walkers. "Many there are," saith he, "that walk, of whom I have told you often, and now tell you weeping, they are enemies of the cross of Christ." The cross of Christ is taken here for the passion of Christ, which suffered on the cross. Whoso offereth up Christ again, once offered and sacrificed for our sins, he is an enemy to the cross of Christ. To seek remission of sins, redemption, justification, satisfaction, or salvation, elsewhere than in Christ crucified, is to be an enemy to the cross of Christ, and to walk not in the high-way of truth, but in the by-paths of wicked men.

Walking after the flesh. Gal. v. [19—21.]

13. St Paul noteth other by-walkers, which walk according to the flesh. In this by-way walked the Sodomites, the Benjamites, yea and David sometimes himself. This was the by-path of the rich glutton, which fed daintily day by day, whose god was his belly: he served no other Lord. In this by-way walk all wantons, flatterers, liars, envious persons, stirrers of strife, makers of division, sectaries, and such like. The end also of this way is perdition.

Walking after covetousness. Ezek. xxxiii. [31.]

14. Ezekiel complaineth of walkers which walk after covetousness. This path is haunted of all sorts of men:

priests, prophets themselves, and prophets' children, yea, kings have been subject to this fault. They are most miserable which take this way. They enjoy no quietness, they tire out themselves with foolish cares, they entangle their hearts with noisome lusts, they grieve the Spirit, their toil and vexation hath neither end nor measure. The prophet therefore beggeth at the hands of God: "Incline mine heart to thy testimonies, and not to covetousness." [Psal. cxix. [36.]

15. Jeremy complaineth of walkers in the hardness of their hearts. They have hearts trampled on with the feet of men, and made as hard as a beaten way. They are become as obstinate against the word and message of God, as ever was Pharaoh. There is planted a prejudice in them, from which they cannot go back. No enchantment, be it never so wise, can have any force upon them; their ears are so cunningly and so closely stopped. [Walking in obstinacy. Jer. xiii. [10.]

16. David complaineth of such walkers as are led by the counsel of the wicked, as Eve by the serpent, Absolon by Achitophel, Saul by Doeg, Roboam by a train of lewd companions' rash heads. The way of all these ungodly ones shall perish. [Walking in the counsel of the wicked. Psal. i. [1.]

17. There is also another kind of inordinate walkers complained of by the apostle; which work not at all, but, under pretence of zeal and religion, forsake all labour, and occupy their heads wholly with searching and sifting other men's doings, their tongues only with barking against such as God hath placed in authority, their ears with nothing but listening after strange and new reports. These are spreaders of bruits, broachers of news, informers of men how the world shall wag. They are still beating and forging out new plots of commonwealths, and undermining the old. They are one of the worst kinds of men that live. The unbridled malapertness of such men the prophet David seemeth to touch, when he saith: "The tongue of them walketh throughout the earth." They make no difference of any person, high or low: they stay no where. David though a king, Paul though an apostle, Christ though the Son of the living God, escaped not the reach of these venomous creatures. Such walking tongues would be tied short. If men cannot bridle them, yet of this we are sure, that " slandering and lying lips the Lord will destroy." [Walking with the tongue. 2 Thess. iii. [11.] [Psal. lxxiii. [9.] [Psal. xxxi. 18.]—

THE SIXTH SERMON.

Walking in treachery. Jer. vi. [28.]

18. Jeremy complaineth also of certain walkers, whom he termeth "rebellious traitors, walking craftily;" flattering them whom they purpose to undermine. These be cunning court-like men, whose countenance will never bewray that which lieth secretly hid within their hearts. Of

[2 Sam. xvi. 1—4.]

this crew was Siba, who pretended great good to his master Mephiboseth, but, spying a time, begged his whole inherit-

[Matt. ii. 7, 8.]

ance of the king; and Herod, that fox, which made a shew of religious worshipping him, whom his meaning was

2 Sam. iii. [27.]

cruelly to destroy; and Joab, which fraudulently bare Abner in hand, that he came to talk with him as a friend, but, getting opportunity, stabbed him to the heart; and

Gen. xxxiv. [13, 25, 26.]

the sons of Jacob, who under pretence of friendship, marriage, and joining in religion with the Sichemites, caused them to be circumcised, and when they were sore, fell upon them and murdered them without compassion or pity.

1 Thess. iv. [6.] [Heb. xi. 32.]

"Let no man defraud or circumvent: for the Lord is the avenger of all such things." "But," as St Paul saith, "what should I say more? Time would be too short, if I should" remember unto you all the by-ways wherein the wicked do walk.

The preferment of evil men the cause why evil walkers do abound in the clergy. Psal. xii. [8.]

19. The prophet David seemeth to be much grieved at the great swarms of bad walkers in his days. "The wicked," saith he, "do walk on every side." And he yieldeth the reason: "Because they are exalted." When bad men are placed in great rooms, when the base are exalted and lifted up into places of authority, then the bounds of wickedness are enlarged, and sin, going on without controlment, gathereth strength. Christ therefore requireth careful choice of ministers in his church: his de-

[1 Tim. iii. 2.]

sire is to have them faithful and wise. Paul would place none but such as were well testified to be blameless in life, and apt to teach with wholesome doctrine. The admitters of ministers are too lavish in our days: they have little regard or care whom they take: St Paul's lesson,

1 Tim. v. [22.]

"Lay not hands on any man rashly," is forgotten. The preferrers unto livings are no less faulty: they choose of the worst: they respect no ability but of the purse. What

2 Mac. iv. [7, 8, 23, 24.]

numbers are there placed this day in the church, as Jason and Menelaus were placed by Antiochus in the priest's office, not for learning, but for money; not for desert, but for reward! It goeth full hardly with the church of God, when Balaam is the bishop, Judas the patron, and Magus the minister. This merchandise will make the house of God a den of thieves. No one thing this day more necessary to be reformed in the church of God.

20. It were happy if the temporal policy were faultless in this behalf, and in choice respected only the worthiness of such men as are chosen to bear office in the commonwealth. The prince, as Jethro said truly, cannot bear the burden of the commonwealth alone. The prince must needs have inferior officers, as eyes to see withal, ears to hear withal, tongues to speak withal, hands to work withal, shoulders to bear up the burthen withal, and legs also to walk withal. If the eyes be blinded or look asquint, if the ears be deaf or hard of hearing, if the tongue cannot speak, or else do stammer, if the hands be numbed, the shoulders weakened, and the legs lamed; it must needs make a lamentable body and a monstrous commonwealth. For, such guides, such people. If officers be ill chosen, men of small wit and less wisdom, weak-hearted and feeble-handed, men not religious, but popish, not favourers, but haters of the gospel, lovers not of truth, but of themselves, partially affected, corruptly minded, such as be mates with thieves, partakers of spoils with extortioners, maintainers of evil men and of evil matters, having their share with malefactors, pretending justice, and doing manifest wrong, not haters of covetousness, but takers of bribes, lingering out causes that are brought before them in hope of commodity, dispatching no matter but for money, such as are not ashamed to suck profit with Vespasian from the homeliest things, such as would sell their very souls for money, such as will not stick, if nothing else may be had, to cut off even the coats of men by the skirts; if such be exalted, is it marvel if the wicked do walk on every side? King David was so careful of this, that he would not suffer a wicked person, a back-biter, an haughty-hearted man, a subtile deceiver, a flatterer, or a liar, to remain in his court. Constantius would not suffer a dissembler in religion, a server of times, a nullifidian, an atheist, an idolater to be about him. For so it hath been always, and so it will be: when the

In the temporalty the reason why wicked men abound is because wicked men bear rule. [Exod. xviii. 18.]

vile are in credit, wicked men will hold up their heads: they will band themselves in companies: all corners will be pestered with them.

Church robbers under the name of church visitors.

21. Wherefore it greatly behoveth them that are in highest authority to bear a watchful eye over those, which deal in causes of importance under them, that such by-walkers be not countenanced with authority, as they are that trot from one diocese to another, prying into churches. The pretence is reformation; but the practice is deformation. They reform not offences, but for money grant licences still to offend. These surveyors are spoilers of the patrimony of Christ. When Moses took upon him to build the ark of God, the princes and the people so plentifully of their own accord gave gifts thereunto, gold, silver, precious stones, scarlet, silk, and cedar, that Moses was forced to make proclamation, and cry, *Sufficit:* "it is enough." I shall most humbly beseech our most mild Moses, the queen's majesty, and that in the blood and bowels of Jesus Christ, as her highness tendereth the glory of God, and the continuance of learning and religion, and her own salvation, to make proclamation not to the ark builders, but unto these church robbers, to stay their hands. Truly *Sufficit:* "it is enough." For there is no more to be had, except, as the prophet speaketh, they will "pull their very skins off their backs." Wo be to that commonwealth, where they are made overseers and examiners of other men's ways, whose own footsteps are uneven. May not the wicked be bold to walk on every side, when so vile persons do bear such sway?

Exod. xxxvi. [5, 6.]

[Mic. iii. 2.]

It is not sufficient to talk of truth: we must walk in it.

22. But the way, wherein the prophet promiseth to walk, is "truth." I will walk in thy "truth:" I will embrace it with my heart, I will frame my life after it, I will profess it sincerely, and be zealous for it. I will not be a knower, but a doer of thy law. They which know it and do it not, deserve not praise, but stripes. For Christianity doth not consist in loud and shrill crying, "Lord, Lord," but in doing the will of our heavenly Father. This toucheth us very near, which content ourselves with the bare profession of the name of Christ; as if it were sufficient to make a flourishing shew, as trees do, which are fair to the eye, but fruitless. The gospel of Christ hath been long taught

amongst us: we have long heard it, the sound hath filled our ears: but whose heart hath it pierced? whose life hath it bettered? Sin is sharply reproved; yet iniquity doth still abound. We have often promised with the prophet, saying, "We will walk in truth;" but we never set forward. Towards God we are hypocrites, towards men deceitful, double-faced, double-tongued, double-hearted. Where should one find a faithful man? It is to us that the prophet Esay speaketh: "Hear this, O house of Jacob, which are called by the name of Israel, and are come out of the waters of Judah, which swear by the name of the Lord, and make mention of the God of Israel, but not in truth, not in righteousness." We are very counterfeits, we use religion but for a policy and for a cloak; we talk, we hear, we pray, we fast: but what truth, what sincerity is there in our doings? We would seem to seek reformation in religion: the pretence is good, many things may be bettered, and we ought to strive unto better things: but God grant that we have not a meaning rather to part the garments of Christ amongst us. We will seem to be careful of civil reformation, and to desire that all abuses in the commonwealth may be redressed: but our intent is in deed to make our gain by corrupt and partial execution of penal statutes; our purpose is only to benefit ourselves by pinching others, and by impoverishing many to enrich a few. Thus the world is full of by-ways; and they are many that walk corruptly. Yea, we have all declined, every one hath stepped aside: "from the sole of the foot to the crown of the head there is no soundness." Prince and people, and priest and prophet, all have strayed from the way of truth, though not all alike. [Isai. xlviii. [1.]] [Isai. i. 6.]

23. Let us therefore return from the paths of iniquity; let us inquire after the good way that we may walk in it. Let us not make courtesy who shall begin, but strive rather every man to be first; the pastor, because he hath the greatest skill; the prince, because he hath the highest room; the people, because they are most in number. If the pastor go before, the sheep will be the readier to follow after: if the fountains be sweet, the rivers that flow from them will not be sour: if there be darkness in the hills, there will be more in the vallies: if those that should give *This duty belongeth unto all, but principally to such as are in authority, because what way they take, in the same others will tread after them.*

light unto others, be turned into darkness, how great shall the darkness of others be! Examples have a marvellous force to lead men. The whole world is led as they have others, especially their superiors, for examples. And therefore you that be chiefest in authority, should by reason be foremost in the way of truth. Walk in what way you will, you are sure to have followers. Josias walked in the strait way to heaven, and the people followed; Jeroboam in the broad way, and the people were carried after in heaps. If you live in security, careless for God's matters, careless for the causes of the commonwealth, careful to feed upon pleasures and fancies, careful to pass over your own times in ease and quietness; the people will easily take after you: your towns and cities will soon be made [Judg. xviii. 27.] like to that secure and careless city of Lais. If ye will have the people of the land watchful, you yourselves must not slumber. If you make light of the word of God, the people will learn by your example to despise it: if you embrace the truth, they also will love it. You, my lords, you whom God hath placed before, you must go before: for God's love strive no longer, take your places and go on, that the people of God, being guided by you, as by lights, may follow after in the way of truth. It is a monstrous thing to see the basest lives in the highest rooms. Your conversation must be a glass for others to look into. Others shall answer for their own faults, but you for your own faults, and for others, who through your example are faulty. To conclude: let us all so walk as becometh the children of the light: let it suffice that in times past we have walked according to the vanity of the Gentiles: let us now return unto the Lord: let us cast away impiety and worldly concupiscence, and live a sober, a righteous, and a godly life: let us with true repentance crave pardon and mercy at the hands of God, and hereafter walk humbly before him, not for a day, or for a month, or a Lent season, but continually all the days of our pilgrimage upon earth. He only shall be saved, that continueth walking in truth to the end. God, for his mercy sake, let fall plentifully the drops and dew of his heavenly grace upon the hill of Hermon, and the mountains of Sion, to the fruitful watering of the whole land of Israel! Teach us,

O Lord, even our princes, our prophets, and our people, thy ways: direct all our goings, that we may walk for ever in thy truth. This that we may do, all and every of us, in our several callings, God the Father grant, for his Son Christ's sake: to whom, &c.

THE SEVENTH SERMON.

A SERMON

PREACHED BEFORE THE QUEEN.

JAMES IV.

8. *Draw near to God, and he will draw near to you. Cleanse your hands, ye sinners; and purge your hearts, ye double-minded.*
9. *Suffer affliction, and be sorry, weep. Let your laughter be turned into mourning, and your joy into heaviness.*
10. *Cast down yourselves before the Lord, and he will lift you up.*

The wisdom that should be in teachers to apply rightly the words of doctrine and exhortation. In this exhortation of St James, three things are contained. Heb. v. [12—14.]

GOD requireth in his household steward, the minister of his blessed word, fidelity and discretion; fidelity, to deliver to God's family such meat, without mingling, as he hath received at his Lord's hands; discretion, to give it fitly in due season, by respecting the time, place, auditory, and like circumstances. All men are not of one kind of constitution. Some are able to receive and digest strong meat, high mysteries, deep secrets of God: others must be fed with milk, simple and plain lessons, yet available to their salvation. These differences are in the food itself. The manner of dividing it standeth in doctrine and exhortation. Doctrine is for the ignorant, to instruct them; exhortation for the learned, to monish and strengthen them: both may most profitably be joined together. Paul, having to do with the ignorant Gentiles (learned in profane arts, but barbarous in true religion), is full of doctrine. James, dealing with the learned Jews, travaileth more in exhortation. Our times are learned times: God *1 Cor. i. [5.]* hath blessed our days with understanding: "We are enriched by him in all speech, and in all knowledge." But we know, and do not; and that deserveth stripes. Miserable is it to be ignorant of Christ, not to know the *[2 Pet. ii. 21.]* path which leadeth to heaven: "Yet better it were not to know the way of truth, than not to walk in it being known." I will therefore follow the wisdom of St James, and with his own words exhort you: "Draw near to God, and he will draw near to you," &c. In which words, first, he exhorteth us to draw near unto God: secondly, he sheweth us the means how we may so do: lastly, he telleth what commodity we shall reap thereby.

2. He exhorteth sinners and double-hearted men to draw near unto God. Sinners are such as be notable and open offenders; who make all the world witnesses of their wickedness. Mary Magdalene is called a sinner, because she was known to be a great offender: "Behold, a woman that was in the city, a sinner." The Sodomites, and the Amalekites, are likewise termed sinners for the excessiveness of their sin, because their sins were notorious and manifest. Double-hearted men are hypocrites, resembling painted sepulchres, beautiful without, and within full of rottenness; such as say, and do not; pretending holiness for advantage, and working mischief in their hearts. [mg: 1. Sinners are exhorted to draw near to God. Luke vii. [37.] Gen. xviii. [20.] 1 Sam. xv. [18.]]

3. This exhortation is general, it reacheth to all; for we are all offenders, even against the majesty of Almighty God, although not all in the same degree. "All have sinned, and do need the glory of God." Every man's ways are corrupt. "The imagination of man's heart is evil, even from his youth." What man living can say, "My heart is pure"? Between an open sinner and an hypocrite there is a difference in their sight, which take them as they seem: there is no difference before God, who beholdeth them as they are. As God will not hear the prayer of the open obstinate sinner, so doth he pour his grievous curse upon all hypocrites and counterfeit Christians. "Wo be to you, ye hypocrites!" [mg: All are sinners, though not all notorious. Rom. iii. [23.] Gen. viii. [21.] Matt. xxiii. [13.]]

4. David, when he committed that great folly, was an open sinner, and gave great offence. It was told him by Nathan, "Thou hast made the Lord's enemies to blaspheme." Marriage is honourable in the sight of all men; but fornication and adultery the Lord doth abhor, and the offenders therein the Lord shall judge. This one sin drowned the whole world: it called fire out of heaven to burn up cities: it destroyed the tribe of Benjamin. "Let it not be once named amongst you." "They that are such [mg: David an open sinner in committing adultery. 2 Sam. xii. [14.] Gen. vi. Gen. xix. [1—29.] [Judg. xix. xx.] Eph. v. [3, 5.]]

shall not inherit the kingdom of God." These foul offenders are here termed "sinners."

<small>The Jews, in cruel dealing with the prophets of God.</small> 5. The Jews were grievous sinners, which slew their prophets, and stoned such as were sent unto them. But they escaped not his heavy hand, whose servants they did so cruelly entreat. God plagued this their sin with strange desolation. He made their house like Shilo, and their city a curse to all the nations of the earth. The Lord hath also sent wise men, scribes and embassadors unto us: of them in these our days we have killed and crucified none: we have scourged none of them in our synagogues: we have persecuted none from city to city: we have not beaten one, and stoned another: we have not dealt thus cruelly with any one of them; but we have dealt hardly and unkindly with more than one. No man's life hath been touched: many men's livings are. They have not been murdered and slain: they are defaced, reviled, and made contemptible to the whole world. These messengers ought to be better esteemed for their master's and for their message sake. But the Son of God, whose servants they are, will in his good time revenge it: he will not <small>[Luke x. 16.]</small> bear this injurious ignominy done to himself. "He that despiseth you despiseth me." Such contemners of Christ and of his ministers may most justly be called "sinners."

<small>Achab, in robbing Naboth. 1 Kings xxi.</small> 6. Achab gave great and open offence in robbing Naboth of his vineyard; and God did revenge this open sin with an open plague, punishing the devourer with devourers, blood with blood. The vineyard of the Lord is set over to the spoil: it is the only prey that is left for greedy cormorants to raven upon. The hedge is broken; wild boars are entered in for to destroy it. If God had not set his elect over it, no doubt ere this day it had been utterly laid waste. You could have looked for no grapes of piety, of learning, or of religion of it; but, being rooted up by these violent boars, it would have brought out nothing but sow-thistles, ignorance, superstition, and <small>Isai. xxxiii. [1.]</small> gross idolatry. But, "Wo be to thee that spoilest! shalt not thou be spoiled?" How both the church and commonwealth are spoiled, all men see it; but few will tell it, and no man goeth about to redress it. These greedy gleaners

are also in the number of them whom our apostle here nameth "sinners."

7. The sin of king Saul was heinous, in consulting with a witch that had a familiar spirit, inquiring of her what chance should befall him. This grievous sin God grievously and without delay plagued. On the next morrow he and his sons were slain; all Israel discomfited, murdered, and put to flight. If every good gift come from God, shall we seek help at devils' hands? If only God knoweth the heart of man and things to come, shall we inquire of secrets at the mouth of Satan? "The devil is a liar;" and shall we believe him? He is our adversary; and shall we seek aid of him? He is a deceiver; and shall we trust in him? "There is no fellowship between Christ and Belial;" neither ought the servants of Christ to communicate with such servants of Satan. "Let witches, sorcerers, and soothsayers, die the death," saith the Lord. Such as communicate with them communicate with devils; and such also are "sinners." *Saul, in consulting with a witch.* 1 Sam. xxviii. [7, 8.] *John viii. [44.] 2 Cor. vi. [15.] Levit. xx. [27.]*

8. Doeg sinned greatly in accusing faithful David and the good high priest Ahimelech to king Saul; who, being light of belief, persecuted the one, and murdered the other. Haman, dealing so with godly Mardocheus, brought him almost to the gallows, and his people to great confusion. The Arians accused the right christian bishop Athanasius of incontinency before the emperor Constantinus; but his innocency, through the providence of God, cleared him[1]. Christ was charged to be a drunkard, a companion of sinners, a destroyer of the law, and of the temple, an enemy to Cæsar. Such false accusations are more current in these our evil times and latter days than ever. If the heathen accounted it a discredit to be termed an accuser, may we not justly call false accusers sinners? By whose means, if false accusations may get credit, innocency shall be condemned, Christ shall be crucified as a malefactor, and Barabbas as an innocent shall be let loose. Wherefore the civil law hath well provided, that the false accuser receive as much damage as he seeketh to bring upon another. And this law hath been sometimes executed. He that falsely accused Apollonius was so served. For, failing in *Doeg, in accusing David and Ahimelech unjustly.* 1 Sam. xxii. [9, 18.] Esther iii. *Matt. xi. [19.] Eus. lib. v. cap. 21.*

[[1] Theod. Hist. Eccl. Amst. 1695. Lib. i. c. 30. pp. 63, 4.—Ed.]

his proof, sentence was given that both his thighs should be broken[1]. This is another kind of "sinners."

Double-minded men.
Gen. xxxiv. [24.]

9. Now, as our apostle remembereth unto us open sinners, so doth he also covert sinners, whom he calleth "double-minded." The Sichemites were "double-minded" in matters of religion, who in respect of gain and profit were content outwardly to yield to Jacob and his sons, to receive the Jews' religion, and to be circumcised. Men for commodity can transform themselves into all colours and conditions, and in open shew profess any religion, inwardly keeping their false hearts to themselves.

Such are they of the Family of Love.

10. Which practice the Family of Love[2] hath lately drawn to a precept, and hath newly broached it as saleable doctrine, that men need not openly be of any religion whereby they may endanger themselves; that it is good christendom to lie, swear, and forswear, to say and unsay to any, saving such as be of the same family, with whom they must only use all plainness, and keep their mysteries secret from all others to themselves. These men may do any thing to avoid affliction, and they have scripture for that purpose: "Your bodies are the temples of the Holy Ghost:" you may not suffer God's temples to be touched. As fitly alleged, as *scriptum est* by the devil.

1 Cor. vi. [19.]

Such they which term themselves the only catholics.

11. In a paper which of late came from the pope as a token to his dear children, there were printed the five wounds of Christ with this posy: *Fili, da mihi cor tuum, et sufficit:* "Son, give me thy heart, and it sufficeth." Whether his holiness did mean thereby to allow dissimulation or no, I will not define. His practices are mystical, and his brood is so throughly framed in this way, that they seem to take the pope's emblem in no other meaning. They halt on both sides: they serve all times, and turn with all winds. By professing all religions, they shew themselves plainly to be of none. They have double hearts, one heart for the prince, another for the pope; one for Christ, and another for Baal; one for a communion, and another for a mass. These dissembling wolves put upon themselves sheep's skins, to deceive withal. Now

[1 Euseb. Pamph. Hist. Eccl. Amst. 1695. p. 153.—ED.]

[2 The Family of Love were a sect of anabaptists, of which Henry Nicolai or Nicholas, a native of Munster, was the founder.—ED.]

are they mild and gentle, flattering, and promising all loyalty to the prince, conformity to government, and consent to religion. But if the times should turn, they would turn off the sheep's coat, and play the wolf in his right kind. They would shew their ravenous nature by their cruel deeds: then would they fill their bellies with that after which they now thirst: they would find swift feet to shed the blood of innocents. From the mouth of the lion, O Lord, deliver us! This sort of people our apostle calleth "double-hearted."

12. Herod was a double-hearted man, who, calling the wise men to him, bade them go and search out Christ, return and bring him word, that he also might go and worship him. He intended to kill whom he pretended to worship. Judas was like affected: he kissed and betrayed. Cain's mind was as double, when he spake fair unto his brother, enticed him into the field, and there villainously murdered him. Joab dealt even so with Amasa and Abner, whom, under pretence of friendship, traitorously he slew. Absolon invited his brother Ammon to a feast, and in the midst thereof suddenly bereaved him of his life. [Such a one Herod, Cain, Joab, Absolon. Matt. ii. [8.] Matt. xxvi. [49.] Gen. iv. [8.] 2 Sam. xx. 8—10.] 2 Sam. iii. [27.] 2 Sam. xiii. [28.]]

13. These double hearts died not with these men: they live still in their posterity. With Herod, all men pretend to worship Christ: but most part also, with Herod, in truth, in heart, in life, kill him, and trample under their feet the precious blood of his testament. Whom we profess in word, we deny in deed: whom in doctrine we follow, him in life we forsake: thus in doubleness with Judas we flatter, we dissemble, we courtesy, we kiss; but the inward heart is full of malice and treason. Faithful friendship hath taken his flight away: "There is no truth in the earth." We speak them full fair, whom we hate full deadly. Whom we kiss, we can sell to death for a piece of money. Judges can talk of justice, and for money pervert judgment. For money the vineyard of the Lord is laid waste by them who profess themselves the keepers of it. By them for money the flock of Christ is scattered, and left to the wolf to be devoured: for money an idol is made a pastor: Judas selleth, Magus buyeth, and a thief by a thief is placed. Beware of these double-hearted men. Cain is a murderer, speak he never so fair. If Absolon [Such are all they towards God, who profess the truth in word, and in life deny the power of it; towards men, they which fawn upon them whom in heart they abhor. Hos. iv. 1.]

9—2

feast thee, yet fear lest thou find sour sauce to thy sweet meat. The bond of brotherhood is not of strength sufficient to retain these double hearts. Take heed of Joab, howsoever he fawn; for he carrieth inwardly a big and haughty mind. It is death to him that any should be in credit, or direct David, besides himself. He must do all alone. His outward speech is fair; but his inward thought is full of hatred, envy, and wrath.

Double-minded men are also commonly double-tongued. Psal. xii. [2.]

14. Such as the fountain is, such is the river that runneth from it. A double heart maketh a double tongue. They which think deceitfully, speak deceitfully, and flatter with their lips." The disciples of the Pharisees and the Herodians, as they had double hearts, so had they double tongues. Before Christ's face they could say: "Master, we know that thou art true, and teachest the way of God truly, neither carest for any man, nor respectest the person of men:" but behind his back they termed him a "seducer, a companion of publicans and sinners, a wine-bibber," and most spitefully railed against the righteous Lord of glory. All flatterers are double-tongued. Whom they praise excessively, being present, of him their manner is, being out of sight, to speak most slanderously and vilely. So unlike they are to our Saviour Christ, who would not praise John to John's disciples, but after their departure commended him to the people. It is St Augustine's judgment, "that the hand of no persecutor is more grievous than is the tongue of a flatterer[1]."

Matt. xxii. [16.]

Luke vii. [34.]

All these are exhorted to draw near unto God.

15. These sinners and double hearts our apostle doth here reprove: using withal an earnest exhortation unto them to draw near unto God, from whom they have so far strayed. All sinners are strayers: for sin maketh a division between God and man. "Your iniquities have made a separation between me and you." To sin is to depart and fall away from God: the more we sin, the faster and farther we fly from him. Judas sinned deeply and deadly: having sinned, he could not abide the presence of that innocent whom he had betrayed; but went out and unrecoverably fell away. The prodigal child, being

Isai. lix. [2.]

[1 Plus persequitur lingua adulatoris, quam manus interfectoris.—August. Op. Par. 1681. Enarratio in Psal. lxix. 5. Tom. iv. col. 714.—Ed.]

loosely given, waxed weary of his father's virtuous house, ranged abroad, fell to folly, fed on filthiness, and bathed himself in all loathsome sin: yet, being touched with God's hand, he repented and drew near. What should I name this or that man which hath gone astray? It is most true, that the prophet saith: "We have all erred and gone astray like sheep." Not one hath remained within the sheepfold. Every one hath either skipped over the hurdles, or crept through the hedge. "All have sinned, there is not one innocent." He that saith he is no sinner, is a sinner, because he is a liar. Our sin therefore hath separated us from God, who hateth and abhorreth sin. Our doubtful double hearts have carried us into many crooked and dangerous ways. Our apostle doth call us home again, as sheep that have strayed, saying, "Draw near unto God." [Isai. liii. 6.] [Rom. iii. [23.]]

16. But what, is it in our own will and power to return? or doth God command that which is impossible for us to perform? Truth it is, "All our sufficiency is of God. Of ourselves we are not able to think a good thought." "It is God that giveth both to will and to perform." "Without me," saith Christ, "you are able to do nothing." No doubt we have power and free will to run from God but to draw near unto him is his grace and gift. *Ad malum sufficit sibi liberum arbitrium, ad bonum non*[1]: "Free will hath in itself ability enough to evil, but not to good." He commandeth us therefore to do that, which of ourselves we are not able to do; that, seeing our want, we may crave his grace and help, which will enable us to draw near unto him. This grace is not in vain: by it we are that we are; when we be, as we should be, near unto him. If he that commandeth us do not reach us his hand, when we are bidden to draw near, we go farther off. "But let God give that which he commandeth, and then command whatsoever he will[2]." "Convert us O Lord, and we shall be converted." If he convert us [To draw near unto God is not in our power without his grace.] [2 Cor. iii. [5.]] [Phil. ii. [13.]] [John xv. 5.] [Aug. de can. no. cap. 8.] [Psal. xix. [7.] [Jer. xxxi. 18.]]

[¹ Quid enim valeat liberum arbitrium non adjutum, in ipso Adam demonstratum est. Ad malum sufficit sibi; ad bonum non, nisi adjuvetur a Deo.—August. Op. Par. 1685. De Cantico Novo c. 8. Tom. vi. col. 596.—ED.]

[² Da quod jubes, et jube quod vis.—August. Op. Par. 1679. Confess. Lib. x. 40. Tom. i. col. 184.—ED.]

not, we shall remain as we are, or rather proceed to worse. "No man cometh unto me," saith Christ, "except the Father draw him." The Spirit and grace of God, of untoward and unwilling, maketh forward and ready; and so, by the efficacy of the Spirit being changed, we which were far off are drawn near.

John vi. [44.]

17. The way to draw near unto God our apostle setteth down at large: "Cleanse your hands, purge your hearts, be afflicted, mourn, weep: let your laughter be turned into sorrow, and your joy into grief. Humble yourselves in the sight of the Lord." Esay the prophet teacheth the self-same in few words: "Let the wicked forsake his ways, and the unrighteous his own imaginations, and return unto the Lord." St Paul meaneth the same thing, when he speaketh of "denying ungodliness and worldly lusts, and living soberly, righteously, and godlily, in this present world." But our Saviour Christ shutteth up the whole in one word: "Repent."

2. The way how to draw near unto God.

Isai. lv. [7.]

Tit. ii. [12.]

Mark i. [15.]

18. The order of our repentance, set down by the blessed apostle, is this. First of all, we must remove evil from us. "Cleanse your hands: purge your hearts:" wash and scour both body and soul: make yourselves clean, both from outward and inward sins. For it is not sufficient to abstain from evil in our external actions, but we must also chase from our hearts evil cogitations. The proud Pharisee seemed to have a pure life, but he had a polluted heart. If the fountain and spring be not pure and sweet, the rivers that issue from it must needs be unsavoury. "From the heart there proceed evil cogitations, murders, adulteries, fornications, false witnessings, revilings." These are the fruits of an impure heart; and these are the works of unclean fingers. The hand is but the servant, to execute that which the heart hath devised. It was folly in Pilate to wash his hands in token of his purity, when his heart had consented to shed the blood of that innocent.

Our hands must be cleansed.

Luke xviii. [11, 12.]

Matt. xv. [19.]

19. The hand hath sundry significations in the scriptures. Sometime it is taken for counsel, as, "Is not the hand of Joab with thee in all these things?" And again: "They met together to do whatsoever thy hand and thy counsel had before decreed to be done." Evil hands are

Hand taken for counsel. 2 Sam. xiv. [19.]

Acts iv. [27, 28.]

the breeders of all mischievous practices; but such counsel is commonly worst to the giver. David prayed to God to confound the traitorous counsel of Achitophel, who conspired against his master and king. And it came to pass that his fingers did knit a rope about his own traitorous throat, to strangle himself withal. It is written of David, that "he fed his people in the singleness of his heart, and led them forth in the discretion of his hands." The sword of government is an edged tool: it requireth the hand of wise counsel discreetly to wield it. Roboam, being guided by the unwise hands of those lusty young counsellors, who advised him to oppress his people with heavy burthens, to bring them into bondage, and to give them short and sharp answers, wrought in the people discontented minds, alienated their hearts from their prince; which in the end was the tearing of his kingdom into pieces. Of twelve parts he lost ten and better. _{2 Sam. xvii. [23.] [Psal.lxxviii. 72.] 1 Kings xii. [13—17.]}

20. The word *hand* is also taken for cruelty and oppression, because the hand is the instrument to work these things. "Your hands," saith the prophet, "are full of blood." Such hands had Herod. And such have they, not only which kill, but which hate, malice, and slander their brethren: for "he which hateth his brother is a man-slayer." _{Hands full of blood. Isai. i. [15.] [1 John iii. 15.]}

21. Finally, because the hand worketh most of all the members of the body in the necessary actions of man's life, therefore all pollutions in our outward deeds are contained in the name of unclean hands. _{All pollutions under the name of unclean hands.}

22. The slanderer and libeller hath bloody hands: his tongue cutteth like a sharp razor: his pen writeth in blood. For he killeth whom he defameth. _{Slander.}

23. The oppressor with his bloody fingers pulleth the skin off the people's backs. Æmilius, being placed by Tiberius Cæsar over Egypt, oppressed the Egyptians with great and unwonted exactions. The emperor hearing of it was wroth, and wrote unto him, "that he would have his sheep to be shorn, but not flayed." Such oppressors of the people greatly wrong the prince, who, being faultless, yet is forced to bear the burthen of that blame. Such gleaners of other men's goods, and pillers, and purloiners, although they join house to house, yet, the foundation of them being laid in blood, that building shall not continue. "That which _{Oppression.}

cometh ill, shall go worse away: they lose as much in their consciences, as they gain in their coffers."

Bribes. 24. Rewards likewise do not only blind the eyes, and pervert the words, but they also defile the hands of the wise and righteous.

Simony. 25. All such as enter into the church of God by corrupt means, defile their hands, and destroy their souls. "That," saith St Ambrose, "which the man gave when he was ordained bishop, was but gold; and that which he lost, was his soul[1]."

Usury. 26. The usurer doth so mire his fingers in money, that with his foul filthy fists he can never take hold upon the tabernacle of God.

Our hands foul even when they are cleanest. 27. It were infinite to go through all particulars. We defile our hands, whensoever our actions are corrupted, infected, and polluted with sin; seem they unto us never so perfect, holy, and good. Things highly esteemed before *Isai. lxiv. [6.]* men are found to be as vanity before God. Our very righteousness in his sight is polluted. Yea many times, even when we do good, then we do ill: in our prayer by coldness, in our alms-deeds by vain glory, we defile the hands which we lift up unto God, and put forth unto men. These foul hands our apostle biddeth us wash: *Mundate manus vestras, O peccatores*[2].

The heart must be purged. Jer. xvii. [9, 10.] 28. And as we must wash our foul hands, so must we purge our infected hearts. "The heart of man is not searched by man. Who knoweth it? Only God is the searcher of hearts." The hypocrite seemeth holy in the face of the world; but his inward man is poisoned with sin. Of men he is commended and reverenced; but his false impure heart the Lord doth abhor. Thy heart must be purged, before thy hands can be washed to any purpose. For as all impurity riseth from the heart, and so polluteth the hands; so must first thy heart be purified, and that *Luke xi. [34.]* will make all clean: "If thine eye be right, all thy body will be clear," saith our Saviour. The stomach well confirmed, all the body will be in good estate. But our hearts *Prov. xx. [9.]* are impure: neither can any man say, "My heart is clean." The Pharisee said, that he was righteous; but he looked

[1 See before, p. 44.—ED.]
[2 Cleanse your hands, O sinners.—ED.]

only upon his hands, and did not see into his proud and malicious heart. The penitent publican wisely knocked upon his heart; for there lay the disease. Every sin breedeth in the heart: from thence it hath his original; and every heart is possessed with sundry sins, and hath need carefully to be purged.

29. Pride polluteth man's heart. This venom poisoned the heart of the great angel of God; of Adam, the most perfect man of God; of Nabuchodonozar, the great and mighty emperor; of Ozias the king. Their hearts were lifted up; and therefore God threw them down. "Pride is the first and greatest sin[1];" and therefore with chiefest care to be shunned. This hidden poison cannot be smothered: it will burst forth into the outward parts. It will appear in thy countenance, in thy pace, and in thy apparel. Monstrous attire doth shew a monstrous mind. A mincing tripping pace, as the prophet doth note, argueth a proud and an unstable heart. A lofty countenance, a stretched-out neck, and a wandering eye, are the pictures of an haughty and a wanton mind. "Unchaste looks are tokens of unchaste thoughts." *It must be purged of pride.* *Isai. iii. [16.]*

30. Saint Paul hath made mention of three great and pestilent infections of the heart. The first is banqueting and drunkenness. "Beware your hearts be not overcharged with surfeiting and drunkenness." Meat and drink are ordained for man, and not man for them: we should eat to live, and not live to eat. Nature is content with little, and by much the health is impaired. A full belly dulleth the senses; and the more wine, the less wit. The judgment of Plato is, that he which filleth his belly twice a day, shall never prove but a sot. Too much drink laid Noah naked, and made him ridiculous to his own son. "Drunkenness is a fawning devil, a sweet poison, a pleasant sin: which whosoever hath, wanteth himself; and whosoever committeth, doth not commit sin, but is altogether very sin itself[2]." Let not your hearts therefore be oppressed and defiled with surfeiting, nor with drunkenness. *It must be kept from being overcharged with surfeits.* *Luke xxi. [34.]* *Gen. ix. [21.]*

[1 Maximum peccatum in homine superbia est; quandoquidem inde manavit nostri origo delicti.—Ambros. Op. Par. 1686. In Psal. cxviii. Expos. Tom. I. col. 1046.—Ed.]

[2 Ebrietas cædis mater, parens litium, furoris genitrix, petulantiæ deformiter est magistra: hanc qui habet, se non habet: hanc qui habet,

From chambering and wantonness.
Hieron. sup. ep. ad Tim.

31. Another poison of the heart is chambering and wantonness. The former breedeth the latter. And "where fulness is, there filth reigneth[1]." These are commonly linked together; and where the one is near, the other is not far off. Ezekiel the prophet addeth another cause of this vice, and that is idleness. A full belly and an idle body make an unchaste heart. David taking an afternoon's vacation, and walking idle in his gallery, fell shamefully away from his former purity, and dangerously from God. Idleness and riotousness are the fuel of uncleanness, which St Jerome considering, breaketh out into these words: "O infernal fury, the matter whereof is gluttony; pride, the flame; the sparks, lewd words; the smoke, infamy; the ashes, impurity; the last end, hell, misery." Our bodies are made unto sanctification, and not to fornication: let us use them to that end to which they were created, that we may bring them to that joyful end of eternal blessedness.

[Ezek. xvi. 49.]

From emulation and contention. [Phil. ii. 3.]

32. The third bane of the heart is emulation and contention. "Let nothing be done through contention and vain glory." Pride causeth emulation, and of emulation cometh strife; so that the cursed generation of vice is fruitful. Pride made the devilish angel envy that his Lord and God should be above him: it made Adam desire to be as full of knowledge as his Creator; Absolon to emulate his father, and to thirst after his kingdom. Cæsar was so proud, that he could not abide a superior: Pompey could not bear an equal. Corah, Dathan, and Abiram,

Num. xvi. [1—3.]

habet, homo non est; hanc qui habet non peccatum facit, sed est ipse peccatum. Ebrietas est dæmon blandus, venenum dulce, rabies voluntaria, invitatus hostis, illecebra honestatis, et pudoris injuria: hanc nullus noverit Christianus, ne auditu quidem sacerdos attingat: ne qui est forma virtutum, vitiorum inde fiat et inveniatur exemplum.—Pet. Chrysolog. Sermo xxvi. De Fidel. Dispensat. in Max. Biblioth. Vet. Patrum. Lugd. 1677. Tom. vii. p. 865.—Ed.]

[1 "Cum enim luxuriatæ fuerint in Christo, nubere volunt." Cum sub eo tempore religionis abundantiam habuerint: quæ sæpe solet generare luxuriam.—Hieron. Op. Par. 1706. Comment. in Epist. I. ad Timoth. Cap. v. Tom. v. col. 1092.—The Benedictine editors prefix to this and some other commentaries the following notice: Commentarii...consequentes licet Hieronymo tribuantur in MSS. Codd. Pelagiano tamen vel ipsi Pelagio adscribendi sunt.—Ed.]

in the pride of their hearts, sought to displace Moses and Aaron, the chief magistrate and the chief minister. They set down a handsome platform of equality; and many of the multitude allowed of it, as well pleased with a popular estate, where the worst of them might be as good as the best. But God brought their device and themselves to nought. This emulation is ever contentious; and contention bringeth dissipation. A kingdom divided will not endure. "Our God is the God of peace, and not of contention." In peace then we shall have safety, and be followers of our God. We ought therefore to be mild and quiet, like sheep; and not contentious and biting, like dogs. "Whilst one of you doth bite another, take heed ye be not devoured one of another." Therefore let every man be content with his own estate. For God hath ordained distinct estates; and by his providence men are placed in them. Pride, surfeiting, and drunkenness, chambering, and wantonness, emulation, and contention, are infections of the heart, and dangerously defile the same: we must purge our hearts of them. ^{1 Cor. xiv. [33.]} ^{Gal. v. [15.]}

33. Thus, if we with a simple eye behold our hands, and take a view of our souls, we shall easily espy foul fingers and polluted hearts. We are bid by our apostle to wash the one, and purge the other; but this is not in the ability of sinful man: it is the work of our gracious God. Christ is the only physician to heal this our disease. Only God remitteth and easeth us of our sin. Therefore our defiled hands and depraved hearts cannot otherwise be washed and made clean, but only with the blood of that immaculate Lamb. For so the scripture witnesseth: "The blood of Jesus Christ doth make us clean from all sin." "If he wash us, we shall be whiter than snow." Otherwise our filthy sin will stick to us for ever. And thus we see that evil must be taken away from all parts, both inward and outward: our hands must be cleansed, and our hearts purged. This is the first part of our repentance. ^{Our hearts and hands are not purged but by Christ.} ^{1 John i. [7.]} ^{Psal. li. [7.]}

34. But this will never be done, unless we conceive unfeigned and hearty sorrow for sin. Wherefore it followeth in the words of the apostle: "Be afflicted, be sorry and weep: let your laughter be turned into mourning, and ^{Christ doth not ease us of the burthen of sin, unless he see us mourn under it.}

your joy into heaviness." "It is heard," saith the apostle to the Corinthians, "and that for certainty, that there is fornication among you, and such fornication as is not once named among the Gentiles. And ye are puffed up, and have not rather sorrowed." They shewed, as he thought, little token of an intent to cleanse themselves, who saw such filth, and laughed at it. If we have purpose indeed to draw near unto the Lord, our hearts must be resolved into tears, and our hands washed in the water of our eyes. Have we sinned with David? Let us cry *peccavi* with as grieved an heart as David did. Have we denied Christ with Peter, not with our lips, but in our lives? Let us then weep for it with Peter bitterly. Have we in transgressing followed the wanton steps of Mary Magdalene? Let us follow her steps also in pouring out tears plentifully for our offences. Have we wandered, and gone astray with the prodigal child? Let us with him likewise turn into ourselves, and behold our defiled souls: let us with him return home at the length with a contrite heart, bursting out into that confession full of sorrow: "Father, I have sinned against heaven and against thee." "A bruised and humbled heart, O God, thou wilt not despise." "Repent you therefore of your sins," saith Peter, "that your sins may be done away." Let your tears shew that ye do repent; and let your lives declare that ye are converted. "When evils past are bewailed, and things bewailed are not committed again, this," saith Ambrose, "is to repent. It is a vain repentance, which is bye and bye sullied again by transgressing. Tears avail nothing, if we fall afresh into our sins. It is bootless to ask pardon for evil deeds, and when we have done, to do them again[1]." This is plain: "The dog to his vomit, and the swine to his mire." Let us therefore wholly cast away all impiety and worldly concupiscence: let us change this idle, vain, wanton, and profane life, with sober, righteous, and godly behaviour. "Let your laughter be turned into mourning,

[[1] Pœnitentia vera est dolor cordis et amaritudo animæ pro malis, quæ quisque commisit. Pœnitentia est et mala præterita plangere, et plangenda iterum non committere.—Ambros. Op. Par. 1690. Sermo xxv. De Sancta Quadrages. ix. Tom. ii. Appendix, col. 425.—This sermon is placed by the Benedictine editors among the Tractatus Supposititii.—ED.]

and your joy into heaviness." For our God seeth all our thoughts: he heareth all our words: he beholdeth all our works. There is no wantonness nor wickedness, but our God, who doth hate it, seeth it (the Lord be merciful unto us); yea, our just God, who will judge us according unto our deeds, seeth it. O Lord, be merciful unto us. O Lord, who shall stand in that most dreadful day? Lord, grant us true repentance, that, forsaking ourselves and detesting our sins, we may fly so unto thy mercy, that we may taste of thy tender compassions, and not receive according to thy justice and our most sinful deserts. "Enter not, Lord, into judgment with thy servants." O [Psal. cxliii. 2.] let us at the length wash our hands and purge our hearts. Let us mourn and bewail our sins; that so, being clean, we may approach and come near unto our God.

35. The only thing which hindereth and keepeth us back from this, is that overweening which we have of ourselves. Whereby it cometh to pass that, when we should be sorrowful, we are puffed up. The apostle therefore, to meet with this fault, and remove this let, addeth: "Cast down yourselves: humble yourselves in the sight of God." 'The country which we seek for is on high, but the way is below, that leadeth unto it. He that seeketh the one, must not refuse the other.' The publican, humbling himself before God, drew near unto him and was received. To whom hath God regard? on whom doth he look? to whom is he near? "Even unto him that is poor and of a contrite spirit, and that trembleth at my words," saith the Lord. Manasses, notwithstanding his idolatrous sinfulness, yet by humility drew near unto God, and found his saving mercy. And all that are or shall be his, must learn of him to be mild, as he is mild; to humble themselves unto Christ's mercy, who humbled himself unto man's cruelty. *We must be humbled and thrown down.* *Isai. lxvi. [2.]*

36. What hath man wherein of right he can boast himself, or whereof he may be proud? It is God who hath given us those good gifts which we have: we have them not of ourselves; and he hath given them us not to pride ourselves in them, and so to make them ill, but humbly to be thankful for them, and to dispose of them well to his glory, knowing and remembering that we must *There is nothing in us why we should not carry humble and lowly minds.*

straitly reckon for them. "Render an account," will one day be a fearful speech. For why? Doth thy nobility, power, and authority lift up thy mind? These are given thee from above. " By me kings reign : by me princes bear rule." "There is no power but of God." He that setteth up, can likewise cast down. Nay, "He hath cast down the mighty from their seat, and hath exalted the humble and meek." And what he hath done once, he can do again. The highest place is not the sweetest nor the safest place : much authority is cumbered with many cares. Such as have entered into a great charge must enter into a great account. And greater cause have they to fear their reckoning, than to be proud of their ruling. The more that God hath lift thee up, the more thou oughtest to humble thyself before him, lest he eternally cast thee down.

Prov. viii. [15.]
[Rom. xiii. 1.]
Luke i. [52.]

37. A christian heart must be an humble heart; and the way to humble ourselves is to know ourselves. For if we did look upon our black feet, our fair peacock feathers no doubt would soon fall down. If we did cast our eyes upon our foul hands and polluted hearts; if we did sift ourselves, and search our souls, and see how ugly we had made ourselves in the sight of God, having blotted out his gracious image in us, and clothed ourselves with the maculate coat of sin, the reward whereof is that eternal death of hell; this sight would terrify us, this consideration would pull down our haughtiness, and cause us to mislike and utterly deny ourselves, and fly only unto God's mercy. Our cheerful countenance would be changed into an heavy, our mirth into sighing, our pastime into prayer. It would make our sorrowful hearts to water our wanton eyes with bitter tears. It would cast down our big and high looks flat upon the earth, and turn our curled frizzled writhen hair into a baser use, even into a towel to wipe the feet of Christ withal. In the stead of monstrous apparel, we would put on sackcloth and ashes; and cry with St Paul, "Miserable man that I am! who shall deliver me?" This sight of ourselves would humble us in the sight of God. This humility would cause us to draw

The cause of our loftiness is the want of looking into ourselves.

Never more abused than now¹.

Rom. vii. [24.]

[¹ This side note is in the edition of 1616, but not in that of 1585.—ED.]

near unto him: if we drew near unto him, he would draw near unto us: if we did cast ourselves down, he would mercifully lift us up.

38. For so it followeth in the last part. This commodity remaineth to such, as in such humble sort draw near unto him. "He will draw near unto you: he will lift you up." If we sinners and double-hearted men wash and purge our hands and hearts, if by faith and unfeigned repentance we draw near unto him, he will meet us in the way, embrace us with his arms of mercy, kiss us with the kiss of peace and reconciliation, put on our spousal ring upon our finger, as fully restored unto our gracious and blessed spouse in that perfect spiritual marriage. He is as ready to forgive our sins, as we are to ask forgiveness: if we turn unto him by repentance, he doubtless will turn unto us in mercy. "He will refresh us; and we shall find eternal rest for our wearied souls." Be our sins as bloody as scarlet is red, he will make them as white as snow. Though they now press sore upon us, yet he will remove them as far from us, as the east is from the west: yea, he will drown them in the very bottom of the sea: he will wholly blot them out of his book, forgive them, and forget them for ever. This our gracious God hath promised: this our true God, who cannot deceive, will perform. Lastly, if with penitent and humbled hearts for our sins we cast ourselves down before God, our God will lift us up. If we condemn ourselves with trust in his mercy, our God will justify us. If we die unto sin, we shall be raised up unto happy righteousness. The more we humble ourselves, the more he will exalt us; not for our own deserts, but for his promise sake, of free mercy, and his Son's complete merits. To conclude, if here we be humbled with Christ, hereafter we shall be exalted with Christ, even into the high heavens; and there be placed in the joyful presence of God our Father: to whom, with his Son Christ Jesus our Saviour, and the Holy Ghost our Sanctifier and Comforter, be all honour and praise now and for ever. Amen.

3. What commodity unto us by drawing near unto God.

Matt. xi. [28, 29.]

Mic. vii. [19.]
Ezek. xviii. [22.]

1 Cor. xi. [31, 32.]

THE EIGHTH SERMON.

A SERMON

PREACHED BEFORE THE QUEEN.

Esay LV.

6. *Seek ye the Lord while he may be found: call upon him while he is near.*

7. *Let the wicked forsake his ways, and the unrighteous his own imaginations, and return unto the Lord, and he will have mercy upon him; and to our God, for he is very ready to forgive.*

<small>Why, how, and with what fruit, God is sought.</small> HERE we learn by the prophet, that salvation is not sold, but freely given of God to as many as hunger and thirst after it; that they which seek the Lord shall find him, so that they seek him in due and seasonable time; and that the time of seeking the Lord is now: "Seek the Lord," &c. In this exhortation of the prophet let us, first, consider why; secondly, how God is to be sought; and, thirdly, what gain doth grow to the seeker. If I should particularly prosecute this distribution, and follow it at large, as every part shall minister occasion of speech, I should be too long for this place. But I mind brevity, because I know before whom I speak. Few words will be sufficient for the wise; and to a mind well instructed already a short putting in mind will serve. If I chance to say what other men have said before me, (for what can be said which hath not been said before?) I must beseech you to remember the words of the blessed apostle St Paul, which was not ashamed <small>Phil. iii. [1.]</small> to tell even his own tale twice: "To write unto you the same things, to me it is not tedious, and to you it is necessary."

<small>1. God commandeth us to seek him.</small> 2. God preferreth obedience before sacrifice. He accounteth it better to obey than to offer. For as all vice is contained in the name of disobedience, because that only

is naught which God misliketh, and that which he misliketh, he hath forbidden so I may be bold to say with St Augustine, that "there is no virtue but obedience only[1]." If therefore the centurion's soldiers obediently went, came, and did what he commanded; if the Israelites were so dutiful unto Josua, that they said, "All things which thou hast commanded us we will do; he that shall not obey let him die the death;" if mortal men for conscience sake must be obeyed; shall we despise the voice of him that saith from heaven, "Seek ye the Lord"? When God doth bid us go, we may not stand still. And that which his prophets in his name command us, he commandeth himself.

^{Luke vii. [8.]}

^{Josh. i. [16, 18.]}

3. But, lest that the majesty of him which commandeth should rather astonish men than set them forward to seek the Lord, with rough commandments he joineth oftentimes sweet allurements: "Come unto me;" come, "and ye shall find rest for your souls;" not enticing men with fair and sweet words only, but pouring his benefits also plentifully upon them. So he dealt with his old and ancient people, whom by his prophet Micheas he putteth in remembrance of three especial blessings, whereby they were provoked to serve the Lord: "Surely I have brought thee up out of the land of Egypt, and redeemed thee out of the house of bondage; and I have sent before thee Moses, Aaron, and Miriam. O my people, remember now what Balak king of Moab had devised, and what Balaam the son of Peor answered him from Shittim unto Gilgal, that ye may know the righteousness of the Lord."

God allureth us by benefits to seek him. Us as Israel, by three especial blessings.

Mic. vi. [4, 5.]

4. The chiefest benefit which the Lord poured upon his people, and the first whereby he allured them to seek him, was this: with an outstretched arm he brought them forth from the land of Egypt, the house of bondage, where their dwelling-place was a prison, and a long life, long misery. No doubt a mighty and a merciful work of God to deliver his people out of such thraldom, and to set them at such liberty as they afterwards enjoyed.

Deliverance out of thraldom.

[1 Oportebat autem ut homo sub Domino Deo positus alicunde prohiberetur, ut ei promerendi Dominum suum virtus esset ipsa obedientia, quam possum verissimè dicere solam esse virtutem omni creaturæ rationali agenti sub Dei potestate.—August. Op. Par. 1680. De Genesi ad litteram Lib. viii 12. Tom. iii. Pars i. col. 230.—Ed.]

[SANDYS.]

Bondage is an heavy yoke, an exceeding plague; freedom and liberty a great benefit, a sweet blessing. The like benefit, in as great a measure of love, favour, and power, we have received at the hands of our merciful God. He hath done that for us, a rejected nation, which he did for his own inheritance. He hath delivered us from the tyranny and thraldom of that great Pharaoh, from Satan, sin, hell, death, and condemnation, by the mighty hand of our Moses, our grand captain, Christ Jesus, who on the cross gat the victory, spoiled our enemy, cancelled the writing of our bondage and servitude, brought us through the Red Sea, and by his bloodshed wrought our perfect and full deliverance. Again, when we groaned under the heavy burthens of a second, the child of the former Pharaoh; when the tyranny of antichrist lay grievous upon our souls, constraining us by force unto those things, in comparison whereof the gathering of stubble, or making of brick, the sustaining of burthens far heavier than the Egyptian laid any upon Israel, would have seemed tolerable, light, and easy; in the midst of these insufferable griefs, even then, when these Egyptians were most fiercely and eagerly bent, when they thought their kingdom most strongly established, and us past looking for any deliverance (and what else could the reason of man suppose?); even then our mighty and merciful God, (to whose works man's thoughts aspire not) by the hand of his mild and faithful servant delivered his people out of that thraldom, of bond made us free, discharged us from the intolerable tyranny of antichrist, delivered us from the usurped power of popery, from the Romish yoke of servile superstition, that we might serve no longer that man of sin, but our God; not with a slavish mind, but in perfect freedom of conscience, according to his most holy word, and not man's blasphemous doctrine. If we did not pass over this blessing of God with blind or closed eyes, surely the consideration thereof would move us, it would force us to break into words of wonderment, and to cry out with the prophet, "How great is thy goodness!" It would stir up in us an earnest desire to seek our gracious Lord, and, when he is found, for ever to cleave fast unto him.

Psal. xxxi. [19.]

5. God, further provoking his people Israel to seek him, putteth them in mind of a second benefit, of sending Moses, Aaron, and Mary[1] before them: Moses to be their magistrate, and Aaron to be their priest; the one to judge, and the other to teach; the one to punish sinners, the other to pray and to offer for them. These two were brethren, that the bond of nature might unite their minds in government; and that their unity might more advance God's glory, and procure the tranquillity and safety of their country. So Joas the king and Jehoiada the bishop joining hands, and drawing in one line, man's policy giving place to the word of God, the only fountain of true honourable policy, Israel had a prosperous and happy state. *The benefit of giving Moses, Aaron, and Mary.* *2 Kings xii. [2.]*

6. Moses was a worthy magistrate. And his greatest commendation is, that he was no less sharp and severe in God's cause, than mild and gentle in his own. His mildness caused him many times to put up other private injuries: it never caused him to spare such as attempted the overthrow of true religion, or made the people to bow themselves unto strange gods. In such cases the very heads and princes of the people escaped not his just hands. He did wisely consider that, as it is a point of mercy to pardon private wrongs, so not to punish public transgressors against God and the state were great injustice; it being in doubt whether their deeds were more pestilent, or their example, if it were strengthened by impunity, would be more pernicious. "The sceptre of thy kingdom," saith the prophet, "is a sceptre of righteousness." And he proveth it thus: "For thou lovest righteousness, and hatest iniquity." Wilt thou know what is good, and what the Lord requireth of thee? "Surely," saith the prophet, "to do justice, and to love mercy." The song of David had these two parts, "mercy" and "judgment." Princes are God's lieutenants: his person they bear, and his image they must resemble. In him both these are joined together: "I am the Lord which shew mercy, judgment, and righteousness on earth." "Mercy without justice is not mercy, but folly," saith St Chrysostom. And again, "Mercy is then rightly termed mercy, if it be shewed *Moses severe in punishing public offenders, easy in pardoning injuries done to himself.* *Num. xxv. [4, 5.]* *Psal. xlv. [6, 7.]* *Mic. vi. [8.]* *Psal. ci. [1.]* *Jer. xi. [24.]*

[¹ Mary—Miriam.—ED.]

so, that justice be not thereby brought into contempt[1]." And St Augustine saith, that "As it is mercy sometimes to punish, so sometimes to spare is cruelty[2]." Concerning ourselves thus much I can say, that if care be not had thereof in time to keep back the rage of sin by repressing sinners, it will be too late, when the land doth flow with blood, to think upon it. Moses so loved the safety of his people, that he cried: "Lord, spare them, or wipe me out of the book of life." To have a governor like to Moses, mild and merciful, yet not careless to be zealous in God's cause, nor unmindful in justice to punish great transgressors, is a great and a rare blessing. Which if our God have bestowed upon us (for unto him we must acknowledge it, although in this place I pass it over, because my desire is not to please, but to teach, neither did I ever use flattering words, as ye know), but if God have been merciful to us herein, the Lord make us thankful for it.

Aug. ep. 54.

Exod. xxxii. [32.]

Aaron and Mary.

7. Together with Moses God gave his people Aaron the priest; which gift he accounteth also as a great blessing. Yet Aaron was a man, though of great virtue, not altogether without blemish. We see how, for fear of the people more than of God, in the absence of Moses, he played the milksop, erected an idol, and with his body, wheresoever his heart was become, either committed idolatry, or at least permitted it, persuaded hereunto, as some suppose, by Mary the sister of Moses. We have too many followers of the steps of Aaron in this weakness. Howbeit unto some God hath given a greater measure of strength and courage: some there are more bold and constant in God's cause and their duty; some that will not

[1 Misericordia tunc vera est misericordia, si sic facta fuerit, ut justitia per eam non contemnatur: si autem contempta justitia misericordia observetur, ipsa misericordia non est misericordia, sed fatuitas. Nam justitia non est vera justitia, nisi habuerit in se et misericordiam: sic et misericordia non est vera misericordia, nisi habuerit in se justitiam.—Chrysost. Op. Par. 1724. Opus Imperf. in Matt. Hom. XLVI. pp. cxciv. cxcv.—The Benedictine editors, in their prolegomena to this work, say: Imperfectum illud opus nec esse, nec esse posse, Chrysostomi certum est.—ED.]

[2 Sicut enim est aliquando misericordia puniens, ita et crudelitas parcens.—August. Op. Par. 1679. Epist. cliii. Tom. II. col. 530.—ED.]

bow their knees to Baal, that will not displease God for the pleasuring of man; some whose liberty and lives are not so dear unto them, but that they can be contented not only to be bound, but also to die for the testimony of Christ. Of this better sort, although in comparison of the worse the number be not so great as good, yet I suppose that few nations under heaven have more faithful and able ministers than this land hath. Beg we at the hands of the Lord of the harvest, to send more pastors and fewer hirelings, more labourers and fewer loiterers. For, in respect of the greatness of the harvest, these workmen, though they be many, yet are but few. When God doth give his people good governors and wise teachers; when he maketh their men to excel in wisdom, their princes to be as Moses, and their priests as Aaron; and, besides all this, raiseth up women like to Mary amongst them, pouring out his Spirit, not only upon their sons, but upon their daughters also, choosing out of them, notwithstanding their weakness, mighty instruments of his power; surely a benefit so rare and precious should win men's hearts unto God for ever.

8. But the prophet goeth forward, and maketh mention of a third thing, which is, that God did turn the cursings of Balaam into blessings. "Remember what Balak king of Moab had devised, and what Balaam the son of Peor answered him from Shittim to Gilgal, that ye may know the righteousness of the Lord." It fretted the heart of that profane king Balak, to behold the flourishing prosperity of God's people, to see Og the king of Bashan, and Sihon king of the Amorites, conquered and slain by them. "This multitude," saith he, "will lick up all that are about us, as an ox licketh up the grass of the field." Wherefore, mistrusting his own strength, and having seen trial of theirs, he devised to hire Balaam the wizard to curse them, and thought by that mean, without all peradventure, to prevail over them. But ye know Balaam's answers; the first, "How shall I curse, where God hath not cursed?" the second, "God hath blessed, and I cannot alter it;" the third, "How goodly are thy tents, O Jacob, and thine habitations, O Israel! As the valleys are they stretched forth, as gardens by the river's side, as the aloe-

[The enemy's curse turned into blessing. Num. xxiii. [Mic. vi. 5.]

[Num. xxii. 4.]

trees which the Lord hath planted, and as the cedars beside the waters." When he saw that God would not suffer his tongue to curse Israel, though it were hired, he gave Balak this advice, to cause the daughters of Moab to steal away their hearts by carnal pleasure, and so to allure them unto the sacrifice of their gods, that, they forsaking the true God, he might also forsake them. This practice was a stumblingblock in their way: whilst they abode in Shittim, they committed fornication: they coupled themselves unto Baal Peor, and ate of things sacrificed unto idols and devils. Wherefore God plagued them, and laid his heavy hand upon them: howbeit he withdrew not his mercy and kindness wholly from them, but in Gilgal took away this their shame, and sealed again the covenant of reconciled love. So that, as there was no curse which could take away his blessing, so there was no counsel that could hinder his good purpose towards his people. Ye are not ignorant how the Balaamite of Rome hath cursed us, our prince, our prophets, and our people, even as "the Philistine cursed David by his gods." But we have found the promise of Christ most true: "Blessed are ye when they shall revile you." Our God hath turned all his curses into blessings: his name be blessed for it. The pope, that Balaam, hath bitterly cursed the ground whereon we go, and the whole land wherein we live. But hath there grown a briar or a thorn the more upon it, for all that man's curse? He that shall survey it and view it well, and mark the plentifulness of these latter years, must needs confess that God hath bestowed upon it more than ordinary or usual blessings. As the blessings of that man are by God accursed, so where he curseth, there the Lord blesseth; and, to the eternal reproof of that our enemy's unjust and uncharitable execration, he hath in these our days opened his bountiful hand far wider than in former times, when those antichristian blessings came posting yearly from Rome, and embraced our land so kindly, that they sucked the sap of wealth both from branch and root. The land of Canaan was a pleasant and a fruitful land, flowing with milk and abounding with honey: truly it was barren, and almost beggarly, in respect of our abundance and store. God may justly say to us, "What could I have done more unto my vineyard, which I have not done unto it?" He hath miraculously given and continued with us that grand blessing of his glorious gospel: he hath wonderfully preserved our sovereign, his servant: he hath kept her safe, as Moses, and David, from Pharaoh, from Dathan, and from Amalek, from Goliath, from Saul, from Absolon, from the hands of her open enemies, and treasons of her deceitful friends:. he hath not only given her a circumspect heart to foresee and to prevent, and, I trust, to cut off all intended destruction; but also hath more than miraculously abated the pride, and confounded the manifold counsels, of her and our enemies, and, contrary to all expectation, kept us in peace and safety. God make us thankful and give us hearts sincerely bent to seek him, which so mercifully by his benefits and graces hath sought us! "How great is thy goodness, O Lord, which thou hast laid up in store for them that fear thee!" "For this shall every one that is godly make his prayer unto thee in a time when thou mayest be found," and call upon thee while thou art near. [Psal. xxxi. [19.] Psal. xxxii. [6.]]

9. If this way will not serve to bring us unto God, another must be assayed: if we will not be led by fair means, we shall be drawn by foul: God hath blessings for them which are of a pliable mind, but for the froward rods. Them he first threateneth, as having no delight or pleasure to punish: he punisheth as one unwilling to destroy. God's correction is for our reformation; but, if it will not reform us, for our confusion. This self-love of ours, this senseless security, this contempt of God's word, this want of godly zeal, these contrivings of treason and conspiracy, are tokens that God hath bent his dreadful bow, and is preparing to make his arrows drunk with our blood. If he spared neither Israelites nor angels, doubtless neither will he spare us, except unfeignedly we seek him, and seek him now. [Them, whom benefits will not win, plagues must constrain to seek the Lord.]

10. For "now is the acceptable time:" now is grace offered: the Lord now stretcheth out his hands of mercy: this is the day wherein the Lord may be found of them that seek him. But some stop their ears at this, and will not hear: they are too wise to be enchanted with these times. If ye tell them of seeking the Lord, their answer [Now is the time to seek the Lord. [2 Cor. vi. 2.]]

[Exod. v. 2.] is, "Who is the Lord?" They say plainly in their foolish
[Psal. liii. 1.] hearts, "There is no God." But the just God will one
Luke xiv. day shew himself to their confusion. Others have their
[18—20.] excuses of worldly hinderances and lets: farms, or oxen, or wives, have tied them by the leg, when they should go and seek the Lord. Others have a mind not utterly unwilling to seek after him; but they would fain stay awhile, and seek him hereafter. Youth, they say, must have his swing: let old age wax holy. Such novices there were, of whom Chrysostom[1] writeth, that they would not be baptized until they were in their death-beds, lest baptism should be as a bridle to hold them in. They were desirous to have their forth[2] in their carnal desires, and at the end of their days by baptism to wash away all at once. But God shall mock such craft; and they, who will not come when he calleth, when they call shall not be heard. Beware of these delays. Let us not defer and put off till to-morrow; but while it is called to-day, even whilst this acceptable day is, let us seek the Lord, that we may find him. Now he is ready to meet us by the way, and lovingly to embrace us with the arms of his eternal mercy.

2.
The Lord is sought and found by faith.

11. The second thing to be considered is, how we may seek the Lord, and in seeking him be sure to find him. I will omit to shew how vainly the gentiles in their idols, the Jews in their ceremonies and traditions, the papists in their superstitions, do seek the Lord. They seek him and find him not, because they seek him where he is not, not where he is; as themselves have imagined, and not as he hath prescribed. The first entrance into the way

[1 Ὅταν γάρ τις διὰ τοῦτο ἁμαρτάνῃ, ἵνα τὸ ἅγιον βάπτισμα πρὸς ἐσχάταις λάβῃ ταῖς ἀναπνοαῖς, πολλάκις οὐ ἐπιτεύξεται. καὶ, πιστεύσατέ μοι, οὐ φοβῶν ὑμᾶς λέγω, ὃ μένω λέγειν. πολλοὺς οἶδα τοῦτο παθόντας ἐγώ, οἳ προσδοκίᾳ μὲν τοῦ φωτίσματος πολλὰ ἡμάρτανον· πρὸς δὲ τῇ ἡμέρᾳ τῆς τελευτῆς ἀπῆλθον κενοί. ὁ γὰρ θεὸς διὰ τοῦτο τὸ βάπτισμα ἔδωκεν, ἵνα λύσῃ τὰς ἁμαρτίας, οὐχ ἵνα αὐξήσῃ τὰς ἁμαρτίας. εἰ δέ τις τούτῳ κεχρημένος εἴη πρὸς ἄδειαν τοῦ πλείονα ἁμαρτάνειν, ῥαθυμίας λοιπὸν τοῦτο γίνεται αἴτιον. εἰ γὰρ μὴ λουτρὸν ἦν, ἀσφαλέστερον ἔζων ἄν, ὡς οὐκ ἔχοντες ἄφεσιν.—Chrysost. Op. Par. 1735. In Epist. ad Heb. Hom. XIII. Tom. XII. pp. 135, 6.—Ed.]

[2 Forth—free way or course.—Ed.]

where God will be found, is faith: *Fide tangitur Christus, fide videtur*[1], saith St Ambrose: "By faith Christ is handled, by faith he is seen." By faith he is found. All our travail in seeking without faith is but a fruitless wearying of our deceived souls: for he that cometh unto God must believe. Ambr. in Luc. lib. vi. cap. 8.

12. And the way to believe is hearing; for by hearing cometh faith: the word is that star which guideth and directeth us unto Christ. "Search the scriptures;" for to this end they are written, "That ye might believe that Jesus is Christ the Son of God, and that believing ye might have eternal life." They were written to be read: and therefore St Paul chargeth Timothy straitly, "Give attendance to reading." They were written to be read, not of him only, but of us also, in what condition or estate soever God hath placed us. Princes are not exempted more than others: no, they above others are especially charged to travail herein. What charge can be devised more effectual than that which is given unto Josua: "Let not this book of the law depart out of thy mouth, but meditate thou therein day and night, that thou mayest observe and do according to all that is written therein; for then shalt thou make thy way prosperous, and then shalt thou have good success"? Good reason it is, that as kings do reign and hold their power by him, so his will, revealed in his word, should be the rule and direction of their government. If they think to establish their thrones better by their own wise and politic devices, they are greatly deceived. There is no policy, no wisdom, like the wisdom of God. The commonwealths which Aristotle and Plato have framed in their books, otherwise full of wisdom, yet compared with divine policies, with that city for whose sake and benefit the Lord doth watch, what are they but fancies of foolish men? As for Machiavel's inventions, they are but the dreams of a brain-sick person, founded upon the craft of man, and not upon godly wisdom, which only hath good effect. Godly princes have no need to seek for counsel at these men's hands; the mouth of the Lord is sufficient for them. "Thy testimonies," saith David, "are my counsellors." Their counsel was to him Faith cometh by hearing the word of God.
John v. [39.]
John xx. [31.]
1 Tim. iv. [13.]
Josh. i. [8.]
Psal. cxix. [24.]

[[1] Ambros. Op. Par. 1686. Expos. Ev. sec. Luc. Lib. vi. 57. Tom. i. col. 1397.—ED.]

sufficient. He read not the scriptures at idle times, or at leisure: they were his meditation continually. Reading was not irksome and tedious unto him: his eyes did prevent the night-watches to meditate in the word. The time was not lost which was so bestowed. For "by thy commandments," saith he, "thou hast made me wiser than mine enemies." The diligence of that noble eunuch, chief officer to the queen of Ethiopia, is greatly commended, as a worthy precedent for christian courtiers to behold and follow. Many cannot read, yet all ought to hear: "I will hearken," saith David, "what the Lord God will say." Who doth not rejoice to hear a prince speak gracious and favourable words? "But I will hear the Lord speak," saith the prophet; "for he will speak peace unto his people." A bad servant, an evil wife, a cursed child, a damnable creature, that will not gladly hear the voice of the Lord, the husband, the father, the Creator. Christ taught daily in the temple; and doubtless he was daily heard. But hearing of the word may not daily be attended, lest it hinder more weighty affairs. Is there any thing more weighty than the matter of salvation? Is the earth of more account than heaven? a short miserable life, than a blessed and immortal? Philip of Macedonia casting off the suit of a poor woman with a short answer, that he had no leisure to hear her cause, she answered boldly, "Why then hast thou leisure to be a king?" I may as boldly ask of them which say they have no leisure to hear God's word, how they will find the leisure to be saved? This word only saveth. Receive ye therefore "the word engrafted, which is able to save your souls."

[Psal. cxix. 98.]

Acts viii. [27, 28.]

Psal. lxxxv. [8.]

James i. [21.]

The want of teachers, at whose mouths the word should be heard.

13. If there be no salvation but by faith, no faith but by hearing the word of God, how should the people be saved without teachers? The mother-city of the realm is reasonably furnished with faithful preachers: certain other cities, not many in number, are blessed too, though not in like sort. But the silly people of the land otherwhere, especially in the north parts, pine away and perish for want of this saving food: they are much decayed for want of prophecy. Many there are that hear not a sermon in seven years, I might say safely in seventeen. Their blood will be required at somebody's hands. The Lord

deliver us from that hard account, and grant redress with speed!

14. But why doth the country want preachers? The people pay tithes of that they have; therefore there must needs be sufficient to maintain them. If things were well ordered, this sequel were good. But the chiefest benefices were by the pope long since impropriated unto monks, which devoured the fruits, and gave a silly stipend unto a poor Sir John to say mass; and as they left it, so we find it still. Where livings were not impropriated by the pope, there they are for the most part so handled, that patrons maintain themselves with those tithes which the people give, and ministers have that which the patrons leave. The world dealeth with God's clergy, as Dionysius the tyrant with Jupiter's idol. They make themselves as merry with spoiling Christ's patrimony, as he with robbing Jupiter of his golden cloak; which, being too heavy for summer, and too cold for winter, he took away, and left instead of it a cotton coat, light for the one time and warm for the other. To take from them which live idly and superstitiously in the church, they plead it to be lawful, because those unprofitable members were unworthy to enjoy the fat of the earth. Abbeys being eaten up, and other profits gone, now as greedy cormorants they seize also upon the church of Christ. It is not fit forsooth that men sanctified unto heavenly things should be overmuch encumbered with these earthly commodities; and therefore even of great devotion and zeal they will ease the church of these her burthens. Thus by men that cannot stand without the fall of the church of God, all means are invented to beggar the ministry. A device no doubt of Satan, and a practice of his imps, to cause a famine of the bread of life by starving the ox that should tread out the corn, and to withdraw God's people from seeking the Lord by weakening and discouraging such as should guide them in the way of life. Thus you see how God must be sought in his word, which word because all men must hear and learn, therefore many must be sent to teach it.

The cause why there are so few sufficient men to teach the people.

15. But because the seed which is cast into the earth groweth not up unless it be watered with the dew of heaven, neither doth the sound of the word bring any man unto

The Lord must be sought by prayer also, and not by hearing only.

Christ, except the grace of the Spirit be with it; which grace God offereth so freely unto men, that there needeth no more but "ask" and "have;" for this cause it followeth in the prophet, "Call upon him while he is near." We may read and hear of God as of one far off. But when we pray unto God, we acknowledge that he is as it were within sight: when we call upon him, we speak to him as unto one which is present. He is never so clearly and plainly found, his presence is never so familiarly enjoyed, as by hearty prayer. Prayer consisteth of two parts; thanksgiving for that which we have received, and requesting of that whereof our souls or bodies have need.

<small>Thanksgiving for benefits already received. Psal. cxvi. [12, 13.]</small>

16. The good king David, falling into consideration of the infinite mercies of God, bursteth out into these careful words: "What shall I render to the Lord?" Finding no way to requite, he resolveth thus: "I will take the cup of salvation, and call upon the name of the Lord." Perhaps the prophet had the more care to shew himself thankful towards God, by reason of the grief which himself sustained through men's ingratitude towards him. He maketh pitiful complaint that his familiar friends, who ate bread at his table, who took sweet counsel with him, whom he had many ways benefited, were unthankful, and requited him with treacherous dealing. An honest-hearted man is never so grieved as when his friendliness is requited with ingratitude. "If it be," saith St Ambrose, "a fault to be matched even with murder, not to requite man with thankfulness, what a crime is it to deal unthankfully with God[1]?" *Dixeris maledicta cuncta, cum ingratum hominem dixeris*[2]: "We have named all the naughtiness that can be objected when we have termed a man unthankful," saith another. Lycurgus, being asked why in his laws he had set down no punishment for ingratitude, answered, "I have left it to the gods to punish." All the punishment which man could devise he thought too easy for a fault so heinous. The ingratitude of Jerusalem did more wound the heart of the Son of

[1 Quod si homini non referre simile homicidio judicatum est; quantum crimen est non referre Deo?—Ambros. Op. Par. 1690. De Excess. Frat. sui Satyri, Lib. I. 44. Tom. II. col. 1126.—ED.]

[2 Pub. Syr. v. 250.—ED.]

God, Christ Jesus, than the spear that pierced him through the heart upon the cross. He hath dealt as mercifully with us as with them: if we deal as unkindly as they with him, we, which know what befel them for it, cannot be ignorant what is likely to befall us, except we take the cup of salvation betimes, and call upon the name of the Lord while he is near.

17. And as his benefits do require thanks, so our own estate doth need succour. Our necessities therefore should make us earnest suitors unto God, that he would be our reliever. Our ship is in peril of tempest, the ragings of the sea do threaten it; yet who crieth, "Help, Lord"? What man is there that weepeth bitterly with Peter, or nightly watereth his couch with tears, as David? Yet all have sinned and offended the Lord of glory. It is high time therefore to call upon God, and that earnestly. The superstitious prayed without understanding. Wherein are we better, if our prayers be without feeling? The fountain of prayer is the feeling of the heart. Pour out that before the Lord: call upon him from thence: cry from the depth, and he shall answer, "Here I am, thy ready helper in time of need." *Craving of help in present necessity.* [Matt. viii. 25.] [Matt. xxvi. 75.] [Psal. vi. 6.] [Isai. lviii. 9.]

18. But withal take this: "Let the wicked forsake his ways, and the unrighteous his own imaginations, and return unto the Lord," that is to say, repent. Paul to Titus useth the like description of repentance, saying, "The grace of God teacheth us that we should deny ungodliness and worldly lusts, and live soberly, and righteously, and godlily, in this present world." Peter out of the psalm, in fewer words, saith the same: "Decline from evil, and do good." The papists set repentance upon three feet, confession, contrition, and satisfaction. But two of them are of wood without life. Their confession is to a priest, whereas the scripture maketh God, and not the priest, our confessor. *Confitemini Domino,* saith the psalmist: "Make confession to the Lord." Their satisfaction is but money matter, and God is satisfied not by gold, but by blood; and with us he is pleased when our lives are amended. *Deus nostrorum emendatione placatur, et qui peccare desinit iram Dei mortalem facit*[1]: "God is pacified by the *Prayer is fruitless where repentance is not.* [Tit. ii. 11, 12.] [1 Pet. iii. 11.] [Psal. cv. 1. Vulgate.] [1 Pet. i. 18, 19.]

[1 Lactant. Op. Lut. Par. 1748. Liber de Ira Dei, c. xxi. Tom. II. p. 173.—ED.]

mending of our manners; and he that ceaseth from sin, bringeth the wrath of God to an end," saith Lactantius. We must forsake therefore our own ways, our own cogitations: they are wicked and ungodly. There is nothing ours but imbecility and naughtiness, which with ourselves we must utterly renounce and forsake, and fly to God's mercy, that in mercy he may accept us. No doubt we have all wandered out of the way, all have started aside, every man hath wandered his own fond and sinful way: we have provoked God's wrath, our ingratitude hath grieved him: we have wickedly profaned his sacred gospel, his word we have contemned and abused, using it as a cloak to cover our deep hypocrisy. Christ was never more professed, and never less obeyed. It is truly verified in our times which the prophet Oseas[1] complained of in his: "There is no truth, there is no mercifulness, there is no knowledge of God in the land: cursing and lying, and murder and theft, and whoredom, have overflowed: blood hath touched blood." Ezekiel teacheth that the sins of Sodom, that sink of sin, were idleness, fulness of bread, pride, and unmercifulness towards the poor. Are not these the sins of this land, of this city, of this court, at this day? Are not these bad ways our ways? Half England liveth idly or worse occupied: we are fed to the full; and who is not puffed up with pride? or who relieveth his neighbour's want? No man is contented with his own estate, but every one striveth to climb higher, to sit aloft. There is want of the true fear of God in all sorts, estates, and ages. Yet we please ourselves, and walk on, as if God either saw not our sin, or else in his justice could not punish it. Are the eyes of the Lord shut up? or hath God forgotten to be just? Surely our sins will not suffer his plagues to stay long from us. What plagues, I dare not presume to prophesy: for God hath kept that secret to himself. But I stand in fear that we are the men to whom Christ saith, "The kingdom of God shall be taken from you;" that we are they, whose sins will bring the sceptre of this kingdom into the hands of an hypocrite. If God in his justice do this, wo worth us most wretched men! The loss of the gospel is the loss of our souls; and

Hos. iv. [1, 2.]

Ezek. xvi. [49.]

[Matt. xxi. 43.]

[1 Oseas—Hosea.—Ed.]

the loss of our sovereign the loss of our lives. Truly, when I fall into consideration of the wickedness of this world, that all sorts of men fall to sinning with greediness, that there is scant one left, as Elias complaineth, that truly seeketh after God, that in all conditions iniquity doth abound and charity wax cold, that the zeal of God is utterly dried up in the hearts of men, that God is served for fashion's sake and not in truth; what should I think but that God hath gathered his lap full of plagues, and is ready to pour them down upon us? There is but one way to stay him, for which he himself doth stay and wait. Do ye not know that the lenity of God inviteth you to repentance? If we will save our Nineveh, we must repent and turn to our God: we must seek him, both prince and people.

19. The benefit which cometh unto those that seek him is this: "he will have mercy on them." Although the house of Israel rebelled against the Lord, as a froward woman rebelleth against her husband, yet he ceased not to call upon them still by the voice of his prophets: "O ye disobedient children, return, return, and I will heal your rebellions." "Surely it pertaineth unto God to say, I have pardoned, I will not destroy." "He looketh upon men; and if one say, I have sinned, and perverted righteousness, and it did not profit me, he will deliver his soul from going into the pit, and his life shall see light. Lo, all these things will God work twice or thrice with a man." He desireth not our destruction, but our conversion, be we never so great sinners. "For he is very ready to forgive." Ask pardon, and thou shalt have it. Return to the Lord unfeignedly, and he will mercifully accept thee.
_{3. The fruit that cometh by seeking the Lord.}
_{Jer. iii. [22.]}
_{Job xxxiv. [31. Geneva version.] Job xxxiii. [27—29.]}

20. And if he be ready to forgive us, let not us be loth to give unto him. We need not ask where he is, or what he wanteth, that we may give unto him. He is near at hand, straying and starving in the streets; naked, hungry, cold, harbourless, sick, and diseased, ruthfully moaning and crying for relief. Let the pitiful cry of our Christ move our hearts to mercy. "He that shutteth his ears at the cry of the poor, shall cry himself and not be heard." Let the merciless Moguntine[1] terrify men of hard and stony
_{Our thankfulness towards God whom we seek must be shewed by our mercifulness to the poor.}
_{Prov. xxi. [13.]}

[[1] The archbishop here refers to the well-known and then popular legendary story of bishop Hatto.—ED.]

hearts, who was devoured of rats, the vilest vermin, for his cruel heart, void of all compassion upon the poor. Let us seek up Christ, and provide for him. He sought us and found us, when we were robbed, spoiled, and deadly wounded: let not us turn away our faces from him, seeking and craving so small help at our hands. He became poor to make us rich: let us out of the abundance of our riches spare somewhat now to the relief of his poverty. He will well requite it. It is not lost which is bestowed upon him in his poor afflicted members: that which we put in the hands of the poor, we lay it up in the Lord's bosom; where neither dice nor cards, hawks nor hounds, horses nor harlots, can consume it; rust and canker cannot eat it, thieves cannot rob and bereave us of it. Unworthy we are to be called Christians, if we suffer our head, Christ Jesus, to be naked, and clothe him not; if we see him hungry, and give him no bread. Worse we are than Jews, if we suffer this ignominy to be done unto Christ, this ingratitude to be shewed to so gracious a God. O let us be merciful; that as children we may resemble our heavenly Father, for he is merciful. Unto this merciful God the Father, the Son, and the Holy Ghost, be honour, glory, and praise now and ever. Amen.

THE NINTH SERMON.

A SERMON

MADE IN PAUL'S, AT THE SOLEMNIZATION OF CHARLES THE NINTH[1], THE FRENCH KING'S FUNERAL.

JOB XIV.

14. All the days of this my warfare do I wait, till my changing come.

THE custom of funerals, as it is ancient, so is it commendable. Abraham, the father of our faith, purchased a piece of ground to bury his dead in. And in that place he himself, Sarah, Isaac, Jacob, and Joseph, were buried with great solemnity and much mourning. Tobias is commended for burying the dead. So is Mary Magdalene for preparing of ointment for the burying of our Saviour. So is Joseph, and also Nicodemus, for the care that they had about Christ's funeral. *The custom of funerals ancient and commendable. Gen. xxiii. xxv. [9; xlix. 30, 31]; and l. [13.] Tob. ii. [9.] John xii. [7, 8.] John xix. [38—42.]*

2. Causes of funerals St Augustine giveth three. First, it is the office of humanity, the duty of charity, decently to commit the dead corps to the earth, out of which they came. This charitable duty is commended in Toby and others, whose names I mentioned before, and was of the very heathen religiously observed. Secondly, it is a thing very seemly and convenient, with reverence to lay the corps in grave; because our bodies are the temples of the Holy Ghost, wherein and by which, as by lively instruments, both God hath been glorified, and his people have received good. "Know ye not that your body is the temple of the Holy Ghost which is in you?" That which hath been so notable an instrument, would not be unreverently entreated, though dead. Thirdly, our faith is hereby confirmed touching the article of our resurrection. For we *Three causes of solemnizing funerals. 1 Cor. vi. [19.]*

[1 Charles IX. died May 30, 1574.—ED.]

[SANDYS.]

lay down the body in the earth, under hope that "this mortal must put on immortality:" as confessing with Job, "I believe that my Redeemer liveth, and that I shall see God in my flesh: mine eyes shall behold him, and none other." But the christian church doth not, neither ought to use funerals, thereby to relieve or benefit the dead. "All these things," saith St Augustine, "furniture of funerals, order of burying, and the pomp of exequies, are rather comforts to the living than helps to the dead[1]." The glutton, of whom St Luke speaketh in the gospel, was buried no doubt with pomp enough; yet his wicked soul was plunged into hell. There cometh therefore no part of blessedness to the dead by funerals: but "blessed are the dead that die in the Lord." Lazarus wanted (as it is to be thought) his funeral; but the want thereof bereaved him not of his happy estate: he died in the Lord, and so was blessed.

3. Sith therefore death bringeth with it our particular judgment; sith "he that believeth on the Son hath everlasting life; but he that believeth not on the Son shall not see life, but the wrath of God abideth on him;" let us live as we will die, and die as they that hope to rise again and live with Christ hereafter. "As every man departeth hence, so shall he be judged at the last day." And, "Every man shall sleep with his own cause, and with his own cause rise again[2]." At our particular death is our particular judgment: at the glorious coming of Christ shall be the general revelation of the judgment of the whole world. After this life there is no help remaining to the dead: to the living there is mercy offered, to the dead there remaineth only judgment. He that is not purged here shall be judged as filthy there.

4. Vain therefore and dangerous is the opinion of purgatory. Vain, because it hath no foundation at all in God's word. Moses, prescribing all kinds of sacrifices in the old

[1 Proinde omnia ista, id est, curatio funeris, conditio sepulturæ, pompa exsequiarum, magis sunt vivorum solatia quam subsidia mortuorum.—August. Op. Par. 1685. De Civitate Dei, Lib. ɪ. 12. Tom. vii. col. 13.—Ed.]

[2 In quo enim quemque invenerit suus novissimus dies, in hoc eum comprehendet mundi novissimus dies: quoniam qualis in die isto quisque moritur, talis in die illo judicabitur.—August. Op. Par. 1679. Epist. cxcix. Ad. Hesych. Tom. ii. col. 743.—Ed.]

law, maketh no mention either of sacrificing or praying for the dead. Paul, instructing the Thessalonians what they ought to do in funerals, neither doth remember unto them sacrifice, nor prayer. Just Simeon never dreamed of purgatory, when as he said, "Lord, now lettest thou thy servant depart in peace according to thy word." Small peace is there in purgatory, as papists report. It never came into St Paul's mind when he said, "I desire to depart hence, and to be with Christ." It was not revealed to the angel when he said, "Blessed are the dead which die in the Lord: they rest from their labours." There is no rest but intolerable pain imagined in purgatory, even to them which die in the Lord. Neither Lazarus, nor the rich man, were acquainted with it: the one was immediately carried into heaven, the other cast into hell. He which said to the thief, "This day thou shalt be with me in paradise," knew only two ways, the strait way to heaven, the broad way to hell: he who knew all things, was ignorant of this third way; for there is no such way to know. This opinion is perilous. The hope of help in purgatory hath sent many deceived souls into hell. This opinion is injurious to the blood of Christ. For if any sin remain to be purged by these after-pains, then "the blood of Christ doth" not "cleanse us from all sin;" and then we make God a liar. It destroyeth repentance; without which there is no remission of sins here, and with which satisfaction for sins afterward cannot stand. For faith and repentance cease with this life. He that hath not his pardon here, deceiveth himself, if he hope to have it hereafter elsewhere. Every man after life shall bear his own burthen, as every man hath wrought in his body. There cometh nothing to the spirits of them that be dead, but that which they wrought while they were alive. "Work thou righteousness before thy death:" for in the grave it is too late. And thus it doth appear that, although the use of funerals be ancient, and that for good causes they are to be celebrated, yet neither purgatory nor prayer, neither any other after helps can be available for the party departed; and therefore we must now sow, as hereafter we will reap. "Cast away impiety, and worldly concupiscence, and live a sober, a just, and a godly life; looking for the blessed hope, and the

[1 Thes. iv. [13—18.]]
[Luke ii. [29.]]
[Phil. i. [23.]]
[Rev. xiv. 13.]
[Luke xvi. [22, 23.]]
[Luke xxiii. [43.] Matt. vii. [13, 14.]]
[1 John i. [7.]]
[Ecclus. xiv. [13.]]
[Tit. ii. [12, 13.]]

THE NINTH SERMON.

appearance of the glory of the great God and of our Saviour Jesus Christ." Here we are, as Christ's soldiers, appointed to "fight a good fight, to fulfil our course, to keep the faith;" and so to look for the promised crown of glory, which God will give to such as look for and love his coming.

<small>2 Tim. iv. [7.]</small>

5. Whereof Job is a good remembrance unto us: "All the days of this my warfare do I wait, till my changing shall come." In which words we have three things chiefly to be considered: first, that our whole life is a warfare; secondly, that this war will have an end; thirdly, that this end is daily to be looked for.

<small>Three things contained in the words of Job.</small>

6. He which saith here, "I wait all the days of this my warfare," saith otherwise also, "Man's life is a warfare upon earth." In this christian war some be generals, some captains, some trumpeters; the rest be common and ordinary soldiers. Every one must keep his standing, answer his calling, fight, and manfully strive for the victory.

<small>1. Man's life a warfare. [Job vii. 1, marginal rendering.]</small>

7. Kings and princes are generals, God's lieutenants upon earth; to defend God's people, to set them in order, to see them well governed, to fight in God's quarrel, to prefer and promote God's cause. They should serve the Lord, the King of kings, "in fear, embrace the Son," advance true religion, "seek the kingdom of heaven;" wherein doth consist their victory and glory. This they will do, if they be zealous in God's cause: if they be indeed the "nurses of his church," they will "hate his enemies with perfect hatred:" they will punish transgressors, protect the innocent, execute justice and judgment, without respect of persons. So shall they *militare Christo*, do the office of a good general in God's war. Such generals were David, Jehosaphat, Ezekias, and Josias. These generals are placed of God, and therefore of duty to be obeyed. "Let every soul be subject to the higher power; for there is no power but of God." God giveth good princes as a blessing; and the same God giveth evil princes as a curse. He gave Samuel in his favour; and in his wrath he gave Saul. He maketh an hypocrite to reign for the sins of the people. These generals have authority from the Lord of hosts, to draw the sword against transgressors, and to execute martial law, according to such limitation as God hath prescribed.

<small>Kings and princes, God's generals.</small>

<small>Psal. ii. [11, 12.]</small>
<small>Matt. vi. [33.]</small>

<small>Isai. xlix. [23.]</small>
<small>Psal. cxxxix. [22.]</small>

<small>Rom. xiii. [1.]</small>

<small>Job xxxiv. [30.]</small>

8. The captains are the nobility, put in their several

<small>The nobles, captains.</small>

authorities over several bands. They must valiantly go before, strive and stand for God's cause, give good example to their soldiers, in honest behaviour, in painful travail, according to their callings; so upright in all their doings, that the people may be enforced to justify them, as the Israelites did their Samuel. Good captains make good soldiers. [1 Sam. xii. [4, 5.]]

9. The trumpeters are the ministers of God's word; by the blast of the trump both to give warning of the enemy, and also to order the going forward of the army. To these men God saith, "Cry out aloud, leave not off, lift up thy voice like a trumpet, and shew my people their offences." If these men be dumb dogs, and sound not the trumpet, as well to forewarn as to guide God's army, the perishing blood shall be required at their hands by whom it hath been betrayed. Paul was faithful and skilful to sound this trump, and to sound it in season, to strive for the truth, and to pour out his blood in God's quarrel. He ended his days like a man full of valour. "I have fought a good fight, I have fulfilled my course, I have kept the faith." His faithful heart was careful for the whole army of God: "I have care of all the churches." *The ministers, trumpeters.* [Isai. lviii. [1.]] [Ezek. xxxiii. [8.]] [2 Tim. iv. [7.]] [2 Cor. xi. [28.]]

10. The common soldiers must keep their stand and station in all obedience and readiness: stoutly they must fight under Christ's victorious banner. They are not trifles for which they strive. Therefore let them not shrink, nor cowardly run away; but with an invincible courage, in an assured hope of the victory, abide all warlike miseries, sustained with the comfort of that reward which no man shall receive, "except he strive lawfully." No man, that "layeth his hand to the plough, and looketh backward," is worthy of the kingdom of heaven. "But he that endureth to the end shall be saved." *The rest, common soldiers.* [2 Tim. ii. [5.]] [Luke ix. 62.] [Matt. x. [22.]]

11. Now we must strive for Christ, and not for antichrist; for the truth, and not against it: "I can do nothing against the truth, but for the truth," saith St Paul. For the gospel, and not for the doctrine of man; for true religion, and not for superstition, must we strive. But our striving for the most part is all awry and wicked. We strive who may be the proudest: pretending equality, we strive in deed for superiority. Neither equal nor superior can we abide: we strive how to supplant and overthrow *They which war under Christ must strive for the truth, and not against it.* [2 Cor. xiii. [8.]]

one another. Envy hath made men impudent, striving to undermine and cast down the walls of innocency, striving how to place and how to displace, how to disgrace and how to bring into favour, how to set up and how to throw down. And in so doing we strive against ourselves, and for the advantage of our deadly foes. This war is not christian: this is not to strive "lawfully." This is not to fight "a good fight." This victory shall not be crowned.

^{2Tim. iv. [7.]}

^{The enemies against whom we must strive, the devil, the world, and the flesh.}
^{1 Pet. v. [8.]}
^{Rev. xii. [9.]}
^{Ecclus. ii. [1.]}
^{Matt. iv. [1.]}

12. Our principal and common enemies, against whom we must all jointly fight, are the devil, the world, and the flesh. The devil is strong and subtile, a roaring lion, and an old serpent, of long and great experience. So soon as we profess to be Christ's soldiers, as a malicious and fierce enemy he invadeth us. "My son, if thou wilt come into the service of God, stand fast in righteousness, and fear; and arm thy soul to temptation." Christ himself was tempted immediately after that he was baptized. His ways of assault are these. He persuadeth to evil: he either hindereth or infecteth that which is good, that no action which we do may be pleasant in the sight of God. He tempteth and overcometh even the perfectest, as he did Adam; the strongest, as he did Sampson; the wisest, as he did Solomon. "He therefore that standeth, let him take heed that he do not fall." No perfection, no strength, no wisdom, ought to free us of this care. But we need to pray continually, "Lead us not into temptation." And yet we, being in the midst of the battle with such an enemy, still sleep in security. But the devil sleepeth not. And this malicious adversary hath spials in our army: he laboureth by corruption to make a mutiny amongst us, that, whilst we strive amongst ourselves, he may more easily eat us up. He setteth the generals together by the ears. The captains they envy one another. The soldiers take parties and are divided. The generals, captains, soldiers and all, contemn the watchmen, and will not give ear, or regard the sound of the trump. The kingdom, the city, the house thus divided, can it, think you, stand long? The devil playeth his part, and plieth it busily; but we like cowards yield, and do not resist; are at variance amongst ourselves, and thereby at agreement with that adversary, whom whoso hateth his brother serveth. Our second

^{Gen. iii. [1—6.]}
^{Judg. xvi. [15—17.]}
^{1 Kings xi. [1—8.]}
^{1 Cor. x. [12.]}

^{Mark iii. [24, 25.]}

enemy is the world; the world, which is altogether set on all wickedness. The third, our flesh; our flesh, which rebelleth, and "lusteth contrary to the Spirit." Fleshly lusts "fight against the soul." And thus we have enemies on every side, yea, and that which is most dangerous of all within us, which daily give us sore assaults. For love of the victory, and shame of this cowardiness, and fear of that dreadful and eternal captivity, let us put on our armour, the girdle of truth, the breastplate of righteousness, the helmet of salvation, and the buckler of faith, a sure defence against all the fiery darts of Satan; and let us take in our hand the sword of the Spirit, the word of God, the dint whereof he dare not abide. "Resist the devil, and he will flee from you." Resist him in faith, in prayer, and in the word. "Be crucified unto the world," even as strangers which are not of the world. "For we have here no abiding city." Chastise the body with watchings, with labour, with fastings. It is a great victory to overcome the devil, a greater to overcome the world, and the greatest of all to overcome thyself, even thine own flesh. To him that overcometh shall be given a crown. But he that is overcome shall be the continual bondman of Satan, our vile and cruel enemy. Let us so strive that we may overcome. He only that "striveth lawfully" shall be crowned.

_{Gal. v. [17.]}
_{1 Pet. ii. [11.]}
_{Eph. vi. [13—17.]}
_{James iv. 7.}
_{Gal. vi. [14.]}
_{Heb. xiii. [14.]}
_{2 Tim. ii. [5.]}

13. This war at length will have an end, a change. Man is mutable; subject to change, and desirous of change. No man is long contented with his own estate, be it never so excellent. The angel would change, to be like unto God. Adam would change, to be as wise as he that made him. Absolon would change, and sit in his father's seat. Solomon would have change of wives. The Israelites would change Moses and Aaron, both magistrate and minister. They would needs change their judge for a king, their Samuel for Saul. The Sichemites would change their religion. The Israelites would change manna, the food of angels, for the fleshpots of Egypt. The wavering Jews changed Christ for Barabbas, their Saviour for a murderer. We are like affected to them, in liking and loving change; change of meat, change of apparel, change of manners. We change simple dealing into crafty undermining, faithfulness into treachery, truth into falsehood, liberality into

_{2. Our warfare shall have a change. Change desired of all men.}
_{2 Sam. xv. [10.]}
_{1 Kings xi. [3.]}
_{Num. xvi. [3.]}
_{1 Sam. viii. [5.]}
_{Gen. xxxiv.}
_{Exod. xvi. [24.]}
_{Num. xi. [3. 4—6.]}
_[Matt. xxvii. 21.]

covetousness, humility into pride, chastity into lewdness, mercy into malice, light into darkness, day into night, all virtue into all vice. And, that which is more monstrous, sheep are changed into goats; shepherds into wolves; and, as Bernard saith, "prelates into Pilates; nurses of the church into robbers of the church[1]." The hearts and tongues of men are changed, and of single both made double. Our times breed men of the nature of the fish polypus, which can change itself into all colours to deceive. And, as he saith in the comedy, "There is a change of all things[2]."

The change which Job looked for.

14. But while we are thus occupied about these choppings and changings, we seem never to remember that great change whereof Job here speaketh; which he daily looked and longed for. And that is the change of this mortal life, looking for that great and glorious resurrection. Death is here termed a change. This change is certain: all flesh must die. The time till this change doth come, not long: the days of man are short and miserable. The time when this change will come, uncertain.

Unto this change all are subject.

15. We all must die. God gave a law to our father Adam, forbidding him to eat of the fruit; adding the penalty of death if he did. Adam transgressed: the penalty [Gen. iii. 19.] was inflicted. The sentence of death was this: "Dust thou art, and into dust thou shalt return." In our father's fall we fell; and of his punishment his children are Heb. ix.[27.] partakers. This is a statute made by the three states: "It Job xiv.[5.] is appointed to all men once to die." "Thou hast appointed 1 Kings ii. man his bounds, which he cannot pass." This is "the [2.] J'sal. lxxxix. way of all flesh:" "what man is he that liveth and shall [48.] not see death?" Neither king nor kesar could ever be 2 Kings xx. dispensed withal from this statute. The good king Ezekias [3, 6.] sought and sued unto God for a dispensation; but it would not be granted: only he obtained the prolonging of his days for a few years. This law standeth fast: this debt

[1 Papæ, cardinalium, episcoporum, aliorumque pontificiorum satellitum multiplicem impietatem graviter reprehendit, eos antichristi ministros, non doctores, sed seductores; non pastores, sed impostores; non prælatos, sed Pilatos appellans.—Bernard, Lib. II. cap. 8, De Vita ejus.—Such is the reference given in Catal. Testium Veritatis, Genev. 1608, cols. 1379, 80: but in Bernard. Op. Par. 1690, which has been consulted, the passage does not appear in the place indicated.—ED.]

[2 Ter. Eun. II. ii. 45.—ED.]

is due unto all flesh. And the time that we have before the day of payment is not long.

16. The days of man are short: the number of his months is known only to the Lord. All creatures now wax old with the aged world. This is even the last hour: the world cannot continue long. Mathusela lived 969 years. If in our age we reach to 80, it is with sorrow and labour. "Thou hast made my days as it were a span long," saith David. "All flesh is grass," saith the prophet, "and all the glory thereof as the flower of the field:" both the grass and the flower quickly fade and fall away; and the flower sooner than the grass. *No man far from the time of his change.* *Gen. v. [27.]* *Psal.xc.[10.] Psal. xxxix. [5.] Isai. xl. [6, 7.]*

17. The people are the grass, and will abide the withering. The flower is the nobility, set aloft in great beauty: yet every frost causeth the flower to fade, and every blast of wind ruffleth the leaves, and even shaketh them off. This all times do teach; and the action we have in hand doth presently put us in mind thereof. This mighty king, this great prince, Charles the French king, whose funeral we now celebrate, in his young years, in his flourishing age, in the perfect strength of his body, when he minded weighty matters and great attempts, even then was he stopped in the midst of his race, and the line of his life cut off. This glorious flower is faded and fallen away. How soon! How suddenly! It falleth out in experience true which is written by Ecclesiasticus: "The life of potentates endureth not long." Some, though few, are consumed with the cares of the commonwealth. The good king David complaineth that his bones were even dried up with the cares he took for his country. Some are wasted away by wantonness, as Commodus, Claudius, Nero, Alexander the Great. Some are shortened by ambition: they will never leave climbing till they catch a fall. That cut off the days of Absolon: that brought Haman to the tree. Some God taketh away because the world is not worthy of them; and some, because they are not worthy of it. He cut off Josias; for "his soul pleased God; therefore he made haste to take him away" from the midst of iniquities. He cut off Achab, Agag, and Herod, because they were "bloody" and "wily" men; therefore they did "not live out half their days." *The mightiest soonest changed.* *Ecclus. x. [9.]* *Psal. cii. [3.]* *2 Sam. xviii. [14, 15.] Esther vii. [10.]* *2 Kings xxiii. [29.] [Wisd. iv. 14.] 1 Kings xxii. [35.] Psal. lv. [23.]*

18. So true it is: "Man that is born of a woman hath but a short time to live;" and it is even as true that followeth in the same sentence, that "his few days are full of misery. He cometh up, and is cut down like a flower: he fleeth as it were a shadow, and continueth not." Man's life is as unlasting as a flower. He cometh up, and is cut down as a flower. He vanisheth away like a shadow of a flower. And while he liveth, he is full of misery. He cometh into the world with sorrow and weeping: whilst he liveth in the world he is hated of the world, or else (which is worse) of God; assaulted of Satan in continual war; subject to the manifold diseases both of the body and of the soul, the one truly miserable, but the other most intolerable. He never continueth in one state. To-day in his princely throne, to-morrow in his dusty grave; to-day placed in great authority, to-morrow cast out of countenance; to-day in high favour, to-morrow in high displeasure; now rich, now poor; now in wealth, now in wo; now sound, now sick; now joyful, now full of sorrow; to-day a man, to-morrow nothing. O how short, how changeable, and how miserable is the state of mortal man! which we neglect, but Jacob well considered, when he answered Pharaoh of his age, "The days of my peregrination are *pauci et mali;* few and evil." "Walk therefore circumspectly," saith St Paul, "for the days are evil." We are fallen into those evil days and perilous times, of the which both Paul and Peter forewarned us. These may be rightly called dismal days. The god of this world hath blinded the eyes of men. "Let him therefore that standeth (I say it again) take heed that he fall not." Let us expect our change, and pray the Lord to increase our faith; that we may be able to stand before him in that day, that dreadful day of his just judgment.

19. As our days here are short and evil, so is the time of our change either to better or worse uncertain. "What is most certain? Death. What most uncertain? The time of death," saith Bernard[1]. We are all tenants at will, uncertain how long to remain in this our earthly

---

[1 Nil mortalibus vel morte certius, vel incertius horâ mortis: siquidem tamquam fur in nocte, ita veniet.—Bernard. Op. Par. 1690. Epist. cv. Tom. I. Vol. I. col. 109.—ED.]

tabernacle. Of this we are put in mind in the Lord's prayer. Give us "this day" our daily bread. We say "this day," as uncertain of to-morrow. It is written of one that, being invited to a dinner on the morrow by his friend, he answered: "These many days I never had to-morrow." Therefore saith St James, let us not appoint for to-morrow, but with conditions: "If the Lord will," and "if we live." The Egyptians, considering the uncertainty of man's days, were accustomed at their great feasts in the midst of their jollity to have one suddenly come forth with an image of death, and shewing it to the guests to pronounce this speech: "Eat, drink, be merry: within a while thou shalt be such as this." And the Israelites dwelt in tents, uncertain of their abode, ever ready to shift: whereby they represent unto us our peregrination in this mortality; wherein because we are uncertain to stay long, we ought at all times to be ready to depart, so that we may enter into that celestial Canaan. This time of man's life and death God hath made uncertain for two causes; the one, that his mind might not be troubled; the other this present text giveth, and it is the last member of our division. James iv. [15.]

20. This end or change is daily to be looked for. Seeing that death is certain, our days short, and the time of our dissolution unknown; wisdom would have us to put ourselves in readiness, looking for our change, the end of this bad life, that it may be to us the beginning of a better. It is good counsel which St Augustine giveth: "Death looketh for thee every where: if thou be wise, look thou every where for him." The remembrance of this our end would bridle sin well in us. "Remember thy end; and thou shalt never do amiss." Christ saith, "Watch; for you know not at what hour he will come." He cometh suddenly as a thief in the night. "The Lord will come when thou lookest not for him, and in an hour that thou knowest not." Let us watch therefore with the wise virgins, having our lamps continually burning, waiting for the coming of the bridegroom, that we may enter with him into his joy. 3. The change of this life continually to be looked for; the first change by death.

Ecclus. vii. [36.]
Mark xiii. [35.]
Luke xii. [46.]
Matt. xxv. [4.]

21. And as man's life is short, so is the coming of Christ at hand. Wait; for it "will surely come, and will The second, by the second coming of Christ.

not stay." "The time is short." This we know; though it be not in us to know the definite point of time, which to the angels of heaven is unrevealed. But Christ hath set down certain tokens of the end, which all are fulfilled; and amongst others he saith, "Iniquity shall abound: charity shall wax cold: the gospel shall be preached in all the world; and then shall come the end." Never more iniquity; never less charity; the gospel never so liberally taught: behold the end. Peter saith, "The end of all things is at hand." If then at hand, how much nearer now! If those were the latter times, surely these are the last times, the very end of the end. Hear the counsel of a wise man: "Make no tarrying to turn unto the Lord, and put not off from day to day; for suddenly shall the wrath of the Lord break forth, and in thy security thou shalt be destroyed, and thou shalt perish in the time of vengeance."

Hab. ii. [3.]
1 Cor. vii. [29.]
1 John ii. [18.]

Matt. xxiv. [12, 14.]

1 Pet. iv. [7.]

Ecclus. v. [7.]

The first danger of not expecting continually our change.

22. By procrastination, driving off, and forslowing our turning to the Lord and looking for our change, three great dangers do ensue. First, if we slumber and sleep in security, if we accustom ourselves with sinning, not looking for our change, neither remembering the fearful coming of our Lord; our custom will wax to be our nature, and hard will it be for us to rise from sin, in which we have been so long and so deeply buried. After that Lazarus had lain four days in the grave, Christ used many circumstances for the raising of him again, who raised others with a word.

John xi. [39—44.]

The second danger.

23. Secondly, it is dangerous in respect of the sudden taking away which happeneth to many, insomuch that they have not time sufficiently to think upon God, or once to cry, "Lord, help." The first age, in all their jollity, not thinking on death, were suddenly drowned; the Sodomites suddenly by fire consumed; Pharaoh with his army swallowed up in the sea; the Israelites gnawn of deadly serpents; Dathan with his complices eaten up of the earth; Herod suddenly devoured with lice; the rich man, after all his provision, suddenly smitten with death; lying Ananias suddenly fell down dead; Eglon the Moabite, Abner the captain, suddenly murdered by the sword of Aod[1] and Joab. All histories, all ages, are full of like examples.

Gen. vii. [22.]
Gen. xix. [24, 25.]
Exod. xiv. [28.]
Num. xxi. [6.]
Num. xvi. [31—33.]
Acts xii. [23.]
Luke xii. [20.]
Acts v. [5.]
Judg. iii. [20—22.]
2 Sam. iii. 27.]

[1 Aod—Ehud.—ED.]

24. The third danger is, that, in driving off to the last day, we shall find hard time then to turn unto our God. Sickness will sore disquiet us, Satan will extremely tempt us, our friends with talking and craving will molest us, the terror of our ugly conscience will astonish us: so that hard it will be for us then to be rightly mindful of our end, and so in this extremity to turn to God, that he in our extreme case may turn his mercy towards us. And, as St Augustine saith, "The remedies come too late when peril of death is near[1]." Remember that which he also saith elsewhere: "He that hath lived well cannot die ill; and he can hardly die well that hath lived ill[2]." He saith hardly, not unpossibly, but questionless very hardly.

The third.

Aug. de doct. Christ.

25. "Put thine household in an order, for thou shalt die, and not live," saith Esay to Ezekias. Give thy goods whilst they be thine, for after death thou hast no interest in them. "Stand with your loins girded and your shoes on your feet, and your staff in your hand; that you may be ready." We have slept too long in sin, to our great danger. Let us now awake to our speedy deliverance. It is sufficient for us that we have spent the time that is past of our life after the will of the gentiles. Let us now imitate that worthy soldier, who, after long warring under Adrian the emperor, returned home, and lived as Christ's soldier a most godly life, and after seven years died, and caused to be written on his tomb, "Here lieth Similis, a man that *was* many years, and *lived* but seven." Let us, these few years that we have,

Motives to wishing and looking for our change.
2 Kings xx. [1.]
Exod. xii. [11.]

1 Pet. iv. [3.]

[1 The passage intended here, to which also the reference is made in page 171, is probably the following: Quotidie expavescenda transitûs nostri et commigrationis incerta hora; quæ et modò vel insperata vel subita sunt, et in æternum remediis caritura sunt. Præveniendus est dies, qui prævenire consuevit.—August. Op. Par. 1683. Sermo cliv. 10. De Passione Domini. Tom. v. Appendix, col. 272. The Benedictine editors do not consider this sermon a genuine work of Augustine, but say, Non indignus est Fausto Semipelagiano.—ED.]

[2 The reference to the treatise De Doctrina Christiana appears to be inaccurate: the following is doubtless the passage quoted: Mori malè times, malè vivere non times. Corrige malè vivere, time malè mori. Sed noli timere: Non potest malè mori, qui benè vixerit.— August. Op. Par. 1685. De Disciplina Christiana 13. Tom. vi. col. 588. —ED.]

live them to God. For that only is worthy to be called a life, which bringeth us from a transitory life to an eternal, from a miserable to a most blessed and glorious. Let the trump ever sound in our ears: "Rise, you dead, come unto judgment." Let us daily remember that we must die; and so shall we contemn these things present, and make haste to things to come. Truly, if we shall rightly consider the vanity of the world, the miserable estate of man, that we are here but pilgrims, "and have no permanent city," that whilst we live in this rotten tabernacle we are mere strangers and men from home, that we daily slide, yea and fall into sin, that our righteous God hateth it, and that the stipend thereof is eternal death, and withal propose before our eyes the celestial kingdom, the crown of glory, the eternal felicities which the Lord hath prepared in heaven for such as love his coming, we will not only watchfully look for, but most greedily desire the same: in our heart we will daily cry with St John, "Come quickly, Lord Jesu:" we will be like affected to St Paul, desiring to depart hence and to be with Christ: we will sigh and mourn as he did, "O wretched man that I am, who shall deliver me from the body of this death?" We will, with Job, even be weary of our lives; and cry, with Elias, "It is enough, O Lord, take my soul:" it will be with us as it was with all the blessed patriarchs, and prophets, and apostles, and holy men, now glorious saints in heaven; who continually being here thirsted after God, and now most blessedly have enjoyed him: we will utterly contemn this earthly trash, worldly vanities, and transitory things, and desire and "seek those things which are above, where Christ sitteth on the right hand of God:" we will, whilst we have our being here, which is but a while, humble ourselves to walk with our God; and although we tread this earth, yet "our conversation will be in heaven; from whence also we look for the Saviour, the Lord Jesus Christ, who will change our vile body, that it may be fashioned like to his glorious body, according to the working whereby he is able to subdue all things unto himself."

Heb. xiii. [14.]
2 Cor. v. [1.]

2 Tim. iv. [8.]

Rev. xxii. [20.]
[Phil. i. 23.]
Rom. vii. [24.]
[Job vii. 15, 16.]
1 Kings xix. [4.]

Col. iii. [1.]

Phil. iii. [20, 21.]

A repetition of that which hath been spoken.

26. Thus we see that funerals are christian, ancient, and commendable; that the causes are sundry, good, and

godly; yet neither our preaching nor prayer, neither any other ceremony nor circumstance, can profit the dead, but are helping comforts to such as live; that only in this life mercy remaineth for man, and after this life only judgment. As we now sow, so we shall then reap. Here we are Christ's soldiers to fight a good fight; so we may hope for the crown of glory. Which thing Job doth well declare unto us: first telling us that we are in continual war; wherein both the generals, the captains, the trumpeters, and common soldiers, that is, the prince, the nobility, the ministers, and the people, must take to them a good courage, be faithful, dutiful, and manful, in fighting the battle of the Lord; every man keep his standing and answer his office. But we must all strive for God's truth, and not struggle against it, not ambitiously contending for superiority, or maliciously how to undermine and wrong one another. This is no lawful combat, no christian war: this is not to fight a good fight. But we must wage war against our common and our deadly enemies, the devil, the world, and the flesh. The devil is a roaring lion, a subtile serpent, who hath overcome the perfectest, the strongest, the wisest. The world is all wrapped in wickedness. The flesh wrestleth against the Spirit. We must put on the armour of God, resist the devil and he will fly from us, crucify the world, chasten our flesh, and bring it into subjection unto the more noble part, our spirit. At length this our warfare will come to an end: we may look for a change. All the world is mutable, and of all the things in the world man most mutable. We would change our condition, our magistrates, our ministers, our religion, all things. But the change that Job speaketh of we least remember: we little think upon the change of this mortal life. We may assure ourselves that we all shall die. It is an act of parliament that shall never be repealed: it is the way of all flesh. The days of man are short, and wretched: short, a span long; wretched, full of miseries. All flesh is as grass, and as a flower: both do fade, but the flower sooner. Cares, wantonness, ambition, yea, God in sundry respects cutteth off both the good and the bad, good flowers, and bad flowers; but all as flowers. The time of our change is uncertain, and often sudden; that our mind be not troubled, that we always be in readiness. Job's example admonisheth us of this: "I look still when my changing shall come." Let us after his example daily look for our change. Let us expect the coming of Christ. He cometh in post: the forewarnings are fulfilled: iniquity aboundeth, christian charity is frozen, the gospel is preached: then is the end. Let us not slumber in security, or drive off to return unto our God. For it is hard for the buried in sin to rise. Man often is suddenly smitten, that he hath no time to repent. In his last day he is disquieted by sickness, by Satan, yea, by his friends, yea by his own conscience. Let us live in reverent expectation of the Lord, with our loins girt, and with our lamps light, and let the trumpet of judgment ever sound in our ears: it will well stir up our hearts. Let us live these few days that remain unto the Lord, whom we ought to have served all our days. And lastly, recounting the vanity of the world, the miserable state of this life, and the inestimable blessedness of the life to come, let us, with John, Paul, Elias, the blessed servants and saints of God, look for the appearance of the coming of Christ Jesus; who will place us upon the right hand of his Father, and give us possession of our inheritance, that we may have the perfect fruition of all the treasures prepared for us by our God in heaven. To him even the Father, the Son, and the Holy Ghost, three Persons, and one God of eternal majesty, be all honour, &c.

THE TENTH SERMON

A SERMON

PREACHED AT HIS FIRST COMING TO YORK.

LUKE I.

74. *That, being delivered out of the hands of our enemies, we may serve him without fear,*
75. *In holiness and righteousness before him all the days of our life.*

THE greater and better part of holy scripture either setteth forth God's goodness towards us, or our duty towards him. In these few but most pithy words of Zachary both are comprehended. The great benefit we receive from God is our redemption in Christ. The duty which we owe to him again is in holiness and righteousness of life continually to serve him. He toucheth our redemption in one word, but in many words explicateth the duty which we owe for it unto our Redeemer; giving us hereby secretly to understand, that men are easily taught to know, but hardly brought to do, their master's will. We are rich in all speech and understanding, but in deeds full poor and barren. We know much, but little do we; although, amongst other things known, this be one, that "he which knoweth his master's will, and doth it not, shall be beaten with many stripes;" and this another, that "not every one that saith, Lord, Lord, but he which doth the will of the Father, shall enter into the kingdom of heaven." We are for all this such as those Pharisees were whom Christ reproveth, because they said, and did not. Even such we are become, as Jude doth describe: "Wells without water, clouds without rain, trees without fruit, dead;" though not as yet "pulled up by the roots." We are hearers of the word, and yet scantly that: but workers of the word we are not. God grant that the word wherein we now glory, be not one day to our shame; that the gospel of salvation

As we have redemption at the hands of God, so he at ours should have the duty of continual holiness and righteousness of life.

1 Cor. i. [5.]

Luke xii. [47.]

Matt. vii. [21.]

Matt. xxiii. [3.]

Jude [12.]

bear not witness against us, and condemn us; that the words which Christ hath spoken unto us heap not judgment upon our heads; that this be not our condemnation also, "that, light being come into the world," we "love darkness more than light." Surely, if we continue to profess in words and deny in deeds, to crucify to ourselves our Saviour Christ afresh, to feed upon our vomit, and to welter in the loathsome mire of our filthy sin; we shall make ourselves "unworthy of the kingdom of God," we cannot claim the benefit of Christ's merits, neither be partakers of that glorious redemption which Zachary here remembereth unto us: but the blood of Christ shall be upon our heads, and we shall perish in our sin as being guilty of our own damnation. "Thy destruction, O Israel, is of thyself."

John iii. [19.]
Heb. vi. [6.]
2 Pet. ii. [22.]
Acts xiii. [46.]
Hos. xiii. [9.]

Our redemption, the end thereof, to serve him; the manner of service, in holiness, &c.

2. Wherefore, to avoid God's perpetual indignation and our perpetual confusion, let us follow the counsel of Zachary; who, instructed by the Spirit of wisdom, teacheth us, first, that we are redeemed; secondly, that the end of our redemption is that we may serve him that hath redeemed us; thirdly, after what sort we should serve him. Where he saith, that we are delivered out of the hands of our enemies, it argueth that we once were in their hands. We are freed; therefore we were bond. And in this point we have to consider, first, our bondage; then, the mean of our deliverance; and lastly, the cause by which we were delivered.

1. All men by nature bondmen.
Psal. li. [5.]
Rom. vi. [23.]
Rom. v. [12.]

3. Adam through his rebellion lost his freedom, and became a bondman; and all we through him and in him are bond, "conceived and born in sin," the children of wrath, bond unto Satan, and servants unto wickedness; the deserved "reward" whereof is "death," even double death, this our present mortality, and everlasting damnation. "As by one man sin entered into the world, and by sin death; so death went over all men, inasmuch as all men sinned." With Adam we lost God's first favour and protection: with him the gracious image of God was blotted out in us also: with him we were expelled out of paradise, cast upon the face of the cursed earth, thrown into the hands of our cruel enemy, whose livery we did put on, and under whose miserable thraldom we lived. In this fall

from God we lost our immortality, we lost our free will, we lost our wisdom, our virtue, our light, our glory, our joy, our heaven, our God. Our perverse heart became prone to all evil, and full of all sinfulness: we became unwise in our judgment, disobedient to our God, deceived and deceiving, serving lusts and deadly pleasures, living in maliciousness and envy, hateful and hating one another. We were " without hope, and without God in this present world;" all blinded in ignorance, and wrapped in all sin. For as we changed our master, so changed we our minds and manners also, and for Christ we served antichrist; we threw away the love of God's eternal truth, and, according to the ignorance of our blinded hearts, hungerly fed upon all poisoned error, and plunged ourselves into all wickedness. This was our most miserable estate: thus we were; and thus we are by nature. This was the pitiful condition of all human flesh. [Eph. ii. [12.]]

4. Let us now see the mean of this our deliverance from this deadly captivity. We are ransomed out of the hands of our enemies, pulled out of the jaws of Satan, freed from the servitude of antichrist, of ignorance, and of sin, only by the mediation of our Redeemer Jesus Christ. He is the Lion of the tribe of Judah, which alone hath trodden the wine-press, alone hath fought the battle, in fighting achieved the victory, and by vanquishing brought our enemy Satan under our feet for ever. On the cross with his blood he blotted out the handwriting that was against us: he spoiled our foes of their prey: he took even captivity itself captive: in a word, he wrought our full and complete deliverance. The price of our redemption was not gold, but blood; the precious blood of our blessed Saviour. The blood of Jesus Christ doth deliver us from all sin. And as he died to redeem us, so rose he again to justify us. In rising again he triumphed over death now conquered: he burst the gates and chains of hell, and set our feet in a place of great liberty: he clothed us with his righteousness; reconciled us to his Father; of enemies, made us friends; of no people, the people of God; of strangers, citizens with angels and inhabitants of heaven, free denizens with the children of God, and heirs of his everlasting kingdom. This deliverance out of [By Christ we are redeemed out of bondage.] [Col. ii. 14.] [Eph. iv. [8.]]

bondage, this redemption, this kingdom of God, and everlasting inheritance, our Christ hath purchased, and God hath granted to all such as thankfully will receive him. ^{John i. [12.]} "As many as received him, to them he gave power to be made the sons of God;" and to receive him is to believe in him; for so it followeth, "to them which believe in his name." Faith therefore is the mean to make us partakers of that great redemption in Christ Jesus. Hereunto ^{Acts x. [43.]} "all the prophets bear witness, that whosoever shall believe in him, by his name he shall receive remission of sins," and withal eternal life.

^{Us he hath delivered after a more peculiar and special manner.} 5. And as Christ hath delivered all his out of the captivity of Satan and sin, so hath he also us after a more special and peculiar manner out of that den of thieves, out of that prison of Romish servitude, out of the bloody claws of that cruel and proud antichrist. Our God hath used our Moses to deliver us from Egyptiacal servitude, that we may serve him henceforward in freedom of conscience: he hath led us out of a marvellous darkness into a marvellous light: he hath given us (for his gift it is) an understanding heart to know God the Father, and him whom he hath sent, Jesus Christ, unto whom by this star, his shining gospel, he hath conducted us. This truth of God hath discovered, yea, and discomfited also gross error. For the want of this light was the cause of all our blindness, which is the mother of all superstition, which is the enemy to all religion. That now we have eyes to see, and hearts to understand, there is no other cause besides the mercy of our Redeemer.

^{The cause of our deliverance is the mercy of him who hath delivered us.} 6. For of the cause of our gracious deliverance thus Zachary recordeth. It was, saith he, "that he might shew mercy towards our fathers." God made a covenant with our father Abraham, confirmed it with an oath, not that it might be surer, but that we might be more assured of it: the covenant was that he would shew mercy, and in mercy work our deliverance. To perform this covenant of grace and mercy made unto our fathers, and comprehending also us, he gave up his only-begotten Son in the fulness of time to death. There was no other motive why he should work our deliverance but only this, his mercy. "God therefore, ^{Eph. ii. [4, 5.]} which is rich in mercy, for the great love wherewith he

loved us, even when we were dead by sin, revived us with Christ." The cause of our redemption was his good-will only. For "by grace" we are delivered. He did it according to the good pleasure of his own will, according to the riches of his grace. So that all the steps to this our redemption are built upon mercy only. God in mercy made covenant of our deliverance, in mercy confirmed it with an oath, in mercy through the merits of Christ performed his promise to us; so that our whole redemption is free, not due; of mercy, and not of merits: "Not by works which [Tit. iii. [5.]] we have wrought, but according to his great mercy he hath saved us." Man never brought one stone to this building: man never laid one finger to this work: it is the only building and work of God, who in tender compassion hath both begun and finished it. We may well wonder that God with so merciful eyes looked upon so miserable and so sinful creatures, that the Son of God would die for the redemption of his enemies. This doth indeed commend his love; seeing that all which he hath done is of mere mercy in himself, without any shadow of merit in us.

7. Now that Christ hath delivered us from Satan, [2. We were redeemed to the end we might serve him.] and that with so dear a price, let us fall no more into the claws of that roaring lion, lest he utterly devour us. He is cast out of our house: let him enter in no more, lest he bring seven with him worse than himself, and then our evil end be far worse than our bad beginning. Now that Christ hath cleansed us from our sin, let us not, swine-like, return to wallow in that slime again. "Thou [John v. [14.]] art made whole," saith Christ: I have washed away thy sin with my blood: "Go and sin no more, lest a worse thing happen unto thee." Now that Christ in a mighty arm hath freed us from Pharaoh, from the house of bondage, let us return no more to the flesh-pots of Egypt: let us not lust after quails; for if we feed upon them, we shall surfeit of them to our destruction. Let us serve no more him that serveth Satan, that undoubted man of sin. And lastly, now that Christ hath opened our blinded eyes, and hath poured understanding into our hearts, now that he hath given us a lantern to guide our feet, let us tumble no more in darkness; but as the children of

light walk in the light honestly, as becometh men in so clear noon-day. For the end of our redemption is that we may serve him without fear, that hath so dearly redeemed us.

Man born unto labour and service.

8. First, we must serve. Secondly, we must serve no other but him. Thirdly, him we must serve without fear. We were created, man is born unto service and labour, as birds unto flight. We were not redeemed and bought with a price to be idle and do nothing, but to glorify him in body and spirit that hath bought us. We are not called to stand or sit still, but to walk every one in that vocation wherewith he is called. The scriptures are full of such speeches as these, "Go," "walk," "work," "sweat," "why stand ye idle?"—to teach us that service is required at our hands.

Matt. viii. [4.]
John xii. [35.]
2 Tim. ii. [15.]
Gen. iii. [19.]
Matt. xx. [6.]
We must serve him, and no other.
Matt. vi. [24.]

9. God delivered us, to the end that being delivered we might now serve him, as heretofore we served Satan. We are not now our own men to serve whom or how we list; but we are his to serve him as he prescribeth. "No man can serve two masters:" we have yielded and promised our service to him; therefore besides him we may serve no other.

Not mammon, as covetous men and usurers do. Eph. v. [5.]

10. We may not serve mammon; for that is made to serve us. The covetous man, which serveth his money, is justly called of Paul "an idolater." For he is our God, not whom we profess, but in whom we repose our trust, and whom we serve and obey. When the Lord commandeth one thing, and his money persuades another, will not his obedience declare whom he maketh his God? God saith,

Luke vi. [35.]

"Lend freely, and look for no gain." But will the usurer, whose money is his God, remit his interest because of this, because the Lord hath so charged him? No: he will not so let go his ten, or twenty, or thirty in the hundred. To him the glory of God, yea, and his own soul, is vile: nothing is precious but only money. What the prophet speaketh of putting forth money to usury, he full little regardeth; but feedeth still upon his mast, and blesseth himself when he waxeth fat, not perceiving that God hath already plagued him with a plague of all plagues, the obduration of his heart. And although that God hath given him over into a dull and senseless mind, his ears being so dammed up that nothing can have entrance to move or touch his hard heart; yet he still blesseth himself and his accursed soul. Thou usurer, thou idolater, that dost glory in thy shame, in thy evil-gotten gold, dost thou not know that thy wealth shall melt like snow before the sun? thinkest thou still to hold it? "O fool, this night shall they take away thy soul," perhaps this instant; and then whose is all this? After that Zaccheus fell to the service of Christ, and that Christ entered into his house, he presently forsook the service of mammon, made a large restitution of that which he had gained by such unlawful means, and then began to be liberal, not only to lend freely, but to give for nothing: he gave the one half of all his goods to the poor. If God would at this day work thus in the heart of one Zaccheus, a rich usurer, how many poor might be relieved by such a restitution! He might maintain many a needy man, and save his own soul. Well, this one thing we know. This word, that proceedeth out of God's mouth against usury, "shall not return in vain:" if it cannot work reformation, it will work confusion. *Luke xii. [20.] Luke xix. [8.] Isai. lv. [11.]*

11. As these serve their money, so there are some *Domino non servientes sed suo ventri*, "servants to the belly, and not to the Lord." He serveth the belly who frameth himself to be of any religion, so that in this world he may live by it; when popery hath the upper hand, then a papist; when the gospel is in due estimation, a protestant; all things to all men, that somewhat may be gained or saved to himself. He maketh no difference between the mass and the communion, Christ and Belial; but for his belly sake will halt on both sides, serve all times and turns. Such a one was Leontius bishop of Antioch; who, being in heart an Arian, covered his religion, and joined with the council of Nice in outward profession of the truth[1]. So his soul was led by the devil, and his body by the world. *Not the belly, as time-servers. Theod. lib. ii. cap. 24.*

12. Some, and those many, are servants of men, as those which in matters of religion wholly hang their souls upon human authorities and judgments. So did the Corinthians: "I hold of Paul, I of Cephas, and I of Apollos." So do all the pope's favourites. And so do those that choose to themselves new masters, new teachers, according to their itching and wandering ears, esteeming such and *Not men, as the popish faction, &c. 1 Cor. i. [12.] 2 Tim. iv. [3.]*

[¹ Theod. Hist. Eccl. Amst. 1695. p. 106.—ED.]

despising others. So do they which praise and flatter men in their folly, thereby to win themselves estimation with them which have men's persons in admiration for gain's sake. Finally, so do they which repose their trust in the merits of men, that seek justification or remission of sins either by their own works or by the deserts of others. For to know that he is our redemption, sanctification, and justice, is no small part of God's service: to give this to any other is to take it from him; which whoso doeth is not worthy to be named his servant. He that serveth him must serve him alone.

Not the world, sin, and Satan.
Rom. vi. [12.]

13. Not him and the world; for the world is wholly set on vanity and mischief: it hateth him, and therefore we must hate it. If ye be his servants, let not sin bear rule in your bodies, or have dominion over you. We must die unto sin, that we may live unto God through Jesus Christ our Lord. He that doth sin is the servant of the devil: the devil is but a bad master to serve: he is a liar, a thief, and a murderer; and he entertaineth no servants but such as be like himself, whose wages are fire, chains, brimstone, darkness, wailing, howling, and gnashing of teeth, in a word, everlasting death and damnation. We are not ransomed out of the hands of our enemies, to serve these masters, mammon, the belly, men, sin, the world, or the devil; but we are redeemed to serve him only, to serve our Christ, our Redeemer, that hath full dearly bought us.

Deut. vi. [13.]

"Thou shalt worship the Lord thy God, and him only shalt thou serve."

We must serve with fear, child-like, not slavish.
Psal. ii. [11.]

14. Him we must serve "without fear." In the psalm it is said, "Serve the Lord with fear, and rejoice unto him with reverence." And here we are taught to serve him without fear. As there is but one God, so the scripture is always one. There is a fear which children have towards their parents, and a fear of servants towards their masters. God will be feared of us as children, but not as servants; or if as servants, not as slaves. The believing Christian, the regenerate child of God, who through faith in Christ is certain of his deliverance from the devil and from hell, assured of remission of sins and of life everlasting in the death and resurrection of Jesus Christ our Saviour, he serveth in the reverent fear of love, and not

in that dreadful fear of death and everlasting damnation, wherewith the reprobate mind is daunted. He feareth not death, for he is sure of life: he feareth not damnation, for he is assured of salvation: he believeth that which Christ hath promised, and doubteth nothing of the obtaining of that which Christ hath procured for him. He is surely persuaded with St Paul, that "neither death, nor life, nor tribulation, nor affliction, nor any thing present, or to come, shall separate him from the love of God, which is in Christ Jesus." He feareth therefore neither the sting of death, nor the power of Satan. But this certainty of God's love towards him in Christ, and the testimony of his love towards God again, casteth out all fear of eternal punishment. "For ye have not," saith the apostle, "received again the spirit of bondage unto fear; but ye have received the Spirit of adoption, by which we cry Abba, Father." The Spirit testifieth with our spirit, that God is our gracious Father; and if he our Father, we his children; and if his children, heirs of his glorious kingdom. The preaching of the law letteth us see our sin, but no remedy against the sting thereof; so that it maketh us fear, and with trembling look for the reward of sin, which is everlasting death. But the Spirit of adoption by the preaching of the gospel telleth us that in Christ we have remission of sins; we are reconciled unto God, and adopted by him; we are his chosen children, and may boldly and joyfully call him Father. And this certainty of our salvation the Spirit of God testifieth to our spirit, whereby we put away all servile fear of punishment, being assured of God's constant favour and eternal love towards us; who never leaveth unfinished that which he hath begun, nor forsaketh him whom he hath chosen.

Rom. viii. [38.]

1 Cor. xv. [55.]

Rom. viii. [15.]

15. Therefore dangerous and desperate is that doctrine of the papists which doth teach us ever to be doubtful and in suspense of our salvation. A lamentable, discomfortable, and miserable estate. Here it is in one word confounded. For Zachary saith, "we are redeemed to serve him without fear or doubtfulness." For where doubt is, there is fear; and what greater fear, than of a thing so fearful? He that will serve God, must serve him in a quiet and joyful conscience, with a sure and undoubted

Popery teacheth, instead of fear, distrust.

confidence of mercy and salvation in Christ the Lord of mercy. "With thee is mercy," saith the prophet, "that thou mayest be feared." As if he should say: Thou art full of clemency and compassion, and therefore we serve thee with a reverent, and without a servile fear; being persuaded of thy great mercy.

Psal. cxxx. [4.]

Inferiors must fear superiors.

16. Fear is ever of the inferior to the superior. It is not required in the prince to fear the subject, the master the servant, the father the child, or the husband the wife; but contrary in all. God feareth not man, his creature: man ought to fear God, who hath created him; to fear him as a loving father, and not as men do fear a fierce tyrant.

Our fear must be joined with love.

17. The true fear which is required of us is ever joined with love. The good child feareth to offend his father, for that love and reverence he beareth to him, and not in respect or for fear of punishment. The honest and well-natured wife, that truly loveth her husband, for the same cause feareth and taketh great heed lest in any thing she should offend him. Even with such fear ought we to serve our God, who is our father; our Christ, who is our spouse. Of this godly fear the prophet David saith, "Serve the Lord in fear." And again: "Fear the Lord, all ye his saints." Of this Christ speaketh: "Fear him which can destroy both body and soul." This fear great goodness and happiness do accompany. It is the beginning of true wisdom. For all wisdom without the fear of God is but earthly, fleshly, and devilish. They that have it shall be satisfied with all good things: "There is no want to them that fear him." It causeth men to decline from evil: it banisheth sin, worketh repentance in man's heart; and happy are all they that fear the Lord, as they cursed which fear him not. If the angel had feared the Lord, he had still kept his place and glorious estate, and not been made of an angel a devil, cast out of heaven into hell. If Adam had loved and feared God, he had not been banished out of paradise, and thrown upon the face of this cursed earth. If the fear of God had not of old wanted, the whole world had not been drowned. If the city of Sodoma had feared God, they might have remained in prosperity until this day. If Cain had feared God, he

Psal. ii. [11.]
Psal. xxxiv. [9.]
Matt. x. [28.]

Psal. xxxiv. [9.]

Gen. iii. [22—24.]
Gen. vii. [17—24.]
Gen. xix. [24, 25.]
Gen. iv. [8.]

had not so treacherously murdered his brother. If Cham, [Gen. ix. 22.] he had not so shamefully discovered his father. If Laban, [Gen. xxix. 23—27.] he had not so deceitfully dealt with Jacob. If Pharaoh, he would have let Israel depart when God commanded. If Israel had loved and truly feared God, they would not have [Num. xi. 4—6.] loathed manna, despised magistrates, followed fleshly lusts, murdered the prophets, crucified Christ, and persecuted his apostles. If the Corinthians had feared God, they would not have been so contentious, so proud, so adulterous; neither would they so uncharitably have judged their brethren in things indifferent: they would not have condemned marriage, the institution of God, neither in such sort profaned the holy sacraments of Christ. The fear of [1 Cor. xi. 21, 22.] God would have brought forth better fruit in all these; and the want thereof brought forth this bad fruit.

18. If the fear of God dwelt in our hearts, the gospel so truly and plentifully preached among us would no doubt bring forth far more fruit: after so many monitions, persuasions, and entreaties, we would lead a better life. When there are amongst us many that breed contention and make division, that lend out their money upon usury, that pollute their neighbour's bed with adultery, that shut up the bowels of mercy and compassion, and suffer Christ to beg, cry, and starve in the streets, that neither regard the heavenly message of their salvation, nor esteem the messenger by whom it is brought, that shew no reverence to the word of God, but manifestly hate, loathe, and despise it, is it not too clear and manifest that we fear not the Lord? *The preaching of the gospel with so little fruit is a token that the true fear of God is wanting.*

19. If the fear of God were in us, would we deal with the servants of God as we now do? The dealing of Hanun, the son of Nahash, towards David's servants was not more villainous, than the dealings of the world are with the honourable embassadors of the most high God at this day. David sent his servants to the king of the children of Ammon to comfort him, straight upon the death of his father. The malicious Ammonites, misconstruing their intent, whispered in the ear of their lord: "Thinkest thou that David doth honour thy father, or [2 Sam. x. 3.] that he hath sent comforters unto thee? Are they not rather sent as spies to search the city, and so to over- *The cruel entreating of God's messengers.*

throw it?" He had no sooner heard the name of a spy, but hands were laid upon David's servants: they were sent away with their beards half shaven, and their coats cut off in the unseemliest place, to his own everlasting ignominy and shame, which so despitefully used men sent unto him of mere love and hearty meaning. For the good king had no other drift or purpose in his heart but this: "I will shew kindness to Hanun, as his father shewed kindness unto me." The true David, the most mighty Prince, the King of all kings, hath in favour, mercy, and reconciled love, sent his embassadors, his ministers unto you, to comfort you in your griefs, and to bring you joyful tidings of a kingdom which it hath pleased his Father to bestow upon you. These messengers ought of right to be honourably received. "Entreat such with honour," saith the apostle. Nay, such messengers "are worthy of double honour." But behold, they are taken as if they were spies: they are accounted as the offscourings, refuse, and baggage of the world; not as the embassadors of the great King, but as contemptible peasants and base outcasts of men. Away they are sent loaden with spiteful words, with slanderous reproaches, injurious dealings, all kinds of contumely and disgrace. But note, of whom; of the Ammonites which fear not God, of the profanely minded atheist, of the carnal gospeller, of the zealous hypocrite, of such in whom the fear of God or the care of their souls remaineth not, of such as also spoil the patrimony of Christ, such as would not stick, I think, to sell Christ himself if they might for money, as Judas did, and to cast lots for his coat with Pilate's soldiers. This robbery and spoil, this despitefulness and ignominy, done unto David's messengers, he took in such sort as done unto himself. For the wrong or ignominy done to the messenger is done to the master who sent him, and on whose business he goeth. David would not put it up so, but revenged it. He comforted his faithful messengers, sent them new apparel, and caused them to remain at an appointed place, Jericho, until their beards were grown again; for it was ignominious to the Jews to be beardless. Afterward he addresseth forth an army of strong soldiers, who set upon the Ammonites, put them to flight,

Phil. ii. [29.]
1 Tim. v. [17.]
1 Cor. iv. [13.]

and made great mortality. And doth not Christ our king esteem the ignominy done to his messengers, as if it were done to himself? Hath he not said, "He that despiseth [Luke x. 16.] you despiseth me?" No doubt he shall comfort his afflicted and despised messengers. As they suffer for him, so shall they reign and shine in glory: "It is a righteous thing [2 Thess. i. [6—8.]] with" him to render unto them that are despised rest, but unto despisers tribulation and vengeance in the day when he shall shew himself from heaven with armies of angels in flaming fire, to the confusion of his enemies. And if in this world also he take from such unthankful Ammonites the gospel, religion, all knowledge and learning; if for the light he give them darkness, for truth lies, for knowledge blindness, for learning barbarism, for Christ Belial; they have the just reward which is due unto them that truly fear not the Lord. We must serve, we must serve him, we must serve him without servile fear.

20. But after what sort? "In holiness and righteousness before him all the days of our life." Here we are to note, first, that God himself prescribeth how men shall serve him; then, what service it is which he prescribeth. God accepteth of no service, but such as he commandeth. "Ye shall not do every one that which seemeth right [Deut. xii. [8, 32.]] unto you; but ye shall do whatsoever I enjoin you," saith the Lord. Our service is limited to that which God liketh. Their worshipping and serving of God "is in vain, which [Mark vii.[7.]] teach doctrines the precepts of men." That which men think highly of, that doth God abhor. Saul thought that [1 Sam. xv. [20—22.]] sacrifice had been service: God had liked better of his obedience. Oza[1] supposed he had done God very good [2 Sam. vi. [6, 7.]] service in holding up the ark which was like to fall: but God taught him that it was far otherwise. The scribes and Pharisees thought themselves the only men that served God, because of their long and often praying, their much fastings, their washings, their tithings, their giving of alms; but who required these things at their hands? Where hath God prescribed these kinds of outward service and worship to be done, as being acceptable to him without inward holiness and true righteousness? In the same rank with these pharisaical devices we may place those papal inventions of

[1 Oza—Uzzah.—ED.]

3. It belongeth to God to prescribe how he will be served.

masses, pilgrimages, vows, auricular confessions, and whatsoever man hath invented without the warrant of God's word, seem it never so godly and holy unto them. For the word of God is the only rule of our religion, our only direction in the service of God.

<small>He will be served in holiness and righteousness, sincerely and continually.</small>
21. The service which God hath here prescribed us is this, "To serve him in holiness and righteousness before him, all the days of our life." Herein is contained whatsoever God commandeth in his law. This is the brief of both the tables. Holiness hath relation to the former table, and righteousness to the latter: in holiness is set forth our duty towards God, in righteousness towards man. We must serve God in holiness in respect of himself: we must serve man in righteousness in respect of God. For that which we do to men, if he command it, we do it unto him. <small>[Matt. xxv. [40.]]</small> "In as much as ye have done this," saith Christ, "to one of these little ones, ye have done it to me."

<small>Our election, his will, commandment, example, calling, requireth holiness at our hands. Eph. i. [4.] 1 Thess. iv. [3, 7.] [1 Pet. i. 16.]</small>
22. Holiness is the end of our election: "He chose us before the foundations of the world, that we might be holy." Our holiness is a thing which God doth greatly desire: "This is the will of God, even your holiness." Unto holiness we are not only constrained by his commandment, but allured also by his example: "Be holy, because I am holy." Unto this we are called: "For God did not call us unto uncleanness, but unto holiness." So that, unless we esteem vilely of our own election, unless we refuse to satisfy the will, to obey the commandment, to follow the example, and to answer the vocation in which God hath called us, we must be holy.

<small>Our holiness must appear.</small>
23. And this our holiness in serving of him must not be smothered in our mind, or concealed in our chamber, but be shewed in open place. As his benefits towards us are more clear than the noon-day, so our confession of him and praise of his name must be openly in the face and eyes of the world, especially in the congregation <small>[Luke ix. 26.]</small> of his saints. "For whosoever," saith Christ, "is ashamed of me before men, I will be ashamed of him before my Father." Christ hath given us example: he made a good <small>1 Tim. vi. [13.]</small> and an open confession unto Pontius Pilate. Daniel, being <small>Dan. vi. [10.]</small> forbid by the king, prayed openly thrice a day to the God of Israel. God commanded Solomon to build him a

temple, wherein publicly he would be served and worshipped of all his people. All the people ascended up to Sion, to the house of the Lord of hosts, there publicly to serve and praise their God. Such as will be members of Christ must be knit together in one body, and in one place, with one mind and one mouth, glorify the Lord.

24. It is true that, when the church is infected and polluted with idolatry and superstition, when the house of prayer is made a den of thieves, the temple of God a synagogue of Satan, when the truth of God is persecuted with the professors thereof, then we are to serve him as we conveniently may. When public service is public idolatry, then we are to listen unto those admonitions: "Avoid the worshipping of idols:" "Bear no yoke with infidels:" "Depart, go out. Touch not that which is polluted." Rather celebrate the passover in the wilderness with Christ, than in a temple profaned and defiled with idolatry. When the gospel is persecuted, secret congregations are allowed. When Christ was crucified, the disciples kept themselves secretly together in a parlour at Jerusalem, for fear of the Jews, and there served God. Such private congregations the ecclesiastical histories plentifully set forth and commend. In such tempests, to serve our God in deserts, in hills, in dens, and holes of the earth, we must be content. But conventicles or private meetings, when the gospel of God, being strengthened with the civil hand, hath his free and safe passage, is publicly and sincerely preached, when all persecution and fear thereof is wholly vanished, have been ever suspicious, and they are the nurses of all errors. It is the property of froward sectaries, whose inventions cannot abide the light, to make obscure conventicles, when the doctrine of truth is set at liberty. The Donatists, the Arians, the Anabaptists, the Family of Love, with all others of the like sort, fostered up their errors in secret and dark corners. But such as be of the flock of the great shepherd Christ ought to assemble themselves in one sheepfold. Perversity never wants excuses, neither is satisfied with any reason; but no man can in right refuse to communicate with us in our church. It is the sanctuary of the Lord, the house of God, the ark of God, wherein the treasures of heaven are laid open for our use,

When christian assemblies to the serving of God may be secret, and when not.

1 Cor. x. [14.]
2 Cor. vi. [14.]
Isai. lii. [11.]

Acts ii. [1.]

Heb. xi. [38.]

no other than such as God hath commanded. The golden pot with manna, the flourishing rod of Aaron, and the tables of Moses; these are no bugs[1] to fray away God's children. They have nothing offered them but the heavenly food, whereupon the elect of God should feed, even that bread which Christ hath sanctified and broken unto us for our comfort.

Christian magistrates may constrain their subjects unto open assemblies where God is served.

25. Such stray sheep therefore, as will not of their own accord assemble themselves to serve the Lord in the midst of his holy congregation, may lawfully and in reason ought to be constrained thereunto. For though religion cannot be driven into men by force, yet men by force may be driven to those ordinary means whereby they are wont to be brought to the knowledge of the truth. Parents cannot constrain their children to be learned; but parents may constrain them to repair thither where they may be taught. Thus you see that God must be served of us in holiness; holiness openly declared and professed, not secretly kept and laid up only in our hearts and bosoms.

With holiness, righteousness must be joined.

26. It followeth in the words of Zachary, "And in righteousness." This righteousness hath chiefly respect to the second table, and putteth us in mind how we ought to use our neighbour. In doing right unto him, we serve the Lord Jesus, whose commandment this is, in righteousness. One lesson well observed were sufficient for this matter. If we could love our neighbours with that kindness which we do ourselves, which is the precept of the law, we would not want in any part of righteous duty towards men. "Render unto every one that which is due:" this is righteousness.

Rom. xiii. [7.]

Righteous magistrates.

27. They which are in authority are called "justices," to the end that their name might put them in mind of that duty which they owe to the commonwealth. If they do not see that laws be put in practice and execution; if in judgment they do not justly punish transgressors, and deal in deciding matters of controversy between man and man with an even hand; if for fear they cruelly cast away the innocent (for cowards been ever cruel), or for favour spare the rich; if they be men of corrupt minds, patrons of evil men, and of evil causes, for their own commodity; if they be not wise with Solomon; if they fear not God with

[1 Bugs—bugbears, objects of terror.—ED.]

Moses; if they love not the truth as David; if they hate not covetousness as did Samuel; surely they do not serve God in righteousness and justice, because they are injurious towards their neighbours.

28. The minister of God's word is also a servant. *Righteous ministers.* We are your servants, brethren, for Christ's sake, whose embassage we bring. If we be fraudulent or negligent in performing the parts of this duty, we are most unrighteous.

29. To serve in justice is the duty of every man. *Righteous rich men.* The rich man is a servant to the poor, to relieve and comfort him as he is able; for that is right, and to that end God hath made him rich, that he as a faithful steward might bestow those rich blessings upon the family and household of God. John the bishop of Constantinople, who for his liberal relieving of the needy was surnamed the Almner[1], was wont to provide daily meat for the poor, and when it was made ready, to come forth, and himself see it served. This service is of us very slenderly and slackly done: Christ's impotent and miserable members are sent away not relieved. To suffer him in his members so to beg, who hath given thee all that thou hast, is horrible ingratitude: it is not the part of a christianly affected heart, of one that serveth his Lord in righteousness.

30. The counsellor at the law is a servant to his client, *Righteous lawyers.* whom he ought to serve in righteousness. Take not excessively of the poor; for that is not right and equal. Of right you should even without money plead his cause: so God commandeth, who will no doubt in that respect pay you your fees with a bountiful hand. Take not of both parties; for that is treachery and not justice. Thou takest not those fees, but stealest them. Neglect not thy client's cause: if thou promise, perform: neither take upon thee more than thou canst well answer. If with words and subtile handling thou winnest an evil cause to another man's wrong, thou art guilty of that wrong: if thou dost by negligence lose a good cause, thou art guilty of that

[1] The archbishop probably means Joannes Eleemosynarius Alexandrin. Episc. See Annal. Eccles. Auct. Cæs. Baronio Sorano, Rom. 1599. Anno 610. Tom. VIII. pp. 212-14.—ED.]

loss, and servest not thy client nor thy God in righteousness.

Righteous men of what estate soever.
Tit. ii. [12.]

31. To conclude and knit up all in a word: of what trade or vocation soever we be, this we must know, that he only serveth God in holiness and righteousness who, denying impiety and worldly concupiscence, liveth "soberly, justly, and holily in this present world;" soberly as touching himself, justly towards his neighbour, and holily as concerning God; he that casteth off the old Adam, and putteth on Jesus Christ; he that truly repenteth, that leadeth a new life, who heareth the word and worketh it, who knoweth the will of God and doth it.

Our holiness and righteousness must be in zeal.
Rev. iii. [16, 17.]

32. And this we must do *coram ipso*, "before him." The service which we do before him must be zealous, hearty, and sincere. We may not serve God with lukewarm service, as the Laodiceans did. For then God no doubt will vomit out us, as he threatened to do them. Vehement therefore and zealous must we be for the house of God, for the glory of God, and in God's service.

With what kind of zeal we must serve.
1 Tim. i. [13.]
Rom. x. [2.]
[1 Cor. ii. 8.]

33. But every zeal God doth not accept or like of. For as there is a zeal according to knowledge, so there is a blind heady zeal, void of true knowledge, and therefore of true faith. St Paul, in his blind zeal, persecuted the church of God. The Jews, in their blind zeal, crucified their Lord Christ. "They have a zeal," saith the apostle, "but not according to knowledge." "If they had known the Lord of glory, they would never have crucified him." This blind zeal causeth poor deceived souls to think themselves zealously affected towards Christ, when they are stubbornly set for antichrist. Zeal without knowledge is not zeal, but stomach. It is not true zeal, but rather a brain-sick giddiness, which causeth many to forsake their natural home, and to wander to Jerusalem, there to worship God: as if they thought, with Benadab[1] king of Syria, that God were the God of the hills and not of the valleys. It is another thing to be eager, and another thing to be zealous. They deceive themselves which think they do the duty of servants zealously bent in their master's cause, when they are sharp without all sober and stayed consideration, reproving them openly whom they ought

1 Kings xx. [23.]

[1 Benadab—Ben-hadad.—ED.]

privately to admonish, rashly condemning them whom they ought charitably to judge as brethren.

34. We must be zealous in God's cause. For angels themselves without zeal are nothing. But our zeal must be, as I said, with judgment. Ye are not ignorant what heroical zeal there was in Moses, in Elias, in Jehu, in Phinees, in Mattathias, in Christ. This zeal, this love, this true holiness and hearty fear of God, is abated in the best, and utterly banished out of most men. Where now, in what corner of this earth, shall we find a man in zeal comparable unto David, whom, when the word of God was contemned, and his ministers despised, the grief thereof had like to have wasted away? "My zeal," saith he, "hath even melted me, because mine enemies have forgotten thy words." What a cross, what a torment was the sin of Sodom to the heart of just Lot! The small remorse which we have for sin sheweth our zeal is not very great. Let us pray therefore to God, as to increase our faith, so to kindle true zeal in us, that we may, as Phinees, with the sword of the Holy Ghost, the word of God, run through, cut asunder, and destroy all the filth and uncleanness which lieth lurking in our hearts; that we cut off all our lewd affections, our carnal lusts, our lascivious thoughts; that we may so mortify the members of the body, and rectify the affections of the mind, that with a chaste life, in body and soul, we may glorify our God. Let us pray for the zeal that was in Christ Jesus, that we may with the sharp whip of unfeigned repentance drive out of our bodies, which are the temples of God's Holy Spirit, all buying and selling, all covetousness, usury, envy, lying, deceit; that we give not our bodies and souls to any such profane use, but to be kept uncorrupt and pure, as beseemeth the temples of his Holy Spirit; that we may offer up unto God, in the midst of these temples, the sacrifice of an humble and of a contrite heart, the sacrifice of righteousness, the sacrifice of praise. Let us beseech him, I say, to inflame our hearts with true zeal, that, earnestly seeking our own salvation and the safety of others, we may be zealous, as the blessed apostle was, with the zeal of God; even holy and zealous before the Lord.

Examples of true zeal in God's service.
Exod. xxxii. [19—29.]
1 Kings xviii. [40.]
2 Kings x. [18—28.]
Num. xxv. [6—13.]
1 Mac. ii.
John ii. [13—16.]
Luke xix. [45, 46.]
Psal. cxix. [139.]

Psal. li. [17.]

2 Cor. xi. [21—23.]

Our zeal must be, as in knowledge, so in sincerity.

35. For, as our zeal must be coupled with judgment and knowledge, so with truth and sincerity. God will not be served with feigned holiness and with counterfeit religion, with outward shews and with the lips, but with the heart. In our prayers we must pour out our hearts before him: in repentance our hearts must be rent asunder: in our alms we must keep a single heart: when the word is preached, we must open our hearts to receive it: whatsoever we do in his service, we must do it heartily, as to the Lord. For all our serving of him is in vain, nay, it is damnable, if we seek only which way we may appear holy and righteous unto men. Such as we would seem to be, we must be indeed; such we must appear in truth before that Lord who seeth our very hearts, and examineth our inmost reins. Let us ever remember that God looketh upon us with open eyes, he beholdeth in greatest darkness, he seeth the unsearchable heart and thought of man: no secret can be kept secret from him. This would bridle in us all inward wicked cogitations, all outward wicked works, if we could well, and as we should, consider it. For if we be ashamed and afraid to offend in the sight of man, who hath only power over our mortal body, how much more should we be overcome with shame and fear to sin in the sight of that eternal God, who hath power over body and soul, to cast them both into eternal fire!

Our serving of God must continue all the days of our life.

36. Thus we are to serve our Redeemer: we are ransomed and bought to serve, not for a day, but for all our days: we are redeemed for ever, to serve him for ever. He that runneth is not crowned till he have ended his race, and then beginneth his glory. Judas and Demas began to serve the Lord; but they were soon weary: their service was unrewarded, because it was uncontinued. Only he that continueth to the end shall be saved: which salvation of our souls and bodies the Lord of his infinite mercies grant, that we may aspire unto him in this life, and attain unto him in the life to come, through the merits of Jesus Christ: to whom, with the Father, and the Holy Ghost, &c.

THE ELEVENTH SERMON.

A SERMON

MADE AT YORK.

Rom. XIII.

8. *Owe nothing to any man, but this, to love one another; for he that loveth another hath fulfilled the law.*
9. *For this, Thou shalt not commit adultery, Thou shalt not kill, Thou shalt not steal, Thou shalt not bear false witness, Thou shalt not covet, and if there be any other commandment, it is briefly comprehended in this saying, even in this, Thou shalt love thy neighbour as thyself.*
10. *Love doth not evil to his neighbour: therefore is love the fulfilling of the law.*
11. *And that considering the season, that it is now time that we should arise from sleep; for now is our salvation nearer than when we believed it.*
12. *The night is past, and the day is at hand: let us therefore cast away the works of darkness, and let us put on the armour of light;*
13. *So that we walk honestly as in the day.*

Our apostle, in the former part of this chapter, hath diligently set down as well the office and authority of a magistrate, as also what duty and obedience the subjects do owe unto him. He was occasioned hereunto, for that the Jews, the elect nation of God (who therefore claimed to be a free people) could not abide so to subject themselves, as to live obediently under foreign princes. The gentiles which now were become christians, thought it not agreeable to their holy profession to yield obedience unto wicked magistrates, persecutors of true religion, who, by evil means had attained unto that authority, and behaved themselves as ill in it. Paul, in this treaty of a magistrate, meeteth with both these errors. He layeth down this foundation for an absolute and a general rule: "Let every soul be subject to the higher powers." This obe- Magistrates ought to be obeyed, whether they be heathen or christian.

dience he requireth both of Jew and gentile, of prophet and priest, in sum, of every Christian; and this position he proveth by sundry forcible reasons.

<small>Why obedience should be yielded unto magistrates.</small>

2. First, "there is no power but of God. The powers that are, be ordained of him." Be the magistrate Jew or gentile, christian or heathen, good or bad, he hath his authority from God, the Magistrate of all magistrates. God hath placed him and ordained him to be thy governor; in respect whereof thou art bound for thy conscience sake towards God for to obey him. Another reason why every soul should live in subjection to the higher power is, because whosoever resisteth the ordinance of God, provoketh the judgment of God against himself. If God for thy sin set a wanton, an hypocrite, yea, or an infidel over thee, thou must obey that wanton, that hypocrite, and that infidel, and not rebel against him. God hath ordained him: to resist that power is to resist the ordinance of God: to conspire against him is to conspire against God: to reject him is to reject God. Christ submitted himself to the authority of Cæsar, and to Pilate's judgment. Resisters and rebels receive to themselves condemnation: they never have, neither ever shall, escape the heavy hand of God's wrath: they feel it often in this life; but in the life to come, if they escape it here, they are sure to feel it. A third reason why we should live obediently is, because there is no reason why we should do otherwise. For why should any man desire not to be subject? Because he is afraid of the power of kings and rulers? Princes are a terror, not to them that do well, but to evil-doers. Wilt thou then be without fear of the power? Withdraw not thyself from obedience, but do well: so shalt thou have praise, and be without fear. For this end magistrates are appointed of God to maintain the good, and repress the evil. And the magistrate is so necessary in respect hereof, that no commonwealth can be safe or long stand without him. For if the bad were not bridled more by the authority of the magistrate, than by any moderation in themselves, they would eat up the good; and a wonderful confusion would soon follow. A fourth reason may be this. God hath put a sword in the magistrate's hands, to shew that he hath appointed

him as his vicegerent to take vengeance on them which do evil. So that the very sight of the sword ought to put us in mind of his power and our obedience. For God hath not delivered him a sword for nothing: he is the minister of God's wrath: he hath not received the sword in vain, it is given him to smite the wicked withal.

3. Wherefore "ye must be subject, not because of wrath only, but also for conscience sake." The apostle concludeth upon the former reasons, that we must submit ourselves obediently unto the magistrate, and attempt nothing against him, not only for fear of punishment, he being the minister of God's displeasure, but also for conscience sake, in that God requireth this obedience at our hands. All this notwithstanding, if magistrates should command that which is impious, and which God forbiddeth, in such cases we have our answer well warranted: *Melius est obedire Deo quam hominibus:* "It is better to obey God than men." _{Magistrates to be obeyed in the Lord, for conscience sake, and not for fear only.} _{Acts v. [29.]}

4. In token of this obedience we pay them tribute, as acknowledging them to be God's ministers. It is not a strange or a new custom to pay custom to princes: all nations, all people, have ever used it and yielded it; and magistrates well deserve it. For their office is both painful and chargeable; they ever caring for the benefit of the commonwealth, to repress the evil, to strengthen the good, to set up virtue, to cast down vice, to defend their people and country, and in well governing, as the good ministers of God, to spend both their goods and lives. These magistrates must be supported, and may lawfully receive the reward of their labours: nay, they must receive it. Wherefore, unless ye will be injurious, and withhold back from them that which is theirs even by debt, and not by courtesy, give to all men their duty, "tribute to whom tribute, custom to whom custom, fear to whom fear, and honour to whom honour is due." We must have magistrates in great estimation and reverence: we must fear them as the ministers of God's wrath: we must honour them, for that they occupy God's place for our benefit: we must readily and willingly pay unto them tribute and custom; for God hath so appointed, and they have so deserved. And therefore the apostle saith, *Red-* _{Tribute due to princes.}

dite: "Pay it." Whereupon St Chrysostom fitly noteth, "We do not give it unto magistrates, but we pay it unto them[1]." It is as due as debt.

<small>What we owe to men, and what to God.</small>

5. Upon this particular touching our duty towards magistrates, our apostle inferreth a general exhortation: "Owe nothing to any man but this, to love one another," &c. This exhortation compriseth two things; our duty to our neighbour, our duty to God. Our duty to our neighbour consisteth in paying him what we owe him, and in loving him as we love ourselves.

<small>1. Examples of them which have well or ill discharged the debt they owe to magistrates.</small>

6. Owe nothing to any man, pay thy debt: pay unto the magistrate obedience, fear, honour, tribute, custom: all this is due unto him, all this is thy debt. The people of Israel bound themselves with solemn promise to pay this debt to their magistrate Josua, whom the Lord had given

<small>[Josh. i. 16 —18.]</small>

to be their governor: "All things which thou hast commanded us, we will do; and whithersoever thou wilt send us, we will go: as we obeyed Moses, so will we also obey thee. Only let the Lord thy God be with thee as he was with Moses. Whosoever shall rebel against thy commandment, and will not obey thy words in all that thou commandest him, let him be put to death." This is the debt we owe to magistrates. Miriam would not pay this debt to her brother Moses; and God plagued her with a foul leprosy: so that she, which had separated herself from common obedience, was separated from all company. Dathan and Abiram, with their complices, rebelliously murmured against their magistrate; and God made the earth open and swallow them up; and a number of that conspiracy he consumed with fire. Absolon rebelled, and would not pay this debt of obedience to his father: but God quickly paid him that which was due to his rebellious and disloyal attempts. God is still the same God: he hateth iniquity, and will not suffer conspiracy, rebellion, or treason against lawful magistrates either unrevealed or unrevenged. And therefore let all subjects, as well to avoid the wrath of God, as also for conscience sake, pay

[[1] Καὶ οὐδὲ εἶπε, δότε, ἀλλ' ἀπόδοτε, καὶ τὰς ὀφειλὰς προσέθηκεν.—Chrysost. Op. Par. 1731. In Epist. ad Rom. Hom. xxiii. Tom. ix. p. 689.—Ed.]

this debt of true obedience in all lawful causes to their lawful magistrate.

7. Let the magistrate pay unto the people the debt which he oweth them. The debt of the magistrate is the just execution of lawful punishment against transgressors. The sword is delivered unto him for that purpose: neither is any open transgression of any kind, whether it concern the first or second table of the law of God, or any man of any calling, be he prophet or priest, exempted from this judgment. Solomon deposed Abiathar the high priest: Jehu slew the false prophets; Elias the Baalites. This sword is given of God to magistrates, to execute just judgment against all sins and all sinners; and this part of debt is to be paid. It is also a part of the magistrate's debt to give upright sentence in matters of controversy between parties. For which cause the poets feign justice to carry a sword in the one hand, and a balance in the other; to kill sin with the one, and with the other to weigh litigious and controversed causes. *The magistrate is a debtor to the people, as they are debtors unto him; he of justice, as they of obedience.*

8. Such as are magistrates, to whom the deciding of causes and punishing offences is committed, should be chosen out of all the people, the best and fittest men for their wisdom and courage, their religion and hearty affection to the truth, and for the hatred which they bear to covetousness. For this is no office for a fool; and he that feareth not God will shew partiality: he that loveth not the truth will justify the wicked, and condemn the innocent: he that hateth not covetousness will take rewards, and be corrupted with bribes, as the sons of Eli, which received gifts with the one hand, and with the other perverted judgment. The eyes even of the wise are blinded herewithal. Fear also, affection, and commiseration, with desire to please men, are great hurts unto justice. Pilate, for fear of Cæsar, gave sentence against Christ: for fear of displeasing a man on earth, he murdered the King and God of heaven. Whom money cannot corrupt, affection will carry away: it is the cut-throat of all justice: the people daily both feel it, and rue it. Pity, or commiseration, made Josua spare the miserable Gabionites, contrary to the express commandment of God. Desire to please caused Pilate to send Jesus over unto Herod; who *Qualities required in a magistrate. Exod. xviii. [21.] Luke xxiii. [7—11.]*

together with his band despised and mocked him. It caused Herod to imbrue his hands in the Baptist's blood. It causeth many, even against the light of their own consciences, to justify the wicked, and condemn the man whom they find innocent. Such do very ill discharge the debt which they owe unto their brethren.

The debt of the minister to his flock. [Rom. i. 14.]
1 Pet. v. [2.]

9. The minister is also a debtor to the people committed to his charge. "I am a debtor," saith the apostle, "both to Greeks and barbarians, to learned and unlearned." The pastor is a debtor unto his flock, to feed it so much as in him lieth, to feed it both spiritually and corporally; spiritually by life and doctrine, corporally with hospitality according to his ability. Woe be to that pastor that payeth not this debt! For if the flock perish for want of food, all that perishing blood shall be required at his hands. A hard reckoning for him to answer, and a sharp punishment to sustain for not answering.

Theirs to him.

10. The flock is indebted to their pastor, to honour and to reverence him as their father, to hear him as their schoolmaster, to obey and submit themselves unto him as to one whom God hath set over them for to rule them, to observe his wholesome precepts, to follow him in life as he followeth Christ, to love him, and to minister necessaries unto him for his convenient sustentation. All this debt is set down in the scriptures; and God requireth payment of it.

The debt of husbands, wives, masters, servants.

11. The husband doth owe unto his wife due benevolence, tender and faithful love, provision for things needful and honest, wise government, good instruction, protection, custody, and honour: the wife is indebted unto her husband to honour him, to love him, to obey him, to learn of him, to be governed by him, to live under him in silence with all subjection, to ease him in the orderly nurturing of his children and the wise governing of his house, to be not only an help, but a credit unto him, by her keeping home, by her industry and painfulness, by her sober, holy, and discreet behaviour. The master oweth to his servant meat, wages, correction, instruction: the servant to his master honour, obedience, faithful service, and whatsoever he is able by labour to perform.

Usurers bad paymasters

12. Every man is to his neighbour a debtor, not

only of that which himself borroweth, but of whatsoever his neighbour needeth; a debtor not only to pay that he oweth, but also to lend that he hath and may conveniently spare; to lend, I say, according to the rule of Christ, "Lend, looking for nothing thereby: and your reward shall be much: you shall be the sons of the Most High." So that these over-payments, the usury which hath spoiled and eaten up many, the canker of the commonwealth, is utterly both forbidden to man, and abhorred of God. To bargain for lead, grain, or leases, with such as have neither lead, grain, nor lease to pay, neither any such matter meant, but only unlawful gain of money, the party to forfeit his obligation, because he neither can nor meaneth such payment, and the lender not content to receive less advantage than thirty at the hundred; this is but a patched cloak to cover this vile sin withal. Whatsoever thou receivest upon condition, or by what means soever thou receivest more than was lent, thou art an usurer towards thy brother, and God will be a revenger against thee. He whom thou shouldst obey, if thou wilt be saved, doth in express words command thee not to lend thy money for usury. "If thou lend money to my people, to the poor with thee, thou shalt not be as an usurer unto him." "If thy brother be impoverished, and fallen into decay, thou shalt relieve him, and as a stranger or sojourner, so shall he live with thee." And again: "Thou shalt not give to usury to thy brother, usury of money, usury of meat, usury of any thing that is put to usury." This word of God man cannot dispense withal; and it shall not return in vain. If it cannot be a converting commandment, it shall be a confounding judgment. The reasons of men for usury must give place to the precept of God against it. What man art thou that wilt be wiser than thy Maker? Hath God condemned it, and darest thou defend it? Is it in his judgment injurious, and doth thy censure think it equal? Hath he seen reason to prohibit it, and dost thou see reason why thou mayest use it? Such reasons, with the makers and users of them, the Lord's justice shall destroy. And yet, in truth, all reason and the very law of nature is against it: all nations at all times have condemned it, as the very bane and pestilence

of that which they owe.

Luke vi. [35.]

Exod. xxii. [25.]
Levit. xxv. [35.]

Deut. xxiii. [19.]

of a commonwealth: whereof the old Roman both history and practice is an often witness. These secret shifts are seen of God, and abhorred, and will be revenged. Well mayest thou escape the hands of man, by thy coloured delusions, yet canst thou not escape the sharp and swift judgment of God; who, accordingly as he hath threatened, will exclude thee out of his kingdom, interdict thee his tabernacle, and hurl thee into hell, where thy evil-gotten money can neither redeem nor help thee. A just reward for thy unjust usury! Our apostle requireth that we pay unto every man the thing that we owe. And we are as much debtors to lend freely, as others faithfully to pay the thing which is lent.

Falsehood in merchants' payments.

13. The merchant is indebted to his neighbour, the seller to the buyer, to deal truly with him; not to defraud him by false weights, false measures, false lights, false words, by swearing and forswearing, or by any such usual but unlawful mean. One lesson observed serveth this matter: lend as thou wouldst borrow; sell as thou wouldst buy; do as thou wouldst be done unto. This is duty, this is debt. Pay it, and "owe nothing unto any man but this, that ye love one another."

The debt of love is general and continual. All men owe it, and no man payeth it so but that still he oweth it.

14. The debt of love is natural and continual. We all owe it, and we owe it unto all. And unto whom we owe it we never pay it, except we acknowledge that we owe it still. In this debt of love we must consider why we must love, whom we must love, and lastly, how we must love.

Reasons why love is due debt.

15. To omit the reasons drawn from nature, this one taken from the God of nature shall suffice. We must love because God hath so commanded, and because it is

[John xiii. 34.]

the fulfilling of all his commandments. "I give you a new commandment," saith Christ, "that ye love one another." In our new birth or regeneration we are made brethren and fellow-heirs with Christ of God's kingdom. As God therefore for ever loveth us in Christ, so we ought to love our brethren for God, and in Christ, for ever. If ye will be known to be his servants, by this men shall know you. If ye will be counted not hearers only, but also doers of the law, the law is love. He that loveth another fulfilleth the law. Which the apostle proveth thus. The law saith: "Thou shalt not kill, thou shalt not steal, thou shalt not bear false witness, thou shalt not covet:" that is to say, Thou shalt no way harm thy brother. Love doth no evil or hurt to any: he that loveth his neighbour will not take away his life, will not defile his bed, will not steal or rob him of his goods, will not witness untruly against him, will not in his heart covet any thing that is his; and he that doth any of these things against him beareth not indeed hearty and true love towards him. "Therefore is love the fulfilling of the law." So that you see great cause why we should enter into this holy and christian band of love.

16. But whom must we love? "Thou shalt love thy neighbour. And who is our neighbour?" Not he only to whom we are joined by familiar acquaintance, by alliance, or nearness of dwelling; but whosoever doth need our help, he is our neighbour, be he Jew or gentile, Christian or infidel, yea, friend or enemy, he is our neighbour. To him we ought to be near to do him good. It is frivolous for thee to object, He is mine enemy, he hath many ways wronged me, he hath raised slanderous reports of me, he hath practised against me, spoiled and robbed me: how can I love him? If Christ had loved his friends only, he had never loved thee, whosoever thou art. Look upon him, whose hands were stretched out upon the cross for his enemies, and for thee when thou wast his foe. No man proposeth him as a pattern to be followed, whom in his heart he doth mislike. Thou mislikest thine enemy because he hateth thee: if thou hate him, then dost thou imitate the very thing which thou hatest. Love thy neighbour therefore without exception, and love him as thyself. *Love is due to our neighbours; and who they be.*

17. For after this manner we ought to love. No man hateth his own flesh: no man is envious of his own commodity or preferment. Nature breedeth a self-love in every man. And as this law of nature doth work in us a very fervent and careful desire, both to procure unto ourselves whatsoever we are persuaded is good, and to avoid whatsoever seemeth hurtful or noisome; so the law of charity requireth at our hands like readiness and cheerfulness to benefit others. Of love towards ourselves, we hide and very warily cover all such faults as might any way work *How we ought to love others; namely, as ourselves.*

our discredit or disgrace. If we love our brethren as ourselves, we will no more blaze their offences than our own. "Charity doth hide the multitude of sins." But when we enlarge the sins of other men, that they may seem great; or reckon them up by one and one, to make them appear as if they were many; how fulfil we the law of charity? Would we do this in our own transgressions? We are never weary in doing good to ourselves; but to do good to others we have no sooner begun but we are even tired. Ourselves we love not in word and shew, but in truth and in deed. If we speak deceitfully every one to his neighbour; if we flatter with our lips; if we carry in our heads a double tongue, and in our bodies a double heart, and say we love, we lie. Which of us being in his right mind doth lift up his fist to strike himself? If any part of our bodies be out of frame, any bone out of joint, we seek by and bye all the help we can to set it in. The name of strife and contention would never be heard of, if we were thus affected towards others. The only breach of peace is the want of love: he that loveth all men will have peace with all men.

[1 Pet. iv. 8.]

A caution to be observed in loving one another. Rom. xii. [18.]

18. Yet this doth suffer a kind of exception. "Have peace with all men," saith the apostle; but he addeth, "if it may be, and as much as in you lieth." It may not be, which may not be lawfully. We may not so yield unto love, that we yield unto sin withal; not so have peace with our neighbours, that, to continue love with them, we depart from the faith and love of God; or that, for peace sake, we flatter and follow our neighbour in his evil. That were to fall out with Christ, that we may keep in with men. If thy hand or eye offend thee, cut the one off, pluck the other out: love God's creation, but hate all sinfulness: the Lord also doth abhor it. And therefore we must be well content to lose the love and bear the enmity of the whole world, for the love we bear to God and his truth. With that strife to keep this peace the Lord is pleased.

The great want of love in these our times.

19. But we are fallen into these evil times, wherein iniquity aboundeth, and charity waxeth cold. Hearty love is turned into hearty hatred: our hands are bloody, and our hearts malicious. He liveth not, that loveth his neigh-

bour as himself. If we did love our neighbours as ourselves, we would not oppress them with extortion and usury: we would not undermine them, and wring them in bargaining: we would not so proudly contemn them, so spitefully envy them, so impudently slander them, or so greedily practise for their infamy and discredit: we would not speak them fair, and mind them evil; fawn on them, and betray them; seek our credit by their reproach, our gain by their loss: when we see their necessities, we would relieve and succour them, bind up their wounds with the good Samaritan, and charitably provide for them. When we suffer them for want to perish in our streets, this is an evident token and manifest argument that we neither love God, neither them that are of God; neither him, nor his. If the virtues which are in love be not found in us, but if contrariwise we abound in those vices from which love is free; if we be void of patience and courtesy, full of envy and froward dealing; if we swell in pride, and care not what we do to advance ourselves above others; if every man's care be only for himself; if our wrath be kindled with every light occasion, and any thing suffice to make us always think the worst that can be surmised, and do the worst that can be invented; if we rather be glad at the fall of our brethren, than rejoice when they constantly abide in the truth; if we be come to that pass, that we can in a manner suffer nothing, believe nothing, hope nothing, bear and endure nothing; what should we say, but acknowledge the arrearages in which we are cast, and confess that we have left that debt of love which we owe to our brethren undischarged? God grant us grace to amend this bad payment, lest he pay us our due punishment! Thus much of our duty towards our neighbour set down in these words. "Owe nothing," &c.

20. Now followeth the duty which we owe unto God. "And that, considering the season, that it is now time we should arise from sleep; for now is our salvation nearer than when we believed. The night is past, and the day is at hand. Let us therefore cast away the works of darkness, and let us put on the armour of light; so that we walk honestly as in the day." Two things are here required at our hands; to cast off the works of darkness, to put

2. Our duty to God, repentance and newness of life.

on the armour of light; to put off the old man Adam, and to put on the new man Christ; to shake off the ragged coat of sin, and to clothe ourselves with the comely vesture of innocency; to abstain from evil, and to do good; in a word, to repent and amend. Why we should thus do, our apostle giveth reasons: the time doth require that now we should arise from sleep: our salvation is near: the night is past, and the day hath dawned.

The time requireth the payments of this debt.

21. This time requireth a new life. For this is the last hour; the acceptable time, the day of salvation; the day when as God doth visit us in his mercy, calling us to the knowledge of him and of his Son Christ, by the preaching of the gospel to the saving of our souls. O that we could know the day of our visitation, and would take hold of this gracious time of mercy! Arise at length, arise from sin, and redeem the time past and lost. We have long, yea too, too long slumbered: it is now more than high time to arise, to arise from sleep of error, of sin, and of security.

The blindness in which the world sleepeth, although the night be past.

22. Many are fallen asleep in the blind errors of man's doctrine: many are yet drowned in the dregs of popery, preferring dreams, fancies, lies, and fables, before the heavenly doctrine of God's everlasting truth. The cause of this their blindness is ignorance of the scriptures: the cause of their ignorance is the hardness of their hearts. They neither know, they are so ignorant; nor will know, they are so stubborn. When they are exhorted to read, they close their eyes; when to hear, they shut their ears; when to come, they draw back their feet. If the sun shine never so bright, they see it not: if the trump sound never so loud, it will not waken them. Christ compareth them very aptly to the hard stony way, whereon what good seed soever is cast, is lost: it can take no root; for either it is eaten up by birds, or trodden down by men. The stubborn-hearted and stiff-necked Jews were cast into this dead sleep, establishing their own righteousness, and rejecting the righteousness that is in Christ Jesu, reposing salvation in their external sacrifices and ceremonies; not seeking it there where it was only to be found, in Christ, which was the sacrificed Lamb from the beginning of the world, that only taketh away the sins of the world. As those were then,

[Luke viii. 5.]

so now these are; who with the proud Pharisees justify themselves by their own defiled works; not regarding the true justification which we have in Christ through faith; preferring the sacrifice of the blasphemous mass, the mere invention of man, or of Satan, before the sweet and acceptable sacrifice which Christ made for us upon the cross once, not to be renewed, and sufficient, not needing help. Men they are of dull ears and of hard hearts, a rebellious and froward generation, to whom whatsoever we speak, this account we may make beforehand: "Surely they will not hear," neither will they arise from the error wherein Satan hath rocked them asleep, cry the prophets never so loud and so often, "Rise, O Jerusalem, be enlightened, for thy light is come, and the glory of the Lord is risen upon thee." "The light is come into the world." Therefore, considering the season, it is time we should awake, lest we be unseasonably taken asleep, and so judged as we are taken. *Ezek. iii. [7.]* *Isai. lx. [1.]* *John iii. [19.]*

23. Arise, thou that sleepest, whether it be in error, or in "sin." This sleep is so pleasant, that all the world lieth in it, and hardly can shake it off. King David fell into it, and continued in it, sleeping very soundly, never lifting up his head for two years' space, till at the length Nathan the prophet, at the commandment of God, awakened him. Zaccheus slept a long time pleasantly in his usury with heaps of evil-gotten goods under his head, till the Son of God himself called upon him and lifted him up, by whose voice he was effectually and throughly wakened; insomuch that his eyes being now opened to see the ugliness of his sin, wherein he had so long time before slumbered, he not only made restitution, but also gave the one half of all his goods to the poor. This man awaked in an happy time. It is most dangerous to slumber long in sin. Custom of sin maketh sin familiar, so that at the length we learn not to fear it at all, but rather to take delight and pleasure in it, to commit it, as the apostle saith, with a kind of "greediness," to count sin no sin, to swallow it down without any remorse or contradiction. Their case is lamentable which are thus fallen asleep, and for the most part their end miserable. Such was the sleep of that rich man, who, having filled his barns, and provided *As many sleep in error, so the most in sin.* *[Eph. iv. 19.]* *Luke xii. [18, 19.]*

14

[SANDYS.]

store for many years, encouraged himself to sensuality: "Soul, take thy rest." You that love the rest of your souls in deed, keep your souls waking, and do not suffer them to take rest. "Awake, thou that sleepest," and takest thy rest: "stand up from the dead, and Christ shall give thee light." It is time to awake: we have slept too long. God would not have us to sleep unto death, but to awake unto life: for he will not the death of a sinner: his desire is rather that we should repent. Now is the time, now Christ calleth thee, now he stretcheth out his arms, now he offereth mercy: come unto him, and thou shalt find true rest for thy wearied soul. Long hath been thy sleep, great hath been thy sin: but God is full of compassion, prest[1], and ready not only to grant, but to offer pardon. If now we refuse it offering itself to us, it will refuse us hereafter when we offer ourselves to it.

<small>Eph. v. [14.]</small>

<small>Sleeping in security.</small>

24. Of this we are not afraid; because we sleep as well in security as in sin. We must therefore be raised out of this sleep also. Man's life is a warfare, and men are soldiers: we must keep our standing and watch, lest we be unawares both assaulted and surprised. We have both many and mighty and fierce adversaries; the devil, who is violently and greedily set as an hungry lion, that roareth for his prey; the world, which hath infinite sleights to deceive us; the flesh, which mightily striveth and wrestleth against the Spirit. There is no place of security left for a christian soldier, there being so many great dangers. There is nowhere any place wherein it is safe to be secure. "Not in heaven," saith Bernard, "nor in paradise; much less in the world[2]." In heaven the angels fell from the very presence of the Godhead: Adam fell in paradise from the place of pleasure; and Judas in the world from the school of our Saviour. In the time of Noe they lived in great security; and the flood suddenly overwhelmed them. In the time of Lot the Sodomites lived in as great security, and were as suddenly consumed with fire. Thus with fire and water security hath been plagued. God hath

<small>Bernard.</small>

[1 Prest—earnest.—ED.]

[2 Nusquam est securitas, fratres, neque in cœlo, neque in paradiso; multo minus in mundo.—Bernard. Op. Par. 1690. Sermo xxx. De Diversis. Tom. III. Vol. I. col. 1147.—ED.]

armed the very elements against that thing, wherein notwithstanding we continue, as if we would try whether he, which wakened them by sending water upon the one, and fire upon the other, would waken us by causing the earth to swallow us up. What we should look for, God doth best know: our security, being the same with theirs, can denounce no less to us than it brought to them. We cry, Peace, peace: what more evident token can there be, that our sudden destruction is at hand? Men are commonly nearest unto peril, both corporal and spiritual, when their minds are furthest from thinking of preventing it. It is written of the people which were in Laish, that because they had no business with any body, nor any body with them, no man raised any tumult, or usurped any dominion in their land, and the place which they inhabited was good and lacked nothing, therefore they dwelt careless, quiet and sure. Which when the spials sent forth from the children of Dan had once perceived, they made no doubt of conquering the land, but encouraged their brethren and set them forward: "Be not slothful to go and enter to possess the land. If ye will go, ye shall come unto a careless people: the country is large: surely God hath given it into your hands." They went up, being only six hundred men, came to Laish, found the people without all mistrust of danger, put them to the sword, and burnt up their city. Their peace bred plenty; their plenty, security; their security, their destruction. And as in dangers of the body, so likewise, or rather much more, in perils which beset the soul, we shall find those temptations most grievous which assault us at unawares. For this cause we are in scriptures so often called upon to be watchful. "Watch and pray," saith our Saviour, "that ye fall not into temptation." He that falleth into temptation asleep, hardly riseth out of temptation alive. For if they that watch continually be not conquerors but with much ado, what shall become of them, upon whom Satan then layeth hands, when, being lusty and strong, having whatsoever their hearts can wish, they are at peace, take their rest, and because they have no change, therefore fear not God? Surely their destruction is as the swelling of an high wall: it cometh suddenly down, and they are fearfully consumed.

[Judg. xviii. 9, 10.]

[Matt. xxvi. 41.]

Watch therefore, and sleep not in security. Blessed is he that watcheth.

Because our salvation is nearer, therefore we ought not to sleep still in darkness.

25. "Our salvation is nearer than when we believed." This is the second reason why we should "cast away the works of darkness, and put on the armour of light." We have entered our names into the profession of christianity in our baptism: we have received the truth by it: we seek salvation: we have been long scholars, we ought now to grow to some good perfection: we draw now near unto the end, therefore we should amend our pace in this our course. The nearer we come to the end of our race, the faster we should run, if we desired to get the reward we run for. Let us do so. And seeing the race that we have to run is even in a manner finished, and the crown we run for is immortal, let us be earnest in the cause; let us cast off all hinderances, and strive industriously unto that salvation which is set before us. Now that we are almost as it were within the reach of the crown of glory, let us take strength unto us, let us double our courage, increase our zeal, add more and more unto every good and perfect gift which we have received from the Father of light. This the nearness of our salvation doth now especially require.

The night is past.

26. Let them that sit in darkness, and in the shadow of death, sleep on. But unto us "the night is past." Night in the scriptures is taken for ignorance, the times whereof are now past. The day-star is risen, and hath appeared unto us. Christ, the true light, is come into the world: he that now will walk in darkness is not blind but wilful, and runneth with open eyes to his own damnation. [John xv. 22.] If the light had not come into the world, "if I had not spoken unto them," saith Christ, "they might have pleaded ignorance:" but I have told them the truth; therefore they are left without excuse. Christ, that light of the world, hath appeared: his cross is painted out before our eyes. [2 Cor. iv. 4.] "If our gospel be hid, it is from them that perish, whom the god," or rather the devil, "of this world hath blinded." We are in the light: the way of truth lieth plain and open before our faces. Let not us walk now as the children of darkness. For darkness and the night are past.

27. "The day draweth near." The day of every man's particular dissolution, and the day of that general judgment of all men. Although the day of our death be uncertain; yet, because all our days are few, our first day is no sooner come, but we are sure and certain that the last draweth near. Wherefore it behoveth us continually to watch, to look for our end, and to put ourselves in a readiness for it. For as we are found in that day, so shall we find in the day after that, the day of the glorious appearing of Christ, when all secrets shall be unsealed, all faults made manifest, and every man receive a blessing or a curse, as he hath wrought in his body good or bad. Many days are past since Christ and his apostles did count it near; therefore now it must needs draw much nearer, and be even at the door. We may now say justly, "It is time to rise from sleep. Our salvation is nearer than when we believed. The night is past, the day draweth on."

The last day draweth near.

28. "Let us walk honestly therefore, as in the day." We are created and redeemed to walk and serve God, in whose service, if we go not forward, we go backward: we may neither lie down nor stand still, but take pains and walk. And that "honestly," having our conversation according to our good profession. We are set as it were upon a stage: the world, angels, and men, fix their eyes upon us. And if the eyes of all these were closed, yet he to whom the night and the light are all one in clearness, our eternal God, he seeth our cogitations, and searcheth our heart: he understandeth all our ways. All things lie open and uncovered unto him: he beholdeth all practices, all devices, all treacheries, all treasons, all sin. Let us walk uprightly and live honestly, as in his sight.

We must therefore walk honestly, as in the day.

29. This we shall do, if we follow the counsel and exhortation of St. Paul; that is, if we first "cast away the works of darkness." Sinful actions are called works of darkness. First, because much sin springeth out of ignorance, which is blindness and darkness; wherefore St Paul allegeth ignorance to be the cause why he persecuted the church of Christ. Secondly, for that sinners, because their works are evil, hate the light which discovereth them, and love darkness wherein they may conceal them. Thirdly,

We must cast off the works of darkness.

because the works of sin are to be cast into that perpetual and utter darkness of hell, and bound in everlasting chains of darkness, unto the judgment of that great day.

We must put on the armour of light.

30. Howbeit, for that it sufficeth not to abstain from evil, but it is required that we should do good; therefore the apostle exhorteth us not only to "cast away the works of darkness," but "to put upon us the armour of light." Wherein look, what was said why sin should be called by the name of darkness, the like may on the contrary side be said why righteousness should be termed by the name of light. First, for that good works are the fruits of the light of knowledge, wherein if we "increase more and more in love, and in all spiritual understanding, we shall not only put a difference between those things that are more excellent, but be pure also and without offence unto the day of Christ, filled with the fruits of righteousness which cometh by Jesu Christ, unto the glory and praise of God." Secondly, because they that walk honestly as in the day-time delight in the light: "For he that doth the truth cometh to the light, that his deeds may be made manifest, that they are done in God," "who is light, and in him is no darkness at all." And therefore, insomuch as they well understand that the night will come, wherein nobody shall be able to work, while they have the light they give themselves to walk in the light, that they may be the sons of the light. And thirdly, because, as Bernard saith, *Bona opera non sunt causæ regni, sed via regnandi*[1]; "Good works are not the causes of, but the way unto the kingdom," so they lead us the way to the inheritance of saints in light, and to the fruition of that God, who as he is "the Father of lights, in whom there is no variableness nor shadow of change," so he dwelleth in a light that cannot as yet be comen[2] unto: we

Phil. i. [9—11.]

John iii. [21.]

1 John i. [5.]

[James i. 17.]

[1 Alioquin si proprie appellentur ea, quæ dicimus nostra merita; spei quædam sunt seminaria, caritatis incentiva, occultæ prædestinationis indicia, futuræ felicitatis præsagia, via regni, non causa regnandi. Denique quos justificavit, non quos justos invenit, hos et magnificavit. —Bernard. Op. Par. 1690. Tractat. de Grat. et Lib. Arbit. cap. XIV. Tom. II. Vol. I. col. 624.—ED.]

[2 Comen—the old form of the participle of to come.—ED.]

shall come to it hereafter, when we shall drink of the well of life, when in his light we shall see light. To the which everlasting life and light he bring us, who is not only the way, the truth, and the life, but God of God, Light of Light, even Jesus our Saviour: to whom, with the Father, and the Holy Ghost, three Persons, and one God, &c.

THE TWELFTH SERMON.

A SERMON

PREACHED AT AN ASSIZES.

MICAH VI.

8. *He hath shewed thee, O man, what is good, and what the Lord requireth of thee: Surely, to do judgment and to love mercy, to humble thyself, and to walk carefully with thy God.*

The occasion of the above written words of the prophet. For the better understanding of the prophet in these few words recited, it shall be requisite to open unto you a few circumstances concerning them, wherein I will be short. We learn in the text that goeth before in this chapter, that God was displeased with his people the Israelites. And that it might appear how just cause he had of offence given him, he challengeth them, that his graciousness towards them, and their unthankfulness towards him, might be examined and tried in just judgment. And God appointeth the mountains to be judges herein, that is, as Jerome[1] expoundeth it, the angels of heaven, whom God often useth as ministers for his glory and for the benefit of man. God declareth therefore here by his prophet, first, that he never wronged them, and therefore they had no cause to complain; secondly, that he hath bestowed his manifold benefits upon them; that he delivered them out of the house of bondage, from the tyrannical hands of cruel Pharaoh, whose slaves their fathers were; that he had given them worthy magistrates, and good priests, to rule, direct, and instruct them, Moses, Aaron, Miriam;

[1 Judicio contende adversum montes, quos non alios significari puto quam angelos quibus rerum humanarum commissa est procuratio.—Hieron. Op. Par. 1704. Comment. Lib. II. in Michææ Proph. Cap. VI. Tom. III. col. 1538.—ED.]

and lastly, that he had turned Balaam's cursings against them into blessings towards them. Now, after that God had thus set forth his great goodness towards them, he chargeth them with their great unkindness towards him; how they fell from the serving of him to the worshipping of false gods, by running a whoring after idols, and sacrificing on their hill-altars, committing most gross idolatry, and foolish superstition; how altogether they contemned the word of the Almighty, the preaching of the prophets, were drowned in sinful security, and fed themselves with their own phantasies, the inventions and vain conceits of man. These and such like were their faults, as may appear in the life of king Achaz, in whose time and reign the prophecy was written. The people, unable to gainsay so manifest a truth, were forced to plead guilty, and to acknowledge their offences, and therefore went about to seek out means how to pacify God's wrath, and to satisfy for their sins; and being doubtful by what means, or with what sacrifice, to please God and appease his anger, inquireth, "Wherewith shall I come before the Lord?" The prophet Micheas directeth the doubtful minds of the people in this behalf, and saith, "He hath shewed thee, O man, what is good, and what the Lord requireth of thee." Thus in few, ye see the occasion of these words, which I have taken in hand to expound unto you.

2. And it shall not be unprofitable with like brevity to apply the circumstances to us and to our times. If God should in like case contend in judgment with us, the law would accuse us, heaven and earth would bear witness against us, and our own consciences would condemn us. For great and manifold are God's mercies towards us; and we render nothing again but mere and extreme ingratitude. "What have I done to thee, or wherein have I grieved thee?" saith the Lord. *[Mic. vi. 3.]*

The likeness between the occasion offered to the prophet of those words then, and of the like now.

3. God hath not envied us: he oweth us nothing, but he giveth us much: he hath not been grievous unto us, but mercifully considered of us. He hath kept promise with us, and performed his word, though we have neglected our faith towards him. We have often tasted of his bountiful goodness, of us altogether undeserved. Polycarpus, being required by an infidel judge to blaspheme

The mercies of God towards the church of England.

Euseb. lib. iv. c. 15.

Christ, made this answer: "Fourscore and six years have I served him, neither did he once harm me in any thing; how then can I blaspheme my king, that hath saved me[1]?" We cannot charge our just God with any wrong, our gracious Lord with any unkindness towards us; but must with Polycarpus ever acknowledge his unspeakable mercy and exceeding goodness. For as he bestowed upon his people the Israelites sundry great benefits, so hath he blessed us with the like or greater. God with a mighty arm hath delivered us out of Egypt, from the tyranny of Pharaoh, not only out of the chains and deadly thraldom of Satan and sin by the death and blood of Jesus Christ our Redeemer, but also out of the servile bondage of the great Pharaoh, though lesser than the former, the Romish antichrist, who villainously bereaved us of our spiritual liberty, robbed us of that inestimable treasure the word of God, and oppressed us with the intolerable burthen of unprofitable labours, trained us up in ignorance, forced us in idolatry and superstition, the ways to hell, to seek our safety and everlasting life. But God in his mercy hath remembered us to do us good, and to work our deliverance, of bondslaves to make us free men, of the children of darkness to make us the sons of light in him, and to restore us to the comfortable freedom of conscience by the gracious liberty of the gospel. God hath also blessed us with good magistrates: he hath not only given us his Son Christ, the Prince of his people, who, by offering up himself a sacrifice for our sins, procured unto us free remission of them; but hath also blessed us with worthy rulers under him, which govern in equity, and sincerely seek the glory of God. He hath given us Moses our sovereign, a prudent and a gentle magistrate, who seeketh not revenge, but beareth with the muttering of the people; yea, with the rebellious Dathan and Abiron, choosing rather to put up any tolerable wrong, than to see the ruin and subversion of men, though they seek it themselves. He hath also given us Aaron and Miriam, priests and prophets, to minister unto us the heavenly bread, the food of our souls, the word of God, the sacraments of Christ;

[[1] Euseb. Pamph. Hist. Eccl. Amst. 1695, p. 107.—Ed.]

and that most faithfully and sincerely, without changing or mingling. And as I said of late in this place, so I say again, England hath at no time heretofore been blessed with so many and so faithful preachers of God's word. Surely God mindeth your salvation, in that he so plentifully offereth unto you the word of salvation; nor that only, but therewithal peace, plenty, and rest, such as our fathers never tasted of in their ages.

4. Which mercies and blessings poured upon us in so great measure should in reason enforce us to praise him our God, and to serve him in true holiness all the days of our life, from the fountain of whose unspeakable goodness we have received them. The Israelites (their strange deliverance out of Egypt, their good magistrates, their manifold blessings, benefits, and graces notwithstanding) were found unthankful. And if God shall enter into judgment with us, and throughly examine us (as one day he will), may we not be accused, and shall we not be found guilty, of the like ingrateful crime? Have we not a longing, as they had, unto that from which the Lord hath delivered us in great mercy? God hath blessed us with both magistrates and ministers of great value; but so thankful are we to him and to them his servants, that we can easily abuse both, mutter against the one, and despise the other: neither is obeyed, neither reverenced, according to the word and will of God. But such as cannot away with Samuel, God in his wrath shall give them a Saul; and such as mislike of the true preacher shall be rewarded with a false prophet. The word is loathed: men are full of the gospel; and of many it is professed without all fruit: we shall therefore hunger for this bread, seek it, and not find it: in the stead hereof, we shall surfeit upon the fruit of our own desires: yea, God in his justice shall take his word from us, and give it to a people that will bring forth better fruits, and more worthy of so precious a blessing. Thus truly considering our case, and entering into judgment with God, we must with the Israelites plead guilty, and, as profess his mercies, so confess our faults.

Our evil requiting of the Lord for his goodness.

5. The guilty Israelites sought means how to satisfy for their sins. Their means were to sacrifice to God, and

The way which men have devised for remedy of this.

to offer up calves, rams, and goats; yea, some have not shrunk to pour the blood of their own children upon the altar, as Moab, who offered up his eldest son to pacify the wrath of God, when in battle he was besieged and brought into straits. Even by like means, when our conscience hath accused us of sin, many have sought to make satisfaction to God for it: some have sought remission of sins in a great number of prayers uttered in a strange tongue without either sense or zeal, neither made in faith nor charity, procuring hatred in God's sight, while they looked to be heard by their much babbling: some have sought to pacify God by hearing and buying of many masses, wherein God was blasphemed, and foul idolatry committed; some by killing of Christ, the first-begotten Son, again, sacrificing him afresh, as they thought, upon their hill-altars for the dead and the quick; but they were deceived: some by the mediation of saints departed, robbing Christ of his office, who is the only mediator and intercessor between God and man: some have thought to make amends for their sins by buying popish pardons, by taking their walks in long pilgrimages to dumb and senseless idols, and in such like not only vain but impious devices of man's foolish brain. Thus sundry have sought out sundry ways, some blasphemous, and some of them ridiculous, to appease the wrath of God provoked by their sin. The Israelites doubted by what mean to satisfy for their sin: what God would accept, they could not tell: they were altogether uncertain which way to please him; and truly it is lamentable that there be so many even now in the clear light of the saving gospel, which doubt by what means they may be saved; and in this doubtfulness many still follow their own phantasies, and through ignorance are led into the highway of damnation. Wherefore such as are doubtful, our prophet Micheas clearly resolveth: such as are out of the way, he calleth into the right path: such as are ignorant, he instructeth; and such as will learn, he offereth to teach what the good will and pleasure of the Lord is.

[2 Kings iii. 27.]

The way which God hath prescribed by his prophet.

6. "He hath shewed thee, O man, what is good and acceptable to him;" surely not to take upon thee to satisfy for sin thyself, for that passeth thy power, all thy

righteousness being but filthiness in the pure sight of God; not to offer up any sacrifice, as being in itself propitiatory for sin, for that Christ only hath done on the cross, and that but once, and that for all: he is the only sacrifice, the only priest, the only mediator, the only Redeemer. The price of our salvation is neither gold nor silver, but the precious blood of the innocent Lamb of God, Christ Jesus, shed for the sins of the world: "there is no other name under heaven, whereby we can be saved." God requireth therefore no satisfaction for sins at thy hands, but at his he hath required it to the uttermost: Christ is thine: God hath freely given thee both him, and with him all things that are his. If thou receive him through a true faith, thy salvation is sealed, and thou art safe. "For as many as have received him, to them he hath given power to be the sons of God, even to them that believe in his name." If thou confess with thy mouth, and believe in thy heart, that thou art delivered from thy sin by that one oblation of Christ, offered upon the cross; that his merit hath made thee the child of his Father, and the inheritor of that kingdom which he hath prepared for as many as are his; then apply thyself to live after the will and commandment of him that hath done so great things for thee: shew thy faith by thy life: let it appear and be seen in thy works, that thou art indeed the loving and the justified child of God, ready and desirous to obey and do his will. And lest in thy working thou shouldest follow thine own phantasy, and do that which is not acceptable in the sight of God, he hath laid out thy way before thee. ^{Acts iv. [12.]} ^{Rom. viii. [32.]} ^{John i. [12.]}

7. "He hath shewed thee, O man, what is good, and what the Lord requireth of thee: surely, to do judgment and to love mercy, to humble thyself, to walk carefully with thy God." Wherein we first learn this lesson, that no service we do to God can please him, but such as himself in his word hath prescribed: he will be served as he hath commanded in his law, and not as thou hast devised with thyself. That service which God in his word doth not require at thy hands, if thou offer it him, it is in vain thou offerest. The Lord hath not asked it, and he will not accept it of thee. "In vain they worship ^{No service pleaseth God, but such as God prescribeth.}

me, teaching doctrines the precepts of men." It is not for nothing that God was so curious in platting forth the tabernacle, and so precise in commanding that all things without exception should be done according to that pattern. Was God so careful over an earthly and a corruptible house, think you? No: his meaning was to teach us that in the spiritual tabernacle, in matters of religion, pertaining to the service and worship of God, all things should be done according to the rule of his own will, which is set down in his written word. For hath he not said in the law, "What I command thee, that only shalt thou do: thou shalt neither add nor diminish"? He that addeth, God shall add unto him all the plagues; he that taketh away, God shall take from him all the blessings, contained in that book. "The doctrine of Christ," saith Clemens Alexandrinus, "is most absolute, neither wanteth it any thing[1]." God is well pleased, when men are so religiously affected, that they dare not swerve a hair's breadth from his word. St Cyprian saith, "The foundation of all religion and faith is laid in the word of God[2]." And St Jerome, "That which hath not authority out of the word of God is altogether as easily refused as proved[3]." Which rule of religion if the Latin church had as well observed, as it is both in the scriptures often given, and often commended by the godly fathers, the church of Christ had never been burthened with so many unprofitable traditions and new inventions of men: so many superstitions, so great idolatry, so ugly pollutions, had never found entrance into

Margin: Deut. xii. [32.] Rev. xxii. [18, 19.] Clem. Alex. Cyprian. Hieron.

[1 Αὐτοτελὴς μὲν οὖν καὶ ἀπροσδεὴς ἡ κατὰ τὸν Σωτῆρα διδασκαλία, δύναμις οὖσα καὶ σοφία τοῦ Θεοῦ.—Clem. Alex. Op. Oxon. 1715, Strom. Lib. I. Tom. I. p. 377.—ED.]

[2 Hæc sunt quæ patres intra canonem concluserunt; ex quibus fidei nostræ assertiones constare voluerunt.—Cypr. Op. Oxon. 1682. Expos. in Symb. Apost. p. 27.—Bishop Fell places this treatise at the end of the volume, and prefixes this notice to it: Ruffino Torano, Aquil. Eccl. Presb. auctore.—ED.]

[3 Alii Zechariam, patrem Johannis, intelligi volunt, ex quibusdam apocryphorum somniis approbantes, quòd propterea occîsus sit, quia Salvatoris prædicarit adventum. Hoc quia de scripturis non habet auctoritatem, eadem facilitate contemnitur, qua probatur.—Hieron. Op. Par. 1706, Comment. Lib. IV. in Matt. xxiii. Tom. IV. col. 112.—ED.]

the house of God. In the scriptures, wherein is contained all that is good, and all that which God requireth or accepteth of, we find no mention either of the name or of the thing of the mass, the pope, purgatory, praying on beads, hallowing of bells, either any such like popish trash: in sum, few parts of their religion have any one stone from thence to be founded or built upon. For where doth God require any one of these or the like at our or their hands? That which is required in his name is this: "To do judgment, and to love mercy," &c. Wherein is fully comprised our whole duty both to God and man.

8. "To do judgment." This sentence receiveth sundry expositions; and each of them yieldeth us sundry good lessons. Jerome[1] understandeth, by doing of judgment, doing all things with reason and ripe consideration. God himself giveth an example hereof, and applieth himself to our senses, that he may instruct our minds herein. For, minding to pour his plagues upon Sodoma and Gomorrah, those sinful cities, he saith first with himself, "I will go down now, and see whether they have done altogether according unto that cry which is come unto me or not, that I may know." It was rashness in Jephthe to promise without exception whatsoever should meet him first, and he paid full dearly for it. Herod, without all reason and judgment, promised to his dancing daughter whatsoever she should demand; and his keeping of promise was even as unadvised. They want judgment that forsake the fresh living springs, and drink of a puddle; that contemn the saving word of God, and be altogether addicted to man's vain and deceitful doctrine; that forsake Christ's merits by sticking to their own. They want judgment that call upon dead saints, when they may and should call only upon the living God; who hath promised, when we cry, both to hear and to help us. They are destitute both of reason and judgment, who vow that which lieth not in their power to perform. The world is not ignorant, how these holy ones performed their vows of chastity and of single life. How

God prescribeth doing of judgment, and what it is to do judgment.

Gen. xviii. [21.]

[Judg. xi. 30, 31.]

[Matt. xiv. 6, 7.]

[1 Ut faciamus judicium, id est, ut nihil absque ratione et consilio faciamus: ut antè mens judicet quid factura sit, et postea opere compleat.—Hieron. Op. Par. 1704. Comment. Lib. II. in Michææ Proph. Cap. vi. Tom. III. col. 1542.—ED.]

unable to bear this yoke the pope's own legate was, which forced this thing here in England upon others, they well knew which took him in the midst of his filth, to his own everlasting infamy, and the great dishonour of Honorius the second, from whom he was sent. *Res notissima negari non potuit*[1]: "the thing was famously known, and could not be denied." Dost thou teach another, and dost not teach thyself? Dost thou forbid marriage, and thyself commit adultery? Dost thou force that yoke upon others, which thyself so shamefully shakest off? What is emptiness of reason and judgment, if this be not? The murder which Theodosius rashly committed without advice or judgment, put him to great penance, and wrought him much sorrow: whereupon he gave his royal assent unto a law, that afterwards he should do nothing without deliberation beforehand taken[2]. The man that is hasty and rash, as he doeth others much wo, so wants no wo himself. St Paul would have our serving of God for to be "reasonable," that is, to be such as that a good and a just reason may be rendered of it; not such reasons as Durandus giveth of popish rites and ceremonies, in a book written purposely of this matter[3], but written in such sort, that a man unacquainted with the strange blindness of their darkened minds would certainly think that such a work was rather published to move laughter amongst companions, than to breed knowledge in the minds of religious Christians. So void they are in all their doings even of common sense and reason, not only of true piety and obedience to God's word.

9. Another interpretation of "doing judgment" may be given, and that is, if we take judgment for the administration of justice; and so it hath a special respect to such as are set in place of deciding causes and repressing sins, who are required by our prophet to give righteous and just judgment. "Give thy judgments to the king, O God," saith the prophet, "and thy righteousness

---

[1] Matt. Par. Hist. Major. Lond. 1640, p. 70.—Ed.]

[2] Theod. Hist. Eccl. Amst. 1695, Lib. v. c. 18. p. 222.—Ed.]

[3] Rationale Divinorum Officiorum. Per Johannem Fust Civem Maguntinum, 1459. This is the first edition, of excessive rarity. The author was made bishop of Mende in 1286, and died in 1296.—Ed.]

to the king's son. Then shall he judge the people in righteousness, and the poor in justice." Justice and judgment are commonly in the scriptures joined together; because, if there be a divorce at any time between these two, God's family and the commonwealth go to wrack and ruin. The psalmist seemeth to note a separation to have been between these two in his time, when he saith, "Judgment shall return to justice." But these may also be so distinguished, that judgment have his especial respect to the execution of the sword, to the punishing of transgressors; justice to the righteous deciding of matters which are in controversy. I need not travail much herein: I speak to wise and learned men, which well know their duty; and I trust that the fear of God will direct them christianly to discharge the same. Ye do not forget that ye are called in the scripture "gods:" not only because ye are set in God's seat, but because ye are the mouth and the hand of God; the mouth to speak in awarding true sentence, the hand to strike in executing judgment without respect of men's persons. Wherein it behoveth you to take good heed, and to beware what ye do. For ye exercise the judgment not of man, but of God. If the seat be his, if ye be his mouth and hand, if sentence be his, if his be the judgment; then see to it that ye judge uprightly as the ministers of that upright Judge. For there sitteth a Judge also upon you: what measure you give, you shall receive, when the great Judge shall proceed to his last and everlasting sentence. He that truly feareth God, and considereth these things, will not swerve from justice, for fear or favour of any man or thing. [Psal. xciv. 15.] [Psal. lxxxii. 6.]

10. I will briefly touch certain properties which should be in such as are placed in God's judicial seat, and leave the rest to your wise considerations. The first thing that judges are especially to take heed of is, that they be not receivers of bribes. Beware of rewards: they are the very bane of upright judgment. *Judges free from taking of bribes.*

11. In God, whose seat ye sit in, there is no iniquity. Such therefore as correct faults ought themselves to be faultless. In condemning others we condemn ourselves, if we ourselves do that for which we condemn others. A *They that judge others must themselves be faultless.*

certain pirate, being charged with his fault by Alexander the great conqueror, made him this answer: "I rob indeed with one little ship, but thou robbest with a whole navy." It is not for him to reprove, that is reprovable.

Acceptation of persons.

12. God is no accepter of persons: neither must you in judgment either favour the rich because of his wealth, or spare the poor for his misery's sake; but weigh their causes in the balance of equity, with an even and steady hand.

Foolish pity.
Josh. ix. [1—15.]

13. The judge may not give place to commiseration: his place is a place of equity, and not of foolish pity. The pitiful and deceitful cry of the Gabionites, the appearance of their miserable estate and condition, made the wise and worthy judge Josua to swerve from justice, and to break the commandment of the Almighty. The exclaiming of the people hath many times as much cause as had the harlot's complaint made unto Solomon, that her child was taken from her, which herself had smothered.

Judgment neither too hasty nor too slow.
1 Kings iii. [16—28.]
Acts xxiv. [22—27.]

14. In proceeding in judgment, beware of swiftness and much speed. It is good for a judge commonly to have leaden feet. Yet, as a judge may be too swift, so he may be too slow. Delatories and shiftings off wear out many a just cause, and beggar many a poor man. The cause standing clear, further pleading should cease, sentence should not be delayed. Solomon set not over the harlots to the next term, but seeing by his wisdom the truth of the cause, proceeded forthwith to judgment. Paul was set over from place to place, from term to term, and could not receive justice: the cause is declared: Felix hoped for a fee. But this fault of delaying justice is laid upon the attorneys and proctors, the counsellors and advocates in the law; who seek their greater gain and wealth through the greater trouble and loss of the people. If they would learn two short lessons of St Paul, and learn withal to follow them, the matter easily might be amended. The one is to love men, and not their money. *Non quæro quæ vestra sunt*, saith St Paul: "I seek not yours, but you." This lesson is hard, but good; and the other is like it. "I can do nothing against the truth, but for the truth," saith the apostle. Nothing in a bad cause, but in a good cause all things. These les-

2 Cor. xii. [14.]
2 Cor. xiii. [8.]

sons well learned would quickly cut off many evil pleas, and drive back causeless controversies.

15. You, to whom the sword of justice and judg- *Partiality.* ment is committed, take heed unto it. Let it not spare mighty men; for their sins are mighty sins. If such offend, their fall draweth down others with them. God therefore commanded Moses to hang up the princes of the people upon gibbets, that they might be examples of punishment who had been examples in sinning. The good consul Junius Brutus spared not his own sons, but cut off their conspiring heads; and Aulus Fulvius, in the like case, did the like thing. Pilate abused his office, when upon suit he spared captain Barabbas the murderer, and killed Christ our Saviour. Spare not traitors, murderers, or thieves, lest you be partakers of their sins. Your lenity towards them is cruelty towards the commonweal, the enemies of whose peace they are. Serve God in fear, love his truth, promote his gospel. The seat, the judgment, the sword, is the Lord's: defend therefore his cause, see to the keeping of his statutes, enlarge his kingdom, advance his glory: for he hath promised to glorify them [1 Sam. ii. 30.] that honour him, but they that despise him shall be full base: he shall make them vile and contemptible.

16. "Doing of judgment" may also generally be taken *Judgment and justice* for just dealing. Justice is a virtue which giveth every *must be in all the deal-* man his own. Render unto every man that which is his. *ings gene-rally of all* Let every man perform his office and fulfil his duty: let *men.* every man do right one to another: do as you would be done unto. If this law were observed, the people should be eased of great expences, judges and justices of great travail. Christ saith, "If a man take thy coat from thee," [Matt. v. 40.] rather than strive, "give him also thy cloak." "There [1 Cor. vi. [7.]] is verily a fault amongst you, because ye go to law one with another: why do you not rather suffer wrong?" Why do ye not rather sustain any kind of tolerable harm? Abraham gave place to Lot, and would not contend: his only reason was, "we are brethren." But brotherhood is [Gen. xiii. [8.]] now-a-days no argument of agreement: our times are so unlike their times, and we so unlike them. There were no better mean in my opinion to bridle these quarrelling and contentious minds of wranglers, than to burthen such

as fail in their cause with great expences and amerciaments. It would make them beware of quarrels and unjust contending, if they were sure to pay well for it. Do judgment: deal justly one with another: pay unto all men that which is due: that which is not due seek not to have at any man's hands.

<small>As we must do judgment, so we must also love mercy; which he that loveth doth not rashly judge others. Luke vi. [36, 37.]</small>
17. The second duty to our neighbour is "mercy:" "He hath shewed thee, O man, what is good, and what the Lord requireth of thee: Surely, to do judgment, and to love mercy." "Be merciful," saith our Saviour, "as your Father is also merciful." This mercy, as Christ there teacheth, will shew forth itself in three properties. First, it will bridle that uncharitable rashness of judging and condemning others. *Nolite judicare:* "judge not." Mercy will not be hasty to judge. There be judgments civil, and judgments ecclesiastical; judgments public, and private judgments. Christ neither forbiddeth the magistrate, neither the public minister, to judge according to the law; neither the parent or master, to judge and correct their offending children or servants. It is uncharitable private judgment which God forbiddeth, when men unadvisedly take upon them to give sentence of others, as if God had resigned his own right into their hands: they condemn whom they list, and say what they list: even as they fancy, so they judge. This man is a saint, and that man a sinner; he the servant of God, and he the child of death. Who art thou that so judgest another's servant? Is it not to his own master only to whom he stands or falls? Who art thou that takest such severity upon thee? that dealest so unmercifully with thy brother? He is a sinner: so thou either art, or hast been, or mayest be: judge therefore thyself, try and examine thine own works. Judge, I say, thyself, and judge not him, lest thou be condemned of the Lord for both not judging <small>Gal. vi. [1.]</small> and judging. "If a brother be overtaken with a fault, ye that are spiritual shew mercy: restore him with the spirit of meekness, considering thyself, lest thou also be tempted." Verily this merciless judging of others is the cause why we fall into many perils and secret temptations. Love mercy therefore; and judge not. He that judgeth with the Pharisee with the Pharisee shall be judged.

18. Another fruit of "mercy" is forgiveness. They who are hasty to judge are for the most part in forgiving slow. But "forgive, and ye shall be forgiven." Howbeit, such as sit in judgment ought to correct and not to remit; because they deal not with injuries done to themselves, but to the laws and commonwealth, or church: but in private injuries we must all remember the words, and follow the example of our Saviour: "Be merciful and forgive." Christ forgave them that put him to death; Stephen, them that stoned him; Joseph, them that sold him; the king, his unthrifty servant one thousand talents. If we forgive not others, it is in vain to pray that which we daily pray: "Forgive us." For so doth Ecclesiasticus well teach us: "He that seeketh vengeance shall find vengeance of the Lord; and he will surely keep his sins. Forgive thy neighbour the hurt that he hath done to thee: so shall thy sins be forgiven thee also, when thou prayest. Should a man bear hatred against man, and desire forgiveness of the Lord? He will shew no mercy to a man that is like himself; and will he ask forgiveness of his own sins? If he that is but flesh nourish hatred, and ask pardon of God, who will entreat for his sins?" And our Saviour's commandment is: "If thou bring thy gift to the altar, and there rememberest that thy brother hath ought against thee; leave there thine offering before the altar, and go thy way: first be reconciled to thy brother, and then come and offer thy gift." Whereunto St Chrysostom alluding saith, "That God had rather want thy sacrifice due to him, than reconciliation should not be made between thee and thy brother[1]."

Lovers of mercy are ready to pardon and put up injuries. [Luke vi. 37.]

Ecclus. xxviii. [1—5.]

Matt. v. [23, 24.]

19. The next and third fruit of "mercy" mentioned by our Saviour is, "Give, and it shall be given unto you." He that loveth mercy giveth alms; but the covetous man is cruel. God is so careful to have the poor relieved, that he hath bound himself by promise to make alms most gainful to the giver: so that it is not in this as in other common expences, but "whatsoever we lay out, that we

Merciful men are bountiful. [Luke vi. 38.]

[1 Τί γὰρ ἂν γένοιτο τούτων ἡμερώτερον τῶν ῥημάτων; ἐκκοπτέσθω, φησίν, ἡ ἐμὴ λατρεία, ἵνα ἡ σὴ ἀγάπη μείνῃ· ἐπεὶ καὶ τοῦτο θυσία, ἡ πρὸς τὸν ἀδελφὸν καταλλαγή.—Chrysost. Op. Par. 1727. In Matt. Hom. xvi. Tom. vii. p. 216.—Ed.]

lay up." "He that giveth to the poor lendeth to the Lord," a sure discharger of his debts to the uttermost: for he leaveth not a cup of cold water given in his name unrewarded. The occasions which we have to shew forth this fruit of mercy are very many and great: we have the poor with us, and we have them with us in great numbers. Are we not worse than Jews, if we suffer our Christ, at whose hands we have received all our riches, in his naked and hungry members to beg his bread at our doors, and pitifully to die even in the midst of our streets for distress, for cold and hunger? If our gospel bring forth instead of mercy this cruelty, instead of kindness this hardness of heart, doubtless God will take his precious gospel from us, and give it to a people that will bring forth better and sweeter fruit. Now, if the love of God and mercy towards our brother cannot pierce our flinty hearts, yet let shame of the world compel us, and our own commodity induce us well to consider of this lamentable case. If that which is given were given in good order, it would ease this common grief. By good order and wise provision the impotent might be so relieved that they should not need to beg, and such as are able might be forced in the sweat of their brows to eat their own bread. And if the matter were taken in hand by them by whom it should, I do not doubt but God would touch the hearts of many a man with tender mercy, that they would both cheerfully and liberally contribute to this work of mercy, which God doth more esteem than any other sacrifice: nay, he refuseth sacrifice and craveth this. The Lord loveth a cheerful and a bountiful giver, and will plentifully reward him. Let every good man set forward this work; it is the work of the Lord, the fruit of mercy, good and gainful, not only to others, but also to ourselves. For behold how the works of mercy do return back again unto them from whom they proceed. "Judge not, and you yourselves shall not be judged. Forgive, and ye shall be forgiven yourselves: give, and it shall be given unto you."

20. All which notwithstanding, the bowels of compassion are in some men so marvellously dried and closed up, that they turn away their faces from all men that desire any thing at their hands, though they ask it not

[Prov. xix. 17.]

Usurers are altogether merciless men.

of gift, but of loan, unless they ask to buy the loan with usury. The Jews even to this day will not lend upon usury among themselves, but lend freely to their brethren and without gain. Judas himself, that sold his Master for money, was not more cruel hearted, I suppose, than these men are, who for money devour their brethren. Their hearts are iron hearts. They have no spark of pity or compassion left in them. Let them not think but that one day their gain shall be their exceeding loss. If Chrysostom thought that one evil-gotten groat laid up amongst a chest full of money would be as a canker to fret out and eat up the rest, what shall become then of so much gotten by so unmerciful and ungodly means? Where is love, where is mercy, when lending of money is become merchandise? Enough hath been said in this place of this matter: which if it be not amended, be ye assured that the Lord God in his just wrath will plague you both in yourselves and in your posterity for it.

21. Now that we have seen what duty we owe to men, let us see what God requireth to be performed unto himself. "He hath shewed thee, O man, what is good." Our duty towards him is to humble ourselves, and to walk carefully with our God. He that will walk with God must be of an humble heart. It is the mild-hearted, and not the proud-minded; the publican, and not the Pharisee, that walketh with him. *The duty towards God which the prophet requireth at our hands.*

22. To walk with him is to be sincerely and heartily careful to set forward his cause, to promote his gospel, to defend his truth to amplify his kingdom to the uttermost of our powers. Princes and they that judge the earth, whom God hath blessed with so high an honour, especially should in fear and reverence serve their God, love his word and gospel, earnestly and cheerfully advance, maintain, and defend true religion. They are able to do most good; and therefore most is required of them. Bishops and ministers, the dispensers of God's blessed mysteries, should carefully travail in their Lord's cause and glory, in season and out of season to preach the gospel, even so much as in us leth: or else the *væ*[1] of God, which hangeth over our heads, shall be poured down upon us. But the *What it is to walk with God.*

[¹ Wo.—Ed.]

saying of St Paul is verified in these our days upon all sorts of people: "All men seek their own." The preferring of true religion, the seeking of God's glory, is the least part of men's care or thought. It was otherwise with Moses, who both loved God's service with perfect love, and hated superstition with perfect hatred. Theodosius, for want of this warmness and zeal in God's quarrel, suffered by his too much lenity the Arians, who denied Christ to be God, quietly to spread abroad their heresies in his dominions, without check or controlling. The good bishop Amphilochius upon this occasion repaired to the emperor, who had at that time with him his son and heir Arcadius. The bishop did his obeisance and duty to the emperor, but saluted not his son; wherewith the emperor finding fault, said, Why salute ye not our son, who shall sit on our seat? No, emperor; for so much as thou dost not care for the Son of God, but sufferest him to lose his honour and place, neither shall thy son be regarded or sit on thy seat. Here, at his own cause called into question, he waxed warm, and forthwith expelled the Arians out of his dominions[1]. Many of them who are hot in their own matters, are cold in God's cause. Yet our prophet biddeth us carefully to walk with our God, and to be earnest in seeking of his kingdom and glory.

[Phil. ii. 21.]

He which walketh with God must walk carefully, especially if God have made him as it were a god amongst men.

23. Be careful over your conversation: give no cause of slander to them which are without, or of offence to the little ones: let not the gospel be discredited by your behaviours. Be careful that the light of your life so shine before the world, that therein your heavenly Father may be glorified. Ye ought to shine as lights: take heed that your light be not turned into darkness. Be bright stars, and not misty clouds. If an eclipse fall amongst you, the rest of England will be darkened with it. Ye are seen and marked of men and angels. The world hath many eyes, ears, and tongues. London, Westminster, the inns of court and chancery, from whence the best and most of you do flow, are as a fountain from whence should spring all true religion, all piety, virtue, and godly conversation. If this spring be corrupted, the rivers that flow from it must needs be polluted. If blasphemous popery, full of idolatry

[[1] See before, pp. 41, 73.—ED.]

and superstition, if vain and puffed-up pride, if wicked avarice and intolerable usury, the great canker of the commonwealth, if belly-cheer and filthy whoredom, if subtile and false dealing, if counterfeit and feigned friendship, if flattery and dissimulation, be the water of this your well; doubt you not but that all England will drink thereof, and they being poisoned by your ill example, their blood shall be required at your hands.

24. Walk therefore, and walk on, go forward. For if ye be in the way of life, not to go forward is to go backward. If ye be entered into this happy path, step not aside, give not back. A dog returning to his vomit is a foul and an ugly thing to behold. Take heed, I say, of backsliding. It is a dreadful thing to forsake Christ, and to be ashamed of the gospel. He that tasteth of this sweet gift of God, the gospel of Christ, and falleth back from it, he is a tormenter, as much as in him lieth, and a crucifier of the Lord of glory. Walk therefore, go on from strength to strength, from virtue to virtue. Ye have been heretofore often moved; but what effect hath it taken? God grant that there be not a retiring from strength to weakness, from virtue to sinfulness! It is to be feared that many men's wonted zeal is transformed into cold security, their liberality into greediness and biting usury, charity into envy, sobriety into wantonness, humility into pride and haughtiness. This is the common walking of men, for whom it were far better if they stood still. The apostle could not mention them but with tears. "There are many which walk," saith he, "of whom I have told you often, and now tell you weeping, they are enemies of the cross of Christ: their belly is their god, their glory is in their shame, their end is damnation." [Phil. iii. 18, 19.]

They which walk with God must still walk on.

25. Walk not as these do in darkness, but in light. "God is light:" walk therefore "with God." And then ye do that which he requireth at your hands. Walk with him: for howsoever we walk, we are sure to walk before him. We cannot shun his eye: if we fly up into heaven, he is there: if we go down into hell, there he is also. He seeth things done in light, and beholdeth that which is covered with darkness: he is privy unto men's thoughts: he knew the spiteful and malicious purposes of the scribes and Pharisees; [1 John i. 5.]

We all walk before God, but not all with God.

he espied Adam biting the forbidden fruit: he looked upon Cain shedding his brother's blood: he perceived the secret sins of Sodom: he understood the corruption of Giezi[1], and made it manifest: he saw the double heart of Judas, who kissed his master and betrayed him: he beheld Siba when he falsely and traitorously accused Mephiboseth unto David. The cloaked adultery and murder, which David had covered with clouds of policy, could not be hidden from his eye: the lie of Ananias was written in capital letters before him, plain to be read: the sleights and conveyances of the usurer cannot be covered with fig-tree leaves from the sight of the Almighty: there is neither bribe given nor taken, but God looketh upon it: there is no treachery nor treason that can be hid from him. *Dominus videt*[2], is a short, but a good lesson. I beseech you, learn it and remember it, that it may teach you to walk always as in the sight of the Lord, who will be a swift witness and a fierce judge against evil doers who walk with Satan. Which thing, rightly and duly considered and weighed, would bridle these untamed affections of ours, and terrify men from these heinous and wilful sins. Our Lord grant this good effect for his great mercy's sake!

Thus have you heard the occasion, explication, and application of these the prophet's words; what way we may please God and pacify his wrath; what we owe to our neighbours, namely, to deal justly and mercifully with them, not rashly to judge of them; easily to forgive them, and liberally to give unto them; what we owe likewise to our gracious God, to wit, to humble ourselves lowly before his majesty, and carefully, zealously, and continually to walk in his presence. To this God, even our good and merciful Father, with his Son our Saviour, and the Holy Ghost our Sanctifier, three Persons and one God, be all honour and glory world without end. Amen.

[1 Giezi—Gehazi.—ED.]
[2 The Lord seeth.—ED.]

THE THIRTEENTH SERMON.

A SERMON

MADE IN YORK, AT A VISITATION.

MATT. XXI.

12. *And Jesus went into the temple of God, and cast out all them that sold and bought in the temple, and overthrew the tables of the money-changers, and the seats of them that sold doves,*
13. *And said to them, It is written, Mine house shall be called the house of prayer: but ye have made it a den of thieves.*

THE church and spouse of God hath been ever most dear to the children of God. Godly princes have always carefully travailed for the good preservation and government thereof. David, that princely prophet. Solomon, that wise and mighty king, Jehosaphat, Ezekias, Josias, Zorobabel, with others most religious and worthy men, which bare excellent rule in their dominions, have painfully travailed not only to build, to amplify, and to enlarge the kingdom of God by setting forward true religion, but also to purge and reform his temple by taking away such defilements and corruptions as grew by means of careless government. The apostles of Christ both among the Jews and gentiles did first plant churches by the diligent preaching of the gospel, and afterward with like care and diligence visit them to see in what state they stood, that, if any thing were gone to decay, it might in time be repaired. This is recorded unto us in the history of their acts and deeds, and namely in the fifteenth chapter. Christ the anointed King and Priest, the great Shepherd of the sheep, the perfect example given us to follow, did not only go about through all Galilee and the coasts of Jewry, preaching the glad tidings of the gospel, and confirming his heavenly doctrine with wonderful miracles; but, as it is in this present history declared, perceiving that through

The care which the godly have always had of the church.

Acts xv. [36.]

the subtilty of Satan, and covetousness of the priests, the temple of God was profaned, in his pastoral care he visited it, and in the zeal of God voided them out which did defile it. How the fathers of the church, and chief pastors, have with great care and diligence every where, at all times, in all ages, done the like, I need not declare unto you: the histories are plain and plentiful. And thus considering my calling and the charge committed unto me, I thought myself by these former examples in duty forced and in conscience bound not only, as much as in me lieth, to feed the flock of Christ, but also to view and see in what state the church of God committed to my oversight and government standeth. And as Christ began with the most magnificent temple of Jerusalem, which he found profaned and polluted through the practice of the priests; so thought I it convenient and meet first to visit this most ancient and famous church, the head and example to all the rest, well hoping to find it in better order.

The church purged, and the use thereof shewed, by Christ.

2. That we may learn by the doctrine and example of Christ how we ought to use ourselves in the house of God, as well for the establishing of true religion and of the sincere serving of God, as also for the expelling of that which is vain, corrupt, and counterfeit, there are in this action of Christ two things especially to be considered of: First, he cometh to Jerusalem, entereth into the temple, findeth it full of corruption, and doth purge it: Secondly, he teacheth the true use of it, and sheweth them their fault who did abuse it.

The entertainment of Christ and his ministers in the world, when they go about to do the work of the Lord. Luke xix. [38.]

3. Christ coming towards Jerusalem was at the first highly magnified and received with applause of the people, crying, "Hosanna, Blessed is he that cometh King in the name of the Lord; peace in heaven and glory on high." But this fair weather did not long continue. So soon as he entered into the city and taught, the chief priests, the scribes, and the princes of the people sought to destroy him: yea, the people which before gave so great applause, crying, Hosanna, soon after cried with a loud voice, *Crucifige*[1]. The gospel in prosperity hath many pretensed friends and favourers; but when it is persecuted by the wise and mighty men of the world, then these

[1 Crucify him.—ED.]

counterfeits shew themselves in their own colours: the hollowness of their hearts is then descried. Let the minister therefore, which mindeth indeed the glory of God, beware that he never depend upon men, whose minds are changeable and always wavering; but let him rest upon God, and rely himself wholly upon his providence. Let us all faithfully and painfully travail in our function, making ourselves ready for the cross, patiently to suffer with Christ Jesus.

4. Being come to the city, he straightway entered into the temple, either, as Gregory noteth, to declare *quod ex culpa sacerdotum ruina populi*[1], "that the fault of the priests is the ruin of the people," and therefore his principal care was to correct and reform them; or else to give all men an example of diligence in repairing to the house of God. *Christ's entering into the temple.*

5. Having entered the temple, he findeth there, instead of pastors teaching the word of God, drovers and brokers making sale; instead of pews for prayer, tables for exchange; instead of righteous men, brute beasts; thieves, instead of a sanctified congregation. Thus he found the church of Jerusalem disfigured and forlorn: this was the state of that synagogue, at what time he came to visit it. *The state wherein he found the temple of Jerusalem.*

6. How to proceed in reforming a church so greatly disordered, our Saviour hath taught us by his own practice amongst the Jews. He entered into the temple, threw out the men that bought and sold, whipped out the beasts, poured out the changers' money, turned their tables upsidedown, overthrew the seats of them that sold doves, and withal told them, *Scriptum est*, "It is written." *He endeavoureth to reform the church by purging it.*

7. In that we read how Christ did all these things, we are thereby given to understand, at whose hands we must expect reformation of things amiss in the church of God. Christ had authority to cast out of the temple whatsoever displeased him, because he was supreme Lord over it. The persons therefore to whom this work of reformation belongeth are not all men indifferently, but they only to whom he hath granted the seat of special *By whom the church should be reformed, when things are found to be amiss.*

[1 Greg. Papæ I. Mag. Op. Par. 1705. In Evangel. Lib. II. Hom. xxxix. Tom. I. col. 1646.—ED.]

authority in his church. If they whom he hath set over his house as principal servants, guides and stewards, either civilly or spiritually, as Moses or as Aaron, to rule and govern it until his coming, shall, in such manner as agreeth with their several places and callings, perform his duty in the church of Christ; whosoever in such proceedings withstandeth them, the same undoubtedly rebelleth against God. Yea, I say further, when God hath given his people kings which are as nursing fathers, and queens which are as nursing mothers to his church; when princes are not enemies but professors of the faith, and protectors of the faithful; their hands ought to be chief in this work: neither is it lawful for subjects, of what degree and order soever, by themselves to attempt alteration and change in the church of God, though it be from worse to better. In the days of Josias, Helkiah, although he were the Lord's high priest, and knew things to be very much out of order, did not thereupon, according to the custom of the turbulent and seditious, by word or writing alienate and estrange the minds of the people from the present kind of government either of the church or public weal, but peaceably and orderly he sent Shaphan the chancellor to the king; who, perceiving the things which were amiss, went immediately up to the house of the Lord with all the men of Judah, and the inhabitants of Jerusalem with him, and the priests and prophets and all the people, where, the faults and abuses being clearly set down that every one might see them, he gave commandment to Helkiah the high priest, and the priests of the second order, and the keepers of the door, to bring out of the temple of the Lord all the vessels that were made for Baal. Thus the prince did his duty, and the priests theirs; he by injunction, and they by execution; they instructing him, and he strengthening them in the work of the Lord. Seeing therefore we have on the one side (the name of the Lord be blessed for it!) the highest power zealous for the glory of God, as theirs was; let not us, whom this care ought especially to touch, shew ourselves less ready than they were to bring out of the temple of the Lord all such filthy corruptions, as are crept into it by the wicked dealings of those ungodly men

Isai. xlix. [23.]

2 Kings xxii. [8.]

which care not how shamefully they pollute and defile it; let not us, whom the Lord hath made the overseers of his house, be slothful in proceeding to sweep, cleanse, and purge it, according as laws and statutes have wisely provided in this behalf; let us consider that we are the Lord's labourers, that the work we have in hand is his husbandry, that our duty is as well "to destroy" as "to build," "to root out" as "to plant." Jer. i. [10.]

8. But what is that which we must labour to destroy? what weeds be those which we must endeavour to root out? We read here, that our Saviour did cast buyers and sellers out of the temple, terming them "thieves." For although to buy and sell be actions in themselves lawful and honest, yet the time and place, with other circumstances, may so change their quality, that he which buyeth shall be as one that robbeth, and he that selleth as one that stealeth. They bought and sold in the temple: this Christ condemneth. Yet behold what a beautiful colour they had set upon their wicked practices, to make them seem allowable before men. For of the judgment of God they made no account. It is written in the law, "Thou shalt eat before the Lord thy God, in the place which he shall choose to cause his name to dwell there, the tithe of thy corn, of thy wine, and of thine oil, and the first-born of thy kine, and of thy sheep, that thou mayest learn to fear the Lord thy God alway. And if the way be too long for thee, so that thou art not able to carry it, because the place is far from thee, where the Lord thy God shall choose to set his name, when the Lord thy God shall bless thee, then shalt thou make it in money, and take the money in thine hand, and go unto the place which the Lord thy God shall choose; and thou shalt bestow the money for whatsoever thine heart desireth, and shalt eat it there before the Lord thy God, and rejoice both thou and thine household." Under pretence of providing that, according to this law, men which dwelt far off might always, at their coming to the temple, have sacrifices there and offerings in a readiness to present before the Lord, their covetous humour fed itself upon the people without all fear of God, without any reverence at all of his sanctuary. May they not justly be termed "thieves," who, pretending thus to serve

What was reformed by Christ in the temple.

Deut. xiv. [23—26.]

the Lord in his sacrifices, robbed and spoiled him in his saints? No doubt Jerusalem, had she known the things which belonged to her peace, would have blessed the hour wherein the Lord of the house came to ease that holy place of so intolerable burthens, to rid his temple of so noisome filth.

What we should reform in the church, according to Christ's example.

9. Now because the root, from whence these abuses and corruptions grew, was the settled wickedness wherewith the hearts both of the priests and people were possessed, therefore we may, without swerving from the true intent of this history, take occasion here to note some special pollutions of the mystical temple of God, which is his church, and to shew the great necessity of removing them: wherein (as the present occasion of our assembly at this time requireth) I will especially touch such as properly belong to that part of the church which hath the spiritual regiment of the other. This therefore is the principal matter which now we have to observe in the fact of our Lord and Master Christ; that if in visiting our temples we find them possessed with wicked pastors, they are not there to be suffered: the rod of severity must whip them out. Who be good shepherds, and who be thieves, it is soon discerned: ye shall know them by their fruits.

The unkind affection of evil pastors. John x. [1—18.]

10. Unto good pastors our Saviour opposeth hirelings, thieves, and robbers, shewing also the difference between the one and the other. The good shepherd loveth his flock entirely: it grieveth him not to pour out his very soul for their sakes: he gathereth them as lambs into his arms, carrieth them in his bosom, and kindly entreateth them. Contrariwise the hireling careth not for the sheep: he beareth a stern and a stony heart towards them. And as their inward affections are far different, so their outward actions are much unlike, whether we look upon their entering into their function, or their dealing after they are entered.

Their unorderly entering upon the flock, by simony.

11. The true shepherd "goeth in by the door: to him the porter openeth:" he taketh not this honour unto himself, but expecteth a calling from God, as Aaron did: he breaketh not in by violence, but waiteth till the porter open unto him, till they give him entrance, to whom Christ hath given power and authority to ordain. But thieves

and robbers "climb up another way:" they wind in themselves by unlawful means: with money they purchase the rooms which they occupy in the church of Christ. Thus did Menelaus get the priesthood from Jason, at the hands of the king, by giving three hundred talents of silver more than the other; albeit he had nothing in himself worthy of the high priesthood, but bare the stomach of a cruel tyrant and the wrath of a wild beast. Thus Leo the tenth, Innocentius the eighth, Silvester the third, two Gregorys, the sixth and the twelfth, yea, the most part of the bishops of Rome for many years, have obtained their popedoms. Thus do their cardinals, bishops, and prelates: thus do their clergy even to this day. And I would to God this were only their fault! A thing both condemned by the commendable laws, decrees, and constitutions of sundry councils, and also by the blessed apostle St Peter so grievously accursed in him whose heart was first therewith infected, that, in the whole body of the sacred scripture, a note of the like indignation conceived against any other sin (as I am persuaded) can scarcely be found. For why? If they which bought and sold but the beasts of the field and birds of the air, doves, sheep, and oxen, in the place which God had sanctified to himself, were therefore termed by a name that declareth their dealings to have been as much abhorred in his sight, as if they had spent all the days of their life in theft and robbery, how can we think any bitterness of speech, or sharpness of punishment, too great for so extreme licentiousness, as theirs that make sale of the cure of souls, that bargain for the gifts of the Holy Ghost? For so they are. The making of bishops, the bestowing of benefices, the presenting, instituting, and inducting of pastors, the placing of teachers, guides, and overseers in the church, is and should be accounted the very work of the Holy Ghost. "Attend," saith St Paul, "take heed to yourselves, and to the whole flock, wherein the Holy Ghost hath placed you bishops to rule the church of God, which he hath purchased with his own blood." Whosoever therefore be the man that presumeth to stain a thing so holy with the execrable filth of indirect dealing, of buying, selling, covenanting, bargaining either for money, or money worth, may it not as justly be said to him, as

[2 Mac. iv. [24.]]

[Acts xx. [28.]]

Acts viii. [20, 21.] to Magus, "Thy money perish with thee, because thou thinkest that the gift of God may be obtained with money: thou hast neither part nor fellowship in this business; for thine heart is not right in the sight of God." I counsel them, with St Peter, that are in the gall of this bitterness and in the bonds of this iniquity, betime to repent them of their wickedness, and to pray unto God that, if it be possible, the thoughts of their hearts may be forgiven them.

Their evil dealing after they are entered. 12. It is a true saying, *Vix bono peraguntur exitu quæ malo sunt inchoata principio:* "Things ill begun are not commonly well ended;" neither are their proceedings likely to be good, whose beginnings are so greatly out of order. They which enter not into the temple as did Aaron, will hardly behave themselves in the house of the Lord as Aaron did. *2 Mac. iv. [7, 8.]* Jason obtained a superiority in the church by money: but how behaved he himself in this his purchased function? Began he not immediately to draw his brethren to the customs of the gentiles? Did he not by and bye change their laws and policies, and bring up new statutes contrary to their law? As the good shepherd entering in at the door, when he is entered, guideth *[Ps. lxxviii. 72.]* his sheep (as David) in the discretion of his hands, feedeth them carefully with wholesome doctrine, and walketh in all uprightness of holy and undefiled conversation before them; so he that climbeth up another way, after he hath gotten himself in, seeketh nothing but to steal, kill, and destroy. *John x. [10.]* "The thief cometh not but to steal, to kill, and to destroy." He hath no other end or purpose.

They steal. 13. The only thing that should be desired by the pastor is the weal and benefit of his flock. For if the mark whereat we shoot be but to make our commodity by the gospel of Jesus Christ, wherein do we differ from thieves and robbers? Is not our intent and purpose the very self-same with theirs? Wherefore St Peter's exhortation is, *1 Pet. v. [2.]* "Feed the flock of God, caring for it, not for filthy lucre, but of a ready mind." If a man have all knowledge, insomuch that he be able to speak with tongues, yea, and to prophesy; yet if the thing for which he laboureth be his own gain, if he use this vocation, than which nothing is more precious and holy, only as a way or trade to live by, whatsoever he receiveth with such a mind, he stealeth rather than receiveth it. This is that whereof the Lord complaineth so grievously by his prophets: "The priests teach for hire, the prophets prophesy for money: yet will they lean upon the Lord and say, Is not the Lord among us?" And again: "These shepherds cannot understand: they all look to their own way," every one for his advantage and for his own purpose. Moses, blessing Levi before his death, saith first, "They shall teach Jacob thy judgments and Israel thy law, they shall put incense before thy face;" and then addeth, "Bless, O Lord, his substance, accept the work of his hands." As if he should have said: So long as Levi and his sons do not seek their own commodity, but thy glory, thou art righteous, and canst not forget to provide in large manner both for them and theirs. As indeed, till the men of that sacred order took flesh-hooks in their hands, and sought to better their estate by force, till they became like to greedy mastiffs, ravening curs, who ever saw the Levite of the Lord forsaken, or the son of the Levite begging his bread? So likewise the church of God was never spoiled, till her pastors were over careful to be enriched. In the prime and first appearing of christian religion, as long as that heroical contempt of earthly things continued in the guides and leaders of the people, what heaps of worldly treasure were brought and laid down even at their feet! Men thought themselves to perform nothing worthy of that profession into which they were entered, unless they sold away their lands, goods, and possessions, and gave all to make them rich, by whose means themselves were become righteous. The contrary to which affection, as in other parts of the christian world, so in this also, hath taken such root, and is grown now so strong, that God may justly charge us as sometime he did his own people, saying, "Ye have spoiled me, even this whole nation." If therefore we be grieved (as who is not grieved?) to see the havock that is made of the church of God, let us change our earthly and worldly affection, that he may change the condition of his church. God is no purveyor for thieves and robbers. Let us, in sincerity and in truth, heartily and in deed despise our own gain for his glory, and

[Mic. iii. [11.]]
[Isai. lvi. [11.]]
[Deut. xxxiii. [10, 11.]]
[1 Sam. ii. [13, 14.]]
[Mal. iii. [9.]]

prove him if he will not rebuke these devourers for our sakes.

They kill when they teach not the truth which saveth. This some do because they cannot teach, some because they will not.

14. The next thing which Christ observeth in thieves is this, they destroy the flock, and make as little conscience to kill as to steal. They kill not the bodies, but the souls of men. The life of the soul is the word of truth, wherein whosoever hath taken upon him to instruct the flock of Christ, and either cannot or will not do it, what doth he else but kill and destroy? Moses, speaking of the obedience of Israel to the laws and statutes of their God, "This is," saith he, "your wisdom." But [Deut. iv. 6, 10.] how came Israel by that wisdom? Did they naturally know the Lord, as beasts do naturally know their dams? No: "The Lord said unto me," saith Moses, "Gather the people together, and I will cause them to hear my words, that they may learn to fear me all the days that they shall live upon the earth, and that they may teach their children." So they came near and stood under the mountain, and were taught of God, which spake unto them out of the midst of the fire. Thus God taught Israel then. Afterward he raised up prophets among them of their own brethren; and they were taught by men like unto themselves. Neither hath God at any time ceased and left off; but from the beginning of the world to this very hour he hath given men knowledge by instruction, and saved his elect by teaching. Cannot God then give wisdom from above without a teacher? Yes, God is able to maintain the life of man without bread. But why do we talk of his absolute power, when his will is that Cornelius be taught by Peter, Lydia by Paul, Paul by Ananias, the eunuch by Philip, every soul that is wise in [Eph. iv. 11, 12.] the doctrine of salvation by "apostles, prophets, evangelists, teachers appointed for the gathering together of the saints, for the work of the ministry, and for the edification of the body of Christ?" As therefore he that will live must eat, so he that will be saved must have a teacher. Wherefore when the Lord meant a blessing to [Jer. iii. 15.] his people, he made them this promise: "I will give you pastors according to my heart, which shall feed you with knowledge and understanding." When their pastors were void of knowledge and understanding, this was ever a

token that their ruin and destruction was at hand. Come now, saith the prophet, "all ye beasts of the field, come to devour, even all the beasts of the forest:" this people cannot continue now, they must needs perish; for "their watchmen are all blind, they have no knowledge: they are all dumb dogs, and cannot bark: they lie asleep, and delight in sleeping." We are unworthy of our lives, if we do not acknowledge the wonderful blessing of God in our ministry at this day. For howsoever it be debased by some, yet is it so far off, God be thanked, from the state of the Jewish clergy in those days, that I am persuaded there neither is, nor ever was, a more learned ministry in any nation under heaven. Nevertheless I acknowledge, it is much to be lamented, that, the glorious gospel of Christ now shining with so perfect beauty as it doth, in the midst of so great light so many should still remain in darkness, living as men without God in this present world, and perishing through the ignorance of his saving truth. In the mean while, they which are the chief and principal causes hereof think they have very well discharged themselves by accusing others; as if, when they, against all both religion and reason, have drawn unto themselves those possessions which ought to maintain such as labour in the gospel, a bishop by striking the earth with one foot might raise up learned pastors sufficient to furnish a whole province. But, whosoever be the principal cause of this disorder, they undoubtedly cannot wash their hands of it, that presume to take upon them the charge of souls, for which they know themselves unfit and altogether unsufficient. In these which destroy, because they cannot save, there is only a defect which, although it worthily deserve punishment, doth nevertheless move some pity and compassion, if there be a willingness to do that which there wanteth ability to perform. But against such as wittingly and wilfully suffer the sheep, for which Christ died, to die for want of instruction, the souls of them that perish do cry as the blood of Abel against Cain, for vengeance and wrath. "Give attendance" therefore "to reading, to exhortation, to doctrine, exercise these things," and give yourselves unto them, that all may see how you profit, and how the church doth profit by you. Ye are fed by the

[Isai. lvi. [9, 10.]

1 Tim. iv. [13, 15.]

sweat of other men's brows: ye receive things temporal without any corporal labour of your own. But with what conscience do ye this, if they which minister unto your necessities reap not that at your hands for which they minister? You can perhaps allege many colourable excuses for yourselves. But will you allege the same in that day, when a strict account of your stewardship shall be required by him that cometh to judge both quick and dead? Consider these things, and "be ye stedfast, unmoveable, abounding always in the work of the Lord, knowing that your labour in the Lord is not in vain." Is it not better for you to save both yourselves and others, than by not saving others not to save yourselves?

1 Cor. xv. [58.]

15. They which are saved must be sanctified "in truth": they which are of the truth must be consummate and "made perfect in one." They are no better therefore than soul-murderers, be they never so painful in their teaching, that teach such doctrines as do either poison the church with heresy, or dismember and rent it asunder with schism. Of heretics St Paul, forewarning the church of Ephesus, saith, "I know that after my departure there will ravening wolves enter in among you, not sparing the flock." Of schismatics he writeth in most earnest manner as well to the church of Corinth, as of Rome. To the one: "I beseech you, brethren, by the name of our Lord Jesus Christ, that ye all say one thing, and that there be no schisms amongst you." To the other: "Mark them diligently which cause division." These serve not the Saviour, they serve the destroyer of the world. "They have over them a king, to wit, the angel of the bottomless pit, whose name in Hebrew is called Abaddon," that is to say, a destroyer. Their pestilent properties St John sheweth, by comparing the harm which they do in the church to the torments which they suffer that are stung with scorpions.

They kill by teaching which teach pernicious doctrine of heresy or schism. John xvii. [17, 23.]

Acts xx. [29.]

1 Cor. i. [10.]

Rom. xvi. [17.]

Rev. ix. [11.]

16. Now, as these destroy by ill teaching, so likewise there are others who, teaching well but living ill, do more harm by their life in one hour, than good by their doctrine in many years. Sozomene[1] writeth that, when barbarous nations saw how the christian priests, which were captives,

They kill by example, who teaching soundly live disorderly.
Soz. l. ii. c. 5.

[[1] Soz. Hist. Eccl. Amst. 1700, Lib. ii. c. 6, pp. 367, 368.—ED.]

did by their sober and reverend behaviour dam up the mouths of evil speakers, they thought them to be men full of wisdom and understanding, and hoped to find favour at the hands of God, if they should worship him after the manner of those worthy and grave sages. Could the ancient prophets, the blessed apostles, the holy fathers in former times have enlarged the bounds of the church in so strange wise as they did, had they not converted more by the rare integrity of their manners, than by the force and power of their words? Not without cause therefore doth the prophet make request in the psalm, that the priests of the Lord may put on righteousness as a garment; for if their shame be seen, who shall hide the nakedness of the people? Thus we see what should especially be reformed in the principal part of the house of God. [Psal. cxxxii. 9.]

17. It remaineth now that somewhat be spoken of the manner of reformation. Christ in reforming the church proceeded orderly, knowing that disorderly remedies of evils are as dangerous as the evils for which they are sought. His orderly proceeding appeareth in this, that he first visited, and then reformed. Visitations, if they be used according to the true intent and purpose whereunto they were ordained, are needful and profitable in the church. For howsoever they be now abused by men of corrupt minds, the cause for which they were first established was the maintenance of truth, the rooting out of heresy, the confirming of good orders, the redressing of things amiss, the continuing of religion, peace, and innocency amongst men. If we reap not this fruit and commodity by them, the fault is in ourselves; in the parties visited, when they hide and conceal that which should be reformed; in the visitors, when they are careless in admonishing and, if that do not serve, in punishing offenders detected and lawfully convicted before them. Let the one sort therefore remember the sin of Achan, how close it was kept, and how God plagued Israel till it was revealed; and let the other consider the example of Christ, which proceeded no less severely in punishing than orderly in searching out the faults and abuses of the temple. *The manner of reforming. Christ reformed the temple orderly.* Josh. vii.

18. The rod in the hand of the pastor is as necessary *Severely.*

as the staff, yea, perhaps more, because they are more whom fear doth constrain, than whom love doth allure to become virtuous. It is noted that in the days of Jason, a dissolute and careless high priest, the inferior sort of priests being let alone were no more diligent about the service of the altar, but despised the temple, and regarded not the sacrifices: they became frequenters of games and heathenish exercises, not without great disgrace to their calling. When Nehemias, returning from captivity, found that Eliashab the high priest had chambered his kinsman, Tobiah, in the court of the house of God, where aforetime the offerings, the incense, the tithes of corn, of wine, and of oil appointed for the Levites had been laid, by which means it came to pass that they receiving not their portions were fled, and so the temple was left destitute; "this," saith Nehemias, "grieved me sore." But whence grew this fault? Where did Nehemias lay the blame, but in the governors? "I reproved," saith he, "the rulers, and said unto them, Why is the house of God forsaken?" If iniquity do abound for want of punishment, they which have authority, be it civil or ecclesiastical, to repress sin, must answer it.

<small>Nehem. xiii. [7—11.]</small>

19. It is not sufficient for them to mislike sin, but they must proceed against it, and that so far till they have throughly redressed things amiss. Christ did not cease pursuing thieves till their cattle were gone, their tables overthrown, their money scattered, themselves expelled and driven out. Which example Constantine well following, hath made himself a precedent worthy by other christian governors to be followed. He did not content himself with misliking or reproving, or lightly punishing heretics, but quite and clean disburthened the church of them. "Shall we suffer," saith he, "the contagious infection of so great evils to creep further; knowing that long delay may cause even the sound and the strong to be infected with it, as with a plague? Why do we not speedily with rigour of public punishment cut up the very roots of such iniquity[1]?" The angel of the church of

<small>Throughly.</small>

<small>Euseb. de vita Constant. lib. iii. cap. 62.</small>

[¹ Τί οὖν; ἀνεξόμεθα περαιτέρω τῶν τοιούτων κακῶν; ἀλλ' ἡ μακρὰ παρεπιθύμησις ὥσπερ λοιμικῷ νοσήματι καὶ τοὺς ὑγιαίνοντας χραίνεσθαι ποιεῖ. τίνος οὖν ἕνεκεν τὴν ταχίστην τὰς ῥίζας ὡς

Thyatira did not perform his duty in this behalf so long as Jezebel was permitted to teach; nor of Pergamus, so long as any one Nicolaitane was there suffered; nor of Corinth, so long as there was any jot of their corrupt leaven kept. "I would to God," saith the apostle, "they [Gal. v. 12.] were cut off which trouble you;" not rased on the skin, or lanced in the flesh, but cut off.

20. This can never be done where there lacketh zeal; for want whereof in the church of Jerusalem their corruptions grew so fast, that there was no place left free and clear: the leprosy of their sin cleaved even to the walls of the house of God, till he came whom the zeal of that house did as it were consume and devour. If there were any spark of the like zeal remaining in any pope or prelate of the church of Rome, could they choose but bewail the unhallowing of their temple? could they patiently abide to see it possessed by heathenish despisers of God's law, to see it made a den of thieves, a kennel for dogs and unclean beasts? There have not wanted even of their own, which have put them in mind of things to be reformed in the body of their church, in their pope and court of Rome, in their bishops and prelates, in their several orders of religious men, in their clergy, and in their laity: there have not wanted, from time to time, such as have clearly convicted them of spoiling, murdering, and destroying. But the answer of the church of Rome hath been always, I cannot err, "I am rich and increased with goods, and have need of nothing." Thus she refuseth, yea, she hateth to be reformed, not knowing, or at leastwise not acknowledging, that she is "wretched and miserable,

That which moved Christ to reform the church was his zeal.

Petrus de Aliaco, Heructus, Anton. Paganus, &c.[1]

Rev. iii. [17.]

εἰπεῖν τῆς τοσαύτης κακίας οὐ διὰ δημοσίας ἐπιστρεφείας ἐκκόπτομεν;—Euseb. Pamph. De Vit. Constant. Amst. 1695, Lib. III. c. 64, p. 430.—ED.]

[1 Petrus de Alliaco (P. d'Ailly) was born at Compeigne in 1350. He became afterwards a cardinal, and died 1419. His best known work is a treatise on the reformation of the church, published with the writings of Gerson. Gent. Hervetus, doctor of the Sorbonne, was born near Orleans, 1509, and died 1594. His works are numerous. M. Ant. Paganus was a native of Venice; or, as some say, of Forli. He became a member of the order of Fratres Minores, and died in 1587, aged 69. Among his works are a treatise on the order, &c. of bishops, discourse on penitence, &c.—ED.]

and poor, and blind, and naked." To let them go, and to come to ourselves. If God have vouchsafed to choose himself an holy dwelling-place amongst us, ought not we to do the best we can to cast out all that staineth and marreth the perfect beauty of his church?

<small>The rule of reformation which Christ followed was the written word.</small>

21. What to amend, both in ourselves particularly and generally in the body of the whole church, together with the right and orderly means of working this amendment, it is not human policy that can teach us. But *Scriptum est*, "it is written," what God requireth. This is the only rule, as of building, so likewise of repairing

<small>2 Kings xxiii. [1—3.]</small>

the church. Josias heard the words of the book of the law, and then reformed his realm, binding himself and all the people by covenant, "to walk after the Lord, to keep his commandments and his testimonies and his statutes," with all their heart and with all their soul. So in the

<small>Nehem. xiii. [1—3.]</small>

days of Nehemias, when "it was found written in the book, that the Ammonite and the Moabite should not enter into the congregation of God, when they had heard the law, they separated from Israel all those that were mingled with them." The same book was opened and read unto us. It was found that our fathers had not obeyed the words of that book, to do according unto all which is written therein for us. Hereupon our gracious sovereign, well following the blessed example of Christ Jesus, did that in her dominions for which she hath as worthily as ever any prince deserved that praise whereof

<small>Isai. lviii. [12.]</small>

the prophet speaketh, saying, "Thou shalt be called the repairer of the breach, and the restorer of the paths to dwell in." She hath caused the vessels that were made for Baal and for the host of heaven to be defaced: she hath broken down the lofts that were builded for idolatry: she hath turned out the priests that burnt incense unto false gods: she hath overthrown all polluted and defiled altars: she hath abolished darkness, and caused the light of God's eternal truth gloriously to shine, as we see it doth in the

<small>Nehem. xiii. [14.]</small>

church of England at this day. Remember her, O Lord, for this, and wipe not out the kindness that she hath shewed on the house of her God and on the offices thereof.

<small>The use whereunto</small>

22. Our Saviour, alleging the words of scripture

before mentioned, doth not only hereby warrant his own deed, and lay open the grossness of their fault, but also instruct them in the right use of that which hitherto they had so greatly abused. "My house shall be called the house of prayer for all nations." In which words we learn first, that the church is consecrated to the service of God, in respect whereof it is called "his house;" secondly, what service it is which he requireth: "My house shall be called the house of prayer;" thirdly, of whom this service is required, namely, of "all nations." *Christ requireth the temple to be restored.*

23. It addeth much to the wickedness of the sons of Heli, and proveth the sin of the young men to have been very great in the sight of the Lord, that they shewed their ravening nature upon the purest and holiest things; that they made no difference between the offerings of the Lord, and common flesh; that they shamefully abused themselves with women, even in the door of the tabernacle of God. The prophet Daniel hath set it down as a note of extreme impiety in Balthazar[1], that he with his princes, wives, and concubines, drunk wine in the golden and silver vessels which were taken out of the temple at Jerusalem. When the men of Tyrus brought fish and other wares, and sold them on the sabbath to the children of Judah, Nehemias reproved the rulers of Judah, and said unto them, "What evil thing is this that ye do, breaking the sabbath day? Did not your fathers thus, and our God brought all this plague upon us and upon this city? yet ye increase wrath upon Israel, breaking the sabbath." Such traffic is as bad in the house, as on the day, which God hath sanctified. Wherefore in the law these two are jointly coupled together: "Ye shall keep my sabbaths, and reverence my sanctuary." The profaning therefore of the temple, the house of God, the place of prayer, is an evident token, that amongst the Jews all religion was now trodden under feet, all reverence of God abolished. This sheweth that there was now no difference at all: holy and common, pure and profane, clean and unclean, all was one. When they, which ought not to die but without the city, were suffered to live within the temple: yea, of and at the altar, when God's *The temple sanctified to the service of God. Dan. v. [3.] Nehem. xiii. [17, 18.] Levit. xix. [30.]*

[¹ Balthazar—Belshazzar.—Ed.]

own house was made a den of thieves, we cannot easily imagine a degree of profaneness beyond this. At this the Lord himself doth seem to wonder. "Is this house become a den of thieves, whereupon my name is called, before your eyes?" What reverence or service is it likely that they would shew otherwhere unto the Lord, who lived as thieves in that glorious sanctuary where all the earth should tremble before him?

<small>Jer. vii. [11.]</small>

24. In the house of God they had the law both read and expounded, they offered sacrifice, and they prayed. But because the service for which the temple was ordained, though not only, yet principally, is prayer, therefore he hath said, "My house shall be called the house of prayer." In Deuteronomy it is called "the place which God chose to cause his name to dwell there." "It is true indeed," saith Solomon, "that God will dwell on the earth?" No doubt, where his truth is sincerely professed, where his sacraments are rightly and duly ministered, where his name is called upon by hearty prayer, where two or three are gathered together in his name, that is to say, to serve him in these things, there the working of his Spirit is so forcible and effectual, his mercy is so object[1] even unto sense, his grace is in such sort felt, seen, and tasted, that he seemeth as it were to stand before men's eyes, to walk, to inhabit, and to dwell amongst them, when they are thus occupied. The door of the church is the gate of the Lord, and the righteous will surely enter into it. They rejoice when they hear men say: "We will go into the house of the Lord," the house of prayer, where as many as call upon the name of the Lord shall undoubtedly be saved. But because no man can call on him in whom he doth not believe, nor believe without hearing the word of God; requisite therefore it is, that the house of public prayer should also be the house of public preaching. For this cause the Jews heard the law every sabbath day in their synagogues.

<small>The public serving of God in the church consisteth in hearing the word.</small>

<small>Deut. xii. [5.]
1 Kings viii. [27.]</small>

<small>Psal. cxxii. [1.]</small>

25. And as they did not only hear the word, but also offer sacrifice, in the house of God; so we in our churches have both the gospel preached, and the sacraments, which are seals of the gospel, administered, knowing

<small>In receiving the sacraments.</small>

[1 Object—obvious.—ED.]

that Christ hath commanded both alike. He which sent his disciples to teach, sent them also to baptize: he which enjoined them to preach, gave them also another charge: *Hoc facite:* "Do this in remembrance of me." Therefore, as often as we speak unto you out of these places, as often as here we minister the sacrament of baptism to your children, in token of their new spiritual birth, as often as we do here present ourselves at the Lord's table to eat of his bread and to drink of the wine which he hath prepared for the comfortable nourishment of our souls, we keep the Lord's institution, and not our own: we do as he hath commanded, not as we have devised: we use the house of God not as thieves, but as saints.

26. For these things the sanctuary was erected for In prayer. these the house of God was sanctified, and for prayer. Therefore the twelve told the rest of the disciples (as it is in the history of their acts), "We will give ourselves [Acts vi. [4.]] continually unto prayer and ministration of the word." Aaron was appointed under the law, as to offer so also to pray for himself and for the people. "Be this sin [1 Sam. xii. [23.]] against the Lord," saith Samuel, "far from me, that I should cease to pray for you." The request which Solo- [1 Kings viii. [30—53.]] mon made unto God in the first dedication of the temple was, that if his people Israel should at any time for their sins be overthrown before the enemy, or heaven be so shut up that they should be in distress for want of rain, or if there should be famine in the land, or pestilence, or blasting, or mildew, or grasshopper, or caterpillar, if the enemy should besiege them, if they should fall into any adversity, whether it were of body or of mind, his ears might always be open to the prayers, which they should make before the Lord in the house of prayer. Hear the supplications of thy people Israel which pray "in this place."

27. Nor only their supplications, but moreover Solo- Thus God will be served of all nations. mon addeth: "As touching the stranger that is not of thy people Israel, who shall come out of a far country for thy name's sake, and shall come and pray in this house, hear thou in heaven thy dwelling place, and do according to all that the stranger calleth for unto thee, that all the people of the earth may know thy name, and fear thee

as thy people Israel do." Agreeable whereunto are the words of the prophet Esay: "It shall be in the last days, that the mountain of the house of the Lord shall be prepared in the top of the mountains, and shall be exalted above the hills, and all nations shall flow unto it." And again: "*The strangers* that cleave unto the Lord to serve him, and to love the name of the Lord, and to be his servants, every one that keepeth the sabbath and polluteth it not, and embraceth my covenant, *them* will I bring also to mine holy mountain, and make them joyful in mine house of prayer: *their* burnt offerings, and *their* sacrifices shall be accepted upon mine altar. For mine house shall be called an house of prayer for *all nations*." This proveth that article of our christian faith to be most certain, wherein we acknowledge the church of Christ to be catholic and universal. For we must understand that there was a time when the Lord gave express charge and commandment, "No uncircumcised in the flesh shall enter into my sanctuary." "The adoption and the glory of the sons of God, the covenants, the law, the service of God, the promises," and all the riches wherewith the church of Christ is adorned, did belong unto Israel, and unto none else: they were the only people that obtained mercy, all the world besides was "Loammi:" amongst them God was known, but as for the nations, they heard not of him: Judea was the only garden of the Lord, the rest of the earth was a mere wilderness: they were the vineyard, and we the forest; they within the walls of the city of God, and we without; they citizens, and we strangers. But now the bounds of the church are enlarged: her elders, as it is in the book of Revelation, do now sing a new song: "Thou hast redeemed us to God by thy blood out of every kindred, and tongue, and people, and nation." "Wherefore remember," saith the apostle, "that ye, being in time past gentiles in the flesh, called uncircumcision of them which are called circumcision in the flesh made with hands, were at that time without Christ, and were aliens from the commonwealth of Israel, and were strangers from the covenants of promise, and had no hope, and were without God in the world. But now in Christ Jesus ye, which once were far off, are made near by the blood of

Christ. For he is our peace; which hath made of both one, and hath broken the stop of the partition wall." This we are willed to " remember." For is it not a thing very memorable, that in us God should now accomplish the promise which he made to his Son so long before: " Ask of me, and I will give thee the heathen for thine inheritance, and the uttermost coasts of the earth for thy possessions": Is it not memorable that, the furious rage of the whole world mightily opposing itself against the kingdom of Jesus Christ, it should notwithstanding grow so soon to this so exceeding greatness, and that by so weak means, from so small beginnings? Now, sith God hath brought this so strangely to pass for our sakes, sith the Lord hath done it for no other cause, but only to open the door of salvation unto us, with how great joy of heart ought we to hear his voice, when he saith of the gentiles, " Let them ascend to mount Sion;" when he saith of his house, " It shall be called the house of prayer for all nations"! He that will not shroud himself under this vine, he that entereth not into this ark, he that will not be partaker of these celestial treasures, these heavenly mysteries, this true bread of life so largely offered unto all nations, if his soul die the death, who will have pity or compassion of him? Wherefore, to conclude, let us be followers of Christ, as becometh his dear children: let us learn by his example to be careful and zealous for the house of God, to purge and cleanse it as much as in us lieth from all defilements, that as oft as we do reverently and religiously frequent it, to hear the word of salvation, to receive the blessed sacraments of the Lord, to pour out our prayers and supplications before him, his Spirit groaning with our spirits, and our requests ascending through the forcible intercession of that only Mediator which is to be heard for his reverence sake, we may rejoice in our salvation, and he be glorified by our rejoicing. Which God the Father grant for his Son's sake. To whom, &c.

Psal. ii. [8.]

THE FOURTEENTH SERMON.

A SERMON

MADE AT THE SPITTLE IN LONDON.

Acts X.

34. *Then Peter opened his mouth, and said, Of a truth I perceive that God is no accepter of persons, &c.*

<small>The fulness of the gospel most clearly opened in the sermon of Peter, by occasion of Cornelius.</small>

THE doctrine of the prophets and apostles doth wholly tend to this end, to declare unto us, that Jesus Christ crucified is the promised Messias, the Redeemer and Saviour of all that do believe in him. Neither is this matter cleared more perfectly by any prophet or apostle, than by the apostle St Peter in this sermon which now we have in hand. For therein is comprised briefly, but most effectually, the fulness of the gospel, the perfect doctrine of salvation. Now, because the occasion of having it preached was Cornelius the captain, and the preacher of it was Peter the apostle, I will note somewhat in either of them severally for the better understanding of that which the sermon itself shall lay before us. In Cornelius therefore, first, what manner of man he was; on what occasion he sent for Peter; and in what sort he received him at his coming.

<small>The person of Cornelius.</small>

2. The curious description which St Luke maketh of Cornelius here declareth him to have been a notable and rare man, both by other circumstances of his person, and by his manners. The other circumstances which I mean, are his country, his calling, and the place of his abode.

<small>His country.</small>
Touching his country, he was an Italian, an ethnick, bred of ethnick parents, trained up amongst a people drowned in idolatry and superstition, worshipping false gods, being
<small>His calling.</small> ignorant of the true God. By calling, he was a soldier, a captain of the Italian band, a captain over one hundred soldiers. The Romans had soldiers out of all provinces;

but their chief force was of the Italians, whom they trusted best as natural subjects. This Italian captain made his abode in Cesarea, a famous city inhabited by the Jews. The whole land of Jewry was brought in subjection to the Roman empire; and lest the inhabitants thereof should revolt, certain garrisons of soldiers were placed in sundry of the greater cities, to see them kept in obedience, and to repress tumults: Cornelius the captain with the soldiers of his retinue were bestowed in Cesarea. If we look on this man's country, if we consider his calling and vocation, if we call to remembrance in what place he lived, and with whom he was conversant; we shall find nothing but idolatry and superstition; we shall behold nothing but rape, robbery, murder, mischief, spoil, blood-spilling; we shall see nothing but lewdness, profaneness, wicked manners, and cursed company. *His dwelling-place.*

3. All the which occasions of corruption notwithstanding, he was devout, he feared God with his whole family, he gave much alms to the people, and prayed God continually. The mighty and merciful God did gather pearls out of this dunghill. "God can raise up children unto Abraham out of stones." Faith, piety, holiness, and religion, come not by nature, but of grace; of God's free gift, not of our deserving; of mercy, not of merit: "Faith is the gift of God." "He worketh all in all." "He giveth to will and to do." "Not by the works of righteousness which we had wrought, but according to his mercy hath he saved us;" that we may acknowledge our wretchedness and unworthiness, and give all glory unto him. *His godliness, so many occasions of the contrary notwithstanding.* Matt. iii. [9.] Eph. ii. [8.] 1 Cor. xii. [6.] Phil. ii. [13.] Tit. iii. [5.]

4. Here we learn, that neither parentage, nor vocation, nor corruption of place, doth shut us out of the kingdom of God. Ethnicks, even wild olives by nature, are graffed by grace in the true olive. Soldiers that live in order are allowed of by John Baptist. Neither filthy Sodom, nor superstitious Egypt, nor idolatrous Babylon, nor corrupt Cesarea, was able to infect Lot, or Joseph, or Daniel, or Cornelius; whom the Lord had chosen according to his good pleasure, and of his mercy had preserved. The foundation of God remaineth sure, and hath this seal: "The Lord knoweth who are his." "I will have mercy on whom I will have mercy." "It is not in him *What we have to learn by the former circumstances.* Rom. xi. [24.] Luke iii. [14.] Gen. xix. Gen. xlv. Dan. i. 2 Tim. ii. [19.] Rom. ix. [15, 16.]

[SANDYS.]

that willeth nor in him that runneth; but in God that sheweth mercy."

<small>The estate of the Jews, over whom Cornelius was placed.</small> 5. Cornelius, the ethnick captain, being placed in Cesarea over the Jews, putteth us in mind how the kingdom of Israel was taken from the Israelites, and given to others. Israel was the elect and well-beloved people of God, the <small>Rom. ix. [4.]</small> happy seed of Abraham, "to whom pertained the adoption, and the glory, and the covenant, and the law that was given, and the services of God, and the promises." <small>John viii. [33.]</small> A most free people, as themselves boasted: "We are Abraham's seed, and were never bound to any man." A plentiful land, flowing with milk and honey, a most flourishing kingdom, a mighty and victorious people; for the Lord of hosts did fight for them. Yet this elect, beloved, free and mighty people was overthrown, wasted, translated, brought into most miserable bondage and slavery, first by the Chaldees, then by the Medes, afterward by the Grecians, and last of all by the Romans. And this was the Lord's <small>Jer. xxvii. [5.]</small> doing. "I have made the earth" (saith he), "the men, and beasts that are upon the ground, by my great power, and by my outstretched arm; and have given it unto whom <small>Dan. ii. [20, 21.]</small> it pleased me." "The name of God be praised for ever and ever; for wisdom and strength are his, and he changeth the times and seasons: he taketh away kings, and setteth <small>Dan. iv.[17.]</small> up kings." "The Most High beareth rule over the kingdom of men, and giveth it to them whomsoever he will."

<small>What brought the Jews in subjection under others. Ecclus. x. [8.]</small> 6. Jesus the son of Syrach, shewing the causes why God translateth kingdoms, "A kingdom is translated" (saith he) "from one people unto another, because of unrighteous dealings, and wrongs, and riches gotten by deceit, and covetousness, and pride." The things that destroyed Sodom <small>[Ezek. xvi. 49.]</small> were pride, fulness of bread, abundance of idleness, and that she strengthened not the hand of the poor and needy. <small>1 Cor. x. [5—10.]</small> The sins that consumed God's people in the wilderness, and of six hundred thousand left but two alive, was loathing of the heavenly manna, and lusting after the flesh-pots of Egypt, worshipping of idols, fleshly fornication, tempting of God, and muttering against magistrates. The cause why Jewry was laid waste, and Israel carried away cap- <small>Jer. xxv. [3.]</small> tive, was the contempt of God's word preached by Jeremy <small>Hos. iv. [1.]</small> three and twenty years; and that "there was no truth,

no mercy, no knowledge of God amongst them." Swearing, lying, murder, theft, and adultery, had gotten the upper hand; and one blood-guiltiness followed another. Therefore did the land mourn; and every one that dwelt therein was rooted out. God is always a just God, one that hateth all iniquity, having no respect to country or calling. If our faults be like, we may look for like punishment. Let us recount with ourselves, and compare ourselves with others. Are we not as guilty of unrighteous dealing, of oppression, of extortion, are we not as covetous, are we not as proud, as ever any people was? Is there not as much pride, belly-cheer, idleness, unmercifulness, in the city of London, as was in the city of Sodom? Do we not as much loathe the true bread of heaven? Cleave we not as fast unto idolatry and superstition? Commit we not adultery and filthy fornication? Tempt we not God? Do we not mutter against the magistrates, as the Israelites did in the wilderness? Is there more truth, mercy, and knowledge of God, less swearing, lying, murder, theft, adultery, and bloodshed in England, than was in the land of Jewry? If kingdoms then be translated for wrongful dealing, for covetousness and pride; how can unrighteous, covetous, and proud England stand long? If God spared not the flourishing city of Sodom, can he in his justice spare the sinful city of London? If God overthrew the mighty people of Israel in the wilderness for their sins, can he wink at our foul and manifold offences? If the land of Jewry was laid waste, and the elect Israel carried away captive for their ingratitude, will not God punish and plague our shameful contempt, our wilful disobedience? For these examples 1 Cor. x. [6.] are written for us, that we should not offend as they did, lest the like fall upon us, as fell upon them; knowing that, if God spared not the branches of the true olive, he will Rom. xi. [21.] not spare the twigs of the wild olive: if he spared not the transgressing angels, the offending Jews, neither will he spare us most vile and sinful gentiles. Our sin no doubt hath justly provoked our God to anger. Let our sighing and groaning, our earnest prayer and true repentance remove his wrath, lest our Nineveh sink, and perish in her sin. Yet remain there a few days of repentance for the safety of our city.

7. Now to the former circumstances of Cornelius, St Luke addeth also the description of his manners; testifying therein that he was devout, that he feared God with all his family, that he gave much alms, that he prayed God continually. Here is he set forth as a perfect pattern of true christianity, an observer and keeper of the law of the Almighty. And because the law is contained in two tables, his piety towards God is commended first; secondly, his love and duty towards men. So that it is shewed how he lived towards God, how he ordered his family, and how he behaved himself towards his neighbours.

The manners of Cornelius.

8. Towards God he was devout: "he feared God, he prayed continually." The foundation of devotion is faith: the fruits are the fear of God, and prayer. Faith cometh by hearing of the word: he heard (by reason that he remained amongst the Jews) that there was one true God, who was only to be honoured. He had heard of the promised seed, in whom all people should be blessed, of the Messias which should be the Saviour of the people. He believed in this promised Messias, and thereupon he is called devout; for without this faith there is no devotion, no piety, no religion. That fear, that prayer, that cometh not of faith, is but vain: it is rejected as sinful in God's sight. "Whatsoever is not of faith is sin." The tree must be good before it bring forth good fruit. "As the branch cannot bear fruit of itself, except it abide in the vine, no more can ye, except ye abide in me," saith Christ. Cornelius brought forth good fruit; and therefore by faith he abode in Christ, that is, he believed. The fruits of his faith were the fear of God, and prayer unto God; for neither can we fear God as we ought, nor call upon him rightly, except we believe in him. "How shall they call on him in whom they have not believed?" And they believe not in God, that do not fear him, that do not call upon him. For true faith will exercise the faithful herein. This fear of God hath ever respect to religion. "Come, ye children, and hearken unto me: I will teach you the fear of the Lord," saith the prophet. That is, I will instruct you in true religion, I will teach you the true worshipping of God. This is the first lesson that a Christian should learn. And as all Christians, so espe-

His devout and religious affection towards God. His faith.

Rom. xiv. [23.]
John xv. [4.]

Rom. x. [14.]

His fearing of God.

[Psal. xxxiv. 11.]

cially such as have dominion and rule over others. Whereupon the princely prophet doth exhort them: "Ye kings, ye judges of the earth, serve the Lord with fear:" as judging them happy, whose commonwealth is ruled by such as are professors and favourers of true religion, such as fear the Lord. Which is most true. For happy was Israel while David, Jehosaphat, Ezekias, and Josias ruled; because they were religious men, and feared God. But unhappy when as Jeroboam, Achab, Amon, and Manasses, ruled; because the fear of God was far from their hearts: they went a whoring after idols, and made Israel to sin. How much the greater care should christian princes have to place none in authority but such as Cornelius, men that are truly religious and fear God; such as Constantius the worthy christian emperor retained in his court, when he cast out them who forsook Christ, saying, that they could not be faithful to their prince, who were unfaithful to God[1]. Neither only princes, but the people also, to whom the election of magistrates appertaineth, should have the like care; remembering the exhortation that Jethro made to Moses: "Provide thou men fearing God." *Psal. ii. [10, 11.]*

Sozom. lib. i. cap. 6.

[Exod. xviii. 21.]

9. And Cornelius "prayed God continually." Faith and fear of God do break out into his praises, and calling upon him by prayer. Prayer is an acceptable service of God, prescribed by himself, and practised by his servants, to the glory of his name. "Call," saith he, "upon me in the day of trouble; and I will deliver thee; and thou shalt glorify me." Of prayer there are two sorts, private and public; both which Cornelius used: public, with his family, which he brought up in the fear of God; private, in secret place, having his appointed hours to pray. When the angel appeared, he was in private prayer, at the ninth hour, that is, at three of the clock in the afternoon. Now, as Cornelius used them both, so by his example should every Christian do. For touching public prayer, the disciples of Christ continued altogether "with one accord" in it. When Peter was cast into prison, "the church made earnest prayer unto God for him." We read of the Pharisee and publican both, that they "went up into the temple to pray." Whereby we may learn, that they

His continuing in prayer both public and private.

Psal. l. [15.]

Acts i. [14.]
Acts xii. [5.]
Luke xviii. [10.]

[¹ See before, p. 97.—ED.]

who refuse to join themselves in public place, the church of God, to pray with other men, they are worse than either Pharisees or publicans. Cornelius made his house such a public place for his whole family therein to serve God. For as he feared God with his whole family, so is it to be thought that he served God with his whole family too: insomuch that there was a church in his house, as in the house of Philemon. A lesson for all them who have families: that they be religious and fear God indeed, they should use private prayer in their houses, and cause their families to frequent it. So shall they make their houses to be churches. And Christ will be in those assemblies, according to his promise: "I will be in the midst of them." As for private prayer, it is also fruitful and effectuous. For therein without suspicion of pharisaical hypocrisy we pour out our hearts before God. Anna in the temple so behaved herself in her private prayer, that Eli the high priest esteemed her as drunk, and sharply reproved her for it. To whom she answered mildly, "I am not drunk, but in my prayer I do pour out my heart before God." Christ appointed himself certain times of private prayer, as in the garden, where he prayed in such earnest and vehement sort, that there dropped from him both water and blood. David had his private night-prayers, wherein such was the earnestness of his affection, that with his tears night by night he watered his couch. It appeareth that Cornelius prayed earnestly and heartily: for his prayer pierced into the heavens, and was acceptable unto the Lord. But God abhorreth prayer that falleth out of the lips, and proceedeth not from the heart. He detesteth the Pharisees, who worship him with their lips, but their heart is far from him. The Israelites poured out many tears when they prayed in Babylon. The very ethnicks would not dally in their prayer with their false gods. It is written even of the heathenish Romans, that, when they honoured their idols with solemn prayers and procession, the criers said to every one whom they met, *Hoc age:* " Set thy mind on this thing wholly:" be attentive to this, and to nothing else. Prayer is the lifting up of the mind to God. He requireth the heart. But alas! our prayers are for the most part only for a fashion, that men

[Matt. xviii. 20.]

[1 Sam. i. 13—15.]

Matt. xxvi. [39: Luke xxii. 44.]
Psal. vi. [6.]

Matt. xv. [8.]
2 Chron. xxxiii. [12, 13.]

In vita Numæ. Plut.

Matt. vi. [5.]

may behold us. Furthermore, the prayer of Cornelius was continual. "Pray ye continually without intermission." 1 Thess. v. [17.] We must pray still, and not wax faint. Which yet is Luke xviii. [1.] not meant as though we should cease from all other travail, and give ourselves only to prayer. That is the error of the Euchites[1]; whose disciples were the superstitious monks, that made the house of God a den of thieves by their hypocrisy. But we are taught hereby to pray often; for we have always occasion of prayer given us. Daniel Dan. vi. [10.] prayed thrice daily in his house with his windows open towards Jerusalem, yea, though the king forbade it. For he would not be restrained from praying to his God. David testifieth that he prayed unto the Lord seven times Psal. cxix. [164.] every day. Satan ceaseth not to assault our faith: let not us therefore cease to cry unto God, "O Lord, in- Luke xvii. [5.] crease our faith." Our tottering boat is tossed in the stormy seas: let us lift up our voice to Christ, and say, "Save us, we perish." We are in danger of greedy roar- Matt. viii. [25.] ing lions; the world, the devil, and the flesh: let us pray, "O deliver us from the mouth of the lion." Let us cry, Psal. xxii. [21.] and the Lord will hear us. "Prayer is an help unto him August. that prayeth, a sacrifice to God, a scourge to the devils," saith Austin. And thus much of Cornelius, his devotion, fear of God, and continual prayer; the points whereby is shewed how he lived towards God.

10. It followeth to be noted, how he ordered his *The ordering of his family.* family: "he feared God with all his household." He played not Nicodemus, that came to Christ by night: he openly professed his religion and faith, yea, and instructed his whole family therein. Neither did he fear to send for Peter, to teach him the religion and faith of Christ. First, the open profession of his religion is commendable. The Romans had forbid by law that any subject should profess or receive *peregrinam religionem:* "a strange religion." They considered that it was dangerous to their state to suffer diversity of religion. They severely punished the transgressors of this law. Yet Cornelius had learned that it is better to obey God than man, that we

[[1] The Euchites or Messalians were a sect of heretics who maintained that men ought to do nothing but pray. They were censured in the general council of Ephesus held in 431.—ED.]

must obey princes *usque ad aras*[1], as the proverb is; so far as we may without disobeying God. Although the Jewish religion was hateful to the gentiles, yet he followed the example of Daniel, of the three young men, of the blessed apostles, who did boldly preach and profess Christ, when they were charged not to do it. We may not be ashamed of our religion: we may not halt on both sides. "With the heart man believeth unto righteousness; and with the mouth man confesseth unto salvation." "Whosoever shall be ashamed of me and my words, of him shall the Son of man be ashamed, when he shall come in his glory, and in the glory of the Father, and of the angels." Moreover Cornelius instructed his family, and brought them up in the fear of God. A rare example in an ethnick captain; nay, a rare example in such as be Christians, and professs most piety, and by calling should be most religious, yea, and are placed as examples not only to families, but to cities, to countries, to nations. He remembered well, that he that hath a charge must answer for his charge. He could not forget, *Redde rationem:* "Give an account of thy stewardship." He was afraid of the saying of the wise man: "An hard judgment shall they have that bear rule." The sins of the subjects, of the people, of the family, will be punished in the magistrates, in the masters, in the householders. For to every one of these saith the Lord, "I will require the blood of them that perish," if through thy negligence, evil example, or want of correction, any of them shall fall from God. "Not only they," saith Paul, "who commit such things are worthy of death, but also they who consent to such as do them." And he consenteth doubtless, which by office should correct sin, and by negligence or corrupt affection suffereth sin. The scripture chargeth Eli the priest with the sins of his unruly sons, at the which he winked; and he was punished for it. The sin that the people of Israel committed in worshipping idols, is laid to the charge of the kings of Israel, which either instituted them, defended them, or did not pull them down. The queen of Saba commendeth Solomon greatly for the good ordering of his house. "Happy are thy men, happy are these thy

[Dan. iii.]
Rom. x. [10.]
Luke ix. [26.]
Luke xvi. [2.]
Wisd. vi. [6.]
Ezek. xxxiii. [6.]
Rom. i. [32.]
1 Sam. ii. [27—36.]
1 Kings x. [8.]

[1 As far as the altars.—ED.]

servants, which stand ever before thee, and hear thy wisdom." King David was so careful, that he would not suffer as much as a liar to remain within his court. Abraham is commended of God for the good nurturing and godly bringing up of his sons and his household. That magistrate that feareth God will not suffer sin in the city unpunished: the sword is given him to cut it off, and beat it down. That pastor that feareth God will use all means to bring his sheep to the sheepfold, if they go astray. That householder that feareth God will, by good order and due correction, keep it in the fear of God. And so shall both the magistrate, the pastor, and the householder deliver their own souls.

Psal. ci. [7.]
Gen. xviii. [19.]
Ezek. xxxiv. [8, 12.]

11. Again, as Cornelius declared the fruits of his faith towards his family, so was he loving and friendly towards his neighbours. "He gave much alms to the people." This is that sacrifice which God doth require chiefly of a Christian: "I will have mercy and not sacrifice." This is "a sacrifice of a sweet-smelling savour, a sacrifice acceptable to God, and well pleasing him." He that relieveth not his needy brother, being of ability to relieve him, doth neither fear nor love God. "Give alms of thy substance, and turn not away thy face from any poor man, lest the Lord turn away his face from thee." "Give, and it shall be given unto you," saith the Son of God. He that sheweth mercy shall find mercy, and judgment without mercy to the merciless. No treasure so well bestowed as that which is given to the poor. That is laid up in heaven. God doth bind himself to recompense that which is given to the poor: for it is given to himself. The merciful shall receive everlasting life, the merciless everlasting death. God gave a law to Israel: "Let there be no beggar among you." This law the Jews keep inviolate to this day. A great reproach and slander it is to us Christians, that the Lord of Jews and gentiles, the Son of God, our Saviour Christ, who became poor to make us rich, at whose merciful hands of his free gift we have received whatsoever we have, to us a great shame and confusion it is, that we should fall so far from all humanity, so utterly forget our Christianity, to shew ourselves so hard and stony-hearted, so unthankful and without all natural

His liberality in giving alms, and that to strangers.
[Matt. ix. 13.]
Phil. iv. [18.]
[Tob. iv. 7.]
Luke vi. [38.]
Matt. xxv. [34—46.]
Deut. xv. [4. in old translations.]

affection, to suffer our God, our Saviour, our Christ whom we profess, not only to go on begging, but to lie hungry, cold, naked, sick, diseased, pining and perishing in the streets and at our doors. This merciless mind, this great ingratitude will no doubt be requited with *Ite:* "Go your ways, ye cursed, into everlasting fire." If it be not reformed in time, God no doubt will come down and revenge it. Cornelius gave liberal alms unto them which were strangers to him. God is careful for strangers. He putteth the Israelites in mind, not to afflict but to comfort the strangers that dwell among them: "for ye yourselves were strangers too." By the prophet Zacharias, he biddeth us beware lest we grieve them: "Oppress not the widow, nor the fatherless, the stranger, nor the poor." God joineth the widows, the fatherless, and strangers most commonly ever together, as persons most destitute, and such as have most need of help. Egypt was blessed for the strangers that dwelt there; but when the king of Egypt Pharaoh oppressed them, they groaned and called upon God, he delivered them and poured his manifold plagues upon Egypt. The sinful city of Sodom was of long time spared for Lot and his family, strangers there. Such as are strangers for the gospel's sake, for the cause which we profess and maintain, are joyfully to be received, cheerfully and liberally to be relieved. For in receiving them we do not only receive angels, as Abraham and Lot did, but we receive and relieve Christ Jesus, whom they profess, and whose members they are. And whatsoever we give to them, we give it him; and he will reward it. But whosoever shall vex, wrong, or offend any of them, "better it were that a mill-stone were tied about his neck, and he hurled into the bottom of the sea." I speak of godly strangers, that are strangers for the truth's sake; not of such as are of no religion, of no church, godless and faithless people, some papists, some anabaptists, some Arians, some libertines: these are to be expelled and cast out of the country, lest for their wickedness God plague the whole realm. God is wont ever to bless the country, for retaining and relieving godly religious strangers: so is he wont to pour his plagues on them that nourish Canaanites among them. And thus much touching Cornelius, the Italian by parentage, by vocation

Marginalia:
Exod. xxii. [21.]
Zech. vii. [10.]
Mark ix. [42.]

a soldier, placed in Cesarea; who was devout, feared God, and prayed to God; who brought up his family in the fear of God; who was pitiful to the poor, and liberally gave alms even unto strangers.

12. The next point we have to consider of is, upon what occasion he did send for Peter. In his prayer at the ninth hour (which is our three of the clock at afternoon), an angel of God appeared unto him, and told him that his prayers and alms were come up in remembrance before God; and bade him send men to Joppe, and call for Simon Peter, who lodged at a tanner's house near the sea, and he should tell him what he ought to do. After the angel was departed, he sent two of his servants and a soldier that feared God to Joppe for Peter. Here is the cause expressed why he sent for Peter. God by his angel commanded; and he obeyed. In the angel's oration I note two things, in Cornelius other two. The angel comforteth Cornelius, and telleth him what he shall do. Cornelius is afraid at the message, and doeth that which the angel willeth him. *His sending for Peter according to the direction of the angel sent from God to him.*

13. Angels are "ministering spirits, sent forth to minister for their sakes which shall be heirs of salvation." God sendeth his good angels to comfort, nourish, govern, guide, and defend his elect. The evil angels are sent either to try the godly, or to punish, plague, and destroy the wicked. This angel was a good angel of God, sent to comfort and instruct Cornelius, the devout and righteous man. He doth comfort him, declaring unto him that his prayers and alms are ascended up in remembrance before God; which is as much to say, as that God doth accept and allow of them. *The office of angels, good and bad. Heb. i. [14.]*

14. The papists abuse much these words of the angel, striving thereby to set forth their own righteousness, to the overthrow of the merit and righteousness which we have by Christ. For they infer thereof, that our own works before we have faith are preparations to grace. Secondly, they attribute our justification to our works. Things more absurd than that they need confutation. For what preparation can there be in us of ourselves to grace, when St. Paul saith plainly, that "we are not able of ourselves, as of ourselves, to think any good"? "The natural man per- *Popish errors concerning preparation to grace and justification by works rising by false collection out of the angel's words. 2 Cor. iii. [5.] 1 Cor. ii. [14.]*

ceiveth not the things of the Spirit of God." And how can our prayers or alms which are not done in faith please God, when "without faith it is impossible to please him"? And if Cornelius had faith, as it must needs be granted he had, that also was "the gift of God," as St Paul teacheth us. Now to attribute justification to our merits or works is to make "of none effect" the merit of Christ; to make grace no grace. For remission of sins is justification; as the scripture sheweth, saying, "Blessed are they whose sins are forgiven." But we obtain remission of sins, not by our works, but through faith in Christ: we are "justified freely, by the grace of God, through the redemption that is in Christ Jesus, whom God hath set forth to be a reconciliation through faith in his blood; to declare his righteousness by the forgiveness of the sins passed." And our works are such, even the works of the best men, that, when we have done all, "we are unprofitable servants." "Enter not into judgment with thy servants, O Lord; for in thy sight shall no man living be justified." The angel therefore meant not that Cornelius was either prepared to grace, or justified by his works; but that God considered his piety, prayers, and alms, and would increase his good gifts in him. For God both accepteth good works, and will reward them. He accepteth them for the man's sake, in that the man is faithful and therefore accepted. In which sort the sacrifice of Abel was accepted through the faith of Abel. He rewardeth our works, not for their worthiness, but for his own sake, for his love and promise. And he promiseth reward, to provoke us to work: for to that end are we created, and redeemed, even to "serve him in holiness and righteousness all the days of our life." So doth the angel comfort Cornelius, in mentioning his works and God's remembrance of them.

15. As for that he willeth him to send for Simon Peter, and learn of him what he should do; this speech doth import that Cornelius in his prayer had desired to know how, and by what means, he should be saved. Whereupon the angel, God's messenger, telleth him that he must send for Peter, by whom he shall be taught the way of salvation. God ever provideth teachers to such as are desirous to learn, and sendeth the word of truth to such

as love the truth. He sent Philip to instruct the eunuch, the queen of the Ethiopians' chief governor, as he was reading the prophet Esaias touching Christ. He provided Ananias for Paul, and Peter for Cornelius. The angel setteth over Cornelius to Peter to instruct him. To commend the ministry, God will have his gospel preached by men, and not by angels. He will not have us look for revelations from heaven, but to give ear and credit to the voice of his messengers, to whom he hath committed the word of reconciliation, whom he would have esteemed for their office sake: to contemn such is to contemn him that hath sent them. "He that despiseth you despiseth me," saith Christ. *Acts viii. [26—29.] Acts ix. [10, 11.] Matt. x. [40: Luke x. 16.]*

16. At his message Cornelius was afraid. The presence of the angel and the strangeness of the message abashed him. Now, if he heard the voice of the angel with trembling and fear, with what awe and reverence should we give ear to the voice of the Son of God, Christ Jesus! Whensoever the gospel is preached, Christ is present, Christ speaketh to us. The godly tremble at his word, as we read in Esay: "To whom will I look? To him, saith the Lord, to him that is poor, and of contrite spirit, and trembleth at my words." They who despise or disobey the word of God do not fear him. For he that feareth God doth reverence his word. *He feareth. Isai. lxvi. [2.]*

17. And he that doth reverence the word of God truly, will no doubt obey it. Example whereof we have in Cornelius. He obeyed the angel, and straightway sent two of his servants, and a godly soldier that waited upon him, to Joppe for Peter. Even so likewise must we give ear when God speaketh, as it is written, "I will hearken what the Lord God will say." Neither may we "consult with flesh and blood" when God commandeth; but we must obey, we must not deliberate in his causes. Reason and experience would have told Cornelius, how dangerous it was publicly to profess a strange and hated religion: it might not only tend to the loss of his office, but of his life too. He might have disputed also with himself, What is Peter? Some odd sectary fled from Jerusalem, who, for fear lest he, with his errors should be condemned, hideth himself in a tanner's house. What learning, what piety can I look for to come out of such a school, and from such *He obeyeth. Psal. lxxxv. [8.] Gal. i. [16.]*

a schoolmaster? This would worldly wisdom and flesh and blood have said unto him; but faith putteth no such peril, but readily obeyeth whatsoever God commandeth: it doubteth not, it staggereth not: but if God say, Go, it goeth; if God say, Come, it cometh; if God say, Do this, it doth it. "Behold, to obey is better than sacrifice; and to hearken is better than the fat of rams."

^{1 Sam. xv. [22.]}

^{He sendeth his servants, and findeth them willing to be sent to Peter.} 18. He sendeth two of his servants, and a godly soldier that attended upon him. Here was the reward of his labour in bringing up his household in the fear of God. He had taught his servants truly and sincerely to fear God; and God had taught his servants faithfully and willingly to serve him. "For he" (saith the scripture), "that doth serve his master faithfully and heartily, serveth Christ Jesu," who rewardeth all faithful service. Abraham brought up his family in the fear of God; and he reaped the fruit of it: he had a most faithful servant, whom he sent to procure a wife to his son Isaac. Whosoever, therefore, will be trustily served, let him train up his household in the fear of God, and expel out thence all that be not godly, as godly David did. It is dangerous for any man to nourish serpents in his bosom: they will at one time or other sting him. Faithless servants have been the confusion of many good masters; and godless children the destruction of many good fathers. Ophni and Phinees were the death of their father Eli, the high priest. And Judas conspired against his master Christ, the innocent Son of God.

^{Col. iii. [23, 24.]}

^{Gen. xxiv.}

^{Psal. ci. [4, 7, 8.]}

^{1 Sam. iii. [11—14.]}

^{Matt. xxvi. [14—16.]}

^{He receiveth Peter with all reverence, and assembleth many to hear him preach.} 19. But to come to that which I set down for the last. Note in Cornelius with what humanity and reverence he received Peter, the preacher of God's word: he called to him his kinsmen and friends, and expected him: he fell down prostrate to do him honour: he thanked him for his coming, declaring how ready he was to hear him. And because faith doth labour for God's glory, and break forth into love towards our neighbour, he called his friends and kinsmen to be partakers of that great treasure of God with him. He was not Cain-like, who had no care for his brother. Cornelius teacheth us, how desirous we ought to be of God's word, how glad and ready to hear it, and how that in dutiful love we should provoke others to the

^{Gen. iv. [9.]}

hearing and embracing of it. For it is the word of truth and salvation. Which St James considering, exhorteth his brethren to "receive the word that is able to save their souls." "And let us consider one another" (saith St Paul), "to provoke unto love, and to good works, not forsaking the fellowship that we have among ourselves, as the manner of some is, but exhorting one another." The arrogant Jews, puffed up with self-love, would not join themselves in the congregation with gentiles. Which thing the apostle reproveth, exhorting them not to contemn their brethren, but rather one provoke another charitably to join together in piety, in hearing of the word, and receiving of the sacraments. As Esay did foreshew that the faithful in Christ's time should say one to another, "Come, and let us go up to the mountains of the Lord, to the house of the God of Jacob; and he will teach us his ways; and we will walk in his paths." But alas! this zeal of the glory of God, this love towards our brethren, is worn away in us: I fear me we will neither go ourselves to hear the word, neither suffer others, but dehort them so much as we may; pretending I know not what, to cover our arrogant malicious hearts withal. Such a man is an usurper; I cannot hear him with safe conscience: he weareth a surplice; I will neither hear him, nor trust him. Another is a shrinker, another half a papist: leave them, hear them not. This is the common cry: I will not use their own speech, it is too proud and too bitter. I trust we all preach Christ crucified. "Howsoever it be," saith St Paul, "so that Christ be taught, I rejoice in it." If we mislike the minister, shall we mislike the message also? If we cannot brook the messenger, shall we be at defiance with him that sent him? God grant us such hearts as Cornelius had, that in liking and love we may provoke one another to piety and godliness that we may hunger after God's truth, hear the word without respect to the messenger, and so hear it that we may live by it! Cornelius fell down prostrate before Peter. He considered of him as of the ambassador of God: he reverenced him as his spiritual father: he gave unto him that double honour which St Paul saith is due unto him. "The elders that rule well are worthy of double honour; specially they who labour in the

James i. [21.]

Heb. x. [24, 25.]

Isai. ii. [3.]

Phil. i. [18.]

1 Tim. v. [17.]

word and doctrine." He looked not on the man, but regarded his office. "We beseech you, brethren, that you know them which labour among you, and are over you in the Lord, and admonish you; that you have them in singular love for their work's sake." St Paul doth greatly commend the Galatians in this behalf, that they loved him "as an angel of God, yea, as Christ Jesus," yea, if it had been possible, they "would have plucked out their own eyes, and given them him." But our times are altered: men are otherwise affected. They envy and mutter against Moses and Aaron. They are become such of whom God complaineth by his prophet Hosea: "Thy people are as they that rebuke the priest." I would to God they would remember Christ's saying: "He that despiseth you despiseth me."

1 Thess. v. [12, 13.]
Gal. iv. [14, 15.]
Hosea iv. [4.]
[Luke x. 16.]

Cornelius in honouring Peter over-reacheth, and is controlled.

20. But the honour which Cornelius gave unto Peter was more than was fit to be given to a man. For Peter refused it with that reason: "I myself am a man too." This zeal and reverence that he had to the word made him over-reach in honouring the minister of it. So did the men of Lystra honour Paul and Barnabas; but they said in like sort, "O men, why do ye these things? We are men, subject to the like passions that ye be." John would have worshipped the angel likewise; but the angel refused: "See thou do it not, I am thy fellow-servant: worship God." Here we learn, how dangerously religious honour is given to any creature. It cannot be thought that either Cornelius or John would rob God of his glory, and give it to angel or man. But yet they were forbidden to do that which they did, lest they should attribute more to the messenger of God than they ought, through preposterous zeal. It is not so great a danger to honour a prince with all humility: therein men cannot so easily exceed, because the honour is civil. But the danger is in a spiritual person, lest in respect of his holy office they honour him too much. And here is the insolent pride of the pope reproved, who vaunteth himself for Peter's successor. Peter took up Cornelius, and would not suffer him to worship him. His successor compelleth princes to cast themselves down before him, and to kiss his filthy feet. This beastly pride declareth him neither to be

Acts xiv. [15.]
Rev. xxii. [9.]

Christ's vicar, nor Peter's successor, but rather his child who said to Christ in the mount, "All these will I give thee, if thou wilt fall down and worship me." If man, who is the lively image of God, may not have this worship, how much less stocks and stones, the dead images of men! For is it not more reasonable that the image-maker should be worshipped, than the works of his hands? *[Matt. iv. [9.]]*

21. Finally, Cornelius thanked Peter for his coming, and declared with, how ready he was to hear him. For in that he said, " Thou hast done well to come," he shewed a thankful mind for his pains taken. So all should be thankful to such as bring them glad tidings, the word of salvation. " He sendeth his word and healeth them," saith the prophet. " Let them confess therefore before the Lord his loving-kindness, and his wonderful works before the sons of men." The philosophers write, even by the law and rules of nature, that the children can never yield worthy thanks unto their parents for their birth and breeding. Such as beget and breed us spiritually deserve more thanks, even so much more as the soul is better than the body, spiritual regeneration better than natural procreation. Such as will not be thankful for the ministers of the truth shall be requited with deceitful teachers. " For God will send them strong delusion that they should believe lies, that all they may be damned that believe not the truth." *[His thankfulness and good acceptation of St Peter's labour in coming.]* *[Psal. cvii. [20, 21.]]* *[2 Thess. ii. [11, 12.]]*

22. Now, how ready himself and his company were to hear Peter preach, it appeareth by the words following: " We are all present here before God, to hear all things that are commanded thee of God." Wherein both the duties of the hearer and the preacher are plainly set down. The duty of the hearer, first, to be present before God; to remember that he standeth in the sight of God, the seer and searcher of hearts, from whom nothing is hid. To stand before the preacher is to stand before God. The presence of God requireth fear and reverence. Fear and reverence should occupy the hearts of them who stand so. Secondly, to hear and learn. There is none so well learned but he may learn more. For while we live, " we know in part," saith St Paul; and therefore we must give diligent care, and apply our minds to that which is spoken. *[His readiness to hear and learn whatsoever God commanded Peter to preach.]* *[1 Cor. xiii. 9.]*

[SANDYS.]

We must not be as a beaten way, where the seed can take no root. We must not suffer prejudice to tread down and destroy the seed, nor the birds of the air, Satan, to pull it out at the one ear, so fast as it entereth in at the other. We may not let our minds wander; but, coming of purpose to hear to our profit, we must beseech God to give us memory and understanding, to print into our hearts that which we hear with our ears. Thirdly, to hear all things, even all the doctrine of God; not things that do please, but things that displease our flesh; not other men's faults, but our own; not only profession, but also conversation; not only faith, but also works; not only to hear, but also to do. Herod heard John gladly while he carped others; but he could not abide to be rubbed on the gall himself. He heard John in many things, but not in all. The Jews at Rome heard Paul, until he applied the words of Esay unto them: "The heart of this people is waxed fat, and their ears are dull of hearing, and with their eyes have they winked; lest they should see with their eyes, and hear with their ears, and understand with their hearts, and return, that I might heal them." Then they shrunk from him, and would no more hear him. The preacher is gladly heard of the people, that can carp the magistrates, cut up the ministers, cry out against all order, and set all at liberty. But if he shall reprove their insolency, pride, and vanity, their monstrous apparel, their excessive feasting, their greedy covetousness, their biting usury, their halting hearts, their muttering minds, their friendly words and malicious deeds, they will fall from him then. He is a railer, he doteth, he wanteth discretion. Not so Cornelius and his company; but they were ready to hear all, and so fashioned and framed according to all that which God by his word should require at their hands.

Mark vi. [17—20.]

Isai. vi. [10.] Acts xxviii. [27.]

The duty of teachers to teach that which God commandeth.

23. The duty of the preacher is expressed in these words, "That are commanded thee of God." The preacher may teach no other than he hath commission to speak, than is commanded him of God. He may not add to the written word, neither take from it. God's law is perfect: it doth perfectly instruct and teach all things necessary to salvation. The disciples must only break those loaves unto the people, which they have received at Christ's hands.

They may not teach their own dreams, inventions, or doctrines. For God will not have them worship him so, but "thou shalt hear the word (saith he) at my mouth, and give them warning from me." And thus much of Cornelius, what he was, on what occasion he sent for Peter, and how he received him at his coming to him. *Ezek. iii. [17.]*

24. Likewise in Peter three things we have noted: how he was occupied when the messengers came to him, how readily he went with them, and what the sermon was that he preached to them. The messengers found him at the sixth hour (which is twelve, as we count) fasting and praying on the house top; where he saw a vision in his trance, a sheet let out of heaven, knit at four corners, wherein were all four-footed beasts of the earth, and wild beasts, and creeping things, and fowls of heaven. And a voice said, "Arise, Peter, kill and eat." First, we see that Peter had his appointed hours of prayer. Prayer is an acceptable sacrifice to God, and a christian exercise; for the use whereof the godly will prescribe themselves certain times. For man's corrupt nature is easily carried away to worldly affairs. He matcheth fasting with prayer, as needful to stir up our slothful drowsy spirits to pray the more fervently. For a full belly maketh a faint prayer. And he sought also a private place to pray in; because in private places we may pour out our hearts more freely unto God. But of this I have spoken before. *The messengers sent from Cornelius find Peter praying.*

25. The vision that appeared was to teach him, that Christ was born a Saviour to the whole world, that the gospel was to be preached to all, that he would all should be saved and come to the knowledge of the truth. And so was declared the calling of the gentiles. For Peter was commanded to make no difference between Jew and gentile, although the gentiles were esteemed as unclean in the eyes of the Jews. Peter, being commanded to kill and eat, abstained in respect of the law. God told him that he should not take as polluted that which he had made clean. All meats are sanctified by the word and prayer. So are the gentiles as clean as the Jews, whose hearts God hath purified. To forbid meats or marriage as unclean, seeing that the Lord hath purified them by *The vision of Peter.* *Acts xv. [9.]* *1 Tim. iv. [1, 3.]*

Tit. i. [15.] his word, is the doctrine of devils. For "all things are clean to them that be clean," and the believing gentile is accepted of God as well as the believing Jew. While Peter mused at this vision, Cornelius his messengers asked for him at the door; and God spake unto him, and said, "Go with them, and doubt nothing, for I have sent them."

His cheerful obedience, being sent to preach.

26. Peter, having the word of God for his calling, went cheerfully forward on his journey, ready to preach to them to whom God did send him. He alleged not how dangerous it was to preach the gospel in Cesarea, how long and tedious a way thither, how odious to be conversant with the gentiles: he indented[1] not what reward he should have, he asked not who should bear his costs: he alleged not his worn body, his old age: he was void of all such put-offs: he knew that "wo be unto him if he preached not:" he remembered his lesson given to others, "Feed the flock of God:" he forgat not Christ's lesson given unto him: "If thou love me, feed my sheep:" he knew that the minister of the word ought to preach in season and out of season. And he took the thing in hand the more gladly, having hope that he should win unto Christ by the word a captain, a man of might and authority: in getting of whom he should also get a great sort, he should get an hundred soldiers, who easily would be drawn to be like affected with their captain: he should win a great family with the rest of Cornelius' friends and kinsmen; and even so it came to pass. It is a great gain unto the church of Christ, when as a man in authority is won by the word. Therefore St Paul used all persuasion to draw king Agrippa to be a Christian, knowing what great advantage would come thereby to Christ's church. To win a prince is to win a multitude, yea, a nation. The church of Christ increaseth and thriveth apace, when kings and queens become nurses to it.

[1 Cor. ix. 16.]
1 Pet. v. [2.]
John xxi. [15—17.]

Acts xxvi. [27—29.]

His entrance into his sermon.

27. Peter being come now to Cornelius, and perceiving how God had touched his heart with the rest of his company, and made them most ready and greedy of the word of God, opened his mouth and said, "Of a truth I perceive that God is no accepter of persons," and so forth.

[¹ Indented=made an agreement or indenture.—ED.]

Now Peter entereth into his sermon, seeing so wide a door opened unto him, so great an occasion offered, so large and apt a field to sow God's seed in. In which sermon there is enough for a Christian to learn: all matter needful to salvation is comprised in it. He that hath taken out this lesson, needeth not to learn another. And a great occasion of it, as of other excellent sermons, was in the people. For the Holy Ghost soweth seed plentifully, where he findeth a good ground to cast it in; and giveth great utterance lightly to the minister, when he giveth good will to the auditory to hear. If the field be barren, the seed is spared lest it should be spilt. He will not have his seed cast in an unfruitful ground. Surely, when the people are worthy of the word, God will send preachers with abundance of it.

28. "Of a truth I perceive that God is no accepter of persons." This is St Peter's entrance to his matter: wherein he declareth that he hath now learned that the gospel of Christ, the doctrine of salvation, doth as well pertain to the gentiles as to the Jews. For although there was a partition-wall which divided them, now it is taken away. The gentiles were "aliens from the commonwealth of Israel, strangers from the covenant of promise, and had no hope, and were without God in the world: but now in Christ Jesu they which were far off are made near. For he is our peace, which made of both one, and hath broken down the partition-wall, to make of twain one new man in himself, so making peace." "Through him both Jew and gentile have an entrance unto the Father by one Spirit." And Peter, having had this revealed to him before in his vision, doth now affirm to the gentiles in the beginning of his speech; partly, to win favourable hearing in that he envied not their salvation, as other Jews did, but carefully sought it; partly, to make them attentive to hear those things which pertained to their salvation. "Of a truth I perceive." Peter confesseth his former ignorance touching the calling of the gentiles, and that he hath learned that which he knew not before. A token of his great humility. His successor the pope is led by another spirit: he cannot abide to grant ignorance, or that he can err: all knowledge is shut up *in scrinio pectoris*, (as they term it) "in the hutch of his breast." Paul would

Being taught of God, he teacheth others that himself before was ignorant.

Eph. ii. [12—14, 18.]

not arrogate all knowledge, though he were taken up into the third heaven, and saw mysteries not to be revealed unto men; for he saith, "We know in part." These Romish rabbies will be no disciples, but masters. They will answer him that shall take in hand to teach them: "Thou art born wholly in sins, and dost thou teach us?"

1 Cor. xiii. [9.]
John ix. [34.]

29. But what hath Peter learned? "That God is no accepter of persons." "I regard not that which man doth regard," saith God to Samuel: "for man regardeth that which is before his eyes; but God regardeth the heart." The person here is taken for the outward appearance and qualities, as you would say, or circumstances of persons— as circumcision, uncircumcision; man, woman; magistrate, subject; Jew, gentile; Englishman, Frenchman; master, servant; rich, poor; fair, evil favoured; a tall man, a dwarf; a citizen, a countryman; a wise man, a fool; a learned, an unlearned. These and such other things are here meant by the persons of men. God is no accepter of these outward shews: he judgeth not as man judgeth. "There is neither Jew nor Grecian, there is neither bond nor free, there is neither male nor female; for ye are all one in Christ Jesus." There is no respect of persons with God: neither ought we to be carried away with external shews of magnifical pomp, of glorious titles, of great authority, much learning, nor in matter of religion to respect the messenger, but the message. Paul reproveth the Corinthians for respecting of persons in matter of religion: some would hear none but Paul, some liked none but Apollos, others followed after Peter, and would only be his disciples. "Is Christ divided?" saith St Paul. The preacher is to be heard for the word's sake, and not for his own sake. If scribes and Pharisees teach out of the chair of Moses, if Judas teach the gospel of Christ, they are to be heard. To hear or not to hear in respect of the person, is to justify or condemn the word for the person. Respect not persons, but reverence the matter: when thou hearest the minister preaching the truth, thou hearest not him, but the Son of God, the teacher of all truth, Christ Jesus. Plato was as honest a man and as good a philosopher as was Diogenes, for all his pretence of simplicity and contemning of the world. Have no respect to outward pre-

God is no accepter of persons. 1 Sam. xvi. [7.]
Gal. iii. [28.]
1 Cor. iii. [4: i. 12, 13.]

tences. Judge not according to the sight, lest in opinion you condemn the good and justify the evil. In matter of salvation neither ought the child to respect his parent, nor the servant his master, nor the subject his prince, nor posterity the predecessors; for we may not hang upon man, but upon God. "Cursed is he that maketh flesh his arm." Jer. xvii.[5.] We must herein only give ear and respect what the Son of God shall say unto us, who is the wisdom of his Father; whom our heavenly Father hath commanded us to hear, Matt. iii.[17; Luke ix. 35.] saying, " Hear you him."

30. " In every nation he that feareth him, and worketh righteousness, is accepted of him." God respecteth not the outward person, but the inward man. He regardeth not the shape, but his own image that is in man. He is not partial to the Jew, more than to the gentile: rich and poor, learned and unlearned, are all one in his sight. He accepteth of such as fear him and work righteousness. Herein is comprised perfect religion; our duty towards God, and our duty towards man; the former, and the latter table; to believe in God, and to do right to our neighbour; to love God above all, and to love our neighbour as ourself. To fear God is in true holiness to serve God: to work righteousness is not to hurt but to help our neighbour, to do to others as we would be done unto ourselves. He that will be a wise man indeed, must learn to fear God. " The beginning of wisdom is the fear of the Lord." All other wisdom wherein the fear of God wanteth, is but " earthly, sensual, and devilish." Such as fear God shall be strengthened to stand against all assaults of Satan; yea, they shall continue and stand stedfast unto the end, even to the last gasp! Canst thou not away with want? Wouldest thou have plenty? " There is nothing wanting to them that fear him." Canst thou not away with infamy? Wouldest thou be praised? The greatest praise that can come to any man is that he feareth God. " It is the glory of the rich, the noble, and the poor." Wouldest thou have all virtues, and the rewards of them? Wouldest thou be free from sins, and the punishments ensuing them? Follow the example of Cornelius, and fear God. For " they who fear God will honour and obey their parents:" they who fear God will

God accepteth them which fear him in every nation.

Ecclus. i. [15.]

James iii. [15.]

Psal. xxxiv. [9.]

Ecclus. x. [21.]

Ecclus. iii. [7.]

diligently exercise themselves in prayer: they who fear God will search their own hearts, see their offences, and with the prodigal child be sorry for them, confess them, and forsake them. They who fear God will abstain from sin; remembering that the Lord doth hate it, and will punish it; and knowing that their doings cannot be hid from him. If the fear of God were planted in our hearts, we would learn after so many admonitions to lead a better life; we would practise such lessons as we have been so long in learning; we would not live in such careless security as we do; the gospel would take better effect in us, and bring forth more plentiful fruit; we would at the length cast away impiety and worldly concupiscence, and live a sober, just, and godly life; we would repent and forsake sin, lest sin procure God's speedy wrath; the ministers would be more diligent in feeding of the flock, the people more ready to hear the voice of the shepherd, the magistrates more careful over the commonwealth, the subjects more obedient to frame themselves to live under law; the rich would not suffer the giver of their riches to go on begging; the poor would endeavour to get spiritual treasures, and to be rich in Christ; finally, we would not feed our bellies so daintily, nor so vainly and superfluously clothe our bodies, but use temperance in diet and sobriety in apparel; having what to eat, and wherewith to be clothed, we would be content. Verily, to conclude, such as fear God abstain from evil, and do good, and, as our apostle St Peter saith, they do "work righteousness."

31. Righteousness compriseth in it all such duty as we do owe unto our neighbour. Whatsoever is contained in the second table, is comprehended in this word "righteousness." But how can we work righteousness, who are as unclean things, and all our righteousness as a filthy clout? Of whom the prophet saith, "There is not one that doth good, no not one?" In deed we are not able to work perfect righteousness. For if we could, then Christ had died in vain, with whose perfect righteousness we must be clothed by imputation, that we may be accepted as righteous in God's sight. "For God hath made him, which knew no sin, to be sin for us, that we might be made the righteousness of God in him." But when

we are justified so by the perfect righteousness of Christ; we must endeavour to serve God in righteousness, and bring forth good fruits, though they be unperfect, such as in this frailty of the flesh we may. And these are accepted of God for Christ's sake, their weakness and imperfection being pardoned in him. Wherefore in this sort we must work righteousness, and follow sanctification. Hitherto, how all estates must apply themselves to work righteousness.

32. Omitting therefore others whom generally this toucheth, I will at this present remember children only of a point of righteousness which they must work; in giving due honour to their parents. For there is a great fault in many at this day, that, whereas they are specially bound to their parents, both by the links of nature, and by the bonds of God's word, they burst those bonds asunder, and dispose of themselves in marriage as they list, without consent of their parents. A fault, as most heinous in the sight of God and condemned by his law, so condemned too by the law of nature, the law civil, the law canon, and the opinion of the best writers. For the law of God doth not only charge children generally to obey their parents in all things, but also particularly doth shew by sundry examples that children ought to be given by their parents in marriage, and not to be left to their own phantasies. And among the ethnicks, even by the law of nature, as their poets shew, marriages for children were not made by themselves, but by their parents. It is written in the law civil: "If a son marry a wife against his father's will, the child that shall be born of that marriage shall not be counted lawful[1]." In the canon law it is said: "Marriages are then lawful when maidens are asked to wives of their parents, and are given by them openly to their husbands: otherwise they are not marriages, but whoredoms[2]." The best writers both old and new

Children put in mind of a work of righteousness towards their parents; without whose consent to bestow themselves in marriage is a thing unrighteous.

Col. iii. [20.]

In ff, de statu hominis l. Paul.

30 q. 5. c. Aliter.

[[1] Corpus Juris Civilis Rom. Lips. 1720. Digest. Lib. I. Tit. v. De Statu Hominum. 11. Paulus, Lib. xviii. Responsorum. p. 115. See also Digest. Lib. xxiii. Tit. ii. De Ritu Nuptiarum. 2. Paulus, Lib. xxxv. Ad Edictum. p. 440.—Ed.]

[[2] Decretum Gratiani Par. 1583. Decr. Sec. Pars. Causa xxx. Quæstio v. c. 1. cols. 1941, 2.—Ed.]

subscribe hereunto; Tertullian, Ambrose, Chrysostom, Augustine, with all the learnedst of latter times; whose particular sentences I omit to recite for brevity sake[1]. But if youthful children have so little reverence both of God and men, that such admonition will not make them leave such disordered marriages, it behoveth magistrates, who are the common parents of the weal public, to bridle their lusts with severe laws for the redress of this evil and the mischiefs ensuing of it. And thus much of St Peter's entrance into his sermon: the sermon doth follow.

<small>The sum and substance of St Peter's sermon is peace by Christ Jesus.</small>

33. "Ye know the word which God hath sent to the children of Israel, preaching peace by Jesus Christ," and so forth. The sum of the sermon is this. Jesus Christ, which is Lord of all, the preacher and author of peace, did faithfully perform the office for the which he was sent, preaching to the people the glad tidings of the gospel, and healing all their diseases, for God was with him; and he was slain and hanged on tree; the third day he arose again from death: he ascended into heaven: from thence shall he come to judge the quick and the dead: to whom all the prophets bear witness, that through his name all that believe in him shall have remission of their sins. Such as this is were the sermons of the apostles. Here are all things necessary to salvation expressed. This is that which God commanded his great apostle, St Peter, to preach. In this doctrine would he have his people trained up. The people received it as a sufficient doctrine. Peter and Paul were directed by one spirit: they neither esteemed <small>1 Cor. ii. [2.]</small> "to know any thing but Jesus Christ, and him crucified;" neither could they testify or preach ought but him. This <small>The parts of his sermon.</small> sermon is divided into three parts; the first, that Jesus Christ the Lord of all was sent unto the people of Israel to preach peace; the next, that he died and rose again from death to procure us this peace; the last, that we are made partakers of this peace by faith in his name. Jesus Christ the Lord of all was sent unto the people of Israel to preach peace. Let us weigh the words severally: they are most effectuous, fully setting forth the mystery of our salvation.

[¹ See Note C.—Ed.]

34. Jesus, by the interpretation of the angel, is a Saviour: "Thou shalt call his name Jesus; for he shall save his people from their sins." The angel, appearing to the shepherds, said, "Behold, I bring you tidings of great joy, that shall be to all the people; that is, that unto you is born this day a Saviour." The ethnicks do seek their safety in their idols; the Jews in the observances of the law, and traditions; the papists in their pardons, purgatory, masses, merits; the true Christians seek it in Jesus Christ the Saviour, and in none but him. He will not be matched therein with any other; but he is a full, perfect, and only Saviour. He is "the Lamb of God that taketh away the sin of the world." There is neither water nor fire, bulls nor bells, masses nor merits, pope nor pardon, that can save us. There is neither devil, or flesh, nor world, if he save us, that can condemn us. For who can condemn, whom he doth justify? And whom he justifieth not, who can save? Christ is *anointed*: and Jesus is called so, because he was "anointed of God above his fellows." Whereupon Esay the prophet writeth of him: "The Spirit of the Lord is upon me; for he hath anointed me." Anointed he was to be a king and priest: for they among the Jews were wont to be anointed. "He is the King of kings, and the Lord of lords." The wise men of the east did acknowledge him a king: "Where is he that is born king of the Jews?" Zachary sheweth further what manner of king: "Behold, thy King cometh to thee, meek, and riding upon an ass, and upon a colt the foal of an ass." This our king doth govern us with a right sceptre. "The sceptre of thy kingdom is a sceptre of righteousness." He doth defend us with a mighty and stretched out arm, against whose power no power can stand. He is that triumphant prince, which hath most victoriously vanquished and thrown under foot our enemies. They labour in vain that kick against the pricks, that strive against his gospel. For he is a prince of might that doth defend it; and "the gates of hell shall not prevail against it." The sun will run his course: the passage of the gospel cannot be stopped. "The gospel is not bound." While it is persecuted, it is enlarged. "The blood that is spilt for it is the very seed

1. Jesus Christ Lord of all sent from God to preach peace. Matt. i. [21.] Luke ii. [10, 11.]

Acts iv. [12.]

John i. [29.]

Rom. viii. [33, 34.]

Psal. xlv. [7.]

Isai. lxi. [1.]

Rev. xvii. [14.]

Matt. ii. [2.]

Zech. ix. [9.]

Psal. xlv. [6.]

Acts ix. [5.]

Matt. xvi. [18.]

2 Tim. ii. [9.]

Tertul.

of it[1]." Now, as he is our King, so our Priest and Prophet too ; at whose mouth we should require the law of God: that prophet like unto Moses, the searcher of truth: that very Son of God, of whom the Father hath said, *Ipsum audite:* "Hear ye him." He is the Priest, which once for all hath sufficiently sacrificed for our sins; by himself and by none other, once and not often, upon the cross, and not upon the altar; sufficient for all such as shall be saved. He is the Priest, the high bishop that maketh intercession for us; the only mediator between God and man, to teach man the will of God, to reconcile God to man, to make intercession between God and man. These are the peculiar duties of Christ, as we are taught in the epistle to the Hebrews.

<small>Deut. xviii. [18.]
Matt. iii. [17: Luke ix. 35.]
Heb. ix. [26.]</small>

<small>Christ the Lord of all.</small>

35. "Which is Lord of all." Lest the gentiles should conceive that Jesus Christ was promised and sent to be a Saviour only to the Jews, he answereth that objection by a prevention (so to term it) calling him Lord of all: the Lord of the gentile as well as of the Jew. "Christ will that all men be saved," that is, men of all sorts. He was sent to preach peace to all, both Jews and gentiles. He is the Lord over all, even the Lord of glory, to whom all power is given both in heaven and in earth. He hath bought us all with a great price, that we should "serve him in holiness and righteousness." Let us remember therefore that of the prophet: "If I be a Lord, where is my fear? saith the Lord of hosts." "Fear not them which kill the body, but be not able to kill the soul: but rather fear ye him, which is able to destroy both body and soul in hell."

<small>1 Tim. ii.[4.]
Matt. xxviii. [18.]
1 Cor. vi. [20.]
Luke i. [74, 75.]
Mal. i. [6.]
Matt. x.[28.]</small>

<small>Christ sent from God to preach peace.
Gal. iv. [4, 5.]</small>

36. "Which God hath sent." "When the fulness of time was come, God sent forth his Son, made of a woman, and made under the law, that he might redeem them which were under the law." He was made man for us, that in our nature he might suffer for us. He was sent of his Father, "being equal with his Father; and being in the form of God, he made himself of no reputation:" all to lift us up, that were cast down to hell, and to rid us from the

<small>Phil. ii. [6, 7.]</small>

[[1] Nec quicquam tamen proficit exquisitior quæque crudelitas vestra; illecebra est magis sectæ. Plures efficimur, quoties metimur a vobis: semen est sanguis christianorum.—Tertull. Op. Lut. Par. 1641. Apologet. adv. Gentes 50. p. 45.—Ed.]

bondage of Satan and his angels, to whom we were enthralled. For that is imported by the peace mentioned in the words that follow. God preached by him. "He sent me to preach the gospel to the poor," saith Christ himself in Esay. To preach the gospel, even the gospel of peace; not to preach war between God and man, but to preach peace. For the word of the gospel is the word of reconciliation. *Isai. lxi. [1.]*

37. And here by Christ's example all messengers of God and ministers of his word are taught by the way, that before they meddle with doing this office, they must be lawfully sent thereto. Such as deny their lawful sending do also deny their lawful preaching. "For how shall they preach, unless they be sent?" saith St Paul. The prophet complaineth of such runners as be not sent: "I have not sent these prophets, saith the Lord; yet they run." Such are sent as are framed thereunto by the Holy Ghost; whom the Holy Ghost hath furnished with gifts fit for that office: which do not usurp it, but stay till they be lawfully called, as was Aaron. *Such as preach must be sent to preach. 2 Cor. v. [20.] Rom. x. [15.] Jer. xxiii. [21.] Heb. v. [4.]*

38. Christ was not only sent to preach peace, but also to be our peace-maker; for through him "we have peace with God;" and in him we should seek peace with men too, as far as lieth in us. For the gospel is the word of peace, not of contention, tumult, and rebellion, as our adversaries term it: of it[1] own nature it is the word of peace: it cometh otherwhence that contention doth follow it; for as soon as the gospel beginneth to be preached, Satan maketh a stir and laboureth to suppress it. As soon as the wise men asked after Christ, Herod was troubled. As soon as Christ entered into Jerusalem to preach, "all the city was moved." The truth hath many enemies. The light is hated of evil doers: the gospel will ever be persecuted. And in this sense is that of Christ verified, "I came not to send peace, but the sword." Christ was sent to preach peace. He preached peace, and made peace between Jews and gentiles; or rather, between them both and the Lord. "For he is peace, which hath made of both one, and hath broken *The doctrine of Christ is a doctrine of peace. Rom. v. [1.] Rom. xii. [18.] Matt. ii. [3.] Matt. xxi. [10.] [Matt. x. 34.] Eph. ii. [14.]*

[1. "It" for "its"; the latter word being formerly not in use and generally supplied by "his."—ED.]

the stop of the partition wall." "Other sheep I have, (saith Christ to the Jews) which are not of this fold; them must I bring also, and they shall hear my voice; and there shall be one sheepfold and one shepherd." He preached peace amongst men, and brought peace into the world. At the time of his nativity (as appeareth in histories), there was peace amongst all nations and people throughout all the whole world[1]; to shew unto the world, that the Lord of peace was come into the world. Peace is the badge that God giveth to discern his from others. Love is Christ's livery-coat. "By this shall all men know that ye are my disciples, if ye love one another." "He cannot be at peace with God, that is at war with his neighbour. He cannot have concord with Christ, that nourisheth discord with a Christian[2]." God hath made us one: let not the devil sunder us into many. Pride is a peace-breaker: humble and mild hearts are not contentious, but "labour to keep the unity of the Spirit in the bond of peace." God hath given us Christ, the Prince of peace: he hath given us the gospel, the word of peace: he hath given us a peaceful queen, (the Lord bless her!) and common peace in our country: let us be thankful to the Lord for it; and woe to him that shall break it! "Be of one mind, live in peace; and the Lord of love and peace shall be with you." He preached peace, peace between God and man. Sin made division between God and us, as it is written in Esay: "Your iniquities have separated between you and your God." So that God's favour descended not to us; neither could our prayers ascend unto him. But Christ hath removed this wall of division: he hath taken away this stoppage: "he hath cancelled on the cross this writing that was against us:" he hath made us a free access unto God. By him we are reconciled unto God the Father. He hath laid our sins upon his own shoulders:

[1 Oros. Hist. Mogunt. 1615, p. 512.—ED.]

[2 The following is probably the passage referred to: Unde Johannes dicit, Qui enim non diligit fratrem suum quem videt, Deum quem non videt, quomodo potest diligere? Mentiebantur enim quidam dilectionem se Dei habere, et de odio fraterno eam non habere convincebantur.— August. Op. Par. 1680. Expos. Epist. ad Gal. Cap. v. Tom. III. Pars II. col. 970.—ED.]

he hath borne the pese[1] of his Father's heavy wrath and indignation: he hath satisfied God's justice, and pacified his anger, and made a perfect peace between God and us. Man's conscience can never rest nor be at peace, until it be settled in the full persuasion of remission of sins in the death and resurrection of Christ Jesus; whereby God receiveth us into his favour, and is at one with us through him. This is that joyful tidings of peace with God, which Christ was sent to preach unto the world. This is that "peace which passeth all understanding." He that with [Phil. iv. [7.]] patience resteth in this peace doth suffer all things: he rejoiceth in the midst of troubles and afflictions: he is not overcome with the fear of man's malice, but will cheerfully and boldly say with St Paul, "If God be with us, [Rom. viii. [31.]] who can be against us?" And with the prophet, "I will [Psal. iv. [8.]] lay me down, and sleep in peace; for thou, Lord, only makest me dwell in safety." This is that peace which Christ preached, and promised to leave with his elect: "Peace [John xiv. [27.]] I leave with you, my peace I give unto you: not as the world giveth, give I unto you. Let not your heart be troubled, nor fear." This peace is far from the ungodly: "there is no peace, saith my God, to the wicked." They [Isai. lvii. [21.]] are ever restless: the biting worm never ceaseth to gnaw and grate in their cumbered consciences.

39. Christ preached peace, when the Lord sent him. [The diligence of Christ in preaching peace.] He was not negligent in his office; he answered his calling carefully. He "went about doing good, and healing all that were oppressed of the devil." He was not retchless in God's matters. He was no dumb dog, no idle idol. He crept not into a corner, he hid not himself: but he walked, he went abroad: he said to his disciples, "Go ye, preach [Matt. xxviii. [19.]] ye:" he gave the example himself: he lay not out of his diocese: he was resident upon his charge, and looked to every part of it: he made not his continual abode at Jerusalem, nor at Jericho, nor at Capernaum, nor in any one city, town, or village, but he went through all Jewry and Galilee: not to poll and pill, to extort and wring out of the people what he could; but it was to do good, and to heal such as were oppressed of the devil, to preach the word, and to work miracles. He preached throughout his

[[1] Pese—weight.—Ed.]

<small>Mark i. [38.]</small> whole charge: "For I came out," saith he, "for that purpose." Nor only did he gladly teach such as came unto <small>Matt. xi. [28.]</small> him; but he invited also and provoked all that were weary and loaden to come, promising them that he would refresh their souls. And herein he did the office of a priest. And again, he healed all that Satan had afflicted; and herein he <small>Psal. lxxii. [4.]</small> did the office of a king. "He shall judge the poor of the people," saith the prophet: "he shall save the children of the needy, and shall subdue the oppressor." He threw out his enemy, the oppressor Satan, and delivered his people out of that enemy's hands. An example for the magistrate to defend the innocent, to deliver the oppressed, to punish <small>Rom. xiii. [4.]</small> the transgressor: for the sword is given him to this end. An example for the minister to teach the word of God, and confirm it with doing what good soever he may, according to the talents that the Lord hath given him. Finally, an example for every faithful Christian, to shew <small>James ii. [18.] 2 Pet. i. [10.]</small> forth his belief by his conversation, his faith by works, "to make his vocation and calling sure" thereby. "For God was with him." Christ wrought his wonderful works by the power of God, and not (as the scribes falsely charged him) by the power of Beelzebub; "for God was with him." He taught the word that he received of his Father: he <small>Luke xi. [20.]</small> cast out devils by the finger of God. He was no chopper or changer of the word: he used neither witchcraft, sorcery, nor conjuring. He wrought not by the devil, but by the power of God.

<small>2. Christ died to procure the peace which he preached.</small> 40. The next part was, that he died and rose again to procure us this peace. "They slew him, hanging him on a tree. God raised him up the third day." The death and resurrection of Christ is the only mean of our reconciliation <small>Rom. iv. [25.]</small> and peace with God. For "he died for our sins, and rose for our justification." By his death and passion he hath cancelled, and fastened upon the cross, the hand-writing that was against us. He hath pacified God's wrath, he hath procured God's favour; of enemies made us friends, of <small>Eph. ii. [19.]</small> strangers citizens, of the children of wrath the children of God, and fellow-heirs of his eternal kingdom.

<small>God hath ordained him a judge of quick and dead.</small> 41. Before this crucified Christ, that died and rose again, we shall appear to give an account of our whole life, of our thoughts, our works and words. For, as St Peter

saith, "he is ordained of God a judge of the quick and the dead." At the latter day he is appointed to be judge of all flesh: "the Father hath delivered all judgment unto him." And "we shall all stand before his judgment seat, that every one may receive the things done in his body, according to that he hath done, whether it be good or evil." This judge is both judge and witness. "I will come near unto you to judgment; and I will be a swift witness against the soothsayers, and against the adulterers, and against false swearers, and against those that wrongfully keep back the hireling's wages, and vex the widow and the fatherless, and oppress the stranger, and fear not me, saith the Lord of hosts." Nothing is hid from his eyes, he seeth the secrets of all hearts: he will not be corrupted, but give unto every one according to his works. Christ is judge. Wherefore we are taught to leave revenge unto him. "Vengeance is mine, I will repay, saith the Lord." For private men to revenge wrongs is to usurp Christ's office, to take judgment out of his hands whom God the Father hath appointed judge of the quick and the dead. You that be afflicted and oppressed with misery and wrong, lift up your heads; "for your redemption draweth near." You that oppress and wrong your brethren, repent, and desire pardon, lest the sentence of God's justice overtake you. His justice no man can abide; "for in his sight shall none that liveth be justified." Christ therefore is given, as St Peter teacheth, to be our Jesus, that is, our Saviour; our Christ, that is, anointed, a King, a Priest, and Prophet; the Lord of all, whom we ought to serve in holiness and righteousness; sent of God, and made man, he preached peace between God and man, and between men among themselves: he died to be a sacrifice for us: he rose again to justify us: he is made our judge, and doth judge justly.

John v. [22.]
2 Cor. v. [10.]
Mal. iii. [5.]
Rom. xii. [19.]
Matt. xxiv. [31—33: *Luke xxi.* 28.]
Psal. cxliii. [2.]

42. Now we with Peter, or rather with the Holy Ghost, with the prophets and apostles give herein to Christ that which is his own. And here is the controversy between the adversaries of the gospel, the papists, and us. We give unto Christ that which is his right: they rob, and take from him that which is his due. We spoil our-

The honour which St Peter in this sermon giveth unto Christ is by us also given him; but not so by our adversaries.

selves of all righteousness, and seek to be clothed with his righteousness: they clothe themselves with their own righteousness, not caring for that righteousness which is in him. We hope to be saved by him, our only priest, our sacrifice, our mediator: they have shaven priests, and unbloody sacrifices, and infinite mediators both of saints and angels. To be short, we acknowledge Christ our whole Saviour, and all the glory thereof we give unto God: they will be saved by themselves, their merits, their pardons; they impart the glory of God unto dead men, to images, to relics, and to dumb creatures.

<small>3. Of the peace which Christ hath procured we are made partakers by faith.</small>

43. The third and last part of St Peter's sermon was, that we are made partakers of peace by faith in Christ's name. "To him all the prophets give witness, that through his name all that believe in him shall receive remission of sins." Wherein three things are remembered unto us: that remission of sins is free; that we receive it by faith; and that this doctrine is witnessed by all the prophets.

<small>Remission of sins free.
Mark ii. [7.]
Tit. iii. [5.]</small>

44. All flesh hath sinned, and doth need forgiveness. God is the only forgiver of our sins. Neither doth he forgive them in respect of man's merits; but of his mercy, good-will, and free mercy. The only means, that moved God to be merciful freely to sinful man, was that most acceptable sweet bloody sacrifice which the innocent Son of God offered upon the cross for our sins. "All have sinned, and are deprived of the glory of God; and are justified freely by his grace, through the redemption that is in Christ Jesus." He took our unrighteousness upon himself, and clothed us with his justice; and "he, who knew no sin, was made sin for us, that we might be made the righteousness of God in him." In Christ and for Christ we receive free remission of sins. "There is no other name given us under heaven whereby we may be saved." "I am the way, the truth, and the life: no man cometh to the Father, but by me," saith Christ. No sin forgiven but through him; and through him all sins are forgiven freely.

<small>Rom. iii. [23, 24.]
2 Cor. v. [21.]
Acts iv. [12.]
John viii. [19, 24, 36.]
John xiv. [6.]</small>

<small>Of remission of sins we are made partakers by faith.</small>

45. The mean whereby we are made partakers of this free remission of sins, in the death and resurrection of Christ, is faith in Christ. "For all" (saith Peter) "that believe in him shall receive remission of sins through his

name." God doth freely offer unto us remission of sin and peace in Christ: the mean and instrument to receive it withal is faith. He that believeth is made partaker of it; and not of it only, but of eternal life also. "For he that believeth in me hath life eternal," saith our Saviour Christ. But this faith, this justifying faith, doth work through love, and sheweth itself by works. The good tree will be fruitful. The believing justified child of God will fear God and work righteousness. {John iii. [16.] Rom. iii. [28.] Gal. v. [6.] James ii. [18.]}

46. This doctrine of justification by faith in the death and resurrection of Christ Jesu is witnessed by all the prophets. It is no new doctrine, but old; not only proceeding from the apostles, but also from the prophets. For Moses and all the prophets bear witness of him. And as they, so the apostles after them. Whose steps we must follow, and acknowledge that no doctrine is to be established, but that which is testified by the apostles and prophets. The true church of Christ doth build her faith on their foundation. God will be worshipped and served according to his prescript word, and not according to the brain of man. The prophets and apostles, with all such as be ministers of the word, are here and elsewhere called witnesses: yea, Christ himself termeth himself a witness of the truth. "For this cause am I born, and for this cause came into the world, that I should bear witness to the truth." And Christ saith to his apostles, "Ye shall be witnesses unto me both in Jerusalem, and in Samaria; even to the uttermost ends of the earth." {Unto this doctrine all the prophets bear witness. Luke xxiv. [27.] Eph. ii. [20.] John xviii. [37.] Acts i. [8.]}

47. The truth is to be testified by public preaching. Paul commendeth the Thessalonians for believing his testimony. His testimony was the gospel, which he did preach and testify unto them. According to the voice that did speak unto him when he was cast off his horse: "I have appeared to thee for this purpose, to appoint thee a minister and witness both of things which thou hast seen, and of the things in which I will appear unto thee." The truth is also testified by writing. By the writings of the prophets, apostles, and evangelists, the truth of God, Jesus Christ, was most plainly testified. As John, to name one of them among many: "This is that disciple which testifieth of these things." The truth is also witnessed when {Bearing witness to the truth, both by teaching and by suffering for it. 2 Thess. i. [10.] Acts xxvi. [16.] John xxi. [24.]}

as it is testified in blood : for a martyr is a witness. Christ told Peter, that when he was young he girded himself, and walked whither he lusted; but when he waxed old, other should gird him, and carry him whither he would not. "Now this" (saith John) "he spake, signifying by what death he should glorify God." Many martyrs have thus testified the truth with suffering for it. But "they overcame by the blood of the Lamb, and by the word of their testimony, not loving their life," no, not "to the death." That minister which will neither testify it by public preaching, nor by writing, will hardly testify it by suffering; but will rather say with Peter, "I know not the man."

[John xxi. 18, 19.]

Rev. xii. [11.]

Matt. xxvi. [72, 74.]

But I must here make an end, for the time hath overtaken me; and without repetition, as you know the manner is. To God the Father, God the Son, and God the Holy Ghost, three Persons and one almighty and all-merciful God, be rendered all thanks, and all glory given, for ever and ever. Amen.

THE FIFTEENTH SERMON.

A SERMON

PREACHED AT STRAUSBOROUGH, IN THE TIME OF QUEEN MARY'S REIGN.

---

2 Cor. VI.

1. *We therefore, as helpers, beseech you that ye receive not the grace of God in vain.*
2. *For he saith, I have heard thee in a time accepted, and in the day of salvation have I succoured thee: behold, now the accepted time, behold, now the day of salvation.*

The prophet, to abate the haughty conceit which naturally we have of ourselves, in such sort as every man were his own God, and had no other whom to praise for the graces and gifts wherewith he is beautified and set forth as a mirror for all other creatures to behold and wonder at, endeavoureth to turn away our eyes from too much gazing upon our own excellency, by pointing as it were his finger at him who is author of every good and perfect gift, saying, "He made us, and not we ourselves." [Psal. c. 3.] For what end and purpose, Zachary teacheth; namely, "that we might serve him in holiness and righteousness [Luke i. 74, 75.] before him all the days of our life." "For we are his [Eph. ii. 10.] workmanship, created in Christ Jesus unto good works, which God hath ordained that we should walk in them." "Ye are not," saith St Paul to the Corinthians, "your [1 Cor. vi. 19, 20.] own." Why so? "For you are bought with a price: glorify therefore God in your body, and in your spirit; for they are God's." Forsomuch then as we are all of the household of God, all one in Christ, all members of one and the same spiritual body, worshipping one Lord, receiving one baptism, professing one faith, and expecting one glory to be revealed upon us in that great day; it

God hath created men to serve and honour him.

is our duty, in token of our near conjunction in the Spirit, with one heart, one mind, and as it were with one mouth, to present ourselves before his mercy seat, to praise him, to hear his word, to receive the seals of his merciful covenant in the gospel, and to offer him our needful supplications together, that in all things it may appear that we are one, as he and the Father are one, even one God to be blessed for ever.

With what zeal, joy, and gladness the godly do perform their service to the Lord.

2. With what zeal and desire God's people of old were wont to do this, we may guess by that which we read of the prophet David; who, being persecuted of his wicked and unnatural son, and driven from the presence of that glorious tabernacle, which with great triumph and joy himself had placed in the city of David, where he was wont with the rest of the people to call upon the name of the Lord, to hear the law, and to offer sacrifice upon those beautiful altars, conceived such a deep impression of grief by the sorrowful meditation of those sweet and heavenly comforts, whereof his soul had tasted in former times, that, forgetting quite the loss of all other royalties whatsoever, he maketh moan for nothing but only this, that he might not now be partaker of those inestimable benefits, and the comforts of mind and conscience, which he was wont to receive at the hand of God, at such time as with the rest of the Israelites he resorted to the tabernacle, where God promised to be present and favourably to hear the petitions there made unto him. Of this his great misery he complaineth him lamentably in divers of his psalms; but especially in the eighty-fourth, where he breaketh out into these words of great zeal: "O Lord of hosts, how amiable are thy tabernacles! My soul longeth, yea, and fainteth for the courts of the Lord: mine heart and my flesh rejoice in the living God." He goeth on, and magnifieth the blessed estates of those silly birds, which might have their nests and lay their young even close by the altars, from the presence of which he was exiled. In the end, to shew the happy case wherein they are to whom continual and daily access to the house of the Lord is granted, he preferreth one day spent there before a thousand any otherwhere; the meanest room about the house of God before the highest throne in the palaces of

Psal. lxxxiv. [1, 2.]

the wicked. In another psalm he so speaketh, as if every day's absence from that holy place were a thousand years: "When shall I come to appear before the presence of God?" As if he should have said, Shall I never? Never shall I be so happy? So the Israelites, at such time as they were exiles in Babylon, declared their earnest desires this way by their bitter tears; Nehemias, by his heaviness in the presence of the king; Christ, by leaving his mother to present himself at holy exercises in the temple, being but as yet of green and tender age. And with what zeal, joy, and gladness, the disciples of Christ, after the death of their Master, joined themselves together in private houses, when by reason of the cruel persecution by the priests they durst not shew themselves abroad, it appeareth both in the Evangelists and in the Acts of the Apostles. Yea, when afterward the Spirit of God miraculously descending upon them had increased both their zeal and courage, they openly professed him whom before they worshipped in secret places. No fear, no prohibition, no threatening of higher powers was able to withhold them: they spake, they entered into the temple, they taught daily; and being persecuted, were glad that God thought them worthy to suffer for his sake, who had died for theirs. God, according to his promise, is ever present in his congregation. "Wheresoever two or three are assembled in his name, he is with them:" yea, what thing soever his saints so assembled shall lawfully ask, his promise is, it shall be given them. *Psal. xlii. [2.] Psal. cxxxvii. [1.] Acts v. [41.] Matt. xviii. [20.]*

3. With what earnest desire, dear brethren, ought we then to stand in this place before the Lord; being driven from the tabernacle of God, as David persecuted, as the blessed apostles of Christ exiled, as Israel cast out of the churches wherein we were nursed and trained up! How thankful ought we to be to our heavenly Father, who hath in so ample a manner, in the midst of our manifold distresses and griefs, caused the light of his countenance to shine in the faces of us his poor afflicted servants! For although, because we, our princes, our prophets, and our people, have grievously sinned in not esteeming so preciously, nor following so religiously, his blessed gospel as we ought to do, therefore he hath bereaved us of our worldly pros- *The like alacrity in serving God required now especially.*

perity, and brought these miseries upon us, wherein we now are; yet, knowing that we are the sheep of his pasture, howsoever we have wandered and gone astray, it hath pleased him in great abundance of mercy so to temper the sharpness of his correction, that we find him still our present helper at hand, and ready most to succour us in our extremest need. Could we wish for more at the hands of God than, being banished and constrained to forsake all the profits and comforts which we enjoyed at home in our native country, here amongst aliens and strangers to find a city so safe to dwell in, maintenance so competent for our needful and reasonable sustentation, such grace in the eyes of the godly magistrates under whom we live, such favour and respect to our hard estate, such free liberty to come together, to call upon God in our common prayers, to hear his word sincerely and truly preached in our own natural tongue, to the great and unsearchable comfort of our souls; finally, all things so strangely and almost miraculously ministered and brought unto our hands, as doubtless we could never have found here, if the Lord himself had not gone before, as it were, to make ready and to provide for us? O what tokens of mercy and special favour hath our kind and gracious Father shewed us in this our exile and distress for his gospel, in these our sorrowful and afflicted times! We have lost the saving truth at home, and found it abroad: our countrymen are become our enemies, and strangers are made our friends: being persecuted by our native rulers, foreign magistrates have shewed us favour. In banishment we have a place to dwell in: in anguish we abound with comfort; and, as the apostle speaketh, "having nothing, we are as possessing all things." Therefore, dear brethren, having received these so great and rare graces at the merciful hands of our good God, I may justly, as one of your poor helpers in these holy labours, use the words of St Paul, which in the beginning I recited; exhorting and beseeching you, "that ye receive not this grace of God in vain." Be not an unthankful people: neglect not the great benefit now offered unto you: approach with all reverence, and present yourselves as humble petitioners before the Lord, and careful servants before our God. For I say unto you, as Jacob said in his journey towards

[2 Cor. vi. 10.]

Mesopotamia: *Vere Dominus est in loco isto*: ." truly God is here," even present amongst us. We do clearly and plainly perceive that, our fathers and mothers, our friends and familiars, having forsaken us, he hath received us as his dearest.

^{Gen. xxviii. [16.]}

4. Let us now take a view of St Paul's words, which I have propounded to entreat of. In the entrance of which he professeth himself to be our helper, furthering us and setting us forward in the course of our salvation, not only by teaching the word of reconcilement, remission of sins, free mercy in the death and through the merits of Christ crucified; but also by most earnest and vehement exhortation, beseeching us worthily to receive this so freely offered grace and blessing. Now, as Paul was an helper and a mover unto godliness, so no doubt we ought all to be helpers every one to another, according to our calling, in distributing and communicating such gifts as we have received at the bountiful hands of God; "every one," according to that of St Peter, "as he hath received grace himself, so ministering it to another, as good dispensers of the manifold graces of God." For he hath not delivered us our talents to be wrapped up, hidden, and buried in the earth: we are stewards so to use the riches of his grace, as may be most to the advantage of his glory amongst men.

Each man should be another's helper.

1 Pet. iv. [10.]

5. Unto this our blessed apostle exhorting setteth three especial things before our eyes to be considered. First, he putteth us in remembrance of the great mercy of God towards us, whereof we are moved not to shew ourselves unworthy receivers: secondly, he sheweth that this is the acceptable and only accounted time, wherein it must appear whether we receive that grace in vain or no: thirdly, he teacheth wherein and how we must declare ourselves so to have received it as behoveth.

Three things contained in St Paul's exhortation.

6. "Receive not the grace of God in vain." I will not travail to tell you, how diversely the name of grace is taken in the sacred scriptures; but rather note unto you in what sense the Holy Ghost doth chiefly use it in this place. Grace is the favour and mercy of God towards sinful men. "It is called grace, because it is given gratis; freely and undeservedly on our parts, to whom it is given[1]."

1. Of receiving the grace of God in vain. What that grace is.

Aug. in Psal. 30.

[[1] "Miser ego homo, quis me liberabit de corpore mortis hujus? Gratia Dei per Jesum Christum Dominum nostrum." Quare gratia? Quia

For us it is purchased, by the only mean and mere merit of our Saviour Christ; and to us it is both offered and exhibited, by the voluntary and unprovoked operation of the Spirit. This grace in itself being large and more than sufficient for all men, the Holy Ghost divideth and bestoweth upon each, breathing where and as he listeth, according to the secret pleasure of his will. Through it we have salvation, whereas through sin we deserve death. For our iniquity was heinous in the sight of God; first committed by Adam, and since continued in us. But far more exceeding was the mercy of our Lord, who, when we were his enemies, "sent forth his Son, made of a woman, and made under the law, that he might redeem them which were under the law, and that we might receive the adoption of sons." No tongue can express, neither any mind conceive this graciousness. Yet let us ponder it with such consideration as we are able. Great therefore, I say, was the mercy of our Creator, who gave his Son; and great the love of our Saviour, who gave even himself for us. Our thraldom was great, that required a ransom of such value; our guiltiness much, that could no otherwise be washed away, but with the very heart blood of the innocent Lamb of God, Christ Jesus our Lord: yea, inestimable and uneffable was the love of our gracious Lord, who, to spare us, spared not himself. He was content to become ignominious before men, that we might be glorious with his Father; to be condemned, that we might be absolved; to be crowned with thorns, to purchase us a crown of immortality; to lose his life, that we might gain life; to suffer death, that we might escape it; and to become as hated and accursed of God, that we might find favour and eternal grace with him. In his death our sin is pardoned: by his blood our filthiness is washed away: by his resurrection we are reconciled to his Father, and made at one with God. Let us not break this so happy truce betwixt the Lord and us: let us not through sin condemn ourselves again: now that we are justified, let us not walk toward hell, he having made plain and easy the path to heaven.

Gal. iv. [4, 5.]

Quia gratis datur. Quare gratis datur? Quia merita tua non præcesserunt, sed beneficia Dei te prævenerunt.—August. Op. Par. 1681. In Psalmum xxx. Enarrat. ii. 6. Tom. iv. col. 149.—ED.]

The image of God in us, defaced through Adam, is repaired by Christ: let us appear, therefore, in this pure image before God, that we may be acceptable in his pure sight. Through Christ we are called to be citizens with the saints, and God's household servants: let us then put on the garments of truth and innocency, that so it may appear whose servants we are by our Lord's livery. We are made the happy heirs of his glorious kingdom, and fellow heirs with Jesus Christ: wherefore let us not seek so possessions here, that we lose a better inheritance above in heaven. If we do, it is in vain that the grace of our Lord Jesus Christ hath been so largely offered unto us, and plentifully poured on us. Yea, his grace will increase the wofulness of our destruction.

7. Grace is offered and received by two especial outward means; the preaching of the gospel, and the holy administration of the blessed sacraments. These two are the instruments, or rather the hands, by the which the Holy Ghost doth offer, exhibit, seal, and deliver the grace of God unto us. *Grace offered by the word and sacraments.*

8. And there be two sorts of men to whom grace is offered by the word in vain. The one are they which will not give it so much as the hearing, but do utterly contemn and unkindly refuse that which the Lord doth so kindly and so graciously offer to them. The other, they that hear it indeed, read it, but consider it not; receive it, but altogether without fruit, and for fashion's sake. Of the former sort are all such as Pharaoh was, who enjoined Moses to come no more in his sight, for he would not hear him. Such also were the Jews, to whom when Stephen preached, they stopped their ears. Such they of whom the Lord complaineth by the prophet, saying, "I spake and they would not hear." *Grace offered in vain by the word to such as will not hear it.* Acts vii. [57.] Isai. lxvi. [4.]

9. Of the latter sort there be three kinds shadowed in the parable of the sower, which went forth to sow his seed: whereof some fell in the highway side, some in stony and gravelly ground, some also amongst thorns. That which fell by the highway side, either the birds of the air picked up, or men trod upon with their feet. Which our Saviour applieth unto him that heareth the word of the kingdom, and understandeth it not; and by and bye the devil taketh it away, lest he should believe, and so be *To such as hear it, but retain it not.* Matt. xiii. [3—7.]

saved. For it fareth with the word preached, as with the seed sown. Some are so dissolute and retchless, that they let it in at the one ear, and out at the other. The hearts of some be so hardened and parched, because they want the watering of God's Spirit (which doth only mollify), that his word can take no root in them. The devil and his deceitful angels do so bewitch them, and fill their hearts with vain cogitations, so abalienate their minds, and trouble their memory, that they cannot tell what is said: it is forgotten by that it is spoken. Yea, the devil doth so throughly occupy the hearts of many other with superstitious opinions and fond persuasions, or with such worldly desires, such fleshly lusts, such froward affections, that the hearing of the blessed word is a wearisome work unto them: every hour spent that way is as tedious as a year, and thought to be wholly lost. Many likewise both hear the word preached, and read the scriptures, as the Pharisees did hear them; that they may seem to favour the gospel, and so, under pretence of holiness, blind the eyes of others, and purloin commodity to themselves. Such come in amongst the children of God, as did Satan of old: yet God knows them to be children of darkness, not of light; yea, and oftentimes he so shaketh them out of their painted rags, that the whole world may espy their ugly and deformed nakedness. Whilst by their hypocrisy they labour to deceive others, they deceive, yea, and damn themselves. To this sort of men therefore the word is offered; but all in vain. Either they receive it not, or they receive it to their own destruction.

To such as retain it, but not still.

10. The second sort are resembled to the stony soil, which receiveth the seed, and it taketh root for a time; but when the heat of the sun cometh, it withereth away. Many such there be, which have gladly heard the gospel, have frequented sermons with appearance of great devotion, and could freshly talk of the holy scriptures of God. But when the heat of the sun burst out, when persecution and fire followed the professors of it, O Lord, how many have shrunk, yea, and utterly fallen from it! How many persecutors now, which then were professors! Not one amongst forty hath tarried the beam and blaze of his burning and trying sun. O Lord God, wonderful is thy mercy; yet

their estate is pitiful. These our times, dear brethren, have marvellously tried what ground we be, what root God's word hath taken in us. Much gravelly ground doth now appear, which before was thought to be sound and battle[1]. So it is, the timeliest fruit often cometh to least proof. The freshest gospeller in appearance, in experience is found not to be the soundest; and the greatest talkers, oftentimes the idlest workers; and such as have bragged most, when it came to be tried in the field, have first fled. Such are God's judgments; who seeth far otherwise than man can see, and through a fawning face espieth a traitor's heart. How vainly therefore a great sort have received and gloried in this gospel, we now perceive, and with mournful hearts do rue it. The Lord forgive them, and strengthen us with his grace unto the end! Here we learn that persecution followeth this seed of God. Christ testifieth that he came to send the sword amongst us, and not peace; signifying, that the gospel would procure many enemies, and much persecution. Wherefore, "my son," saith the wise man in the book of Ecclesiasticus, "when thou comest to the service of God, stand in justice and fear, and make ready thy soul to trial." Happy is that ground which, being tried, is found good and fruitful. Matt. x. [34.]
Ecclus. ii. [1.]

11. The third sort are compared to ground overgrown with thorns. For as thorns choke the seed which is sown amongst them, so that it cannot bring forth that fruit which it ought to do; so the cares of the world, and the pleasures of this life, which be as thorns to wound, as brambles and briars to entangle the minds and consciences of men, destroy that spiritual seed, which in a heart well prepared and purged from these weeds would grow up unto everlasting life. In this number we may reckon those base-minded worldlings mentioned in the parable; who, being invited, came not, because their farms, their oxen, and their wives, withheld them. The inordinate care that some have for their children and family, how to find them food and raiment more than sufficient; the desire that others have to keep their worldly substance, their possessions and riches, and also to increase the same, and get to live in wealth themselves, and to leave their children To such as receive it and retain it, but unprofitably.

[[1] Battle—rich, fertile.—ED.]

rich; the pleasure that some other have to live in honour, and to be in office, finely to feed, and to go gorgeously, to follow their lusts and the transitory pleasures of this vain world, hath overgrown, yea utterly choked, in a great sort of men, a great deal of good seed. Many there be whom the cares, the riches, and the pleasures of this sinful world have so bewitched and drawn into so corrupt a sense, that even, like the Gadarenes or Girgesites, rather than lose one of their pigs, they will bid adieu to the gospel of Christ, and beseech the Lord of salvation to depart out of their coasts. Most true therefore it is which St Paul noteth in them, whose hearts are possessed with carefulness of this world's good. "They that will be rich fall into temptation and snares, and into many foolish and noisome lusts, which drown men in perdition and destruction." Riches are the nurses of all vain delights and fleshly pleasures. This caused our Saviour so heavily to threaten: "Woe be to the wealthy!" Let us therefore learn, by this warning of our Saviour, when the gospel of Christ is preached, to take heed, that neither it be devoured by birds, nor trodden down with feet, nor withered with heat, nor choked with thorns, and so made unprofitable; but rather, being received, kept, and cherished in the ground of our hearts, it may grow and increase so abundantly, that when the Lord shall see it ready for the sickle, and send his angels to cut it down, it may fill the reapers' hands, and make rich the barns of him that looketh for fruit of it.

Matt. viii. [34.] Luke viii. [37.]

1 Tim. vi. [9.]

Luke vi. [24.]

Grace offered by the sacraments.

12. Now, as the graces of God purchased for us by Christ are offered unto us by the word, so are they also most lively and effectually by the sacraments. Christ hath instituted and left in his church, for our comfort and the confirmation of our faith, two sacraments or seals; baptism, and the Lord's supper. In baptism, the outward washing of the flesh declareth the inward purging and cleansing of the Spirit. In the eucharist, or supper of the Lord, our corporal tasting of the visible elements, bread and wine, sheweth the heavenly nourishing of our souls unto life by the mystical participation of the glorious body and blood of Christ. For inasmuch as he saith of one of these sacred elements, "This is my body which

[Luke xxii. 19.]

is given for you;" and of the other, "This is my blood," [Matt. xxvi.] he giveth us plainly to understand, that all the graces, which may flow from the body and blood of Christ Jesus, are in a mystery here not represented only, but presented unto us. So then, although we see nothing, feel and taste nothing, but bread and wine; nevertheless let us not doubt at all, but that he spiritually performeth that which he doth declare and promise by his visible and outward signs; that is to say, that in this sacrament there is offered unto the church that very true and heavenly bread, which feedeth and nourisheth us unto life eternal; that sacred blood, which will cleanse us from sin, and make us pure in the day of trial. Again, in that he saith, "Take, eat: [Matt. xxvi. drink ye all of this," he evidently declareth that his body 26, 27.] and blood are by this sacrament assured to be no less ours than his; he being incorporate into us, and as it were made one with us. That he became man, it was for our sake: for our behoof and benefit he suffered: for us he rose again: for us he ascended into heaven; and finally for us he will come again in judgment. And thus hath he made himself all ours; ours his passions, ours his merits, ours his victory, ours his glory; and therefore he giveth himself and all his, in this sacrament, wholly unto us. The reason and course whereof is this. In his word he hath promised and certified us of remission of sins, in his death; of righteousness, in his merits; of life, in his resurrection; and in his ascension, of heavenly and everlasting glory. This promise we take hold on by faith, which is the instrument of our salvation: but because our faith is weak and staggering through the frailty of our mortal flesh, he hath given us this visible sacrament, as a seal and sure pledge of his irrevocable promise, for the more assurance and confirmation of our feeble faith. If a prince gave out his letters patent of a gift, so long as the seal is not put to, the gift is not fully ratified; and the party to whom it is given thinketh not himself sufficiently assured of it. God's gift, without sealing, is sure; as he himself is all one, without changing: yet, to bear with our infirmity, and to make us more secure of his promise, to his writing and word he added these outward signs and seals, to establish our faith, and to certify us that his promise is most certain. He giveth us therefore these holy and visible signs of bread and wine, and saith, "Take and eat, this is my body and blood;" giving unto the signs the names which are proper to the things signified by them; as we use to do even in common speech, when the sign is a lively representation and image of the thing.

How grace is received by the sacraments, and not in vain.

13. Let us therefore be thankful unto our Redeemer Christ for these his great benefits, and so unspeakable and undeserved mercies; and let us receive this holy sacrament as a sure pledge, that the virtue of his death and passion is imputed unto us for justice, even as though we had suffered the same which he did in our own natural bodies. Let us not be so perverse, as to draw back when Jesus Christ calleth us so lovingly to this royal feast; but, with good consideration of the worthiness of this gift, present we ourselves with a fervent zeal, that we may come worthily to this holy table. "Let each man try himself, and so eat," saith the apostle. Let us enter into ourselves therefore, and examine the estate of our hearts and souls, and consider in what case we stand. If we be not of the sanctified household of God, not Christ's servants and faithful disciples, shall we dare presume to press in, being aliens and strangers to the Lord's, as most comfortable, so also most dreadful, table? No: let no impenitent blasphemer of God, no whoremonger, or vile and unrepented sinner, presume to touch or taste this food; for such shall not feed upon Christ and his merits, but they receive their own damnation. But such as will worthily feed at this blessed feast must earnestly and truly mourn for their sins past, in a settled purpose and resolution never willingly to defile themselves again. And such as will be partakers of this bread that came from heaven, Jesus Christ, our one and only Saviour, must also be as one bread or loaf, and as one body joined together in brotherly love and all other offices of godly and christian charity. For if thou come to this banquet without this vesture of love, it shall be said unto thee, "Friend, how camest thou hither, not having on thy wedding garment?" A woful speech, and an end most miserable. Let this suffice for the first point, which is the blessed

apostle's exhortation, "not to receive the grace of God in vain."

14. Concerning the second member, wherein we are put in mind that this is the time to shew ourselves worthy receivers of grace; he applieth to his purpose the words of the prophet Esay, who, speaking unto Christ as in the person of his Father, saith, "In an acceptable time have I heard thee, and in a day of salvation have I helped thee." The acceptable time is that whereof St Paul speaketh: "When the fulness of time came, God sent his Son, made of a woman." It was indeed an acceptable time and full of grace, wherein the sacrifice of Christ was so graciously accepted, and his prayers heard of God. And it may well be called "a day of salvation," wherein his Father gave him a triumphant victory over those so bitter torments of death. An acceptable time was it, a day of salvation; not so much in respect of him, who at all times was accepted, as of us, who without him and his death had been refused. For in that day was our redemption wrought by our Redeemer, and sinners saved by his passion who had no sin. And as he died and rose, so he prayed and was heard for us: "I pray for them; I pray not for the world; I pray for them whom thou hast given me," saith our Saviour. Now the acceptable time and day of salvation which Esay spake of, St Paul doth very aptly and effectually apply to his present occasion: "Behold, now is the acceptable time: behold, now is the day of salvation." For the fathers lived in hope of this acceptable day of grace and favour to come: but the very time beginneth from the suffering of Christ Jesus, and continueth even to the world's end. And unto every one of us so much of this acceptable time is granted, as we have time granted here to live. Which being not long (because our life is but as it were a span), it may fitly be called a day, or rather an hour of salvation. This day therefore grace is offered us of God; against whose majesty "forasmuch as all have sinned," and by sin "are deprived of his glory," we must needs acknowledge that for the recovering of our loss we stand all in present need of his grace. Now is the time wherein our souls do groan to be relieved with grace and mercy. For

2. The time to receive grace offered is, when God calleth by the preaching of the gospel.
Isai. xlix. [8.]

Gal. iv. [4.]

John xvii. [9.]

Rom. iii. [23.]

who can say, My heart is sound, I need no physician? What one man is there amongst us all, who hath loved God as he ought to do? or tendered his neighbour's case as he would his own? We may dally with ourselves, and think that we suffer not for our own transgressions, that we are not cause of that great plague and calamity, which presently is come upon our country. Beloved, do not deceive yourselves. Our God is a righteous judge, who blesseth the innocent, and heapeth punishment upon the offending soul. For truly, if we search ourselves as we ought to do with a single eye, if we examine our thoughts, take a reckoning of our words, and peise[1] our deeds and ways in an equal balance; ask our hearts, and they will tell us, inquire of our conscience, and it will declare unto us, that every one of us hath well deserved more than hath happened unto any of us: yea, we shall find that all have not suffered half so much as every one hath deserved.

Gen. iii. Our first parents, for tasting the fruit that was forbidden them, were themselves cast out of their pleasant habitation, and punished in all their posterity to come for ever. Have we, being terrified by the horror of their example, withheld our hands, and bridled our affections from every Num. xvi. [31—33.] unlawful and forbidden thing? Corah, Dathan, and Abiram, with their favourites and confederates, were swallowed up of the earth for whispering against Moses and against Aaron. Did we never once mutter against our good and lawful magistrates, against our judges, and against the Lord's mi- 2 Sam. xxiv. [15, 17.] nisters? David, for numbering of his people, procured such a plague, that seventy thousand were consumed with it; and are we so unspotted, that we have not in as heinous a matter as this offended God? Would to God we were! but the Lord and our own consciences do know, how far otherwise the case doth stand. I will not enter into particulars, nor open the sores of any man, but send you home into the closet of your own hearts to see it. And if we prosecute the comparison in such wise as hath been touched, I nothing doubt but every one of us may justly lay the cause of this heavy displeasure of God, and grievous plague, upon himself: every one may say and cry out with the prophet David, "It is I that have sinned," I that have

[1 Peise—poise, weigh.—ED.]

committed iniquity and deserved this great vengeance. The smart whereof as we do outwardly feel, so, if it inwardly pierce us to the quick of our hearts and souls, if we be truly wounded and humbled in deed with the grievous remembrance of our former sins; this is, of all other, the most acceptable time for us to receive the saving health of God; who as he taketh his time to offer us grace, so we must also take ours to receive it being offered. "To-day," saith the apostle, "if you will hear his voice, [Heb. iv. 7.] harden not your hearts." It is to-day, so long as he speaketh by his prophet, saying, "Return every one from his Jer. xviii. [11, 8.] evil way, make your ways and your works good." "If this nation, against whom I have pronounced, turn from their wickedness, I will repent of the plague that I thought to bring upon them." It is to-day, so long as that voice of John the Baptist is heard, "Repent;" so long as wisdom uttereth her voice in the streets, and crieth, "Turn;" Matt. iii. [2.] Prov. i. [23.] so long as our Lord and Saviour saith, "Come," it is to-day. Matt. xi. [28.] These so often callings and so sweet admonitions ought to be of force sufficient to set us forward to repent, to turn and come to our merciful Saviour in this day of salvation, and to follow the worthy examples of our wise forefathers, who, being stirred up in like sort, have awaked and have been saved. That very day that 2 Sam. xii. [13.]. Nathan the prophet told David of his fault, he repented, and was received to mercy. The Ninevites likewise were a wise and a circumspect people: they took their time, Jonah iii. [5—9.] even the acceptable time of their repentance, which else had come too late. So they, which repented at the preaching Matt. iii. [5, 6.] of John, made speed to retire from their own by-paths, and to turn into the ways of God. As many as received fruitfully and effectually the grace which the Lord did offer by the hands of Peter, preaching the remission of sins, Acts iii.[19.] they also took the opportunity of that self-same hour, and so were saved. All these things (as St Paul witnesseth) "are written for our instruction," that we might learn Rom. xv. [4.] wisely to redeem the time, and to know the day of God's most gracious visitation.

15. Especially now, sith we do not only hear the sound of his voice, but also feel the smart of his correction. There is no hope that ever we will receive the

The most especial time to receive grace is when God afflicteth.

grace of God, if in the midst of our afflictions we refuse it. His case is desperate whom adversity cannot cure, whom eternal death hath so possessed and benumbed, that the very sharpest medicines are unable to work upon him. "Turn you, therefore," saith Wisdom, "at my correction." When men are heavy laden with grief and sorrow, then are they fittest to call for and to receive refreshing. Examples hereof are almost infinite. After Joseph's brethren were brought into comber[1] and into fear of their lives, they remembered their fact committed against their brother; and it grieved them much, which before had much contented them. Whilst men are at ease and have rest in the flesh, grace is no grace; the promises of God cannot have their effectual and powerful operations, no, not in the very elect of God. Look upon Manasses in his throne, and in prison; upon the people of Israel, at home in peace, and abroad in banishment; upon Noah, David, Ezekias, all the saints and servants of God, in their flourishing estate, and in their grievous troubles; and ye shall find that the gracious offers of God were never received worthily in deed, but in great extremities. "When a man is stricken with sorrow upon his bed, and the grief of his bones is sore," saith Elihu in the book of Job, "so that his life causeth him to abhor bread, and his soul dainty meat; if in such a case there be a messenger with him, or an interpreter, one of a thousand, to declare unto man his righteousness, how that God will have mercy upon him, and will say, Deliver him that he go not down into the pit, for I have received a reconciliation;" such a message of grace no doubt will then be heartily accepted, or else be in vain for ever. It is affliction that maketh the kingdom of heaven to suffer violence. When we are in misery, in trouble, in distress of body and mind, then especially is the acceptable time, then is the high day of our salvation. "Thou didst chastise me," saith the prophet Jeremy, "and then I came to understanding." So that the most especial time to shew ourselves worthy receivers of the grace of God is when his chastisements are upon us, and his anger doth afflict our souls. Wherefore most properly, beloved in the Lord, to you it may

[1 Comber—trouble.—ED.]

be spoken, "receive not the grace of God in vain." This is the acceptable time, this is the day of your salvation. Although the grace of God have heretofore been offered and unkindly refused, yet, now that the hand of his heavy displeasure, now that the rod of his correction is laid upon you, O receive it not now in so acceptable a time in vain!

16. The only way to shew ourselves worthy receivers of grace is, by hearty and unfeigned repentance to acknowledge that we have sinned in perverting righteousness, and to amend that which we know and acknowledge to be amiss. If we think to be received into his favour without this, brethren, we deceive ourselves. He is gracious, but to the penitent; and will have mercy upon sinners, but upon sinners which forsake their sinfulness. It is true that he will heal whom he hath spoiled; and whom he hath wounded he will build up: he will quicken the dead, and raise up them that are thrown down; yet so, if they say, "Come, and let us return unto the Lord." The first effect therefore of grace in the heart of man is unfeigned repentance: with the doctrine whereof we are throughly enough acquainted. We have no need to be taught what the name doth signify: the nature, properties, and parts thereof are known. Only the practice wanteth; whereunto we are so slow, and so hardly are drawn, that in this one point we weary out all our teachers: about this one thing they waste, they spend themselves. And in the end we are most commonly as we were at the first, like the leopard that changeth not his skin. To bring men to repentance is such a work of weight, that God himself seemeth as it were tired with labouring so long about it. As appeareth by those passionate and grievous complaints recorded in holy scripture: "I have spoken, they do not hear:" "I have stricken, they are not grieved:" "How often would I have gathered them as a hen her chickens under her wings, and they would not be gathered." "O Ephraim, what shall I do unto thee? O Judah, how shall I entreat thee?" Yet neither were they ignorant, and we do very well know, that there is no other medicine save repentance only, to heal the wounds of our souls; no other way to restore ourselves again to our Father's

3. The right way of worthy receiving grace is by hearty repentance.

Hos. vi. [1.]

[Isai. lxv. 12.]
[Jer. v. 3.]
[Matt. xxii. 37.]
Hos. vi. [4.]

home, but only, "Father, I have sinned;" no other mean to quench the wrathful indignation which our sins have caused to burn and flame as an oven, but only our tears. Though our sins be red as scarlet, or as fire; yet, being bathed with the water of our eyes, they are scoured and made as white as snow. It is written of Mary (not of that virtuous Mary, but of the dissolute), that she was *mulier peccatrix*; notorious for her light and lewd behaviour. Yet by repentance, as she died unto sin, so, the memory of sin being dead unto her, she liveth still in the glorious remembrance of that righteousness which penitent sinners obtain by faith. She is honourably mentioned wheresoever the gospel of Christ is heard: all men speak of her tears, of her sins no one is mentioned or known. The precious oil wherewith she was wont to anoint herself, that she might be more pleasant to the senses of her lovers, she now poureth out, and for love sake bestoweth it upon her Saviour. The eyes, which were wont to cast wanton looks upon the dissolute, did now gush out with water, and served as conduits at the feet of Christ. The hair, which before had been wrapped in gold, had been coloured, pleated, and bordered[1], laid out and beset with pearls, was now employed to a far other use, that the honour received from the feet of Jesus might put out the shame which before it had taken from the eyes of lewd and amorous beholders. Having washed and dried, she could not satisfy herself till she had also kissed her Saviour's feet; whose mercy had now eased her heart of that deadly sting, which the lips of wantons had imprinted and left behind them. O blessed pattern of true contrition, how worthily art thou left for all posterity to talk of, to behold, and to follow! Such converts shew plainly that they are worthy receivers, and that the grace of God hath not appeared unto them in vain. For they who in this sort deny ungodliness and worldly lusts, will surely, according to the blessed apostle's exhortation which followeth, "give offence to none."

17. For although there must of necessity offences rise, yet, "Wo be to him by whom they rise!" Why? Were not the Pharisees offended at the scholars and disciples of

[1 Bordered—broidered.—Ed.]

Christ for not fasting, for eating with unwashed hands, for plucking the ears of corn on the Sabbath-day, and for such like things of their own invention, toys of no importance? Nay, did not the most charitable deeds of Christ himself offend these peevish hypocrites? It is true, they were offended with him and his, as at this day the Romish Pharisees are offended with us and ours. But we must mark and observe, that we are warned only not to give offence to any man. If men be offended with us, which by us are not offended, such offences, being not given of us but taken of them, are not our faults, but their follies. Unto us therefore at this time St Paul's exhortation importeth thus much, that sith God hath granted us favour in the eyes of this people, with whom we presently converse, it were a thing most intolerable for us with Jacob's children to commit such crimes, or give such offences, as might make us odious and loathsome in their sight. The gospel hath now gotten honour and renown by these our sufferings for it: let it not hereafter be ill spoken of and slandered through our disordered conversation. Of all others we had need to walk most warily. We are set as it were a city upon a mountain to be gazed at. Our conversation is marked of all men, and diligent search made of it on every hand. Friends, enemies, and strangers observe our steps; and a little fault in us will be taken as a great offence. "Let the word of Christ dwell richly [Col. iii. 16.] amongst you, with all wisdom;" "that ye may be blame- [Phil. ii. 15, less and pure, as the sons of God, without rebuke; that 16.] we may be as shining lights in the world, holding forth the word of life, that in the day of Christ we may rejoice and be glad," as they who have not received the grace of God in vain. Let us, forsomuch as our heavenly Father, for the merits of his Son, and by the ministration of his Spirit, doth graciously offer and exhibit unto us his manifold mercies and benefits, especially in his holy word and sacraments, thankfully and worthily receive the same; and namely, in this acceptable time, the only time appointed of God for us to receive and for him to offer grace. Finally, let us shew that his grace hath taken root and place in our fleshy, not fleshly hearts, in bringing forth the works of the Spirit, the fruit of true repentance, of sanctification and good life; giving offence to no man, no, not to those which are without; but walking quietly, honestly, and orderly in all things, that men, seeing our blameless and inoffensive conversation, may glorify God the giver of all goodness, and the eternal Father. To whom, with the Son, and the Holy Ghost, one God of most glorious majesty, be all honour and praise rendered in the church for ever. Amen.

THE SIXTEENTH SERMON.

A SERMON

PREACHED AT A MARRIAGE IN STRAUSBOROUGH.

Heb. XIII.

4. *Marriage is honourable in all.*

As God made the world and all the creatures therein contained to serve for the setting forth of his glory and great majesty, so likewise by the forcible and mighty operation of his strength and power he preserveth still the works of his hands; lest, if he should have only builded the goodly frame of this world, and afterward suffered the same to decay, the praise of his name should have lasted but a while, and reached but to a few; which now passeth through many generations, and continueth to all eternity. For this he provided, when, having finished the creation of trees and herbs, and made them both beautiful and good in their appointed seasons, he blessed them with secret virtue, to multiply by bringing forth fruit and seed, each according to his kind; that there might be a continuance and increase of things so behoveful for lively creatures. Also, that the lively and sensible creatures themselves, the birds of the air, the beasts of the field, and fishes in the sea, might yield in all ages the benefit which the children of men do reap by them; he poured into them also the selfsame blessing of increase and fruitfulness. And as unto these, so likewise unto man, the greatest in honour, though in order the last of all his creatures, he gave the same power, to spread out himself by propagation, and to replenish the face of the earth. *Why God blessed plants, beasts, and men, with power to increase themselves by propagation.*

2. For the seemlier and better ordering whereof, to the end that, as God himself is most pure, and therefore hateth all uncleanness, so the actions of men, who in nature *Man's offspring by marriage.*

resemble him, might be framed according to the pattern of his image; he prescribed a way how man, as beseemeth the excellency of his creation and nature, might, not after a brutish and beastly manner, but in all honesty and cleanliness, bring forth the honourable fruit of his body; that so God's creation and work might be continued, his kingdom enlarged, and his name, by reason of the multitude, much more praised. And this mean or way appointed by God was matrimony; a state, whereof the chosen vessel of God writeth this, as the judgment of the Holy Ghost, "Marriage is honourable." Wherein for your better instruction and learning, my purpose is to shew you the reasons of the honour which it should have, and also of the great disgrace which it hath amongst men.

<small>1. Marriage is honourable in respect of the author.</small>

3. - "Marriage is honourable;" first, in respect of the author by whom it was ordained; secondly, in regard of the causes thereof; thirdly, for the duties which are required of the parties married. Touching the first, it appeareth in the beginning of the book of Genesis, how after that God had perfectly accomplished his creation, and had given the lordship over all living creatures unto Adam, he said, "It is not good that man be alone: let us make him an helper that may be before him:" let us make woman. Whereupon our Saviour in the gospel inferreth, "That therefore which God hath joined together, let no man separate;" approving marriage to be the institution of God, and a natural order (proceeding, I mean, from the God of nature) to be observed and used for ever. Neither did he only confirm this law and ordinance of God in plain words and in his teaching, but he also did honest and honour the same with his presence. For being called to a marriage, he, his mother and kinsfolk gladly went, there to feast with others, where it pleased him miraculously to increase their cheer, and withal their honour. For it is not nothing which this doth add to the holy and reverend estimation thereof, that the first miracle which Christ wrought was wrought at a marriage, and is so by the Holy Ghost recorded. Now, besides this, that Almighty God himself ordained marriage, and that in paradise, a most heavenly habitation, and that before the innocency of man was stained with sin; besides this, that

<small>Gen. ii. [18.]</small>

<small>Matt. xix. [6.]</small>

<small>John ii. [1—11.]</small>

Christ did allow and many ways approve the same, yea, and moreover vouchsafed to resemble his spiritual conjunction with his church unto this estate; we find that the patriarchs, the priests, and prophets, the holiest men of God, Abraham, Moses, Aaron, and the rest of that blessed company, have chosen to live rather in marriage than otherwise; acknowledging thereby the state of marriage to be undoubtedly no less allowable, if not more honourable, than single life.

4. Concerning the second point, that is to say, the honour which riseth from the causes for which God did institute the state of wedlock, the scripture noteth especially three. The first is mutual society, help, and comfort. And this were a cause sufficient to esteem of marriage highly, if there were no other. For God hath said, "It is not good that man be alone; let us make him an helper;" an helper, and not an hinderer.

<small>2. Marriage is honourable in respect of the causes for which it was ordained; as comfort, help, and mutual society. Gen. ii. [18.]</small>

5. The second cause why matrimony was ordained, and must be honoured, is increase and propagation. For although that this may be, as we see it is in lewd and shameless persons too often, without this estate of marriage; yet this is so much against the dignity of human nature, that such broods have been always basely accounted of by men which have had but the bare light of natural understanding. Wherefore the blessed apostle hath said, "I will that the younger sort marry, and bring forth children;" giving us thereby to understand, that there can be no seemly propagation of mankind save only in marriage. Children begotten in the state of matrimony are the blessing of God; and "the fruit of the undefiled womb is a reward," as Solomon wisely acknowledged in the psalm. For a man to be honoured with the name of a father, to be renewed and continued in his posterity, if it be not a special blessing of God and a very exceeding great reward, why are men and women so desirous to see the fruit of their bodies? Why was Anna so exceeding in craving children at the hands of God? Why was barrenness so grievous unto Sarah? Why did it seem reproachful unto Elizabeth? Is it a small benefit, that God hath raised out of the body of Abraham so many patriarchs, priests, prophets, judges, and kings; such

<small>Propagation.

1 Tim. v. [14.]

Psal. cxxvii. [3.]

1 Sam. i. [10, 11.]

Luke i. [25.]</small>

a multitude not only of men of reputation on earth, but also of blessed saints and citizens in heaven? If it were an honour unto Abraham to be a father of many nations; surely marriage, which made him a lawful and an honourable father, ought very honourably to be esteemed.

Remedy against concupiscence. 1 Cor. vii. [2.]

6. Another cause of honour given unto marriage is, for that it is a remedy against uncleanness: "Let every man have his wife, and every woman her husband, for the avoiding of fornication." Upon which words of St

Ambrose.

Paul Ambrose writeth very aptly: *Qui abstinent a licitis, in illicita prolabuntur*[1]*:* "They which forbear things lawful to use fall many times to use things which they should forbear." And he bringeth in the Manichees for example; as we may bring in the papists, and namely that pond of Rome, adjoining to a nunnery, wherein were found the heads of seven thousand bastards[2]. It is true that all have not need of this remedy, because all are not subject to the danger and peril of this disease. But if any man be subject to this disease, let him beware how he despise this remedy. There be, no doubt, that have the gift of chastity by birth; and there be that have made themselves

Matt. xix. [12.]

chaste by endeavour: but of this all[3] men are not capable. As it is the gift of God, so it seemeth to be a rare and not a common gift. Such as have it and so live sole, they are more fit to labour in God's church, it must needs be granted, for they are cumbered with fewer cares. But be these cares never so many and great, better it is to marry than to burn, and to be burthened with ordinary and honest cares, than with unordinary and dishonest carelessness to be destroyed. There are many that deceive themselves, thinking a single and a chaste life to be all one. To be pure in body and in spirit, this is

[[1] Ideo ergo non permittit, ne ab licitis se abstinentes, inconcessa præsumerent, sicut faciunt Manichæi.—Ambros. Op. Par. 1690. Comment. in Epist. ad Cor. Prim. Cap. vii. Tom. II. Appendix, col. 132.—This commentary is placed by the Benedictine editors among the Tractatus Supposititii.—ED.]

[[2] The authority on which the archbishop relied for this story was, no doubt, the letter of Volusianus to pope Nicholas, which Fox has printed in his Acts and Monuments, Lond. 1684, Vol. II. pp. 301-3.—ED.]

[[3] The early editions have "all this;" but the transposition seems absolutely necessary to the sense.—ED.]

chastity. He that seeth a woman, and in his heart hath a lewd desire towards her, hath defiled his heart, and is in soul unchaste. If every man try himself according to this rule exactly, peradventure he shall see a disease in himself that needeth remedy; which if he neglect and so perish, whom may he blame? The medicine is commended with a title of honour, that thereby we might be allured to use it. The danger of not using of it, if need require, is death. For harlots and adulterers the Lord shall judge.

7. Thus much being spoken of the causes for which honour is given unto marriage; I will briefly speak of the duties of honour required between parties married. How honourably a man should use his wife, So Paul teacheth plainly in many places, but especially in his epistle to the Ephesians. "Men, love your wives, as Christ hath loved his church." In which place he instructeth not only by precept, but also by setting a pattern before our eyes to follow; and that is Christ, the true spouse to his church the congregation of the faithful. "The husband ought to love his wife, even as Christ did his church." But Christ suffered death to redeem his church: even so truly the husband, if necessity so required, to save his wife should jeopard his own life. His life is well spent in saving of her, and by losing of her ill spared. "Christ purged and made his church beautiful, void of spot or wrinkle," that it might resemble himself, as near as might be, in purity. Even so the husband should labour to reform his wife; to instruct and frame her to discretion, sobriety, all matron-like virtues, and all godliness. A wise wife maketh a happy husband; and in her goodness he shall find gladness. The husband is called "the head of his wife, as Christ is of the congregation." When as the head espieth faults in the members of the body, it doth not study how to cut them off and make separation, but doth muse upon a remedy, and labour to procure a medicine to apply unto the hurt parts, to recover the body, and to cover the fault if he cannot cure it. A good husband is a good head: his endeavour will be to cure his diseased wife, and not to cut her off from him; especially to win her unto Christ, if she wander out of the right way. Her faults

3. Marriage honourable in respect of mutual duties between parties married.

The duties of honour required in the husband towards his wife.

Eph. v. [25—27.]

will make him sorrowful, not furious; and to pity her infirmities, without hating of her person. Wisdom is required in the head, to rule and govern well the body which is placed under it. He that braggeth and boasteth that he is the head, and yet wanteth the prudency which the head should have, is unworthy to be named that which indeed he is not. A wise husband must wink at many faults, and bear with many of his wife's infirmities. He that foolishly champeth upon those griefs, which wisdom would have be swallowed, if he live in continual misery, may say, that he only liveth happily which liveth wisely; no greater wisdom than to devour follies. Yet the husband's lenity ought not to be such as to nourish foolishness. Virtue is always discreet, and in all things the mediocrity. St Paul giveth the reason why men should give this honour to their wives: for "he that loveth his wife loveth himself, they two being one flesh. No man ever hated his own flesh. Our own bodies we love, as Christ hath loved his church." If a man's natural body were never so mangled, so sick, so corrupted, so crooked and evil favoured, he would yet love and feed it, and cherish it so much the more, by how much more it needed comfort. Even so ought a man to nourish, comfort, and help his wife, be she never so deformed or out of fashion, whether it be by nature or by casualty, in body or in mind. We have Christ for our example. When the church ran a whoring, and committed loathsome idolatry, he did not forsake it: neither yet doth our gracious Lord forsake his beloved spouse, wonderfully spotted with sin; but covereth and forgetteth faults, and useth all means possible to reform and make us fit for him. The like should appear in the husband to his wife; seeing Paul setteth forth Christ to be a pattern to follow. This is that which St Peter meaneth, when he exhorteth men to dwell with their wives "according to knowledge." He would have husbands to rule according to wisdom, and not to play the tyrants; not to be sour, cruel, rash and rageful; but to govern them according to the order of God's word, in all sobriety, gravity, gentleness, love and discretion; providing for them by honest means, as for themselves. For, if "he that provideth not for his family be worse than an infidel," there is none so bad as he that is careless for his wife. No infidel neglecteth his own body. And as St Paul in the place above mentioned, so St Peter in this which was last alleged, sheweth reasons why the husband should give this honour to the wife.

8. "Give honour unto her, *velut infirmiori*, as to the weaker." This may seem rather to be a cause to contemn, than to honour. For such is the use. The rich despise the poor, the learned the ignorant, the strong the weak. But this use is wicked. Hath not God "chosen the weak of this world to overcome the strong, the foolish to confound the wise?" Are not the ignorant as well as the learned God's? Have the rich one foot more of possessions in heaven than have the poor? Despise not therefore the weaker creatures, lest thou dishonour the Creator of them. But seeing that man and wife are members of one body, they especially ought to bear one with another's infirmities, to cover, to dissemble, and to forgive each of them other's weakness. Yea, the viler the members of our bodies seem to be, the more careful we are to cover and to honour them: for so St Paul speaketh. In like manner, the more weak the woman is, the more diligent should her husband be to give her this honour, to cover her infirmity, and not to broach it abroad. For, in dishonouring her, he dishonesteth his own body. We easily forgive children when they offend, by reason of their age. The want of discretion is for them excuse sufficient. So a man ought to consider the infirmity of his wife, and to bear with her for it.—The second cause of honouring her is for that God doth give her honour. God maketh her partaker with thee of his spiritual graces, and fellow-heir of everlasting life. Dishonour thou not therefore her on earth, whom God hath honoured with a place in heaven. —The third cause why the wife should be well-esteemed of is for unity's sake. For contempt doth breed contention, and contention is an hinderance to devotion. Honour your wives therefore, *ne preces vestræ interrumpantur:* " that your prayers through strife be not interrupted and broken off." Thus much for the duty of the husband.

Reasons why the wife should be honoured of her husband.
[1 Cor. i. 27.]
[1 Cor. xii. 23.]

9. Touching the duties of honour which the wife doth owe to the husband, we find in the beginning of the book

Duties of honour required in the wife.

of Genesis, that because of her transgression (for Eve seduced Adam, not Adam Eve) God gave her a law of subjection to her husband, that she might ever after be better directed by him, than he had been at that time by her. *Sub viri potestate eris, et ipse dominabitur tui*[1]. St Paul also, in his epistle to the Ephesians and Colossians, putteth wives in remembrance of this subjection: "Wives, be subject to your own husbands, as to the Lord: because the man is the head of the wife, as Christ is the head of the church. And therefore, as the church is in subjection to Christ, so ought wives to be in subjection to their husbands." What should we seek more reasons? this one is sufficient. God hath set the husband over the wife in authority; and therefore she ought willingly and dutifully to obey him: else she disobeyeth that God, who created woman for man's sake, and hath appointed man to be woman's governor. Peter also setteth forth this obedience, and bringeth Sarah for an example: "Wives, be obedient to your husbands," "even as Sarah obeyed Abraham, calling him Sir: whose daughters ye are made in well doing." Yea, we are taught that wives should be of so good behaviour and of such modest conversation, that by their chaste and mild life, and the sweetness of their godly manners, they might win their evil husbands unto God, and of atheists make Christians. St Paul, in his epistle to Titus, also teacheth a wife her duty; that is, that she "go apparelled as becometh holiness; that she be no quarreller, or false accuser; but study to be sober, to love her husband, to love her children, to be discreet, chaste, abiding at home, good and obedient to her husband." "Obey in all things," saith St Paul, "even as it becometh you in the Lord." So that, except it be against God's word, the wife ought in all things to obey her husband. It is the wife's duty, as Theophylact well teacheth, to regard those things that be within the house[2], not lavishingly

[1 Thou shalt be under the power of thy husband, and he shall rule over thee.—ED.]

[2 Κρεῖττον γὰρ οἰκοδεσποτεῖν, τουτέστι, τοῦ οἰκείου οἴκου φροντίζειν καὶ ἐργάζεσθαι, ἢ ἀλλοτρίους οἴκους περιερχομένας φλυαρεῖν καὶ ἀργεῖν.—Theophyl. Op. Venet. 1755. Comment. in I Epist. ad Tim. Cap. v. Tom. II. p. 579.—ED.]

to waste or spoil their goods, but to spare with discretion, by such frugality as is convenient, to see things safe, and set in good order. God hath appointed her to be an helper, not an hinderer. If she cannot get, yet let her save. As he is to follow his affairs abroad, so she is to ease him of care and cost at home. Let her be mild-worded, and mild-mannered. For, *Melius est habitare in angulo domus, quam cum muliere litigiosa:* "It is better to dwell in the corner of an house, than with a contentious woman." An honest and a modest woman is an honour to her husband; but the dissolute wife and undiscreet is a death. She may not be a gadder abroad, a tattler, or a busy-body, but sober, quiet, and demure; not an open teacher, but ready to learn of her husband at home; obedient in all lawful things; taking example of Sarah, and giving example to the younger women of well demeaning themselves. Thus the man and wife joining themselves together in true love, endeavouring to live in the fear of God, and dutifully behaving themselves the one towards the other, either of them bearing wisely the other's infirmities, doubtless they shall reap joy and comfort by their marriage: they shall find this their estate, which "is honourable in all," happy and profitable unto them. [Prov. xxi. [19.]]

10. Now that we see the honour which is due unto marriage in respect of the author, causes, and duties thereunto belonging, it remaineth that we consider by what means that honour is in each of these defaced. The honour of wedlock in respect of the author is diminished, partly by the false persuasions of such as do not think it ordained of God; and partly through their lewd and corrupt affections, who, not denying this ordinance to be from him, enter notwithstanding carelessly into it, without such reverend consideration as is requisite in things which he hath established. Satan, the sworn enemy of all godliness, hath ever by all means laboured to undermine, deface, and overthrow the credit of this kind of life, using the ministry of many wicked and forsaken heretics, by whom it hath been not only misliked as troublesome, but utterly condemned as unclean and beastly. The Manichees condemned marriage, as a thing whereof Satan was the first author: they denied utterly that God created male and female: they affirmed

1. Marriage dishonoured by heretics, that hold it not to be of God.

as many as like the use of matrimony to be imps of Satan, not servants of God. Others, allowing marriage so it were but once, if happily it were iterated, disallowed it: with which error some of the ancient fathers themselves, as it seemeth, were overtaken. "It is," saith one, "a law of matrimony, not to iterate matrimony[1]." A law: but whose law? Sure we are that in the book of the law of God there is no such law. Again, there were that approved wedlock, yea, though it were iterated; but if priests did marry, they held them no better than unclean persons. Finally, there are that say, marriage is, if not honourable, yet tolerable, and that in priests; but so, if they enter into priesthood being once married, not into marriage being once priested[2]. Against these, howsoever in their sole and single life they pretend great purity and perfection, as it were of angels (although their glory most commonly hath been their shame, and the virginity of most of them hath been whoredom and adultery), it sufficeth us that St Paul doth term their lessons "the doctrine of devils;" and that the godly patriarchs and prophets whom I named before, living in the state of marriage, were familiar with God, and most dear in his undefiled sight. Insomuch that by St Augustine[3], speaking of this matter, Abraham is compared with John Baptist for his holiness, and by Chrysostom[4], Moses with Elias.

[1 Tim. iv. 1—3.]

[1 A collection of passages similar to that in the text may be found in SS. Patr. Apost. Coteler. Amst. 1724. Not. in Herm. Past. Mandat. IV. Lib. II. and in Const. Lib. III. cap. 2. Tom. I. pp. 90, 1. 278, 9.— ED.]

[2 Compendious accounts of these various notions may be found in Bingham's Orig. Eccles. See particularly XXII. i. 5; XVI. xi. 7; XXII. i. 10; IV. v. 5.—ED.]

[3 Non est impar meritum continentiæ in Johanne qui nullas expertus est nuptias, et in Abraham qui filios generavit.—August. Op. Par. 1685. De Bono Conjug. 26. Tom. VI. col. 335.—ED.]

[4 Βούλει μαθεῖν, ὅτι οὐδὲν παραβλάπτει ἔχειν γυναῖκα καὶ τέκνα; Μωϋσῆς οὐχὶ γυναῖκα καὶ τέκνα εἶχεν; Ἠλίας οὐχὶ παρθένος ἦν; ...μή τι παρέβλαψε τοῦτον ἡ παρθενία; μήτι παρενεπόδισε τοῦτον ἡ γυνὴ καὶ τὰ τέκνα;—Chrysost. Op. Par. 1718. Cont. Jud. Gent. et Hæret. Hom. Tom. I. p. 821.—The Benedictine editors consider this homily spurious, and call it "inepti hominis Chrysostomo adscriptum opus."—ED.]

11. This state, therefore, whatsoever heretics have taught to the contrary, being, in consideration of the first ordainer thereof, honourable, we ought in no wise unadvisedly, lightly, or wantonly, to take in hand a matter of such weight and of so grave importance, lest we dishonour it by our disordered affections, as heretics by false persuasions have done. In entering therefore into marriage, the first caution is that which St Paul hath to the Corinthians, whom he teacheth how their widows should bestow themselves. For although the rule be in particularity applied to them, yet it serveth not for them alone, but for all, the condition of all being herein like to theirs. Whether it be a widow therefore that bestoweth herself, or a virgin which is bestowed in marriage, the thing she doth is lawful, "only in the Lord." Marriage dishonoured by them that seek it; and not in him whom they acknowledge to be author of it. 1 Cor. vii. [39.]

12. They do not this in the Lord, that marry either whom they should not, or as they should not. Whom they should not, as persons either naturally or spiritually unfit to join in marriage. Of persons unfit to be yoked in wedlock by reason of the natural bonds wherewith they are already coupled, the law hath plainly said, "None shall come near to any of the kindred of his flesh." The unruly desires of men, which presume to go further in these cases than the shamefacedness of natural honesty doth permit, must be restrained and repressed. For this cause John the Baptist told Herod, "It is not lawful that thou shouldst have thy brother's wife." For this cause St Paul dealt so sharply and severely in the cause of that lewd Corinthian, with whose foul and unnatural fault the whole church of Corinth was much disgraced. Marriage between parties too nearly linked by nature. Lev. xviii. [6.] Mark vi. [18.] 1 Cor. v. [1.]

13. In marriage, therefore, there ought to be a reverend regard of nature, that this state be not dishonoured by unseemly copulation, as in like sort it is by the ungodly joining of the faithful with unbelievers. Of this thing holy Abraham, in providing a wife for his son, had as we see an especial care. For the eldest, and therefore by likelihood the discreetest, servant of his house, yea, and the trustiest, as it seemeth (for he had rule over all which Abraham did possess), was not permitted to deal in this matter without taking a corporal oath beforehand. "I will make thee swear," saith Abraham, "by the Lord Marriage without care of religion. Gen. xxiv. [3.]

God of heaven and God of the earth, that thou shalt not take a wife unto my son of the daughters of the Canaanites, amongst whom I dwell." Abraham would not link his son with the wicked. He remembered what had come of such marriages in the age before him, when "the sons of God took them wives of the daughters of men" only for their beauty, without regard of religion or honesty. Their destruction was a lesson unto him: he avoided their sin by fearing their punishment. God gave his people express charge concerning this, that they should beware in joining marriage with Amorites and Canaanites, the indwellers of that profane country; not only forbidding this kind of marriage, but also shewing the reason why his people should forbear it, lest idolatrous wives should make their husbands also to become idolaters: "Lest they make thy sons go a whoring after their gods." Whereof we have a notable example in Solomon; whose pitiful fall, being so wise a prince, to so horrible impiety, ought to be admonition sufficient unto us, to submit our wisdom to the wisdom of the Almighty, and our desires to his commandment. But had Solomon never been, or had his fall been unrecorded, our own times may teach us what fruits have come of such ungodly conjunctions. Man's nature is corrupt and frail: he runneth headlong into wickedness, but to righteousness must be drawn by God; and sooner can the evil pervert the good, than the good persuade the evil. This kind of marriage therefore seemed so wicked unto Esdras, that he caused the Israelites, after their return out of captivity, to put away their strange, not women only, but wives which they had taken to themselves in Babylon. And shall Christians do well in receiving such into marriage, as Jews being married unto did well to put from them?

Gen. vi. [2.]

Exod. xxxiv. [16.]

1 Kings xi. [1—8.]

Ezra x. [10, 11.]

14. But the common sort of men, in making their matches this way, have chiefly two outward untoward respects, regarding nothing in their choice except it be either beauty or money. The sons of God of old, bewitched with the beauty of the daughters of men, procured the general flood to overflow them all, and to wash the defiled world. Sampson took one of the daughters of the Philistines to wife, because she pleased his eye:

The cause of irreligious marriage is the over-great respecting of beauty or wealth.

Judg. xiv. [1—3; xvi. 4.]

but what came of it? It cost him a polling, wherein stood his strength; and it lost him both his eyes, which before were ravished in the beauty of that deceitful woman. Others there are yet of a baser note, whose only care is to match themselves wealthily. Their question is with what money, not with what honesty, the parties whom they seek are endowed; whether they be rich, not whether they be godly; what lands they have on earth, not what possessions are laid up in heaven for them. Such as marry for money, as the money wasteth, so their love weareth; neither is there any love or friendship constant, save only that which is grounded on constant causes, as virtue and godliness, whereof only neither time nor man can spoil us. There was a rich man in Athens which had a daughter to marry, and he asked counsel of Themistocles how to bestow her, shewing him that there was a very honest man that would gladly have her, but he was poor; and there was a rich man which had also desired her, but he was not honest. Themistocles answered that, if he were to choose, he would prefer moneyless men before masterless money. It is true that St Paul saith, "Godliness is great gain." Whether it be man or woman that is godly, they be rich; and, as Solomon saith, "He that findeth a good wife, findeth a good and precious thing:" the value of gold is not to be matched with her. In marriage therefore it behoveth us to be careful, that they whom we choose be of the household of God, professing one true religion with us; the disparagement wherein is the cause of all dissention, true friendship being a loving consent, as in all things, so chiefly in God's true service. [1 Tim. vi. 6.] [Prov. xviii. 22.]

15. But this is not enough. For although the parties married be such as the law of the Lord alloweth to come together, yet can it not be said that they marry in the Lord, except they also marry in such sort as the law prescribeth. For marriage may be as much dishonoured by the one, as by the other. For orderly entering into the state of matrimony, it is required that they, which be under the tuition and government of others, have the full consent of their parents, tutors, or such as have rule over them, to direct and guide them. Abraham provided a wife for his son Isaac: Isaac sent Jacob into Mesopotamia to *Marriage without consent of parents, or such as are instead of parents.* [Gen. xxiv. 2—4; xxviii. 1, 2.]

his uncle Laban, and there commanded him to take a wife, and he did so. In the law of Moses children are commanded to honour their parents. And what honour is given unto parents, if in this chief case, being the weightiest one of them that can happen in all their life, their advice, wisdom, authority, and commandment, be contemned? The law saith, "If a man find a maid that is not betrothed, and take her and know her, then the man that knew her shall give unto the father of the virgin fifty shekels of silver, and she shall be his wife." What? Although the parents be against it? No. For, "If her father refuse to give her to him, he shall pay the money and not marry her." Again the law saith, "Whosoever voweth a vow unto the Lord, or sweareth an oath to bind himself by a bond, he shall not break his promise, but shall do according to all that proceedeth out of his mouth." Nevertheless, "if a woman vow a vow unto the Lord, and bind herself by a bond, being in her father's house, in the time of her youth, and her father disallow her the same day that he heareth all her vows and bonds wherewith she hath bound herself, they shall not be of value, and the Lord will forgive her, because her father disallowed her." If promises made to God without consent of parents are of no effect, can promises made to men be effectual, where the parents' consent is not had? "Children," saith the apostle, "obey your parents in all things." In all things? and not in this the greatest of all? When St Augustine was required to help to make a marriage in the behalf of a young man, and the other party was named, he answered: "I like that match well: *Sed mater adolescentulæ non adest, cujus voluntatem, ut nosti, requirere debemus*[1]: but the mother of the young damsel is not present, whose good will (as you know well enough) we must ask." And, as the parents' or tutors' consent is to be had in all good and lawful marriages, so it is against the duty of good parents, either to keep their children longer un-

[1] Fortassis enim quæ nunc non apparet, apparebit et mater, cujus voluntatem in tradenda filia omnibus, ut arbitror, natura præponit: nisi eadem puella in ea jam ætate fuerit, ut jure licentiore sibi eligat ipsa quod velit.—August. Op. Par. 1679. Epist. ccliv. Tom. II. col. 881.—ED.]

married than is convenient, or through an over-great desire of enriching them (which is the common disease) to marry them against their liking. Such marriages seldom or never prove well, but are for the most part the cause of great sin and much misery. There can be no lawful and commendable match, where there wanteth full consent and agreement of the parties whom it most concerneth. Rebecca was asked, whether she would go with Abraham's servant and be married unto Isaac, or no. Her parents did neither keep her back from marriage when she was fit for it, nor conclude it till her own mind were known. Such then as marry not in the fear of God, making a religious and a godly choice, having the full consent of their parents or tutors; doubtless God is no author of their marriage: it is not he that coupleth and joineth them together: their estate is base, and not honourable, in his sight. Gen. xxiv. [58.]

16. Touching the causes for which God appointed marriage, we have heard that the first is mutual help and comfort. For the man is a "cover" of defence unto his wife, and the woman a "pillar" of rest unto her husband. As a body without a head, so is a woman that hath no husband. And, "As where no hedge is, there the possession is spoiled; so he that hath no wife wandereth to and fro mourning." This is the judgment of the wise. But the mouths of fools are always open to aggravate the incumbrances, troubles, and sorrows, which the married are wont to sustain in the flesh; never remembering the helps and comforts, which notwithstanding men religiously yoked in the Lord must needs acknowledge far to exceed all those grievances, both in number and measure. If any find it otherwise, sith the fault is not in marriage, which was instituted for our help, but in the married, who make it a hindrance to themselves by their own folly, let the men be blamed, let the thing be honoured. *Dishonour done to marriage in respect of the first of those causes for which God appointed it.* *Ecclus. xxxvi. [25.]*

17. But as in this case it fareth, so doth it also in the next. A virtuous son is his mother's glory: they that see him count the womb that bare him blessed. Yea, "though his father die, yet is he as if he were not dead, because he leaveth one behind him, like him. In his life he saw him, and had joy in him, and was not sorry in *The second.* *Luke xi. [27.]* *Ecclus. xxx. [4, 5.]*

his death, neither was he ashamed before his enemies." Thus, when our children do well and prosper, marriage is honoured. But are they dissolute and disobedient? Do they trouble us, as Simeon and Levi did their father? Do they make us abhorred amongst the inhabitants of the land? By and bye we grudge, and think unreverently in our hearts, Behold, this is the fruit of marriage. So that which giveth honour to the birth of man, receiveth dishonour by his lewd behaviour.

Gen. xxxiv. [30.]

The third.

18. To come to the last. The physician must be honoured, because God created him for necessity. In like sort marriage, which God hath given as a remedy, and not only as a mean unto propagation. If therefore we need it, and do not use it, how do we honour it? St Paul was so careful in this respect, that even where he giveth the highest commendation to single life, there he addeth, "This I speak for your commodity, not to tangle you in a snare, but that ye follow the thing which is honest." And again, "He that hath decreed in his heart to keep his virgin, doeth well, yet so, if he stand firm in his heart that he hath no need, but hath power over his own will." Otherwise, were it not better to use an honourable remedy, than to nourish and increase an incurable sore? Let us take heed how we feed the flesh in her unlawful desires. For it cannot be in vain that God should speak so directly, and as it were so particularly, unto every one that lewdly defileth and profaneth the temple of the Holy Spirit: *Perdet te Deus;* "Thee God shall destroy." This the enemy knoweth, and therefore he laboureth so diligently by all means to keep this sore ever festering within itself. For which cause it is strange to consider, how he hath dulled the hearts of many by settling a strong persuasion in them, that, although they fry in the heat of their vile affections, yet their outward continency of body is of itself meritorious before God, their single life of itself acceptable and holy. What a puddle of uncleanness, what a sink of filth, what ugly abominations have grown in the world under this pretence, to the great displeasure of Almighty God, the dishonour of marriage, the slander and shame of christian profession, the enlarging of the kingdom of sin and darkness, the

1 Cor. vii. [35, 37.]

[1 Cor. iii. 17.]

sending of souls innumerable down to hell, time will not suffer me to discourse.

19. 'I will therefore add somewhat concerning the disgrace which cometh unto marriage, in regard of the duties thereunto belonging, and so end. The company and fellowship of married folks, if discreetly, lovingly and religiously they perform those needful duties each unto other which God requireth at the hands of both, then no doubt their estate is blessed of the Lord, and deserveth to be honoured amongst men. But if there want discretion in them, we see what contentions, strifes, and heart-burnings are wont to grow between couples, to the great disquieting of their own minds inwardly, and if things do chance to break out, as such flames commonly do, to the discrediting also of their persons openly in the world. How unsweet and unpleasant such a life is, the wise man sheweth by comparing a troublesome and contentious wife to "a continual dropping;" as contrariwise, "if there be in her tongue gentleness, meekness, and wholesome talk, then is not her husband like other men." [Prov. xix. 13.] [Ecclus. xxxvi. 23.]

Marriage, in respect of the duties thereunto belonging, dishonoured for want of discretion in married folks.

20. Let hearty love and affection be lacking between them; and what enemy can devise so great a torment against them as they exercise continually upon themselves? Do they not find that daily whereof Job complaineth, as of a thing which touched him nearer to the quick than any other cross, though he suffered both many and heavy crosses besides? "My breath," saith he, "was strange unto my wife, though I prayed her for the children's sake of mine own body." [Job xix. 17.]

Want of hearty affection.

21. Take away religion; let their hearts be void of the fear of God; and what sin is there so heinous, what iniquity so huge, whereunto they are not always in danger one to be persuaded by the other? When Satan despaireth of all other means, he useth this as the surest to speed in accomplishing wicked purposes. He found no such instrument as Jezebel to make Achab wallow in blood, as idolatrous women to bewitch Solomon, as the daughters of Moab to steal away the hearts of the children of Israel. It is godliness and religion, conscience and fear of sin, that keepeth them within the limits of their duty. Without this, they are not only careless of that comely

Want of religion and the fear of God.

shamefacedness and sober temperance which beseemeth the honesty of their estate; but, exceeding the bounds of all modesty, they overflow and break out even into extreme lasciviousness with others. Hereby the honourable ordinance of God is loathed and condemned of loose wantons, as a thing which bringeth infinite miseries with it, a thing wherein there is nothing but grief, no quietness of heart, no repose of mind. Thus I have shewed you the author of marriage, God himself; the causes of marriage, mutual comfort and help, procreation, and avoiding of uncleanness; the duties that each party linked in marriage doth owe unto other; the honour which marriage hath by every of these; and in these the ground from whence discredit and dishonour groweth unto marriage. God grant that, whether we be called to this honourable estate of marriage, or have received the gift to live otherwise, we may keep both our souls and bodies unstained, and in all things walk as becometh saints that have betrothed themselves unto Christ Jesus. To whom with the Father and the Holy Ghost, &c.

THE SEVENTEENTH SERMON.

A SERMON

PREACHED AT PAUL'S CROSS, AT HIS FIRST COMING TO THE BISHOPRICK OF LONDON.

JOHN VI.

1. *After these things, Jesus went his way over the sea of Galilee of Tiberias.*
2. *And a great multitude followed him, because they saw his miracles which he did on them that were diseased, &c.*

OUR Lord and Saviour Jesus Christ, the Arch-pastor and great Shepherd of our souls, casting his eyes toward the city of Jerusalem, bewailed the lamentable estate thereof, and that with tears. The like effect, although proceeding from a cause unlike, I find in myself, beholding this Jerusalem of ours, this famous city: the greatness whereof doth add not a little to that exceeding grief of mind which the deep consideration of so weighty a thing must needs work. This office requireth a perfect man to teach, govern, and guide this learned and wise people: this great and large diocese doth wish for one furnished as Samuel, or rather as Solomon, with all graces and gifts of learning, policy, wisdom, and knowledge of things belonging both to God and men. This cumbrous charge hath made many a good and godly man to withdraw himself, to shrink back, utterly to refuse the like place and calling. For although it be a faithful saying, "If a man desire a bishop's office, he desireth a good work;" yet such are the difficulties, so many are the perils whereunto they are subject which labour in it, that the richest in all spiritual graces, the most plentifully endued with rare and excellent gifts of God, might have good cause to fear lest (the frailty of flesh and blood being so great) a burthen so heavy should make them faint.

2. It is no easy matter to till the Lord's ground,

The weightiness of a bishoply charge, especially over a great and a wise people.

1 Tim. iii. [1.]

The hardness of per-

<small>forming the office of a bishop, in respect of the pains in teaching.</small>

to weed his field, to bring in his harvest, to trim his vineyard, to feed his flock, to build his house, to watch over his city, to preach his word, to distribute his sacraments, to execute his discipline, to govern his church, to perform so many parts as are required in him by whom this great and high charge is undertaken. Where should one find a servant of that fidelity and wisdom which the cure of souls doth ask? a servant that knoweth how to minister seasonably unto every soul; to feed infants, novices, little ones, with rudiments of Christianity as with milk, them of better growth with stronger meat; to confirm men established in the truth, and reclaim them that slide from it; to wound and bruise the hearts of the obstinate, who bend themselves wilfully against God; and to comfort such as have heavy hearts, troubled consciences, by reason of sin?

<small>Living.</small>

3. Neither is the pastor pressed only with these burthens which are peculiar and proper to himself, but even those which are common to others with him are also heavier unto him than others. To lead a godly and a righteous life belongeth not to the pastor alone, but unto all. Yet in this which is common unto all, there is more laid upon him than any. Others must be sober, he a mirror of sobriety; they virtuous and honest, he such a pattern of virtue and honesty, that he may say with St <small>[Phil. iii.17.]</small> Paul, "Be ye followers of us, walk as ye have us for an example." St Chrysostom compareth the pastor unto one that wrestleth naked[1]. If there be any deformity at all in the body of a naked man, it is soon espied and faulted. We are naked to the eyes of the whole world: no one in the world which hath not more eyes than one; no eye which is not quick and sharp sighted to espy a blemish; no blemish, be it never so great in others, half so soon found, or half so much pointed at, as the least and lightest thing awry in us; at whose hands notwithstanding it is required to walk unreprovable.

[1 Οὐ γάρ ἐστιν, οὐκ ἔστι δυνατὸν, τὰ τῶν ἱερέων κρύπτεσθαι ἐλαττώματα· ἀλλὰ καὶ τὰ μικρὰ ταχέως κατάδηλα γίνεται. καὶ γὰρ ἀθλητὴς, ἕως μὲν ἂν οἴκοι μένῃ, καὶ μηδενὶ συμπλέκηται, δύναται λανθάνειν, κἂν ἀσθενέστατος ὢν τύχῃ· ὅταν δὲ ἀποδύσηται πρὸς τοὺς ἀγῶνας, ῥᾳδίως ἐλέγχεται.—Chrysost. Op. Par. 1718. De Sacerdot. Lib. III. 14. Tom. I. p. 390.—Ed.]

AFTER THESE THINGS JESUS WENT, &c.   333

4. Now if unto these so many and so weighty con-siderations, to this endless care and thought, which a good shepherd taketh day and night in attending both to himself that he may walk without blame, and to his flock that it may conveniently be governed, we adjoin those continual labours of studying, meditating, reading, and writing, whereunto the depth of the mysteries of God do necessarily enforce him that must lay them open before others (which if he do not, a wo inevitable hangeth over him; if he do, the travail of doing it is such that the apostle himself crieth out, "Who is sufficient for these things?"); all this being duly and throughly weighed, we may well conclude that he, which desireth the room of a bishop in the church, desireth as a good, so also a hard, and undoubtedly a very troublesome office. *Studying.* [2 Cor. ii. 16.]

5. Secondly, it is an office full of peril and danger. For if we preach things pleasant unto men, we discharge not the duty of the servants of God: if we preach his truth, we are hated as their deadly enemies to whom we preach. For not speaking against sin, the Lord threateneth death: "If thou dost not speak to admonish the wicked of his wicked way, his blood will I require at thine hand;" and for speaking against sin, Elias was persecuted, Zacharias stoned, Esaias cut in pieces, Jeremias cast into a dungeon, John Baptist, Stephen, Paul, James, Peter, Justin, Athanasius, Cyprian, Polycarp, of our own bishops and teachers not a few, in other nations huge multitudes, both heretofore and of late, in most cruel and savage manner tormented, with all extremity that might be devised to increase the bitterness of their death. *The peril both of discharging and not discharging their duty.* [Ezek. iii. 18.]

6. Many ancient prophets and worthy fathers of the primitive church, casting these accounts in their minds, have shunned and laboured by what means they could to avoid this office. Doubtless man's flesh is frail; we are all weak and full of infirmity. If this office require a strong man to bear the burthen of so great a travail, certainly it is altogether unfitly cast upon me. I would have wished rather rest for this my wearish body, full of diseases and, as the prophet speaketh, almost worn away like a clout. If this office, in respect of the hardness thereof, of the great dangers incident into it, and in con- *In these considerations good men have rather wished to avoid, than laboured to get the office of a bishop.*

sideration of man's unableness to perform it, have made so many so loth to enter upon a charge of such difficulty and danger before God and the world, what may I then think of myself? From the bottom of my heart I confess with St Paul, *Minimus sum:* "I am the least of the apostles, not worthy to be called an apostle." Wherefore, as Moses was contented to take upon him the charge and keeping of a few sheep in Madian, but, being called to guide the great and mighty people of Israel, answered, *Mitte quem missurus es:* "Send whom thou wilt send;" so, although considering the great want of labourers in the church of Christ, I were contented to undertake the care and charge of a small flock; yet, being called to this great, this wise and rich people, remembering my unfitness thereunto, I saw no answer more convenient for me than that of Moses before mentioned. But God hath his secret and unsearchable working; and I am as clay in the potter's hand. *Si passeres non cadunt in terram absque providentia divina, fortuito fient episcopi*[1]*?* "If sparrows fall not on the ground without the providence of the Almighty, are bishops made at all adventure?" saith St Cyprian. Here I see God hath placed me by the hand of his chief minister, with the advice of her wise and honourable counsellors, and the choice of them to whom it appertaineth; not without your great contentation and liking, as I am given to understand. I have therefore submitted myself, and taken upon me this heavy yoke (as the Searcher of all secrets will bear me record) *unwillingly* and *willingly*. In respect of my many imperfections, my unfitness to execute this great and weighty office in such sort as it ought to be performed, I receive it unwillingly; but in regard of the calling which I am persuaded proceedeth from the determination of Almighty God, I willingly submit myself hereunto. It is you, it is you, dearly beloved, that have drawn me hither. Her ma-

[marginal notes: [1 Cor. xv. 9.] [Exod. iv. 13.] Cyprian.]

[[1] Cum Dominus in evangelio suo dicat: Nonne duo passeres asse veneunt, et neuter eorum cadit in terram sine Patris voluntate? Cum ille nec minina fieri sine voluntate Dei dicat; existimat aliquis summa et magna, aut non sciente, aut non permittente Deo, in ecclesia Dei fieri; et sacerdotes, id est, dispensatores ejus, non de ejus sententia ordinari?—Cypr. Op. Oxon. 1682. Epist. lix. p. 129.—ED.]

jesty could spy nothing in me worthy of this room, but your too much and on my part altogether undeserved liking. The Lord be merciful unto me, and grant me his grace, that in some measure I may answer your expectation!

7. And now to the matter which I have chosen to speak of at this present. Wherein it shall not be a thing unnecessary for your better understanding, somewhat to consider of the circumstances and occasions whereupon the words which I have read do depend. Christ having cured a poor sick man which had been eight and thirty years diseased, whom he found lying by the pond of Bethsaida[1], desirous of remedy, but lacking one to help him into the water where it was to be had, the blind Jews, because this was done upon the sabbath day, found themselves much grieved, and thereupon persecuted Jesus; who, after an apology made in defence of that holy action, perceiving their malice to be increased thereby rather than abated, left them, and went beyond the sea of Galilee. Howbeit, the multitude left not him; but because they had seen the signs and wonders which he wrought, miraculously recovering the sick, and restoring them to perfect health, therefore they flocked after him in great troops. "When Jesus therefore had lifted up his eyes, and saw that a very great multitude came unto him, he saith to Philip, Whence shall we buy bread that these may eat?" *The occasions whereupon Christ forsook Jerusalem, and went beyond the sea of Galilee. John v.*

8. The first reason therefore, why Christ forsook Jerusalem, and went beyond the sea of Galilee, was to the end he might convey himself from the tyranny and persecution of the wicked. So we read in the gospel according to St Matthew, that hearing how his fore-runner was beheaded, he went aside, took boat, and retired into a solitary place apart. Whereby we are given to understand, that if our lives be particularly sought, we may lawfully flee from the cruel and bloody hands of our persecutors. Christ, foretelling his disciples of the grievous and heavy entertainment which they should find at the hands of the world, giveth them this lesson: "Beware of men;" and withal this licence: "When they shall persecute you in this city, fly into another." Herein I need not much to persuade: frail and fearful flesh is ever ready to fly peril. But what scripture those men can allege for *To avoid the hands of the wicked. Matt. xiv. [13.] Matt. x. [17, 23.]*

[¹ Bethsaida—Bethesda.—Ed.]

themselves that fly not for the gospel, but from the gospel, that fly before they be persecuted, or their blood sought, as yet I cannot learn. Belike they fear lest they should be repaid with their own measure. No: our gospel is a doctrine of mercy, and not of malice: they which sincerely profess it are full of clemency, and altogether ruled by piety: our church consisteth of mild sheep, and not of cruel wolves: the popish church is the wolvish and bloody church. We seek reformation, and not destruction; knowing that christian hearts are to be persuaded by the scriptures, and not by fire and faggot to be enforced. Yet do I not mean by this speech, but that the obstinate, the resisters and disturbers of religion, the false prophets and deceivers of the people, may be lawfully cut off: the sword may lawfully be drawn against such as are manifest traitors unto the truth and to the state. But this is not the matter whereof they stand in fear. It is not outward danger, but inward terror, for which they fly. *Fugit impius nemine persequente:* "The wicked man flieth when no man pursueth him": he trembleth where nothing is to be feared: the wagging of a leaf doth make him shake, because his heart is evil.

Prov. xxviii. [1.]

To take some rest.

9. Another cause why Christ went aside into the wilderness may seem to have been a desire of taking some rest after the great and manifold travails that he and his disciples had sustained, as appeareth by the words which he spake to his disciples: "Come apart into the wilderness and rest a while." This lesson is gladly learned, and too much practised. *Requiescite*[1] pleaseth every man. The truth is, that the body and mind of man must after labour be refreshed with rest. But he which laboureth not is altogether as unworthy to rest as to eat. Again, such as will take rest and ease after labours, must learn of Christ as well to measure their ease as their pains. He permitteth his disciples to take their rest; but he limiteth and restraineth his permission, saying, "Rest a while." For by too much rest men are not made the more fit, but the less willing to take pain. There is no one fault from which the wise man doth so much endeavour to withdraw men, as from sloth. For this cause he putteth us so often in mind of the great blessings which God doth heap upon

Mark vi. [31.]

[1 Rest ye.—ED.]

the painful man. "The hand of the diligent shall bear [Prov. xii. 24.] rule." "He that tilleth his land shall be satisfied with bread, [Prov. xxviii. 19.] &c." Again, endeavouring to set out the lively pattern of a perfect woman, such a one as can hardly be found amongst a thousand, he noteth this as a chief and principal virtue in her: "She laboureth cheerfully: her candle goeth [Prov. xxxi. 18, 27.] not out: she overseeth the ways of her household, and eateth not the bread of idleness." As for the slothful, he did not only hate them himself, but laboured by all means to make them odious; sometime by setting their forlorn estate before men's eyes: "I passed by the field of the slothful, and by [Prov. xxiv. 30—34.] the vineyard of the man destitute of understanding; and lo, it was all grown over with thorns, and nettles had covered the face thereof, and the stone wall thereof was broken down;" sometimes by shewing their excuses and shifts to avoid labour: "The slothful man saith, A lion is without, [Prov. xxvi. 13—15.] I shall be slain in the streets;" sometimes by describing their lazy gestures: "As the door turneth upon his hinges, so doth the slothful man upon his bed: he hideth his hand in his bosom, and it grieveth him to put it to his own mouth;" sometimes by deriding their unwillingness to take their leave of their rest: "Yet a little sleep, a little slumber, a little folding of the hands." And what is the end? "Poverty cometh as one that travelleth by the way, and necessity like an armed man." Wherefore, though weariness, though labour and travail do cause thee to desire necessary rest, yet beware that the sweetness of rest do not cause thee to think that labour is unnecessary. Rest, but rest *a little.*

10. The last cause that I gather of Christ's going into [To avoid the feast of Easter.] the wilderness was, as it may be conjectured, to avoid the feast of Easter at Jerusalem. For so the evangelist speaketh: "Easter, a festival day of the Jews, was now at hand." It seemeth strange that Christ, the example of all good order and behaviour, should fly from this solemn feast of Easter, which he himself by his prophet Moses had straitly commanded to be observed and kept. You must therefore consider, that the Jews neglected the commandment of God, and instead thereof set up their own traditions, as St Paul recordeth, so that the temple was now become a den of thieves. Christ therefore avoided too much fellowship with this wicked generation. "For what society hath [2 Cor. vi. 14—16.]

righteousness with unrighteousness? what communion hath light with darkness? what concord hath Christ with Belial? what part hath the believer with the infidel? what agreement hath the temple of God with idols?" In this we ought all to follow Christ; all to fly, as he did, from the place where the service of God is openly profaned, and his name intolerably blasphemed. "Depart, depart, go out from thence." Choose rather to suffer want in the wilderness with Christ, than to enjoy the pleasures of the world with an evil conscience; to be partakers of the word of life in a desert, than to reign where the adversary of Christ and Christianity beareth sway. God be praised for ever! in our churches of England, to our great comfort, God is served even in such sort as himself by his holy word hath prescribed; so that no miscontented person can allege any reason sufficient why to withdraw himself from our assemblies. Our church prayers are the psalms, our lessons the scriptures, our sacraments according to Christ's institution. Which thing, not many years sithence, I alleging unto one of no small account now in Lovain, his answer was, " I must confess, that is good which you have in your churches; but the truth is, you have not enough." Indeed we have less in their eye than enough. But if we weigh things according unto that rule, "Whatsoever I command you, take heed you do it: thou shalt put nothing thereto, nor take ought therefrom;" then can it not be denied but that our *little* is sufficient, and their *more* is too much.

Isai. lii. [11.]

Deut. xii. [32.]

Occasions which moved the multitude to follow Christ. Novelties.

11. As these considerations drove Christ into the wilderness, so the evangelist setteth forth some motives which caused so great a multitude to follow him. Some were drawn with the strangeness of those things which he wrought and taught amongst them. To whom in these our days we may compare them which haunt sermons for no other end, but either vainly to hearken for news, or curiously to note what order and eloquence they may find in the preacher, or maliciously to take hold of things spoken, when they may by froward construction be drawn to an offensive meaning. These labour to their own loss: they are unprofitable followers.

Hunger.

12. Others followed Christ for bread. Such followers our times have brought out too many. So long as the

gospel can feed, cherish and maintain them, they are willing and glad to be professors of it; but when persecution cometh, they shrink. A great sort of halting and dissembling ministers do now occupy rooms in the church, which in heart hate the gospel, yet for bread sake they are contented to go in the same rank with the followers of Christ Jesus. But he knoweth their secret cogitations, and will one day make them known unto others what they are.

13. Sundry there were which followed for a desire which they had of bodily health. For Christ "went about healing every malady, and every infirmity in the people." We see by daily experience, that the body is more cared for than the soul, the flesh than the spirit, the carcase than the mind. If the body be diseased, we seek physic; and are willing to pay well for it: to preserve the body from grief and sickness, who is not careful? But where is he that studieth how to avoid the diseases of the soul, that mortifieth the noisome desires of the flesh, that keepeth his heart in awe and subjection, that dieteth himself according to the rules which that blessed physician hath prescribed? Chrysostom findeth great fault with parents in this behalf, who, if their children fall sick in body, weep and lament; but if they be never so grievously vexed and tormented with sin, they make light or no account of it[1]. These men love the bodies of their children, as it seemeth, better than their souls. So this frail carcase, this body of clay, is much made of. To procure things good and comfortable for it, we can be content to travel sea and land, to be at any cost, to endure any pains. If health may be had, though it be in a wilderness, it will be sought.

Health.
Matt. iv. [23.]

14. The last and best sort of followers were such as followed Christ to hear his word. This is that travail that chiefly is required of a Christian: "Seek first the kingdom of God." This declareth us to be his children, to be his flock. "He that is of God heareth God's word." "My

The word of life.
[Matt. vi. 33.]
John viii. [47.]
John x. [27.]

[1 Πῶς γὰρ οὐκ ἄτοπον; ὅταν μὲν ὑπὸ δαίμονος ἐνοχλῆταί σου ὁ υἱός, πρὸς πάντας τοὺς ἁγίους τρέχεις, καὶ τοῖς ἐν ταῖς κρυφαῖς τῶν ὀρέων ἐνοχλεῖς, ὥστε αὐτὸν τῆς μανίας ἀπαλλάξαι ἐκείνης· ἁμαρτίας δέ, ἢ παντὸς δαίμονός ἐστι χαλεπωτέρα, συνεχῶς ἐνοχλούσης, οὐδὲν πλέον ποιεῖς.—Chrysost. Op. Par. 1735. Eclog. de Liberor. Educat. Hom. xxvii. Tom. xii. p. 633.—Ed.]

sheep hear my voice." Thus you see the causes why Christ was followed of the multitude.

Christ with his disciples quiet in the mount when the multitude came unto him.

15. Christ was quietly set with his disciples in the mount when this people approached. The hill, as St Chrysostom[1] noteth, may represent the kingdom of God; the inheritors whereof are always delighted to climb upward, to seek those things that be above, to take pleasure in nothing but that which is from heaven. Christ and his disciples, being on the top of the mount, were quiet. And the church of Christ, even in the wilderness, in the midst of affliction, doth in him find rest. "In the world," saith our Saviour, "you shall have distress; but have confidence, I have overcome the world: these things have I spoken unto you, that in me you may have peace." Upon this assurance Peter, being in prison and in chains, slept quietly; the prophet David, in the midst of persecution, took sweet and pleasant rest: "I lay me down," saith he, "and sleep in peace; for thou, Lord, only makest me dwell in safety."

[John xvi. [33.]

[Psal. iv. 8.]

The miracle which Christ wrought, and the circumstances which are to be considered in the people, in his disciples, and in himself. The people were the vulgar sort.

16. Now followeth the miracle which our Saviour wrought by occasion of the multitude which was there assembled together with him and his disciples. In this there are many things contained, very worthy of your good and godly considerations; which for order's sake we may reduce to the persons of the people, of the disciples, and of Christ. Concerning the people the words of the evangelist St John are these, *Sequebatur eum turba multa:* "a great troop followed him." But St Mark, more lively expressing the great zeal and desire they had to the gospel of Christ, saith, "They ran flocking thither on foot out of all cities." In whom we have first to observe, that they were not of the princes, nor of the priests, which came unto him, but *turba*, the common and vulgar sort. *Num quis ex principibus?* "Doth any of the rulers or of the Pharisees believe in him?" "Not many noble, not many wise," saith the apostle. The noble and mighty loved liberty of life, and feared mutations. The wise were circumspect, and saw that the gospel would mar their works. Only the

Mark vi. [33.]

John vii. [48.]

1 Cor. i. [26.]

[[1] Παιδεύων ἡμᾶς ἀεὶ διαναπαύεσθαι ἀπὸ τῶν θορύβων καὶ τῆς ἐν μέσῳ ταραχῆς.—Chrysost. Op. Par. 1728. In Joannem Hom. xliii. Tom. VIII. p. 248.—This is Chrysostom's comment on the passage, but it does not seem to convey exactly the idea here attributed to it.—ED.]

people, they which were basely accounted of in the world, they which knew not the law, came unto Christ.

17. The second thing to be observed in them is their cheerfulness, their alacrity, their zeal and courage. They came not dragging their legs after them; they "ran" unto Christ. Neither care of things at home, nor fear of danger abroad, neither the length of the way thither, nor the lack of lodging and food there, neither the fear of the priests, the scribes and Pharisees, the known and professed enemies of Christ, nor any other by-respect in the world was able to stay them. Shall not this people rise up in judgment, think you, against us, whom God hath by so many blessings allured, and as it were enticed to come unto him; and notwithstanding findeth us so far from this cheerful and gladsome following of him, that, when he doth follow and seek after us, we turn our backs and fly from him? Could we do thus, if indeed we did believe that he hath "the words of eternal life," and that as many as "continue with him to the end, they shall be saved?" *They came cheerfully.* *John vi.[68.] Matt. x.[22.]*

18. The third thing especially to be noted in this people is, that their willingness to come was not greater than their readiness to obey him unto whom they came. For when they were willed to "sit down upon the grass," although they were so many and had so little in sight before them, (for what were five loaves and two fishes to relieve almost five thousand men?) nevertheless, they made no answer, they gainsayed not, but without contradiction did that which they were commanded. Elisha prophesied in the name of the Lord, and promised plenty to the people of Samaria, being grievously afflicted with extreme famine. But a prince in great favour and authority with the king replied against the man of God, "Though the Lord would make windows in the heaven, could this thing come to pass?" The same prophet sent one to Naman the Syrian with this message: "Go and wash thee in Jordan seven times; and thy flesh shall come unto thee again, and thou shalt be cleansed." But Naman replied, "Are not Abanah and Pharphar, rivers of Damascus, better than all the waters of Israel? may I not wash me in them and be cleansed?" This is the manner of the wise ones in the world: when they should obey God, they reason and dispute the matter with him, as if he knew not what he *They did obediently as they were commanded.* *[2 Kings vii. 2.] 2 Kings v. [10, 12.]*

did. But the faith of this people did subdue their wit and reason to the sacred word and will of God.

The disciples cause the people to sit down.

19. This may suffice concerning the people. Of the disciples of our Saviour it is said, that "they made the people to sit down." Hence ministers, pastors, and teachers may learn, that, sith God hath ordained them as the means whereby the elect must be brought to the obedience of Christ Jesus, they cannot approve their fidelity unto him, except they be careful to fulfil the work for which he hath appointed them. "I say unto you, that many shall come from the east and west, and shall sit down with Abraham, Isaac, and Jacob, in the kingdom of heaven." In this sense that we might also "sit down," Christ hath established those high and holy functions before mentioned. Wherefore St Paul professeth, that for this cause he received grace and apostleship, that obedience might be yielded to the faith amongst all nations. For this he laboured, as in other places, so in Corinth also, both delivering them the doctrine which he had received, and executing amongst them the discipline which their grievous abuses did deserve.

Matt. viii. [11.]

[Rom. i. 5.]

They divided the bread which Christ appointed to the people.

20. The second thing to be noted in the disciples is, that they neither purloined nor changed the people's food. They received bread, and they delivered bread. But there are deceitful workmen, which have entered by a postern gate into the church, which preach and deliver not what they have received at the hands of Christ, but what antichrist hath delivered them. For sweet bread they give sour leaven; for wheat, darnel; for wholesome meat, venomous poison; for the word of God, the doctrines of man; for truth, fables and vain fancies: for the holy communion, popish private blasphemous masses; for the serving of God, the worshipping of images; for fish and loaves, stones and serpents.

They gathered that which was left.

21. The next thing to be noted in the disciples is, that when the people had eaten sufficient, they gathered up the broken meat which remained. By which frugality of theirs we are admonished to use the creatures of God in such sort, as they may be most beneficial unto many; after we have taken for our own contentment, then to reserve for the use of others, that nothing be wasted which may profitably be saved. God loveth a bountiful, but not a wasteful hand. For although it be true which the prophet saith, that God "hath given the earth to the sons

[Psal. cxv. 16.]

of men;" although it be granted that we may rule over the fish of the sea, and over the fowl of heaven, and over every beast that moveth upon the earth, using them not only for our necessity, but also for our honest delight and convenient pleasure; yet we must remember, that this power is rather a stewardship than a lordship over the creatures of God in earth. We stand accountable for them: we may not lavish them out as we list.

22. That which hitherto we have observed in these disciples is both allowed of God, and written that it might be followed of us. Another thing there is which we may not let pass, although it be a blemish and a stain in them. For when Christ spake unto them of feeding the multitude, one answered, "Two hundred pennyworth of bread is not sufficient for them, that every man may take a morsel." Another said, "Here is a boy that hath five loaves and two fishes: but what are they among so many?" The like we read of the servant of Elisha in the second of Kings. There came a man from Baal-shalisha, which brought the prophet twenty barley loaves and certain corn. The prophet willed it to be given to the people, that they might eat. "But his servant answered, How should I set this before a hundred men? Well, give it, saith the prophet, that they may eat: for thus saith the Lord, They shall eat, and there shall remain. Then he set it before them; and they did eat, and left over." This mistrust of the power and wonderful providence of Almighty God is the very root of all evil. It caused the rich man, spoken of in the gospel, to hoard up corn for many years: it caused Ananias to withdraw a portion of the price of his farm: it caused Vespasian to lay an unsavoury imposition upon the people to pay money (be it spoken with good manner) for their very urine: it caused Judas to betray his master: it caused the Israelites, when their city was besieged, to make their bellies their coffers, to eat their gold.

They doubted how the people could be fed, when they saw not wherewithal.

2 Kings iv. [42—44.]

Luke xii. [19.]

23. But let us now come from the people and disciples to the person of Christ himself; in whom the first thing which we have to observe is his diligence in his office. He preached in the cities, in the temple, in the villages, in the ships, on the shores, in the wilderness: he neither spared any labour, nor omitted any occasion to do good.

Christ diligent in his office.

24. The next thing is his pitiful affection towards the people, upon whom when he looked, his heart was touched with compassion; first, because they were as sheep without a pastor. The high priests, the learned scribes, the holy Pharisees, were their appointed pastors, to govern them, to teach them, and to lead them by example of honest life. Nevertheless Christ saith, they were *sine pastore*: "without a shepherd." The glorious, covetous, deceitful, ceremonial, and superstitious rabble of popish guides, God doth not account amongst the guides of his people: neither are they to be called pastors, but devourers of the flock. Pastors which cannot or will not teach are no pastors. "Because thou hast refused knowledge," saith God by his prophet Ose[1], "I will also refuse thee, that thou shalt be no priest to me." Undoubtedly their hearts are not touched with any pity or compassion at all over God's people, who, for their own private gain and commodity, thrust such pastors upon the church, that when the church hath them, it may justly be said it hath no pastors. This is the plague, the poison, the bane of all religion: it threateneth ruin to Christianity.

Pitiful towards them which had no pastor to feed their souls.

Hos. iv. [6.]

25. The other cause that moved Christ to compassion was, that the people which had tarried long with him were hungry, and in the wilderness could get no meat. By this we learn of our master Christ to bear pitiful hearts towards our needy, naked, and hungry brethren. "For whosoever hath this world's good, and seeth his brother have need, and shutteth up his compassion towards him, how dwelleth the love of God in such a man?" In former times here hath been provision for the poor, and some as yet remaineth; but it is for the most part much abused. I shall therefore exhort you, the citizens of London, and in Christ Jesus require it at your hands, that such order may be taken, that the poor may be provided for, and not suffered to cry in your streets. If you that be magistrates will take the thing in hand, you shall find, I doubt not, a great sort of liberal hearts and helping hands hereunto. The suffering of the people to beg breedeth great inconvenience both in the church and commonwealth. I do therefore in Christ again require you to take due consideration hereof, that this thing may be reformed. So shall you well please

Towards them which wanted food to refresh their bodies.

1 John iii. [17.]

[1 Ose—Hosea.—ED.]

God, ease and profit yourselves, and give a good example to the rest of the realm. God cannot be unmindful of so good a work. It will be an hundred times requited both in this life, and in the world to come.

26. The last thing which I purpose to note in the person of our Saviour is, that he did not only conceive an inward pity and therewith content himself; but his compassion brake out and declared itself in works of mercy. He sent them not away, as the manner is, loaden with words and empty of alms: he fed them largely, and gave them till every man had enough. But first he gave thanks to his heavenly Father; leaving us an example thankfully to acknowledge that, whatsoever we receive, it cometh from him as from the principal author, and whatsoever we bestow, he is the Lord and owner of it. In dividing the bread he used the ministry of his disciples, as the stewards and disposers of his riches. Be it therefore corporal or spiritual sustenance which we receive, although it be at the hands of men, yet is it unto us as if Christ himself in his own person did reach out his hand from heaven to feed us. They are therefore too nice, which refuse their meat because they like not the man by whom it is brought and set before them. They, by whose means we are made partakers of good things, are unto us the angels of God, and ought accordingly to be honoured, of what quality soever they be in themselves. The food which they gave to the people did miraculously grow by diminishing, and by consuming increase. So it was with the meal and oil of that poor widow of Sarephta. It was in sight too little to suffice one: in use it proved more than sufficient for many. So it is with all the graces and gifts of God: they grow in the hands of him that spendeth; and in the coffers of him that saveth they waste. Thus I have briefly gone over such things as I thought most convenient for this time. The Lord bless the seed of his word sown amongst us, and give it a plentiful and a large increase, to his own glory and our comfort, through the merit of Jesus Christ, by the gracious operation of the Holy Ghost: To whom, &c.

He gave thanks, divided bread; and it increased in dividing.

1 Kings xvii. [16.]

THE EIGHTEENTH SERMON.

A SERMON

PREACHED AT PAUL'S CROSS.

Luke XXI.

25. *Then there shall be signs in the sun, and in the moon, and in the stars, &c.*

<small>The excellency of the Jewish nation.</small>

<small>Isai. v. [4.]</small>

<small>Rom. ix. [4, 5.]</small>

<small>Jer. vii. [4.]</small>

God bethinking himself, and as it were musing upon the benefits and blessings which he had, in great abundance of mercy, bestowed from time to time upon the people of Israel, breaketh out by his prophet into these words: "What might I do for my vine, which I have not done?" The graces wherewith he enriched them were infinite: their prerogatives above all other people of the world were manifold, and for the preciousness and rareness of them most wonderful: to them "the adoption, the glory, the covenant, the law, the service of God, the promises were impropriated: of them were the fathers, and of them, as concerning the flesh, Christ came, who is God over all blessed for ever:" they had the ark, the temple, and the oracles, with a promise that God would be their God, and they should be his, even God's own elected and beloved people (if they walked in his ways, and wrought his will) for ever. But this ungracious and unthankful nation was unworthy of such worthiness: they worshipped God with lips, and not with heart; outwardly in shew, but not inwardly in hearty and sincere truth; according to the letter, but not according to the spirit; after their own conceits, but not agreeably to his blessed will revealed in his holy word. Their cry was still, "The temple of the Lord, the temple of the Lord;" but, through their profanation, they made the temple of the Lord a den of thieves. They cried "Lord, Lord," but they did not his will on whom they cried: for sweet grapes, they yielded sour; for hearty and sincere service, hypocritical and painted shews of religion: their glory was in the external beauty of their material temple: they wondered at the stones and goodly buildings, at the gorgeous furniture and precious gifts, wherewith it was both outwardly and inwardly adorned and enriched.

2. Whereupon our Saviour, to take away the cause of this vain hope and foolish joy, took occasion thus to prophesy of that glorious temple: "Are these the things that you look upon? The days will come, wherein there shall not be left a stone upon a stone, which shall not be destroyed." This prophecy was as evidently accomplished as it was made. For thirty-eight years after that they had crucified Christ, their promised Messias, the Lord of glory, God raised up the servants of his wrath Vespasian and Titus, emperors of Rome, who besieged, conquered and rased their Jerusalem, made havock of the people as of dogs, murdered eleven hundred thousand, man, woman and child, of that cursed nation. Then was fulfilled the cry of those crucifiers: "His blood be upon our heads, and upon our children." It hath been, and shall be for ever. Yea, the violence of the Romans proceeded farther, and pulled down the temple, and laid flat with the ground their only glory; insomuch that, according to the express words of our Saviour's prophecy, they left not one stone upon another. The Jews sundry times, having licence thereunto, attempted to build it up again, but it would not be; for what their hand builded in the day, the hand of the Lord most miraculously hurled down by night[1]. Most true it is, that Christ saith, there is not one word that cometh out of God's mouth, not one tittle or jot written in his word, which shall not in his due and appointed time be accomplished.

A prophecy concerning the overthrow of their temple; and the performance thereof. [Luke xxi. 6.]

[Matt. xxvii. 25.]

3. Hence we may take this instruction, that God is not delighted in outward shews, in gorgeous pomps, in beautiful buildings, in painted sepulchres: it is the inward beauty of the king's daughter, and not the outward bravery of the harlot of Babylon, wherewith God is pleased: it is

God delighteth not in the outward beauty of any thing.

[¹ Soc. Hist. Eccl. Amst. 1700, Lib. III. c. 20, pp. 158-9: Soz. Hist. Eccl. Amst. 1700, Lib. v. c. 22, pp. 513-14. To these may be added, besides a host of other authorities, that of Ammianus Marcellinus, Lib. XXIII. 1.—Ed.]

the contrite heart of the prostrate publican, and not the proud ostentation of the Pharisee, wherein he doth take delight. God alloweth as well of Peter in his mantle, as of Aaron in his mitre. All these external shews are but as the beauty of a painted wall, not only not acceptable, but even loathsome unto God, when the soul, the mind, the inward part is polluted.

<small>The cause of their ruin, they knew not the time of their visitation. Visitation in mercy moveth them not. Luke xix. [44.]</small>

4. The causes why this house, this costly building and temple of God, was so miserably destroyed, Christ himself declareth, saying, "Because thou hast not known the time of thy visitation." There is a double visitation; the one in mercy, the other in justice. Our merciful God first visited this people in great and often mercy: he delivered them out of the hands of Pharaoh: he gave them good guides: he delivered unto them his law written in tables of stone: he caused heaven to give them bread, and the hard rock to yield them drink: he made them triumph over their enemies, and possess strange cities: he brought them to a land that flowed with milk and honey, and caused them to reap that which their foes had sown: he gave them priests and prophets, and builded them both an ark by Moses, and a temple by the hands of Solomon, wherein he would be worshipped. All which notwithstanding, this stiff-necked people was obdurate and unthankful: no benefits could ever win them. They provoked their gracious Lord unto most fierce and most just wrath. After their deliverance, they lusted to return to the place from whence they were delivered: they muttered against Moses, and despised holy Aaron. They loathed and misliked the very food of heaven, even the meat of angels: the written law of God they mightily transgressed: his messages they contemned: the prophets and messengers they derided, evil entreated, murdered: lastly, to add a crown to all their former wickedness, their promised Messias, their King, Christ Jesus the Son of the living God, they most spitefully, cruelly, and villainously crucified.

<small>Visitation in justice.</small>

5. This great unthankfulness of theirs did greatly provoke the just Lord to displeasure, and as it were enforce him to visit them in justice sharply, and with the rod of more than usual correction. Wherefore he plagued them with mortality in the wilderness: only two entered the

land of promise, of all the number that came out of Egypt: he gave them over into the hands of their enemies; and they that hated them were lords over them: he cast them into exile and miserable bondage: he burnt up their holy city: he destroyed their glorious temple: he left them to be devoured with pestilence, with hunger, and with the sword, the accustomed instruments of his wrath. Insomuch that even to this day the remnant of that elect and chosen people is scattered far and wide, and doth live in all contempt, hatred, and slavery; marked like Cain to be known as a murdering vagabond upon the earth, to be a bye-word, and an example of God's justice to all the world, throughout all succeeding ages.

6. Now all these things came unto them, not only for their punishment, but also "for examples unto others, and were written to admonish us, upon whom the ends of the world are come." They are patterns for us to look upon, that, seeing their sin and the punishment thereof, we may eschew the one, if we desire to escape the other. And they cry daily in our ears. Let not your faults be like their faults, lest your destruction also be like to their destruction; for God is the same, yesterday, and to-day, and for ever: he hateth sin no less now than before, no less in us than in them. *These things recorded for our benefit. [1 Cor. x. 11.]*

7. He hath visited us in mercy, as he visited them; yea, we have tasted perhaps more abundantly of his goodness than ever they did. And as the benefits we have received do at the least equal theirs, so their unthankfulness is much behind ours, if it be rightly and duly considered. God having so strangely, so far beyond all hope, so much beside our expectation, and more besides our desert, so many times and so many ways delivered us, not out of one Egypt, from under one Pharaoh, through the midst of one sea, but out of sundry places, of most grievous, irksome, and tedious captivity, from under the heavy yoke of sundry cruel tyrants, through the midst of sundry main seas of troubles and afflictions; yet have we for all this buried the memory of our deliverance in forgetfulness, yet do we for all this sin daily, and that with greediness; yea, and spiritually, as far as in us lieth, crucify Christ afresh, and shed his most precious blood again. We are weary *Our blessings as great as theirs, our unthankfulness greater.*

of the gospel: the food of life is rejected as a thing unsavoury: we have no liking to feed at the Lord's table: our desire is rather to frank up ourselves with that which we should abhor and loathe: every house and corner is full of idolatry and superstition, of sin and filthiness, full of murmuring against God, full of grudging and repining against the Lord's anointed. For of his prophets what should I say? was there ever any time, any age, any nation, country, or kingdom, when and where the Lord's messengers were worse entreated, more abused, despised, and slandered, than they are here at home, in the time of the gospel, in these our days? We are become in your sight, and used as if we were, the refuse and parings of the world. Every mouth is spitefully opened, every tooth is sharpened and whetted against us. Hard it is to find one fourth, that will love and reverence us as fathers, obey us as governors, honour us as God's embassadors, learn of us as of schoolmasters, hear and follow us as shepherds, give us worthy wages as workmen that take pains for your salvation. But our expectation is not deceived: Christ our Saviour hath told us long ago that the world should hate us; and our case is no worse herein than the blessed apostles' was: our reward is great in heaven. And it were well if this unkind affection did reach no further than unto us only. But it spreadeth wider, and regardeth as little the throne of David, as the chair of Moses, the sword as the book, the prince as the prophet, the civil as the ecclesiastical state. Some desire a change. Others not only desire it, but conspire for it too; and contrive treachery, greedily expecting their looked for time, the day of their felicity and of their great joy. But if God in his wrath grant such a time, which for his mercy sake I trust he will never do, it will be, even to them who now so earnestly desire it, a day of death and not of life, of lamentation and not of joy. What gained they who desired the change of Samuel for Saul, of Christ for Barabbas? They procured God's wrath, their own confusion, and perpetual slavery. So it fareth with miscontented minds. Their own desires plague them.

Therefore, without repentance, our punish-

8. Thus we cannot but see God's goodness and our unthankfulness, his gifts and our abusing of them, his pa-

tience and our continual frowardness. Our sins are come to the fulness with the Amorites: iniquity hath gotten the upper hand, and crusheth down all piety. Can our God, think you, wink at so manifest, or hold his hand at so grievous sin? If he spared not the branches of the true olive, not his first-born Israel, not his elect people, but often punished, and at length gave them quite over, for that they neglected his word, and despised the preachers of it; if he spared not his own only city, not the holy temple, wherein he would be worshipped, but, for that they were both polluted and profaned, destroyed both for ever; what can we, which are but as wild twigs, whose father was an Amorite and whose mother an Hittite, who have not hearkened to his word sent from heaven, who have defiled his sacred temple, and even crucified his Christ, look for any other but God's great plagues and dreadful vengeance to be poured upon us to our eternal misery? Doubtless we have deeply provoked him unto anger. The only way to pacify and appease his wrath, to mitigate his indignation, and to remove his plagues from us, which even now hang over us, is our earnest repentance; to turn unto our God with our whole heart, that he may turn to us; to lament and forsake our wickedness; to trust in mercy, and to crave pardon; to promise and perform amendment of this sinful life. Thus we must do, and that speedily; or else without doubt and without delay we perish. *[ment cannot be less than theirs.]* *[Ezek. xvi. 3.]*

9. The threatened destruction of the temple hath occasioned me thus much to say. Now, when Christ had uttered the sentence of ruin and desolation against that holy place, the disciples, as Matthew reporteth, came secretly unto him, and asked not only of the time when the temple should be destroyed, but also of the second coming of Christ, and of the end of the world. They enquired as men desirous to learn that whereof they were ignorant. And they asked of Christ, the wisdom of God, the appointed schoolmaster of whom we should seek for knowledge. They asked, as I said, three several things; of the destruction of Jerusalem, of the second coming of Christ, of the end of the world; which two latter are indeed but one. To whom Christ maketh answer, not assigning any certainty of the times when these things should be accomplished, but shew- *[The disciples question concerning both the particular destruction of the Jews and the general consummation of the whole world. Matt. xxiv.]*

ing signs that should go before as well the destruction of Jerusalem, as also his second coming. "It is not for you to know the times and seasons (saith he), which the Father hath put in his own power." No, not the Son of man, as man, knew them.

The time when the end of the world shall be is for two causes concealed from men, to whom notwithstanding the signs that go before it are revealed.

[Mark xiii. 33.]

10. This knowledge is kept from men for two causes, as St Augustine well noteth. The one, lest it should hinder and withdraw us from performing our necessary duties, lest it should terrify and amaze us, and make us careless to provide for ourselves and others. Another reason, why the time both of our own particular end and of the general consummation of all things is left uncertain, is that we might at all times make ready and prepare for it, seeing it might happen at any time, even at any instant. "Watch and pray, because ye know not what hour." God hath therefore kept the time itself secret; but hath revealed certain tokens and signs going before it, that, when we see the messengers and fore-runners of him which cometh swiftly to judge quick and dead, we may lift up our heads, knowing that our Redeemer and redemption is near at hand. Christ foresheweth (as I said) the signs that should happen as well before the ruin of Jerusalem, as also before his second coming in the end of the world. The evangelists have mixed and folded them one within another, so that which do serve for the one, and which for the other, it cannot precisely be discerned. St Chrysostom thinketh, that all the signs, simply and literally understood, have relation to the destruction of Jerusalem; but mystically or spiritually considered of, they may be applied to the end of the world[1]. Others, whom in this I do rather follow, refer the former signs, as false prophets, war, sedition, earthquakes, famine, pestilence, persecution, hatred of the disciples of Christ, and besieging, to the destruction of Jerusalem; and these latter signs in the sun, moon, and stars, &c. to the latter coming of Christ to judgment.

Five things to be noted in the coming of Christ to judgment.

11. In this coming of Christ to judge the quick and the dead, we may for our better instruction consider these things; first, that there shall be a judgment, and who

[¹ A full exposition of Chrysostom's views on this subject will be found in his three homilies on Matthew xxiv.—Chrysost. Op. Par. 1727. In Matt. Hom. lxxv, lxxvi, lxxvii. Tom. vii. pp. 722, &c.—Ed.]

shall be that judge; secondly, the time when this judgment shall be; thirdly, the signs which shall go before it; fourthly, the manner of it; lastly, how we ought to be in perpetual preparation and readiness thereunto.

12. "A day the Lord hath set, in the which he will judge the world in righteousness by that man whom he hath appointed; whereof he hath given an assurance to all men, in that he hath raised him from the dead." Here we see plainly that there is a day appointed for righteous judgment of the whole world; that there is a man appointed to give sentence in that day; that there is an assurance already given to all men of all things that are written concerning both the day, the judgment, and the judge. "With God" (saith the apostle, speaking to the faithful which suffered tribulation for the name of Christ), "with God it is a righteous thing to recompense tribulation to them that trouble you, and to them which are troubled rest." This righteous thing with God is not performed here as yet. For this world is as an hell unto the godly, and an heaven unto them which despise righteousness. Therefore it cannot be but that God hath appointed a day hereafter to judge the world with that justice which shall give unto every man according to that he hath done, be it good or evil, and which shall render vengeance unto them that know not God, but rest unto such as now are troubled for his sake. "Our Lord knoweth to deliver the godly from temptation, but to reserve the unjust unto the day of judgment to be tormented." Wherefore St Peter, threatening false prophets and lying masters, which bring in sects of perdition, and deny him that bought them, even the Lord, saith, that "their judgment long ago was not far off, and their perdition sleepeth not." The day of their eternal condemnation is appointed: the man that shall condemn them is already assigned and well known. "We must all appear before the judgment seat of Christ." "The Father hath given all judgment to the Son." "He is constituted judge of quick and dead."

There shall be a judgment. Acts xvii. [31.]

2 Thess. i. [6, 7.]

2 Pet. ii. [9.]

2 Pet. ii. [3.]

2 Cor. v. [10.]
John v. [22.] Acts x. [42.]

13. This Judge hath three properties. First, he is more privy to our thoughts, words, and deeds, than we ourselves are: he seeth in darkness as well as in light, at midnight as at noon day: no secret is hid from him;

The properties of him that shall judge. His knowledge.

neither can any man convey himself out of his eye-sight. He saw Adam when he ate of the fruit which was forbidden him: he looked upon Cain when he slew his only brother: he beheld Cham when he discovered his father's nakedness: he took a view of Sarah when she laughed behind the door; of the sons of Jacob when they sold their brother Joseph into Egypt. His eye was open upon David's filthy and bloody acts, upon Absolon's treason, upon Achitophel's wicked counsel. The oppression of Achab, the cruelty of Jezebel, the pride of Haman, the covetous heart of Balaam and of Geze[1], the pride and hypocrisy of the Pharisee, could not be kept from him. He seeth all sleights in merchandise, all shifts in usury, all malicious minds, all flattering tongues, all lying lips.

<small>Psal. xxxiii. [13—15.]</small> "He looketh down from heaven, and beholdeth all the children of men: from the habitation of his dwelling-place he beholdeth all them that dwell on the earth: he fashioneth their hearts every one, and understandeth all their works." He shall be both a judge and a witness, in that <small>Jude [15.]</small> day, "of all the wicked deeds which the ungodly have committed, and of all the cruel speakings which wicked sinners have uttered against him and his," who as now they cannot avoid his sight, so neither shall they then be <small>[Psal. l. 22.]</small> able any way to escape his hand. "O consider this, you <small>[Psal. xciv. 9.]</small> that forget God." "He that made the eye, shall not he see?" Can your deeds be concealed from him, that seeth all the children of men, and can call them every one by his name?

<small>His power.</small> 14. Another property of this heavenly Judge is the infinite greatness of his power. He doth what pleaseth <small>Phil. ii. [10.]</small> him: all things are subject unto his will: unto him "every knee boweth, of things in heaven, and things in earth, and things under the earth." He hath power to save and to kill, to lift into heaven, and to cast into hell: heaven is his seat, earth is his footstool. What he willeth is as sure as it were already done. We should fear therefore this mighty Judge, who hath such power to do his will, and who will do that only which is just.

<small>His justice.</small> 15. For his third property is his justice. He taketh no rewards: his sceptre is straight, his judgment right-

[1 Geze—Gehazi.—ED.]

eous, his eye simple: he will not be entreated of the wicked, neither shew them any mercy. In that day every one of them shall receive justice and just punishment. These are his properties; and he changeth them not. He seeth all: he hath all power: he is a righteous judge of all, and over all for ever. By this which hath been spoken, we see that we have to look for a day wherein the world shall be judged; and we see who it is that in that day shall judge the world.

16. Of this the Lord hath sufficiently assured us. For, when divers things are spoken of before they come to pass, the performance of the first is the assurance of the rest. He which promised to raise up Jesus from the dead, hath also promised to judge quick and dead by the same Jesus so raised. Sith the one is performed, how can we stand in doubt of the other? We may assure ourselves that there is a day of judgment to come; because the resurrection of the Judge is already accomplished, past, and gone. "So then every one of us shall give accounts of himself to God." There is no prince, no potentate, no prophet, no apostle, no man, no woman, neither rich nor poor, high nor low, that can escape this judgment. We must answer for our facts, even as every man hath wrought. We must answer for every idle word, for every corrupt and wicked thought. What can the unclean fornicator, the covetous usurer, the mighty oppressor, the proud contemner, the ambitious climber, the envious hypocrite, the bloody murderer, the false deceiver, the cruel prince, the unfeeding pastor, the unjust judge, the deceitful merchant, what may they answer in that day but plead guilty? and what can they look for, but *Ite maledicti*: "Go, ye cursed?" Once again I say, "O consider this, ye that forget God." *The certainty and assurance of these things.* Rom. xiv. [12.] Psal. l. [22.]

17. But when shall this judgment be? As this question is moved by two sorts of men, so there are in scripture two kinds of answers made unto it. There are mockers which walk after their own lusts; and these ask, "Where is the promise of his coming? Since the fathers died which were overwhelmed by the flood of Noah, all things continue as they were from their first creation." To whom St Peter maketh answer, that they err of set purpose. Otherwise they, that are so witty in reasoning against *The time of judgment.* 2 Pet. iii. [4, 5, 7.]

the truth of God's promises, might know this, that the power of the word which created the world, and kept it till the day appointed for the punishment of the wicked by water, doth also now "keep the heavens and the earth in store, and reserve them to fire against the day of judgment and of the destruction of ungodly men." Having stopped their mouths with this answer, he leaveth them without any further instruction, because they were but swine, and the doctrine of the judgment to come is precious. But the disciples of Christ with another mind making this demand, "Tell us when these things shall be, and what sign of thy coming, and of the end of the world," are abundantly instructed by their Lord and Master, which knoweth all things, and withholdeth nothing from his which is any way needful to be known. Touching the time, they are forbidden to inquire about it. "For as in the days before the flood they did eat and drink, marry, and give in marriage, and knew nothing till the flood came and took them all away; so shall also the coming of the Son of man be." "In the hour that ye think not, will the Son of man come; in a day and in an hour which no man knoweth, no not the angels of heaven, but the Father only." It is therefore both vain and dangerous which some have attempted, in setting this and that year, beyond which the world cannot endure. But such is the crookedness of our nature. In watching, which is commanded, how careless are we! and how curious in seeking out "the time and season," which to do we are so oft and so expressly forbidden!

[Matt. xxiv. 3.]

Matt. xxiv. [36, 38, 39.]

Acts i. [7.]

Signs going before the coming of Christ to judgment.

18. Touching the signs and tokens going before the coming of Christ to judgment, they are set down for our benefit and instruction; and therefore let us make some stay in the due consideration of them. "There shall be," saith the evangelist, "signs in the sun, and in the moon, and in the stars," &c. These signs shall appear before the coming of Christ; partly, that the world may be admonished of the fearful judgment that is at hand, and thereby provoked to repentance; partly, that the wicked may in this life be punished by the creatures of God, whom they have abused; partly, that it may appear, that the creatures which have served sinful man against their will

will now no longer serve the enemies of their Creator; and partly, to declare that the world is come to his just old age, and shall have an end. There shall be signs in the sun. What signs these shall be, it is elsewhere in the scriptures declared. "The heavens shall shake: the sun and moon shall be dark; and the stars shall withdraw their shining." Again: "The sun shall be turned into darkness, and the moon into blood, before the great and terrible day of the Lord come." The like we read in the book of Revelation. "I beheld, and lo, the sun was black as sackcloth of hair, and the moon was like blood, and the stars of heaven fell unto the earth, as a fig-tree casteth her green figs, when it is shaken of a mighty wind." Whereunto the words of St Matthew also do agree: "The sun shall be obscured, and the moon shall not yield her light: the stars shall fall from heaven, and the powers of heaven shall be shaken." The simple and literal understanding is, that there shall be wonderful and terrible eclipses in the sun and in the moon: which things, in this last age, in this last hour of the world, since the ascension of Christ, have sundry times and in most strange sort been seen. Or else, even as, when Christ was crucified, the sun lost his light, and darkness for a time was upon the face of the whole earth; so shall it be at his second coming to judge the children of darkness with eternal death. Others expound it that, when Christ shall come in his glory, the beams of his brightness shall so far surmount the shining of the sun, moon, or stars, that in comparison thereof they shall seem dark, and give no light[1]. Of this his brightness he gave a glimpse, when he was transfigured in the mount Tabor. To seek out many expositions of these words, it shall not need. This we may observe in the writings of the prophets, that with them it is usual, when they foreshew great plagues, to use these and the like speeches. So doth Esaias in his prophecy concerning the plagues of Babylon: "The stars of heaven and the planets thereof

Joel ii. [10, 31.]

Rev. vi. [12, 13.]

Matt. xxiv. [29.]

Beda.

Isai. xiii. [10.]

[1 Sidera in die judicii videbuntur obscurari, non deminutione suæ lucis accedente, sed superveniente veræ lucis claritate, quod vero dicit, "Et stellæ cœli erunt decidentes": hoc est, suo lumine carentes.—Ven. Bedæ Op. Col. Agrip. 1612. In Matt. Evang. Cap. xxiv. Lib. iv. Tom. v. col. 70.—Ed]

shall not give their light, the sun shall be darkened in his going forth, and the moon shall not cause her light to shine." Again: "The earth is utterly broken down, the earth is clean dissolved, the earth is moved exceedingly." "The moon shall be abashed, and the sun ashamed, when the Lord of hosts shall reign in mount Sion." The like we read in Ezekiel, threatening destruction and desolation to Egypt: "I will cover the heaven, and make the stars thereof dark: I will cover the sun with a cloud, and the moon shall not give her light: all the lights of heaven will I make dark for thee, and bring darkness upon thy land, saith the Lord." I might allege the like out of Joel, Jeremy, Amos, and Micheas; but the matter is clear enough, and needeth rather to be considered than proved.

<small>Isai. xxiv. [19, 23.]</small>

<small>Ezek. xxxii. [7, 8.]</small>

<small>An allegorical application of the foresaid signs.</small>

19. The words, being literally thus understood, may be morally applied, not without great fruit, unto the understanding and wise hearer, which can discern between interpretation of scripture and application thereof. In the one we give you the bare sense of the scripture: in the other we teach you the profitable use of it. For the use of scripture may be very well shewed, not only by such collections as do probably gather, or necessarily conclude one thing out of another; but also by those allegorical comparisons which shew how in one thing another is shadowed, and a spiritual thing resembled in a corporal. As for example, if here we refer the sun to Christ, that Sun of righteousness, the moon to the church, and the stars to the pastors and doctors of the church.

<small>The darkening of the sun by false doctrine. 2 Thess. ii. [3, 4.]</small>

20. The sun, in this sense, is most evidently in this our age darkened: Christ is obscured by that great enemy antichrist, "the man of sin," who hath set himself in Christ's peculiar place, and will be "exalted above all that is called God." To make any other mediator between God and man, saving only Christ Jesus which is not only man, but also God; to seek elsewhere remission of sins, justification, redemption, sanctification, or salvation, than only in this Jesus, and in him crucified, doth darken and make dim both him and his merits. And of this treason the Romish antichristian church, which they term catholic, is found guilty. For the children of this harlot labour by all means to obscure the Son of God, to rob him of

the glory of his deserts in our salvation. I would never have believed that any professing learning, or having had but a glimpse of the course of the word of God, could have been so gross in such sort to have eclipsed the brightness of Christ Jesus, by giving his glory unto earthly creatures, if of late I had not to my great grief and their great shame heard their own blasphemous confessions thereof. Surely the Romish strumpet hath rubbed her forehead: her children are become altogether shameless: whatsoever she determineth, they make it equivalent with the written word of God. There is no absurdity in popery (in which there are full many and full gross) which they do not defend to be right good and catholic. The pope's pardons, purgatory, masses, merits, prayers both for and to the dead, pilgrimages, images, relics, yea holy water, and holy bread—all these they will have, some one way, and some another, to be forcible remedies against sin and death. This is their religion and serving of God: thus they honour the Lamb that was slain for the sins of all the world. If this do not derogate from him, and stop the brightness of his glory, who is the only once offered propitiation for all our sins, by whose blood we are only purged, whose death only hath made us free from death; if this do not obscure the glorious beauty of Christ Jesus, if this do not deface the worthiness of his merits, what doth? or what can do? Hath the glorious Son of God sacrificed his precious life for our sakes upon the cross, that Thomas of Canterbury's[1] blood, poured out in an earthly quarrel, should make passage to heaven for us? Is there any man in whose heart the light of the glory of God hath shined, which seeth not how this fog doth darken this blessed Sun?

21. Again, this Sun is obscured when as we profess that in our words, which in our lives and deeds we do deny. After that king David had committed adultery, Nathan the prophet charged him therewith in these words: "Thou hast caused the enemies of the Lord to blaspheme." When men profess well and live ill, their life is not tolerated for their profession, but their profession is slandered by their conversation. When the Jews which professed the law did not practise it, the law which they professed heard

The darkening of the sun by corrupt life and conversation.

2 Sam. xii. [14.]

Rom. ii.[24.]

[1 Thomas à Becket.—ED.]

evil thereby. For a bad professor of a good thing is a stain to that thing which he doth profess. This is the special fault of our wicked days: these our times are cloudy, and full of this darkness: our light doth not shine to glorify God, but our darkness doth abound to the obscuring of his Christ. The merciless rich men, which wring and oppress by deceitful and injurious dealing, which neglect and despise their afflicted brethren, the needy members of Christ, "do not they blaspheme the worthy name wherewith both they and we are named?" It were a great deal better never to have professed than not to practise, never to have received than not to observe, never to have known than not to obey, the word of truth. Unto them which hear the word and keep it being heard, a blessing is promised; but unto them of whom it is written, *Dicunt et non faciunt:* "They say and do not," woes again and again are denounced. "This know," saith the apostle, "that in the last days shall come perilous times. For men shall be lovers of themselves, covetous, boasters, proud, cursed speakers, disobedient to parents, unthankful, unholy, without natural affection, truce-breakers, false accusers, intemperate, fierce, despisers of them which are good, traitors, heady, high-minded, lovers of pleasure more than lovers of God, having a shew of godliness, but having denied the power thereof." Let all the world judge whether these be not the clouds which have darkened the sun of our days.

[James ii.[7.]

[Matt. xxiii. 3.]

2 Tim. iii. [1—5.]

The moon turned into blood by cruelty of persecution.

22. Now as the sun resembleth Christ, so the moon his church. For as the moon hath her light from the sun, so the church hers from Christ. And as the sun, being unchangeable, is at all times exceeding bright and glorious; but the moon doth change, and sometimes is at the full, sometimes at the wane, her light to the eye of the world now increasing, and now diminishing, now filling the whole globe, and now in no part thereof appearing; so Christ, and his church. Christ's glory is always great, and always one. His church upon earth doth vary: now she flourisheth, and now is black: sometimes she overspreadeth the face of the whole earth, at other times she is brought to so narrow straits, that mortal eye is unable to espy her. When the church of Christ is persecuted as it was in the days of those cruel emperors which were

of old, and as it is at this day under antichrist and antichristian princes, this is as it were the changing and resolving of the moon into blood. Hereby it cometh to pass, that she which looketh as the morning, and is fair like the moon, changeth her outward shape and figure, and appeareth in the eyes of them that behold her like a garment dyed in blood. By this we see what the spouse of Christ is to look for in this world. Wilt thou be of the number of them that live godly? Prepare thyself to suffer. All that will live godly in Christ must do it: it is their portion. If he were persecuted, why should we be spared; if he despised, why we well reputed of? Let us not therefore be dismayed, though we see the church of God in heavy case. Let her foes debase and oppress her for a while; her king shall at length deliver her, and crown her with eternal glory. She was never, I think, in greater distress, the enemy never more cruelly bent, Christ in his members never more bloodily crucified, than even in these our days, as well by enemies, as by false and bastard brethren, who, pretending the aid and succour of the church, practise nothing but theft and robbery. She is both wounded by her adversaries, and spoiled even by her own children: the one have made her bloody, and the other beggarly. Howbeit, as the ark of Noe was tossed upon the waters, but could not be drowned, the Lord sustaining it with his mighty hand; so the church in the end shall have a glorious triumph over all the enemies of God: hell gates may strive, they cannot prevail: in suffering she shall conquer, and when by persecution she is made most black, then is she in truth most beautiful. "I am black, O daughters of Jerusalem," saith the spouse, "black but comely." Through ignominy she cometh unto glory, by tribulation to a kingdom, by the cross to joy, and by death to immortal and everlasting life. The death of the saints of God is precious: their sufferings are honourable in his sight, for whom they suffer: nay, they are profitable even unto them: it behoveth the moon to be turned into blood. Her restoration shall be much more glorious. [Cant. i. [5.]]

23. It followeth that the stars also shall fall from heaven. Unto stars we may very well compare teachers, *The falling of stars from heaven.*

pastors, and guides, the brightness of whose doctrine and conversation should give light to such as live in this world's misty darkness. [John v. 35.] John Baptist was called *Lucerna lucens et ardens:* "a candle which doth both shine and burn." They which are as stars unto others here [Dan. xii. 3.] "shall hereafter shine as the brightness of the firmament, and as the stars of heaven for evermore." But these dangerous days have made many of these stars to fall from the firmament of heavenly doctrine to the dregs and dreams of man's learning. And one star falleth not commonly alone: Lucifer drew a train of others after him. The star which falleth to the earth becometh earthly, loseth the light which it had, and, like a brand which is smothered, spendeth and wasteth itself to nothing. [Heb. vi. 4—6.] He that hath been once illuminated like a star, and received the heavenly gift, and been partaker of God's Holy Spirit, and hath tasted of the good word of God and of the powers of the world to come, if he fall at any time away, hardly or never doth he rise again. Dreadful examples hereof there are both ancient and late, as Judas, Julian, Arius, Franciscus Spira, Staphilus, Baldwin[1], and such like: whose fearful ends it were to be wished that they which follow their declining steps did well consider. For touching our own countrymen and brethren according to the flesh, the greatest withstanders of the truth at this day are such as have been either preachers, or earnest professors of that which now they hate so deadly, and by impugning so fiercely persecute. They are fallen from heaven to earth: Christ they have forsaken, and betaken themselves to the man of sin, Christ's adversary: they embrace darkness instead of light, error in place of sound doctrine, damnable heresy for the pure and saving truth. Had it not been better that these apostataes had never known this blessed way,

[[1] F. Spira was a lawyer of Padua, who died about 1548, in a state of great mental horror, in consequence of having been induced to recant the reformed faith. F. Staphylus was professor of Greek at Wittemberg. In 1553 he renounced protestantism, and afterwards published a book on the disagreement of doctrine among the protestants. F. Baudouin was professor of law at Bourges and other places. He is said to have four times professed the reformed religion, and as often to have returned to that of his ancestors. The other individuals mentioned in the text are sufficiently well known.—ED.]

than, knowing it, so traitorously and so damnably to shrink from it? But, to leave them to their desperate resolution: others there are that stand in doctrine, but fall in life and manners, whose conversation is not in heaven, but altogether upon the earth, being worldly-minded, not like stars of light, but like clouds of darkness, teaching others and not themselves, that say and do not: they are wholly bewitched with love of this present base world; themselves they seek, (and would to God they sought themselves aright!) but they seek not Christ, without whom themselves are lost. This is the great scandal of the world at this day: wo unto them by whom it cometh! Well, by that which hitherto hath been spoken, we see how Christ (the Sun of righteousness, the brightness of his Father) is obscured as well by false doctrine as by wicked conversation; how the moon (the church) is made black and bloody by cruel persecution; how the stars (the teachers and doctors of the church) are fallen, both by heresy from heavenly doctrine, and by dissolute behaviour from the shining brightness of a sanctified and celestial life. _{Rom. ii. [24.]}

24. The same words might give me occasion to touch sundry other kinds, both of persons and things: I might shew how the spiritual dignity of the pastor, who should be as the sun in the eyes of men, is darkened and obscured by contempt; how the civil authority of the magistrate, which ought to shew itself in exercising just and lawful power upon the works of darkness, and so to bear rule as it were in the night (being in this age in many places used as a sword to slay the innocent and well-meaning man, and as a shield to defend and strengthen sin), hath so clean lost that glorious light of justice, that it seemeth even changed into blood; thirdly, how the people, which are in number as the stars, be in nature and disposition so far removed from heaven, that the very naming of things above, as of things which do not concern them, is become even tedious and odious unto them. Again, I might shew you how faith (which, as the sun, giveth light to other virtues) is itself dimmed; how the ancient virtues, which have been in high and honourable callings, have left their place and are not found: they are fallen,

Other applications of the foresaid signs.

like stars from heaven. Charity, being unto other virtues as the moon in comparison of the rest of the stars, is also changed: her sweet and amiable nature is converted into more than savage barbarity: tender-hearted men are become bloody-minded: every man hunteth after his brother as after a prey: each degree is maliced and hated of other, the clergy of the laity, the shepherd of the sheep, the rich of the poor, yea, the man of the wife, the parents of the children, the master of the servants, all men of some, and some almost of all. The bond of peace, the link of love, that malicious enemy hath burst asunder. What shall I say? Surely all things do shew that the end of all things is at hand.

What these signs shall work in the hearts of men.

25. Now, what effects these signs before mentioned shall have in men's hearts, those words do plainly declare which follow: "There shall be upon earth trouble among the nations, with perplexity." "By the nations (saith St *Aug. ad Hes.* Augustine) he meaneth those that shall stand on the left hand, and not those that are of the seed of Abraham, and shall be blessed[1]." Those dogs, goats, hypocrites, and counterfeit Christians, which are without the fold of Christ, having their own conscience to accuse and bear witness against them, that they have despised the Son of God, even him who should have been their Saviour, Christ Jesus; that they have rejected his gospel, resisted the truth, weltered in all uncleanness and sin, like beasts; shall at that day fall headlong into deep desperation, knowing that at the hands of that just and severe judge they shall receive the due reward of their frowardness and iniquity. These terrible signs shall smite such fear into their hearts, and so wonderfully amaze them, that whatsoever they behold, they shall tremble at it; whatsoever they hear, it shall be in their ears as it were the roaring of the seas. Men's minds shall be troubled: their faith shall wither and waste away as an untimely plant:

[1] Quod ergo dictum est secundum Lucam, "Et in terris pressura gentium", gentes voluit intelligi, non pertinentes ad semen Abrahæ, in quo benedicentur omnes gentes, sed gentes quæ ad sinistram stabunt, quando congregabuntur ante Judicem vivorum et mortuorum omnes gentes.—August. Op. Par. 1679, Epist. cxcix. Ad Hesych. 40. Tom. II. col. 755.—ED.]

they shall utterly fall from God, and all hope of salvation. Yea, the very elect shall quake and tremble: they shall be for the time void of counsel, and as it were men at their wits' end. For if now their minds be troubled, to see the present confusion of things in the world; to see kingdoms and nations in armour one against another; to see so much monstrous cruelty shewed, so much innocent blood poured upon the ground; to see the wicked so prosper, and the godly so trodden under foot like dust; to see the matter of salvation, even the word of God, called into question, so earnestly and doubtfully to be disputed of even amongst the learned sort with most hateful and despiteful contention, whereof there is like to the eye of man to be no end—if this do so much astonish men's minds now, that it maketh them doubtful what to think, or what to do, in what great perplexity shall they be in that day, when false Christs and false prophets, not one nor two, but many, shall arise, so forcible in persuasion, that they might deceive, if it were possible, even the elect of God, and when the powers of heaven shall be moved! When these things are, doubtless men's hearts must needs fail them for extreme fear, and for looking after those things which shall come upon the world. Our merciful Lord comfort us that we do not faint, and strengthen us that we may stand in that day! After all those signs in the sun and the moon and the stars, in the powers of heaven, and in the hearts of men, betokening Christ's approach, "then," saith the evangelist, "they shall see the Son of man come."

26. The manner of his coming is thus described. "He shall come in a cloud with power and great glory." It was told the disciples, before whose faces Christ was received up into glory, "This Jesus, which is taken up from you into heaven, shall so come as ye have seen him go." He went in a cloud, and shall come in a cloud. His first coming into the world was contemptible, but his second coming shall be glorious; his first, to be judged of the world; his second, to judge the world. He shall be accompanied with the angels of heaven, partly to set forth his princely honour and royal majesty; for so it is written: "Let all his angels worship him;" and partly to be his

The manner of Christ's coming to judgment.

[Acts i. 11.]

Matt. xxv. [31.]

Psal. xcvii. [7.]

ministers in things appertaining to this judgment; for so we read: "He shall send his angels with a great sound of a trumpet; and they shall gather together his elect from the four winds, and from the one end of the heaven unto the other." St Paul joineth with these angels flaming fire. "He shall shew himself from heaven with his mighty angels in flaming fire, rendering vengeance unto them that do not know God, and which obey not the gospel of our Lord Jesus Christ; which shall be punished with everlasting perdition from the presence of the Lord, and from the glory of his power, when he shall come to be glorified in his saints, and to be made marvellous in all them that believe." This fire shall (whereof the apostle speaketh) dissolve and melt away the heavens and the earth. Which burning shall be as it were the fining of gold in the furnace, not consuming, but purging the substance of these creatures from the dross of those alterable qualities whereunto they are now subject. So Bede speaketh of them, *Per imaginem transeunt, per essentiam subsistunt: præterit figura hujus mundi, non substantia*[1]*:* "Their shape vadeth, their substance remaineth: the figure of this world doth pass away, but not the nature." "We look for new heavens and a new earth," saith St Peter: "These heavens shall pass away with a noise: these elements shall melt with heat: this earth, with the works that are therein, shall be burned up." Then shall God be glorified, and appear marvellous. Let the mighty remember this, which build their nests aloft; the rich, which join house to house, whose garners, cellars, and pastures are full of grain, wine, and cattle, whose chests are stuffed with money, who wholly apply the world as they should live ever upon the earth. All this gear will be consumed: it is but matter for the flame. Flee therefore, flee from this world, which will suddenly melt away: look not back toward this pleasant Sodoma, which the Lord will shortly set on fire. For what doth it profit a man to gain the world, which, though it

[1 Quæ ergo peribunt, veterascent, et mutabuntur: constat pro certo, quia consumpta per ignem, mox abeunte igne gratiorem resumet speciem. Præteriit enim figura hujus mundi, non substantia.—Ven. Bedæ Op. Col. Agrip. 1612. In II Epist. Pet. Cap. iii. Tom. v. col. 724. See also in Apoc. Cap. xx. Lib. iii. col. 807.—ED.]

be enjoyed for a while, yet at length must needs melt as wax, and to lose his soul, which, if it were not lost, might live in bliss for ever? Love not, seek not the things of this world: look unto that by which we may stand in the day when the Lord shall shew himself from heaven, when he shall come to be glorified in his saints, and to be made marvellous in them that believe. "The wicked shall not be able to stand in that judgment, neither sinners in righteous men's company." At the coming of this power, at the presence of this great God, at the sight of this tribunal seat, so full of glory and of terror, the deriders of Christ, the contemners of his word, the workers of iniquity, shall tremble and quake, and desire through despair that the mountains may fall on them, and cover them from his fearful presence. But the faithful, the elect, shall lift up their heads with joy, and be made partakers of exceeding glory: they shall sit upon the twelve seats, and judge the twelve tribes of Israel. Where the faith of the apostles shall condemn the unbelieving Jews; the piety of the centurion all ungodly magistrates; preaching Paul all unpreaching prelates; Zaccheus all usurers; and Lazarus all repining impatient and wicked beggars. The books shall be laid wide open in the sight of all flesh; the book of God, and the book of man's conscience; the book of his law, and the book of our life. It shall be examined in the one, what God hath commanded; in the other it shall be testified how man hath obeyed: in the one, what works of mercy he hath required at our hands; in the other, what fruits of merciless affection the ground of our stony hearts hath yielded. And according to the evidence both of the one and of the other, the eternal and irrevocable sentence shall pass from the mouth of God. The perjured, the usurer, the adulterer, the liar, the idolater, shall be cast into the lake which burneth with fire and brimstone; into that utter darkness, where shall be wailing, weeping, gnashing of teeth, endless horror, and everlasting wo. But the elect, which have lived a sober, a just, and a godly life, which have loved the coming of Christ Jesus more than this world or their present lives, they shall enter into the kingdom of their Lord; they shall be glorified with Christ, and possess with him that everlasting in-

[Psal. i. [5.]]
[Rev. xx. [12.]]
[Matt. xxv. [34—46.]]
[Rev. xxi. [8.]]

heritance, having heard that most joyful sentence: "Come, ye blessed of my Father, possess the kingdom prepared for you from the first foundations of the world."

<small>Matt. xxv. [34.]</small>

27. Hereupon St Peter inferreth this conclusion: "Seeing all these things must be dissolved, what manner persons ought ye to be in holy conversation and godliness, looking for, and hasting unto the coming of the day of God?" And St Luke this threefold exhortation: "Take heed to yourselves: watch: pray continually." "Take heed of surfeiting and drunkenness, lest your hearts be oppressed; lest that day come upon you at unawares," and unlooked for; lest it happen to you as it happened to the fathers in the days of Noah: they ate and drank, and suddenly the water overwhelmed them; or as to the Sodomites: they burned in lust, and suddenly fire consumed them from heaven; or as to the Israelites: they fed themselves greedily, surfeited, and died with the meat in their mouths. Let their dreadful ends make us eschew their sins. Beware also of the cares of this life. They be perilous thorns, and prick thy heart to death. Judas was careful by any means to gather money; and to what it brought him, ye all know. Ananias and Saphira, caring how to live, made no conscience to lie to the Holy Ghost: their destruction was most sudden. When the rich man was in the midst of his care how to enlarge his barns, that very night his soul was taken from him. Beware therefore, and take heed specially of these two things: let not your hearts be overwhelmed with excess of meats and drinks, nor choked with the cares of this present life.

<small>Our preparation unto this judgment, by heed-taking. 2 Pet. iii. [11, 12.]</small>

<small>[Luke xxi. 34, 36.]</small>

28. Besides this wariness and heed-taking, it is further required that we be also watchful. For sith we know not what time the Lord will come, expedient it is that we should be in continual expectation of him, that, whensoever he come, we may be ready with joy to meet him. Happy is he that watchfully looketh for the coming of Christ Jesus, and he miserable whom the Lord shall overtake unlooked for. St Jerome did so live in continual watching and waiting for this day of redemption, that the sound of that voice was still in his ears, Arise, ye dead, and come to judgment! "I do wait," saith Job, "all the days of my warfare, till my change come." The like we read of the

<small>By watching.</small>

<small>Jerome.</small>

<small>Job xiv.[14.]</small>

prophet David, whose watchfulness was such, that the watchman standing upon his ward, being weary of the discomfortableness of the night, doth not so eye the rising of the morning as he did the glorious appearing of the Lord. "I have waited," saith he, "upon the Lord, my soul hath waited, and I have trusted in his word. My soul waiteth on the Lord, more than the morning watch watcheth for the morning." How happy is their estate, whom the Lord in that day shall find thus ready for him! [Psal. cxxx. 5, 6.]

29. But because we can of ourselves neither rightly beware, nor diligently watch without the special assistance of his Spirit, therefore, as we are exhorted to watch, so are we likewise admonished to pray. The Lord of his infinite mercy grant, that, being thus prepared to meet the Lord in the day when he cometh to judge the quick and the dead, we may be found worthy to enter with him into that rest, which he by the shedding of his most precious blood hath purchased for all the blessed of his Father: To whom, &c. *By praying.*

THE NINETEENTH SERMON.

A SERMON

PREACHED AT PAUL'S CROSS.

Matt. VIII.

23. *And when he was entered into the ship, his disciples followed him.*
24. *And behold, there arose a great tempest in the sea, so that the ship was covered with waves: but he was asleep.*

<small>The state of the church militant figured by a ship tossed upon the waters.</small>

This short history doth by way of a type or figure set forth the state of the church, putting us in mind that the way to the kingdom of God is rough; that we must enter into joy through much sorrow; that here we must be always on the suffering side; that the whole life of a christian man upon earth is a warfare; that such as will be disciples of Christ must bear the cross; that as many as will be in the same ship with him must prepare themselves unto dangerous storms. The sea of this wicked world is troublesome: the church of God is beaten and tossed like a boat: it is disfigured with sharp and stormy weather. Feeble is all flesh, manifold are our infirmities, faint is our faith; and seeing our sin, with the remembrance of the stipend due for the same, we are ready to sink into the bottomless gulf of desperation. In this dangerous estate we find no help in ourselves. But behold, the disciples of Christ have taught us by their example where help is to be sought in the midst of these manifold and great distresses: and that is only in Christ, who is always a present helper of them which seek him in time of need; who hath overcome and victoriously triumphed on the cross against Satan, sin, the world, hell, death, and condemnation. To him all power giveth place: against him no force is able to stand: unto him all things are made subject. He is that Samson which by his own death hath slain his foes; that David which hath dashed out the brains of Goliah, the grand enemy of God's people; that seed which hath bruised the serpent's head; that Almighty which rebuketh winds, ceaseth storms, easeth the burthens of them that mourn, washeth away iniquity, freely forgiveth sin, heareth and delivereth out of trouble. If we cry with the disciples in our distress, "Help, Lord," he will in mercy awake and hear us: through his mighty power he will both cause the raging of the sea to cease, and stay the madness of the people.

2. But, to the end we may more particularly gather such lessons out of this parcel of scripture, as may most tend to God's glory and our edifying, I mean to stand while this time will permit upon these points, shewing, first, that we must follow Christ into the ship; secondly, that as many as will sail with him shall be in danger; thirdly, that in their danger they shall not be destitute of help, if they seek it at his hands. It is not my peculiar conceit, but Tertullian[1] and Chrysostom[2] do note, that this ship representeth the church of Christ tossed with the surges of temptation, with the stormy waves of calamity and trouble in this present world. *Christ must be followed into this ship.*

3. Christ hath always had a church here on earth: it was begun in paradise; sithence it hath remained and continued even unto this day. And as Christ hath his boat, so hath antichrist also his. Wherefore it behoveth us to know and discern the one from the other. The ark of the tabernacle of the Lord hath her true ornaments whereby to be known. Therein are laid up the treasures of God, most precious jewels. St Paul telleth us what they are. In the ark of the testament was "a golden pot having manna, and the rod of Aaron that had blossomed, and the tables of the testament." In the tables was the written word of God: manna was a figure of that mystical *This ship must be known from the ship of antichrist.* Heb. ix. [4.]

[[1] Ceterum navicula illa figuram ecclesiæ præferebat, quòd in mari, id est seculo, fluctibus, id est persecutionibus et tentationibus, inquietatur, Domino per patientiam velut dormiente.—Tertull. Op. Lut. 1641. De Baptismo, p. 261.—ED.]

[[2] Γυμνασίας ἕνεκεν ταῦτα συνεχωρεῖτο, καὶ τύπος ἦν τῶν μελλόντων καταλήψεσθαι αὐτοὺς πειρασμῶν.—Chrysost. Op. Par. 1727. In Matt. Hom. xxviii. Tom. viii. p. 333.—ED.]

food wherewith we are nourished to eternal life: the rod of Aaron resembled the sceptre of discipline. So that where nothing is taught but according to the written word, where the sacraments are sincerely ministered, where the rod and sceptre of government is used, there is Christ, there is the church. And we may thank our God for ever, that in his marvellous great mercy he hath made us partakers of these so rich and precious blessings; whereby we know assuredly that God is amongst us, that he sitteth in the midst of our assemblies, that this church is unto us as the ark of Noah, as the glorious sanctuary of the Lord, as the ship into which Christ Jesus is entered.

When we know the ship where Christ is, thither we must follow him.

4. When the Romans minded to leave the city, Scipio took an ensign in his hand, and set forwards towards the capitol, saying, *Quicunque vult rempublicam salvam me sequatur*[1]: "Whosoever wisheth well to the common state, let him follow me." But most truly it may be said, "Whosoever wisheth well to his own soul, let him follow Christ." He is no servant, that refuseth to follow his master: he that followeth him not is not worthy of him. The sheep when they hear the voice of their shepherd, they go after him. He is no member of Christ, that sundereth himself from the head of that body whereof he professeth himself a member. That branch, that is cut off from the vine, withereth and is fit for nothing but for the fire. After that Judas left Christ, and gave himself to be a sectary of the high priests, his case was lamentable. No man cometh to the haven, but he which followeth Christ to the ship. If we leave him, whither should we go? There is no other that hath the words of eternal life. Let us therefore do as his disciples did, forsake all and "follow." Follow him not only to the ship, but in the ship.

The way to follow him to the ship is by denying ourselves.
Matt. xvi. [24.]
Luke ix. [23.]
Mark viii. [34.]

5. They follow Christ to the ship, which by faith in the gospel are gathered and united to his church; the door and entrance whereunto is narrow. For so Christ describeth it: "If any man will come after me, let him deny himself." This lesson is general: for St Luke saith, *Dixit omnibus:* "He spake unto all;" and St Mark, *Et turbæ et discipulis dixit:* "He spake it both to the multitude and to his disciples." No man therefore can look to come

[[1] T. Liv. Hist. Lib. xxii. c. 53.—Ed.]

unto Christ by any other way. We must begin with the plain denying of ourselves, that is to say, the forsaking of our impiety and fleshly lusts.

6. To deny impiety is to forsake false doctrine, false worshipping of God, and whatsoever is against the first part or table of the law. "The house of God," saith Tobias, "shall be built for ever with a glorious building, as the prophets have spoken of it; and all nations shall turn and fear the Lord God truly, and shall bury their idols:" that is to say, they shall forsake their impiety, and so be numbered with the saints of God. When the Ephesians, which had used curious arts, were converted to the faith of Christ, they brought their books and burned them, as many as were worth by estimation fifty thousand pieces of silver. By the writings of Athenagoras, Clemens, Justin Martyr, Arnobius, Minutius, Lactantius, and many other of the ancients, it appeareth that the very first thing which those men of famous memory did in their conversion from gentility[1] to the truth, was openly to proclaim defiance to that impiety, wherein they had been nursled and trained up. Constantine, considering with himself the lives and doings of former emperors, and finding that their estate had been always worse which had worshipped the gods of the nations, that they which gave greatest credit to idolatrous spirits of divination were but deluded, that none had fairer promises of prosperous events than they whose ends were most infortunate, that his father only amongst the rest putting his trust in the God which created heaven and earth had by experience all the time of his life found him a mighty protector, and a bountiful rewarder of them that fear him; when it pleased God by this mean to bring him to a love and liking of the truth, he began forthwith to shew great tokens of favour unto Christians, to have conference with their bishops and chief professors, to restore them whom cruelty had cast out of their lawful possessions for believing in the name of Christ, to erect houses of great charge for prayer and holy exercises of the church, to do whatsoever might any way be devised, not only for the succour and needful relief, but also for the honour and dignity of

^{Our impiety.}

^{Tob. xiv. [5, 6.]}

^{Acts xix. [19.]}

[¹ Gentility—religion of the gentiles, paganism.—ED.]

Christians. Now by this that Tobias foresheweth how the gentiles, being converted to the truth, shall bury their idols; that St Luke recordeth how the Ephesians burned all their impious books; that the fathers in their first conversion wrote so vehemently against paganism; that Constantine gave so many and so great tokens of a mind detesting all impiety, and burning with the love of Christ Jesus; by this, I say, we may perceive how impossible it is to steal a true denial of impiety, how impossible for a man which indeed hath denied it not to shew his denial in his deeds.

All our worldly and fleshly desires.

7. To deny impiety it is not enough, except we also deny our fleshly lusts. If we look into our evil and corrupt nature, we shall find nothing but that which leadeth us clean from Christ, nothing but rebellion against the Spirit, distrust in the providence of Almighty God, joy and delight in earthly things, blindness of mind, hardness of heart. All this we must mortify: this we must shake off: we must quite relinquish our own wills, and submit ourselves wholly to the will of God. Shall we refuse to do this, when Christ himself hath said, "I seek not to have mine own will, but the will of him that sent me?" And again, "It is meat unto me to do his will." And in his greatest agony, "Not as I will, O Father, but as thou wilt." This is a doctrine hard to practise and put in ure. It is the fault of our corrupt flesh: we think too highly of ourselves: we are too much wedded to our own wills. The blessed apostle (as we think) speaketh like a man besides himself, when he saith, "If any man seem to be wise amongst you in this world, let him be made a fool that he may become wise." This is but the entrance unto Christianity; yet how few are there which be come thus far! The rich young man in the gospel seemed to be very forward in the way; but Christ discovereth his affection, and sheweth, that he had not denied himself, and therefore was no fit disciple for him. It made him heavy and pensive to think of leaving so great possessions, and of weaning his heart so soon from the world. He could have been contented to deny impiety; but Christ would have worldly concupiscence also to be denied. "For the grace of God our Saviour," saith

[John v. 30.]
[John iv. 34.]
[Matt. xxvi. 39.]
[1 Cor. iii. 18.]
[Luke xiv. 18—23.]
[Tit. ii. 11, 12.]

the apostle, "hath appeared to all men, teaching us that denying impiety and worldly desires, we live soberly, and justly, and godly in this present world."

8. This is the way wherein Christ must be followed by as many as desire to be shipped with him, to be of the number of his people. This is the door of entrance into the church. When we are once entered and received into the ship, as we followed him thither by believing the gospel, by "denying impiety and worldly lusts;" so there we must follow him by walking as we have him for our example, purging ourselves "even as he is pure," and "shewing forth the virtues of him that hath called us out of darkness into his marvellous light." "Be ye holy, for I am holy," saith the Lord. As according to his similitude and likeness we were at the first created, so now according to the same similitude we must also be framed and fashioned anew. Sith we were first light, and became darkness afterward, and are made now again of darkness light in the Lord, it is no reason that we should any more frame ourselves unto the lusts of our ignorance; "but, as he which hath called us is holy, so likewise ought we to be holy in all manner of conversation." When the Jews boasted that they had Abraham to their father, their vanity was reproved: "If ye were the sons of Abraham," saith Christ, "ye would do the works of Abraham: but now ye go about to kill me, a man that have told you the truth, which I have heard of God: *Hoc Abraham non fecit:* Abraham did not this." It is in vain for us to boast of the name of Christians, except the image of Christ be seen in our life and conversation. If we follow him not, we are not his.

The way to follow him in the ship is imitation.

1 John iii. [3.]
1 Pet. ii. [9.]
Levit. xi. [45.]

1 Pet. i. [15.]

John viii. [39, 40.]

9. We are exhorted to be followers both of God and of men. "Be ye followers of God, as most dear children." Again: "Be ye followers of them which through faith and patience inherit the promises." God is the rule, as of faith, so of life: wherefore absolutely, "Be ye followers of God;" but of men always with this caution, "Be ye followers of me, as I am of Christ." The Thessalonians St Paul commendeth, forasmuch as they were "followers of him and of the Lord." If our fathers, elders, guides, and teachers, be a "rebellious generation, a generation that set not their

How God is to be followed, and how men.

Eph. v. [1.]
Heb. vi. [12.]

1 Cor. xi. [1.]

1 Thess. i. [6.]

Psal. lxxviii. [8.]

heart aright, and whose spirit is not faithful unto God," then are they no precedents for us to follow: but be followers of us, so long as we are followers of Christ, and are examples unto you, "in word, in conversation, in love, in spirit, in faith, in pureness." Whatsoever things are true, whatsoever things are honest, whatsoever things are just, whatsoever things are pure, whatsoever things pertain to love, whatsoever things are of good report; if there be any virtue, if there be any praise, think on these things, which ye have both learned and received, and heard and seen in me: these things do, and the God of peace shall be with you."

1 Tim. iv. [12.]
Phil. iv. [8, 9.]

10. Their estate in the world which follow Christ in such wise as hath been shewed, is here resembled by a ship tossed and grievously shaken with a tempest. It is and ever hath been, yea, and will be their lot, whether they be upon sea or land, to be in peril, to stand in fear, to have wind and weather against them. As many as follow him must deny themselves, and, having denied themselves, they must take up the cross. The cross signifieth all afflictions; which may be divided into two kinds, afflictions of punishment, and afflictions of trial: the former are common unto all; the latter are proper to the elect of God.

They which are with Christ must suffer trouble and affliction.

11. The sin of Adam brought misery unto man, and a curse unto all the creatures of God. Hence it cometh to pass, that with sorrow and tears we enter into the world; and when we are in it, we have a short continuance: yet in that shortness, good Lord, unto how many chances and changes are we subject! In the end we die; and who doth know what becometh of us? our graves keep us secret. "As the waters pass from the sea, and as the flood decayeth and drieth up, so man sleepeth and riseth not: he lieth in the dust, and shall not be raised from his sleep till the heaven be no more." O how bitter is this to such as put their trust in uncertain riches! how dreadful is the remembrance of death unto the wicked! But they only are not subject unto death: the sorrows of the grave take hold on all, inasmuch as all have sinned. Howbeit, in these afflictions which come as punishments unto all, there is a difference. They come not unto all with like intent of him that sendeth them: they fall upon the godly

Afflictions common unto all men.

Job xiv. [11, 12.]

for their correction, but they bring confusion unto the wicked.

12. There are other afflictions proper to believers, tribulations which God doth send as special tokens of favour to his dearest saints; trials which are, unto them that bear them patiently, seals and assurances, that they are counted worthy of the kingdom of God for which they suffer. For the world, which hateth both the truth and the light, cannot but hate all such as love the truth, and as walk in the light. Out of this fountain spring all those molestations which the godly do suffer for righteousness' sake at the hands of wicked and ungodly men. David saw this when he said, "Many are the troubles of the just." St Paul did consider it, and therefore said, "They that will live godly in Christ Jesus shall suffer persecution." Christ did often put his disciples and scholars in remembrance of it: "If they have persecuted me, they will persecute you." In the world we are sure to find heavy entertainment; but this is our comfort: with whom we suffer, with him we shall reign: we shall live with him in glory with whom now we are in misery, if so be we take up our cross and follow him. Patience perforce is no patience. Not every one which beareth any manner of cross, but he which taketh it up, that is to say, which is willing to bear it, he shall receive an immortal crown of glory. The wild, resty, and unbroken horse, if he kick and fling never so much, yet is he forced to carry his rider; but, being managed and tamed, he passeth on quietly with his burthen. The wicked mutter, they murmur and blaspheme when they are once touched; but the servants of God do not only take that patiently which is laid upon them, but they rejoice that they are thought worthy to suffer. Be they never so much afflicted in body, the end of their affliction is always joy in the spirit. The wicked kick against the prick: the godly submit themselves to the yoke, knowing that they are stricken with a tender hand, that he which humbleth them loveth them, and shall turn all things to their good. Yea, they take up not only their own crosses, but also the griefs and sufferings of others upon their backs: they are content to feel the smart even of other men's stripes, to put their shoulders under the burthens of their brethren, to

Afflictions peculiar unto God's elect.

Psal. xxxiv. [19.]
[2 Tim. iii. 12.]

[John xv. 20.]

weep for the sorrows of other men as much as for their own, when others are bound to be as if they were in chains with them. These are the sufferings of the church of Christ: these are the crosses of his children. As for heretics, they have no portion in this cup. Though they offer themselves unto all kinds of torture, yet because they suffer not for the truth, but against the truth, they cannot look for that rest which is promised to God's afflicted, "when the Lord shall shew himself from heaven, accompanied with his mighty angels." For it is not the cross, but the cause, that makes a martyr. "Blessed are they that suffer for righteousness' sake." There is no cause why that irreligious crew should glory in their sufferings, which fight for antichrist, for heresy, for popery, for superstition, sedition, self-will and singularity: *Non ex passione certa est justitia, sed ex justitia passio gloriosa est*,[1] saith St Augustine: "Our sufferings are no argument of our righteousness, but our righteousness an ornament unto our sufferings."

_{2 Thess. i. [7.]}

_[Matt. v. 10.]

_{Aug. cont. epi. Parmen. lib. i. cap. 7.}

_{Affliction laid upon the general body of the church.}

13. To these afflictions whereof we have hitherto spoken, the church hath always been subject: from the beginning it hath been tossed and much troubled. Abel, the image of the church, was unnaturally murdered by the bloody hand of his own brother. Abraham, the father of our faith, with his family, a figure of the church, lived as a pilgrim, and they as strangers upon earth. The Israelites were in Egypt tyrannized by Pharaoh, in the wilderness many ways chastised of the Lord, afterwards in continual storms, war, and battle, before they could be placed in the land of Canaan: when they were come thither and had dwelt long there, in the end their temple was spoiled, their people murdered, their cities razed, and they led captives into strange countries. This was the lot of God's church, the portion of his elect and chosen people in former times. In the last days, Christ himself was no sooner in the world, but he was by and bye forced to save his life by flight. There was no day, no hour that passed over him without grief, from the time of his birth to that very moment wherein he yielded up the ghost. How it fared with his

[¹ August. Op. Par. 1688. Cont. Epist. Parmen. Lib. I. 15. Tom. IX. col. 21.—ED.]

disciples after him, and after them with the churches which they had planted, it may appear by the history partly of their acts, and partly of those times wherein Nero, Trajan, Domitian, Diocletian, and others of the like disposition lived. But no time so bloody and cruel, as since that Roman strumpet hath usurped authority over Christ and his church. The church could hide itself in no corner of any kingdom in the whole world, but his tyranny found it out, to vex it, to persecute it, and to spoil it. What blood he hath shed, what murders he hath committed in these latter days, England, Scotland, Flanders, and France, can sufficiently record. By this it is evident to all men's eyes, how the church in the midst of this wicked world is tossed like a ship upon the sea.

14. As the whole church of Christ, so every member that truly professeth him, is subject unto great tentation. If the ship be in danger, how can they be without peril that are in it? As soon as we profess the name of Christ, the devil stirreth up his storms and tempests of temptation, to make us deny and forsake our profession; wherein his assaults be most fierce, in which respect the blessed apostle doth call them fiery. So it pleased God to chastise and keep under every son whom he receiveth. And if we would be without affliction, then were we bastards and not children. *Upon every particular member.*

15. If both the whole body and every member thereof be thus devoted unto suffering, the chiefest members must look to be in greatest dangers. That which Christ told his disciples must be verified in all their successors: "The world shall hate them." For why? They which hate to be reformed cannot brook to be reproved; and we must needs rebuke the world of sin. What misery soever cometh to the church, the minister is alway the first that feeleth the smart of it. This we find to have been true in the prophets, in the apostles, and in others, that from time to time have borne the rooms of overseers in the church. *Quem prophetarum non persecuti sunt?* saith Christ: "What prophet can be named which hath not been persecuted?" The time would not suffer me to make but only a bare rehearsal either of the ancient worthy guides of the church, which have been most cruelly en- *Upon the principal members specially.* [John xv. 19.] [Matt. xxiii. 34: Acts vii. 52.]

treated and murdered in former times, or of your own pastors whom our late evil days have seen taken from us in most cruel sort.

The causes from whence such storms do rise as trouble that church.

16. By this it is plain, that the whole church of Christ, and every member of the same, is subject to tribulations, afflictions, and troubles, and the chiefest members most subject. Let us now consider how and why this cometh to pass. The most near and immediate cause of their trouble which are tossed upon the sea, is the rising of winds and the raging of the waters. This is manifest unto sense. They that go down to the sea in ships, and use traffic in great waters, do see that, when the stormy wind ariseth and lifteth up the waves, they which are in the ship mount up to heaven and descend to the deep, so that their soul melteth for trouble; they are tossed to and fro, and stagger like a drunken man, and all their understanding is swallowed up. Wherefore the blustering winds and the stormy seas were the sensible cause, why the ship wherein Christ with his disciples sailed was sore tossed and greatly dangered. Now, if we look into the sea of the world, we shall find that all our grief and vexation cometh from those unquiet motions which are raised by our spiritual and ghostly enemy, who never resteth, but tumbleth to and fro, raising one tempestuous storm in the neck of another. What marvel then if the church be troubled; or rather, how can it be otherwise than troubled and sore assaulted, seeing Satan hath so many ways to molest it, and useth as many as he hath? Sometimes he stirreth up cruel and bloody persecution. If that will not serve, he useth such winds as are somewhat more calm, but no whit less dangerous, the winds of division and contention, than which nothing doth sooner hazard the church of Christ. A kingdom being at unity in itself, though it be small, yet may be strong; but divided and distracted into factions, though it be mighty, how should it stand? This is a thing which I wish greatly that we did throughly consider. Hitherto (such is the mercy of Almighty God) our enemies have not prevailed against us, although they be many, and we but few; they strong, and we weak. But if a few silly weak ones be miserably divided, what may we look for but inevitable

ruin? It is lamentable that the gospel of peace should bring forth schism. This is both slanderous, and undoubtedly perilous to our profession. Unto them whom Satan hath abused, as his instruments to work this evil, I may speak in a manner as the clerk of Ephesus did to the people, when they were in an uproar without cause. There is no idolatry, no impiety, maintained by the laws and orders of this church. If Demetrius and the craftsmen which are with him have any thing concerning other matters, there is authority, we have courts, there are lawful assemblies to hear, to discuss, and to determine them. When they refuse the peaceable means whereby strife may be ended, and will follow no course but that which breedeth confusion and raiseth tumults, may they not justly be accused as clamorous troublers of the church of God, forasmuch as there can be no just and allowable reason alleged of these their troublesome and unquiet dealings? Shall we be followers of men in contention, and that about frivolous and vain things, and leave the walking after Christ in peace and love? "Now the God of patience and consolation grant that at the length we may be like minded one toward another, according to Christ Jesus, that with one mind and one mouth we may praise God even the Father of our Lord Jesus Christ." [Rom. xv. 5, 6.]

17. Thus the church, as a ship, is by outward persecution and inward contention, as it were by storms and tempests, troubled. The storms, which trouble the particular members of the church, are our own rebellious and disordered desires, which never suffer us to enjoy any long rest of mind. Some are troubled with one unquietness, and some with another. Some cannot rest for the cares of the world: some swell with pride and vain glory: some boil in rancour, envy and malice: some fry in lust, some with anger. The best are secretly disturbed with that from which the holy apostle crieth out, "Miserable man, who shall deliver me?" When these things have so shaken us, that our souls are thereby bruised, then doth Satan raise the greatest storm of all other. He layeth our sins before our eyes, and persuadeth with us, as he did with Cain and Judas, that our iniquity is greater than can be pardoned, our sores past cure, our breaches such as are

How the storms which trouble men in particular do arise.

[Rom. vii. 24.]

without hope or remedy. With this blast and puff he overthroweth many; and the dearest children of God are most subject hereunto. It is therefore good to resist sin betimes, lest, when the conscience is therewith overburthened, if the devil cast our sin before us, together with the judgment of God against sin, we make shipwreck of our faith.

<small>Our troubles do grow when the causes that should appease them are asleep.</small>

18. Now, when these troubles are not quieted by such causes as have power to appease them, then are the causes (although not properly, but figuratively) said to be asleep. So the Lord, when he seeth his children to be afflicted, or suffereth the wicked for a time to go unpunished, till he deliver the one, and plague the other, is to our seeming as if he slept. And the grace of God in us, whereby we withstand and resist that which fighteth against the Spirit, may be said to wake as long as it worketh, and to sleep then when it ceaseth working. When we sleep naturally, our bodies are subject to many dangers. Holofernes being asleep, the weak hand of Judith was able to make him shorter by the head. *In corde christiano et tranquillitas erit et pax, sed quamdiu vigilat fides nostra: Si autem dormit fides nostra, periclitamur*[1]. "In a christian heart there shall be both tranquillity and peace, but no longer than our faith is kept waking: if that fall asleep, we are in danger," saith St Augustine. For this cause St Paul crieth out so loud in the ears of men, "Awake, thou that sleepest;" and to Timothy, "Stir up the gift of God which is in thee," but let it not sleep.

<small>Aug. in Psal. 32.</small>

<small>Eph. v. [14.] 2 Tim. i. [6.]</small>

<small>Sleepiness to be shaken off by magistrates.</small>

19. If the master and governor of the ship, who sitteth at the helm, fall asleep, the ship cannot keep her

[1 It does not appear that there is any such passage in the place indicated. The following is probably that intended by the archbishop: Quando ille dicitur dormire, nos dormimus: et quando ille dicitur exsurgere, nos excitamur. Nam et Dominus dormiebat in navi; et ideo fluctuabat navis, quia dormiebat Jesus. Nam si illic vigilaret Jesus, non fluctuaret navis. Navis tua, cor tuum: Jesus in navi, fides in corde. Si meministi fidei tuæ, non fluctuat cor tuum: si oblitus es fidem tuam, dormit Christus: observa naufragium. Verumtamen quod restat fac, ut si dormierit excitetur; dicas illi, Domine, exsurge, perimus: ut increpet ventos, et fiat tranquillitas in corde tuo.—August. Op. Par. 1681. In Psalm xxxiv. Enar. Sermo i. Tom. IV. col. 230.—ED.]

right course unguided, but will fall upon every sand, rush upon every rock, and so hazard whatsoever is in it. The boat of Christ is set over unto two governors, the magistrate and the minister: it is dangerous if either of them be not watchful. When such kings ruled Israel as lived securely, took their ease, and cared not for the public benefit, such as Manasses and Jeroboam, then was there great confusion in the church and commonwealth: God was not served: idolatry every where was committed. It is a great fault in rulers and judges of the earth, when their eyes are not open to behold the disorderly dealings of the wicked, nor their ears to receive the complaints of the poor, the fatherless, the widow, and them which suffer wrong. There was sometime a serjeant that now resteth (I hope in peace), who, when a poor man craved his advice in a matter, and offered him no money, answered, "I hear thee, but I feel thee not." This man's heart was awake unto covetousness, but unto judgment and justice asleep.

20. Ministers are termed by a special name of watchmen, to shew, that they above all others should beware of too much sleep. "Son of man, I have made thee a watchman unto the house of Israel," saith the Lord to his prophet. "Now, if the people take a man from amongst them, and make him their watchman, if when he seeth the sword come upon the land he blow the trumpet and warn the people, then he that heareth the sound of the trumpet, and will not be warned, if the sword come and take him away, his blood shall be upon his own head. For he heard the sound of the trumpet, and would not be admonished: therefore his blood shall be upon him; as contrariwise, he that receiveth warning shall save his life. But if the watchman see the sword come, and blow not the trumpet, and the people be not warned, if the sword come and take any man from amongst them; he is taken away for his iniquity, but his blood will I require at the watchman's hand." Wherefore, there could not a greater plague happen to the people of God, than that whereof the prophet Esay maketh mention: "Their watchmen are all blind: they lie asleep and delight in sleeping." Whilst the husbandmen slept, the evil man

By ministers.

Ezek. iii. [17: xxxiii. 2—6.]

Isai.lvi.[10.]

sowed his darnel, and went his way, and was not seen. Sleepy folk are the cause why the field of the Lord is overgrown with weeds, his church infected with sin and error. When the pastor sleepeth, the wolf devoureth: sin entereth and maketh havock.

It is good that Christ should sleep and we be troubled. [Psal. cxxi. 4.]

21. But, sith "he that keepeth Israel will neither slumber nor sleep," it may be marvelled how that thing which he keepeth can be subject to so many storms and tempests, which might be prevented if he did not suffer himself or us, or them whom he hath set as watchmen over us, to fall asleep. Whereunto I answer, by the same distinction which the spouse herself doth make in the Song of Solomon: "I sleep, but my heart waketh." God suffereth us, that is to say, our outward man, to be molested, troubled, vexed: upon our flesh he seemeth many times to shut his eyes, although in truth the eyes of his fatherly providence be always open even upon that, not permitting us therein to be tried and tempted above our strength. But over our *hearts* we know by manifest experience, and are sure to find, that he still keepeth a continual watch. "The Lord will keep thee (saith the prophet) from all evil: he will keep thy soul." And although it be grievous, yet is it meet and expedient, yea good and profitable for us, that our hearts, our souls, our spirits, being so surely and safely kept, God should sometimes wink at the troubles of our flesh, as if he saw them not.

Cant. v. [2.]

Psal. cxxi. [7.]

He sendeth his disciples help in their troubles.

22. The disciples in their great fear and danger went unto Christ, and wakened him with their cries: "Help, we perish." Dost thou see us cast away, and not consider it? Of the like complaints of the people of God in the midst of their distresses, we read in sundry places, especially of the psalms: "Up, why sleepest thou, O Lord? Awake, be not far off for ever. Wherefore hidest thou thy face, and forgettest our misery and our affliction? Our soul is beaten down unto the dust, our belly cleaveth unto the ground: rise up for our succour, and redeem us for thy mercy's sake." These groans and cries be not poured out in vain. Christ rebuketh the winds and seas: his servants have their wish: their requests are no sooner uttered than granted. If we, as good disciples of these disciples, do in our troubles fly

Psal. xliv. [23—26.]

unto Christ for aid, in his mercy he shall hear us, and deliver us by the strength of his mighty power. He cannot suffer us to be tried above that which we are able to bear. Be our suit never so desperate, he can help it. For nothing is impossible with God. Would you see some fit examples? The Israelites groaned unto him in Egypt: he heard them and delivered them from the tyranny of Pharaoh. The young men in the furnace called upon him, and were preserved. The cry of Daniel stopped the mouths of lions: Paul and Silas being in bonds prayed, and their chains fell loose from them; the doors opened and gave them passage. Although we be plunged never so low, although the floods run clean over us, insomuch that we seem to ourselves as it were past help and recovery, yet we are not past help so long as we are not past desire to be holpen. The greatness of our peril can be no stop to our deliverance, because the power of our deliverer is infinite. In deed we see that men are altogether amazed, and in a manner bereft of wit and understanding, when they feel themselves dangerously tossed to and fro. But do we not also see that, when they cry unto the Lord in their trouble, he bringeth them out of distress, he turneth the storm to calm, so that the waves thereof are still? do we not see how they pass through tribulations to the kingdom of heaven, and through stormy tempests are brought to the haven where they would be? This the Lord doth, that we might confess his loving kindness before him, and his wonderful works before the sons of men. To him therefore, even God the Father, God the Son, and God the Holy Ghost, be all honour and glory for ever and ever. Amen.

THE TWENTIETH SERMON.

A SERMON

PREACHED AT PAUL'S CROSS.

1 Peter IV.

7. *The end of all things is at hand. Be ye therefore sober and watching in prayer.*
8. *But above all things have fervent love among you; for love covereth the multitude of sins.*
9. *Be ye harborous[1] one towards another, without grudging.*
10. *Let every man, as he hath received the gift, minister the same one to another, as good disposers of the manifold graces of God.*

<small>We must live as they that in the end shall give account how they have lived. 1 Cor. iii. [11.] 1 Pet. ii. [5.]</small>

The apostle St Peter, like a perfit[2] workman and a skilful builder, first layeth a sure foundation, and then frameth and erecteth a good building thereupon. The foundation is Christ. "Another foundation no man can lay." He is the rock, the foundation; and we as "lively stones" must be framed thereupon, hewed and squared with the hammer and square of God's word, that we may grow to be "a spiritual house, an holy priesthood, to offer up unto God through Jesus Christ spiritual and acceptable sacrifices" of piety, prayer, and thanksgiving. Through Christ we are brought from darkness unto light, that from henceforth we should walk as the children of that light wherein he hath placed us: of a perverse generation we are through him made an holy people, that we should be <small>Deut. x. [12—16.] 1 Pet. i. [18, 19.] Luke i. [74, 75.]</small> "holy" as he is that called us: we are redeemed, "not by gold and silver," but by the innocent blood of the immaculate Lamb, to "serve him that hath delivered us out of the hands of our enemies in holiness and righteousness all the days of our life:" we are called to be the children of God, citizens of the heavenly Jerusalem, and to be fellow heirs

---

[¹ Harborous—hospitable.—Ed.]
[² Perfit—perfect.—Ed.]

with Christ of that his eternal kingdom; that we should be obedient and loving children, trusty and dutiful citizens, that we may be not only called, but chosen, accepted, and admitted to inherit with Christ, the first begotten of God. What building we be, whether "gold or stubble," what life we lead, it will one day appear. Our conversion will be called unto an hard account. In that day we must stand before the tribunal seat of God, and render a reckoning, yea, and receive as we have wrought in our bodies, good or bad. The judge is even at hand: *Veniens veniet:* "He will come surely without fail, and without stay." "He standeth before the door." This is the last hour: the trump is in a readiness to be blown to judgment. [Habak. ii. [3.] Rev. iii. [20.]]

2. For, saith Peter, "the end of all things hangeth over us." In which words the apostle doth both comfort us, and exhort us. Such as are afflicted, oppressed with wrong, burthened with poverty, vexed with sickness, slandered, persecuted, or hated of the world, here they may receive comfort. Your misery shall be but momentany and short; your joy shall be great and endless. "Lift up your heads, for your redemption draweth near." The end of your affliction, together with the end of all things, is at hand. Again, upon these words a most necessary exhortation is inferred. Christ is coming in the clouds all flesh shall rise and reckon: he only that hath his lamp burning shall enter in with the bridegroom: as we are found, so shall we be taken and judged. "The end is at hand: be sober therefore, and watch unto prayer." [The consideration of the last end doth make them that are heavy joyful, and them that are godly watchful. Luke xxi. [28.]]

3. Whereas the holy scriptures do make often mention of a double end; the one, wherein we are to yield up our mortal lives; the other, wherein Christ at his second coming shall finish the course of all this sinful world; the apostle treating in this place of the latter, I shall at this present follow his footsteps, and speak of Christ his second coming to put an end to all things. For they which say, "Where is the promise of his coming?" deceive themselves. "He hath set a day wherein he will judge the world in justice:" "he is appointed judge of quick and dead." The angel of God beareth witness of his coming. "This Jesus, which is taken up into heaven, shall so come as ye have seen him go." And St John, as if he beheld and saw him coming, [The last end of all things is certain. 2 Pet. iii. [4.] Acts xvii. [31.] Acts x. [42.] Acts i. [11.]]

saith, "Behold, he cometh with clouds, and every eye shall see him."

^{Rev. i. [7.]}

4. But as his coming is most certain, so the hour, day, month, year, or time, is most uncertain. "It is not for you to know the seasons and precise points of time, which the Father hath appointed in his own power." "Of that day and hour no man knoweth, no, not the very angels of heaven, but my Father only." "The day of the Lord will come stealing upon us, as a thief in the night."

The time thereof uncertain. Acts i. [7.] Matt. xxiv. [36.] 1 Thess. v. [2.]

5. Now, as we know not the day and time, so let us be assured that this coming of the Lord is near. He is not slack, as we do count slackness. That it is at hand, it may be probably gathered out of the scriptures in divers places. The signs mentioned by Christ in the gospel, which should be the foreshewers of this terrible day, are almost already all fulfilled. The prophecies of Daniel of the four monarchies, of the little horn, and of the times, weeks, and days, are manifestly come to pass. The defections or fallings away, which are spoken of in holy scriptures, are also in great part accomplished. The provinces, the ten kingdoms, are fallen from the Roman empire, and that wicked one hath wrought the mystery of iniquity. Again, there hath been, in a manner, a general falling from the catholic faith, as the apostle long before foretold us; some unto Mahomet, some unto antichrist his brother. Even about one time Mahomet appeared, and the pope swerved from the true faith of Christ; the one renouncing him in name, the other in deed; the one quite blotting out the mention of Christ, and denying at all to profess him in word, the other keeping his name, but robbing him of his office, and shutting him out of his right place; both falling from the faith. That defection also is come upon us, which St Paul did prophesy of: "In the latter times men shall fall from the faith, giving ear to deceiving spirits and doctrines of devils." And St Peter: "There shall come in the last days mockers, that walk after their own lusts, and say, Where is the promise of his coming?" Thus heretics and atheists have fallen from Christ and christian faith. We that profess Christ and his gospel, are also charged with a defection, a schism, and a falling away. But in every apostasy two things must be considered, from whom and to whom this sliding

The time near at hand, as appeareth by signs, but how near we know not. Matt. xxiv. Dan. vii. 2 Thess. ii. [1—12.] 1 Tim. iv. [1.] 2 Pet. iii. [3, 4.]

is. We gladly grant that we are fallen away from the bishop of Rome, who long ago fell from Christ: we do utterly abandon his usurped and proud authority: we have happily forsaken that synagogue of Satan, that den of thieves, that polluted church, that simoniacal temple; and we joyfully confess that we have no society or fellowship with his darkness. In our sermons we preach Christ, and none else but him: we know nothing, we teach nothing, we believe nothing, but Christ and him crucified. In our sacraments we shew forth the Lord's death in no other sort, than he himself hath done and commanded us to do. In our lives we worship the Lord alone; and, in yielding up our souls, we fly for mercy only to the merits of Christ Jesus, our merciful Saviour. This is our apostasy. We have forsaken him that hath forsaken God, and whom God hath forsaken: we have left that man of sin, that rose-coloured harlot with whom the kings of the earth have committed fornication, that triple-crowned beast, that double-sworded tyrant, that thief and murderer, who hath robbed so many souls of salvation, and sucked so much innocent blood of christian martyrs, that adversary unto Christ, that pretensed vicar, who hath displaced the person, not only taking upon him Christ's room and office, but also boasting himself as if he were a god, and being content of his parasites so to be called. This wicked man of sin is at length revealed by the sincere preaching of the gospel. Daniel in his prophecies, Paul in his epistles, and John in his revelations, have most lively described and pointed him forth even as it were with the finger. Yea, through his pride and ambition, his usurping authority and worldly rule, his tyranny and persecuting of Christ in his members, he hath sufficiently revealed and detected himself, if none had done it for him.

6. This wicked man the Lord shall destroy with the breath of his mouth; and then shall be the end. The blast of God's trump hath made him already stagger: he hath caught such a cramp, that he beginneth now to halt: his long and far-reaching arm is marvellously shortened: his coffers are waxen leaner: his falsehood is espied: many princes refuse to taste any more of his poisoned cup: he is fallen from being the head, and come almost to be the

The destruction of antichrist.

tail: he was too cruel and too violent to continue. There is no counsel nor power against the Lord. And that, as all men, so especially he hath felt. It is too hard for him to kick against the spur, to fight against the Lord of hosts. Seeing therefore that this man of sin is not only revealed, but in a manner overthrown too, doubtless the Lord is coming, and the end of all things draweth near. [Matt. xxiv. 12, 14.] "Iniquity (saith our Saviour) shall abound, and charity shall wax cold: the gospel shall be preached in the whole world; and then an end." Iniquity doth abound: for, as the prophet saith, [Hos. iv. [1, 2.]] "There is no truth, there is no pity, there is no knowledge of God in the earth. Slandering, lying, murdering, stealing, and whoring, have overflowed the world." Charity is frozen up, and become cold as ice. These latter days have bred and brought out swarms of such as love themselves, but neither God nor their neighbours. God's word never sounded more shrill, never was preached more sincerely, than at this day. It is not bound or shut up in straits: it hath free and large passage. Iniquity thus flowing, charity thus ebbing, and God's gospel thus sounding throughout the world, I may conclude with St Peter, "The end is near at hand."

The duties towards God which St Peter inferreth upon this doctrine.

7. This coming of Christ will be a joyful day for God's children: they shall lift up their heads: but to antichrist, to the enemies of God's gospel, to the workers of iniquity, it will be a day of wrath, indignation, and all affliction. But they put far from them the remembrance thereof: they set it aloof, and go still forward, heaping up riches, though they know not how soon they shall depart from them; building, though they know not for what inhabitant; purchasing, though they know not who shall inherit; decking, feeding, pampering themselves, though they know not whether the next or this night, the next or this moment, their soul shall be taken from them. The world is towards an end. [1 John ii. [15.]] "Love not the world therefore, neither the things that are in the world;" but "be ye sober and watching in prayer, and above all things have fervent love amongst you." This is St Peter's exhortation in this place; wherein we learn our duty towards God, and our duty towards our neighbour. Towards God: "be sober, watch, and pray:" towards our neighbour: "have fervent charity."

8. There is an inward and an outward sobriety; "in- Inward sobriety.
ward sobriety," as Origen defineth, "is that whereby we
keep our affections and desires within lists, that no man
take more upon him than is meet, but every one according to the measure of his degree[1]." Which definition that
father seemeth to have drawn out of the words of St Paul:
"Let no man be more wise than behoveth him; but let Rom. xii. [3.]
every man be soberly minded." Angels, having too lofty
a conceit of themselves, were not able to keep their first
estate. Our first parents, for passing the limits of sobriety,
lost the godly possession which God had given into their
hands. Through an unsober desire of knowing all things,
they knew too soon their own misery. This haughtiness
of heart set Absalon so far besides himself, that neither
force of nature, fear of God, nor shame of men and the
world, could withhold him from traitorous attempting to
tear the crown from his father's head. It is strange to
see how Herod was swollen with the arrogant overweening
and proud conceit of his own eloquence. His strange blasphemous pride had a strange and fearful punishment. Na-
buchodonozor, through his affection being not content to
be the highest amongst men, was made the vilest among
beasts. Those are ugly patterns of monstrous minds, void
of that sobriety which was in Paul, who, although God
had exalted him to the third heaven, and there shewed
him more than a man might conceive, thought neverthe-
less modestly and meekly of himself. "I am the least of 1 Cor. xv. [9.]
the apostles, not worthy to be called an apostle." The like
affection was in St Peter: it caused him to loathe himself
at the sight of the majesty of the Son of God: "Depart Luke v. [8.]
from me (saith he), I am a sinful man." It was in that
centurion, which thought himself unworthy to open a door

[1 In his ergo omnibus Paulus nos vult "non plus sapere quàm oportet sapere, sed sapere ad sobrietatem:" quod in Græco dicitur σωφροσύνη, in nostris autem codicibus, hoc est, in scripturis divinis sobrietas à majoribus interpretatum est: ab aliis tamen eruditis viris temperantia ponitur: quæ temperantia una ex quatuor generalibus virtutibus habetur. Et in hoc ergo loco meliùs apostoli dicta lucerent, si haberemus et nos scriptum secundùm Græci sermonis virtutem, "sed sapere ad temperantiam:" hoc est, ut in omnibus vel quæ agimus, vel quæ loquimur, vel quæ sentimus, temperantiam teneamus.—Orig. Op. Par. 1759. In Epist. ad Rom. Lib. ix. Tom. iv. p. 647.—Ed.]

unto Christ Jesus. It was in the publican, that durst not cast so much as an eye up to heaven. Such again pass the bounds of this sobriety, as seek after needless things, neglecting necessary. The philosopher that gazed upon the skies, heeding not the pit that was under his feet, was deservedly laughed to scorn by a girl[1]. We are all tainted with this fault, whereby it cometh to pass, that we waste, saith Seneca, a great part of our life in doing nothing, a greater in doing evil, the greatest of all in meddling with those things which are not for us. They that in matters of religion will know more than God hath revealed, think not soberly, but arrogantly of themselves. Wo be to them which are wise in their own eyes! they are foolish in the sight of God. The root of this vice is a false persuasion which we have taken, that we can stand of ourselves. Wherefore the apostle putteth us in mind of our danger, unless we be supported by other manner strength, than by our own feeble faith. "I would not, brethren, that ye should be ignorant of this secret, lest you should be arrogant in yourselves." We bear not up ourselves: God doth bear up all; and each man is or should be a stay to bear up others. We are all members of one body; and we know we have need one of another. The hand cannot want[2] the help of the toe, though the least and lowest member. Man alone were a miserable creature: he could neither clothe, nor feed, nor defend himself from violence. The wisest man oftentimes needeth counsel. Who was more wise than Moses? yet Moses knew he needed the advice of others, and therefore, occasion serving, disdained it not. Rebecca saw more than Isaac in things nearly concerning their children Esau and Jacob; Sarah more than Abraham in the mother of Ismael. Naaman followed the counsel even of his servants; and it did not repent him so to have done.

Rom. xi. [25.]

9. Now, as this inward sobriety of mind and judgment is required, so are we exhorted likewise to an outward sobriety, which consisteth in diet, in apparel, in gesture, and in speech. Be sober in diet. Nature is contented with a little: but, where sobriety wanteth, nothing is

Outward sobriety in diet.

[[1] The story is told of Thales. Diog. Laert. Lib. i.—Ed.]
[[2] Want—do without.—Ed.]

enough. The body must have sufficient, lest it faint in the midst of necessary duties: but beware of gluttony and drunkenness. And Christ saith, "Take ye heed, overload not your hearts with these burthens of excess." Be not drunken with wine. [Luke xxi. 34.] These lessons are fit for England, where ancient sobriety hath given place to superfluity; where many such rich men are, as fare daintily day by day. God grant their end be not like his, who, riotously wasting here the creatures of God, wanted afterward a drop of water when he would gladly have had it! John Baptist was content with a simple diet, Christ with very slender fare; but there are of us, I fear me, whose god is their belly, and whose felicity is meat and drink. Our excess this way is intolerable and abominable: we strive to equal almost Vitellius, who had served unto him at one feast 2000 fishes, and 7000 birds; and Heliogabalus, that monster of the world, who at one supper was served with 600 ostriches. There is no bird that flieth, no fish that swimmeth, no beast that moveth, which is not buried in our bellies. This excess is an enemy both to wealth and health: it hath cut off much housekeeping, and brought many men to extreme beggary; and as many great diseases are cured by abstinence, so fulness hath been the cause of sundry strange and unwonted sicknesses. Aurelian the emperor did never send for physician in time of his sickness, but cured himself only by thin diet. And as immoderate feeding doth much hurt to the body, so it is more noisome to the mind. For as the ground, if it receive too much rain, is not watered, but drowned, and turneth into mire, which is neither fit for tillage nor for yielding of fruit; so our flesh, over-watered with wine, is not fit to admit the spiritual plough, or to bring forth the celestial fruits of righteousness. The herbs that grow about it will be loathsome and stinking weeds; as brawling, chiding, blasphemy, slander, perjury, hatred, manslaughter, and such like bad works of drunkenness and darkness. Are not these unsavoury fruits enough to make us abhor the tree? A drunken body is not a man, but a swine, fit for devils to enter into. For these sins are against nature, which, being moderately refreshed, is satisfied; being stuffed, is hurt, violated, and deformed. God hath given us his creatures soberly to use, and not so shamefully to abuse: we should, if we did well, feed the body to serve and not to rule, to obey, and not to lead, the spirit. "I chastise my body," saith St Paul, "and bring it into servitude." Is it not perilous, trow you, to pamper and make strong our adversary? or have we a greater or stronger enemy than our rebellious flesh? Full-bellied drunkards are no better than traitors in this spiritual war. Gedeon, a figure of Christ, would no other soldiers to fight against the Madianites, but such as stood and took up water in their hand, and licked it out: of such there were but 300 in number: the rest, that were afraid, or lay down to drink their fill, he sent away: they were not for his purpose. Such filled bellies were not fit to serve God, nor able to fight against the Madianites, Satan, and sin, God's, and God's people's enemies. The Israelites lusted after quails, but to their own confusion. Esau, for his belly sake, sold his birth-right and inheritance. Beware their examples. Lucullus, a Roman, had a servant always at his elbow, to pull him by the sleeve at such times as he poured in too fast. But we have the blessed apostle of Christ, the servant of God, to put us in mind of sobriety in diet. Nor in diet only, but also in attire.

1 Cor. ix. [27.]

Judges vii. [4—8.]

10. "A man's apparel, laughter, and gait, doth shew his nature." In apparel this is to be observed, that, avoiding vanity and pride therein, every man wear according to his calling. John Baptist ware a rough coat of camel's hair; but Solomon used rich and glorious apparel; and yet both used that which did become them. There is no more holiness in a friar's cowl, than in a shepherd's cloak: yet that is comely in one, which is not seemly in another. St Paul is very earnest with women, and requireth them to go in sober apparel, decking themselves "with shamefacedness and modesty, not with broidered hair, or with gold, or pearls, or sumptuous attire, but as becometh women that profess the fear of God." And St Peter telleth them, that their godly mother Sarah went soberly apparelled. Sarah was a good woman, a rich woman, and a noble woman: such as follow her footsteps need not be ashamed. Yet do I not condemn all other apparel: yea,

Sobriety in attire.
Ecclus. xix. [30.]

1 Tim. ii. [9, 10.]

even such apparel as is costly and gorgeous may be fit for some states and personages. I do not doubt but that Hester and Judith did wear gold, and were gorgeously decked. But if Paul and Peter did live in our days, they would not spare the vanity of our women, much less of our men. The vain and monstrous apparel of all other countries and nations England hath scraped together, and in a bravery put it on; the estimation whereof is this: a light wavering mind, matched with a vain proud heart, desireth a light, vain, strange, proud, and monstrous apparel, to cover and clad it withal. But sobriety is content with that which is seemly. Be sober in your apparel.

11. Be ye sober also in your speech and gesture. Be slow to speak; and when you speak, let your words be so seasoned, that they may be wholesome, and not offensive to the hearer. Let no lewd speech proceed from your mouths. A man's speech and gesture will bewray his thoughts. The talk of a fool is unsavoury altogether, and his gesture uncomely; but a wise man's understanding is seen even in his looks. A fool exalteth his voice in laughter; but the man that is soberly minded will scarcely smile to himself. He that is guiltless hideth not his face; but the murderer's head is in his bosom. Our outward actions are lively tokens of our inward disposition from which they proceed. Wherefore it greatly behoveth all estates and conditions of men, both inwardly in mind, and outwardly in diet, attire, speech, and gesture, to be sober. *Sobriety in speech and gesture.*

12. With sobriety St Peter joineth watchfulness. "Be sober and watching." I will not here recite unto you the manifold kinds of watching, whereof the scriptures make mention; but rather note a few unto you most necessary, and such as the apostle chiefly meaneth. Before we can watch, we must be wakened. Wherefore he saith, "Awake, thou that sleepest, and stand up from the dead; and Christ shall give thee light." He speaketh not of natural sleeping, but of a sleep which is in death. He that liveth in pleasures is dead being alive; and they that wake unto sin are asleep unto righteousness. All such as live in error, and lie in sin, are but dead men in the sight of God. Aristotle saith, that seven hours of sleep suffice naturally *Awaking out of error, superstition, and sin.* Eph. v. [14.]

the body. Let it suffice the souls of men to have slept in the lap of antichrist 700 years, and to have been rocked so long in the cradle of that deadly error. It is now high time to awake, and arise from the dreams of popery; for they are not sickly, but deadly. At the length, let Christ shine unto thee: the light of his gospel, if thou embrace it, will drive away the dark clouds of error and ignorance. Awake, I say, at the sound of God's word, from thy former superstition; and at length embrace the truth, which will be as a lantern, nay, as a bright shining star to guide thee unto Christ. St Paul speaketh to the elect of God, who, doubtless will at length awake. As for the reprobate, they still shall sleep on in their errors and sins, unto their eternal death and confusion. But "arise, Jerusalem, and be thou enlightened:" arise, Jerusalem, from death to life, from error to truth, from darkness to light, from antichrist to Christ, who by his Holy Spirit will illuminate thee, that thou mayest know God the Father, and him whom he hath sent, Jesus Christ, and that is the only way to everlasting life. Pliny, reproving our drowsiness, saith, that sleep doth steal away the half of our life. But this sleep whereof we speak stealeth away the whole life of the greatest part of men. David himself lay slumbering in the filthy sleep of whoredom a whole year at the least, and could not awake until Nathan blew in his ear and stirred him. But David's sleep was but a nap in comparison of such as are so hard and fast asleep, that they will never stir, until fire out of heaven flee about their ears to waken them. So were the Sodomites wakened and consumed. Awake therefore; and when ye are wakened, then watch.

Isai. lx. [1.]

Watching that we ourselves be not deceived by false teachers.

13. Watch, that ye be not deceived by false prophets, who watch to deceive you, and teach otherwise than Christ hath taught. The devil is a subtile persuader of men: he is a lying spirit in the mouth of his prophets: his ministers and workmen are crafty companions, such as creep into houses and lead away the simple as captives with them. A man of a watchful eye shall know these wolves by two properties. First, they are ravenous, cruel, bloody: they will persecute and kill: they will be as Cain, and not as Abel; as Ismael, and not as Isaac; as Esau, and not as

Jacob; as Pharaoh, and not as Moses; as Caiaphas, and not as Peter. The second note is that which Chrysostom mentioneth: "Whoso in blasphemy yelleth and howleth with a foul and open mouth against the truth, he is a wolf[1]." Such they were of whom the prophet speaketh in the psalm, saying, "They set their mouth against heaven."

Chrysost.
Psal. lxxiii. [9.]

14. All must watch, that they be not themselves deceived by these deceitful wolves when they put on sheep's clothing. But God giveth charge to such as be the pastors of his people, to be watchful also over others; not only carefully to feed them, as his flock dearly redeemed, in good and wholesome pastures, but also to drive and chase away the wolves, lest God's sheep be devoured by them. And this pastoral office doth not only pertain unto priests and preachers, but also unto princes and temporal governors, whom God hath placed in authority to that end that they should promote his glory. For the which cause God calleth Cyrus the king, his shepherd. *Vigilate:* "watch" the wolf to drive him away: watch the flock to feed it.

Watching that others be not deceived.
Isai. xliv. [28.]

15. Let every one be watchful over his life, that his conversation be according to his profession. If we walk disorderly, we shall not walk alone: our example will draw others after it; and their sins we shall answer for. Lucifer fell not alone: he drew company from heaven with him. Jeroboam, being sinful, made Israel to sin. And he is burned in the hand with that mark of horror, for a warning to all succeeding ages: "Jeroboam the son of Nebat, that made Israel to sin." Let us beware that we play not Simeon and Levi, and so make our father Jacob to be loathed of the Canaanites. We profess Christ and true Christianity: let us not through our lewd life be a slander to our Saviour, and a shame to his gospel. Watch therefore. But because, as St Paul saith, neither planting nor watering will help, except God himself do give increase; because our watching, as the prophet witnesseth, is in vain, neither can sobriety and heedfulness serve to keep a city, "except the Lord himself do keep it;" let

Watching over our lives.
2 Kings xiii. [2, 11.]
Praying. 1 Cor. iii [7.]
Psal. cxxvii. [1.]

[[1] Qui ergo secundum Deum vocem humilitatis et confessionis emittit, ovis est: qui vero adversus veritatem turpiter blasphemiis ululat contra Deum, lupus est.—Chrysost. Op. Par. 1724. Opus Imperf. in Matt. Hom. xix. Tom. vi. p. xciv.—ED.]

us crave help at God's merciful hands, and let us pray as well as watch. When St Paul hath armed God's soldier, [Eph. vi. 18.] he biddeth him "pray." Man, be he never so well appointed for defence, never so strong and perfit, cannot stand without God's strength. He that looketh but a little into the world, shall espy just cause to move us to prayer, if any men; now, if ever. The great devil in these our later days is let loose. Antichrist rageth and seeketh our confusion. The wicked glistering world marvellously deceiveth and bewitcheth. The flesh reigneth and beareth swing. The spirit is faint: sin overfloweth: Christ is coming in the clouds to call us unto judgment. Therefore "be ye sober, watch, and pray." Pray, I say, not in shew, but in deed; not in appearance, but from the heart; not for fashion, but in earnest. Babble not in words like hypocrites, but pour out thy heart before God, as did Hannah. And God grant, for his Christ our Jesus' sake, that in faith and love we may lift up pure hands, sincere affections, and hearty groans unto our Lord, that we may overcome our many and dreadful enemies, purchase pardon, and glorify God. Let us with David, with whom we have sinned, pray for mercy. Let us with the disciples of Christ, with whom we have wavered, pray for the increase of our faith, because the end of all things is now at hand.

The duty towards men, which St Peter inferreth upon his doctrine concerning the end of all things: have fervent charity. [Rom. xiii. 8.]

16. It followeth, "Have fervent charity amongst yourselves." This concerneth our duty towards men, as the other did towards God. All our duty towards our neighbour consisteth in love. "He that loveth another hath fulfilled the law." John, the beloved disciple of Christ, was the preacher of love: it was ever in his mouth, as it is in his writings; insomuch that, lying upon his death-bed, his disciples requesting to have one lesson from him before his departure, he was able to devise no one thing more needful to be spoken of, than this which he had often said: "Love one another, my little children." Peter would have our love to be earnest and hot. Every one loveth himself very vehemently; but our love towards others is very cold and chill. Our love for the most part this way is in word and in phrase, but not in deed and in truth. This world is double-hearted: dissembling is made a trade to live by. There be many Labans, but few Jacobs; many that salute

and say *ave*[1], but their next word is *apprehendite*[2]. If Christ came now, he were like to find little faith. but less charity: yet without charity all that we do is vain: yea it is very sin. Let us therefore love as God hath loved us: he loved us not slenderly, when he took so bitter a death for us: a God for his enemies. See therefore that ye have vehement, sincere, and hearty love among yourselves; not contenting yourselves barely to have it in shew, unless ye shew it by these effects which St Peter in this place setteth down. Vehement love here spoken of is described by these properties. First, it "covereth the multitude of sins:" secondly, it causeth us to be given to "hospitality:" thirdly, it will not suffer men to hide those graces which they have received at God's hands, but is a cause of bestowing the same to the use and benefit of their brethren. [Matt. xxvi. 48, 49.]

17. It is not our charity that can cover our sins from the sight of God. Christ is the propitiation for our sins. "It is I that blot out your iniquities," saith the Lord. But, as God's love to usward covereth our sins, so ours towards our brethren doth cover theirs. If God love us, his mercy is as a cloak that hideth all our shame: he seeth no blemish or deformity in us. If we love our brethren, our charity is as a veil before our eyes: we behold not their faults. Although they be great, we do not weigh them; although many, we reckon them not. For "charity covereth even the multitude of sins." The eye of the charitable man is always viewing his own wounds: as for the scars of other men, he seeth them not. His hand is always occupied, not in picking out motes from other men's eyes, but in drawing out beams from his own. St Augustine, to shew the great dislike he had of such as uncharitably delighted to unfold other men's faults, wrote these verses over his table: Charity hideth sins. [Isai. xliii. 25.]

Quisquis amat dictis absentum rodere vitam,
Hanc mensam vetitam noverit esse sibi[3]. Posidon. in vita August.

Whoso loveth to gnaw upon men in their absence,
Let him know that this table doth not like his presence.

[1 Hail.—ED.]
[2 Lay hold on him.—ED.]
[3 August. Op. Par. 1696. Tom. x. Appendix, col. 272.—ED.]

18. The next fruit of love is hospitality. "Be har-borous one toward another, without grudging." St Paul is of the same judgment; for having used this exhortation, "Let brotherly love continue," he immediately addeth: "Be not forgetful to lodge strangers." Hospitality hath respect unto all men, but chiefly to strangers, namely such as are of the household of faith, and are driven out of their country for the profession of Christ's gospel. Such are chiefly to be relieved. Of such especially it is written and provided for in the law: "The stranger that dwelleth with you shall be as one of yourselves, and thou shalt love him as thyself: for ye were strangers in the land of Egypt: I am the Lord your God." God hath offered us at this time great occasion to shew forth our charity. Many of God's good children are strangers in England. Let us not omit this good occasion to do good. Abraham and Lot were liberal towards strangers; and, when they supposed to have received men, they received angels to their great benefit. But we no doubt, in receiving these strangers which wander from place to place, being cast out of their countries for confessing and professing Christ, receive not angels, but the Lord of angels. "He that receiveth you receiveth me." In doing good to strangers, we do good also to ourselves: for great shall be the benefit when Christ shall say, "I was a stranger, and ye harboured me:" as great the curse to them to whom it shall be said, "I was harbourless, and ye did not lodge me." St Peter would have us given to hospitality without murmuring, and with kindness entertain strangers. For in shewing of benevolence there are three special virtues, which if they be wanting, our benefits lose their grace and goodness. The first is willingness: "God doth love a cheerful giver." The second is bountifulness: for "he that soweth sparingly shall reap sparingly." The third is singleness of heart: for if we give vain-gloriously to be seen of men, we lose our reward at God's hands, as by murmuring we deserve no thanks of men.

19. There be two grand enemies of hospitality. The one is covetousness, the other profuseness. Nigardliness would not suffer Nabal, that rich carl, to bestow a piece of bread to relieve the necessity of David a king. "Shall I take my bread and my water and the flesh of my beasts

that I have killed for my shearers, and give it to men whom I know not either who or whence they are?" Others, with the prodigal son, waste that unthriftily, wherewith they should relieve the poor and comfort strangers: some of them being eaten up, as they say, with three H. H. H. horses, hawks, and harlots; some with vain apparel, casting away as much upon a garment, as would almost ransom a king; some with building, some with banqueting; some by one mean, and some by another: whereby it is come to pass that hospitality itself is waxen a stranger, and needeth harbour: we have shut it quite and clean out of doors.

20. The last fruit of hearty love is the good bestowing of our graces and gifts to the benefit of others. "Let every man, as he hath received a gift, minister the same one to another, as good disposers of the manifold graces of God." The gifts that we have which be good, they be of God; for "every good gift cometh down from the Father of lights." And these gifts we receive to bestow upon others, as good stewards of the Lord. St Peter doth seem chiefly as it were to point unto two sorts of high and principal stewards, at whose hands an especial reckoning of the graces of God will be required; the magistrate and the minister. For God "leadeth his people like sheep by the hand of Moses and Aaron," whose gifts are the sword and the word: whereof the one may not be borne in vain, but drawn to the punishment of evildoers, and to the advancement of them that do well; the other is to be preached in season and out of season, to the confirmation of the truth, the refutation of error, the exhortation to virtue, the dissuasion from vice, that the man of God may be perfectly enabled to every good work. Howbeit, as magistrates and ministers are principally meant in this exhortation, so are all sexes and sorts of people called upon. For we shall all give an account of our stewardship: we must all make a reckoning of the talents we have received; be they five, two, or one. No man is born or brought up to himself, but to the benefit and behoof of another; and as stones in one building, or members in one body, so is every man interested and invested in the possession each one of another, to the end no man should seek his own things, but the things that make for the profiting of another. Which one lesson amongst many,

Charity communicateth every grace and gift of God unto others.

James i. [17.]

if once we would hear to learn it, and learn to remember it, and remember to follow it, and follow to continue and persevere in it, we should not only declare ourselves to be good dispensers of the manifold gifts and graces of God, but hear also that blessed voice, *Euge, serve bone et fidelis:* "Come, my good and faithful servant: I have set thee over a few small things, I will henceforth place thee over more and greater: come and enter into thy Master's joy:" whereunto he bring us, that so dearly bought it for us, even Jesus the price of our redemption: to whom, with the Father and the Holy Ghost, a Trinity in unity, be rendered all thanks, and all glory given from this time forth and for evermore. Amen.

[Matt. xxv. 21.]

THE ONE AND TWENTIETH SERMON.

A SERMON

PREACHED AT PAUL'S CROSS, AT WHAT TIME A MAIN TREASON[1] WAS DISCOVERED.

PSALM IV.

5. Offer the sacrifices of righteousness.

THE occasion why the princely prophet wrote this psalm is the great distress whereunto he was brought by the monstrous and unnatural rebellion, which his ambitious son Absolon raised against him. This forced him to fly unto God for aid, and by earnest prayer to seek help from heaven. The sum and substance of the psalm consisteth in these points. First, he crieth unto God for deliverance from this wicked conspiracy: "Hear me when I call, O God of my righteousness: thou hast set me at liberty when I was in distress: have mercy upon me, and hearken unto my prayer." Secondly, he reproveth the wicked enterprise of his foes, and therewithal moveth them to repentance: "O ye sons of men, how long will ye turn my glory into shame, loving vanity and seeking lies? For be ye sure that the Lord hath chosen to himself a godly man: the Lord will hear when I call unto him: tremble, and sin not: examine your own heart upon your bed, and be still: offer the sacrifices of righteousness, and trust in the Lord." Thirdly, as one assured of present help, he turneth his talk again unto God, and rejoiceth in the sweet and comfortable feeling of his grace, saying, "Many say, Who will shew us any good? but, Lord, lift up the light of thy countenance upon us: thou hast given me more joy of heart than they have had when their wheat and their wine did abound: I will lay me down, and also sleep in peace; for thou, Lord, only makest me dwell in safety."

The occasion and parts of the psalm.

[1 The conspiracy of Babington and Ballard in 1585.—ED.]

The prophet allegeth his innocency and righteousness.

2. The prophet, in calling upon the name of God, maketh mention of his own innocency: "Hear me when I call, O God of my righteousness." Not that he thought himself so just and righteous, that God could not charge him with any sin; for so no man can try his cause and stand in judgment with God: which thing he also confess- [Psal. cxliii. 2.] eth, saying in another place, "Enter not into judgment with thy servant; for in thy sight shall no flesh living be justified." For one duty scarce performed, he is able to charge us with a thousand omitted; nay, we cannot allege him one for a thousand. Why then doth the prophet speak of innocency? Why doth he use this phrase of speech: "Hear me, O God of my righteousness"? Surely he knew that God is a merciful defender of them whom the world doth undeservedly hate and persecute. And in respect of his enemies, for any cause which they had so to conspire and rebel against him, he might justly and truly even in the sight of God protest himself to be innocent. He was a merciful and a just prince, never offering wrong to any: his rebellious son he had sundry times spared, but never offended: he never grieved his wicked counsellor Achitophel, neither yet the raging people which unnaturally opposed themselves against him. In respect hereof he allegeth his righteousness and innocency, his heart being a witness unto him that towards them he had ever shewed himself mild and merciful.

He maketh mention of God's wonted mercies towards him.

3. The prophet, having thus professed his uprightness, urgeth and provoketh God to take the defence of his cause now, as at all times he had heretofore protected him: "Thou hast set me at liberty when I was in distress." David passed through many troubles; but God delivered him out of all. He strengthened him against that huge and monstrous Philistine, far beyond the reason or expectation of man. For, if ye compare a youngling with one of perfect age, a simple shepherd with a soldier exercised in feats of arms, one of small stature with a vast giant, a naked man with one most strongly armed, the combat could not choose but seem in all points very unequal, insomuch that the Philistine plainly contemned him. But God fought for him, and gave him the victory. Besides this, he delivered him also from the fraud and treachery of wicked Doeg, from

the treason of the men of Caila[1] and Ziph, which laboured to give him into his enemies' hands. God delivered him from Achis king of Geth, where he was in great danger. How often, and by what miraculous means he saved him out of the hands of Saul, the histories do manifestly and plainly shew. Therefore he putteth God in remembrance of this his wonted mercy. God is well pleased when his benefits are well remembered. Upon this experience of God's former mercies he conceiveth great confidence and sure hope, that his protector would not leave him now in the briars; that the God of whose mercy he had so often tasted, seeing that his cause was just, would not now leave him as a prey to his enemies, neither suffer them to trample over him.

4. Thus we see, that the security of princes doth not rest upon their power, be they never so strongly guarded, but upon their innocency: we see from whence they ought in their troubles to look for succour: we see by what means they may assure themselves of help from heaven. In the second part of the psalm the prophet reporteth the rebellion of his foes, and withal moveth them to repentance. He reproveth them especially for two causes; first, for that they laboured to displace the prince whom God had set over them, wherein the ignominy which they did unto him was not so great as the injury which they offered unto God. *He reproveth those which conspired against him.*

5. The contrivers thereof were not men of mean calling, but of high place and great authority; and therefore they are not called the sons of Adam, but the "sons of man," *filii viri*, noble personages. Conspiracies are not wont to be bred in the heads of the meanest sort: which thing the prophet noteth in the second psalm: "The princes [Psal. ii. 2.] are assembled together in counsel against the Lord, and against his Christ." Mary, the very sister of Moses, a woman of place and countenance, devised a plot to displace her brother. Moses spared her because she was his sister; but God plagued her because she was a rebel, and cast upon her a most foul disease. Core, Dathan, and Abiram, which conspired also against Moses, were not the meanest men in their tribe. Jeroboam, a man of great might, conspired *What kind of men they were which conspired.*

[¹ Caila—Keilah.—ED.]

against Solomon, and openly rebelled against Roboam. The king's son Absolon, the great wise counsellor Achitophel, rose up against their lawful sovereign, and armed the people against him. If I should enter into profane histories, and recite unto you the authors and contrivers of civil seditions from time to time, it would appear that they were for the most part *filii viri*. It is sometime otherwise. For we read that simple men, that men whose names are not spoken of without some special note of extreme baseness, have notwithstanding stirred up dangerous tumults. But such are either set on by other of greater calling, or else, as heedless men, they soon vanish and come to nothing. But if potent and mighty persons attempt the overthrow of a state, except they be discovered and cut off at the first, they overwhelm all like a main sea. God therefore commanded Moses especially to punish the princes of the people, as the chief authors of all evil. "Take all the *heads* of the people: hang *them* up before the Lord." It is not safe to think of mercy, when the mighty have determined to cast down them whom God hath set up, to displace whom he hath settled, to bring into ignominy whom he hath advanced to the seat of honour.

[Num. xxv. 4.]

Their continuance in their wicked purpose.

6. The continuance of these wicked ones in their traitorous purpose sheweth both their cankered and incorrigible malice, and also the patience and long-suffering of that good king. Wherefore he saith, "O ye sons of man, how long?" Such malice they conceived, such desire they had to advance themselves, so greedy they were of government, and to bear the whole swing, that they ceased not, they gave not over. Men easily stay themselves from proceeding in good things, but hardly are drawn from performing evil. This property the Lord did note in them which sought to make themselves famous by building a tower as high as heaven. "Behold," saith the Lord, "this they begin to do; neither can they now be stopped from whatsoever they have imagined to bring to pass." But God defeated that purpose by dividing their language. Such as love to climb aloft, to build in the skies, to make their dwellingplace amongst the stars, will never stay till God cast them down.

[Gen. xi. 6.]

Their cunning practices against the Lord's anointed.

7. "Ye sons of man, how long?" This rebellion rose

not upon a sudden rage: it was with much consultation first contrived, and so continued from time to time. After Absolon had imbrued his hands in blood, after he had cowardly slain his brother, after his heart was inured with so great and grievous sins, he stayed at nothing, but went on adding blood unto blood. If moderate severity could have bettered him, he was driven out from his father's presence: if unspeakable clemency could have caused him to relent, his murder was pardoned, he called home, and received into favour. But his cankered heart could never be scoured. It is true which the wise man saith, "There is no trusting of a new reconciled enemy." Being now in favour in the court, he sought all means to wreak his wrath, and by conspiracy to compass the kingdom. First, he laboured to win the favour of the people: he was gentle and humble to every one, so courteous that he kissed them: he lamented that they were not well entreated, that their causes were not indifferently heard, that they were oppressed with grants from the king, wherein private men's gain was sought, and the commonwealth much hindered: he wished the public benefit were better considered of. By these means he stole away the hearts of the people; he became popular, and was thought a great good commonwealthsman: if any thing fell out well, he was reputed the only author and occasioner of it. Touching religion, because it was generally well liked, therefore he neglected no occasion wherein he might make any plausible shew of a mind most religiously inclined. He asked leave of his father to go to Hebron, there to pay his vow and to sacrifice unto God. This holy hypocrite would hide his treason under the cloak of religion. While he pretended the serving of God according to the law, he minded a lawless rebellion against God and his anointed, most unnaturally conspiring against his dear father. Many of the nobles, suspecting no treason, liked well of him, honoured him as chief next to king David, and accompanied him to Hebron, the chief city. In the mean while, he sent closely abroad his secret messengers, his sworn men whom he trusted best, in every coast at one certain day and hour to proclaim him king; and the same day, by the subtile advice of crafty Achitophel, who

[Ecclus. xii. 10, 11.]

was grandfather to Bersabe[1], and therefore hated David, he was proclaimed in Hebron. Behold this holy traitor, who chose rather to worship the rising than the setting sun! Achitophel giveth shrewd counsel forthwith to apprehend the king, and to surprise the city with all the treasure, artillery, and other munitions of war that were therein. This counsel was dangerous to king David: howbeit, he being but fainthearted, that purpose was altered. He looked for greater strength both foreign and at home: in the mean time, his counsel was disclosed, and the king by the providence of God delivered. Achitophel for sorrow went home and died: he hanged himself. Treason will not be cured till traitors be extinguished: this hydra hath many heads: if you cut off one, more will start up, unless the neck be seared. The Pharisees and scribes, with the Herodians, never ceased till they brought our Saviour unto his cross. The pope, with that serpentine generation, will never be pacified, but still practise against the Lord and against his anointed. The froward rebellious Israelites could not rest till Samuel was taken from them. It is the nature of the wicked, the longer they continue in sin, the less to be weary of it: they have no sooner brought one thing to pass, but immediately they devise another: there is no end of their malice; and therefore the king asketh, "How long?"

The king's patience.

8. The wonderful patience of the good king in bearing with these rebels, whose former faults he had often winked at and sundry times pardoned, did them no good: his lenity was abused, neither were such men so to be dealt with: it is not the way to seek by benefits to reclaim men so grounded and settled in evil. The obdurate heart of Pharaoh will never be mollified. Tigers will not be tamed: it is almost impossible that one, which hath drunk of the cup of that harlot, should retain in his heart any drop of loyal blood, or any part of a sound and faithful meaning towards such as are not of their own mark, what courtesy or kindness soever be shewed them.

All their devices were but vanity.

9. But the prophet goeth on condemning their madness, forasmuch as the thing which they devised was but

[1 Bersabe—Bathsheba.—Ed.]

"vanity." They might soothe themselves in their purpose for a time; but he sheweth that in the end it should deceive them, as a man is deceived that putteth his trust in a lie. "How long will you turn my glory into shame, loving vanity, and seeking lies?" They pleased themselves in their subtile inventions, devices, and counsels, not considering that there is no device, no counsel, that can prevail against the Lord. The prophet knew that he which dwelleth in heaven did laugh and had them in derision; that he would make Achitophel to snare himself in his own devices; that he would take them in the pit which they had digged for others. This he knew; and this he willeth them also to know, that whom the Lord hath set up he will maintain and defend. "Be ye sure that the Lord hath chosen to himself a godly man: the Lord will hear when I call unto him." The consideration hereof (if we weigh it as we should) may give us courage and strength against that man of blood, which at this day doth so cruelly persecute the professors of the gospel, and so proudly take upon him to depose christian princes and to place hypocrites in their rooms at his pleasure. Let him also know, that the Lord hath chosen to himself godly men: the Lord will hear when they call upon him: he that toucheth them toucheth even the apple of the Lord's own eye. Let him tremble that lifteth but a finger against them.

10. *Contremiscite:* "Be afraid" to set yourselves against God and your prince, to attempt such an overthrow to the common state. Cease from conspiracy: leave your treacherous devices: be not deceived, you cannot prevail: you do but work your own confusion: call yourselves to a reckoning betimes: have some quiet and sober consideration of your doings: when you are in your beds free from all trouble, then commune with your own hearts, weigh the cause that you take in hand. I am your prince, God hath placed me over you: ye are my subjects, God hath so placed you: you should love me, and not seek my shame and subversion: ye owe me obedience and not rebellion, honour and not treason. What occasion have I given you thus to set yourselves against me? I have dealt righteously and graciously with you: I have been merciful, not cruel over you:

They are exhorted to relent and change their minds, to offer the sacrifice of righteousness unto God.

I have sought your safety more than mine own. But whom would ye have to reign over you? A false worshipper, an hypocrite, a murderer of his own brother, an incestuous fornicator, one that will flatter you and deceive you, swear and not perform. Consider these things, weigh what wickedness you have taken in hand, and be quiet, "be still." Cease from rebellion, and obey peaceably the prince whom God hath placed over you. So long as ye continue in the hardness of your hearts, though you offer him all the beasts upon a thousand hills, it is all in vain. Repent, and "offer up the sacrifices of righteousness." The Israelites, when they had sinned, were wont to offer sacrifice to pacify God, as appeareth in the law. But for the most part this was done without feeling of their sin, without true repentance, formally, and for fashion sake only. But outward service, without inward remorse and repentance for sin, God doth abhor. The rebel Absolon offered sacrifice in Hebron; but in vain, because his heart was full of treason. Antichrist reneweth his oblations every day; but to what purpose, so long as he mindeth murder, stirreth rebellion, and maliciously persecuteth the spouse of Christ? " Sacrifice the sacrifices of righteousness:" offer God repentance for your former faults; and "put your trust in the Lord." Thus we see by what occasion the prophet uttereth these words, which I have chosen to speak of at this time.

<small>Levit. iv.</small>

<small>Sacrificing usual in all ages.</small>

11. To offer up sacrifices it hath been usual in all ages, amongst all people, kindreds, and nations of the earth. But I will only speak of such as the people of God have offered up. Before the law, Abel, Abraham, Jacob, Job, and others; in the time of the law, Aaron with the Levites presented offerings before the Lord. In the time of the gospel the apostles had, and at this day also Christians have, their sacrifices, which, being faithfully offered, are graciously accepted in the sight of God.

<small>Sacrifice God requireth.</small>

12. Sacrificing is a voluntary action, whereby we worship God, offering him somewhat in token that we acknowledge him to be the Lord, and ourselves his ser‑

<small>1 Pet. ii. [5.]</small> vants. "Ye are made," saith St Peter, "an holy priesthood, to offer up spiritual sacrifices acceptable to God by Jesus Christ." God therefore doth require this duty at our hands. It was commanded in the law: the prophet

David calleth for it; and St Peter teacheth that even now it is also due unto God from men.

13. Let us now consider who are priests to offer up these sacrifices. For there can be no sacrifice without a priest, as there can be no priest where there is no sacrifice. In the scriptures I find a threefold priesthood allowed of God; a Levitical priesthood, such as that of Aaron and his sons; a royal priesthood, figured in Melchisedeck, and verified in Christ; a spiritual priesthood, belonging generally to all Christians. The Levitical priesthood continued unto Christ, then ceased. For being a figure of the truth which was to come, the truth being come, it could no longer continue. Neither is there in the royal priesthood of Melchisedeck any other that hath succeeded, but only Christ. He is "a priest for ever according to the order of Melchisedeck," a king and a priest, a God and a man, perfect, innocent, undefiled, unspotted, severed from sinners; yet numbered, punished, plagued with the wicked; humbled to the depth, and exalted far above the highest heavens; without beginning, without end, without father as man, without mother as God. The third priesthood is that which is common to all Christians: for "he hath made us kings and priests unto God his Father." [Rev. i. 6.] Where the popish priesthood taketh footing, in what ground the foundation thereof is laid, I cannot find in the scriptures. Antichrist is the author of that priesthood: to him they sacrifice, him they serve.

The priests by whom sacrifice is to be offered.

14. What sacrifices Aaron did offer up, and what sacrifice Christ hath presented to his Father, we all know. It followeth now to be considered, what kind of sacrifice we must offer. Aaron offered sacrifice, which could not in itself be accepted of God, nor take away the sins of them for whom it was offered. For whether they be offerings of thanksgiving, they were not of that value that God should take delight and pleasure in them; or sin-offerings, "it is impossible that the blood of bulls and goats should take away sin"—impossible. But the Priest according to the order of Melchisedeck hath offered the sacrifice of his own flesh, acceptable even for the worthiness of it, and by the virtue which is in it forcible and more than sufficient to wash away all sin. This he did willingly: "He made him- [Isai. liii. [10.]]

The sacrifice which Aaron offered, the sacrifice of Christ, and our sacrifice.

[Heb. x. 4.]

self an offering for sin." He did it perfectly: "With one offering he consecrated for ever them that are sanctified." Where full remission of sin is, there needeth no further sacrifice for sin; and the Holy Ghost beareth us record that we have full remission of all our sins: "Their sins and iniquities will I remember no more." We are healed with his stripes; and where there is no sore, there needs, no salve. Not that we have no sin; but, acknowledging that we have it, it is as if we had it not, because he is faithful to forgive it, and just to cleanse us from it. "The blood of Jesus cleanseth us *from all sin;*" the blood of Jesus once shed, the offering of the body of Jesus Christ *once.* So that there remaineth no other sacrifice to be daily offered, but the sacrifice of "righteousness," which we must all offer.

The sacrifice of the minister.

15. At the hands of the minister it is required that he feed the flock committed unto his charge: this is righteousness in him, it is his sacrifice. God will have no blind, no lame, no unclean thing to be offered: therefore let as many as offer the sacrifice of righteousness take heed to that they do. "The words of the Lord are *pure* words, like silver tried in a furnace of earth fined seven times." He therefore that speaketh, "let him speak as the words of God."

The maintenance of the minister to offer sacrifice.

16. Furthermore, as it is reason that they which sacrifice at the altar should live of the altar, even so it is against all equity and right, that the labour of preaching the gospel should rest upon any man's back, and the maintenance due for the same be withheld and kept from him. It hath been told you often, and some have been angry to hear it so often told, that the ministry is too much pinched, the living of the church so fleeced, that many worthy ministers have scarce, nay, they have not wherewith tolerably to sustain themselves.

The sacrifice of the magistrate.

17. To come from the minister to the magistrate, when heinous crimes are detected and brought to light, there is then a special sacrifice of righteousness required at his hands; such a sacrifice as Joas offered, who, following the good advice of Jehoida the high priest his faithful counsellor, put Athalia, which had murdered the king's children and usurped the kingdom, to the sword. The Lord some-

time doth so deal with his people, that they plainly see his wrath to be kindled, and his heavy indignation impossible to be appeased, till this sacrifice be offered him. The Israelites were overthrown in battle, till Achan was stoned to death. King David found no rest in his kingdom, till Absolon and Adonias had that which their rebellious practices did deserve. God requireth as well the sacrifice of justice, as of mercy: yea, he sometimes accepteth justice for a sacrifice, and plagueth mercy as a grievous sin. If David had not spared his son for murder, his son had not troubled him with rebellion. For rebellion he would also in fatherly pity and compassion have spared him: this God could not suffer, but took execution of justice himself, stretched out the arm of an oak, and strangled the gallant in his own hair. Saul suffered Agag: but he felt the wrath of the Lord for it to the loss of his kingdom. *Qui parcit lupo mactat gregem:* "He that spareth a wolf spilleth the blood of the flock," saith Chrysostom. God appointeth the magistrate to be "a revenger unto *wrath* upon him that committeth evil." They which glory to have the sword rusty in the sheath, when they would draw it out, peradventure shall not so well be able. Let magistrates therefore, from the highest to the lowest, execute justice without fear or favour when need requireth, and so they shall offer up the sacrifice of righteousness. [Josh. vii.] [Chrysost.] [Rom. xiii. [4.]]

18. As this sacrifice belongeth peculiarly to them, so there are others belonging, although to them, yet not to them alone, but to all Christians. We must all sacrifice unto the Lord with our goods, with our minds, and with our bodies. For all these we have received to serve him withal. With our goods the needy must be relieved, the naked clothed, the hungry comforted and fed. For this sacrifice St Paul commendeth to the Philippians: "I was even filled after that I had received of Epaphroditus that which came from you, an odour that smelleth sweet, a sacrifice acceptable and pleasant unto God." The like he hath also to the Hebrews: "To do good and to distribute forget not; for with such sacrifice God is pleased." [The sacrifice of all Christians offering their goods.] [Phil. iv. [18.]] [Heb. xiii. [16.]]

19. To have the sacrifice of the body offered, St Paul is very earnest with the Romans: "I beseech you, brethren, by the mercies of God, that ye give up your bodies [Their bodies.] [Rom. xii. 1.]

a living sacrifice, holy and acceptable unto God." "Let not thine eye behold the thing which is evil, and it is made a sacrifice: let no unclean word escape thy tongue, and it is an offering: let thine hand do no harm, and it is an oblation[1];" saith St Chrysostom. To the like effect Origen: "When thou subduest pride, thou dost offer a calf; when wrath, a ram; when lust, a goat; a dove, when a vain and wandering cogitation[2]." But the most precious sacrifice of the body is, when being mortified it is also offered to the cross for the testimony of Jesus Christ, in whose cause the death of the saints is dear in the sight of God. If the prophets, the apostles, the martyrs of all ages, have offered up the glorious sacrifice of righteousness, why should we be accounted faithful as they were, unless we be willing to do and to suffer as they did? We have a long time had fair weather: wisdom would that we should provide for storms. Christ's church must be tried: such is God's wont. A rough storm was rising; but the Lord (such are his mercies) raised up a wind which scattered the clouds: he hath in great favour and tender love delivered us from the lion's mouth: let us therefore live no longer in this our senseless security, but offer him sacrifice, as of our bodies, so likewise of our minds, repentance and praise.

Their souls in repentance.

20. Our sins no doubt have provoked his wrath: our ingratitude hath grieved him: our iniquities have kindled his indignation: we have grievously offended by despising his word, from the highest to the lowest. The magistrates are for the most part cold in God's cause: they are not eaten up with the zeal of his house: justice and judgment

[1 Καὶ πῶς ἂν γένοιτο τὸ σῶμά, φησι, θυσία; μηδὲν ὀφθαλμὸς πονηρὸν βλεπέτω, καὶ γέγονε θυσία. μηδὲν ἡ γλῶσσα λαλείτω αἰσχρὸν, καὶ γέγονε προσφορά. μηδὲν ἡ χεὶρ πραττέτω παράνομον, καὶ γέγονεν ὁλοκαύτωμα.—Chrysost. Op. Par. 1731. In Epist. ad Rom. Hom. xx. Tom. ix. p. 656.—ED.]

[2 Cum in librum Levitici aliqua diceremus, pro viribus explanare tentavimus quomodo unusquisque rationabili obsequio cultus Dei, si superbiam corporis sui vincat, immolet vitulum; si iracundiam superet, arietem jugulet; si libidinem vincat, in holocaustum offerat hircum; si vagos et lubricos cogitationum resecet volatus, columbas et turtures immolet.—Orig. Op. Par. 1759. In Epist. ad Rom. Lib. ix. Tom. iv. p. 643.— The passage to which Origen here refers as treating the same matter more at large will be found In Levit. Hom. ii. Tom. ii. p. 195.—ED.]

they commonly omit, and wickedly pervert. The guides and pastors of the church seek themselves, and not those things which belong to Jesus Christ. And the people, not well guided nor severely corrected, are of all other farthest out of frame. Now, if the Most High have power over the kingdom of men, to give it to whomsoever he will, and to appoint over it most vile persons when pleaseth him; and if, because of our unrighteous dealing, he should (as he hath done many a time and oft unto nations far greater and mightier than ours) pour us as it were out of one vessel into another, translate the sceptre of this kingdom from hand to hand, instead of a gracious and religious lady cause an hypocrite to reign over us, (which the Lord never suffer these eyes to see!) what could we say, but God were just in all his ways, and had brought that upon us which our sins have deserved? To appease his wrath, and to stay these or the like plagues from breaking in and from overwhelming the land, there is no other way but speedily to offer up the sacrifice of righteousness. This is the sacrifice of righteousness, even a broken and a contrite heart. [Dan. iv. [25.]]

21. The other sacrifice of the mind is praise; which consisteth in thanksgiving and petition. Let us thank our God for his manifold mercies. For "it is the Lord's mercies that we are not consumed; because his compassions fail not, but are renewed every morning: great is his faithfulness." Being mindful therefore of these his mercies, let us as thankful servants offer unto this our merciful God this sacrifice of righteousness, never ceasing to magnify and praise his name. O Lord, we acknowledge this to be thy work, without any merit or desert of ours. We bless thee, we praise thee, we thank thee for it: accept, O Lord, this our service and sacrifice in thy great mercy. [In thanksgiving. Lament. iii. [22, 23.]]

22. The second part of this our sacrifice of praise is to pour out requests and supplications. Let us herein with humble and penitent hearts, with sure trust that God will hear us out of heaven, crave at his merciful hands the deliverance of his anointed, our sovereign lady, out of all distress, from the rebellion of Absolon, from the counsel of Achitophel, from the rage and fury of all that conspire to do her harm. Thou knowest, O Lord, that [In making prayers and supplications.]

she hath not deserved this treachery at their hands, being most mild and merciful, doing good unto all, hurting none. Therefore, O Lord, according to thy merciful wont, as thou hast done hitherto, so deliver, protect, and defend her still: finish that which thou hast most graciously begun: bridle, O Lord, her enemies and ours: let them know their madness: open their eyes and cause them plainly to see, that they cannot prevail against thy chosen servant, that they cannot cast down or bring into ignominy her whom thou hast set up and placed in honour. Give grace, O Lord, if it be thy good pleasure, that they may enter into themselves, examine their own hearts, see their sin, repent them of their wickedness, abstain from farther proceeding, that thou in thy mercy mayest shew them grace and favour in the end. And grant, O Lord, that we which profess thy holy name may still offer unto thee the sacrifice which thou requirest, even the sacrifice of righteousness, that the minister of thy word may sincerely and diligently preach thy gospel; that being a good example to the flock, and leading a godly and an upright life, he may bring thee the offerings of many souls, unto the stretching out of thy glorious kingdom amongst men. Grant that princes and magistrates, whom thou hast set in authority, may without fear or favour offer also this sacrifice in upright deciding of controversed causes, and severe punishing of malefactors. Finally, give this grace, O Lord, we beseech thee, to thy whole flock (for we are thy flock, the sheep of thy pasture), that we all may offer unto thee our goods, our bodies, and our souls; for they are thine. Grant that we may liberally bestow our goods to the needful relief of thy poor saints; that we may mortify our bodies, and cheerfully offer them, if need so require, to any kind of torment for thy sake; that in soul we may offer thee the sacrifice of true repentance for our sins, of hearty thanks for thy great grace, and of earnest suit for continuance of thy mercy and favour towards us. We humbly beseech thee, O Father, for the merits of thy dear Son, upon whom (as upon our altar) we offer up all our sacrifice, bow down thy merciful ear to our petitions: extend thy mercies to thy little flock: preserve our gracious queen; and so direct the hearts of all which bear authority under her, that by their good government we may lead a peaceable and a quiet life in all godliness and honesty. To thee, O merciful Father, with thy Son Christ Jesus our only Redeemer, and that blessed Spirit our sweet Comforter, three Persons and one God, be all honour and praise both now and ever.

THE TWO AND TWENTIETH SERMON.

A SERMON

PREACHED AT PAUL'S CROSS, AT HIS REMOVING TO YORK.

2 Cor. XIII.

11. *For the rest, brethren, fare ye well: be perfit, be of good comfort, be of one mind, live in peace; and the God of love and peace shall be with you.*

<small>St Paul's farewell to the Corinthians.</small>   AFTER that our apostle St Paul, as a faithful teacher, a wise steward, a loving father, a vigilant watchman, a diligent labourer, a severe punisher of all sin, had with a good conscience painfully travailed a long time with the famous city of Corinth; omitting no part of apostolical duty; opening unto them all the mysteries of Christ, the whole counsel of God, all the secrets of his truth; at the length by the goodwill and calling of God being elsewhere appointed to preach the gospel, he forgetteth them not in the time of his absence, but as by word afore, so still by writing endeavoureth to lead them on. Wherefore, being now to make an end both of speaking and writing unto them, he most lovingly taketh his leave, and with his farewell giveth them this sweet exhortation: "Be perfit, be of good comfort, be of one mind, live in peace; and the God of love and peace shall be with you."

<small>The same applied to the present occasion.</small>   2. My present case is not much unlike, although I myself be most unlike; for happy were he that might follow so blessed a guide, though it were with far unequal paces. The city is like, the people are like, my departure from you is like; but the performing of my office amongst you, I must confess, hath been much unlike. And good cause why: for God alike hath not bestowed his gracious gifts. Yet my conscience beareth me record, I have en-

deavoured to tread in the same steps. And in doctrine, which is the chiefest point, I dare affirm even the same which the holy apostle doth, I have delivered no other unto you than that which I have received of the Lord: yea, safely in the sight of the most high God, I may say with him, you have received of us "not the word of men, but, as it was indeed, the word of God." In distribution whereof, neither have I used flattery, as you know; neither coloured covetousness, the Lord will testify; neither have I sought mine own praise, my heart is witness. And this testimony of conscience that I have dealt sincerely in the house of God, as touching doctrine, hath been my great relief and comfort in all the stormy troubles which by the mighty assistance of almighty God I have waded through. Concerning diligence in the execution of mine office, although I have had a ready will, yet my weak body being not answerable to my desire, as all flesh herein is faulty, so for my part I must plead guilty. One debt and duty with St Paul I protest I have truly paid you; for with a tender affection I have loved you. The nurse was never more willing to give the breast unto her child, than I have been that you should suck, not only milk, but also blood from me, if it might stand you in stead, or serve to your safety. God he knoweth that with this love I have loved you. In using correction I have sought reformation, and not revenge: to punish hath been a punishment to myself: I never did it but with great grief: I have always laboured rather by persuasion to reclaim transgressors, than by correction: with which kind of dealing because stubborn minds will not be bowed, my softness, I grant, hath rather deserved reproof than praise. My life and conversation amongst you I leave wholly to your secret judgments. I cannot say (for who can?) that my heart is clear. If "in many things we offend all," how can any man say he is no sinner, except he say also that God is a liar? Howbeit, this the God of my righteousness knoweth, that wittingly and willingly I have wronged no man: if I have, *reddam quadruplum*, "I will render four times" so much good. If any have wronged me, I heartily forgive, and will forget it for ever. While I live, I will acknowledge that I have received more good liking, favour, and friendship at your hands, than

1 Cor. xi. [23.]

1 Thess. ii. [13.]

James iii. [2.]

I could either look for or deserve. God no doubt hath his people, he hath many a dear child in this city. But now that by his providence, not by my procurement, I am called from hence, to serve elsewhere in the church of Christ, I will with St Paul take my leave of you; and that the more willingly, as well because it is God's good will and appointment, as also for that I trust the change shall be good and profitable unto you. My hope is, that the Lord hath provided one of choice to be placed over you; a man to undertake this great charge so well enabled for strength, courage, gravity, wisdom, skill in government, knowledge, as in many other things, so especially in the heavenly mysteries of God, that I doubt not but my departure shall turn very much to your advantage: amongst whom sith a great part of my life is now spent, and a few evil days do remain otherwhere to be bestowed, I must use the words of the blessed apostle: "For that which remaineth, my brethren, fare ye well:" my dear and faithful flock, farewell: my crown and my joy, farewell: again (with grief I speak it) farewell. I must in body go from you, yet in heart and good will I shall ever be with you: you shall ever be most dear unto me, and I shall not cease (God forbid I should!) to pour out my prayers before the Almighty in your behalf, that the great Shepherd of the sheep of the Lord Jesus Christ may take charge of you, and by his Holy Spirit direct and govern you in all your ways. In like sort, I most heartily crave at your hands, that ye be not unmindful to pray also for me, that I may walk worthily in my calling, and fulfil the ministry which I have received; that God may open unto me the door of utterance, to speak the mysteries of Christ as becometh me to speak; that I may in faith and boldness do his message; that he may deliver me from the disobedient, and that my service may be accepted of the saints; that the word of the Lord may have his free passage, and that I may finish the residue of my course in the gospel of Christ to the glory of God and profit of the church.

An exhortation to perfection.

3. And now, brethren, for my last and long farewell, I can use no fitter words of exhortation than these are: "Be perfect, have consolation, be of one mind, live in peace; and the God of charity and peace shall be with

you." Two special things there are comprised in these words, an exhortation and a promise. We are exhorted to be perfect, to be of good comfort, to live in unity and peace; and we are promised that, so doing, the God of love and peace shall remain with us. The first part of the exhortation is as it were the root and fountain of the second, and the second likewise of the last. For perfection breedeth comfort, and comfort causeth peace. But let us particularly consider of every branch of the exhortation. "Be perfect."

4. Integrity or perfection is of two sorts: the one is divine, the other human. That which pertaineth unto God is absolute: that which is of men is not without defect. In God there is full and absolute perfection. "Your heavenly Father is perfect," saith our Saviour: so perfect, that there is not so much as any shadow of imperfection at all in him. "He is light," perfect light, "there is no darkness in him." He is the fountain from whence all perfection floweth: "every perfect gift is from above." "He which planted the ear, shall not he hear? he that formed the eye, shall not he see? he that teacheth man knowledge, shall not he understand?" saith the prophet. "Shall I cause to bring forth, and shall I be barren?" saith the Lord. He cannot but be perfect in himself, which is the cause of all perfection in others. *Perfection in God.* *Matt. v. [48.]* *1 John i. [5.]* *James i. [17.]* *Psal. xciv. [9, 10.]* *Isai. lxvi. [9.]*

5. And as he is perfect, so all things are perfect which are his. His law is perfect, and maketh them perfect which fulfil it. "O that my ways were directed according to thy statutes: then should I not be confounded," saith the prophet. His commandments are "holy, and just, and good." *Scimus quia bona est lex:* the goodness and perfection of it is apparent, clear, and manifest: "We know the law is good." But St Paul seemeth to charge the law with imperfections. "The law," saith he, "brought nothing unto perfection." It is true that the law in itself is perfect, able to save and make perfit all such as are able perfitly to observe it. For what saith the law? "Do this, and thou shalt live." Yet no man liveth by the law: why so? Because the law is unperfit? God forbid. The cause then, why being perfit it bringeth nothing to perfection, is the weakness and infirmity of our flesh. *In his word.* *Psal. cxix. [5, 6.]* *Rom. vii. [12.]* *1 Tim. i. [8.]* *Heb. vii. [19.]* *[Lev. xviii. 5. Luke x. 28.]*

<small>tom. viii. 3, 4.</small> "Wherefore that which was impossible to the law, inasmuch as it was weak because of the flesh, God, sending his own Son in the similitude of sinful flesh and for sin, condemned sin in the flesh; that the righteousness of the law might be fulfilled." Although no man therefore be brought to perfection by the law, yet the law remaineth perfit; even as he is perfit which gave the law.

<small>In all his works.</small> 6. Every work of the mighty God is perfit. When he had made heaven and earth, sea and land, fish, fowl, man, beast, and whatsoever is contained within the compass of the whole world, having finished all, he beheld the <small>Gen. i. 31.</small> works of his own hands, and saw they were all "exceeding good." If there be this perfection in the works of God, then whatsoever he do in heaven or in earth, seem it unto us never so much out of order, yea, although it be even against all reason in our eyes, yet must we always set our hands unto this: it is of God, therefore perfit. For, <small>Isai. xlv. 10.</small> "Wo be to him that saith to his father, What hast thou begotten? or to his mother, What hast thou brought forth?" Shall the clay say to the workman, What makest thou? dust and ashes to the Creator of heaven and earth, It is not good and perfit which thou doest?

<small>Perfection in us by imputation.</small> 7. As God is perfit in himself, in his word, and in all his works; so we are exhorted to fashion ourselves according to that similitude and likeness which is in him, and to become perfit as our Father in heaven is perfit. There is a perfection which all believers have by imputation; whereof although St Paul do not speak directly in this place, yet, because it is the root of that perfection whereof he speaketh, it is not besides the purpose for me to put you in mind of it. Unto every son of Adam it <small>Ezek. xxviii. [15.]</small> may justly be said, "Thou wast perfit in thy ways from the day that thou wast created, till iniquity was found in thee." But our sanctification being once defiled and polluted with sin, he which liketh no unclean or unperfect thing, if he look upon us as we are in ourselves, cannot but loathe us. Wherefore, except the perfection of righteousness which is in Christ be imputed unto us and accounted as ours, except in him we be made the righteousness of God, how should we ever hope to appear without spot and wrinkle in the sight of God? He therefore is perfect, whose

imperfections Christ with his perfection hath covered. This is a secret, which because the Jews were not able to comprehend, therefore they stumbled. Israel sought perfection, and found it not. Wherefore? Because they sought it by the works of the law, and not by faith: they thought perfection by imputation to be a mere fancy. Contrariwise the gentiles, not following that perfection which is by the law, attained unto that which is by faith: which St Paul did so esteem, that although he were, concerning the righteousness which is in the law, unreprovable, yet he thought all the labour and travail lost which he had spent about attaining perfection that way, and desired nothing more than to be found, not having his own perfection which was of the law, but that which is through the faith of Christ.

8. But the perfection, whereof St Paul here speaketh, is nothing else but the finishing of that which the grace of Christ hath already begun to work in our hearts, our growing and increasing in true godliness, our proceeding and going forward from virtue to virtue, from strength to strength, till we come unto that whereunto we strive. "Brethren," saith the apostle, "I count not myself as if I had attained it, or were already perfect: but one thing, I forget that which is behind, and endeavour myself unto that which is before, and follow hard towards the mark for the prize of the high calling of God in Christ Jesus. Let us therefore, as many as be perfect, be thus minded:" let as many as have attained the former perfection, strive unto this which is the latter. *Perfection to be sought for by industry and labour.* *Phil. iii. [12—15.]*

9. For this cause apostles, prophets, evangelists, pastors, and teachers at the first were given: unto this all doctrine and exhortation doth tend, that, being "builded together to be the habitation of God by the Spirit," we might "rise to a perfect man unto the measure of the age of the fulness of Christ," and "in all things grow up into him which is the head;" in all things, whether they be inward virtues, or outward duties, which God requireth at the hands of men. Touching inward virtues, although we have knowledge, and be established in the present truth; although our faith be such, that it be known and spoken of throughout the world; although we abound in *Inward perfection.* *[Eph. ii. 22.]* *Eph. iv. [13, 15.]*

godliness, in brotherly kindness, and in all love; it is nevertheless a thing needful as long as we are in this tabernacle, that we be always put in mind, stirred up, and provoked to endeavour that in these things we may abound more and more, and go forward in them to perfection.

In knowledge.
Col. i. [6.]
10. The word of truth, which is the gospel, was fruitful among the Colossians, from the very first day that they heard and truly knew the grace of God. Yet St Paul ceased not still to pray for them, and to desire that they might be fulfilled with the knowledge of his will in all wisdom and spiritual understanding, that they might increase in the knowledge of God, and so be perfect. The Hebrews no doubt were not utterly ignorant in the highest mysteries of their salvation: yet are they sharply reproved for their rawness, and exhorted to proceed from the doctrine of the beginning of Christ, and from the first principles of the word of God, that at the length they might [Heb. vi. 1.] come to some "perfection." We must all confess, even the best learned amongst us all, that as yet we are but beginning to learn, we know but little, our skill is of small and tender growth. It behoveth us therefore to pray continually with the prophet: "Lord, teach us thy statutes:" [Psal. cxix. 12.] make us to understand the way of thy precepts, that we may profit in meditating of thy law: lead us on in our way by the gracious conduction of thy Holy Spirit: so direct our course that we may run out the race into which we are entered, not ceasing till thou hast brought us into all truth, fully instructed us in thy righteousness, made us absolute and perfect unto all good works.

In faith.
11. Where there is backwardness in knowledge, there must needs be also weakness of faith: if we grow in the one, we are the nearer to perfection in the other. How great care the blessed apostle had, that the faith of as many as did believe through his preaching might be perfited, let that one speech of his to them of Thessalonica 1 Thess. iii. [7—10.] serve to shew, instead of many: "Brethren, we had consolation in you, in all our affliction and necessity, through your faith. For now are we alive, if ye[1] stand stedfast

[[1] The ancient editions have "we;" but this is probably a mistake for "ye."—ED.]

in the Lord. What thanks can we recompense to God again for you, for all the joy for which we rejoice for your sakes before God, night and day praying exceedingly that we might see your face, and might accomplish that which is lacking in your faith?" If he were thus careful for the faith of others, shall we neglect to make perfect our own? When we hear that this is the victory which overcometh the world, even our faith; that by faith all the fiery darts of Satan are expelled and driven back; that unto believers all things are possible; that he which believeth cometh not into judgment, but hath passed from death to life; are we not glad to say in our hearts, Lord, we believe? If we be, then considering that by how much our faith is more stedfast, by so much we are the more certainly assured of all these things, let us join in request with the disciples of Christ, and beg of him to "increase faith in us:" let us cry even with tears, Lord, help our incredulity. 1 John v. [4.] [Eph. vi. 16.] [Mark ix. 23.] John v. [24.] Luke xvii. [5.]

12. "But how can you believe," saith our Saviour, "that receive glory one of another, and the glory which is of God only ye seek not?" How should we grow unto fulness of faith, which are so empty and void of godliness? The complaint of the prophet might never be more truly and generally applied: "there is no fear of God." Zeal is even quenched, religion almost dead, true devotion abolished from the hearts of men: there is not a godly man left upon earth; or if there be, if God have reserved to himself at this present many thousands (as I doubt not but he hath) of godly men, yet how hard is it to find one amongst those many thousands which daily goeth forward profiting and perfiting himself in godliness! In godliness. John v. [44.] [Psal. xxxvi. 1.]

13. Whereat we cannot greatly marvel. For if men grow so cold as we daily see they do in charity, love, and brotherly kindness towards men whom they see, they must needs be colder in love towards God, whom no man ever saw. Thus because our profiting in all these parts of inward perfection hath been hitherto very slow, it is therefore needful to put you in mind of this present exhortation: "concerning that which remaineth, brethren, be perfect." In brotherly kindness and love.

14. It is not enough to seek for inward perfection, Outward perfection in doing.

unless we also endeavour to be outwardly perfect. If we have the ripeness of men in knowledge, we may not shew the fondness of children in behaviour. To say we have faith, what availeth it, except we have works also? See we not that the faith of Abraham was effectual, and wrought with his works, and that through his works his faith was made perfect? Are we sincerely religious towards God? [James i. 27.] "Pure religion and undefiled before God even the Father is this, to visit the fatherless and widows in their adversity, and to keep ourselves unspotted of the world." Do we profess love and charity towards our brethren? Let the whole course and practice of our life, as near as possibly we can, be sincere, upright, sound, and perfect. For broken dealings are as odious in the sight of God, as they are grievous and offensive towards men. Let your love appear by your good fruits, your works of charity. And if ye have laid a good foundation of this already, finish the work which ye have begun: in that which ye do, study how to abound. Be not weary of well doing. As in that which is past, so "for that which remaineth, brethren, we [1 Thess. iv. [1.]] beseech you and exhort you in the Lord Jesus, that ye increase more and more;" not only coveting spiritual gifts, and being studious of good works, but also seeking to excel in them, that in all things ye may be made rich in Christ, in all virtue, and in all speech.

In speaking. Prov. xv. [14.] Col. iv. [6.]
15. "The mouth of the fool (saith Solomon) is fed with foolishness:" but "let your speech (saith the apostle) be gracious always, and powdered with salt." Perfection herein ought so much the more earnestly to be desired, by how much it is the more hardly obtained in this than in other things. As by using the bit in the mouth of a horse his whole body is turned about; and as by moving the rudder a ship is directed whithersoever it pleaseth the mind of the governor; so he that is perfect to rule the tongue with skill is able to rule all the body with ease. "But [James iii. [8.]] the tongue is an unruly evil, full of deadly poison." Therefore as many as desire to be perfect must keep a continual watch before their lips, that, if an unsavoury word escape them, they may lay their hands on their mouths betimes; that, if they have spoken unadvisedly once, they may answer no more, or if twice, yet proceed no further. This use shall

breed such perfection in the end, that all our talk shall be gracious, all our words well seasoned, all our speech and communication become such as that whereof the wise man speaketh in the book of Ecclesiasticus, saying, " The talk of him that feareth God is all wisdom." [Ecclus. xxvii. [11.]]

16. With these things if we join that perfection also [In suffering.] which St James mentioneth : " Let patience have her perfect [James i. [4.]] work," we shall then fully answer our apostle's exhortation, we shall " be perfect and entire, lacking nothing." " Now [1 Pet. v. 10.] the God of all grace which hath called us unto his eternal glory by Christ Jesus make you perfect, confirm, strengthen and stablish you."

17. Our apostle very fitly, having exhorted us to be perfect, addeth in the next place, *Consolationem habete:* " Be of good comfort." For as many as seek to be perfect shall find many grievous hinderances to stay them in their course : necessary therefore it is that in this respect they should be comforted. There is no one part or degree of perfection wherein the righteous and godly do not find many great occasions offered, quite to discourage and daunt their hearts. St Paul was perfect and ripe in the knowledge of Jesus Christ; and it was objected against him as a token of extreme fury, *Multæ literæ te ad insaniam redigunt :* [Acts xxvi. [24.]] " Much learning makes thee mad." Abraham, for the great perfection of his faith, is called the father of them that believe : but how sore were those assaults that withstood his hope and assurance in the promise! The godliness of Job was so absolute and perfect, that God himself doth as it were make a vaunt of him unto Satan : " Hast [Job i. 8.] thou not considered my servant Job, how none is like him in the earth, an upright and just man, one that feareth God and escheweth evil?" Yet how near was he brought to the gulf of destruction, both of body and soul! The love, wherewith the holy apostle embraced the church of Corinth, was so strong and perfect, that he wished even to be bestowed and spent for their souls : but what a discouragement was this unto him, that the more he did love, the less he was loved! Touching the prophet Jeremy, whether we consider his dealings, his speakings, or his sufferings, we see there was great integrity in all; but his wrestlings and strivings with the wicked were so irksome and tedious

[An exhortation to rejoice and be of good comfort.]

[2 Cor. xii. [15.]]

unto him, that he seemed sometimes more than half resolved to give over all, as if it were but bootless to strive longer. All which notwithstanding, we are here exhorted to be of good comfort, forasmuch as, although our hinderances be great, yet sure we are safely to pass through them: they cannot dam up the way between us and the kingdom of heaven. Through this strait way our brethren have passed before us; and we need not fear to follow after. Christ himself hath gone before by a far harder passage than his meaning is to lead any of us by. Think it therefore no strange thing for the perfect to suffer: be not discomforted or dismayed at it, "knowing that the same afflictions are accomplished in your brethren which are in the world." If we patiently suffer with him and them, we shall gloriously be crowned with him and them. It is true that the godly, the just, and perfect, have fierce adversaries, mighty enemies, the devil with his lost and forsaken train, the world full of baits and allurements unto evil, the flesh ever ready and greedy to take them. "But have confidence (saith our Saviour), I have overcome." Although ye travail and be heavy laden for a while, yet comfort yourselves, knowing that your anguishes, griefs, and molestations shall have an end, your tears shall be wiped away and dried up; but the joy which shall be given you is everlasting. The seed of tears which ye sow now is nothing to that harvest of joy which hereafter shall be reaped. Again, whatsoever doth befall us here, it cometh not unto us by hap or chance; but all is disposed by the will and providence of Almighty God: when we are chastised, we are chastised of the Lord: it is of mere love and perfect righteousness that we are corrected: it is not for our harm, but to our good, either for the trial of our faith, or for the reformation of our life. So that the man which feareth God, which walketh uprightly in his sight, having the testimony of a good conscience, cannot want matter of consolation: he hath wherefore in the Lord to rejoice always: God hath given enough for his continual comfort. "For that which resteth" therefore, brethren, lift up your heads and "be comforted."

18. Finally, to come to the last branch of this present exhortation, "be of one mind, live in peace." These

fruits of unity and peace are not gathered, but where integrity and comfort have taken root. One temple was builded for the people of God, one law written by the finger of God, that the church of God might in all things be one. The bond of unity is verity: neither can they be truly one, which are not one in truth. And therefore, although an angel should come from heaven with all shew of learning, and all appearance of unspotted and undefiled purity, teaching things contrary to that one truth which you have received, reach him no hand, salute him not in token of consent: unity with him is enmity with God. But if all be builded upon the settled foundation of God's truth, if all be members of one body, servants to one master, soldiers fighting under one banner, children of one and the same father; then is the name of unity and peace amiable. "Behold," saith the prophet, "how good and how sweet a thing it is for brethren to dwell together in one." It is good like the dew which watereth the hills, sweet like that oil which was poured upon the head of the high priest. Oil is pleasant, and dew profitable: the one giveth a most fragrant smell, the other maketh the ground fruitful: but the goodness and sweetness of unity, of peace, no tongue is able sufficiently to express. If this oil and dew of peace, unity, and concord shall be poured, as upon Hermon and Aaron, so likewise upon the tops of our mountains, upon the heads of our guides, upon our magistrates, and upon our ministers, and shall thence distil to the lower parts, as it were to the valleys that lie under the one, and to the skirts of the other's garments, the fruit that shall thereby grow unto us, and the pleasure which all beholders shall conceive of it, is unspeakable. Wherefore, with St Paul, "I beseech you, brethren, by the name of our Lord Jesus Christ, that you all speak one thing, and that there be no dissentions among you, but be ye knit together in one mind and in one judgment." And, as it is said that the last lesson which St John the evangelist gave to his disciples was, *Filioli, diligite vos invicem:* "my little children, love one another;" so, my dear brethren, receive you also this last lesson at my hands: "Be perfect, be of good comfort, be of one mind, live in peace."

Psal. cxxxiii. [1.]

1 Cor. i. [10.]

19. And then I dare conclude and promise with St *The promise made to*

them which do as they have been hitherto exhorted.

Paul, "the God of love and peace shall abide with you." That God which hath so much commended peace unto us, that God who is so much delighted in love, that God which is the author of love and peace, that God which is peace and love itself, he will be with you; a sure tower for your defence, against whose power no power is able to stand; a present help in all necessities; a loving Father which cannot forget you; a merciful God; a faithful Schoolmaster; a good Shepherd. He will feed you with the food of life: he will augment and increase your faith, confirm and stablish you in all truth: his love to the end shall continue with you: his peace he will give you, and leave among you: he will stand always at your right hand, maintain your lot, lead you through this vale of tears, and conduct you safely to the land of promise: he will pull from your shoulders this miserable coat of your corruption, and clothe you with the robes of immortality: he will change this vile body, and make it like the glorious body of Jesus Christ. All this that God, which cannot lie, hath promised: all this that omnipotent, mighty, and merciful God will perform even to all such as labour to become perfect, as joy in the Holy Ghost, as have comfort in Christ, as consent in true religion, and live in peace and brotherly concord. To that God immortal, invisible, and only wise, be all honour, glory, and praise, now and ever. Amen.

MISCELLANEOUS PIECES

OF

ARCHBISHOP SANDYS.

MISCELLANEOUS PIECES

OF

ARCHBISHOP SANDYS.

ADVICE CONCERNING RITES AND CEREMONIES IN THE SYNOD, MDLXII.

From Strype's Annals, Vol. I. Part I. Chap. xxix.

[HERE bishop Sandys brought in his paper; wherein his advice was to move her majesty,]

First, That, with her majesty's authority, with the assistance of the archbishop of Canterbury, according to the limitation of the act provided in that behalf, might be taken out of the Book of Common Prayer *private baptism*, which hath respect unto women: who, by the word of God, cannot be ministers of the sacraments, or of any one of them. Potest fieri in Synodo. Bishop Grindal's marginal note.

Secondly, That, by like authority, the collect for crossing the infant in the forehead may be blotted out: as it seems very superstitious, so it is not needful.

Thirdly, That, according to order taken by her majesty's father, king Henry VIII. of most famous memory, and by the late king Edward, her majesty's brother, certain learned men, bishops and others, may by her majesty be appointed to set down ecclesiastical orders and rules in all ecclesiastical matters, for the good government of the church of England, as shall be by them thought most meet; and the same in this present session of parliament, whatsoever they shall order or set down, within one year next to be effectual, and for law confirmed by act of parliament, at or in this session.

ORDERS FOR THE BISHOPS AND CLERGY.

Id. Chap. xxx.

[SANDYS, bishop of Wigorn, drew up orders] to be observed by the bishops and other ecclesiastical persons, by their consents and subscriptions in this present synod.

First, Forasmuch as bishops are not born for themselves, but for their successors, and are only possessors for their own time; every bishop, by the subscription of his hand, promiseth that he shall not either by lease, grant, or any other means, let, set, or alienate any of his manors, or whatsoever heretofore hath not been in lease, except only for his own time, and while he is bishop.

Item, That no bishop, dean, or chapter, shall give or grant any advowson of their prebend, parsonage, or vicarage, after the date hereof.

Item, That no bishop shall admit any into the ministry, who hath not good testimony of his conversation; who is not learned, fit to teach the people; and who hath not presently some appointed place, cure, and living to serve. And that he do not admit the same without the consent of six learned ministers; who shall all lay their hands upon his head at his admission.

Item, That every bishop by himself, or by his officer, shall see that every curate, parson, vicar, or other, do catechise the children and youth of his parish every Sunday, according to the injunction in that behalf.

Item, It is ordered, that no minister shall marry any other than be within his parish, the woman-party at the least; and that he do it not, except the banns be openly thrice proclaimed in the same parish, and that he knew that the parents of the party consented thereto.

Item, That no bishop, dean, or chapter, shall bestow their benefices, whereof they be patrons, but upon such as be learned and fit for the office, and such as will subscribe to sound religion now by authority set down.

Item, That every bishop take order, that whosoever is a common swearer in his diocese, if after two admonitions by the minister he will not leave the same, that then it shall be lawful for the minister to exclude him from the communion, until he shall find reformation in him.

ADVERTISEMENT TO THE TRANSLATION OF LUTHER'S COMMENTARY ON GALATIANS.

To the Reader.

This book being brought unto me to peruse and to consider of, I thought it my part, not only to allow of it to the print, but also to commend it to the reader, as a treatise most comfortable to all afflicted consciences exercised in the school of Christ. The author felt what he spake, and had experience of what he wrote, and therefore able more lively to express both the assaults and the salving, the order of the battle and the mean of the victory. Satan is the enemy, the victory is by only faith in Christ, as John recordeth. If Christ justify, who can condemn? saith St Paul. This most necessary doctrine the author hath most substantially cleared in this his commentary: which being written in the Latin tongue certain godly learned men have most sincerely translated into our language, to the great benefit of all such as with humbled hearts will diligently read the same. Some began it according to such skill as they had. Others godly affected, not suffering so good a matter in handling to be marred, put to their helping hands, for the better framing and furthering of so worthy a work. They refuse to be named, seeking neither their own gain nor glory, but thinking it their happiness, if by any means they may relieve afflicted minds, and do good to the church of Christ, yielding all glory unto God, to whom all glory is due.

Aprilis 28, 1575.

Edwinus London.

EPISTOLA PASTORALIS EPISC. CESTRENS[1].

E MSS. Caio-Gonvill. Cantab. 197. pp. 471—4.
(MSS. More, A. 27. in the printed Catalogue.)

Archiepiscopus Eborum Cestrensi Episcopo.

GRATIA, pax, et salus, a Deo Patre et Domino nostro Jesu Christo. Intuenti mihi, frater venerande, cursum et conditionem hujus impietate perditi sæculi, quantos agat triumphos Satan, quam longe lateque dominetur scelus, quam innumeri sint ac frequentes improborum hominum flagitiosi greges, quam exilis, quam arida, vel potius quam nulla sit in terris fides, nulla pietas; videmur in ultima et impia mundi hujus jam interitui vicina tempora devenisse. Cum porro mihi in mentem venit zizaniam, horum peccatorum semen, nulla re magis in agro Domini vel spargi vel succrescere, quam agricolarum somnolentia, colonorum desidia; nec aliunde tantam cladem invectam esse Hierosolymæ nostræ sanctæ civitati (qua et muri ejus evertuntur, et ipsa pene capta cedit inimicorum violentiæ) quam quod excubiæ, quæ deberent vigilare, somno sopitæ, suis muneribus desunt: ad hæc cum recolo nos etiam ipsos, quibus curam suæ vineæ commisit Dominus, officio nostro parum satisfecisse, vitas nimium secure tanquam in alta pace transegisse, neque hostibus Christi satis fortiter resistendo, neque Domini fundum arando satis diligenter, neque pascendo gregem satis fideliter, neque satis vigilanter in specula consistendo, munus nostrum prout decuit adimplevisse: uti meipsum negligentiæ coarguo[2], testeque conscientia cogor succumbere veniamque petere, (quanquam dissolutum et penitus desidem me nunquam fuisse novit Dominus;) ita, charitate pia fraternaque benevolentia commotus, meum esse duco te cohortari: uti quemadmodum idem nobis incumbit onus, eadem est administrandæ provinciæ reddenda ratio; sic conjunctis animis

[[1] This pastoral epistle has been printed, but with some variations, by Strype, Annals, Vol. III. Book I. Chap. 15. Appendix, No. XXIX.—ED.]
[[2] Coargo, MS.—ED.]

quales nos esse decet ponderemus, securitatem et somnolentiam discutiamus, redimamus tempus, accingamus nos ad prœlium, gladios et arma Spiritus capiamus, hostem communem profligemus, et Christi fidem vel ad sanguinem et cædem defendamus. Præfecit enim nos Deus gentibus et populis, ut extirpemus et eradicemus, ut perdamus et ejiciamus, ut ædificemus et plantemus. Ideoque nostrum est, fibras superstitionis et idololatriæ radices falce divini verbi resecare, bonas etiam fruges evangelii propagatione per animos hominum conserere, arces et turres Jerechuntis tuba cœlestis Spiritus evertere, muros autem Jerosolimæ sacrumque templum, quantum in nobis est, erigere; sævitiam et tyrannidem Antichristi summa contentione convellere, regnum autem et imperium Filii Dei sedula prædicatione stabilire. Neque vero solum hunc in pascendo suo grege laborem videtur Dominus a nobis postulare, verum etiam flagitat, ne solutis legum sacratarum vinculis impune peccatum volitet. Vult enim Dominus libidinem comprimi, scelus constringi, dissolutos mores contineri, quæque dilapsa jam diffluxerunt, severis legibus et dignis suppliciis coerceri. Ita et saluti præcipitantis patriæ melius consulemus, et eorum furorem qui afflictam eam cupiunt opprimere fœlicius concutiemus. Hic igitur fideles et justos nos esse convenit, æqua lance quod suum est cuique tribuentes. Non enim debemus nos quenquam, vel ob opes divitem, vel ob auctoritatem potentem, vel ob amicitiam charum, vel ob commoditatem utilem, sic respicere, quo minus opus Domini strenue compleamus. Qui ergo sunt contumaces et præfracti hostes virga sunt ferrea comminuendi, saltem, ne lepra sua sanos inficiant, constringendi: capiendæ sunt vulpeculæ quæ demoliuntur vineam, et pandenda venabula quibus errones papani, seditionum faces et ecclesiæ pestes, irretiti cadant. Hoc enim genus hominum pessimum est, et nostri fundi calamitas, qui nimia licentia fiunt deteriores, et impunitate jam feroces, audacter cum summo discrimine bonorum omnium insolescunt. Est misericordia crudelis, et cur non cogeret ecclesia perditos filios ut redirent, si perditi filii coegerunt[1] alios ut perirent? Ut autem hæc omnia facilius eveniant, ac partitis operibus facilius optatos exitus sortiantur, non alienum arbitror, si pro auctoritate nobis con-

[[1] Cogerunt, MS.—ED.]

cessa quisque nostrum quos apud se noverit pietate præstantes et fide sanos convocet, eorumque strenuam et diligentem operam in his ecclesiæ reique publicæ tam incertis et dubiis rebus exposcat. Lumbis enim succinctis, frater, oportet nos sedulo negotium Domini conficere: multi sunt hostes, multa nobis quærenda sunt consilia; nec in hisce difficultatibus omittendum quicquam quod ullo modo saluti communi possit conducere. Neque enim debemus extimescere quenquam, cujus est in naso ipsius spiritus. Dominus omnipotens nobis aderit et dux et vindex, simus modo pro domo Dei zelo ferventes, flagrantes studio, neque aliqua necessitudine complectamur, quos aliena in Dominum nostrum et suam ecclesiam esse mente[1]   ; nam qui perfidi sunt in Deum, in principem fideles esse non possunt. Quas nacti sumus provincias, ornemus eas, nobisque ipsis et universo gregi diligenter caveamus. Aderit enim proculdubio brevi Dominus, qui nos præfecit ecclesiæ suæ, proprioque sanguine redemptam eam e gehennæ faucibus eripuit, ante cujus tribunal stare nos oportet, nostræque dispensationis districtam rationem reddere. Qua tempestate fœlix ille qui intrepide coram Filio Dei, mortuorum et viventium judice, poterit consistere. Hæc mihi in mentem venerunt, de quibus tuam dominationem admonere mei esse officii putavi, sperans humanitatem tuam fidele hoc meum consilium et amicum animum bonam in partem esse accepturam. Deus Opt. Max. ecclesiam suam protegat, hostes veritatis conterat, nostrisque piis studiis fœlices et prosperos exitus concedat. Amen.

Bushopthorpiæ, 13 Februarii 1583

Tuus in Christo frater

E. Ebor.

To the Right Reverend
in Christ, my very
good Lorde the
Bushopp of
Chester.

[1 A word omitted in MS.—Ed.]

[*The same Translated.*

A PASTORAL EPISTLE TO THE BISHOP OF CHESTER[1].

The Archbishop of York to the Bishop of Chester.

GRACE, peace, and salvation from God the Father and our Lord Jesus Christ. When I look, venerable brother, at the course and condition of this world lost in impiety; what triumphs Satan obtains, how far and wide vice bears rule, how numerous and crowded are the wicked assemblies of ungodly men, how weak, how withered, or rather how entirely gone from the earth is faith, is piety; it seems to me that we are now arrived at the last and ungodly times of this world, drawing near to destruction. When, moreover, I have reflected that tares, the seed of these sins, are scattered and grow in the Lord's field by nothing more than by the drowsiness of the husbandmen and the sloth of the cultivators; and that from no other cause has such misfortune come to our holy city Jerusalem (by which her walls are overthrown, and she is almost fallen a prey to the violence of her enemies), than that the watchmen who ought to have watched, overcome with sleep, have been wanting to their duties; when besides I remember that we ourselves, to whom the Lord has committed the care of his vineyard, have little satisfied our charge: that we have passed our lives too securely, as if in a time of profound peace, that we have not as we ought fulfilled our duty either by resisting the enemies of Christ boldly enough, or by tilling the Lord's field diligently enough, or by feeding the flock faithfully enough, or by standing with sufficient vigilance upon our watch-tower; as I condemn myself of negligence, and by the testimony of conscience am compelled humbly to

[1] Bishop Chaderton.

implore forgiveness (though utterly careless and sluggish
the Lord knows I never was); so, moved by dutiful love
and brotherly kindness, I think it my duty to exhort
you, that whereas we have the same burden laid upon us,
and the same account to render of the administration of
our charge, so with united hearts we should consider
what manner of persons we ought to be, should throw off
carelessness and drowsiness, should redeem the time, should
gird us for the battle, should take the sword and armour
of the Spirit, should defeat the common foe, and defend the faith of Christ even unto blood and unto death.
For God has set us over the nations and peoples, to
pluck up and to root out, to destroy and to cast away, to
build and to plant. It is therefore our part to cut off
the fibres of superstition and the roots of idolatry with the
sharp sickle of the divine word; to sow also good corn by
the propagation of the gospel in the minds of men, to overthrow the citadels and towers of Jericho by the trumpet
of the heavenly Spirit, but as far as in us lies to build the
walls and sacred temple of Jerusalem; to shake down with
the utmost vigour the cruelty and tyranny of antichrist,
but to stablish by diligent preaching the kingdom and dominion of the Son of God. For not only does the Lord
seem to require this labour of us in feeding his flock, but
he also demands that sin should not be permitted to burst
the bonds of established laws and fly abroad with impunity. For the Lord would have lust to be repressed,
wickedness to be checked, licentious manners to be restrained, and those things which have utterly fallen asunder
to be bound up by severe laws and condign punishments.
So we shall better provide for the safety of our sinking
country, and more happily disappoint the madness of those
who desire to crush her in her depressed state. We must,
then, be faithful and just, giving with impartial balance to
every one his due. For we must not so regard any one,
either the rich man for his wealth, or the mighty for his
influence, or the friend for his love, or the man who is
serviceable to us for the convenience he may afford, as not
strenuously to fulfil the work of the Lord. Those who are
stubborn and inveterate foes are to be bruised with a rod
of iron, at least to be restrained that their leprosy infect

not the sound: the little foxes which destroy the vineyard must be taken, and nets must be spread by which the papal stragglers, the fire brands of seditions, and the pests of the church, may be snared and fall. For this kind of men is the worst, and the very destruction of our field, who by too great liberty become worse, and, already fierce through impunity, grow boldly insolent to the great danger of all good men. Mercy is cruel; and why should not the church compel her abandoned children to return, if her abandoned children compel others to perish? But that all these things may more easily come to pass, and by the labour thereof being shared may more readily obtain the wished for results, I think it proper, that, according to the authority committed to us, each of us should collect those whom he knows about him to be eminent in piety and sound in the faith, and that he should require their strenuous and diligent assistance in these so uncertain and doubtful circumstances of church and state. With our loins girt, my brother, we must diligently accomplish the Lord's work: the enemies are many, many counsels must be sought by us, nor in these difficulties must any thing be omitted which can in any way conduce to the common safety. For we ought not to fear any man whose breath is in his nostrils. The Almighty Lord will be present to us, both a leader and an avenger, if we only be fervent in zeal for the house of God, burning with desire, nor receive into any friendship those whom [we know], to be of hostile mind towards our Lord and his church; for those who are faithless toward God cannot be faithful to their prince[1]. The stations we have attained let us adorn; and let us take diligent heed to ourselves and to the whole flock. Soon, no doubt, the Lord will come, who has placed us over his church, and has redeemed it by his own blood, and snatched it from the jaws of hell, before whose tribunal we must stand and give a strict account of our stewardship. At which time happy is he who can fearlessly stand before the Son of God, the judge of quick and dead. These things I have thought it my duty to advise your lordship, hoping that your kindness will take in good part this my

---

[1] See before, p. 97.

counsel and friendly mind. The most high and good God protect his church, overthrow the enemies of the truth, and grant to our pious desires happy and prosperous results. Amen.

Bishopthorp, 13 February, 1583,

Your brother in Christ,

E. EBOR.]

PRAYERS TO BE USED AT HAWKSHEAD SCHOOL.

From Abingdon's Antiquities of the Cathedral Church of Worcester, corrected by an original preserved at Hawkshead.

Also I ordain and constitute, that certain godly prayers hereafter set down, and immediately following in these constitutions, be made in the said school by the schoolmaster for the time being, the usher, and scholars of the same school, every morning before the said schoolmaster and usher begin to teach the said scholars, and every evening immediately before the breaking up of the said school, and every day before they go to dinner to sing a psalm in metre in the said school.

A PRAYER FOR THE MORNING.

Most mighty God, and merciful Father, we sinners by nature, yet thy children by grace, here prostrate before thy Divine Majesty, acknowledge our corruption in nature by reason of our sins to be such, that we are not able of ourselves to think one good thought, much less able to profit in good learning and literature, and to come to the knowledge of thy Son Jesus Christ, our Saviour, except it shall please thee, of thy great grace and goodness, to illuminate our understandings, to strengthen our feeble memories, to instruct us by thy Holy Spirit, and so to pour upon us thy good gifts of grace, that we may learn to know, and know to practise those things in these our studies, that may most tend to the glory of thy name, to the profit of thy church, and to the performance of our christian duties. Hear us, O God, and grant these our petitions, and bless our studies, O heavenly Father, for thy Son Jesus Christ's sake, in whose name we call upon thee, and say, Our Father, &c.

[Here follows the prayer for the Queen's Majesty in the form of common prayer, beginning, " O Lord our heavenly Father, high and mighty, &c.]

EVENING PRAYER,

AT THE BREAKING UP OF THE SCHOOL.

Most gracious God, and most merciful Father, we acknowledge how much we are bound to thy Divine Majesty for all those great gifts and manifold mercies, which thou of thy mere grace and favour hast bestowed upon us, as well for our election, creation, redemption, justification, and sanctification, with all other good gifts of body and mind; and what else soever we have, of thy grace and favour we have received it; as also for that thou hast moved the mind, and stirred up the heart of Edwin Archbishop of York, our founder, to purchase and provide this Free Grammar-School for us, for our education and breeding in good literature and learning. Grant, O God, that we may ever be thankful for the same; and give us grace not to abuse this great gift of mercy, but that we may so apply our studies, holpen and directed by thy Holy Spirit, that we may increase in all good knowledge and learning, to the glory and praise of thy name. Grant this, O God, for thy Son Jesus Christ's sake, our only Redeemer and Saviour. Amen.

ANOTHER PRAYER FOR EVENING.

All honour, glory, and praise be given to thee, most merciful Father, and gracious God, for all thy loving-kindnesses and manifold graces poured down upon us, namely, that it hath pleased thee to protect us this day from all dangers of the enemy, bodily and ghostly, and to increase thy gifts of knowledge and godliness in us. Grant us, O good God, to love thee, and for these thy great mercies still to grow in thankfulness more and more towards thee. And, forasmuch as thou hast appointed the night to rest in, and the day to travail in, give unto us such quiet and moderate sleep, as may strengthen our weak bodies to bear those labours whereunto thou shall appoint them. Suffer not the prince of darkness to prevail in the darkness of this night, nor for ever against us. But watch thou still over us with thine eye, and guard us with thy hand against all his deceits and assaults; and though our bodies do sleep, make thou our souls to watch, looking for the appearance of thy Son, Jesus Christ, that we may be waking to meet him in the clouds, to enter with him into eternal joy and blessedness. These things we crave at thy hands, for thy Son, Christ Jesus' sake, to whom with thee and the Holy Ghost be rendered all praise, glory, and majesty, for ever and ever. Amen.

PREAMBLE TO THE ARCHBISHOP'S WILL.

Dated August 1, 1587.

Extracted from the Registry of the Consistory Court of York.

In Dei nomine, Amen. I, Edwin Sandes, Minister of God's holy word and sacraments, Archbishop of York, although most unworthy, often minding the frailty and uncertainty of man's life in general, and withal feeling mine own manifold infirmities in particular both by my years and for my sins; and also remembering, that, when the Lord shall say, *Redde rationem villicationis tuæ*[1], I amongst other shall appear before the tribunal seat of Christ, to receive in this body according to that I have done, be it good or evil: I reckon it in myself a christian duty, with Ezekias, *disponere domui meæ*[2]; and, considering that as I brought nothing in this world, for naked I came out of my mother's womb, so can I carry nothing thereout, but naked must I return again, even earth to dust, and carcase to worms, the way of all flesh; while the Lord God hath lent me the leisure, being presently in sound health of body and perfect memory, (I humbly thank him for both) even thus I discharge myself of those talents, which the Lord hath committed to my charge, and make my last Will and Testament in such sort as followeth:

First, and above all, my soul and spirit I commend, with David and Stephen, into the merciful hands of my gracious God and loving Father; assuredly believing by faith, and certainly trusting by hope, that he in the fulness of his good time, best known unto himself and least unto me, will receive the same unto himself, not in respect of any my deserts, (for my righteousness is but a very dunghill and defiled cloth,) but of his own free mercies, and for the alone merits of his only Son, mine only Saviour Jesus Christ;

[[1] Render an account of thy stewardship.—Ed.]
[[2] To set my house in order.—Ed.]

who, being without any sin, was made a curse and sacrifice for all my sins, that I might be made the righteousness of God in him; who in his own body bare all my transgressions upon the tree, that by smart of his stripes, and blood of his wounds, I might be healed; who hath cancelled upon the cross the whole hand-writing that was against me, that I might not only be entertained as a servant and reconciled as a friend, but adopted as a son and accepted as an heir with God the Father, and an heir together with Jesus Christ, who is also made unto me wisdom, righteousness, sanctification, and redemption. And as in this faith and full assurance of my perfect redemption by the death and only deserts of Jesus Christ, the true Lamb of God, and very Lion of the tribe of Juda, I have and do live; so in the same firm and stedfast faith and hope I end my sinful life, and gladly yield up withal my soul immortal and mortal body.

Secondly, although this body of mine is but a clod of clay, a prison of my soul; my will is, it shall be buried neither in superstitious nor superfluous manner; yet, for that it hath been and is, I trust, not only a vessel of the gospel, but likewise a temple of the Holy Ghost, I require that the same be so decently and conveniently brought to ground, as appertaineth to a Christian, a servant of Almighty God, and a man of my calling; putting no doubt but that I shall see my Redeemer with mine own eyes, and be covered with mine own skin, and that the Lord Jesus shall make this my vile body like unto his glorious body, whereby he is able to subdue all things unto himself: *Reposita est hæc mihi spes in sinu meo*[1].

Thirdly, because I have lived an old man in the ministry of Christ, a faithful disposer of the mysteries of God, and to my power an earnest labourer in the vineyard of the Lord, I testify before God, and his angels, and men of this world, I rest resolute and yield up my spirit in that doctrine which I have privately studied and publicly preached, and which is this day maintained in the church of England; both taking the same to be the whole counsel of God, the word and bread of eternal life, the fountain of living water, the power of God unto salvation to all them

[[1] This hope I have laid up in my bosom.—ED.]

that believe, and beseeching the Lord besides to turn us unto him that we may be turned, lest, if we repent not, the candlestick be moved out of it place, and the gospel of the kingdom for our unthankfulness taken from us and given to a nation that shall bring forth the fruits thereof; and further protesting in an upright conscience of mine own, and in the knowledge of his majesty, before whom I stand, that in the preaching of the truth of Christ I have not laboured to please man, but studied to serve my Master, who sent me not to flatter either prince or people, but by the law to tell all sorts of their sins, by the Spirit to rebuke the world of sin, of righteousness, and of judgment, and by the gospel to testify of that faith which is in Jesus Christ and him crucified.

Fourthly, concerning rites and ceremonies by political constitutions authorized amongst us, as I am and have been persuaded, that such as are now set down by public authority in this church of England, are no way either ungodly or unlawful, but may with good conscience for order and obedience sake be used of a good Christian; for the private baptism to be ministered by women I take neither to be prescribed nor permitted; so have I ever been and presently am persuaded, that some of them be not so expedient in this church now, but that in the church reformed, and in all this time of the gospel (wherein the seed of the scripture hath so long been sown), they may better be disused by little and little, than more and more urged. Howbeit, as I do easily acknowledge our ecclesiastical policy in some points may be bettered, so do I utterly mislike even in my conscience all such rude and indigested platforms as have been more lately and boldly, than either learnedly or wisely, preferred, tending not to the reformation, but to the destruction of the church of England. The particularities of both sorts reserved to the discretion of the godly wise, of the latter I only say thus, that the state of a small private church, and the form of a learned christian kingdom, neither would long like nor can at all brook one and the same ecclesiastical government.

Thus much I thought good to testify concerning these ecclesiastical matters, to clear me from all suspicion of double and indirect dealing in the house of God, wherein

as touching mine office I have not halted, but walked
sincerely according to that skill and ability which I received
at God's merciful hands. Lord, as a great sinner by reason
of my frail flesh and manifold infirmities, I flee unto thee
for mercy. Lord, forgive me my sins, for I acknowledge
my sins. Lord, perform thy promise, and do away all
mine iniquities. Haste the coming of thy Christ, and
deliver me from this body of sin: *Veni cito, Domine Jesu*[1].
Clothe me with immortality, and give that promised crown
of glory. So be it.

[[1] Come quickly, Lord Jesus.—ED.]

NOTES.

NOTES.

Note A. (See p. 88.)

Ὡς γὰρ ἀπὸ γῆς ἄρτος προσλαμβανόμενος τὴν ἔκκλησιν τοῦ Θεοῦ, οὐκέτι κοινὸς ἄρτος ἐστὶν, ἀλλ' εὐχαριστία, ἐκ δύο πραγμάτων συνεστηκυῖα, ἐπιγείου τε καὶ οὐρανίου· οὕτως καὶ τὰ σώματα ἡμῶν μεταλαμβάνοντα τῆς εὐχαριστίας, μηκέτι εἶναι φθαρτὰ, τὴν ἐλπίδα τῆς εἰς αἰῶνας ἀναστάσεως ἔχοντα.—Irenæi Op. Par. 1710. Cont. Hæres. Lib. iv. Cap. 18. p. 251.

Vani autem omnimodo, qui universam dispositionem Dei contemnunt, et carnis salutem negant, et regenerationem ejus spernunt, dicentes non eam capacem esse incorruptibilitatis. Si autem non salvetur hæc, videlicet nec Dominus sanguine suo redemit nos; neque calix eucharistiæ communicatio sanguinis ejus est, neque panis quem frangimus, communicatio corporis ejus est[1].—Id. Cont. Hæres. Lib. v. Cap. 2. p. 293.

Professus itaque se concupiscentia concupisse edere pascha ut suum (indignum enim ut quid alienum concupisceret Deus), acceptum panem, et distributum discipulis, corpus illum suum fecit, "hoc est corpus meum" dicendo, id est, figura corporis mei. Figura autem non fuisset, nisi veritatis esset corpus. Ceterum vacua res, quod est phantasma, figuram capere non posset. Aut si propterea panem corpus sibi finxit, quia corporis carebat veritate; ergo panem debuit tradere pro nobis. Faciebat ad vanitatem Marcionis, ut panis crucifigeretur. Cur autem panem corpus suum appellat, et non magis peponem, quem Marcion cordis loco habuit? non intelligens veterem fuisse istam figuram corporis Christi, dicentis per Hieremiam, Adversus me cogitaverunt cogitatum dicentes, Venite, conjiciamus lignum in panem ejus; scilicet crucem in corpus ejus. Itaque illuminator antiquitatum quid tunc voluerit significasse panem, satis declaravit, corpus suum vocans panem. Sic et in calicis mentione testamentum constituens sanguine suo obsignatum, substantiam corporis confirmavit. Nullius enim corporis sanguis potest esse, nisi carnis.—Tertul. Op. Lut. 1641. Adv. Marcionem, Lib. iv. 40. p. 571.

Nempe sæpe ita loquimur, ut pascha propinquante dicamus, crastinam vel perendinam Domini passionem, cùm ille ante tam multos annos passus sit, nec omnino nisi semel illa passio facta sit. Nempe ipso die dominico dicimus, Hodie Dominus resurrexit; cùm ex quo resurrexit tot anni transierint. Cur nemo tam ineptus est, ut nos ita loquentes arguat esse mentitos, nisi quia istos dies secundùm illorum, quibus hæc gesta sunt, similitudinem nuncupamus, ut dicatur ipse dies qui non est ipse, sed revolutione temporis similis ejus; et dicatur illo die fieri, propter sacramenti celebrationem, quod non illo die, sed jam

[1] This passage is not extant in Greek.

olim factum est? Nonne semel immolatus est Christus in seipso; et tamen in sacramento non solùm per omnes paschæ solemnitates, sed omni die populis immolatur; nec utique mentitur, qui interrogatus eum responderit immolari? Si enim sacramenta quamdam similitudinem earum rerum, quarum sacramenta sunt, non haberent, omnino sacramenta non essent. Ex hac autem similitudine plerumque etiam ipsarum rerum nomina accipiunt. Sicut ergo secundùm quemdam modum sacramentum corporis Christi corpus Christi est, sacramentum sanguinis Christi sanguis Christi est, ita sacramentum fidei fides est. Nihil est autem aliud credere, quàm fidem habere. Ac per hoc cùm respondetur parvulus credere, qui fidei nondum habet affectum, respondetur fidem habere propter fidei sacramentum, et convertere se ad Deum propter conversionis sacramentum, quia et ipsa responsio ad celebrationem pertinet sacramenti. Sicut de ipso baptismo apostolus, "Consepulti," inquit, "sumus Christo per baptismum in mortem." Non ait, sepulturam significavimus: sed prorsus ait, "Consepulti sumus." Sacramentum ergo tantæ rei nonnisi ejusdem rei nuncupavit.—August. Op. Par. 1679. Ad Bonifacium Epist. xcviii. Tom. II. cols. 267, 8.

Hæc enim sacramenta sunt, in quibus non quid sint, sed quid ostendant semper adtenditur: quoniam signa sunt rerum, aliud exsistentia, et aliud significantia.—Id. Par. 1694. Cont. Maximin. Arianum, Lib. II. Cap. xxii. 3. Tom. VIII. col. 725.

Postquam typicum pascha fuerat impletum, et agni carnes cum apostolis comederat, assumit panem, qui confortat cor hominis, et ad verum paschæ transgreditur sacramentum; ut quomodo in præfiguratione ejus Melchisedec, summi Dei sacerdos, panem et vinum offerens fecerat, ipse quoque veritatem sui corporis et sanguinis repræsentaret.—Hieron. Op. Par. 1706. Comm. Lib. IV. in Matt. Cap. xxvi. Tom. IV. Pars I. col. 128.

Τί δέ ἐστι τὸ σαρκικῶς νοῆσαι; τὸ ἁπλῶς εἰς τὰ προκείμενα ὁρᾶν, καὶ μὴ πλέον τι φαντάζεσθαι. τοῦτο γάρ ἐστι σαρκικῶς. χρὴ δὲ μὴ οὕτω κρίνειν τοῖς ὁρωμένοις, ἀλλὰ πάντα τὰ μυστήρια τοῖς ἔνδον ὀφθαλμοῖς κατοπτεύειν· τοῦτο γάρ ἐστι πνευματικῶς.—Chrysost. Op. Par. 1728. In Joannem Hom. xlvii. Tom. VIII. p. 278.

Τί οὖν; ἡμεῖς καθ' ἑκάστην ἡμέραν οὐ προσφέρομεν; προσφέρομεν μέν, ἀλλ' ἀνάμνησιν ποιούμενοι τοῦ θανάτου αὐτοῦ . . . οὐκ ἄλλην θυσίαν, καθάπερ ὁ ἀρχιερεὺς τότε, ἀλλὰ τὴν αὐτὴν ἀεὶ ποιοῦμεν· μᾶλλον δὲ ἀνάμνησιν ἐργαζόμεθα θυσίας.—Id. Par. 1735. In Epist. ad Heb. Cap. x. Hom. xvii. Tom. XII. pp. 168, 9.

Si enim vasa sanctificata ad privatos usus transferre peccatum est et periculum, sicut docet nos Balthasar, qui bibens in calicibus sacratis de regno depositus est et de vita; si ergo hæc vasa sanctificata ad privatos usus transferre sic periculosum est, in quibus non est verum corpus Christi, sed mysterium corporis ejus continetur; quanto magis vasa corporis nostri, quæ sibi Deus ad habitaculum præparavit, non debemus locum dare diabolo agendi in eis quod vult?—Id. Par. 1724. Op. Imperf. in Matt. Hom. xi. Tom. VI. p. lxiii.

Note B. (See p. 90.)

Πῶς δὲ τοιαύταις ὑποδέξῃ χερσὶ τοῦ δεσπότου τὸ πανάγιον σῶμα; πῶς δὲ τῷ στόματι προσοίσεις τὸ αἷμα τὸ τίμιον, τοσοῦτον διὰ τὸν τοῦ θυμοῦ λόγον ἐκχέας παρανόμως αἷμα;—Ambros. in Orat. ad Theodos. in Theod. Hist. Eccl. Amst. 1695. Lib. v. c. 18. p. 220.

Sacerdotes quoque qui eucharistiæ serviunt, et sanguinem Domini populis ejus dividunt, etc.—Hieron. Op. Par. 1704. Comment. in Sophon. Proph. Cap. iii. Tom. iii. col. 1671.

Οὐ καθάπερ ἐπὶ τῆς παλαιᾶς, τὰ μὲν ὁ ἱερεὺς ἤσθιε, τὰ δὲ ὁ ἀρχόμενος, καὶ θέμις οὐκ ἦν τῷ λαῷ μετέχειν ὧν μετεῖχεν ὁ ἱερεύς. ἀλλ᾽ οὐ νῦν· ἀλλὰ πᾶσιν ἓν σῶμα πρόκειτα, καὶ ποτήριον ἕν.— Chrysost. Op. Par. 1732. In Epist. II. ad Cor. Hom. xviii. Tom. x. p. 568.

Comperimus autem, quod quidam sumpta tantummodo corporis sacri portione a calice sacri cruoris abstineant. Qui proculdubio (quum nescio qua superstitione docentur obstringi) aut integra sacramenta percipiant, aut ab integris arceantur: quia divisio unius ejusdemque mysterii sine grandi sacrilegio non potest provenire.—Gelasius Papa Majorico et Joanni episcopis.—Decret. Gratian. Par. 1583. Decret. Tert. Pars. De Consecrat. Distinct. ii. Cap. 12. cols. 2363—5.

Ubi vero solennibus adimpletis calicem diaconus offerre præsentibus cœpit, et accipientibus ceteris locus ejus advenit, faciem suam parvula instinctu divinæ majestatis avertere, os labiis obturantibus premere, calicem recusare. Perstitit tamen diaconus, et reluctanti licet, de sacramento calicis infudit.—Cypr. Op. Oxon. 1682. De Lapsis, p. 132.

Quo modo ad martyrii poculum idoneos facimus, si non eos prius ad bibendum in ecclesia poculum Domini jure communicationis admittimus?—Id. Epist. lvii. p. 117.

In calice Dominico sanctificando, et plebi ministrando, non hoc faciunt, quod Jesus Christus, Dominus et Deus noster, sacrificii hujus auctor et doctor, fecit et docuit.—Id. Epist. lxiii. p. 148.

Note C. (See p. 282.)

Nam nec in terris filii sine consensu patrum rite et jure nubunt.— Tertull. Op. Lut. 1341. Ad Uxor. Lib. ii. c. 8. p. 191.

Consulitur puella non de sponsalibus, nam illa judicium exspectat parentum; non est enim virginalis pudoris eligere maritum.—Ambros. Op. Par. 1686. De Abraham, Lib. i. 91. Tom. i. col. 311.

Μηδὲν ἐῶμεν αὐτοὺς τῶν ἡδέων καὶ βλαβερῶν ποιεῖν, μηδὲ ὡς παισὶ χαριζώμεθα· ἐν σωφροσύνῃ μάλιστα διατηρῶμεν αὐτούς... ταχέως αὐτοῖς γυναῖκας ἄγωμεν.—Chrysost. Op. Par. 1734. In I. Epist. ad Tim. Cap. iii. Hom. ix. Tom. xi. p. 597.—There is a similar passage in Matt. Hom. lix. Tom. vii. p. 604. These expressions of Chrysostom inculcating on parents the duty of providing wives for their sons are doubtless those referred to by the archbishop; as they are expressly quoted by other writers of the same age when speaking on the same subject. See Becon's Works, Lond. 1564. The Boke of Matrimony. Vol. I. fol. DCXXI. 2.

A passage from St Augustine is given in the text, p. 326.

ERRATUM.

In p. 168, l. 24, *omit* return.

INDEX.

AARON, a good priest, 148.
Absolon, his rebellion, 407.
Abuses in attire, diet, &c. to be repressed, 49.
Adrian the emperor, 173.
Æmilius oppressed Egypt, 135.
Afflictions, common to all, 376; peculiar to God's elect, 377; on the body of the church, 378; on particular and principal members, 379.
Alexander the great, 169; answer made to him by a pirate, 223.
Alliaco, Petrus de, 249.
Alms, duty of giving, 265.
Amasis, his law against idleness, 117.
Ambrose mentions Herod's burning books of the Jews, 116; touches bishops of his time with simony, 44, 136; brought emperor Theodosius to repentance by ecclesiastical discipline, 72; says pride is the greatest sin, 137; describes true repentance, 140; says Christ is handled and seen by faith, 153; reprobates unthankfulness towards God, 156; shews the evil result of forbearing things lawful, 316; his testimony that the cup was given to the laity, 455; says that a virgin is dependent on the judgment of her parents in respect to marriage, 455.
Ammianus Marcellinus referred to, 347.
Amphilochius, zealous against the Arians, 41, 73, 232.
Anabaptists, 191, 266.
Angels, their office, 267.
Antichrist, sells for money, 11; and Christ, difference between, 12, 20, 28; his destruction already begun, 389.
Antigonus, his speech when he should put on a diadem, 36.
Antiquity, argument from, made by Romish foxes, 66.
Apollonius falsely accused, 129.
Apostates notorious, 362.

Apostasy of the reformed, what, 389.
Arcadius, not saluted by Amphilochius, 232.
Aristotle says, seven hours' sleep suffice the body, 395.
Arius, banished by Theodosius, 41; his dreadful end, 362.
Armour of light to be put on, 214.
Assemblies, solemn, ordained in church for special benefits, 55; christian, when they may be secret, 191, 192.
Athanasius, falsely accused by Arians, 129.
Attire, sobriety in, 394.
Augustine says, it cannot be grace which is not every way free, 11; requires a doctrine to be recited from scripture that it may be believed, 14; Petilian's charge against him, 16; says, princes must forbid things whereby the commands of God are broken, 41; speaks of those compelled to come in, 46; says, pastors must recall wandering sheep to the fold, 72; quotes the opinion of Socrates on worship, 87; asserts that by faith we eat the body of Christ, 88; says, we must hear only, This saith the Lord, 95; shews we must be ready to excuse our brethren, 106; condemns the flatterer's tongue, 132; defines the ability of free-will, 133; his desire that God give what he commands, and command what he will, 133; says, there is no virtue but obedience 145; says, it is sometimes cruelty to spare, 148; mentions three causes of funerals, 161; considers order of burying, &c. as comforts to the living, and not helps to the dead, 162; asserts that as every man departs hence, so shall he be judged at the last day, 162; reccmmends men to look for death, 171; says that remedies are too late when death is near, 173; asserts that he cannot die ill who has lived well, 173; says,

prayer is a sacrifice to God, a scourge to the devils, 263; enforces brotherly love, 286; says, grace is so called because given gratis, 297; compares Abraham with John Baptist for holiness in respect of marriage, 322; says, the mother's consent must be asked for a damsel's marriage, 326; explains why the knowledge of the time of the world's end is kept from us, 352; explains the meaning of nations (Luke xxi. 25), 364; says, sufferings are no argument of righteousness, 378; warns that if faith fall asleep we are in danger, 382; the verses he wrote over his table, 399; says, the sacraments are called by the names of the things they signify, 453, 454; declares sacraments signs of things, being one thing and signifying another, 454.

Authorities must be prayed for, 82.

Aylmer, succeeds Sandys in the see of London, xxii.

Babington's and Ballard's conspiracy, sermon preached on occasion of, 403.

Baldwin, or Baudouin, an apostate, 362.

Baptism, by the sacrament of, we are incorporated into the church of Christ, 87; of persons delayed till their death-beds, 152; outward washing of the flesh in, declareth inward purging of the spirit, 302; private, of women, disliked by Sandys, 433, 448.

Baronius, referred to, 193.

Bartie, a fellow prisoner of Sandys, xii.

Becket, 359.

Becon's works referred to, 456.

Bede, his interpretation of the sun and moon being obscured, 357; his opinion of the dissolution of the heavens and the earth, 366.

Benefits by which God allures men, 145.

Benjamin, a tailor, helps Sandys to escape, xiii, xiv.

Bernard calls idleness the mother of toys, 117; says, prelates are changed into Pilates, 168; speaks of the time of death as most uncertain, 170; says, it is nowhere safe to be secure, 210; calls good works not the causes of, but the way unto the kingdom, 214.

Bertram, or Ratramnus, says the elements remain after consecration the same in substance as before, 89.

Bill, Dr, ii, v.

Bingham's Orig. Eccles. referred to for accounts of different notions respecting matrimony, 322.

Bishop's charge, its weightiness, 331; its hardness, 332; peril of discharging and not discharging duty of it, 333; many good men have endeavoured to avoid it, 333.

Bishops, not made by chance, 334; orders for, 434.

Bishopric of London, Sandys took unwillingly and willingly, 334.

Bland, Sandys' schoolmaster, i.

Boasting, nothing in us to authorize, 102.

Bondage, we are redeemed from by Christ, 179; of Romish servitude, Christ hath delivered us from, 180.

Bondmen, all men are by nature, 178.

Bountifulness, a fruit of mercy, to be shewn, 229, 230.

Bourne, Sir J., his dispute with Sandys, xviii.

Bowler, converted by Sandys and Bradford in prison, vii, viii.

Bradford, in prison with Sandys, vii, viii.

Brotherly concord, St Paul exhorts to, 92; arises of unity in religion, 97; illustrated by a comparison, 98, 99; —kindness, we must abound more and more in, 424, 425.

Brutus, 110; spared not his own sons, 227.

Burghley, Cecil, lord treasurer, instrumental in Sandys' promotion, xix; Sandys writes to him, xx, xxi, xxiii, xxv, xxvi.

Cards, dice, &c., recreation with, 118.

Care for others, a mean to maintain concord, 107; in some merely pretended, 107, 108; must be hearty, 108; specially concerns princes, counsellors, &c., 108–110.

Cartwright, Sandys conplains of, xx.

Chaderton, bishop, letter to, 436, 439.

Change, desired of all, 167; of this

INDEX. 459

mortal life, all subject to, 168; to be daily looked for, 171; dangers of not expecting, 172.

Charity, exhortation to, 398; hideth sins, how, 399; prone to hospitality, 400; communicates gifts and graces to others, 401.

Charles IX., funeral sermon for, 161.

Children, not to marry without their parents' consent, 50, 281, 282, 325, 326.

Christ, foretold, 7; his coming and designations, 8; men invited to him, 8, 9; thought highly of office of a minister, 35; died for all, 79; alone purges our hands and hearts, 139; his second coming, tokens of, 171, 172; and his ministers, how received in the world, 236; Lord of all, 284; sent from God to preach peace, 284; peace throughout the world at his coming, 286; died to procure peace, 288; ordained judge of quick and dead, 288; honoured by us, but not by Papists, 289, 290; why the multitude followed, 338, &c.: diligent in his office, 343; pitiful, 344; good that he should sleep and we be troubled, 384; the foundation, 386; his coming joyful to God's children, 390; his righteousness to be imputed to us, 422; his coming near, 438, 441; by his merits alone Sandys looked for salvation, 446, 447.

Christians, their sacrifice, 413, &c.

Chrysippus, 36.

Chrysologus reprobates drunkenness, 137.

Chrysostom says that he who lives other than he speaks teaches God to punish him, 71; asserts that if we were spiritual we should not need corporal signs, 87; says that mercy without justice is folly, 147, 148; speaks of men deferring baptism to their death-beds, 152; says, we pay, not give, tribute to magistrates, 200; enforces reconciliation, 229; thought an evil-gotten groat would be a canker, 231; compares Moses with Elias for holiness in respect of marriage, 322; compares a pastor to one that wrestles naked, 332; blames parents who make little account of their children's sin, 339; thinks the hill on which Christ sat may represent the kingdom of God, 340; his view of the signs mentioned by Christ, 352; thinks the church represented by the ship into which Christ went, 371; describes a wolf, 397; cautions against sparing a wolf, 413; defines a sacrifice, 414; says, we must view all mysteries with inward eyes, 454; declares that we make in the eucharist not so much a sacrifice as the commemoration of a sacrifice, 454; says, there is in the eucharist not the true body of Christ, but the mystery of his body, 454; his testimony that the cup was given to the laity, 455; says that parents must provide wives for their sons, 455.

Church, called a vineyard, 57; means used by foxes to destroy it, 65; purged, and use thereof, 236; by whom to be reformed, 237, 238; figured by a ship, 370; whence such storms arise as trouble it, 380.

Church of England, purged of idolatry and superstition, 58, 59; nothing in it ordained wicked or contrary to the word, 95; mercies of God towards it, 217, 218;—ill-requited, 219; no reason sufficient to withdraw from it, 338; doctrine in it the whole counsel of God, 447; rites and ceremonies in it not ungodly, though in some points might be bettered, 448.

Church robbers under name of church visitors, 122.

Cicero, 45, 110.

Claudius, 169.

Clemens Alexandrinus declares the doctrine of Christ most absolute, 222.

Codrus, 53, 110.

Comfort, exhortation to, 427, 428.

Commodities received by coming to water of life, 31.

Commodus, 169.

Conspiracy, who are mostly contrivers of, 405, 406.

Constans wrote a menacing letter to Constantius, 109.

Constantinus required that matters might be decided according to things which were written, 15; enjoined the synod to order all things by book of God, 40; his inauguration celebrated by a sermon by Eusebius, 56; wrote letters in behalf of Christians persecuted in Persia, 109; Athanasius accused before him, 129; disburthened the church of heretics, 248; shewed favour to Christians, 373.

Constantius said those who were faithless to God could not be faithful to their prince, 97, 261, 438, 441; received a menacing letter from Constans, 109; would not suffer a dissembler in religion to be about him, 121.

Contention, a hinderance of unity, 100; vain-glory the breeder of, 101.

Cornelius, his character, 256, &c.; he had faith, 260.

Corpus Juris Civilis, 281.

Cotelerius, referred to for passages against second marriages, 322.

Counsel, evil, has wrought ruin, 39.

Covetous men serve mammon and are idolaters, 182.

Creatures, religious honour not to be given to, 272.

Crœsus, 53.

Cross, to be taken up, 377.

Crossing on the forehead, 433.

Crying to the Lord will bring help in trouble, 384.

Curtius, 53, 110.

Cyprian says he is not joined to the church who is sundered from the gospel, 94; declares the foundation of all religion to be laid in the word of God, 222; says, bishops are not made without the providence of God, 334; his testimony that the cup was given to the laity, 455.

Cyrus, 53.

Dandelot, said to have been poisoned, 66.

David, why he wrote Psalm iv., 403; alleges his innocency, how to be understood, 404.

Death, our state not changed after, 162; all subject to, 168.

Decius, 110.

Deering, suspended, xxi.

Deliverance from popery, God's mercy the cause of our, 180.

Demosthenes, 36.

Diligent man blessed, 337.

Diogenes, 278.

Disciples question Christ about the destruction of Jerusalem and end of world, 351.

Discipline ecclesiastical, 71, 72.

Dissent from church of England to be lamented, 95.

Doctrine, pernicious of heresy or schism, those which teach are soul-murderers, 246.

Donatists, 191.

Double-minded men, 130, &c.

Drunkenness reproved, 137.

Durandus, his Rationale Divinorum Officiorum, 224.

Duty of holiness and righteousness owed to God, 177.

Ecclesiastical orders to be made by learned men, 433.

Egyptians, a custom of at feasts, 171.

Election requires holiness, 190.

Elizabeth, queen, her character, 57, 58, 80, 81; prayer for her, 415, 416.

Emulation a bane of the heart, 138.

End of all things certain, 387; consideration of it makes the heavy joyful and godly watchful, 387; time of it uncertain, but by signs may be thought to be near, 388.

Enemies, against whom we must strive, 166.

Erasmus says every body's dreams are at this day read amongst divine scriptures, 18.

Eucharist, we are fed by it, 87; how inward grace is reaped in it, 88; a sign, memorial, figure effectual of body of Christ, 88; visible elements in it are not changed in substance, 89, 90; preparation required to the worthy receiving of it, 90; Christ's body and blood in it are in a mystery not represented only but presented to us, 302, 303; we must try ourselves before receiving it, 304; opinions of fathers respecting it, 453, &c.

Euchites or Messalians, a sect of heretics, 263.

Eusebius referred to, 38, 109, 130, 218, 248; preached at the inauguration of Constantine, 56.

Evaristus declares marriage not wedlock if consent of parents be wanting, 50.
Exiles, English, found many tokens of mercy, 296.

Fabius, 45.
Faith cometh by hearing the word of God, 153; we are made partakers of peace by it, 290; we have remission of sins by it, 290; justification by it an old doctrine proceeding from prophets and apostles, 291; perfection in it to be sought, 424; victory only by it, 435.
False teachers, how they may be known, 396, 397.
Family of Love, a sect, 130, 191.
Families to be instructed in the fear of God, 264, 270.
Fathers do sometimes check and contradict one another, 20; the first thing they did on their conversion was to proclaim defiance to paganism, 373.
Fear must be joined with love, 186.
Flatterer, his tongue is grievous, 132.
Forgiveness of injuries a fruit of mercy, 229.
Foxes, enemies of the church so called, 62, &c.; the means they use to destroy the church, force and fraud, 65, &c.; must be taken and how, 69, &c., 437, 441.
Free-will, 133.
Fulvius, his impartiality, 227.
Funeral, Sandys' directions for his, 447.
Funerals, causes of solemnizing, 161.

Gates, Sir John, ii, iv.
Gelasius, pope, his testimony that the cup was given to the laity, 455.
Gentile and Jew, no difference between, 275, 277.
God, how to draw near unto, 134, &c.; comfort in drawing near unto him,143; to be sought and found by faith and prayer, 152-155; fruit of seeking him, 159; forsakes not whom he has chosen, 185; his messengers cruelly intreated, 187; must prescribe how he will be served, 189, 221; our duty to, is repentance and newness of life, 207; various ways devised of pacifying his wrath against sin, 219, 220; the true way of pacifying him, 220, 221; what it is to walk with him, 231; walkers with him must walk on, 233; public serving of him in the church consists in hearing the word, prayer, and the sacraments, 252; will be served of all nations, 253, 254, 279; neither parentage nor vocation shuts us from his kingdom, 257; no accepter of persons, 278; his fear should be planted in the heart, 280; created men to serve and honour him, 293; as the perfect rule to be followed absolutely, 375.
Godliness, perfection in, to be sought, 425.
Godly have always had a care for the church, 235.
Gospel, the little fruit of, a token that the fear of God is wanting, 137; while persecuted, it is enlarged, 283; men may lawfully flee from persecutors of it, 335.
Grace of God free, 11, 21, 297; needed that we may draw near unto God, 133; works a preparation to it, a popish error, 267; receiving it in vain, what, 297, &c.; offered by the word and sacraments, 299, &c.; time to receive it when offered by gospel,305;—when God afflicts, 307, 308; right way of receiving it by repentance and walking without offence, 309, &c.
Graces and gifts grow in the hands of him that spendeth, 345.
Gratiani Decretum, quoted in regard to marriages without parents' consent, 281; quoted for decree of Gelasius, 455.
Gregory Nazianzen says, a kingdom grounded on good will stands fast, 53; declares unity and peace the best thing, 93.
Gregory, pope, declares universal bishop a proud name, 101; explains why Christ entered into the temple, Matt. xxi. 12, 237.
Grindall, archbishop, comes to England with Sandys, xvi; consecrated to see of London, xviii; translated to York, xix; granted some liberty to opposers of liturgy, xx; translated to Canterbury, xxi; disagreement with Sandys, xxii; dies, xxv.

Hand, significations of, in scripture, 134, 135; must be cleansed, 134.

462   INDEX.

Hatto, bishop, legend of, referred to, 159.
Hawkshead school, founded by Sandys, xxvi; prayers to be used at it, 443.
Hearer of the word, his duty, 273, 274.
Heart must be purged, 136, &c.
Heavens and earth shall be dissolved, 366.
Heliogabalus, his gluttony, 393.
Henry the emperor received poison in the sacrament, 66.
Hervetus, 249.
Hilary, his answer to Constantine, 15, 16; his description of peace, 94.
Hill on which Christ sat, what it denotes, 340.
Holcroft, Sir T., procures the liberation of Sandys, x, &c.
Holiness the end of our election, 190; must appear, 190.
Homer quoted, 48.
Honorius II., pope, 224.
Honour to God, what, 27, 28.
Hooker, recommended by Sandys to mastership of Temple, xxvi.
Hospitality to be shewn to godly strangers, 266; charity is prone unto it, 400.
Huddlestone, Mr, takes one of Sandys' horses, vi.
Humbled, necessary to be, 141.
Humbleness of mind, a mean to preserve unity, 103.
Humility, divers kinds of, 103, 104.
Hurlestone, an acquaintance of Sandys, xiii, xiv.
Husbands, duties of, 317, &c.
Hutton, dean of York, his disputes with Sandys, xxiii, xxvi.

Idleness, no such bane as, 117.
Idol, and image, no real difference between, 28.
Idolatry and superstition to be rooted out, 437, 440.
Ignorance the mother of superstition, 113.
Inferiors must fear superiors, 186.
Ingratitude a foul crime, 156.
Innocency, security of princes rests upon, 405.
Irenæus, his testimony on the eucharist, 453.
Isaac, Mr, a friend of Sandys, xv, xvi.

James, bishop of Jerusalem, his continual praying, 38.
Jerome counsels to be always occupied, 117; says, where fulness is filth reigns, 138; denounces idleness and riotousness, 133; explains what is meant by mountains (Micah vi. 2), 216; insists on the authority of the word of God, 222; expounds the doing of judgment, 223; had always the sound of call to judgment in his ears, 368; says that Christ in the eucharist gave a representation of the truth of his body and blood, 454; his testimony that the cup was given to the laity, 455.
Jerusalem destroyed by contentions of John, Simon, and Eleazar, 101.
Jewish nation, excellency of, 346; temple, overthrow of, predicted, and fulfilment of it, 347; cause of this ruin, 258, 348; a warning to us, 259, 349, &c.
John, bishop of Constantinople assumes the title of universal bishop, 101; the Almner, 193.
Judas, his dreadful example, 362.
Judges must be free from bribes, faultless, &c., 225; to be neither hasty nor slow, 226.
Judgment, what it is to do, 223, 227; must be administered by magistrates, 224; shall certainly be, 353, 355; who shall be judge, his properties, 353, &c.; time of it not to be enquired into, 355, 356; signs going before it, 356, &c.; warnings and preparation for it, 368, 369.
Julian, his dreadful example, 362.
Justice to be in dealings of all, 227.
Justification by faith witnessed by all the prophets and apostles, 291.
Justinian deposed Sylverius and Vigilius, 40.

Knowledge, means whereby God leadeth to it, 113; contempt of means whereby it is attained, 113; prayer and meditation needful in order to it, 114; God the only teacher of it, 114; perfection to be sought in it, 424.

Labour, man born unto, 182.
Lactantius says, God is pacified by the mending of our manners, 157.

INDEX. 463

Last day draweth near, 213.
Laws to be executed and kept by authorities, 51.
Lawyers must be righteous, 193.
Leaver, Mr, ii, iii.
Legends thought true in time of popery, 18.
Leontius, bishop of Antioch, an Arian, 183.
Levites, blessing upon, till they became depraved, 243.
Life of man a warfare, 164, &c.
Lock, Mr, xv.
London, magistrates of, charged to relieve the poor, 344.
Lord's supper—see Eucharist.
Love, the livery coat of Christ, 98; fear must be joined with it, towards God, 186; debt of it natural and continual, and reasons why, 204; due to neighbours, and who they be, 205; caution in respect to it, 206; great want of it in these times, 206, 207.
Lusts to be denied, 374.
Luther on Galatians, a comfortable treatise, 435.
Lycurgus set down no punishment for ingratitude, 156.

Magistrates should be chosen for worthiness, 47; may constrain their subjects to open assemblies for God's service, 192; ought to be righteous, 192; to be obeyed whether christian or heathen, 197; why obedience to be yielded to them, 198; tribute a debt due to them, 199; examples of those who have well or ill discharged the debt they owe them, 200; qualities required in them, 201; their sacrifice, 412.
Mammon, not to be served, 182.
Marcion, a heretic, 15.
Marriage not lawful without consent of parents, 50, 281, 325, 326, 455; honourable for the author, 314;—for causes why ordained, 315;—for mutual duties, 317; dishonoured by heretics, 321; not to be carelessly or improperly entered on, 323; beauty or wealth in it, not to be too much respected, 324, 325; must be affection and religion in it, 329; not to be solemnized except in the parish where parties, or woman at least, reside, 434.
Martyr, Peter, Sandys dwelt in his house, xvi.
Mary, queen, consents to Sandys being set at liberty, x.
Matthew Paris, referred to, 224.
Mass, no foundation for, in scripture, 223.
Men to be followed with a caution, 375.
Merchants must deal truly, 204.
Mercies promised to David, 32.
Mercy without justice is folly, 147; to be loved, 228.
Merits, popish doctrine of, 25.
Ministers, office of, thought highly of by Christ, contemned by men, 35, 350; their duty to pray and teach, 38, 39; those who neglect their duty should be deposed, 40; provision to be made for them, 45, 96; their debt to the flock, 202; the means whereby the elect are to be brought to obedience of Christ, 342; their sacrifice and maintenance, 412.
Ministry, a learned, in England, 245.
Miracles, no infallible proofs of true doctrine, 17.
Mistrust of God's providence a root of all evil, 343.
Mitchell, Mr, apprises Sandys he may escape from the Tower, vii.
Mitch, Mr, tries to pull Sandys from his vice-chancellor's chair, v.
Moon, representing the church, turned into blood by persecution, 360, 361.
Moore, Mr, a friend of Sandys, iii, vi.
Moses, a worthy magistrate, 147.
Mouse, Dr, one day a protestant, the next a papist, iv.
Mower, James, Sandys lodged at his house, xv.

Neighbours, who they be, 205.
Nero, 169.
Nets to be used by ministers, 70, &c., 437, 441.
Nicholas or Nicolai, founder of Family of Love, 130.
Northumberland, duke of, ii, iii, iv.

Obedience to be at once given to God's commands, 269.
Offence, we must walk without, 310, 311.

Origen defines sobriety, 391; expounds what a sacrifice is, 414.
Original sin, man humbled by true doctrine of, 21.
Orosius referred to, 186.

Paganus, 249.
Parker, archbishop, with the duke of Northumberland, ii; consecrates Sandys, xvii; displeased with him, xviii; dies, xxi.
Parents, some love the bodies of their children better than their souls, 339.
Parliaments, use of, 34.
Partiality not to be shewn by judges, 226.
Pastors too careful to be enriched, and then the church spoiled, 243; that cannot, or will not, teach, no pastors, 344.
Paul's farewell to the Corinthians, 418.
Peace, the fruit of the gospel, 60, 61; by Jesus Christ, 282; the badge of God's people, 286; Christ's diligence in preaching it, 287; Christ died to procure it, 288; we are made partakers of it by faith, 290; exhortation to it, 428, 429.
Peaceably, what it is to live, 86.
Pelagius, 24.
People, to be constrained to hear the word, 46; their duty towards God, higher powers, &c., 52; their duty under princes, 85, 86; when they are worthy the word, God will send preachers of it, 277.
Perfection, exhortation to, 420; of two kinds, 421; in God, what, 421; in us by imputation, 422; to be sought for industriously, 423; inward, 423, &c.; outward, 425, &c.
Persecution, cruelty of, 361.
Persons not to be respected in execution of laws, 85; God no acceptor of, 278; not to be respected, 437, 440.
Philip of Macedon, answer made to, 154.
Plagues must constrain those whom benefits will not win, 151.
Plato, 278.
Pliny says, sleep steals away half our life, 396.
Poison has been administered in the sacrament, 66.

Polycarp, his answer to an infidel judge, 217, 218.
Pope, authority of, papists' argument from, 67; paper which came from him, 130; has frequently obtained the popedom by simony, 241; his haughtiness in requiring his feet to be kissed, 272; has not the humility that Peter shewed, 277; always practising against the Lord and his anointed, 408.
Popery, difference between it and true Christianity, 12, 20, 28; grounds of it, 16, &c.; doctrines of it opposed to scripture, 19; teaches not fear but distrust, 185; absurdities of it defended to be catholic, 359.
Popish guides no pastors, 344.
Poor, rebuke for not relieving them, 51; mercifulness to, 159, 160.
Prayer, to be made for kings and for people, 38, 78, &c.; to or for the dead not to be taught, 39; what, and its parts, 76, 77; why it is to be made for princes and people, 83, &c.; fruitless where repentance is not, 157; two sorts, public and private, 261; a christian exercise, 275; needful in conjunction with watchfulness, 397, 398; for the queen, 415, 416.
Prayers to be used at Hawkshead school, 443, &c.
Preacher, his duty, 274.
Preachers, seditious at Paul's Cross, Sandys complains of, xx.
Precepts of men, religion not to be built on, 17.
Pride, a great sin, 137.
Priesthood, a threefold, in the scriptures, 411.
Priests, christian, their sober behaviour made a favourable impression on barbarous nations, 246, 247.
Princes, their duty towards God and commonwealth, 41; how they serve God as princes, 41, &c.; they are to purge and cleanse the church, 42, 43; they must provide that people be taught, 44, 45; their duty towards the commonwealth, 46, 47; their power to provide good laws, 48, &c.; they must execute laws, 51, 52; must study to make people live in peace, 83;—in piety and honesty,

84; they must themselves be examples, 84, 85; must care for others, 108, 109; must be foremost in the way of truth, 123, 124; to win them to the truth is great gain, 276.

Profanation, open, of the service of God we must fly from, 338.

Professors, many have fallen in time of persecution, 300.

Prophecies concerning Christ accomplished, 7; feigned, a means used to deceive the people, 67.

Punishments to be inflicted on foxes that spoil the church, 72, &c.

Purgatory, the opinion of it vain and dangerous, 162, 163; has no foundation in scripture, 253.

Queen, prayer for, 415, 416.

Ratramnus, see Bertram.

Rebellion in the northern counties of England, 65.

Redemption of men by Christ free, not due, 180, 181; was that they might serve him, 181.

Reformation of the church, the proper manner of it, 247, &c.; the rule to be followed in it is the written word, 250.

Religions, liberty of professing divers, dangerous to the state, 49.

Remission of sins free, 290.

Repentance necessary, 139, 140, 207; the right way of worthy receiving grace, 309.

Revelations, dangerous to look for instruction by them, 115.

Rites and ceremonies in the church of England not ungodly, 248.

Rome, church of, seeks her own glory and gain, 23; her evil doctrines, 23, &c.; robs God of his honour, 27.

Sacraments, two, 87 grace offered by, 302, 303.

Sacrifices usual in all ages, and God requires them of us, 410; the priests by whom they are offered, 411; what offered by Aaron, what by Christ, and what by us, 411, &c.

Samuel, a minister, magistrate, prophet and prince, 35, 36; a pattern herein to be followed, 37.

Sanders, Mr, a fellow prisoner with Sandys, ix.

Sandys, archbishop, his birth and education, i; vice-chancellor of Cambridge, where he preaches at proclamation of queen Jane, ii; prepares his sermon for the press, iii; his answer to the duke of Northumberland, iv; expostulates with the university, v; resigns his office of vice-chancellor, v; carried to the Tower, vi; refuses to escape, vii; removed to the Marshalsea, viii; released, xii; goes into Essex, xiv; sails to Antwerp, xv; goes to Strausborough and Zurich, xvi; loses his wife and child, xvi; returns to London, xvi; in commission for revising Common-Prayer, xvii; has some scruples about rites and ceremonies, xvii; consecrated bishop of Worcester, xvii; displeases archbishop Parker, xviii; has a dispute with Sir John Bourne, xviii; married a second time, xviii; employed on bishops' bible, xix; translated to London, xix; issues injunctions, xix; complains of seditious preachers, xx; has a dispute with Deering, xxi; recommends a national synod, xxi; receives a legacy from archbishop Parker, xxi; translated to York, xxi; disputes with Grindall, and Aylmer, xxii; opposed by Whittingham, xxiii; gives an account of his visitation to lord treasurer Burghley, xxiii; is plotted against by Sir R. Stapleton, xxiv, xxv; answers in parliament the petition of sixteen articles, xxvi; has a controversy with his dean, xxvi; dies and is buried at Southwell, xxvii; his epitaph, xxvii, xxvii; notice of him from Catalogue of bishops, xxix, xxx; his works xxx, xxxi; excellence of his sermons, 3; bids farewell to London, 419, &c.; his hope of his successor, 420.

Schism, lamentable, no just cause for it, 381.

Scilurus, the Scythian, story of, 49.

Scipio, his saying to the Romans who wished to leave the city, 372.

Scripture the foundation and rule of

religion, 12, 222; true professors have rested their faith on it, 13, 14; pope will not have his doctrine tried thereby, 15, 16; commendation of it, 113.

Security, sleeping in, dangerous, 210.

Seneca describes how life is wasted, 392.

Sermons, many men haunt them for vain reasons, 338.

Service, to be paid only to God, 182; with childlike, not slavish fear, 184; God must prescribe it, 189, 221.

Ship of the church must be distinguished from that of antichrist, 371; we must follow Christ into it by denying ourselves and imitating him, 372, &c.; those that are in it with Christ must suffer trouble, 376.

Sigismund, emperor, 102.

Signs of Christ's coming, 356, &c., 388, &c.; strike terror into men's minds, 364, 365.

Silvester, pope, believed to be a magician, 66.

Similis, his epitaph, 173.

Simony, the church to be purged from, 43, 44, 136; thieves break into the church by it, 240, 241; those that enter by it deal evilly after they have entered, 242.

Sin, most sleep in, 209.

Sinners exhorted to draw near to God, 127; different kinds of, 127, &c.

Sleepiness to be shaken off by magistrates and ministers, 382, &c.

Sloth reproved, 337.

Sobriety, inward, 391; outward, 392, &c.

Socrates, his opinion of worship, 87.

Socrates, Eccles. Hist. referred to, 109, 347.

Solon describes the chief safety of a commonwealth, 52.

Southwell, Sandys buried at, xxvii.

Sozomen, Eccles. Hist. referred to, 97, 109, 246, 261, 347, 441.

Spira, his dreadful end, 362.

Spirits foul, testimony of refused, 17.

Staphilus, 362.

Stapleton, Sir R., his foul plot against Sandys, xxiv, xxv.

Stars falling from heaven signify pastors falling away, 361, 362; another application of, 363.

Stewardship, account to be given of, 401.

Subsidies due to the prince, 53.

Syrus, P., denounces ingratitude, 156.

Sylverius, pope, deposed by Justinian, 40.

Tanner, bishop, his account of Sandys' works, xxx, xxxi.

Tares, by what fault they grow in the Lord's field, 436, 439.

Teachers, the want of, and why so few, 154, 155; needful, 244; God provides them for such as desire to learn, and honours them, 268, 269.

Teaching, to be in the good and right way, 39, 40.

Temple, use to which Christ required it to be restored, 251.

Temporal blessings, why God sends them, 61; if they are abused, plagues will follow, 62.

Terence, quoted, 108, 168.

Tertullian says that Christians prayed for persecuting emperors, 80; asserts that the blood spilt for the gospel is the seed of it, 283, 284; likens the ship (Matt. viii. 23, 24), to the church, 371; says that Christ called a figure of his body, his body, 453; forbids sons to marry without consent of their parents, 455.

Thales, story of, 392.

Thankfulness due to those who bring the word of salvation, 273.

Themistocles, 36, 53, 325.

Theodoret, Eccles. Hist. referred to, 72, 73, 109, 129, 183, 224, 455.

——— says the mystical tokens in the eucharist do not leave their proper nature, 89.

Theodosius rebuked by Amphilochius, 41, 73, 232; brought by Ambrose to repentance, 72; gave his assent to a law to do nothing without deliberation, 224.

Theophylact says the wife must regard the things within the house, 320.

Thraldom of will, 21.

Traditions, a ground of popery, 16, 19.

Transgressions, the cause of plagues, 306.

Treason will not be cured till traitors be extinguished, 408.

Tribute due to princes, 53, 199.

Trip. Hist. referred to, 41.

Troubles, causes from which they arise, 380, 381; they grow when causes which should appease them sleep, 382; Christ sends help to his disciples in them, 384, 385.

Truth throws down men and advances Christ, 22, 23; to be walked in, 117, 122, 123; to be testified by public preaching, 291.

Unity, the scripture exhorts to, 93; description of the best kind of it, 94; of religion in the church of England, 95; hinderances to it, 100, &c.; preservatives of it, 103, &c.

Unwritten verities, dangerous to admit, 14, 15.

Usury, Sandys remonstrates against, xxvi; to be repressed, 50, 136; ten, twenty, thirty in the hundred taken, 182; a vile sin, 203.

Vain-glory, a hinderance to unity, 101; hardly bridled, 102, 103.

Valentinus, a heretic, 15.

Valerius Maximus, referred to, 36, 52, 53.

Vengeance, to be left to God, 289.

Victor, pope, received poison in the sacrament, 66.

Vigilius, pope, deposed by Justinian, 40.

Vitellius, his gluttony, 393.

Vives condemns the golden legend, 18.

Volusianus, his letter to pope Nicholas, 316.

Walkers in by-paths complained of, 118, &c.

Wantonness, a poison of the heart, 138.

Waste must be avoided, 342.

Watching, most necessary kinds of, 395, &c.

Waters of life, men are invited to, 10; how men must come to them, 30.

Way, keeper of the Marshalsea, viii.

Way, how taken in scripture, 116.

Whittingham, dean of Durham, xxiii, xxiv.

Wicked abound because wicked bear rule, 121.

Wife, to be honoured of her husband, 317, &c.; honour she owes her husband, 320.

Wilford, Sir T., Sandys marries his daughter, xviii.

Winchester, Gardiner, bishop of, x, xii.

Will, thraldom of, 21.

Word of God, a precious jewel, 113.

Word, scruples against hearing it reproved, 271.

Works of men are imperfect and evil, 22; justification by them a doctrine of popery, 25; of supererogation not to be allowed, 25; of darkness to be cast off, 213; good, the fruits of the light of knowledge, 214.

World, its blindness, 208.

Wyat, his rebellion, viii, ix.

Zeal, necessity and nature of, 194; examples of it, 195; must be in knowledge and sincerity, 196; moved Christ to reform the church, 249; none in church of Rome, 249; of the godly to serve the Lord, 294.

www.ingramcontent.com/pod-product-compliance
Lightning Source LLC
Chambersburg PA
CBHW071221290426
44108CB00013B/1242